THE EXCEL SPREADSHEET
FOR ENGINEERS
AND SCIENTISTS

Irvin H. Kral

CAD/CAM
General Dynamics
Air Defense Systems Division
Pomona, California

PRENTICE HALL
Englewood Cliffs, New Jersey 07632

Library of Congress Cataloging-in-Publication Data

KRAL, IRVIN H.
The Excel spreadsheet for engineers and scientists / Irvin H.
Kral.

p.   cm.
Includes bibliographical references and index.
ISBN 0-13-296765-0
1. Engineering—Data processing.   2. Microsoft Excel (Computer
program)   I. Title.
TA345.K73 1992   90-28472
620'.00285'5369—dc20   CIP

Editorial/production supervisor
  and interior designer: **Karen Bernhaut**
Cover designer: **Lundgren Graphics, Ltd.**

Prepress buyer: **Mary McCartney**
Manufacturing buyer: **Susan Brunke**
Acquisitions editor: **Michael Hays**

© 1992 by Prentice-Hall, Inc.
A Simon & Schuster Company
Englewood Cliffs, New Jersey 07632

The publisher offers discounts on this book when ordered in bulk quantities. For more information, write:

Special Sales/Professional Marketing
Prentice-Hall, Inc.
Professional & Technical Reference Division
Englewood Cliffs, New Jersey 07632

Microsoft® is a registered trademark of Microsoft Corporation. Screen shots Microsoft® Excel © 1987–1990 Microsoft Corporation. Reprinted with permission from Microsoft Corporation.

Printed in the United States of America

10 9 8 7 6 5 4 3 2 1

ISBN 0-13-296765-0

Prentice-Hall International (UK) Limited, *London*
Prentice-Hall of Australia Pty. Limited, *Sydney*
Prentice-Hall Canada Inc., *Toronto*
Prentice-Hall Hispanoamericana, S.A., *Mexico*
Prentice-Hall of India Private Limited, *New Delhi*
Prentice-Hall of Japan, Inc., *Tokyo*
Simon & Schuster Asia Pte. Ltd., *Singapore*
Editora Prentice-Hall do Brasil, Ltda., *Rio de Janeiro*

Contents

7 Function Macros   229

8 Command Macros, Menus, and Dialog Boxes   292

Preface

Computers are important to technical disciplines for the computational support they provide. Engineers, scientists, and other technically trained persons are familiar with programming computers in high-level languages or with running professionally prepared application programs for which they must supply input data only. In the former case, ability to develop algorithms for solving the problems is required, knowledge of the language statement syntax and structure is required, and techniques for obtaining graphical and numerical output must be adopted. In the latter case, limitations for applying the application program must be known, some familiarity of the underlying algorithms must be acquired to appreciate the computed output, and input data requirements must be known. An intermediate case is also available whereby a data structure, a graphics interface, and the means for incorporating high-level program-like statements are provided that allow one to quickly prepare the semblance of a custom-made program. This case arises because of developments that advanced the capabilities of spreadsheet programs. Yes, we are referring to a program that has its origin in business applications. However, we will show that at least one modern spreadsheet program can be applied to many engineering tasks without requiring that the user first become skilled in computer programming to benefit from its use.

A spreadsheet program is an application program. Like many high-level programming languages, it was developed to fill a need in an application area (business) not otherwise well addressed by existing programming languages. This need, characterized by data visually presented in tabular form that often is also required in graphical form, is shared by professionals in the engineering and scientific community. Therefore, it is reasonable to believe that a spreadsheet program will be useful in technical applications also. Such must be the case, as evident from articles appearing in the technical literature. However, tutorial material for engineers and scientists is needed; hence, the reason for writing this text.

Our evaluation of spreadsheet programs convinced us that the most advanced program for engineering applications is Microsoft® Excel. We make extensive use of its capabilities and present in an engineering context nearly all of its features. Currently used versions are 3.0 and the 2.xx series. We are sympathetic with users who resist upgrading to a new version for the sake of being current. Observing that most new versions of software provide only small increments of improvement over their immediately preceding version, we have segregated the discussion on version 3.0 improvements into a separate section in each chapter. This gives us the opportunity to highlight those new features that truly provide new capability for engineering application. Updating to new versions is not always as simple as buying and installing the new version, even if its purchase can be justified. Upgrading usually is an expensive, time consuming, and frustrating experience. Often one must buy new versions of supporting software, in this case Microsoft® Windows and new printer drivers, and probably additional computer memory and supporting accessories. Upgrading to a new version of Windows also impacts other software which will not run under the new version. We run all Excel examples for version 2.10 under version 3.0 and discuss any differences in operation. We run Excel under the DOS operating system on an IBM PC/AT compatible computer with an EGA monitor, a mouse, a dot matrix printer, and a hardware accelerated laser printer.

This text is written for persons with a technical background, such as engineers, scientists, students in a technical discipline, and persons working in a technical capacity in industry. It is written at the undergraduate level and is suitable for a one-semester course on Excel. No prior computer programming experience is assumed or required for using the text. However, the reader is assumed to be familiar with operation of the computer on which the spreadsheet program is to be run. The text is for use in university and college courses in engineering, engineering technology, industrial technology, and computer science courses, for courses on spreadsheet use by industrial companies, and for self-study.

New material is introduced incrementally, and its understanding depends only on the material of previous chapters. We discuss the worksheet first, then graphs, then macros, and finally the database and features for using Excel with other applications. This ordering of material allows us to maintain the incremental introduction of new material in such a manner that its re-introduction is thereafter unnecessary. It allows the reader to learn as much as possible about using Excel in the shortest time and still be functional with all the material learned during that time. We do as much with worksheets as is possible before covering graphs and before continuing into the power of macros.

Chapter 1 contains an overview of the spreadsheet program and places in perspective its application to engineering problems. We discuss educational prerequisites for using spreadsheet programs and the programming philosophy of the text. We explain our choice of Excel and describe the system of notation used to present the material.

Chapter 2 covers spreadsheet basics, the mechanics of entering data, elementary worksheet commands, the construction of simple formulas, program testing and debugging, and printing of results. The reader should now feel comfortable working with spreadsheets, should be able to handle most applications requiring computations with the basic mathematical operators only, and should have some idea of problems that arise when using spreadsheets. Thus far the reader should be able to solve with a spreadsheet program all problems that can be solved with a hand calculator of limited capability.

Chapter 3 introduces the student to Excel built-in mathematical functions. Also, use of variables is introduced, worksheet editing commands are presented, formatting of documents is discussed, and more debugging techniques are described. The reader now will be able to work with formulas of arbitrary complexity.

Chapter 4 explores the use of arrays in worksheets. Mathematical operators applied to arrays are discussed and built-in matrix computational functions are described. The class of problems that the reader can now solve with a spreadsheet program is greatly enlarged. Discussions on debugging worksheets apply to the special considerations when working with arrays.

Chapter 5 explores the complex computational structures possible with Excel's decision making and iteration control structures. The logical data type is introduced and logical expressions and functions are discussed. More complex computations are now possible with a spreadsheet program, so special debugging considerations are presented for this purpose. The student should now be able to solve problems for which the result is dependent on computational paths determined during run time.

Chapter 6 covers the preparation of graphs and the generation of data to plot. Graphs are called charts in Excel. Certain features of Excel make it easier to generate tables of data, manipulate them, and compute with them. We seize this opportunity for help with our work. However, we do not discuss in detail all the graphing capability, since certain types of graphs are seldom used in engineering work.

Chapter 7 introduces the concept of user-developed function macros. Macros are very important to the Excel user because they allow one to incorporate modularity and hierarchy in spreadsheet work and because they allow certain program constructs not allowed in worksheets. Their use also serves as a vehicle by which some structured programming techniques may be employed. However, the Excel language cannot be considered a structured programming language. With the material presented in this chapter, the student should be able to apply spreadsheet techniques to virtually any engineering problem.

Chapter 8 covers command macros and custom menus and dialog boxes. These Excel features, used principally for convenience, allow us to incorporate preferences into the way spreadsheet programs run and the way the user interacts with them. We can also save ourselves time with the command macros, and we indeed use them thereafter in our examples.

Chapter 9 is devoted to the database feature. Although it does not have extensive capabilities, we find this feature convenient for creating limited engineering databases and for manipulating them.

Chapter 10 deals with the subject of interacting spreadsheets and other applications. Multiple applications can be linked with Excel for static and dynamic sharing of information. With this feature, seldom should it be necessary to manually intervene in transfer of information between applications, thus saving time, reducing errors, making data-sharing temporally current, and providing entry for others to otherwise restricted applications.

Chapter 11 contains comprehensive examples of Excel use in engineering. Not only can the power of Excel be appreciated, but some of its limitations also become evident.

This text is intended for classroom use, but it may also be used for self-instruction. To appreciate the contents, the student should have a substantial mathematical background. For students having less mathematical ability, the examples can be modified for their level of knowledge and some sections of the text may be treated lightly or omitted. The material should be covered in chapter order with frequent discussions of proper program construction and error elimination.

Problems should be run on a computer as study progresses. There is no alternative to learning than by structuring problems for spreadsheet solution, becoming involved with the mechanics of preparing and running the program, debugging the program, and verifying program output. The Microsoft® Excel *Reference Guide* and *Functions and Macros* manuals should be available while running version 2.xx, and the *User's Guide* and *Function Reference* manuals should be available while runing version 3.0.

Irvin H. Kral
San Antonio Heights, California

CHAPTER 1

Introduction

This text is about using a spreadsheet program for engineering applications. In this chapter, we discuss the characteristics needed in such programs to serve our purpose because engineering requirements of computer programs often differ substantially from those of other disciplines. We also discuss the prerequisites for using spreadsheet programs, principally from a hardware viewpoint, in order to assemble a system that meets our needs.

1.1 THE SPREADSHEET PROGRAM

The computer program called a spreadsheet is an application program for which the user supplies data and instructions in the form of commands and formulas to make the desired computations. It is not a computer language in which to write a program. Its physical appearance resembles its namesake, the business spreadsheet, which is the organization of a procedure to perform computations in a tabular layout. Despite its name origin, a tabular organization of data with an implicit computational procedure applies to many disciplines, including engineering. Because of the program's constraint of displaying information in tabular form, we can structure a problem so that both its data structure and its computational methodology conform with spreadsheet characteristics. Thus, we may choose to alter our thinking on solving a problem because we have a ready-made

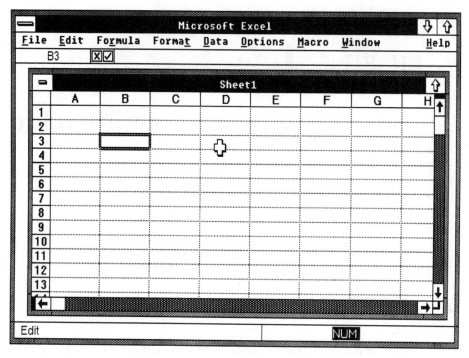

Figure 1.1   Spreadsheet screen presentation.

scheme for organizing our solution technique and have the power of the computer to make the computations.

Although we will later discuss in detail the parts of a spreadsheet program, let us briefly review its organization now to prepare us for explanations later. Physically, we see on our computer screen a presentation like that of Figure 1.1. First, we see a physical layout of a worksheet-like presentation on which we enter our problem-input information. This is the rectangular gridded layout of cells for which the program is named. Then, we identify means for communicating with the functioning of the program. These are the menus with predefined commands that operate on the information we enter into the worksheet. We call this a menu-driven program. We are given limited freedom to tailor the command meaning through submenus and a question/response type dialog. Finally, there is the workspace itself, a rectangular area within which the gridded layout appears. The results appear within the cells of the worksheet in which formulas are entered. Thus, the worksheet appears as an on-screen storage area. Of course, we are able to save our work for rerun later or for other purposes.

1.2 SELECTING PROBLEMS FOR SPREADSHEET APPLICATION

The spreadsheet program has been available for personal computers for several years. Although initially applied to business applications, its use in engineering is expanding. Various applications of the program have been reported in the literature, as can be seen in the bibliography at the end of this chapter.

Not all spreadsheet programs are created equal, however. Real-time applications of computers are prominent in engineering, and because of this, problems in transferring data from the application to the spreadsheet program may arise. One software product to enable such data transfer has been described in the literature. But, as we will see later in this book, such software is unnecessary when a spreadsheet program is used that allows communications with other applications.

Because of the unique presentation of a spreadsheet program, we must alter our way of thinking about how to enter data into the program and how to control its execution. Upon becoming familiar with the program layout, it should be evident that certain problems fit the layout format naturally. But the form of other problems will seem to defy solution by the spreadsheet program, while still others will be totally unsuited to this form of solution. Therefore, we should attempt to classify problems for spreadsheet solution. We must remember that the spreadsheet functions like an imperative language (FORTRAN, PASCAL, etc.). The basic concept is to store and command. In short, we specify in great detail how the desired values are to be computed, not just what they must be.

We will point out the principal characteristics of various problems and associate them with the features of the spreadsheet program that allow their solution with this computer technique. Because much explanation and illustration of characteristics is involved, this process will be a continuing one throughout the text.

Each chapter of this book presents new spreadsheet program features. Therefore, the capability for recognizing candidate problems for this solution technique is continually being expanded. Finally, it must be presumed that improvements in spreadsheet programs will continue and that these programs will become appropriate solution vehicles for a wider class of engineering problems.

1.3 SPREADSHEET PROGRAM REQUIREMENTS FOR ENGINEERING APPLICATIONS

Engineering applications involve mathematical computations of arbitrary complexity with results often displayed in tabular or graphical form. Computations are routinely made with logical, complex, and character data types as well as with the usual real and integer forms. Manipulation of equations in matrix and vector form is often required, and nearly all computations use a variety of elementary functions based on trigonometric, statistical, series, logical, or special forms. Graphs are routinely prepared that display data on linear and nonlinear rectangular axes, or in polar form, to show relationships in linear or logarithmic form, to emphasize angular characteristics, to show discrete properties, or to otherwise accentuate characteristics not evident from data present in other forms. Engineering applications of computers also involve real-time data acquisition and control of experiments and real-time signal processing.

Selecting a computer language to serve an application area first requires an evaluation of the language to determine whether its features fulfill the requirements that the application will impose on the language. We seek answers to such questions as

1. Are the desired data structures available?
2. Are the required data types available?
3. Are suitable built-in and application-specific functions available as part of a library?
4. Are the necessary decision structures provided?
5. Are suitable control structures available?
6. Are there modularity and hierarchical structuring capabilities?
7. Can real-time applications be implemented in the language?
8. Can formatted reports be easily prepared?
9. Can graphical entities be conveniently displayed?
10. Are convenient file-handling procedures available?
11. Are comprehensive diagnostics provided?

The availability of required features contributes to the ease with which the language can be learned. More importantly, the complexity of the application determines its ease of use.

Comparable considerations apply in selecting a spreadsheet program. Although not a language, its application depends on control through command selection and formula computation. Therefore, some factors for language selection also apply to spreadsheet selection. The user interface to the program is also a contributing factor in the selection.

For engineering applications, we want the following features:

1. *The ability to conveniently express mathematical relationships.* Look for convenience in preparing formulas, especially with respect to their natural construction and interpretation. Look for common symbol use and formula formatting. Avoid programs that require preparation and formatting that would lead to errors on entry. Look for error-checking features and help in locating formula-syntax errors.

2. *A generous supply of built-in, or library, mathematical functions.* As a minimum, look for functions that you expect in a high-grade scientific hand calculator. Expect built-in physical constants appropriate to an engineering field (e.g., pi, *e,* electron charge, Boltzman's constant, Planck's constant, gas constant, gravitational constant, etc.), unit conversion functions, trigonometric and hyperbolic functions, probability and statistical functions, curve-fitting functions, and logical functions.

3. *The capability for hierarchical modularity with provision for user-defined modules.* Look for the ability to define and use program modules (subprograms, or functions, or macros). These must accept arguments and return values with data types appropriate for the nature of the subprogram, and one must be able to use them in a hierarchical manner.

4. *A supply of data types common to engineering computations.* Look for real, integer, multiple precision, complex, logical, vector, and matrix typing. Expect number formatting for user-specified precision. Look for character and string typing and manipulation. Expect automatic type recognition and conversion in formula and subprogram argument contexts.

5. *An automatic graphing facility.* Look for the common engineering graph formats (linear-linear, log-linear, and log-log) with interchangeable axis orientation. Expect automatic scaling with user override capability. Look for polar, probability, bar (horizontal and vertical orientation), contour, and surface (with and without hidden line removal) plot capability. Expect to combine curves onto a single graph.

6. *An ability to make decisions.* Look for IF-THEN-ELSE constructs that accept relational, arithmetic, and logical expressions individually or in combination. Expect default value assignments and flexibility of outcome assignment.

7. *The capability to control the flow of statement execution.* Look for statements that permit branching and looping, for example, FOR-NEXT, WHILE-NEXT, GOTO, and so on. Require that iteration control be inherent to the program. Determine the amount of loop nesting permitted and the range of control. Look for structured programming type constraints.

8. *A user-oriented natural screen presentation.* Look for screen layouts that conform with the natural way of performing tasks. Expect convenient and consistent layouts, menu locations, terminology, and user interaction. Avoid presentations that require constant keyboard entry. It is a distraction from the engineering task-thought sequences, and it unnecessarily demands concentration and memory recall by the occasional user. Select a screen pointer device that does not require unnecessarily precise pointer positioning. A mouse is recommended. Use a color display with a program that allows user setup options for customizing the presentation. Follow the guidelines presented later for color assignment and coordination.

9. *The capability to communicate with other applications.* Look for features that allow one to import and export data with other applications. Seldom is the spreadsheet result used in an isolated context. Often it must be used for computation by another program and it may be incorporated in a report prepared with a word processor program. Look for dynamic data exchange as well as static exchange. Be sure that linkages to other documents are possible for merging of information and coordination of project type activity.

1.4 PREREQUISITES FOR USING A SPREADSHEET PROGRAM

We assume that the reader of this text has an engineering background, or at least a technical background, so as to recognize the context in which we discuss problem solution techniques. One must be able to project a spreadsheet feature into the application in order to use it. We intend to explain the feature; the reader will be expected to place it in context with little further discussion on our part.

We expect the reader to be familiar with the operation of a personal computer. Only basic operation is required for this book. But some knowledge of the computer directory structure and of file management techniques with basic commands is essential. The spreadsheet program must already be installed on the computer, or the reader must know how to install it. It is essential that one program in the spreadsheet language in order to learn it. Although one can engage in textbook-only study, learning comes quickest and the knowledge becomes permanent when the computer is used to learn the concepts.

With experience in using a program, one soon learns that a certain hardware complement is necessary for full use of the program and for acquiring skill in its use. For a spreadsheet, we recommend the following:

- The maximum high-speed memory recommended for the program by its developer.
- A color monitor.
- A mouse-pointing device.
- A coprocessor accelerator chip.
- A hard disk for storage of the program and related files.

1.5 WHY EXCEL?

We analyzed the available spreadsheet programs for features that meet the requirements of Section 1.3. The evolution of the program implies that only the most recent version of a program warrants consideration. We eliminated all programs but Microsoft® Excel. Even then, after working with it for a substantial time, we still discovered deficiencies in it. We mention them as we discuss the features.

Excel is an extensive program that shares at least one characteristic with all large computer programs, namely, that there are many details that qualify the range of application of the features. We do not attempt to describe all exceptions and special conditions under which a feature can be used. Instead, we rely on the reader consulting the Excel reference documentation for further information.

1.6 "WHAT IF" AND PRODUCTIVITY

The importance of the computer for engineering computation was established several decades ago. Numerous work procedures, computational algorithms, and hardware improvements are reflected in productivity achievements when using the computer. The user interface has improved so that the user can concentrate on application of problem solutions rather than on understanding how to use the computer. The graphical interface has been simplified and improved to allow complementary presentation insight. More than ever, the engineer now enjoys the opportunity to think creatively while at the computer rather than just reacting to cryptic passive-responses output by or expected as input to the computer. Emphasis has shifted to productive engineering time at the computer. The engineer is able to rapidly iterate the design cycles based on output from the computer.

Considerable insight into the problem solution is possible through these iterations. The iterations are often made for exploratory reasons, and thus they become part of a crude optimization effort. Were this effort to be systematized, a useful algorithmic approach would ensue that would cause convergence to an acceptable solution in a reduced time period and therefore lead to an increased productivity endeavor. Work of this kind is often called a "what if" analysis because one seeks answers to questions that arise after having obtained a solution, or an analysis is made to reveal the effects of our decisions. We try to gain intuition into our problem or to seek answers to questions we cannot provide purely by judgment. Unfortunately, the "what-if" analysis often becomes a cut-and-try procedure that does not follow a converging path. Convinced that there is already too much time and effort spent in pursuing cut-and-try analyses, we advocate instead an organized approach in which some effort is spent in determining the direction of the outcome and order-of-magnitude results first. Then the computer is used to provide accurate numerical confirmation, or not, of our investigative suspicion. Producing large volumes of numerical results without a converging process can easily overwhelm one and obscure the implications of the analyses. Therefore, in this text, our examples are prepared under this philosophy whenever a "what-if" analysis is suggested.

1.7 SYSTEM OF NOTATION USED IN THIS TEXT

Throughout the text, the typographic conventions of Table 1.1 are followed for the presentation and discussion of statement elements, function formats, formulae construction, keystroke combinations and sequences, and file references. This convention conforms to the Excel documentation for continuity to the extent that the feature appears in the documentation.

Examples:

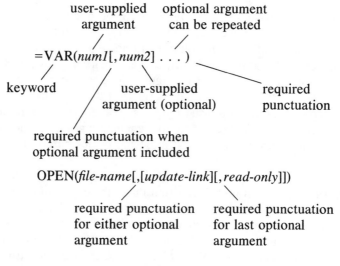

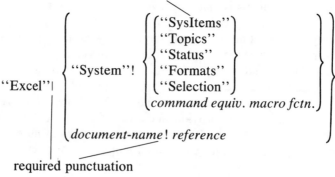

TABLE 1.1 TYPOGRAPHIC CONVENTIONS

Feature	Format
Keynames	Capital letters.
Key combinations	Two keys must be pressed simultaneously when their keynames are separated by a plus sign (+).
Key sequences	Two keys must be pressed in sequence when their keynames are separated by a comma.
Keywords (with preassigned meaning)	Capital letters, e.g., function names such as SQRT, EXP, etc.
User-supplied words for text and formulas	Lower case, with possibly upper case for selected letters when appearing in worksheet context. Italics, when appearing in statement format.
Punctuation and special characters	Essential where shown and must be included, except for the following: { } Choices in a required portion of a format are enclosed within braces. One and only one of the choices must be selected, the others omitted. [ ] Optional portions of a format are enclosed within brackets. These may be included or omitted as required to express the desired function. When choices are available within the optional portion, one and only one of the choices must be selected, the others omitted. All punctuation must be included.
Command references	Boldface, spelled and capitalized as appear in menu or dialog box.
Menu paths	Boldface, a sequence of commands, possibly separated by commas, as through a hierarchy of menus and/or dialog boxes.
Matrices	Boldface, upper case.
Vectors	Boldface, lower case.
. . . (ellipsis)	Preceding argument can be repeated.

BIBLIOGRAPHY

Chemical Engineering

[1] Cheng, S., "Trilinear diagram revisited: Application, limitation, and an electronic spreadsheet program," *Ground Water,* July/August 1988, pp. 505–510.

[2] El Shayal, I., "Rigorous engineering calculations on a spreadsheet," *Chem. Engrg.,* January 18, 1988, pp. 117–119.

[3] Ferrall, J. F., A. W. Pappano, and C. N. Jennings, "Process analysis on a spreadsheet," *Chem. Engrg.,* March 3, 1986, pp. 101–102, 104.

[4] Ghare, S. K., "Use of electronic spreadsheet in chemical engineering design calculations," *Proc. Annual Computer Aided Engrg. Conf.* (Atlanta, GA), June 16–20, 1985, pp. 704–706.

[5] Goldfarb, S. M., "Spreadsheets for chemical engineers: Design calculations," *Chem. Engrg.,* April 15, 1985, pp. 91–93.

[6] Grulke, E. A., "Using spreadsheets for teaching design," *Chem. Engrg. Ed.,* Summer 1986, pp. 128–131, 153.

[7] Heck, G. F., "Simulating feedback control," *Chem. Engrg.,* May 9, 1988, pp. 99–101.

[8] Hein, M., "Pipeline flow analyses employ spreadsheet concept," *Oil & Gas Journal,* February 11, 1985, pp. 68–70, 72–74.

[9] Hirschel, R., "Spreadsheets for chemical engineers: Solving differential equations by the relaxation method," *Chem. Engrg.,* April 15, 1985, pp. 93–94.

[10] Holmes, J. W., "Fluid-flow analysis with spreadsheets," *Chem. Engrg.,* December 19, 1988, pp. 166–168.

[11] Johnson, T. S., "How spreadsheets aid process and control engineering," *Hydrocarbon Proc.,* February 1985, pp. 61–63.

[12] Julian, F. M., "Flowsheets and spreadsheets," *Chem. Engrg. Prog.,* September 1985, pp. 35–39.

[13] Kauffman, J. M., "Chemistry calculations using MULTIPLAN and the Macintosh," *J. Computers in Math & Sci. Teaching,* Spring 1987, pp. 38–42.

[14] Schmidt, W. P., and R. S. Upadhye, "Material balances on a spreadsheet," *Chem. Engrg.,* December 24, 1984, pp. 67–68, 70.

[15] Selk, S., "Spreadsheet software solves engineering problems," *Chem. Engrg.,* June 27, 1983, pp. 51–53.

[16] Sowa, C. J., "Engineering calculations on a spreadsheet," *Chem. Engrg.,* March 2, 1987, pp. 61–63.

[17] Tucker, M. A., "Refinery spreadsheet highlights microcomputer process applications," *Oil & Gas Journal,* January 23, 1984, pp. 68–70, 73.

[18] White, J. R., "Use spreadsheets for better refinery operation," *Hydrocarbon Proc.,* October 1986, pp. 49–52.

Civil Engineering

[19] Anderson, M. L., et al., "Lotus 1-2-3 applications in civil engineering education," *Proc. 1988 Ann. ASEE Conf.* (Portland, OR), June 19–23, 1988, pp. 1516–1524.

[20] Brown, K. G., and A. D. Koussis, "Lotus spreadsheet design for storm drain network," *J. Computing in Civil Engrg.,* July 1987, pp. 197–213.

[21] Casas, A., "Spreadsheets: A new design tool," *Civil Engrg.,* December 1986, pp. 66–67.

[22] Chao, A. C., Y. Liu, and W. J. Rasdorf, "Spreadsheet approach for the design of air stripping of volatile organic contaminants (VOCs) from water," *Proc. 5th Conf. Computing in Civil Engrg.* (Alexandria, VA), March 29–31, 1988, pp. 731–741.

[23] Chong, A. K., and S. A. Veress, "Cost estimates of photogrammetric related ser-

vices using electronic spreadsheets," *Photogramm. Engrg. & Remote Sens.,* January 1988, pp. 47–50.

[24] Farid, F., "Sensitivity analysis of construction contract prices using spreadsheets," *J. Computing in Civil Engrg.,* July 1989, pp. 238–252.

[25] Harrison, C., "Spreadsheets for input and output," *Proc. 5th Conf. Computing in Civil Engrg.* (Alexandria, VA), March 29–31, 1988, pp. 693–699.

[26] Jewell, T. K., "Applications of the spreadsheet Multiplan and equation solver TK! Solver in civil engineering education," *Proc. Annual Computer Aided Engrg. Conf.* (Atlanta, GA), June 16–20, 1985, pp. 463–476.

[27] Kleiner, D. E., "Engineering with spreadsheets," *Civil Engrg,* October 1985, pp. 55–57.

[28] Lefter, J., and T. Bergin, "Structural analysis by spreadsheet," *Civil Engrg.,* May 1986, pp. 76–77.

[29] Malasri, S., and V. Chowdhary, "Prestressed concrete beam design using a spreadsheet program," *Proc. 1988 Ann. ASEE Conf.* (Portland, OR), June 19–23, 1988, pp. 1536–1540.

[30] Malasri, S., and S.-R. Syed-Mohammad-Ridzuan, "Education software development using spreadsheet program," *Int. J. Applied Engrg. Ed.,* v. 3, n. 1 (1987), pp. 55–58.

[31] Mortimer, K., "Spreadsheets ain't just for bean counters," *Proc. 1987 Ann. ASEE Conf.* (Reno, NV), June 21–25, 1987, pp. 1529–1533.

[32] Neis, M. E., J. M. Wigham, and V. V. Neis, "Macro-spreadsheet programming applied to well drawdown," *J. Computing in Civil Engrg.,* April 1988, pp. 121–135.

[33] Shoemaker, W. L., and S. Williams, "Prestressed concrete design using spreadsheets," *PCI Journal,* March/April 1988, pp. 110–129.

[34] Stiemer, S. F., and D. Lo, "Formatted spreadsheets for engineers," *Microcomputers in Civil Engrg.,* June 1988, pp. 145–156.

[35] Tootle, G., and K. Hatfield, "Spreadsheet applications to stormwater management," *Proc. 5th Conf. Computing in Civil Engrg.* (Alexandria, VA), March 29–31, 1988, pp. 700–709.

[36] Urzua, A., "One-dimensional rate of consolidation settlement using Lotus 1-2-3," *Proc. 5th Conf. Computing in Civil Engrg.* (Alexandria, VA), March 29–31, 1988, pp. 779–782.

[37] Yarmus, J. J., "Use of spread sheets in small firms," *J. Computing in Civil Engrg.,* July 1987, pp. 217–219.

[38] Yu, L. S., and T. S. Tisdale, "Application of Lotus Symphony in water quality modeling," *Proc. 4th Conf. Computing in Civil Engrg.* (Boston, MA), October 27–31, 1986, pp. 98–109.

Electrical Engineering

[39] Bredenkamp, G. L., "Use of spreadsheets in electrical engineering," *IEEE Cir. & Dev. Mag.,* September 1987, pp. 27–35.

[40] Cortesi, D. E., "Dr. Dobb's Clinic," *Dr. Dobb's Journal,* September 1983, pp. 12–14, 16. Simulation of digital logic circuits.

[41] Goodlet J., "Parametric electrical and mechanical design using an electronic spreadsheet," *Proc. Ann. ASEE Conf.* (Cincinnati, OH), June 23–26, 1986, pp. 152–157.

[42] Hills, A., "Use of a spreadsheet program in an antenna design application," *IEEE Trans. Ant. & Prop.,* April 1986, pp. 585–587.

[43] Huelsman, L. P., "Electrical engineering applications of microcomputer spreadsheet analysis programs," *IEEE Trans. Ed.,* May 1984, pp. 86–92.

[44] Linder, K. W., "MHD design exercise using spreadsheets," *Proc. 1988 Ann. ASEE Conf.* (Portland, OR), June 19–23, 1988, pp. 2146–2150.

[45] Lofy, F. J., "Design of electronic circuits using spreadsheet techniques," *Proc. 1988 Ann. ASEE Conf.* (Portland, OR), June 19–23, 1988, pp. 1567–1579.

[46] Monssen, F. J., "The use of the Visicalc spreadsheet in the analysis of the RC lead and lag networks," *CoEd,* April/June 1986, pp. 13–16.

[47] Nagurney, L. S., "Using a spreadsheet in receiver design," *CoEd,* October/December 1988, pp. 51–55.

[48] Oman, H., "Power budgets with a personal computer," *Proc. 21st Intersociety Energy Conversion Engrg. Conf.* (San Diego, CA), August 25–29, 1986, pp. 1690–1692.

[49] Peabody, F., D. W. Nyberg, and W. G. Dunford, "The use of a spreadsheet program to design motors on a personal computer," *IEEE Trans. Industry Appl.,* May/June 1987, pp. 520–525.

[50] Rao, N. D., "Microcomputer spreadsheet calculations for application in power systems," *IEEE Trans. Power Apparatus & Sys.,* September 1984, pp. 2537–2543.

[51] Rao, N. D., "Typical applications of microcomputer spreadsheets to electrical engineering problems," *IEEE Trans. Ed.,* November 1984, pp. 237–242.

Industrial Engineering

[52] Bankes, W. F., "Automated system for scheduling pipeline time for small batch production using a Symphony spreadsheet," *Computers & Ind. Engrg.,* v. 11, n. 1–4 (1986), Proc. 8th Ann. Conf. Computers & Ind. Engrg. (Orlando, FL), March 19–21, 1986, pp. 303–307.

[53] Bankes, W. F., "Automated system for machine tool capacity and utilization," *Computers & Ind. Engrg.,* v. 11, n. 1–4 (1986), Proc. 8th Ann. Conf. Computers & Ind. Engrg. (Orlando, FL), March 19–21, 1986, pp. 308–311.

[54] Chong, A. K., and S. A. Veress, "Cost estimates of photogrammetric related services using electronic spreadsheets," *Photogramm. Engrg. & Remote Sens.,* January 1988, pp. 47–50.

[55] Coleman, H. W., "A PC spreadsheet application for safety stock calculation," *Prod. & Inventory Mgmt. Journal,* 2nd qtr, 1987, pp. 110–116.

[56] De Lurgio, S. A., and J-G Zhao, "Teaching integrated production and information control system principles using a spreadsheet simulator," *Prod. & Inventory Mgmt. Journal,* 1st Qtr. 1989, pp. 29–35.

[57] Diaz, I., and S. Lezman, "Material handling simulation: Minimizing bottlenecks and improving product flow using Lotus 1-2-3," *Ind. Engrg.,* June 1988, pp. 40–46.

[58] Dix, R. C., "Electronic spreadsheets in manufacturing," *Production Engrg.,* April 1985, pp. 78–81.

[59] Earnest, D. L., "Capital equipment justification: A spreadsheet application template," *Computers & Ind. Engrg.,* v. 13 (1987), Proc. 9th Ann. Conf. Computers in Ind. Engrg. (Atlanta, GA), March 18–20, 1987, 341–345.

[60] Evans, J. R., "Spreadsheets and optimization: Complementary tools for decision making," *Prod. & Inventory Mgmt. Journal,* 1st qtr, 1986, pp. 36–46.

[61] Fargher, J. S. W., Jr., "Industrial engineering spreadsheet applications from a manufacturing resource planning (MRP-II) system," *Computers & Ind. Engrg.,* v. 13 (1987), Proc. 9th Ann. Conf. Computers in Ind. Engrg. (Atlanta, GA), March 18–20, 1987, pp. 100–106.

[62] Fields, F. E., "Industrial engineering use of a spreadsheet," *Computers & Ind. Engrg.,* v. 11, n. 1–4 (1986), Proc. 8th Ann. Conf. Computers & Ind. Engrg. (Orlando, FL), March 19–21, 1986, pp. 312–315.

[63] Godin, V. B., "Solving decision tree analysis using IFPS or Lotus," *Ind. Engrg.,* April 1987, pp. 20–21, 24–25, 27.

[64] Godin, V. B., and A. Rao, "Lotus 1-2-3 can produce dynamic graphic simulation without stops in the program." *Ind. Engrg.,* March 1988, pp. 42–43, 45–46.

[65] Graff, L., "Spreadsheet applications in benefit/cost analysis," *Computers & Ind. Engrg.,* v. 17 (1989), Proc. 11th Ann. Conf. Computers in Ind. Engrg. (Orlando, FL), March 15–17, 1989, pp. 293–297.

[66] Hamilton, W. R., and K. E. Rothe, "Computerized cost estimation spreadsheet and cost data for fusion devices," *Fusion Technology,* v. 8, n. 1, pt. 2(A), July 1985, Proc. 6th Topical Meet. on Tech. of Fusion Energy (San Francisco, CA), March 3–7, 1985, pp. 356–361.

[67] Hong, S., and J. Maleyeff, "Production planning and master scheduling with spreadsheets," *Prod. & Inventory Mgmt. Journal,* 1st qtr, 1987, pp. 46–54.

[68] Kennedy, S., and J. R. Martinez, "Spreadsheet application to labor determination," *Computers & Ind. Engrg.,* v. 13 (1987), Proc. 9th Ann. Conf. Computers in Ind. Engrg. (Atlanta, GA), March 18–20, 1987, pp. 317–318.

[69] Kleinfeld, I. H., "General purpose software adapted for IE applications," *Ind. Engrg.,* February 1984, pp. 18–20.

[70] Kuo, W., and R. Folkers, "Mini-micro computers: Spreadsheet programs solve systems dynamics problems," *Ind. Engrg.,* November 1986, pp. 24–26, 28–29, 31.

[71] Liu, M.C., "Using spreadsheet to teach on-line statistical process control," *Computers & Ind. Engrg.,* v. 17 (1989), Proc. 11th Ann. Conf. Computers in Ind. Engrg. (Orlando, FL), March 15–17, 1989, pp. 191–195.

[72] Lue, T.W., "Using integrated spreadsheets for production and facilities planning," *Computers & Ind. Engrg.,* v. 13 (1987), Proc. 9th Ann. Conf. Computers in Ind. Engrg. (Atlanta, GA), March 18–20, 1987, pp. 88–91.

[73] Martin, J., "Multi-machine assignment workload calculation sheet. A Lotus 1-2-3 program for calculation of randomly serviced multi-machine assignments for measured daywork systems," *Computers & Ind. Engrg.,* v. 11, n. 1–4 (1986), Proc. 8th Ann. Conf. Computers & Ind. Engrg. (Orlando, FL), March 19–21, 1986, pp. 346–350.

[74] Masri, S., and C. Moodie, "Using an electronic spreadsheet to analyze manufacturing flow systems," *Computers & Ind. Engrg.,* v. 9, n. 2 (1985), pp. 183–193.

[75] McDermott, K. J., "Microcomputer and spreadsheet software make time studies less tedious, more accurate," *Ind. Engrg.,* July 1984, pp. 78–81.

[76] Mendenhall, C. M., and G. E. Whitehouse, "Electronic spreadsheets ease microcomputer use for IE's," *Ind. Engrg.,* September 1984, pp. 22–24, 26.

[77] Morse, L., and G. E. Whitehouse, "Electronic spreadsheets evaluated for IE applications, Part 1 of 2," *Ind. Engrg.,* February 1985, pp. 17–18, 20–22, 24, 26, 28.

[78] Morse, L., and G. E. Whitehouse, "IEs must look at equipment, needs in choosing spreadsheets," *Ind. Engrg.,* March 1985, pp. 21–22, 24–31.

[79] Oden, H. W., "An interactive productivity measurement model using spreadsheet software," *Computers & Ind. Engrg.,* v. 11, n. 1–4 (1986), Proc. 8th Ann. Conf. Computers & Ind. Engrg. (Orlando, FL), March 19–21, 1986, pp. 325–329.

[80] Oden, H. W., "Developing flexible productivity measurement models using spreadsheet software," *Computers & Ind. Engrg.,* v. 14, n. 2 (1988), pp. 161–170.

[81] Parlar, M., "Dynamic programming on an electronic spreadsheet," *Computers & Ind. Engrg.,* v. 10, n. 3 (1986), pp. 203–213.

[82] Pemberton, R. G., "A Lotus 1-2-3 model for airline level of operations planning," *Computers & Ind. Engrg.,* v. 11, n. 1–4 (1986), Proc. 8th Ann. Conf. Computers & Ind. Engrg. (Orlando, FL), March 19–21, 1986, pp. 330–334.

[83] Rickles, H. V., and K. A. Elliott, "Spreadsheet programs enable quick custom analyses of material handling problems," *Ind. Engrg.,* February 1985, pp. 80–83, 85.

[84] Sitton, R. W., "How microcomputers and electronic spreadsheets can be used to educate industrial engineering students," *Computers & Ind. Engrg.,* v. 17 (1989), Proc. 11th Ann. Conf. Computers in Ind. Engrg. (Orlando, FL), March 15–17, 1989, pp. 175–179.

[85] Sounderpandian, J., "MRP on spreadsheets: A do-it-yourself alternative for small firms," *Prod. & Inventory Mgmt. Journal,* 2nd qtr, 1989, pp. 6–11.

[86] Taylor, D. D., "Using Lotus 1-2-3 to generate random numbers and record observations of a system," *Ind. Engrg.,* August 1987, pp. 46–47, 49–50, 52, 96.

[87] Terry, W. R., K. W. Cutright, and W. J. Herald, "Spreadsheet template approach for nonlinear regression estimation," *Computers & Ind. Engrg.,* v. 11, n. 1–4 (1986), Proc. 8th Ann. Conf. Computers & Ind. Engrg. (Orlando, FL), March 19–21, 1986, pp. 335–339.

[88] Trevino, J., and L. F. McGinnis, "Electronic spreadsheet implementation of a lot sizing procedure for a single-card kanban system," *Computers & Ind. Engrg.,* v. 11, n. 1–4 (1986), Proc. 8th Ann. Conf. Computers & Ind. Engrg. (Orlando, FL), March 19–21, 1986, pp. 340–345.

[89] White, B. E., "Using electronic spreadsheets to analyze real world capital expenditures," *Proc. Int. Ind. Engrg. Conf. & Societies' Mfgrg. & Productivity Symp.* (Toronto, Ont., Canada), May 14–17, 1989, pp. 99–104.

[90] Whitehouse, G. F., "Electronic spreadsheets and their applications," *Proc. Ann. Int. Ind. Engrg. Conf.* (Chicago, IL), May 6–10, 1984, pp. 57–63.

[91] Whitehouse, G. E., and G. W. Hodak, "A spreadsheet-based macro manpower

model," *Computers & Ind. Engrg.*, v. 11, n. 1–4 (1986), Proc. 8th Ann. Conf. Computers & Ind. Engrg. (Orlando, FL), March 19–21, 1986, pp. 316–320.

[92] Zimmerman, S. M., and D. R. Gibson, "A proposed method to use electronic spreadsheets to develop quality control charts, *Computers & Ind. Engrg.*, v. 17 (1989), Proc. 11th Ann. Conf. Computers in Ind. Engrg. (Orlando, FL), March 15–17, 1989, pp. 384–389.

Mechanical Engineering

[93] Cress, D., "Integrating spreadsheet modeling into a fluid mechanics course," *Proc. 1988 Ann. ASEE Conf.* (Portland, OR), June 19–23, 1988, pp. 2141–2145.

[94] Eid, J. C., "Spreadsheets for thermal analysis," *Machine Design,* October 23, 1986, pp. 121–125.

[95] Eid, J. C., "A methodology and tutorial for thermal modeling with PC spreadsheets," *Heat Transfer Engrg.*, v. 8, n. 2 (1987), pp. 95–107.

[96] Frielich, S. D., "Computer modeling helps choice of DC servo motors," *Robotics World,* August 1987, pp. 28–29.

[97] Gillett, J. E., "Better heat flow analysis on spreadsheets," *Machine Design,* January 12, 1989, pp. 127–132.

[98] Goodlet J., "Parametric electrical and mechanical design using an electronic spreadsheet," *Proc. 1986 Ann. ASEE Conf.* (Cincinnati, OH), June 23–26, 1986, pp. 152–157.

[99] Isakower, R. I., "Stress analysis with spreadsheets," *Machine Design,* July 23, 1987, pp. 120, 122.

[100] Palmer, M. E. III, M. G. Pecht, and J. V. Horan, "Adapting the spreadsheet to engineering problems," *Computers in Mech. Engrg.*, September 1985, pp. 49–56.

[101] Thompson, T. R., "Spreadsheet analysis of heat conduction problems," *Proc. 1987 Ann. ASEE Conf.* (Reno, NV), June 21–25, 1987, pp. 287–294.

[102] Thompson, T. R., "Spreadsheet analysis of heat conduction problems," *CoEd,* July/September 1988, pp. 47–51.

[103] Work, R. E., "Psychrometric analysis with an electronic spreadsheet," *Heating, Piping & Air Cond.*, February 1986, pp. 99–102.

Miscellaneous Engineering

[104] Conger, J. L., "Using financial tools for nonfinancial simulations," *BYTE,* January 1988, pp. 291–292, 294, 296. Poisson distribution in a Monte Carlo simulation.

[105] Croskey, C. L., "Spreadsheet illustration of engineering economics," *IEEE Trans. Ed.,* November 1988, pp. 270–275.

[106] Douglas, R. E., and G. E. Whitehouse, "Use of spreadsheets to evaluate the importance of competition in bidding for government contracts," *Proc. 1987 ASEE Ann. Conf.* (Reno, NV), June 21–25, 1987, pp. 107–111.

[107] Fetters, J. L., "Monitoring and forecasting spreadsheet for a large industrial facility," *Energy Engrg.*, August/September 1987, pp. 56–61.

[108] Finley, H. F., "Monitor maintenance performance with an electronic spreadsheet," *Hydrocarbon Proc.,* January 1985, pp. 66–68.

[109] Hannaford, B., "The electronic spreadsheet: A workstation front end for parallel processors," *Proc. COMPCON, Spring '86* (San Francisco, CA), March 3–6, 1986, pp. 316–321.

[110] Holm, R. A., "Personal microcomputers—the worksheet," *Tappi Journal,* May 1983, pp. 122–123.

[111] Holm, R. A., "Personal micros—the process flow as worksheet for a secondary fiber system," *Tappi Journal,* November 1983, pp. 92–93.

[112] Holm, R. A., "Personal micros—worksheet methods for process simulation," *Tappi Journal,* March 1984, pp. 106–107.

[113] Matheny, A., "Simulation with electronic spreadsheets," *BYTE,* March 1984, pp. 411–412, 414. Simulation with finite difference approximation.

[114] Mayer, R. H., "Spreadsheet simulation to enhance the ocean engineering design experience," *Proc. 1988 Ann. ASEE Conf.* (Portland, OR), June 19–23, 1988, pp. 2151–2153.

[115] Nicholas, K. W., "Designing cathodic protection systems using electronic spreadsheets," *Materials Performance,* September 1986, pp. 25–33.

[116] Pardoen, G. C., "SRS—Spreadsheet response spectrum," *J. Environmental Sci.,* September/October 1987, pp. 31–32.

[117] Robbins, R. M., "Using a computerized spreadsheet: Calculating the heating value of a waste," *Pollution Engrg.,* December 1987, pp. 58–60.

[118] Robbins, R. M., "Using a computerized spreadsheet: Part II—Cyclone separator design," *Pollution Engrg.,* March 1988, pp. 66–68.

[119] Rushton, J. D., "Microcomputer spreadsheet calculations for a bleach plant," *Tappi Journal,* August 1985, pp. 132–135.

[120] Soubra, D., "Link between measurement and spreadsheet," *IEEE Cir. & Dev. Mag.,* January 1988, pp. 66–67.

[121] Tan-atichat, J., "Spreadsheets: A new nontraditional engineering tool," *Int. J. Applied Engrg. Ed.,* v. 3, n. 6 (1987), pp. 551–558.

[122] Valstar, J. E., "Expert system development on a spreadsheet," *Proc NAECON 86: Nat. Aerospace Electronics Conf.* (Dayton, OH), May 19–23, 1986, pp. 1218–1225.

[123] Wells, H. A. Jr., M. R. Gordon-Clark, and G. Abbott, "Process simulation using spreadsheets," *Tappi Journal,* March 1986, pp. 98–101.

Mathematics and Science

[124] Barnes, S. J., "Automated plotting of geochemical data using the Lotus Symphony package," *Computers & Geosciences,* v. 14, n. 3, 1988, pp. 409–411.

[125] Benenson, G., "Using spreadsheet software to do math experiments in the classroom," *Proc. 1988 Ann. ASEE Conf.* (Portland, OR), June 19–23, 1988, pp. 654–659.

[126] Conger, J. L., "Using financial tools for nonfinancial simulations," *BYTE,* January 1988, pp. 291–292, 294, 296. Poisson distribution in a Monte Carlo simulation.

[127] Dory, R. A., "Spreadsheets for physics," *Computers in Phys.*, May/June 1989, pp. 70–74.

[128] Dory, R. A., "Matrices and contour plots," *Computers in Phys.*, May/June 1989, pp. 84–87.

[129] Dory, R. A., "Ordinary differential equations," *Computers in Phys.*, July/August 1989, pp. 88–91.

[130] Dory, R. A., and J. H. Harris, "Fourier analysis using a spreadsheet," *Computers in Phys.*, November/December 1988, pp. 83–86.

[131] Enloe, C. L., "Solving coupled, nonlinear differential equations with commercial spreadsheets," *Computers in Phys.*, January/February 1989, pp. 75–76.

[132] Eriksen, S. E., "Regression analysis using Lotus 1-2-3," *Collegiate Microcomputer*, November 1988, pp. 324–328.

[133] Eriksen, S. E., "Regression diagnostics using Lotus 1-2-3," *Collegiate Microcomputer*, February 1989, pp. 61–68.

[134] Ferrini-Mundy, J., and L. L. Zia, "Project calculate: Computer aided learning of calculus using spreadsheets," *Collegiate Microcomputer*, November 1989, pp. 300–304.

[135] Hagler, M., "Spreadsheet solution of partial differential equations," *IEEE Trans. Ed.*, August 1987, pp. 130–134.

[136] Hoffman, D. B., "The evaluation of forecasting models by using Lotus 1-2-3," *Collegiate Microcomputer*, v. 5, n. 2 (1987), pp. 165–173.

[137] Hsiao, F. S. T., "Micros in mathematics education—Uses of spreadsheets in CAL," *Int. J. Mathematical Ed. in Sci. & Tech.*, November/December 1985, pp. 705–713.

[138] Hsiao, F. S. T., "A computational design of some matrix iterative methods using spreadsheets," *Ind. Engrg.*, May 1987, pp. 17–18, 23–26.

[139] Hsiao, F. S. T., "Implementation of the Gauss-Jordan method of matrix inversion by spreadsheet macros," *Int. J. Mathematical Ed. in Sci. & Tech.*, September/October 1988, pp. 729–737.

[140] Hsiao, M. C. W., "Teaching regression analysis with spreadsheets," *J. Computers in Math. & Sci. Teaching*, Summer 1985, pp. 21–26.

[141] Joshi, B. D., "Lotus 1-2-3: A tool for scientific problem solving," *J. Computers in Math. & Sci. Teaching*, Winter 1986/1987, pp. 28–36.

[142] Kari, R., and Y. Dubreuil, "Use of a spreadsheet to collect large quantities of student experimental data," *J. Computers in Math. & Sci. Teaching*, Fall 1987/Winter 1987/1988, pp. 16–21.

[143] Kolodiy, G., "Studying projectile motion with a spreadsheet," *J. Computers in Math. & Sci. Teaching*, Summer 1987, pp. 40–42.

[144] Kuo, Y-L, and W. Kuo, "Application of electronic spreadsheets to linear and integer programming," *Int. J. Applied Engrg. Ed.*, v. 3, n. 6 (1987), pp. 563–575.

[145] Landram, F. G., J. R. Cook, and M. Johnston, "Spreadsheet calculations of probabilities from the F, t, χ^2, and normal distribution," *Comm. of ACM*, November 1986, pp. 1090–1092.

[146] Lee, P., "Lotus 1-2-3 model generates normal random numbers," *Ind. Engrg.*, December 1988, pp. 16–18.

[147] Misner, C. W., "Spreadsheets tackle physics problems," *Computers in Phys.*, May/June 1988, pp. 37–41.

[148] Pardoen, G. C., "Spreadsheeting power spectral density calculations," *J. Environmental Sci.*, July/August 1987, pp. 26–29.

[149] Silvert, W., "Teaching ecological modeling with electronic spreadsheets," *Collegiate Microcomputer*, May 1984, pp. 129–133.

[150] Treat, C. H., "Using spreadsheets to teach finite-differences," *Proc. 1987 Ann. ASEE Conf.* (Reno, NV), June 21–25, 1987, pp. 1051–1057.

[151] Treat, C. H., "Using spreadsheets to teach finite-differences," *CoEd*, July/September 1988, pp. 12–19.

[152] Watkins, W., and M. Taylor, "A spreadsheet in the mathematics classroom," *Collegiate Microcomputer*, August 1989, pp. 233–239.

[153] Wells, G., and C. Berger, "Teacher/student-developed spreadsheet simulations: A population growth example," *J. Computers in Math. & Sci. Teaching*, Winter 1985/1986, pp. 34–40.

Engineering Education

[154] Basu, P. K., A. D. Koussis, and N. B. Fancher, "Role of spreadsheets in computer aided course development," *Proc. 1987 Ann. ASEE Conf.* (Reno, NV), June 21–25, 1987, pp. 1990–1997.

[155] Baxter, H. R., and E. F. McBrien, "Grading using Lotus 1-2-3 and the IBM/PC," *CoEd*, April/June 1988, pp. 27–30.

[156] Genalo, L. J., and B. R. Dewey, "Spreadsheets for engineering freshmen," *Proc. 1988 Ann. ASEE Conf.* (Portland, OR), June 19–23, 1988, pp. 1138–1141.

[157] Huelsman, L. P., "Electrical engineering applications of microcomputer spreadsheet analysis programs," *IEEE Trans. Ed.*, May 1984, pp. 86–92.

[158] Malasri, S., "Student advising using spreadsheet program," *Int. J. Applied Engrg. Ed.*, v. 3, n. 6 (1987), pp. 559–562.

[159] Schalkoff, R. J., "A note on the effective use of PC-based spreadsheets for course grading," *IEEE Trans. Ed.*, February 1986, pp. 42–45.

[160] Ward, T. L., "Spreadsheet software: Puissance in practice," *Proc. 1987 Ann. ASEE Conf.* (Reno, NV), June 21–25, 1987, pp. 104–106.

[161] Ward, T. L., "Spreadsheet software: Puissance in practice," *CoEd*, July/September 1988, pp. 101, 104.

[162] Wiggins, E. C., "A spreadsheet based electronic gradebook," *CoEd*, January/March 1986, pp. 24–27.

[163] Wiggins, E. C., "The electronic spreadsheet gradebook—an update," *CoEd*, October/December 1987, pp. 26–28.

CHAPTER 2

Basic Computation

The material in this chapter is fundamental to the remainder of the text. It includes an introduction to the spreadsheet. An example is presented on how to read a simple spreadsheet before anything at all is described about the spreadsheet. This is to demonstrate the ease with which spreadsheets can be understood. This chapter includes terminology on spreadsheets, procedures for creating new spreadsheets, and a discussion on entering data into them.

We begin with the application of spreadsheets to simple formulas. Simple, as used here, merely means that computation is performed using the basic arithmetic operators only. We describe the various parts of a formula and the mechanics of constructing formulas, and provide information on understanding the spreadsheet computational process. Finally, we discuss how to verify a spreadsheet by testing it, how to debug it, and how to obtain a printed listing of the results.

The material to be described provides comprehensive coverage of a spreadsheet from a beginner's viewpoint. It is basic to the remainder of the text and must be thoroughly understood.

Upon completing the material in this chapter, the reader should feel comfortable using a spreadsheet to solve simple formulas. We introduce mathematical functions and other mathematical topics later.

2.1 EXAMPLE

Example 2.1: A Simple Formula

In this example, we compute the dc resistance of an aluminum strand of wire in an electrical cable consisting of aluminum strands over a steel stranded core. The formula below ignores the conductance of the steel core but includes the effect of the

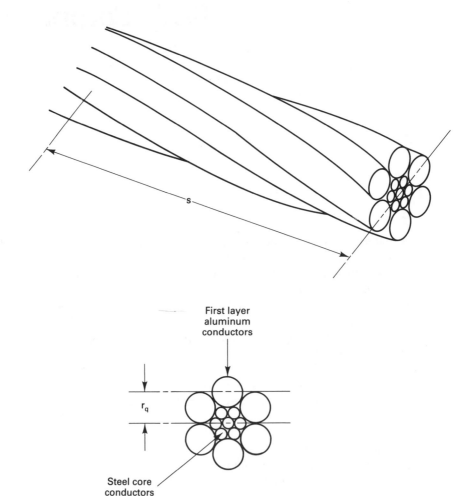

$$r_{dc} = \frac{5280\,\rho}{A}\sqrt{1 + \left(\frac{2\pi r_q}{s}\right)^2}$$

r_q = radius of centers of strands in layer
s = length of lay (in same units as r_q)
ρ = resistivity in (ohm-cir mil)/ft at 25° C
A = area of aluminum conductor in cir mils

Figure 2.1 Construction of stranded electrical cable.

	A	B
1	rho	17.07
2	area	44478.66842
3	dia ctr	0.4221
4	s	7.91
5		
6	rdc	2.054633234

Figure 2.2 Example 2.1 spreadsheet results.

helical lay of the aluminum conductor. The construction of the cable is shown in Figure 2.1, where a single layer of aluminum strands is shown.

The formula for a single strand of the aluminum conductor, in ohms per mile at 25°C, is also given in Figure 2.1. For a cable constructed as shown in the figure, where there are 7 steel strands and 6 aluminum strands, we could have the following values for the variables:

diameter of centers of the strands in the layer = .4221 in.

diameter of the aluminum strands = .2109 in.

length of helical lay = 7.91 in.

resistivity = 17.07 (ohm-cir mil)/ft

The cable, of about 270,000 cir mils, will carry about 480 amps at 100°C at 60 Hz.

A solution using the Microsoft® Excel spreadsheet program is shown in Figure 2.2. It consists of text (entries in cells A1 through A6), numerical input values (entries in cells B1, B3, and B4), and the solution (value in cell B6). The result, r_{dc} = 2.0546 ohms, can easily be verified by hand computation. Blank cells (A5, B5) are allowed in the cell area within which computations appear. We also must enter the formula. It is shown in cell B6 in Figure 2.3, which is a printout of formulas for this example. One other formula, in cell B2, converts wire area from square inches to circular mils (1 cir mil = 0.0000007854 sq in.). The values in cells B1, B3, and B4 are constants.

The spreadsheet program computes values for formulas. In the formula for r_{dc} (cell B6 of Figure 2.3), we have constants (5280, 2, 3.14159, .5), operators (+, *, /, ^), and memory locations (cells) within which variable values are found. The cells are specified by their column and row coordinate designators. For example, the value for rho is referenced by its cell coordinates (cell B1) as are the area (cell B2), the conductor center diameter (cell B3), and the lay length (cell B4). We use coordinate

	A	B
1	rho	17.07
2	area	=3.14159*0.2109^2/(4*0.0000007854)
3	dia ctr	0.4221
4	s	7.91
5		
6	rdc	=5280*B1/B2*(1+(2*3.14159*B3/2/B4)^2)^0.5

Figure 2.3 Example 2.1 spreadsheet formulas.

references only in Chapter 2. Beginning in Chapter 3, we use names for the locations of variable values.

The objective in constructing a formula for spreadsheet computation is to assemble constants, operators, and memory references on one line in spreadsheet syntax so that the desired computation is correctly performed. Parentheses are used for grouping purposes. For now, it suffices to associate the mathematical representation with its spreadsheet equivalent as follows:

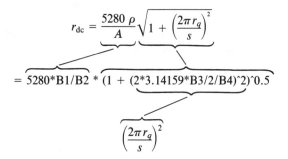

Multiplication is designated with the asterisk (*), division with the slash (/), and exponentiation with the caret (^). Our objective for the moment is to exhibit the readability of simple spreadsheet formulas. It suffices, then, to settle for mere identification of the components within the formula. A full explanation of the computation procedure for this formula is given in Section 2.3.

2.2 SPREADSHEET BASICS

This section includes an introduction to the spreadsheet window, descriptions of mouse and keyboard use, a discussion on selecting cells and making entries (except for formulas, which are described in Section 2.3), and a description of some basic commands. Although the Microsoft® Excel spreadsheet is illustrated, the discussion applies to other manufacturers' spreadsheets with minor modification.

2.2.1 The Spreadsheet Window and Workspace

Figure 2.4 shows the Excel spreadsheet window, hereafter referred to as the Excel window. It is organized with a menu bar across the top, with a combined reference area and formula bar immediately below the menu bar, a status bar across the bottom, and a large workspace just above the status bar. For the moment, we limit our discussion to a second window, the worksheet window, that occupies the workspace as shown in the figure. We later introduce other types of windows for the work space.

The worksheet window is a rectangular structure organized into cells, each of which is at the intersection of a column (labeled alphabetically) with a row (labeled numerically). Usually, a grid is made visible to delineate the cells. A

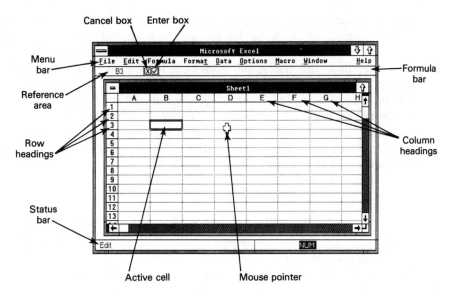

Figure 2.4 Excel spreadsheet window.

selected cell is referred to as an *active cell*. It is highlighted with a bold border for its cell outline. The one shown in Figure 2.4 is cell B3, named by virtue of the column and row intersection from which it is formed. Entries will be placed in chosen cells on the basis of the application problem needs. For Excel, the maximum size of the array of cells is 256 columns by 16,384 rows. Column labeling is with double letters after the first 26 columns. For now, the important parts of the worksheet window are the column and row headings, the array of cells, and the active cell identification.

The Excel window, occupying the entire screen, enables us to direct spreadsheet activities via menu commands. We monitor our dialog with messages in the reference area, formula bar, and the status bar. When menu commands are chosen, drop-down menus appear from which further commands can be executed. These commands are described in this text as the need arises. The reference area shows the cell address, or addresses for multiple cell selection, of the active cell. The formula bar displays the formula in the active cell. It is useful for monitoring the progress of formula entry and for inspection purposes and is further described in Section 2.3. The status bar displays messages identifying the state of the spreadsheet, errors, and the like.

2.2.2 Creating a New Spreadsheet and Entering Data

On entering the spreadsheet program, we find the worksheet cells empty. We have a choice of beginning a new worksheet, which we are about to do, or requesting the retrieval of another one we have saved. A new worksheet lies in the workspace and appears as shown in Figure 2.4, where it is named Sheet1. We have the option of changing this name, which we will do in Section 2.2.3.

The empty worksheet is ready to be used. We will select cells into which we will enter data and ready the worksheet for the formulas to be prepared and entered as described in Section 2.3. For interaction, we prefer to use the mouse for the reasons given in Chapter 1. Keyboard-only interaction is always possible, however. A brief introduction to the mouse, its operation, and the cursor shapes is given in the box on page 25 entitled Mouse Operation. Assuming this box has been read, we proceed with the worksheet development. A keyboard interaction procedure will also be described for this task.

To select a cell, we do either of the following:

Mouse action	Keyboard action
• Position the insertion pointer at the desired location, then click.	• Use the arrow keys to select the cell to edit.
• Type the edit: backspace to delete, character keys to enter.	• Press F2 (function key 2) to activate the formula bar.
• Click the enter box to complete the change.	• Move the insertion pointer with the left/ right arrow keys to the desired location.
	• Type the edit: backspace to delete, character keys to enter.
	• Press ENTER to complete the change.

We can enter as many as 255 characters per cell in Excel. Should we change our mind about the contents of a cell, or should we wish to correct an entry, we can perform simple editing as follows:

Mouse action	Keyboard action
• Move the pointer to the desired cell then click. It becomes the active cell.	• Use the up, down, left, and right arrow keys to move to the cell to be made active.
• Type the desired data with the keyboard. Watch the characters appear in both the cell and the formula bar. The insertion pointer moves as characters are entered to show where the next character will go. Use the backspace key to erase characters.	• Type the data to be entered. See the corresponding step for mouse action.
• When finished, click the enter box. The data is now entered in the cell. If the data is not to be entered, click on the cancel box. The data is cleared from the formula bar and active cell.	• When finished, press the ENTER key to enter the data into the cell. Press the ESCAPE key to clear the data from the formula bar and active cell.

MOUSE OPERATION

The mouse is a small hand-held input device that is used to control the position of a pointer on the screen. It operates on an optical or a mechanical principle. It is grasped palm down and moved over a flat surface, after which at least one of its buttons is pressed to activate a function as directed by the program using the mouse.

Excel is controlled by only one mouse button, the left one for a multiple-button mouse. When pressed, hereafter referred to as *clicked*, a programmed action takes place. This may be a menu entry selection, a cursor positioning action, a window controlling movement, or the like. The mouse may be moved while a button is held down, an action called *dragging*. It may also have to be clicked twice in rapid succession, an action called *double clicking*.

The cursor controlled by the mouse is moved on the screen in a direction corresponding to the direction the sensing element of the mouse is moved. This movement usually conforms with the orientation of the mouse when held in a natural position with the fingers on its buttons, that is, it moves left when the mouse is moved left, and so on. If the motion of the mouse is restricted to a small area, it may be lifted, moved back, placed down again, and moved again to create the effect of a long continuous movement. Usually, the pointer is disturbed only slightly by this action.

Numerous pointer shapes are used by Excel. The commonly appearing shapes are shown below. They are each described in this chapter in the context of their use. The hourglass shape, not shown here, appears when Excel is busy. Its meaning is to wait until Excel is finished.

Pointer shape	Meaning
⌖	Click to select menu choices and window functions.
⌖	Click to select cell or drag to select range of cells.
I	Click to position insertion point in string of characters, such as in the formula bar.
⇳	Drag to vary the height of a row.
⇔	Drag to vary the width of a column.

We can now make simple entries in the worksheet cells. Because we haven't yet discussed the entry of formulas, the data we may enter would be text. The text is useful to us because it allows our worksheet to be commented. The entries in column A of Figures 2.2 and 2.3 are text data. The text is not used for computation, but it does help us identify the meaning of the adjacent numerical values.

2.2.3 Important Basic Worksheet Commands

The purpose of this section is to introduce some basic commands in order to become functional with Excel immediately. We describe the commands to start a new worksheet, to open existing worksheets, to save worksheets for use in other Excel sessions, to delete and close worksheets, and to exit the Excel program.

The procedure for the above-mentioned tasks is to first choose **File** from the menu bar, then to make a selection from the drop-down menu, and perhaps to complete a pop-up dialog box. Menu bar and drop-down menu entries chosen are displayed in inverse video. Figure 2.5(a) shows the drop-down menu. The contents of this menu are actually context dependent, but the menu shown in the figure contains all of the choices we need now. Some of these choices, the commands followed by ellipsis (. . .), produce pop-up dialog boxes in which further information is given or in which a selection must be made from choices. See the box titled The Dialog Box on page 28 for further information on its use.

File New

   This command, via its dialog box of Figure 2.5(b), is used to create an empty worksheet. We choose **Worksheet,** then **OK,** and proceed as when we first enter the Excel program.

File Open

   This command, via its dialog box of Figure 2.5(c), is used to open an existing worksheet. We enter its name in the **File Name** box either by typing it in or by choosing its name from the **Files** display box. It may be necessary to specify a different directory to retrieve the worksheet by first selecting an entry from the **Directories** box, then selecting **OK** (selecting [. .] takes us to the preceding level of the directory). By this means, we can traverse the directory structure as we wish. By default, Excel assigns type .XLS to worksheet files. Optionally, to display just those names whose type is .XLS, we use the wildcard (*) and type *.XLS in the **File Name** box. We then choose a file name from among those in the list. When we select **OK,** the chosen worksheet is displayed on the screen. We can double-click on the entries with the mouse and thus eliminate the need for selecting **OK.**

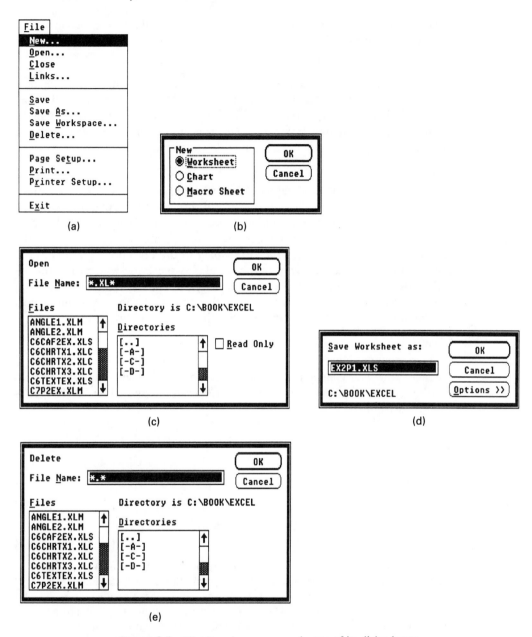

Figure 2.5   File drop-down menu and some of its dialog boxes.

File Save

This command saves changes made to the active worksheet under the same name in which it was opened. The worksheet remains open and ready for use. This command is useful for saving the worksheet as progress is being made on its development in order to have a copy available in case the one on the screen becomes lost or corrupted for any reason.

File Save As

This command, via its dialog box of Figure 2.5(d), is used to save new worksheets or new versions of existing ones. One must type the new name in the dialog box and select **OK.** The worksheet's current name will be displayed in the dialog box. Overtype this name with a new one before selecting **OK.** The worksheet is saved in the current directory.

File Delete

This command, via its dialog box of Figure 2.5(e), is used to delete files from the disk. The names of files in the current directory appear in the **Files** list box. The file to be deleted is either typed in the **File Name** box or selected from the **Files** list. It may be necessary to specify a directory from the **Directories** box to locate the files to display in the **Files** box. Optionally, to display just those names whose type is .XLS, we use the wildcard as for the **File Open** command. When we select **OK,** the chosen file is deleted from the disk. Because we cannot reverse the action of the command, Excel prompts for confirmation of the deletion in another dialog box.

File Close

This command closes the active worksheet. Should it contain unsaved changes, the user is prompted for confirmation to save with changes, to save without the changes, or to cancel the **Close** command. The worksheet is removed from the screen.

THE DIALOG BOX

Choices from the menu bar in Excel produce drop-down menus which often reveal further commands to choose from. Some of these command names are followed by ellipsis (. . .). Choosing one of these commands produces a pop-up dialog box, in which further information must be entered or additional choices selected in order to complete the command. One such box appears below, for which the various parts of the dialog box are identified. We have the list box (a list of choices for a command), the text box (in which information is entered for the command), the check box (a toggle for turning an option on or off), the option button (a toggle for selecting from among related choices), and the command button (for carrying out a command, that may lead to another dialog box).

Action	Mouse	Keyboard
Choose in a list box	Click on the choice. If necessary, click on arrow box to scroll, or drag box in scroll bar.	Tab to desired list box. Press ALT+*key* for underlined letter or number of choice (*key* toggles choice on or off). Use arrow keys to scroll within the box.
Edit in text box	Click for insertion point position, edit as in formula bar.	Tab to desired text box. Position insertion point with arrow keys, edit as in formula bar.
Toggle check box	Click on the box.	Tab to desired check box. Use arrow keys or press ALT+*key* for underlined letter.
Select option button	Click on the box.	Tab to desired option button. Press ALT+*key* for under-lined number or letter.
Execute command	Click on the button.	Tab to desired command button. Press ALT+*key* for under-lined letter.
Choose OK or Cancel	Click on the desired button.	Press ENTER for OK, ESCAPE for Cancel.

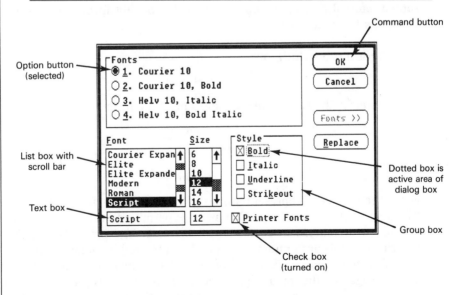

Command button

Option button
(selected)

List box with
scroll bar

Text box

Fonts
◉ 1. Courier 10
○ 2. Courier 10, Bold
○ 3. Helv 10, Italic
○ 4. Helv 10, Bold Italic

OK
Cancel
Fonts >>
Replace

Font   Size   Style
Courier Expan 6   ☒ Bold
Elite   8   ☐ Italic
Elite Expande 10   ☐ Underline
Modern   12   ☐ Strikeout
Roman   14
Script   16

Script   12   ☒ Printer Fonts

Dotted box is
active area of
dialog box

Group box

Check box
(turned on)

File Exit

This command ends the Excel session. Should the worksheet contain un-saved changes, the user is prompted for confirmation to save the changes, to save without the changes, or to cancel the **Exit** command. The user is re-turned to the operating system.

2.3 SIMPLE FORMULAS

An arithmetic formula in a spreadsheet context is the equal sign and the right-hand side of a mathematical formula written to accurately express the mathematical meaning in the symbols of the spreadsheet language and contained on one line. The equivalent of the variable on the left-hand side of a mathematical formula is the cell in which the formula is contained. The result of a computation becomes the value of the cell. A formula is constructed in the formula bar and stored in a cell.

2.3.1 Parts of a Formula

The formula always begins with the equal sign (=). The expression that follows it is composed of a sequence of constants, cell references, arithmetic operators, parentheses, or functions.

Numerical constants may be represented in either integer or real-number form, since the spreadsheet does not differentiate between the two number forms and treats all constants as real floating-point quantities. That is, they are repre-sented internally in signed coefficient and exponent form. Allowed formats for constants are as follows:

Signed magnitude only.

$$[\pm]\ coeff$$

where *coeff* is the real or integer constant of the form

$$n$$
$$n.$$
$$.m$$
$$n.m$$

and where *n* and *m* represent strings of decimal digits for the integral part and fractional part, respectively. Commas are permitted in the strings of digits. We will not use commas in constants of this text. The brackets indicate that the polarity symbols are optional except when required by actual value.

Constants may include a + or − sign as a unary operator. When the con-stant is negative, the minus sign is required. If no sign is present, the constant is assumed to be positive. Leading zeros before the decimal point for numbers less than 1 are optional, as are trailing zeros following the last nonzero digit to the right of the decimal point. Constants may also be replaced by scalar variables (names, in spreadsheet terminology) as described in Chapter 3.

Examples:

Valid: 413
2.81
-1.9066
0.00002
$-.0607$
$+55$
-239.0
61,420

Exponential form.

$$[\pm]coeff\ E[\pm]exp$$

where *coeff* = real constant of the form

n.
.m
n.m

$$exp = n \text{ (exponent, integer only)}$$

All comments following the signed magnitude description also apply to the exponential form. The exponential form represents a constant (the coefficient) multiplied by 10 raised to an integer constant (the exponent) where 10 is replaced by the letter E and the multiplication is implied. The following illustrates the conversion.

$$-3,415,000 = -34.15 \times 10^5 = -34.15E5$$

$$0.00000737 = 7.37 \times 10^{-6}\ \ = 7.37E-6$$

Examples:

Valid:	15.8E-6	$=$ 0.0000158
	.619E5	= 61,900
	920.E-7	= .000092
	7.22E05	= 722,000
	$-.296E+06$	= $-296,000$
	$-176.E-08$	= -0.00000176
	$+82.E+05$	= 8,200,000
Invalid:	6193E-2	No decimal point in coefficient
	$-.0027E3.$	Decimal point in exponent

The exponential form is recommended only for numbers greater than 100,000 or less than 0.00001, since it is difficult to construct (mathematical conversion is necessary and varied characters are used) and since it leads to errors in reading (mathematical conversion is necessary and character combination is confusing). It is used to advantage when large numbers contain many following zeros before the decimal point and when very small numbers contain many leading zeros after the decimal point.

Arithmetic operators are special characters used as binary (requiring two operands) or unary (requiring a single operand) operators in arithmetic expressions. The following is a selection of Excel arithmetic operators:

Symbol	Binary operation	Unary operation
^	Exponentiation	
/	Division	
*	Multiplication	
+	Addition	
−	Subtraction	Negation

Arithmetic expressions.   An arithmetic expression may consist of a single simple operand, such as a constant or cell reference, or it may consist of a collection of operands separated by arithmetic operators. An expression may never contain adjacent operators or adjacent operands.

Single constants or cell references are expressions that may appear by themselves as the expression in a formula. Here are some examples.

$$= 4.78$$
$$= C13$$
$$= -R6$$

In the first formula, the value +4.78 is assigned as the value of the cell. When the second formula is executed, the current value of cell C13 is assigned as the value of the cell containing this formula. The third formula indicates that the negative of the current value of cell R6 is to become the new value of the cell containing this formula.

Constants and simple cell references may be combined with arithmetic operators to form more complex expressions as follows:

$$= A1 + .119 - C15/36$$
$$= 3.3*X5^2 + 1.06*X5 - 4$$

In the first formula, the value of C15 will be divided by 36, and this result will be subtracted from the sum of 0.119 and the value of cell A1. The final value will then be assigned to the cell containing this formula. If C15 = 72 and A1 = −6.3, then the containing cell is assigned the value −8.181. Note that integer and real numbers may be mixed in an expression. The second formula is in the form of a

TABLE 2.1

Operator	Priority
^	1 (highest)
*, /	2
+, −	3 (lowest)

quadratic equation as follows:

$$y = ax^2 + bx + c$$

Also, note that multiplication is never implied but always requires use of the multiplication symbol.

The order of evaluation of an expression is governed by the hierarchy of arithmetic operators and proceeds from left to right among operations of the same priority as modified by use of parentheses. The hierarchy is given in Table 2.1. This hierarchy will be expanded in Chapter 3 to include functions and in later chapters to include logical operators. For the quadratic form shown above, the evaluation would proceed as follows (the W_i indicate intermediate evaluation results):

$$
\begin{aligned}
\text{value} &= 3.3*X5^2 + 1.06*X5 - 4 \\
&= 3.3*W_1 + 1.06*X5 - 4 \\
&= W_2 + 1.06*X5 - 4 \\
&= W_2 + W_3 - 4 \\
&= W_4 - 4 \\
&= W_5 \quad \text{(evaluation completed)}
\end{aligned}
$$

The order of evaluation may be modified with parentheses. Although parentheses are not operators, they override the precedence order and function as if they had a priority higher than any operator. Note the differences in the following, where X1, Y1 and Z1 are cell references:

Algebraic notation	Suitable Excel formula
$w = \dfrac{xz}{y}$	= X1/Y1*Z1
$w = \dfrac{xz}{y}$	= (X1*Z1)/Y1
$w = \dfrac{x}{yz}$	= X1/(Y1*Z1)
$w = \dfrac{x}{yz}$	= X1/Y1/Z1

The second formula requires that X1*Z1 be evaluated prior to the division. The third formula requires that Y1*Z1 be evaluated prior to the division. We cannot substitute brackets [ ] or braces { } for parentheses.

Parentheses are required where shown in the following examples, where cell references are implied in the expressions:

Algebraic notation	Excel formula
$l = \dfrac{ij + k}{h}$	= (I2*J2 + K2)/H2
$b = (x + y)(w - v)$	= (X4 + Y4)*(W4 − V4)
$k = \dfrac{d}{-f}$	= D3/(−F3)
$r = a + \dfrac{b + d}{c}$	= A1 + (B1 + D1)/C1
$r = a + \dfrac{b}{c + d}$	= A1 + B1/(C1 + D1)
$s = \dfrac{t^{k+1}}{w}$	= T3^(K3 + 1)/W3
$g = t^{k/w}$	= T5^(K5/W5)
$f = (a + b - c)^3$	= (A7 + B7 − C7)^3

Expressions may be nested within other expressions by enclosing them within parentheses. The evaluation of nested expressions begins with the innermost expression and progresses outward. Evaluation of an expression is always from left to right and according to the operator hierarchy rule unless modified by parentheses. Following are examples of nested expressions, where cell references are implied in the expression:

Algebraic notation	Excel formula
$h = \dfrac{r}{g + k(x - y)}$	= R2/(G2 + K2*(X2 − Y2))
$m = \dfrac{p + \dfrac{q}{a - b}}{xy - z}$	= (P4 + Q4/(A4 − B4))/(X4*Y4 − Z4)
$y = a + bx + cx^2 + dx^3 + ex^4$	= A1 + X1*(B1 + X1*(C1 + X1*(D1 +E1*X1)))

The second formula will be evaluated as follows, where the W_i indicate intermediate evaluation results:

$$\begin{aligned}
\text{value} &= (P4 + Q4/(A4 - B4))/(X4*Y4 - Z4) \\
&= (P4 + Q4/W_1)/(X4*Y4 - Z4) \\
&= (P4 + W_2)/(X4*Y4 - Z4) \\
&= W_3/(W_4 - Z4) \\
&= W_3/W_5 \\
&= W_6 \quad \text{(evaluation completed)}
\end{aligned}$$

Redundant sets of parentheses, those not used for altering operator precedence or for changing the result of a computation, may be used to effect program clarity and understanding.

2.3.2 Mechanics of Constructing Formulas

The procedure for preparing the formula for a cell is to activate the cell, type the formula in the formula bar, then select the enter box in the formula bar.

When a cell is activated by choosing it (made visible because it is surrounded by a dotted outline), the word Enter is displayed in the status bar at the bottom of the worksheet, signifying that the worksheet is in the enter mode. Simultaneously, the formula bar is activated and the chosen cell number appears in the reference area of the formula bar. Formula entry begins by pressing the "=" key. The symbol appears in the formula bar and in the chosen cell.

Action within the formula bar is limited to entering and editing, or correcting, formula characters and symbols. The formula is typed, beginning from the equal sign and progressing to its end. Mouse and keyboard procedures are as follows:

Action	Mouse	Keyboard
Activate the cell	Click on it	Use arrow keys to position the bold box outline on the cell
Begin formula entry	Type "="	Type "="
Continue entry	Type remainder of formula	Type remainder of formula
Make corrections	Click to position insertion point cursor, then delete and/or enter desired characters	Position insertion point cursor with arrow keys, then delete and/or enter desired characters
Enter formula	Click on enter box	Press ENTER key

If, before entry, it is determined that the formula is not wanted in that cell, it can be canceled by clicking on the cancel box (mouse) or pressing the ESCAPE key (keyboard). This action restores the previous contents of the formula bar. If the formula has already been entered, an edit menu selection is needed to undo the entry. Editing a formula in this manner is discussed in Chapter 3.

Additional techniques for working in the formula bar are shown in the following table. Excel must be in the edit mode to conduct the actions, that is, Edit must appear in the status bar.

Action	Mouse	Keyboard
Turn on edit mode	Click in the formula bar	Press F2
Move character positions left or right	Click to position the insertion point cursor	Use arrow keys
Move one word left or right	"	CTRL+arrow keys
Move to beginning of line	"	Press HOME
Move to end of line	"	Press END
Select characters	Drag through the desired characters	SHIFT+arrow keys
Select word	Double click the desired word	SHIFT+CTRL+arrow keys

A combination of mouse and keyboard techniques is often found useful when working with formulas.

Example 2.2

Given the formula

$$w = ax - \frac{42.81x^2 + c}{\sqrt{b^2 - \sqrt[3]{a}}}$$

where the value for a is in cell B3, b in C9, c in B6, and x in B4. The correct formula is

$$= B3*B4 - (42.81*B4^2 + B6)/(C9^2 - B3^{(1/3)})^.5$$

However, assume the following was typed in the formula bar and has not yet been entered:

$$= \underbrace{B33}*B4 \underset{\uparrow}{+} \underbrace{(4.281}*C9^2 + \underbrace{B6}/C9^2 - \underbrace{B3^1/3})^.5$$
$$\quad 1 \qquad 2 \quad 3 \qquad 4 \qquad 5 \qquad 6$$

Sight checking shows errors at locations 1 through 6 as marked. We proceed with the corrections.

1. Remove one of the 3's by (mouse) relocating the insertion pointer to either of the 3's and pressing the DELETE key or (by keyboard) relocating the insertion pointer with arrow keys and pressing the DELETE key.
2. Delete the plus sign and replace it with a minus sign by (mouse) relocating the insertion pointer to immediately follow the + sign, then pressing the BACKSPACE and − keys in sequence or (by keyboard) relocating the cursor on the + sign, then pressing the DELETE and − keys in sequence.
3. Remove the ".2" characters and reenter them in the correct order by (mouse) selecting both characters with the drag motion, pressing DELETE and reentering the two characters in the right order or (by keyboard) selecting both characters with the SHIFT+arrow keys, then deleting and entering as for the mouse.

4. Remove cell reference C9 and replace it with B4 by (mouse) double clicking on C9 to select it as a word, by pressing DELETE, then typing B4, or (by keyboard) selecting C9 as a word with the SHIFT+CTRL+arrow keys, then deleting and entering as for the mouse.

5. Remove the division sign and enter the three characters ")/(" by (mouse) selecting the /, pressing DELETE, then typing)/(, or (by keyboard) selecting with the arrow keys, pressing DELETE, then typing)/(.

6. Insert the left and right parentheses by (mouse) placing the insertion pointer between the appropriate characters, clicking the mouse, typing the desired parenthesis key, then repeating this process for the other parenthesis or (by keyboard) proceeding as for the mouse but by using the arrow keys to position the cursor.

The formula for an active cell is always visible in the formula bar. No other formulas are visible at that time when operating in the values display mode. Instead, the value contents of the cells are displayed. To see all formulas simultaneously, one must change the display for this purpose. This is done with the **Options** drop-down menu of Figure 2.6(a). Choose **Display,** for which the dialog box of Figure 2.6(b) appears, choose **Formulas,** at which time an X appears in the box, then **OK** to execute the command. The formulas for all cells are now visible in their cells. If necessary, adjust column widths to see the complete formulas. A simple procedure for adjusting column width with the mouse is as follows:

Place the cursor on the desired column boundary within the column heading. Note the change in cursor shape (see figure in Box titled Mouse Operation on page 25). Drag horizontally to move the boundary.

The widths of columns for any display may be adjusted in the above described manner. Row heights may be similarly adjusted by working with the boundary in the row heading. The dialog box **Display Formulas** choice is a toggle. To revert to a normal display, toggle it to remove the X, then choose **OK.**

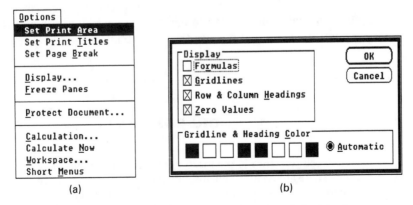

(a)   (b)

Figure 2.6 Options drop-down menu and the Display dialog box.

Other possibilities for altering the worksheet appearance from the dialog box exist. The reader is encouraged to experiment with the other toggle choices as well as with color settings.

2.3.3 Remarks on the Computational Process

The order in which calculations are made in a worksheet is based on formula dependency. Usually, the value of a formula of a cell is directly dependent on the values of cells that it references. The referenced cells, in turn, may be dependent on the values of other cells. Eventually, no more precedent cells can be found that contribute to the value of the original formula. Therefore, the calculation must begin with the most precedent cells and work through the dependency relationships until the desired value is computed. See the box titled Cell References on page 38. The computations of a worksheet may also be called demand-driven. Demands for values for parts of the worksheet (initially the whole worksheet) generate demands for values of expressions. The demands propagate through the worksheet like an infection, then gradually the required values flow back in the opposite direction until all demands are satisfied.

The first time a calculation is made, it is made automatically on completion of a formula and a numerical value is produced, provided its precedent cell references have values. Thereafter, calculations are made when changes are made that affect formulas through the dependency relationship. Changes made to constants that are the single entry in a cell are changes when used as references in formulas and thus invoke recalculation.

Calculations are based on the stored values of cells, not on their display formats. Numbers are stored to 15 digits of accuracy. The number of the cell being calculated appears in the reference area of the formula bar, as can be seen in Figure 2.4. For an involved worksheet, this display may be dynamic and too rapid to visually follow.

Control of the calculation is automatic as previously described, but it may be changed to manual. The simple problems we are working with now do not require manual control, so we will discuss this feature later.

CELL REFERENCES

A cell reference is the location of a cell or a group of cells on a worksheet. There are relative and absolute types of references, each of which may be represented in A1 or in R1C1 reference style. References in both styles are based on designations of the column and row headings of the worksheet.

The *absolute* type of reference specifies the location with respect to the origin of the worksheet coordinate system. Each coordinate of the reference is preceded by the $ sign.

Example:

$D$6   This A1 style reference, used anywhere on the worksheet, is the cell at the intersection of column D with row 6.

The *relative* type of reference specifies the location with respect to the origin of a local coordinate system centered at the cell containing the reference. It is prepared similar to the absolute reference except that the $ signs are omitted. Although its row and column specification resembles that for an absolute reference, it is converted to an internal representation for use in, say, a formula. Thereafter, Excel accesses the reference in a row and column incremental manner with respect to the local coordinate system.

Example:

D6   If the cell containing this A1 style reference is $B$3, then D6 is located two columns to its right and three rows below it.

References can also be mixed absolute and relative. For example, $C5 has an absolute column reference and a relative row reference, while E$9 has a relative column reference and an absolute row reference. Figure (a) shows several A1 style references and the locations they reference. The formula of cell B3 has been copied into cell F5.

The R1C1 reference style uses numerically labeled rows and columns. Column labeling is set by toggling the **Options Workspace** dialog box **Display R1C1** text box on. The cell reference is constructed by preceding the row and column numbers by R and C, respectively. The absolute type of reference appears as R3C8 (for row 3, column 8), while the relative reference has the numbers within brackets, such as R[2]C[−1] (for two rows down, one column to the left). The numbers for the absolute reference are the actual row and column numbers, while for the relative reference they are the signed increments. An R1C1 style reference may also be constructed as a mixed R1C1 style reference, such as R9C[3] or R[−2]C4. Figure (b) shows R1C1 style references for the formulas of Figure (a).

From a user's perspective, there are two factors that govern the choice between using an absolute or a relative reference. One is the need to compute row and column positions for cell access, the other is to ensure that correct cell locations are accessed when formulas are moved or copied from one cell to another. In the first case, available only for macros, the decision can be made on whether to use global or local coordinate systems. For the former use, it requires absolute references; for the latter, it requires relative references. In both instances, the R1C1 style must be used, often in conjunction with arrays.

In the second case, the decision must be made on the need for a relative address with respect to a new cell location, or on the need to reference an absolute location regardless of the containing cell's location. Excel automatically changes the relative references to reflect the move.

The **Formula Reference** command is used to convert a selected reference in the formula bar to any of the other types of the same style. The accompanying figures illustrate both types and styles of references and the consequences of their movement in the worksheet.

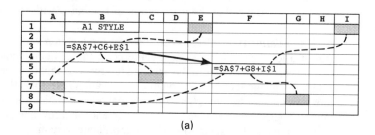

(a)

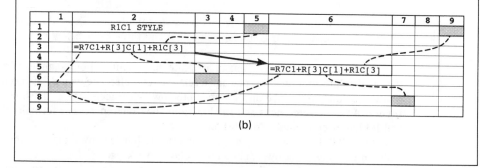

(b)

Worksheets containing much involved mathematics, or even just a large number of elementary computations, may require much calculation time. While the calculations are in progress, it is permissible to engage in other activities, such as issuing commands or constructing other formulas. For these purposes, calculation is momentarily interrupted to service the request, thus extending its calculation time slightly. Computations with the operators *, /, and ^ and with functions using these operators are speeded up with the math coprocessor chip installed in the computer. This chip is recommended for engineering calculations.

Example 2.3

The sum of the series given by the left-hand side expression below is the right-hand side expression:

$$\frac{3}{1 \cdot 2 \cdot 4} + \frac{4}{2 \cdot 3 \cdot 5} + \frac{5}{3 \cdot 4 \cdot 6} + \cdots (n \text{ terms})$$

$$= \frac{29}{36} - \frac{1}{n+3} - \frac{3}{2(n+2)(n+3)} - \frac{4}{3(n+1)(n+2)(n+3)}$$

	A	B
1	n	4
2	n+3	7
3	(n+2)(n+3)	42
4	(n+1)(n+2)(n+3)	210
5		
6	sum	0.620634921

(a)

	A	B
1	n	4
2	n+3	=B1+3
3	(n+2)(n+3)	=(B1+2)*B2
4	(n+1)(n+2)(n+3)	=(B1+1)*B3
5		
6	sum	=29/36-1/B2-3/(2*B3)-4/(3*B4)

(b)

Figure 2.7   Worksheet for Example 2.3 in (a) values mode and (b) formulas mode.

This sum, computed by the Excel program, appears in Figure 2.7. For a value of n, entered in cell B1, a value for each following formula will be calculated and displayed in the worksheet. We chose to compute the denominator factors individually to speed up the calculation, to allow incremental verification, and to insert the text in column A as documentation. We have intermediate results that allow convenient checking against our hand calculation. Repeated calculations, such as the kind found in the denominators above, should be separated and performed individually with the results used elsewhere. There is no advantage to including all calculations in one involved formula. The simple formulas that we are discussing in this chapter are not demanding of computer time or amount of memory. But one error in the formula will cost more to discover and correct than any perceived savings in using the program.

Example 2.4

For the transistor circuit of Figure 2.8, and with some usual circuit operation assumptions not stated here, we have for the dc collector current this equation:

$$I_c = \frac{R_e + R_b}{R_e + R_b + h_{21}R_b} I_{co} - \frac{h_{21}E_{bb}}{R_e + R_b + h_{21}R_b}$$

where

$$I_{co} = \text{grounded-base cutoff current}$$

$$h_{21} = \text{grounded-base short-circuit current gain}$$

The stability factor S is given by

$$S = \frac{\Delta I_c}{\Delta I_{co}} = \frac{R_e + R_b}{R_e + R_b + h_{21}R_b}$$

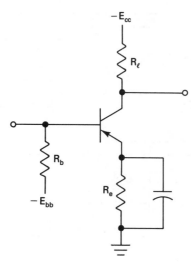

Figure 2.8 Schematic diagram for Example 2.4.

which shows how the collector current I_c, and hence the operating point, varies with a given change in I_{co}. Given a set of numerical values for R_e, R_b, and h_{21}, we can readily compute S. Then, by varying any of these circuit or device parameters, we can determine the resulting effects on S. This procedure is, at times, called performing a "what-if" analysis. However, in Chapter 1, we were critical of this brute force method because it resembles a cut-and-dry procedure that often leads to the collection of much data but few significant conclusions. Instead, we rewrite the stability factor equation as follows:

$$S = \frac{\Delta I_c}{\Delta I_{co}} = \frac{1}{1 + h_{21} - \dfrac{h_{21}R_e}{R_e + R_b}}$$

We see that the stability is improved (numerically made smaller) because of the last term in the denominator which contains R_e, the symbol for the emitter resistor. This resistor causes the circuit to have negative feedback which, in turn, is responsible for the improved stability. Without this resistor, by letting $R_e = 0$, then

$$S = \frac{1}{1 + h_{21}}$$

This is the stability of the grounded-emitter circuit. A "what-if" analysis now is reduced to determining numerical values, if they are wanted. From the rewritten equation above, we know the influence of the factors contributing to the stability factor, so no "what-if" analysis is needed for that purpose. All we have to do is consider the influence of R_e and R_b in the last term of the denominator. We see that R_e should be increased and R_b decreased, but not indefinitely, of course, since circuit specifications other than the stability factor must also be considered.

To finish this example, we will compute S given the following values: $R_e = 1000$, $R_b = 15,000$, and $h_{21} = -.98$. The worksheet is shown in Figure 2.9.

	A	B
1	Re	1000
2	Rb	15000
3	h21	-0.98
4		
5	S(feedback)	12.30769231
6		
7	S(w/o feedback)	50

(a)

	A	B
1	Re	1000
2	Rb	15000
3	h21	-0.98
4		
5	S(feedback)	=1/(1+B3-B3*B1/(B1+B2))
6		
7	S(w/o feedback)	=1/(1+B3)

(b)

Figure 2.9 Worksheet for Example 2.4 in (a) values mode and (b) formulas mode.

For comparison purposes, we computed values for S with and without the feedback resistor R_e. The influence of R_e in lowering the stability factor is dramatic. Should we want graphical evidence of this, we could change the value of R_e and recompute S. Several pairs of values could then be plotted to see the effect. We discuss plotting in Chapter 6.

2.4 TESTING, DEBUGGING, AND PRINTING

Testing is the process of proving the results of the formulas. Special case values may have to be entered to verify the correctness of the various paths that a computation sequence may follow. At the moment, this should not be a problem, since we have constructed only single-path formulas.

We should attempt, within our ability, to prepare a hand calculation of the formula so that we may check the results obtained from the run. Do not use special cases for the verification except as noted earlier. For example, in the expression $a + b*x$, do not set $x = 0$, since there is no way to determine whether b has the right value. Similarly, for the expression $a + b*(x - 1)$, do not set $x = 1$. Other areas to watch are (a) in exponents, where they should not be driven to 0 or 1, (b) adding two terms whose values differ by many orders of magnitude, since the influence of one will be masked by the other, (c) subtracting two nearly equal terms since their difference may be in substantial error, and (d) the use of the same numerical values for several constants and variables, since an error in a cell reference may be overlooked.

The problem should be simplified to yield simple formulas. If necessary, build up the problem in increments by adding a new increment with each partial verification. All formulas do not have to be general purpose. Constants can be written into the formula: they do not have to be stored in cells and their cell then referenced in the formula. In this way, errors of cell entry can be avoided.

Organize the computational sequence in the natural order in which hand computations would be performed. A modest, straightforward approach is easier to understand and debug.

Debugging—the process of removing errors from the worksheet—requires knowledge of the function of the mathematics of the formulas and familiarity with the preparation of Excel formulas. Some clues to debugging a worksheet follow.

Errors may be in the computed value and arise from the problems of formula construction described earlier, in which case they may not be evident. Sometimes they may be obvious because of an error value displayed. Error values begin with the number sign (#) and are followed by a short string of characters whose meaning is suggestive of the type of error. For now, we should consider the following error values.

#DIV/0!

This error value in a cell means that a divide-by-zero condition occurred while computing the formula for that cell. The values of all denominators should be checked. Unusual values causing this condition may have propagated into the cell from a precedent cell's computation.

#N/A

This error value means that no value was available for a cell reference used in the formula of that cell. For the simple formulas we are working with, it probably means that we referenced a blank cell in the formula.

#NUM!

This error value in a cell may mean that an inappropriate computation was attempted, such as raising a negative number to a fractional exponent during exponentiation, or that the size limit of a number has been exceeded, possibly during an intermediate computation sequence. The maximum positive number is 1.789E305, the minimum positive number is 2.225E-307.

#VALUE!

This error value in a cell means that its entry cannot be converted to a numeric data type. Check the entry for invalid characters that produce a text value rather than a numeric value.

Error values may appear any time, but are most likely to do so just as one attempts to enter the formula. Running in the automatic calculation mode will reveal many such errors immediately, thus enabling immediate correction. Remember that a string of # symbols in the cell is not an error. It just means that the column is not wide enough to display the number. The cell should be widened as described in Section 2.3.2.

Consider impossible mathematical situations such as, for example, attempting to extract the root of a negative number. Excel only works with real numbers, not complex quantities.

Do not bypass worksheet safeguards during entry and execution time. They are there to detect problems and, although they may slow computation, are invaluable during the early stages of formula verification.

For various reasons, one of which is for verification and debugging purposes, printouts of the worksheet and/or formulas are desired. Before printing in Excel, we must be sure that our printer is set up and that the page is set up for printing according to our preferences. From Figure 2.10(a), we first execute the **File Printer Setup** command. The dialog box of Figure 2.10(b) appears, from which we select the printer to be used, if more than one printer is available. Then, we choose the **Setup** button to display the dialog box of Figure 2.10(c). We set up particulars regarding the printer and type of printout, then choose **OK.** Default values are shown in Figure 2.10(c).

We must also set up the page display by executing the **File Page Setup** command and making the proper entries in the dialog box of Figure 2.10(d), where default values are shown. One must type in new margin values if needed and toggle on or off the text boxes at the bottom of the dialog box for the additional printout desired. The **Header** and **Footer** text box values shown cause the name of the document and the page number to be printed, respectively. When the values are entered as desired, choose **OK.**

Executing the **File Print** command of Figure 2.10(a) produces the dialog box of Figure 2.10(e). We must then enter the desired number of copies and pages to print, set the toggle for draft or letter quality, and choose the proper **Print** button for **Sheet** (worksheet), **Notes,** or **Both.** If we want to see a reduced version of our printout on the screen before printing, we toggle on the **Preview** button. Upon choosing **OK,** we begin printing unless the **Preview** toggle is on, in which case we wait for its presentation on the screen.

The preview display for Example 2.4 is shown in Figure 2.11. From this window, we can print the document by selecting the **Print** button. Meanwhile, if there is more than one page to print, we can toggle among them for inspection purposes with the **Next** and **Previous** buttons, and we can expand the view either with the **Zoom** button or by positioning the magnifying glass cursor with the mouse and clicking on it. The display is enlarged for detailed inspection and scroll bars appear that allow movement of the view across the screen. Choose the **Cancel** button to cancel the **Print** command.

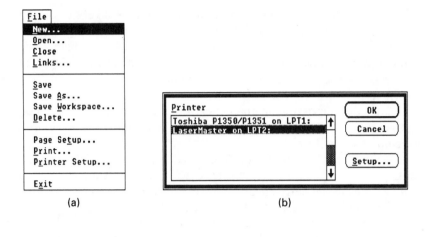

(a)   (b)

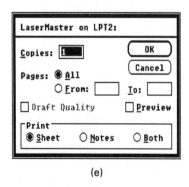

(c)   (d)

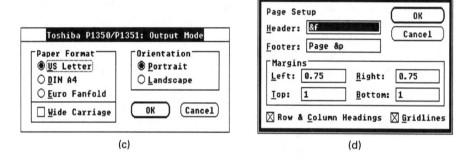

(e)

Figure 2.10 (a) File drop-down menu and dialog boxes for (b) and (c) Printer Setup, (d) Page Setup, and (e) Print commands.

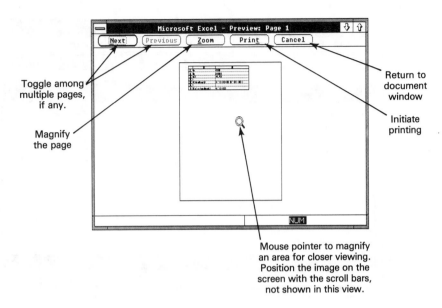

Toggle among
multiple pages,
if any.

Magnify
the page

Return to
document
window

Initiate
printing

Mouse pointer to magnify
an area for closer viewing.
Position the image on the
screen with the scroll bars,
not shown in this view.

Figure 2.11 Print command Preview display.

2.5 ABOUT VERSION 3.0

When we first enter Excel version 3.0 we see the window of Figure 2.12. It contains the tool bar, which is the display of buttons immediately below the menu bar. None of these buttons help us with the material of this chapter. We can turn off the tool bar (make invisible) with the **Tool Bar** check box in the **Options Workspace** dialog box of Figure 2.13 and, in this way, gain additional worksheet display area.

Computational results from Excel version 3.0 are identical to those from version 2.2. Therefore, all worksheets of this chapter run under version 3.0 without change. Since we are working with simple formulas that depend on arithmetic operators only, this should be no surprise. Otherwise there would be something drastically wrong with at least one of the two Excel versions.

New capability in version 3.0 that applies to the material of this chapter is the adjustable margin and column spacing feature in the print preview window. It is enabled by choosing the **Margins** button in the print preview window of Figure 2.14, which also shows the margins and column widths as dotted lines. This window is displayed with the **File Print Preview** command or through the **File Print** dialog box. Often the material is not printed out exactly as displayed. There may be column spacing differences or the printout may not appear in the desired location on the paper. The margins and column spacing may be adjusted by dragging with the mouse the handles at the ends of the dotted lines. Also, the **File**

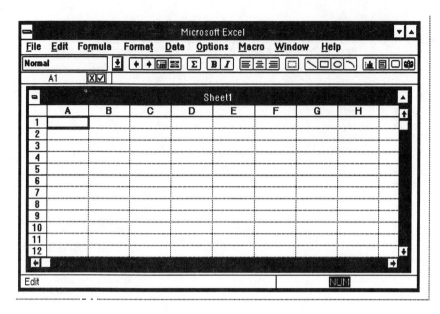

Figure 2.12   Excel version 3.0 window.

Page Setup dialog box can be displayed from this window by choosing the **Setup** button. This provides speed and convenience in making changes to entries of that dialog box.

Numerous menus and dialog boxes discussed in this chapter have been changed slightly in version 3.0. Some changes to note are:

1. The **Print Preview** command has been added to the **File** menu of Figure 2.5(a).

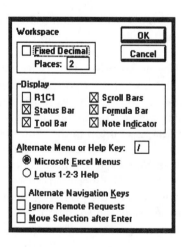

Figure 2.13   New Options Workspace dialog box.

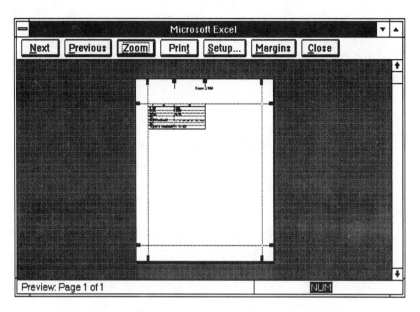

Figure 2.14   Print Preview window with Margins button selected.

2. A directory list box is included in the **File Save As** dialog box of Figure 2.5(d).

3. There are horizontal and vertical centering choices, portrait/landscape orientation buttons, and an echo regarding paper size and other printer characteristics in the **File Page Setup** dialog box of Figure 2.10(d).

4. Upon entering a right parenthesis in the formula bar, the parenthesis and its matching counterpart are momentarily made boldface for recognition as a matched set. This should help to identify immediate hierarchical errors of formula construction by comparing Excel recognized structures with that believed to be entered. It can also provide confidence that entries are without such errors.

PROBLEMS

Write spreadsheet programs using mathematical operators and cell references to solve the following problems:

2.1 Given the three sides of a triangle, a, b, and c, solve for its area with the formula below. Let the three sides have the values 10.5, 6.3, and 15.2.

$$area = \sqrt{s(s - a)(s - b)(s - c)}$$

where $s = (a + b + c)/2$

$$ans = 26.13197275$$

2.2 The gravitational force of attraction is given by the formula below. Compute it for the values $m_1 = 44 \times 10^8$, $m_2 = 81.7 \times 10^{10}$, and $d = 176 \times 10^6$.

$$f = \frac{km_1m_2}{d^2}$$

where

$$f = \text{force in dynes}$$

$$m_1, m_2 = \text{masses, grams}$$

$$d = \text{separation distance, cm}$$

$$k = \text{gravitational constant, } 6.67 \times 10^{-8}$$

$$ans = 0.007740611$$

2.3 Compute the body surface area for a height of 5 ft 9 in. and weight of 170 lbs by the following formula (BSA in square meters):

$$\text{BSA} = 0.007184W^{.425}H^{.725}$$

where

$$W = \text{body weight, kg}$$

$$H = \text{height, cm}$$

$$ans = 1.927791684$$

2.4 The current efficiency for electrolytic deposition is given by the formula below. Compute it for depositing 0.5 g of metallic silver (atomic weight $= 107.88$) from a nitric acid solution of silver nitrate (deposition factor $= 1$) in 21 min with a current of .65 amps.

$$\eta(\%) = \frac{161000F_dD}{tiA}$$

where

$$F_d = \text{deposition factor}$$

$$D = \text{amount deposited, grams}$$

$$t = \text{time, minutes}$$

$$i = \text{current, amps}$$

$$A = \text{metal atomic weight}$$

$$ans = 54.66662864$$

2.5 The current passing through an n-type semiconductor is given by the equation below. Compute it for $\mu_n = 3600$, $E = 100$, and $n_n = 1.75 \times 10^{15}$.

$$i = q\mu_n n_n E$$

where

$$i = \text{current, amp/cm}^2$$

$$q = \text{electron charge, } 1.6 \times 10^{-19} \text{ Coulomb}$$

$$\mu_n = \text{electron mobility, cm}^2\text{/volt-sec}$$

$$n_n = \text{electron density, number/cm}^2$$

$$E = \text{electric field, volts/cm}$$

$$ans = 100.8$$

2.6 The thermal conductivity of oil shale is given by the equation below. Compute it for an oil shale whose oil yield is 30 gal/ton at a temperature of 47°C.

$$k_t = 0.57827(1.8081 - 0.03698F + 0.00198T + 0.0003056F^2$$

$$- 0.000005184T^2 - 0.00001872FT)$$

where

$$k_t = \text{thermal conductivity, Btu/hr-ft}^2 \text{ °F/ft}$$

$$T = \text{temperature, °C}$$

$$F = \text{oil yield, gal/ton}$$

$$ans = 0.59501285$$

2.7 The combined resistance of three resistors in parallel is given by the formula below. Compute it for three resistors whose values are 220, 470, and 330 ohms.

$$R_t = \frac{1}{\dfrac{1}{R_1} + \dfrac{1}{R_2} + \dfrac{1}{R_3}}$$

$$ans = 103.0564784$$

2.8 Use the equation below to compute a value for y given that $x = 2.5$, $a = -1.4$, $r = 3.2$, $t = .075$, $p = 151$, $v = 11.3$, $b = -5.67$, and $w = .808$.

$$y = \left(\frac{(x + a)/r}{t + 1}\right)^{1.6} \left(p^{1/3} + \frac{v(t - x)^2}{ab + w}\right)^3$$

$$ans = 348.1931572$$

2.9 One procedure for evaluating the polynomial

$$y = a_5x^5 + a_4x^4 + a_3x^3 + a_2x^2 + a_1x + a_0$$

uses a method called nesting, whereby we set up the computation as follows:

$$y = ((((a_5x + a_4)x + a_3)x + a_2)x + a_1)x + a_0$$

Compute a value for y in its nested form given that $a_5 = -8.8$, $a_4 = 3.5$, $a_3 = .1$, $a_2 = -7$, $a_1 = 6.3$, $a_0 = 10.5$, and $x = 14.3$.

$$ans = -5116827.446$$

2.10 Let (x_1, y_1) and (x_2, y_2) denote the coordinates of any two points in the xy-plane. Compute the distance between the points $(-3, 1.5)$ and $(4, -5.5)$ with the following formula:

$$D = \sqrt{(x_2 - x_1)^2 + (y_2 - y_1)^2}$$

ans = 9.899494937

CHAPTER **3**

Numeric Functions

We now introduce more computational aids provided by spreadsheet programs that will expand our formula preparation capability. One such very important feature is called built-in functions. These are mathematical functions that provide numerical results. The functions help us avoid preparing complex computational structures to determine numeric results. They are called "built-in" because they are provided with the spreadsheet program.

It is time to consider mature ways to prepare a worksheet. So, we introduce names for the variables (cell references), we show how to select ranges of cells and perform operations on them as a group, and we further explain techniques for streamlining our worksheet procedures.

Because properly documenting our work offers the advantages discussed in Chapter 1, we also discuss ways to format our worksheet for readability, understanding, and reporting. This helps in verifying and debugging our worksheet. We also offer more debugging procedures.

Upon completing this chapter, the reader will be able to solve the most complex of formulas and will obtain hard-copy output that will be suitably formatted for the application.

3.1 MATHEMATICAL FUNCTIONS

Various mathematical operations, which are more complicated than those performed by the operators discussed in Chapter 2, are so useful and often needed that they are provided as predefined formulas always available to the user. These are called *functions*. They have the same meaning in worksheet computation as we are accustomed to in ordinary mathematics. This is, they express a mathematical relationship by which the value of a dependent variable, called the *function value,* is determined for values given to one or more independent variables, called the *arguments*. Without their availability, the worksheet user would have to develop an algorithm for each function required, consistent, of course, with convergence and accuracy requirements sufficient to satisfy the problem. A list of some functions available in Excel is given in Table 3.1.

A function reference is an expression of the form

$$name(list)$$

where *name* is a unique spreadsheet word and *list* is a list of one or more arguments required by the function. When used, *name* acts as a scalar variable that is assigned a value upon evaluation of the function. Each argument is an arithmetic expression that may be a numeric constant, a cell reference, or a complicated expression containing arithmetic functions and nested expressions. Arguments must be separated from each other in *list* by commas.

The functions are used by typing their assigned name, with associated argument list, in the proper location of an expression just as any cell reference is used in an expression. The evaluation of expressions containing functions is subject to the hierarchy rules of Table 3.2, where it is seen that functions are assigned a priority higher than that of arithmetic operators. The result from evaluating a function is the substitution of a computed value in the position in the expression where the function appears. The evaluation of the expression is then completed using this value. Of course, the arguments of the function must be computed before a value is returned for the function.

The following table of examples use functions in the construction of formulas. Cell references are implied in the expressions.

Algebraic notation	Excel formula
$\alpha = \arctan 63.49$	= ATAN (63.49)
$r = \sqrt{x^2 + y^2}$	= SQRT(X1*X1 + Y1*Y1)
$\text{area} = \dfrac{ab}{2} \sin \theta$	= .5*A6*B6*SIN(T6)
$a = \sqrt{b^2 + c^2 - 2bc \cos \beta}$	= SQRT(B2*B2 + C2*C2 − 2*B2*C2*COS(B3))
$w = t - k \sin \left(\beta + \arctan \dfrac{y}{x} \right)$	= T7 − K7*SIN(B3 + ATAN(Y7/X7))
$t = \dfrac{\log \sqrt{a^2 - x^2}}{x^2}$	=LOG10(SQRT(A9*A9 − X9*X9))/(X9*X9)
$w = e^{at} \left(\dfrac{1}{t} + \ln t \right)$	= EXP(A2*T2)*(1/T2 + LN(T2))
$d = 7.5a^{-|x^2-3.6|} \tan^2 \theta$	= 7.5*A4^(−ABS(X4*X4 − 3.6))*TAN(T6)^2

TABLE 3.1 SOME EXCEL BUILT-IN FUNCTIONS

Name	Algebraic notation	Symbol	Comments
Arithmetic			
Absolute value	$\lvert x \rvert$	ABS(x)	Function value is positive x.
Square root	$\sqrt{x}$	SQRT(x)	x must be nonnegative.
Natural logarithm	$\ln x$	LN(x)	Base e.
Common logarithm	$\log x$	LOG10(x)	Base 10.
Exponential	e^x	EXP(x)	e is base of natural logarithm.
Factorial	$n!$	FACT(n)	n must be nonnegative; it is truncated.
Sign	$\mathrm{sgn}(x)$	SIGN(x)	Function value is 1, 0, −1 if argument is +, 0, −, respectively.
Integer	$\mathrm{int}(x)$	INT(x)	Truncates fractional value.
Modulo division	$\mathrm{mod}(a,b)$	MOD(a,b)	Function value is remainder of $a \div b$, with sign of b.
Random number	rand()	RAND()	Function value is random number between 0 and 1.
Pi	π	PI()	Function value is the constant π accurate to 15 digits.
Statistical			
Average	$\bar{x}$	AVERAGE($x_1, x_2, \ldots, x_n$)	Average of the x_i.
Sum	$\Sigma\, x_i$	SUM($x_1, x_2, \ldots, x_n$)	Sum of x_i.
Algebraic minimum	$\min\{x_1, x_2, \ldots, x_n\}$	MIN($x_1, x_2, \ldots, x_n$)	Function value is algebraically smallest value from argument list.
Algebraic maximum	$\max\{x_1, x_2, \ldots, x_n\}$	MAX($x_1, x_2, \ldots, x_n$)	Function value is algebraically largest value from argument list.
Standard deviation	σ	STDEV($x_1, x_2, \ldots, x_n$)	Unbiased value.

Trigonometric:

Name	Algebraic notation	Symbol	Comments
Sine	$\sin \alpha$	SIN(α)	α in radians.
Cosine	$\cos \alpha$	COS(α)	α in radians.
Tangent	$\tan \alpha$	TAN(α)	α in radians.
Arcsine	$\arcsin x$	ASIN(x)	Function value is angle in radians normalized to 1st or 4th quadrant.
Arcosine	$\arcos x$	ACOS(x)	Function value is angle in radians normalized to 1st or 2nd quadrant.
Arctangent	$\arctan x$	ATAN(x)	Function value is angle in radians normalized to 1st or 4th quadrant.
Arctangent	$\arctan(a/b)$	ATAN2(a,b)	Function value is angle in radians in correct quadrant; a and b must not both be zero; 1st and 2nd quadrant angles are measured CCW, 3rd and 4th quadrant angles are measured CW.

TABLE 3.2

Operator	Priority
Functions	1 (highest)
^	2
*, /	3
+, −	4 (lowest)

Example 3.1

To illustrate the use of functions, we will solve this equation

$$\alpha = \frac{\dfrac{a^2}{2}|x - a| + \sqrt{\dfrac{x}{n^{1.5}} + n^2}}{15.8 \sin(\pi - \theta) - \left(\dfrac{a^2}{3} - x\right)^{1.5}} - \frac{21.3a^{n-2}\sqrt{a - \dfrac{\cos(\theta^2 + \pi/2)}{x}}}{e^x|x - a^2 + .07|\sin^2\theta}$$

for input values of $a = 4.5$, $x = -1.2$, $n = 4$, and $\theta = 65$ deg. First, we determine if the functions we need are available in Excel. From Table 3.1, we see that ABS, SQRT, SIN, COS, EXP, and PI are available. The PI function returns the value for π. All else in the above formula can be computed using the basic operators. We choose to group the input values together at the beginning of the worksheet layout. We must also convert θ from degrees to radians, which we will do in a formula at the time we enter θ. Because the formula for α is not very complicated, we choose to compute only four intermediate values that are also easily hand calculated. These are the two numerators and two denominators, which will then be used in the formula for α. The results are shown in Figure 3.1. The text values in column A serve as comments.

The numerator and denominator factors for each term are computed in cells B6 through B9. The value for α is computed in cell B11. Simple hand calculations verify the results. New values can be substituted for the independent variables, and recalculations can be easily made. However, precautions are required to avoid negative radicands.

3.2 VARIABLES (NAMES)

It is now time to learn something that will make working with formulas much easier for us. We will not add new computational capability, but we will learn some of the Excel convenience features.

We have used exclusively the cell coordinate reference scheme in our formulas. But using any reference scheme that depends on position within the worksheet is an inflexible, inconvenient, and error-prone scheme. We prefer the traditional method in computer program languages of assigning a name to the variable or constant. We usually choose names that convey the purpose of the variable and use these names wherever the variable must be referenced in a formula. A basic procedure to follow is to select a cell, assign it a name, then use the name as a cell reference. We may choose to work with more than one cell at a time and therefore assign several names simultaneously.

A variable name must begin with a letter, which may be followed by characters that are letters, numbers, the underscore (_), a period, or some combination of these characters, but it cannot contain spaces or resemble a cell reference. Here are examples of names:

Valid:	Stress	
	X.1	
	OHMS	
	New_ Value	
Invalid:	C	used in Excel for R1C1 style references
	A1	resembles coordinate reference
	23K6	doesn't begin with a letter
	W(6)	invalid characters

	A	B
1	a	4.5
2	x	−1.2
3	n	4
4	theta	1.134464014
5		
6	alf1n	61.69370585
7	alf1d	−8.095953731
8	alf2n	829.6700361
9	alf2d	5.289391897
10		
11	alpha	−164.4757805

(a)

	A	B
1	a	4.5
2	x	−1.2
3	n	4
4	theta	=65*PI()/180
5		
6	alf1n	=B1^2/2*ABS(B2−B1)+SQRT(B2/B3^1.5+B3^2)
7	alf1d	=15.8*SIN(PI()−B4)−(B1^2/3−B2)^1.5
8	alf2n	=21.3*B1^(B3−2)*SQRT(B1−COS(B4^2+PI()/2)/B2)
9	alf2d	=EXP(B2)*ABS(B2−B1^2+0.07)*SIN(B4)^2
10		
11	alpha	=B6/B7−B8/B9

(b)

Figure 3.1   (a) Values display and (b) formulas display for the worksheet of Example 3.1.

Because we are working with entities used in formulas, we will learn to use some commands of the **Formula** drop-down menu. It is shown in Figure 3.2 together with a selection of dialog boxes. The commands of this menu that we need to learn now are

Formula Define Name

Formula Apply Names

Formula Create Names

Formula Paste Name

Formula Paste Function

Our discussion of the pertinent dialog boxes is brief because a general discussion of working with them appears in the box titled The Dialog Box on page 28. Here is what the above commands do.

Formula Define Name

This command, via its dialog box of Figure 3.2(b), is used to create a name for a cell, cell range, value, or formula. You can also delete or change a name with it. First, select the cell to be named, then type the name in the text box labeled **Name** and choose the **OK** button. If the chosen name has already been defined, no error may be issued for its redefinition. Therefore, anomalous results should be expected. Often, the user is prompted for verification of name redefinition. You can edit in the **Name** box as you would in the formula bar. All names currently defined will appear in the **Names in Sheet** list box. Upon selecting a name from this box, you may delete it by choosing the **Delete** button.

To define a name for a value, first type the name in the **Name** box, then type its value in the **Refers to** box, then choose **OK**. The value is named without being placed in a cell. Use this procedure to define a common constant, such as Avogadro's number.

To name a formula, first type the name in the **Name** box, then type its formula in the **Refers to** box, then choose **OK**. The formula is named without being placed in a cell. Use this procedure to define a conversion factor, such as =9/5*DegC + 32, which converts the value for DegC, assumed to be in units of °C, to °F.

Formula Apply Names

This command, via its dialog box of Figure 3.2(c), is used to replace cell references with names. Because we advocate beginning the worksheet with names, we find no need for a replacement command. This command is not discussed further.

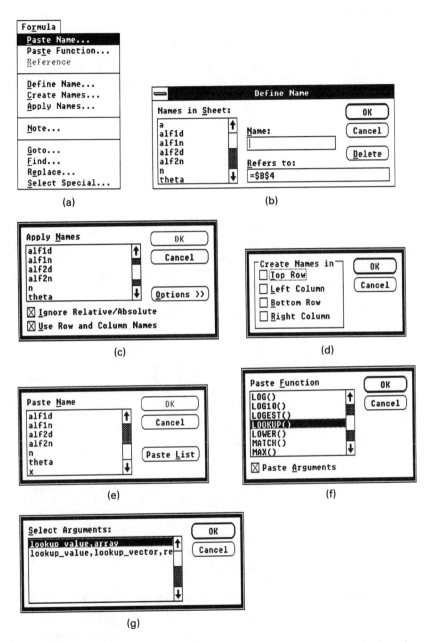

Figure 3.2   (a) Formula drop-down menu, and (b) through (g) a selection of dialog boxes displayed by commands of the menu.

Formula Create Names

This command, via its dialog box of Figure 3.2(d), is used to name several areas of a worksheet at one time by using text in a column or row adjacent to the areas to be named. Application of this command requires that we first select an area (see Box titled Cell Selection on page 60) that includes the text that will become variables for the adjacent cell(s). Then, in the dialog box, we toggle our choice in the **Create Names in** box and choose **OK**.

CELL SELECTION

A single cell selected as described in Section 2.2 is subject to the effects of the next command executed. It is possible to select more than one cell at a time. For example, we can select a rectangular array of cells, a single row of cells, or a single column of cells as shown in Figure (a). We can also make a multiple selection, which is any combination of single cells or ranges of cells not all contiguous, as shown in Figure (b). All selected cells are subject to the next command to be executed. The procedures for making the various types of selections are as follows:

Selection type	Mouse	Keyboard
Single cell	Position the cursor on the desired cell, click the button.	Position the cursor on the desired cell with the arrow keys. It is automatically selected.
Range	Position the cursor on a corner of the range to be selected, press the button, drag to the opposite corner and release the button. In the case of a single row (column), position the cursor in the row (column) heading, and click.	Select one corner of the range, press F8, select the other cells with the arrow keys. For a single row (column), select one cell in the row (column), press CTRL+SPACEBAR (SHIFT+SPACEBAR).
Multiple	Click the first cell or drag through the first range, hold down CTRL, click each additional cell or drag through each range.	Select the first cell or range as described above. Press SHIFT+F8. Use arrow keys to move to each additional cell or start of range and select as described above.
Entire worksheet		Press CTRL+SHIFT+SPACEBAR

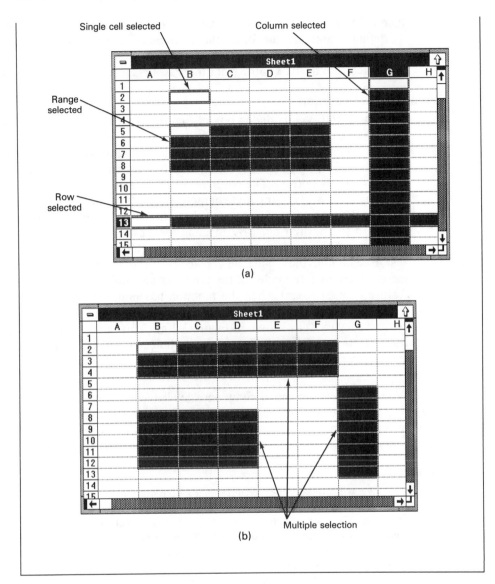

(a)

(b)

Formula Paste Name

This command, via its dialog box of Figure 3.2(e), is used to paste a name into the formula bar at the insertion point when the formula bar is active; otherwise, it activates the formula bar and then pastes the name into it. It is an alternative way to enter names into the formula bar, other than by typing them. The **Paste Name** box lists all names defined on the active worksheet. To define a name, use any of the three commands described above. To paste a name, position the insertion point at the desired location in the formula bar, select the desired name from the **Paste Name** box, then choose **OK**.

Formula Paste Function

This command, via its dialog box of Figure 3.2(f), is used like the **Formula Paste Name** command, but it pastes the name of a function into the formula bar. The **Paste Function** list box contains the names of all available functions. Scroll the list box to locate the desired function name, select it, then choose the **OK** button. The parentheses are pasted also. To accelerate the scrolling process, type the first character of the function name to display the first function name beginning with that character. Then, step through the names to the desired one. By toggling the **Paste Arguments** box, text descriptions of the function's arguments are included between the parentheses. Eventually, they must be replaced by the actual arguments and are merely there as a reminder of the type and position of the arguments. This feature is most useful when the function has multiple arguments or when there are alternative sets of arguments to choose from. Multiple argument choices may exist as shown in Figure 3.2(g). This latter dialog box appears from functions with multiple argument choices when **OK** is chosen for the dialog box of Figure 3.2(f).

With the above described commands available, we can choose from a variety of techniques to construct a formula. The **Formula Paste** commands are useful whenever the names are long, because long names could be misspelled while typing them, and whenever one is not sure of the exact formula spelling.

Example 3.2

We will convert the cell references of Example 2.1 to variable names and reconstruct the formula for the resistance. Figures 2.2 and 2.3 show the data and formulas. We used text in column A to remind ourselves of the meaning of the values in rows 1 through 6 of column B. With the **Formula Create Names** command, we will create names for the values in column B from the text given in the corresponding rows of column A.

We need create names only for cells B1 through B4. Because we do not reference cell B6 a name is not needed for it. First, we change the text in cell A3 from "dia ctr" to "dia_ctr", since blanks are not allowed in names. Then we select the rectangular area bounded at the opposite corners by cells A1 and B4. In the **Create Names** dialog box, we toggle on the **Left Column** choice, because the text is to the left of the cells to be named, and choose **OK**. The corresponding cells in the B column have now been named. To check this, invoke the **Formula Paste Name** command and look in the **Paste Name** list box. The created names will appear there. If we want to name cell B6, we can repeat the above procedure or execute the **Formula Define Name** command and type its name in the **Name** text box.

At this time, we could use the **Formula Apply Names** command to change the cell references to names in the formula for cell B6. Also, we could individually change the cell references to names by using editing techniques in the formula bar. Instead, we will reconstruct the formula as if it did not exist.

First, select the formula and delete it by any convenient way while in the formula bar. Then, begin typing in the new formula. Whenever a name is needed, execute the **Formula Paste Name** or **Formula Paste Function** command to enter the desired name. Complete the formula in the usual manner. This is what it will look like:

$$=5280*rho/area*SQRT(1+(2*PI()*dia\_ctr/2/s)\string^2)$$

Example 3.3

We now apply the procedure of Example 3.2 to Example 3.1. Figure 3.1 shows that numerous variable names can be applied to input values for a, x, n, and θ. They can then be used in the numerator and denominator factors which, in turn, can be named and used in the final formula. The **Formula Create Names** command is ideal for this example, since we can name all cells in one operation. The intervening blank cells do not cause problems for this purpose. Figure 3.3 shows the result after we use the **Formula Apply Names** command.

	A	B
1	a	4.5
2	x	−1.2
3	n	4
4	theta	1.134464014
5		
6	alf1n	61.69370585
7	alf1d	−8.095953731
8	alf2n	829.6700361
9	alf2d	5.289391897
10		
11	alpha	−164.4757805

(a)

	A	B
1	a	4.5
2	x	−1.2
3	n	4
4	theta	=65*PI()/180
5		
6	alf1n	=a^2/2*ABS(x-a)+SQRT(x/n^1.5+n^2)
7	alf1d	=15.8*SIN(PI()-theta)-(a^2/3-x)^1.5
8	alf2n	=21.3*a^(n-2)*SQRT(a-COS(theta^2+PI()/2)/x)
9	alf2d	=EXP(x)*ABS(x-a^2+0.07)*SIN(theta)^2
10		
11	alpha	=alf1n/alf1d-alf2n/alf2d

(b)

Figure 3.3   (a) Values mode and (b) formulas mode worksheets for Example 3.3.

3.3 WORKSHEET EDITING COMMANDS

Some skill in using a worksheet is required to develop one properly for a new problem. Otherwise, rework may be needed because of new thoughts on layout, partitioning the problem into its mathematical parts, expansion of the problem to accommodate new requirements, and so on. In this section, we introduce some worksheet features that enhance our ability to quickly proceed to a preferred solution.

Some basic worksheet editing commands are described below. They should be learned and used to organize and revise a worksheet for documentation purposes. Hereafter, using these commands will be implicit during any discussion involving changes to the worksheet. Figure 3.4 shows the **Edit** drop-down menu and some associated dialog boxes.

Edit Undo

This command reverses the effect of certain commands or actions. Only the last command or the last cell entry typed can be reversed. This command reverses all **Edit** commands, the **Formula Apply Names** command, the **Paste List** in the **Formula Paste Name** dialog box, and the typing in the formula bar after it is entered into a cell. Use this command when discovering that the last action should not have been taken. The wording of the command in the drop-down menu is context sensitive.

Edit Clear

This command, via its dialog box of Figure 3.4(b), clears a cell of its formats, formulas, or notes, or all three items depending upon the toggle setting of the **Clear** list buttons. Only formulas apply to our needs at this time. If the formula bar is active, this command clears only that part of it that is selected. Choose the **OK** button to execute the command. Contrast the action of this command to the **Edit Delete** command. **Edit Clear** removes only the contents of cells while **Edit Delete** removes the cells and readjusts cell boundaries of the worksheet to close up the space between cells.

Edit Delete

This command, via its dialog box of Figure 3.4(c), removes the selected cell(s) from the worksheet and readjusts cell boundaries to close up the space between cells as denoted by the toggle setting of the **Delete** list box. Choose the **OK** button to execute the command. Contrast the action of this command with that of **Edit Clear**.

Edit Insert

This command, via its dialog box of Figure 3.4(d), inserts a blank cell or range of cells into the worksheet. The insertion action is governed by the selection of cells preceding execution of the command. If an entire row (or column) is selected, the command is automatically executed and the row (or

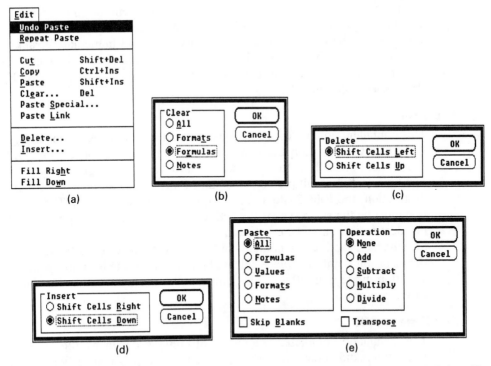

Figure 3.4 (a) Edit drop-down menu and dialog boxes for the (b) Clear, (c) Delete, (d) Insert, and (e) Paste Special commands.

column) is inserted by adjusting the remainder of the rows (or columns) of the worksheet. The dialog box appears when the selection is smaller than an entire row or column. In this case, execute the command by choosing the **OK** button.

Edit Copy

This command initiates the action for copying the contents of cells or characters of the formula bar to a destination via the **Edit Paste** or **Edit Paste Special** commands. Before invoking this command, the cells or formula parts must first be selected; that is, the area to be copied must be identified. Excel may use a temporary storage area called Clipboard which, at times, can be referred to directly. This command does not in any way disturb the information to be copied.

Edit Cut

This command initiates the action for moving the contents of cells or characters of the formula bar to a destination via the **Edit Paste** or **Edit Paste Special** commands. Before invoking this command, the cells or formula parts must first be selected; that is, the area to be cut and moved must be identified. Excel may use a temporary storage area called Clipboard which, at times, can be referred to directly. This command immediately removes the selected parts of a formula bar but merely highlights cells to be cut. The movement of cell contents occurs when invoking the **Edit Paste** or **Edit Paste Special** commands.

Edit Paste

This command completes the actions of copying or moving as begun by the latest **Edit Copy** or **Edit Cut** command. Before invoking this command, the destination, the cells or formula location into which pasting is to occur, must first be selected. Multiple copies of **Edit Copy** areas can be made when the destination, the **Edit Paste** area, is larger than the copy area. The destination must be the same size as the **Edit Cut** area, or only the upper left cell of the destination should be selected for complete copying to occur. If the formula bar is active, the contents of Clipboard are inserted at the location of the insertion point or replace selected characters in the formula, whichever selection mode is in effect. This command is not a substitute for the **Edit Insert** command.

Edit Paste Special

This command completes the action of copying begun by the latest **Edit Copy** command subject to the selections in the dialog box of Figure 3.4(e). Before invoking this command, the destination cell or formula location into which pasting is to occur must be selected and choices in the dialog **Paste** and **Operation** boxes must be toggled on. This command allows portions, or all, of the copied cells to be pasted with the possibility that selective combination of the copied contents with the destination contents should occur according to the **Operation** box toggle. The **Transpose** toggle of this command is used to transpose a matrix in the mathematical sense.

Because of our preoccupation with formulas, we should be aware that alternatives now exist for editing in the formula bar. Once a cell has been selected, its contents appear in the formula bar. Any rework of that formula can be done by any one, or a combination, of the following Excel features.

1. Direct editing with the keyboard only, and maybe using the mouse for selection, as described in Chapter 2.
2. Using commands from the **Formula** drop-down menu, as described in Section 3.2.
3. Using commands from the **Edit** drop-down menu, as described above.

The message area of the status bar should be observed often. It contains information pertinent to the operating mode of Excel and to the activity in the worksheet. Messages related to editing that are displayed there and their interpretation are as follows:

Message	Interpretation
Edit	Excel is in the Edit mode. The formula bar may be edited.
Copy (Select destination and press Enter or choose **Paste)**	A copy operation is in progress. Complete it by selecting the destination and invoke the **Paste** command.
Cut (Select destination and press Enter or choose **Paste)**	A move operation is in progress. Complete it by selecting the destination and invoke the **Paste** command.

Example 3.4

The purpose of this example is to illustrate the use of some of the commands discussed in this section and to introduce a method for iterative computing.

A magnet and a structure for shaping the magnetic flux path are shown in Figure 3.5. The design goal is to determine the length L_m and thickness t of the magnet, given the dimensions in the figure and the need for 2000 Gauss flux density in the air gap.

We choose Hyflux Alnico V for the magnet material and operate the magnet at the maximum energy product with $B = 10,200$ Gauss and $H = 515$ Oersteds (graphical computation not shown here). The formulas for the length L_m, in inches, and cross-sectional area A_m, in square inches, of a magnet necessary to produce a given flux density in the air gap are

$$L_m = \frac{H_g L_g r_f}{H_d} \tag{3.1}$$

$$A_m = \frac{B_g A_g \sigma}{B_d} \tag{3.2}$$

where

H_g = field strength in the air gap, Oersteds

L_g = length of the air gap, in.

r_f = reluctance factor (increase in magnetomotive force over air gap requirements), dimensionless

H_d = magnetizing force, Oersteds

B_g = flux density in the air gap, Gauss

A_g = area of the air gap, sq in.

σ = leakage flux factor, dimensionless

B_d = operating flux density, Gauss

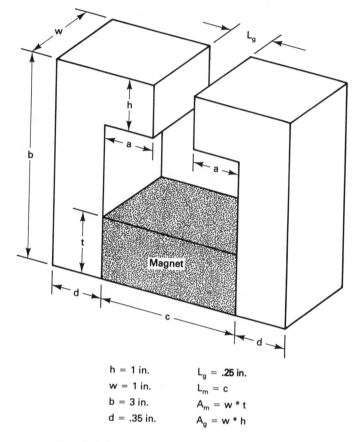

h = 1 in. L_g = .25 in.
w = 1 in. L_m = c
b = 3 in. A_m = w * t
d = .35 in. A_g = w * h

Figure 3.5 Magnet and structure for Example 3.4.

For the magnet configuration shown, the formula for the leakage flux factor σ is

$$\sigma = 1 + \frac{L_g}{A_g}\left[1.7U_a\frac{a}{a + L_g} + 1.4b\sqrt{\frac{U_b}{c}} + .67U_c\right] \qquad (3.3)$$

where

a = length of part a, in.

b = length of part b, in.

c = length of part c, in. (same as L_m)

U_a = perimeter of cross-section of part a, in.

U_b = perimeter of cross-section of part b, in.

U_c = perimeter of cross-section of part c, in.

A_g = cross-sectional area of air gap, sq in.

Because we must know σ to compute A_m, and hence the magnet thickness t, and because we must know U_c, and hence t, to compute σ, no direct computation of the magnet width t is possible, so we will organize our computations to manually iterate until we converge to a self-consistent value for σ, after which time we compute the final value for t.

The computational procedure is as follows:

1. Compute the length of the magnet from equation (3.1).
2. Assume a value for σ and compute the magnet cross-sectional area from equation (3.2).
3. Compute the magnet thickness t from the relationship $A_m = w*t$.
4. Use the value of t from step 3 to get U_c for equation (3.3) and compute a value for σ.
5. Compare the assumed value of σ in step 2 with that computed in step 4. If their difference is not acceptable, go back to step 2, use the value of σ from step 4, and repeat steps 3 and 4 until a self-consistent value for σ is obtained, at which time we will stop.

The output from Excel is shown in Figure 3.6 for the first iteration. We made 5 iterations before stopping, entering the value from location B10 into B4 each iteration. The values for σ were as follows:

	Values for σ	
Iteration	Step 2	Step 4
1	3.5 (initial)	4.262666276
2	4.262666276	4.312762982
3	4.312762982	4.316053648
4	4.316053648	4.316269800
5	4.316269800	4.316283998 (final)

We will automate this problem in Chapter 5, where we let Excel make the substitutions for σ and iterate to an acceptable difference. Meanwhile, let us discuss this solution for a moment before working it over to illustrate some editing commands.

1. We deliberately avoided defining some variables until later. This means we entered many numerical values in formulas. L_m (row 1) is a straightforward implementation of equation (3.1), a (row 2) is a combination of variables and numerical values, A_g (row 3) is precomputed from the dimensions of Figure 3.5, and σ (row 4) is the assumed value. The value for σ is entered in B4 as a constant, not as a formula. We copy into this cell the new value for σ as computed in row 10.
2. A_m (row 5) is a straightforward implementation of equation (3.2). Because $B = \mu H$, then $B_g = H_g$, since $\mu = 1$ for air. Also, t (row 6) is a trivial computation for the magnet thickness, since $w = 1$.

	A	B
1	Lm	1.165048544
2	a	0.457524272
3	Ag	1
4	sigma	3.5
5	Am	0.68627451
6	t	0.68627451
7	sig1	4.397255575
8	sig2	6.393801686
9	sig3	2.259607843
10	sigma'	4.262666276

(a)

	A	B
1	Lm	=2000*0.25*1.2/515
2	a	=(Lm-0.25)/2
3	Ag	1
4	sigma	3.5
5	Am	=2000*Ag*sigma/10200
6	t	=Am/1
7	sig1	=1.7*4*a/(a+0.25)
8	sig2	=1.4*3*SQRT(2.7/Lm)
9	sig3	=0.67*2*(1+t)
10	sigma'	=1+0.25/Ag*(sig1+sig2+sig3)

(b)

Figure 3.6 Worksheet for Example 3.4 in (a) values mode and (b) formulas mode.

3. The bracketed part of equation (3.3) is partitioned into three parts (rows 7, 8, and 9) with U_a and U_b precomputed and with various numerical values entered into the computations. The new value for σ, called σ' in row 10, is equation (3.3).

Let us now illustrate some of the commands introduced in this section. We will reorganize the worksheet of Figure 3.6 to produce the ones shown in Figure 3.7. We will enter the numerical values into named cells so that formulas can be constructed with symbolic references. We will also partition the worksheet to better identify the computations.

1. Select row 1 and **Edit Insert** 4 lines. Manually enter new rows 1 through 4 of Figure 3.7(a) and apply **Formula Create Names** to columns A and B of these four rows. **Edit Clear All** the contents of cell B5 and enter the formula shown in Figure 3.7(a).

2. Select row 6 of Figure 3.7(a) and apply **All** of the **Edit Clear** command. With row 6 still selected, **Edit Insert** 3 lines. Manually enter new rows 7, 8, and 9 of Figure 3.7(b). **Edit Clear All** the contents of cell B10 and enter the for-

mula shown in Figure 3.7(b). Apply **Formula Create Names** to columns A and B of these four rows.

3. Select row 12 of Figure 3.7(b) and **Edit Insert** one line. Manually enter the information shown in new row 12 of Figure 3.7(c) and apply **Formula Create Names** to columns A and B of this row. **Edit Clear All** the contents of cell B13 and enter the formula shown in Figure 3.7(c). Select row 14 and **Edit Insert** one line to get Figure 3.7(c).

4. Select cell B15 of Figure 3.7(c) and edit it in the formula bar to look like cell B15 of Figure 3.7(d). Select row 16 of Figure 3.7(c) and **Edit Insert** 9 lines.

	A	B
1	Hg	2000
2	Lg	0.25
3	rf	1.2
4	Hd	515
5	Lm	=Hg*Lg*rf/Hd
6	a	=(Lm-0.25)/2
7	Ag	1
8	sigma	3.5
9	Am	=2000*Ag*sigma/10200
10	t	=Am/1
11	sig1	=1.7*4*a/(a+0.25)
12	sig2	=1.4*3*SQRT(2.7/Lm)
13	sig3	=0.67*2*(1+t)
14	sigma'	=1+0.25/Ag*(sig1+sig2+sig3)

(a)

	A	B
1	Hg	2000
2	Lg	0.25
3	rf	1.2
4	Hd	515
5	Lm	=Hg*Lg*rf/Hd
6		
7	Bg	2000
8	h	1
9	w	1
10	Ag	=h*w
11	sigma	3.5
12	Am	=2000*Ag*sigma/10200
13	t	=Am/1
14	sig1	=1.7*4*a/(a+0.25)
15	sig2	=1.4*3*SQRT(2.7/Lm)
16	sig3	=0.67*2*(1+t)
17	sigma'	=1+0.25/Ag*(sig1+sig2+sig3)

(b)

Figure 3.7 Rework of the worksheet shown in Figure 3.6(b).

	A	B
1	Hg	2000
2	Lg	0.25
3	rf	1.2
4	Hd	515
5	Lm	=Hg*Lg*rf/Hd
6		
7	Bg	2000
8	h	1
9	w	1
10	Ag	=h*w
11	sigma	3.5
12	Bd	10200
13	Am	=Bg*Ag*sigma/Bd
14		
15	t	=Am/1
16	sig1	=1.7*4*a/(a+0.25)
17	sig2	=1.4*3*SQRT(2.7/Lm)
18	sig3	=0.67*2*(1+t)
19	sigma'	=1+0.25/Ag*(sig1+sig2+sig3)

(c)

	A	B
1	Hg	2000
2	Lg	0.25
3	rf	1.2
4	Hd	515
5	Lm	=Hg*Lg*rf/Hd
6		
7	Bg	2000
8	h	1
9	w	1
10	Ag	=h*w
11	sigma	3.5
12	Bd	10200
13	Am	=Bg*Ag*sigma/Bd
14		
15	t	=Am/w
16		
17	a	=(Lm-Lg)/2
18	b	3
19	cc	=Lm
20	d	0.35
21	Ua	=2*(w+h)
22	Ub	=2*(w+d)
23	Uc	=2*(w+t)
24		
25	sig1	=1.7*Ua*a/(a+Lg)
26	sig2	=1.4*b*SQRT(Ub/cc)+0.67*Uc
27	sigma'	=1+Lg/Ag*(sig1+sig2)

(d)

Figure 3.7 Continued

Manually enter in new lines 17 through 21 the information shown in Figure 3.7(d). Excel will not let us give cell B19 the name "*c*" (it considers it to be an invalid reference name because it conflicts with the R1C1 naming convention), so we choose the name "*cc*." Also, enter the information in cells A22 and A23. Select cell B21 and execute the **Edit Copy** command. Then, select cell B22 and execute the **Paste All**, **Operation None** toggles of the **Edit Paste Special** command. Select cell B23 and repeat the **Edit Paste Special** command. Edit cells B22 and B23 in the formula bar to appear as in Figure 3.7(d).

5. Edit cells B25 and B26 in the formula bar to appear as in Figure 3.7(d). Select row 27 and execute the **Edit Delete** command to remove sig3 from the worksheet. Edit new cell B27, the formula for σ', in the formula bar to appear as in Figure 3.7(d).

On completing the above changes, the numerical values should appear as in Figure 3.8(a). The worksheet is now ready for the iterative computations, with

	A	B
1	Hg	2000
2	Lg	0.25
3	rf	1.2
4	Hd	515
5	Lm	1.165048544
6		
7	Bg	2000
8	h	1
9	w	1
10	Ag	1
11	sigma	3.5
12	Bd	10200
13	Am	0.68627451
14		
15	t	0.68627451
16		
17	a	0.457524272
18	b	3
19	cc	1.165048544
20	d	0.35
21	Ua	4
22	Ub	2.7
23	Uc	3.37254902
24		
25	sig1	4.397255575
26	sig2	8.653409529
27	sigma'	4.262666276

(a)

	A	B
1	Hg	2000
2	Lg	0.25
3	rf	1.2
4	Hd	515
5	Lm	1.165048544
6		
7	Bg	2000
8	h	1
9	w	1
10	Ag	1
11	sigma	4.3162698
12	Bd	10200
13	Am	0.846327412
14		
15	t	0.846327412
16		
17	a	0.457524272
18	b	3
19	cc	1.165048544
20	d	0.35
21	Ua	4
22	Ub	2.7
23	Uc	3.692654823
24		
25	sig1	4.397255575
26	sig2	8.867880418
27	sigma'	4.316283998

(b)

Figure 3.8 Numerical results for the edited worksheet of Example 3.4 (a) after the initial computation and (b) after several iterations.

$\sigma = 3.5$ as the starting value in cell B11. This time, during the iterations, we will copy the value from cell B27 into cell B11 with the **Paste Values**, **Operation None** toggles of the **Edit Paste Special** command. After several iterations, we have the results of Figure 3.8(b).

3.4 FORMATTING A DOCUMENT

We consider documenting our work an important part of the engineering task. Thus far, we used text in a cell adjacent to a value as a description of the value. Later, we defined that text as the name of the value and then worked in a more natural engineering context. We now learn of other ways to improve the appearance of our worksheet to contribute to the documentation process. We will learn how to prepare report quality output and to develop good work habits, so that proper documentation is a natural outcome of problem preparation, solution, and display. In this section, we concentrate on the Excel features to use for this purpose. We do nothing to compromise accuracy of the problem solution. As a first step, we consider the worksheet features that affect the following:

1. The arrangement, through alignment, of text and numbers within cells to create a favorable impression of the worksheet as a whole.
2. The highlighting of cells, and thus data, with shading, outlining, and otherwise introducing a form of obvious tabular structure to the worksheet.
3. The size of cells by varying their dimensions to accommodate, for display purposes, varying quantities of data within the cell.
4. The appearance of the display, and printed report, by adding, or eliminating, visual effects caused by color, gridlines, row and column headings, and the like.

Features of Excel that allow us to perform the above effects are invoked with some of the commands of Table 3.3. These commands are briefly discussed below. Several commands affect both the display and printer, others affect only the display unit and thus allow the user to customize the worksheet for preferential appearance, while the remainder of the commands are associated with obtaining printed output.

The following commands control certain features via the **Format** drop-down menu of Figure 3.9.

Format Number

This command allows us to specify the appearance of numerical values with respect to number of digits displayed, the location of the decimal point, the color of the characters displayed, the conversion to percentage, and so on.

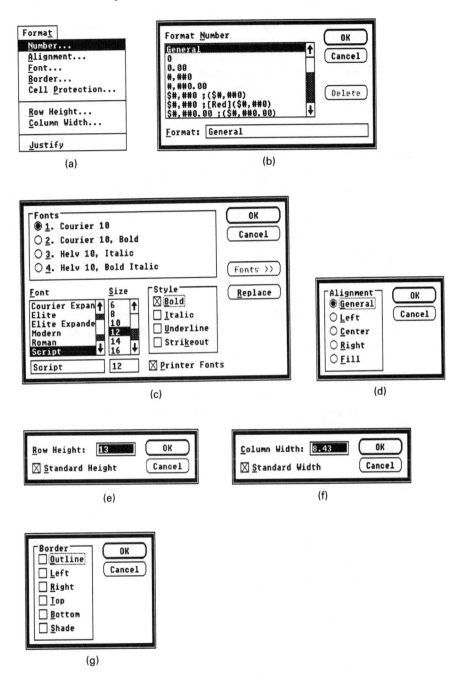

Figure 3.9   (a) Format drop-down menu and dialog boxes for the (b) Number, (c) Font, (d) Alignment, (e) Row Height, (f) Column Width, and (g) Border commands.

Except for graph axis tick mark labeling, this menu selection is usually not important for most engineering work because we can accept full numerical precision of the values without concern for their appearance. The dialog box of Figure 3.9(b) shows a selection of formats, for which the default one is called General. More information on numerical formatting is given in the Number Formats Box on page 77. It is possible for the user to define a custom format.

Format Font

This command, via the dialog box of Figure 3.9(c), allows a variety of text fonts to be chosen and applied to different cells as desired. The size and style of character are also available for assignment to the font upon selecting and toggling the desired choice. The fonts are applied to selected cells by choosing the **OK** button. Font size is measured in points, where 72 points = 1 inch.

Format Alignment

This command, via the dialog box of Figure 3.9(d), allows the contents of the selected cell(s) to be aligned horizontally within their confines. It is used to position the contents for association or demarcation purposes. The default selection is General.

TABLE 3.3   COMMANDS FOR FORMATTING A DOCUMENT

	Output unit affected	
Command	Display	Printer
Format Number	X	X
Format Font	X	X
Format Alignment	X	X
Format Justify	X	X
Format Row Height	X	X
Format Column Width	X	X
Format Border	X	X
Formula Note	X	
Window Show Info	X	
Options Display	X	
Control Run/Control Panel/Preferences/Colors	X	
File Page Setup		X
File Printer Setup		X
File Print		X
Options Set Print Area		X
Options Set Print Titles		X
Options Set Page Break		X

Format Justify

This command is used to left- and right-align paragraphs of text evenly within a chosen range of cells over one or more columns. The effect is to ignore intercell boundaries, when more than one cell is chosen horizontally, and to spread out the text over the space available with multiple lines of text, if necessary. With this command, it is not necessary to resize individual columns to make room for a pleasing paragraph of text. Numbers must not be included in the selection for justification.

Format Row Height

This command, via its dialog box of Figure 3.9(e), is used to specify a new height for a selection of cells, or to return to the default height by toggling **Standard Height** on. The height measurement is in points, as for fonts (72 points = 1 inch). With the mouse, row heights may be adjusted by dragging the row boundary as explained in Section 2.3.2.

Format Column Width

This command, via its dialog box of Figure 3.9(f), is used in a manner similar to **Format Row Height**, except that the width measurement is in number of characters. Column width may also be adjusted with the mouse as described in Section 2.3.2.

NUMBER FORMATS

A number format is a picture assembled from symbols. It specifies how the value of a cell is to appear. The picture may have up to four sections, each separated by semicolons. The general form of the format is

$$[section\text{-}1][;[section\text{-}2][;[section\text{-}3][;section\text{-}4]]]$$

where *section-i* is used to format the cell contents according to the following table, given that the contents is positive, negative, zero, or text, and according to the number of sections used in the format.

Number of sections used	Format application			
	section-1	*section-2*	*section-3*	*section-4*
4	positive no.	negative no.	zero	text
3	non-negative	negative no.	text	
2	all nos.	text		
1	all nos.			

Each section is optional, but the position of an omitted section prior to the last section used must be indicated by including the corresponding semicolon. An omitted section inhibits display of that type of value.

The allowed symbols are shown in the accompanying symbol table. Their use is illustrated in the example table. The procedure for setting the display format is as follows:

- Select the cells to be formatted alike.
- Execute the **Format Number** command.
- Select a built-in format from the Format Number list box (scrolling may be necessary to see them all), edit an existing format, or type in a new one in the **Format** text box.
- Choose the **OK** button.

The display format of a cell may be changed at any time by following the above procedure again.

Symbol	Numeric interpretation
0	Digit placeholder, no suppression of leading and trailing zeros in this position.
#	Digit placeholder, suppresses leading and trailing zeros in this position.
.	Display the decimal point.
,	Thousands separator, visible when needed.
E− E+ e− e+	Exponent indicator for scientific notation.
: $ − + ( ) space	Given character to be displayed.
"text"	String within quotation marks given as *text* to be displayed.
@	Text placeholder.

Symbol	Action interpretation
%	Multiply preceding value by 100 and display it with a trailing % character.
\	Display the next character following this backslash.
*	Repeat the next character following this asterisk so as to fill the column width.
[color]	Change the color of the characters displayed in the cell to color = BLACK, WHITE, RED, GREEN, BLUE, YELLOW, MAGENTA, or CYAN.

Value entered	Format applied	Displayed value	Comments
26.438 −.29 0	0.0#	26.44 −0.29 0.0	Digits always show in 0 positions; all digits show to left; rounding in rightmost 0 or #.

Values	Format	Result	Explanation
.0382 −16.1447 0	#.00	.04 16.14 .00	# needed to show digits to left of decimal point.
62748.6 −933.4 0	#,#00	62,749 −933 00	Show integers without decimal point in format; separate thousands with comma.
.1432 −3.6 0	0.0%	14.3% −360.0% 0.0%	Values multiplied by 100; % sign added on right.
606.488 −.000939 0	0.000E+00	6.065E+02 −9.390E−04 0.000E+00	Scientific notation, decimal point adjusted automatically; rounding if necessary.
.933 −28.6 0	0.#;0.00	0.9 28.60 0.	Interpret as for three-section format without text section.
.0066 −85.2 0 This is text	0.##;(0.##);0;@	0.01 (85.2) 0 This is text	Four-section format; negative numbers enclosed within parentheses; @ for text display.
13.84 −42 0 Overflow	"R = "0.0;"Imaginary";@	R = 13.8 Imaginary R = 0.0 Overflow	Three-section format; combine text with number format in *section-1*.
1 0 −1 IHK	"Left";"Right";	Left Right IHK	Four-section format (no @ in *section-3*); zero values not displayed; display text for 1 and −1; display text since @ not needed for *section-4* and *section-4* not omitted.
1 0 −1 IHK	"Left";"Right";;	Left Right 	Four-section format; zero values not displayed; display text for 1 and −1; text not displayed because *section-4* is omitted (it would show if @ were there).

Format Border

This command, via its dialog box of Figure 3.9(g), is used for adding solid lines as borders for cells and for shading their interior for contrast with neighboring cells. The toggle choices within the dialog box allow the periphery or individual sides of the cells to have added borders. The borders or sides of cells can also be deleted with this command.

It is important to work with a display presentation that suits the preferences of the user. Not everything we do to the worksheet has to show in a printout. We can use color to advantage and we can simplify the screen appearance. The following commands affect the worksheet appearance on the display unit and, in the case of Notes, contribute to documentation of the work.

Formula Note

This command, shown with the Cell Note window in Figure 3.10, allows text, called notes, to be attached to a cell. These comments add to the documentation of a worksheet. They may also be viewed with this command, and they may be printed out with the **File Page Setup** command described below. Notes can be added, deleted, and edited in the window. The influence of this command depends on the range of cells selected.

Window Show Info

This command, shown with its Info window in Figure 3.11, is used to display information about the selected cell, including its note. When executing this command, the menu bar changes to the Info menu bar. The Information available for display is indicated by the designations shown in Figure 3.11(b). The designations, selected from the **Info** menu, are toggled on or off to show, or hide, the information. They are all toggled on for the figure.

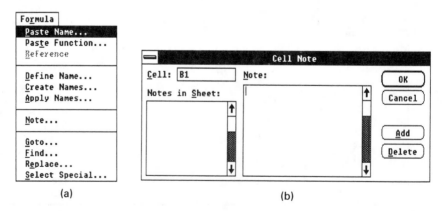

(a)   (b)

Figure 3.10   (a) Formula drop-down menu and (b) Note dialog box.

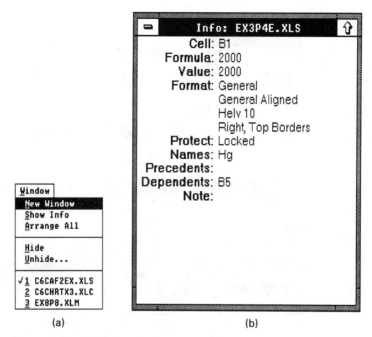

Figure 3.11   (a) Window drop-down menu and (b) Show Info output box.

Options Display

This command was introduced in Section 2.3.2, where we discussed its use in showing formulas on the screen. The drop-down menu and its dialog box are shown in Figure 2.6. Now, we feel the other choices given in the dialog box of Figure 2.6(b) are important for setting up the display to suit personal preferences. We can, via the toggles, show (or hide) gridlines, row and column headings, zeros in blank cells, and we can choose the gridline and heading color for color displays. Use of these features is recommended to establish a comfortable working environment that contributes to accuracy in development of the worksheet. These options do not control the printed output.

Screen Colors

This command, via its dialog box, is used to specify the colors for various screen areas. The series of menus that one must follow to access the colors dialog box is shown in Figure 3.12. We begin by choosing the **Control** menu icon, the upper left corner of the Excel window, to get the **Control** drop-down menu, Figure 3.12(a). We then select **Run** to display the **Run Application** dialog box, Figure 3.12(b). Choosing the **Control Panel** toggle and the **OK** button exposes the Control Panel window from which we select **Preferences**, Figure 3.12(c). Another drop-down menu appears, Figure 3.12(d),

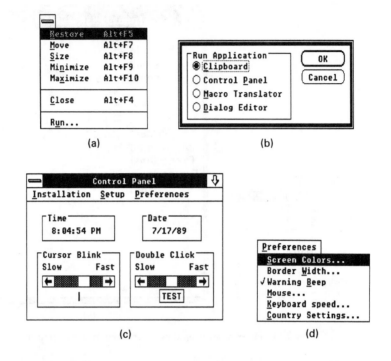

(a)   (b)

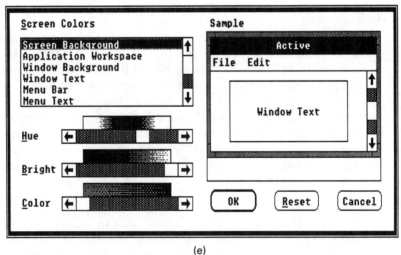

(c)   (d)

(e)

Figure 3.12 Series of menus, dialog boxes, and windows that must be activated
to reach the Screen Colors dialog box.

from which we select **Screen Colors** after which, finally, the **Screen Colors** dialog box appears, Figure 3.12(e). It is now possible to adjust the hue, brightness, and tint of the screen, workspace, window text and background, menu text, menu bar, title bar text and selected/unselected background, the active/inactive border, scroll bars, and the window border. The user is encouraged to experiment with various color combinations to achieve satisfying screen presentations. Comments on the use of color appear in the Box titled Effective Use of Color on page 83.

To get printed output, we must specify the appearance of the printed document, specify which printer to use, and execute the print command. We can accept default appearance settings so that a minimum of effort is required to get a printout. Optionally, we may define a print area smaller than provided for by the default setting, we may define text for a page title, and we may set manual page breaks for large worksheets. The commands that we are concerned with are shown in Figure 2.10. We discussed printing briefly in Section 2.4.

File Page Setup

This command, via its dialog box of Figure 2.10(d), is used to specify headers and footers, which are text printed at the top and bottom of the sheet, respectively, the sheet margins, and toggles for row and column show (or hide) and gridlines show (or hide). Some leeway is provided for special formatting of the header and footer content.

File Printer Setup

This command, via its dialog boxes of Figures 2.10(b) and 2.10(c), is used to specify which printer to use and, optionally, to change settings in the **Setup** box. When only one printer is installed with your computer, no multiple choices will be available.

File Print

This command, via its dialog box of Figure 2.10(e), is used to print the document according to the settings of the **File Page Setup** and **File Printer Setup** dialog boxes. Other selection choices and toggles govern what and how much, numbers of pages and number of copies, are to be printed. The worksheet and/or notes are selected by toggles.

EFFECTIVE USE OF COLOR

The user of Excel is permitted to alter the color of various features of chart, worksheet, and macro windows and their contents. Choosing colors is not a matter of esthetics. Effective use of color provides more information, since we can use it qualitatively (to differentiate among) and quantitatively (to

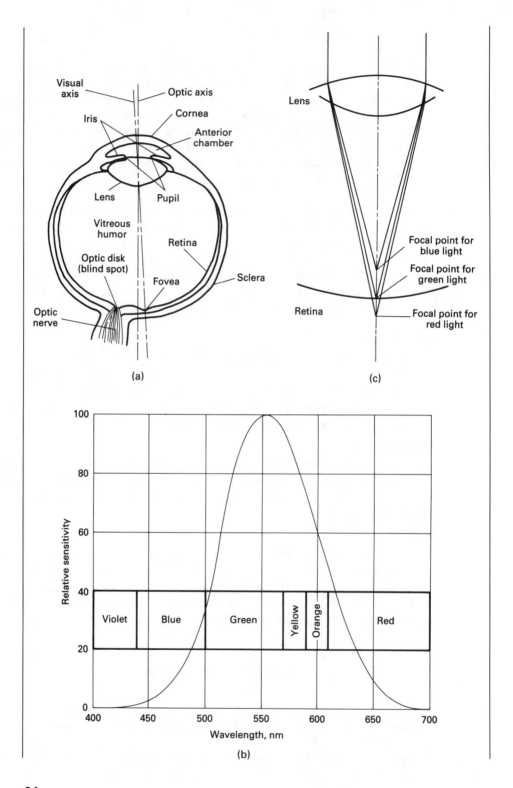

(a)

(c)

(b)

display relationships of degree). We can use color to differentiate among top-ics and functional areas on the screen and to focus attention on action items at the expense of background information. For these purposes, we rely on its *hue* (color sensations reported by observers for wavelengths between 400 nm and 700 nm), *brightness* (correlation between light intensity and visual stimulus ordered from light to dark), and *saturation* (chromatic purity contributing to the color sensation—narrow band of wavelengths corresponds to more color saturation). This presentation is for users of color systems rather than for designers of such systems. We address topics for using color to discriminate and inform, to avoid fatigue, and to avoid errors.

Color sensations result from the nervous system response to stimulation by light waves of nerve terminations (rods and cones) on the retina within the eye. Some important parts of the eye are shown in the structure of Figure (a), a horizontal cross-section of the right eye viewed from above. The response to light is governed by characteristics of the components in the light path within the eye, namely, the cornea, lens, fluids, and retina. The sensitivity of the eye to light in the visible spectrum is wavelength dependent, as shown in Figure (b) for a "standard" observer. This curve represents an averaging of the re-sponses of the three types of photopigments (red, green, and blue) that are most sensitive to color. Nominal focusing of images on the retina is produced through muscular forces acting to shape the lens. But lack of lens color correc-tion causes nonuniform diffraction of light rays at different wavelengths to cause convergence problems. The result is that images produced by different wavelengths are focused by the lens at distances different from the retina, as shown in Figure (c). The eye *accommodates* such differences by refocusing to enable one to see each color sharply. Constant refocusing for this purpose causes eye fatigue.

The eye is an imperfect optical system whose performance degrades with time. The lens yellows with time and absorbs light at short wavelengths (blues) more than at the long wavelengths (reds and yellows); fluids in the eye reduce the transmittance of short wavelength light (thus filtering out blue light more than light at longer wavelengths); the three photopigments are not equally distributed in the cones of the retina (red 64%, green 32%, blue 2%); the rods and cones are not evenly distributed over the retina (cones are more dense in the center, rods more dense in the periphery); the cones in the center of the retina have little blue photopigment (and hence this area, the fovea, is least sensitive to small blue objects); and an unfortunate recombination of the signals from the photoreceptors takes place in the optic nerve path to produce color and brightness signals such that the blue signal does not contribute to the brightness and, hence, does not help produce sharp edges. The above deficien-cies are not present to the same extent in all individuals.

Rules for the proper use of color are developed because of the deficien-cies in the human visual system. Color photography and color television de-velopments are partly based on the need to allow for such deficiencies. We can adopt and apply many rules for display of color images on a computer monitor that were long ago applied in these other fields. The hue, brightness, and color (saturation) controls of the Excel dialog box shown in Figure 3.12 and the opportunity to display characters in color as indicated in the Number Formats

Box on page 77 allow such rules to be applied in spreadsheet work. Within the limited range of colors available for most personal computers, the following rules can be applied in Excel:

1. Use white, black, or gray for very small features (small text, thin lines, and very small areas), since the eye distinguishes such features only in terms of brightness, not color. This implies that color discrimination should not be used for such features.

2. Avoid eye fatigue, and possibly reduce errors, by minimizing lens accommodation (refocusing). Use colors not far removed from each other in the spectrum [see Figure (c)].

3. Use the short wavelength limitations of the eye to your advantage by selecting blue for backgrounds, large objects, and for objects at the periphery of the display.

4. Use color only for the qualitative and quantitative purposes mentioned above. This usually requires that few different colors be used at a time and, usually, that color not be used when edge detection is required.

5. Choose background colors from near the ends of the spectrum (blue, red, etc.) to emphasize brightness contrast for small features in spectrally centered colors.

The following references are recommended for in-depth application information on the use of color in computer displays.

1. P. English-Zemke, "Using color in online marketing tools," *IEEE Trans. Prof. Comm.,* vol. 31, no. 2, June 1988, pp. 70–74.

2. G. M. Murch, "Physiological principles for the effective use of color," *IEEE Computer Graphics & Appl.,* vol. 4, no. 11, November 1984, pp. 49–54.

3. G. Murch, (a) "The effective use of color: Physiological principles," *Tekniques,* vol. 7, no. 4, Winter 1983, pp. 13–16; (b) "The effective use of color: Perceptual principles," *Tekniques,* vol. 8, no. 1, Spring 1984, pp. 4–9: (c) "The effective use of color: Cognitive principles," *Tekniques,* vol. 8, no. 2, Summer 1984, pp. 25–31 (published by Tektronix, Inc.).

Example 3.5

We now use some of the commands discussed in this section to alter the appearance of the worksheet for Example 3.4. We start with the worksheet of Figure 3.8(a).

First, we insert a new first row. Then, we select cell A1 and type in Magnet Design with extra blanks so that it is centered within cells A1 and B1. Now, by multiply selecting columns A and B in rows, 6, 14, 16, and 28, executing the **Format Border** command, and toggling the **Shade** text box on, we will lightly stipple the selected cells. Upon printing the worksheet without row and column headings and without gridlines, we get the presentation of Figure 3.13(a).

We can select the range A1:B28, execute **Format Font**, toggle **Style Bold** on, choose **OK**, and print out the worksheet to get Figure 3.13(b). In Figure 3.13(c), we turned on the **Border Outline** toggle of the **Format Border** dialog box for the multiply selected cells as above before printing the worksheet. Now, after toggling on the **Row & Column Headings** and **Gridlines** text boxes of the **File Page Setup** dialog box, we print out Figure 3.13(d).

Example 3.6

In this example we will describe how to print out information on a cell. Recall that we can enter our own information into a cell with the **Formula Note** command. Also, we can display additional information about a cell with the **Window Show Info** command. Since we opened another window with this latter command, we have menu selections that apply only to that window, one of which is the **File** drop-down menu that is exactly like the one for the worksheet. Because it contains a **Print** command, we can print out the contents of the Info window, which we have done in Figure 3.14, using cell B28 of Figure 3.13.

	Magnet Design			Magnet Design	
Hg	2000		**Hg**	**2000**	
Lg	0.25		**Lg**	**0.25**	
rf	1.2		**rf**	**1.2**	
Hd	515		**Hd**	**515**	
Lm	1.165048544		**Lm**	**1.165048544**	
Bg	2000		**Bg**	**2000**	
h	1		**h**	**1**	
w	1		**w**	**1**	
Ag	1		**Ag**	**1**	
sigma	3.5		**sigma**	**3.5**	
Bd	10200		**Bd**	**10200**	
Am	0.68627451		**Am**	**0.68627451**	
t	0.68627451		**t**	**0.68627451**	
a	0.457524272		**a**	**0.457524272**	
b	3		**b**	**3**	
cc	1.165048544		**cc**	**1.165048544**	
d	0.35		**d**	**0.35**	
Ua	4		**Ua**	**4**	
Ub	2.7		**Ub**	**2.7**	
Uc	3.37254902		**Uc**	**3.37254902**	
sig1	4.397255575		**sig1**	**4.397255575**	
sig2	8.653409529		**sig2**	**8.653409529**	
sigma′	4.262666276		**sigma′**	**4.262666276**	
	(a)			(b)	

Figure 3.13   Various worksheet printouts for Example 3.5

	A	B
1	Magnet Design	
2	Hg	2000
3	Lg	0.25
4	rf	1.2
5	Hd	515
6	Lm	1.165048544
7		
8	Bg	2000
9	h	1
10	w	1
11	Ag	1
12	sigma	3.5
13	Bd	10200
14	Am	0.68627451
15		
16	t	0.68627451
17		
18	a	0.457524272
19	b	3
20	cc	1.165048544
21	d	0.35
22	Ua	4
23	Ub	2.7
24	Uc	3.37254902
25		
26	sig1	4.397255575
27	sig2	8.653409529
28	sigma'	4.262666276

Magnet Design (c):

Hg	2000
Lg	0.25
rf	1.2
Hd	515
Lm	1.165048544
Bg	2000
h	1
w	1
Ag	1
sigma	3.5
Bd	10200
Am	0.68627451
t	0.68627451
a	0.457524272
b	3
cc	1.165048544
d	0.35
Ua	4
Ub	2.7
Uc	3.37254902
sig1	4.397255575
sig2	8.653409529
sigma'	4.262666276

(c)   (d)

Figure 3.13 Continued

```
       Cell: B28
    Formula: =1+Lg/Ag*(sig1+sig2)
      Value: 4.262666276
     Format: General
             General Aligned
             System 10
             No Borders
             Shaded
    Protect: Locked
      Names:
 Precedents: B3,B11,B26:B27
 Dependents:
       Note: Sigma' is the final leakage factor computed from the
             iterative procedure.  It is not used to compute the magnet
             thickness (t).
```

Figure 3.14 Printout of the Info window.

3.5 DEBUGGING

Much of the new material of this chapter concerns layout and display presentation techniques that enhance problem documentation and provide a more friendly atmosphere for working on the problem. An important secondary result of practicing these good work habits is a reduction in errors because an organized work procedure inherently introduces fewer bugs into the work. Should there be bugs to remove, abundant documentation reduces the time for this task because less time is needed to understand what has been done and to comprehend its implication. Thus, we feel strongly that adopting a consistent documentation style that incorporates many of the built-in documentation aids of Excel will produce better quality and more accurate results in shorter work sessions. We say this even though, in this text, we omit much of the worksheet document for conservation of space and because we supplement our examples through discussion.

It is important to work in the context of the engineering discipline. Retain the engineering nomenclature rather than using computer style acronyms, use variable names rather than cell coordinate references, and partition the problem into logically related parts to reduce the burden of trying to understand complex mathematical relationships confined to the constraints of the viewing screen size.

The new computational capability introduced in this chapter is the use of built-in functions. Sources of errors in using functions include:

1. Entering argument values in the wrong units, for example, entering degrees when radians are needed in the trigonometric functions.
2. Using the wrong function when multiple similar choices exist, such as LN instead of LOG10, STDEV instead of STDEVP, and so on.
3. Failing to convert the units of values returned by a function, for example, failing to convert radians to degrees for the inverse trigonometric functions, when degrees are needed for the formula.
4. Ignoring the range of values over which the formulas apply, for example, computing negative arguments for the square root and logarithm functions and thus obtaining errors.

We also advocate using names for cells instead of using their coordinate references. For debugging purposes, these advantages are realized:

1. Inadvertent cell references are avoided because we would not assign names to blank cells, but the cell coordinate reference is a legitimate reference even when the cell is blank and wrongly entered.
2. We can conveniently obtain a list of names used in the worksheet via the **Formula Define Name** command. From this list we can choose the name and not rely on entering it into the formula via the keyboard, thus avoiding typos. We do not advocate mixing names and cell coordinate references in the same worksheet.

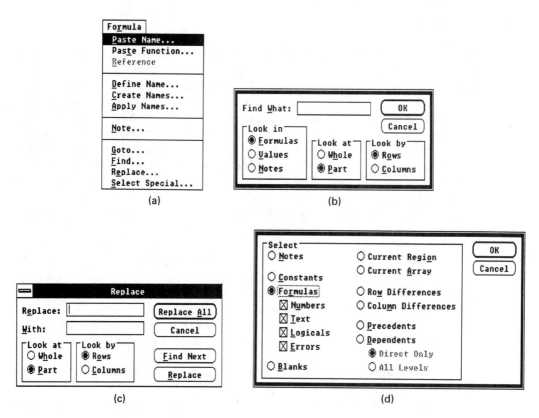

Figure 3.15 (a) Formula drop-down menu with dialog boxes displayed by the (b) Find, (c) Replace, and (d) Select Special commands.

3. User chosen names are more distinctive in formulas than cell coordinate references because of their uniqueness, thus making sight checking of formulas easier, since there is no blending of characters as would occur when cell coordinate references only are used. Unusual entries are thus easier to discover.

It is very important to select proper test values when functions are used in formulas for reasons given above. Special cases must be carefully selected to ensure that all parts of the formulas are verified. Watch for multiplication by zero as was discussed in Section 2.4. Cases that test problem boundary values must be used so that the formula is verified over the limits of the variables. Complex formulas entered in numerous cells are especially difficult to debug. For these cases, it is wise to use Excel features that inform and display attributes of the formula. Some of these features from the **Formula** drop-down menu of Figure 3.15(a) are now described.

Formula Goto

This command selects a named area or a reference from the list box or it can be typed in. It is used to locate and scroll to a desired part of the worksheet. Because it remembers the last goto selection by having entered two cell references successively, one can toggle back and forth between the two parts of the worksheet. This is a convenience feature that should be used with large worksheets.

Formula Find

This command, via its dialog box of Figure 3.15(b), is used to search for text or a number in a cell or selected range of cells. The text can be a variable name. This command is useful in locating #NAME? and #REF! error values. One can search formulas, values, and notes and request a match with the entire cell contents (**Whole**) or with any portion of the cell contents (**Part**). This command is useful with large worksheets.

Formula Replace

This command, via its dialog box of Figure 3.15(c), is used to search for and replace characters in the worksheet or within a selected range. It is useful when making corrections that require changes to other parts of the worksheet. It should always be used to make substitutions when there are multiple values to replace in a complex worksheet, since it is more thorough during the search than a human usually is.

Formula Select Special

This command, via its dialog box of Figure 3.15(d), is used to select cells that have a specified set of characteristics. The search for cells with the chosen characteristics is over the entire worksheet or over a selected range. Some of its search features are similar to those of the **Formula Find** and **Formula Replace** commands but more possibilities are provided. The **Precedents** and **Dependents** choices should be considered for tracing the cell references to determine their implications on the computations.

Special effort should be made to obtain as much information about error conditions as possible in order to locate the trouble spot. For this purpose, one should use the **Window Show Info** command of Section 3.4, since information related to a cell is easily obtained and displayed with this command. Having so much information automatically displayed in one location with this command allows visual correlations to be made among diverse data about a cell that potentially allows focusing on the solution.

3.6 ABOUT VERSION 3.0

New capability in version 3.0 that applies to the material of this chapter incudes the built-in functions of Table 3.4. Of course, all worksheets of this chapter run under version 3.0 without change.

In this chapter we have worked with numerous commands of the **Formula** menu since our formulas contained built-in functions and user named variables. Any version 3.0 changes to the associated dialog boxes of Figures 3.2 and 3.10 are minor.

Numerous other menus and dialog boxes discussed in this chapter have been changed slightly in version 3.0. Some changes to note are:

1. The **Edit Delete** and **Edit Insert** command dialog boxes of Figures 3.4(c) and 3.4(d), respectively, now contain **Entire Row** and **Entire Column** buttons.
2. The **Patterns** command has been added to the **Format** menu of Figure 3.9(a). Its dialog box is shown in Figure 3.16. Each button associates with a drop-down list of choices (not shown) for use in formatting a cell or cell range.
3. The **Format Number** dialog box of Figure 3.9(b) now contains a **Sample** box that shows the number in the selected cell as formatted by a choice made from the list in the box. Numbers can now be formatted as fractions.
4. The **Format Font** dialog box of Figure 3.9(c) now contains a **Sample** box that shows characters chosen from the **Font** list box.

TABLE 3.4 ADDITIONAL BUILT-IN FUNCTIONS OF VERSION 3.0

Name	Algebraic notation	Symbol	Comments
Hyperbolic			
Sine	$\sinh x$	SINH (x)	
Cosine	$\cosh x$	COSH (x)	
Tangent	$\tanh x$	TANH (x)	
Arcsine	$\sinh^{-1} x$	ASINH (x)	
Arcosine	$\cosh^{-1} x$	ACOSH (x)	
Arctangent	$\tanh^{-1} x$	ATANH (x)	$-1 < x < 1$
Statistical			
Median*	median $(x_1, x_2, \ldots, x_n)$	MEDIAN $(x_1, x_2, \ldots, x_n)$	

* For the x_i in algebraically ascending order, the function value is $x_{\left(\frac{n+1}{2}\right)}$ for n odd,

$\frac{1}{2}\left[x_{\left(\frac{n}{2}\right)} + x_{\left(\frac{n}{2}+1\right)}\right]$ for n even. The x_i need not be ordered for this function, it will be calculated correctly.

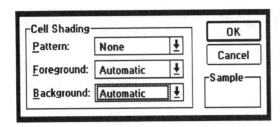

Figure 3.16 Format Patterns dialog box.

5. The **Format Row Height** and **Format Column Width** dialog boxes of Figures 3.9(e) and 3.9(f), respectively, now contain **Hide** and **Unhide** buttons. To hide a row, select at least one cell in the row to be hidden, then choose **Hide**. To unhide a row, select at least one cell in each of the rows adjoining the hidden row, then choose **Unhide**. A comparable procedure applies to columns.

6. The path of windows and dialog boxes given in Figure 3.12 to modify colors for various screen areas should be modified by replacing Figures 3.12(c) through 3.12(e) with Figures 3.17(a) and 3.17(b). The path denoted by Figure 3.12, and also as modified by Figure 3.17, relies on capability provided by Windows, not by Excel.

7. The **Formula Find**, **Formula Replace**, and **Formula Select Special** dialog boxes of Figure 3.15 each have been enhanced slightly with additional button choices.

8. The **Format Patterns**, **Control Run/Control Panel/Color**, and **File Print Preview** commands now allow us to format the document for screen display and the **File Print Preview** command also allows us to format for printer output. These new commands should be added to Table 3.3

3.6.1 Goal Seeking

A computational aid called *goal seeking* is offered to solve a direct formula for an inverse solution. Whereas normally we enter equations that solve for the dependent variable, given that we have values for the independent variables, the goal seeking routine attempts an inverse solution. That is, it tries to obtain a value for a single independent variable that yields a specific dependent variable value without altering the structure of the worksheet. For example, given the equation

$$y = (x - 4)(x + 9) = x^2 + 5x - 36$$

and a numerical value for x, say 3, Excel will compute $y = -12$. However, with the **Goal Seek** command, we can instruct Excel to compute a value for x that yields a specific value of y, say -22. Through a variation procedure (varying x, the independent variable) Excel attempts to converge to the desired dependent variable value. The physical steps for invoking this procedure are as follows:

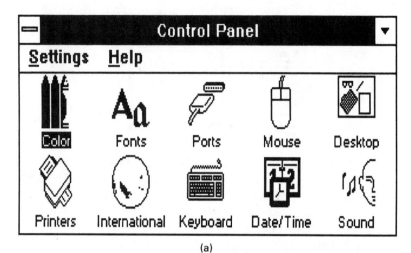

(a)

(b)

Figure 3.17   (a) Windows Control Panel and (b) the Color settings window.

1. Enter the direct equation in a cell, or cells, with dependency relations tracing back to the independent variable, which must be a constant in its own cell.

2. Execute the **Formula Goal Seek** command of Figure 3.18(a) to display the setup dialog box of Figure 3.18(b).

3. Complete the dialog box entries for the address of the dependent variable "**Set cell:**", the desired dependent variable value "**To value:**", and the ad-

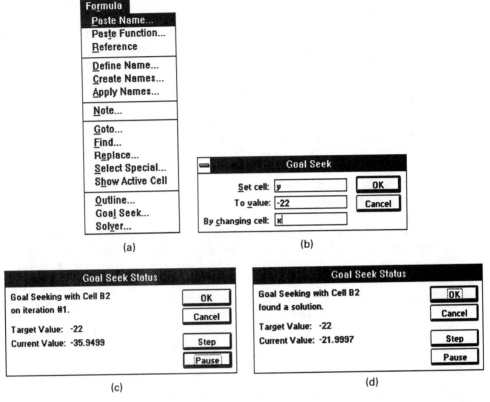

Figure 3.18 (a) Version 3.0 Formula menu and (b) Goal Seek entry, (c) Goal Seek status, and (d) Goal Seek results dialog boxes.

dress of the independent variable for this run "**By changing cell:**", then choose **OK**.

4. Excel attempts to solve the inverse problem. The dialog box of Figure 3.18(c) is displayed to provide occasional updates of its progress and with buttons to interrupt the computation.

5. Upon completion of the attempts, the dialog box of Figure 3.18(d) is displayed with the solution reached, if any, or a message to the contrary. The solution obtained may be substituted into the worksheet as the new solution, if desired, through button selection.

The goal seek routine has unspecified limitations. It appears to vary the independent variable within a limited range of its current value only. Since we have the roots from the factored form of the equation, our starting value for x determines which root will be found, if we seek a dependent value of zero. With the formula of Example 3.1, goal seek requires few iterations to reach a solution in most cases. Some conditions may be impossible, such as dividing by zero, computing a negative radicand, etc. Although a warning that a possible solution may not have been found, even the results from using goal seek should be verified before serious use is made of them.

3.6.2 Solver

The Solver application program is included with version 3.0 to provide an alternative technique for solving a variety of problems. Upon or after installation with Excel version 3.0, it modifies the **Formula** menu to include the **Solver** command used to run the program as shown in Figure 3.18(a). For this discussion, we assume that it is installed.

1. Introduction.   Solver is used for solving linear or nonlinear problems with or without constraints. It does this numerically, not analytically. Thus, its solutions are approximations controlled by tolerance specification. It can be applied to problems that are implicitly or explicitly stated, are single variable or multivariable, are constrained or unconstrained and that have equality or inequality constraints that are linear or nonlinear, and that have linear or nonlinear objective functions. It is useful for finding minimum or maximum values, for finding a specific value, or for finding a feasible solution from some solution space. We apply Solver to worksheet problems.

In this section we explain how to describe our problem to Solver and how to use it to obtain a solution. Because Solver can be applied to problems more general than those of this chapter, we will revisit it later in other application settings. Meanwhile, we can use it to solve problems such as these:

1. Solve for the three roots of $w^3 - 5w - 1 = 0$.

2. Solve $2y - \log_{10} y = 7$ for y.

3. Minimize $f(x, y) = x^3 + y^3 - 3xy$ such that $x \geq 0$ and $y \geq 0$.

2. Problem entry and execution.   We first prepare our problem on a worksheet. The nature of Solver requires us to structure the problem as an optimization problem. That is, we must designate a cell as containing the objective function and we must specify its type of outcome (maximum, minimum, or equality), we must identify cells containing the independent variables to be adjusted during the optimization run, and we must construct solution constraints. With our worksheet as the active document, we enter Solver by executing the **Formula Solver** command of Figure 3.18(a), which produces the dialog box of Figure 3.19. We define the problem to be solved with entries in this dialog box and in those of Figure 3.20, which are the constraints entry and modification dialog boxes.

After we enter the dialog box of Figure 3.19 we can begin problem setup by entering the objective function cell (by selecting it or by typing its name or refer-

Solver Parameters

Se_t Cell: `$C$1`   OK

Equal to: ○ _Max   ● Min   ○ _Value of: `0`   Cancel

By Changing Cells: `$B$1:$B$2`

Subject to the Constraints: _Solve

```
$B$1 <= 10
$B$1 >= -10        Add...
$B$2 <= 10
$B$2 >= -10        Change...    Options...
                   Delete       Reset
```

Figure 3.19   Formula Solver dialog box.

ence) in the **Set Cell** box and clicking the desired **Equal to** button, and entering a value in the **Value of** box if needed. The **Set Cell** entry must be that cell in which the objective function calculation culminates. We can then enter the independent variable cells (by selecting them or typing their names or references) to be adjusted in the **By Changing Cells** box. The independent variables must directly, or indirectly, affect the objective function or the constraints. Finally, we must enter the constraints as relational expressions, which will appear in the **Subject to the Constraints** box.

To add new constraints, we click on the **Add** button of Figure 3.19, then make entries in the dialog box of Figure 3.20(a). The left side of the expression, the **Cell Reference** box, must be a cell or cell range (select it or type in its name or reference), the relational operator must be chosen from the drop-down list (choices being <=, =, and >=), and the right side of the expression, the **Constraint** box, must be a number, cell reference, or formula (none of which must contain cell names). Edit the left and right hand sides as in the formula bar. Add additional constraints with the **Add** button of Figure 3.20(a). Upon completion, click on the **OK** button to return to the Solver dialog box. Proof-read the constraints in the **Subject to the Constraints** box of Figure 3.19. To make corrections, select the constraint to be changed and click on the **Change** button to get the dialog box of Figure 3.20(b), which will contain the constraint selected for change. Enter the changes as described above for the **Add** constraint dialog box. Choose the **OK** button to return to the Solver dialog box. Clicking on the **Delete** button of Figure 3.19 causes the selected constraint to be deleted. With the problem now set up, we start computation by choosing the **Solve** button.

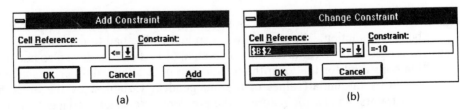

(a)   (b)

Figure 3.20   (a) Solver Add constraints and (b) Change constraints dialog boxes.

	A	B	C
1	x		=(3*x^2+12*y^2-18*x+96*y+239)/4
2	y		

(a)

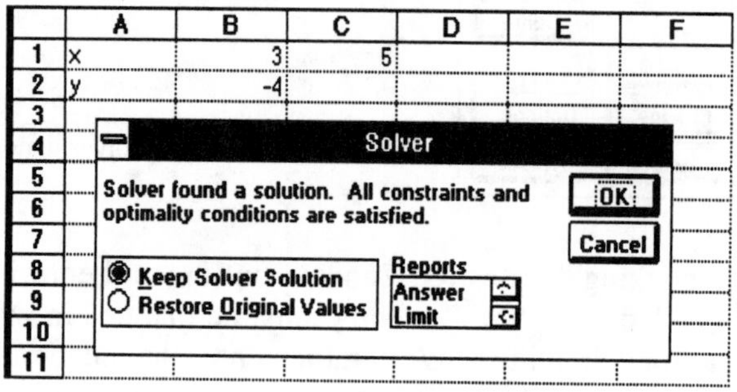

	A	B	C	D	E	F
1	x	3	5			
2	y	-4				
3						
4		Solver				
5		Solver found a solution. All constraints and	OK			
6		optimality conditions are satisfied.				
7			Cancel			
8		● Keep Solver Solution Reports				
9		○ Restore Original Values Answer				
10		Limit				
11						

(b)

Figure 3.21 (a) Example worksheet in formulas mode and (b) a Solver completion dialog box on the worksheet in values mode.

We will illustrate Solver with this example:

Minimize the elliptic paraboloid

$$z = (3x^2 + 12y^2 - 18x + 96y + 239)/4$$

subject to

$$-10 \le x \le 10$$

$$-10 \le y \le 10$$

We assigned the names in column A to adjacent cells of column B and entered the formula in C1 of the worksheet shown in formulas mode in Figure 3.21(a). Upon entry to Solver we prepared the dialog box as shown in Figure 3.19. Although we entered the x and y variables by name, Solver insisted on converting them to absolute references as shown. We did select cell C1 for entry into the **Set Cell** box. This dialog box is ready to run. We clicked on the **Solve** button to run Solver and waited for it to finish. We could see values changing in the cells as Solver made its trials. A short time later the screen looked like Figure 3.21(b), the worksheet in values mode, where we see the dialog box message to which we must respond and values for x, y, and the objective function, which is the minimized value for z.

3. Guidelines for use.   Solver easily solved our problem, which was a well behaved function. We aren't always so lucky. We had to narrow the constraints to get the last two roots for the polynomial of 1. above, and we also had to narrow the constraint for the logarithmic equation of 2. above. Its performance is influenced by the initial values of the independent variables, by the breadth of the constraints, and by the nature of the problem. We suggest giving it as much help as possible by narrowing the constraints ranges, especially to avoid regions with singularities. It works very well on worksheets set up for traditional spreadsheet analysis, those that primarily use arithmetic operators for calculation, but it is not the solution to all our problem solving needs.

Here are some operational characteristics of Solver that should help determine its use.

1. When no constraints are entered, and **Max** or **Min** are chosen, it operates in the unconstrained mode.

2. When constraints are entered, and **Max** or **Min** are chosen, it operates in the constrained mode.

3. When **Value of** is chosen and an entry made in its box, and when equality constraints are entered, it operates in the goal seeking mode that we discussed in Section 3.6.1.

4. When the **Set Cell** box is left empty, it seeks the first feasible solution.

We saw a Solver completion message in Figure 3.21(b). There are other messages in its repertoire for successful and unsuccessful completion attempts, the latter for improving its performance and converging to a solution. But, there also are other opportunities to extract improved performance from it. We can control some of its operational parameters via its **Options** dialog box, shown in Figure 3.22 with default parameters. We can set its maximum run time, the maximum number of iterations to attempt, the precision of solution values, and choices for internal operation.

The **Max Time** entry is the maximum time allotted for the run after clicking on the **Solve** button. It is not wall clock time. The progress made toward a solution during this time period depends on the speed of the computer, the size and complexity of the problem, the number of independent variables, the constraint precision value, the time spent on concurrent activities, and the time spent responding to planned interruptions. Its readjustment is often made to satisfy the special needs for debugging and for allowing long run-time problems to complete.

The **Iterations** entry sets the maximum count of iterations that Solver attempts on the problem. This is a limit imposed on Solver's internal iteration

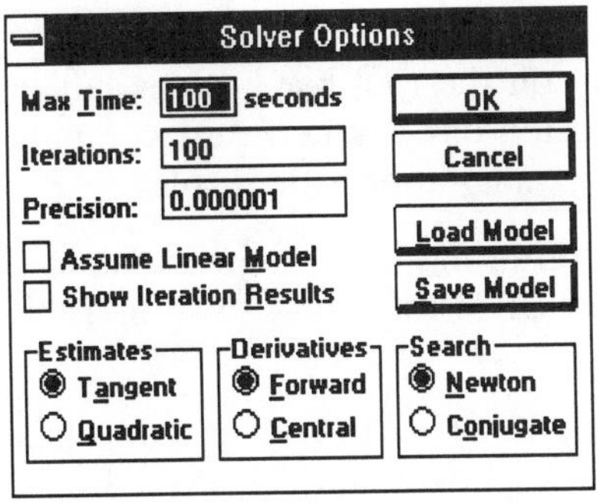

Figure 3.22 Solver Options dialog box.

structure. It is often used while debugging to limit the number of attempts Solver makes to reach a solution. At other times it is necessary to increase this count to give Solver an opportunity to finish its job. The **Precision** entry is a value applied to each constraint cell to determine whether it satisfies the constraint imposed on it. It establishes a band of acceptance on the constraint value that affects the accuracy of the solution. Higher precision (a smaller numerical value) implies greater accuracy.

We advocate giving Solver as much help as possible through careful constraint specification and initial value entry. However, when our problem is linear and has linear constraints, we can turn on the **Assume Linear Model** check box of the **Solver Options** dialog box to enter a speed-up mode of operation. If your problem is, in fact, not linear, Solver will notify you to turn off the **Assume Linear Model** check box and restart the run. It will then apply its general algorithm to the problem.

Control of Solver via the options buttons in the **Estimates**, **Derivatives**, and **Search** boxes of the **Solver Options** dialog box apply to the numerical methods used by Solver. Familiarity with numerical methods is required for proper application of these choices. Whenever Solver has difficulty with a problem, and you have either no inconsistent contraints or an ill-behaved problem, option choices other than the default ones should be considered. Problems detected during setup are reported as error messages. After that time, useful error messages are scarce and you have no knowledge of where Solver encountered difficulty in the solution phase. Guidelines for selection of options are context dependent and will not be discussed further.

A solution can be saved or discarded. When Solver completes its run, the worksheet or macro sheet objective function and independent variable cells contain the final values of the computation. These may be retained by choosing the **Keep Solver Solution** button of Figure 3.21(b) or discarded, and the starting values may be restored in those cell locations by choosing the **Restore Original Values** button. The **Reset** button of Figure 3.19 is used to clear entries from that dialog box and to restore default settings elsewhere in order to place Solver in its original starting condition.

3.6.3 The Tool Bar

In this section we comment on the tool bar buttons labeled in Figure 3.23. Of these, only the auto-sum button directly performs computation. The remainder are for document formatting, annotation, and display.

1. The *Auto-sum* button brings us no new capability. It is a convenience feature for limited use of the SUM function shown in Table 3.1. The procedure for using it is as follows:

> Select the cell into which the SUM function is to be placed and click the *Auto-sum* button, or press its keyboard equivalent ALT+EQUAL.

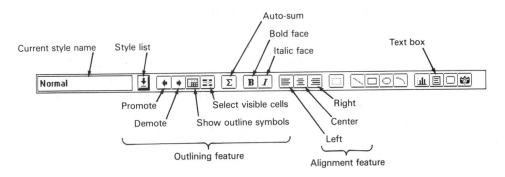

Figure 3.23 Excel tool bar.

Excel inserts the SUM function (with a preceding equals sign) into the selected cell with the proposed argument being a cell range with values that could be summed. It first reaches upward from the selected cell but if column summing in this manner is not possible, it will reach to its left for row summing. The formula appears in the formula bar with the proposed argument selected. The chosen range is indicated on the worksheet, or macro sheet, with a dotted outline box. This is all that the *Auto-sum* button does. At this time, accept the formula as is, edit it if desired, or cancel it. Once in the formula bar, the formula must be treated as if it were entered in any of the ways discussed thus far.

The Auto-sum button cannot be used to paste the SUM function into a partially constructed formula. To combine it with other elements of a formula, first enter it into the cell, then manually enter the remainder of the formula.

2. All characters of a cell, cell range, or the entire worksheet or macro sheet, can be formatted for bold, italic, or both faces of type with the *Bold face* and *Italic face* buttons. Simply select the cells to be formatted and click on the desired button. The effect can be undone by clicking the button again. These buttons are simply a convenience feature since we can already format with bold and italic faces from the **Format Font** dialog box.

3. All text and numbers of a cell, cell range, or the entire worksheet or macro sheet, can be aligned within their cell with the *Left, Center,* or *Right* alignment buttons when the formulas check box of the **Options Display** dialog box is off. These alignment buttons are simply a convenience feature since we can already align text and numbers this way via the **Format Alignment** dialog box.

4. Comments can be added to a worksheet or macro sheet with the *Text box* button. There is no other way to generate the text box. We create it as follows:

1. Activate the window on which the text box is to be placed.
2. Click on the *Text Box* button. The cursor changes to a cross-hair symbol for drawing a rectangular box.

3. Position the cross-hair cursor to the location for one corner of the text box. Press the mouse button and drag it to shape and size the ensuing box, which will become the text box. Pressing SHIFT during this operation will generate a square box; pressing CTRL will align the box to the cell grid. When the mouse button is released, the box will resemble the selected one shown in Figure 3.24, but without the text. The black squares, or handles, surrounding the box indicate that it is selected.

4. With the text box still selected, type the desired text into it. Text automatically wraps to fit the box width. Start a new line by pressing ENTER. When finished entering text, click outside the text box, which now will resemble the unselected box shown in Figure 3.24.

We can customize the text box by resizing it, by changing its shape, or by altering its text or text font after we have selected it (by placing the cursor within its border and clicking the mouse button). Then, the **Format Text** and **Format Font** commands can be used to alter the box text in the usual manner. Also, when the box is selected, it can be deleted with the **Edit Clear** command or by pressing the BACKSPACE or DELETE key. The box can be sized by dragging a handle, on the side or corner, while observing the dotted outline of its new dimensions. Pressing SHIFT while dragging a corner handle will keep the box proportioned; pressing CTRL while dragging will align the box frame to the cell grid. The box can be moved to a new location by dragging it there after first clicking on its border with an arrow cursor. If not already selected, it becomes selected upon doing this.

The amount of text within a text box can exceed the size of the box. In this case, the text wraps to fit the box width with excess lines hidden from view. To see the hidden lines, select the box, place the cursor within it, and nudge it against the top or bottom edges to cause up or down scrolling, respectively.

5. A combination of formats for a cell, when named and saved for later application, is called a *style*. A style allows us to apply the combination of formats to a cell, cell range, or the entire worksheet or macro sheet all at once. This is a convenience feature that saves us work and time when much styling must be

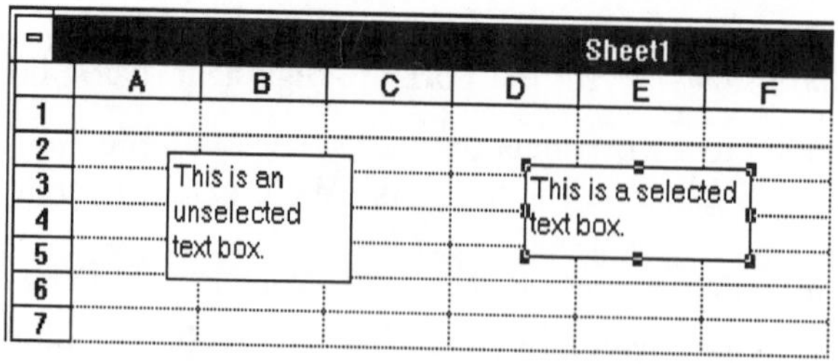

Figure 3.24 Unselected and selected text boxes.

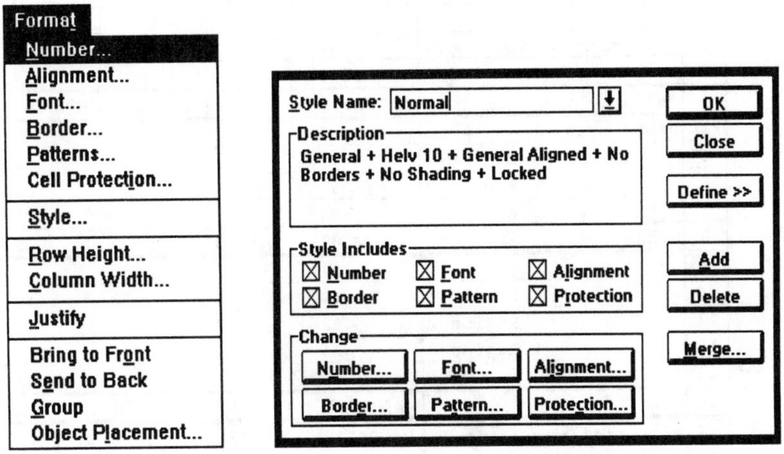

Figure 3.25   (a) Version 3.0 Format menu and (b) Format Style expanded dialog box.

done. The concept of a style is also used with many word processing programs. In Excel, we can apply styles with a tool bar button or with menu commands.

The tool bar *Current style name* box shows the name of the style applied to the current selection of cells. A list of available styles is made visible in a dropdown list box by clicking on the *Style list* button. From this list, we can choose styles from those supplied with Excel (Comma, Currency, Normal, or Percent) or from custom styles that were added to the list, by clicking on the name of style displayed. Immediately, the selected cells are restyled to the chosen format.

We can create our own style with the **Format Style** command of Figure 3.25(a), which leads us to the dialog box [shown in Figure 3.25(b)] that we obtained from the first level box by expanding it with the **Define** button. It shows that check boxes allow us to include, or remove, style features. Included style features can be specified in detail by making choices in other dialog boxes via buttons at the bottom of the figure.

Since cell styling is a matter of preference and not calculation oriented, we choose not to discuss it further, but do encourage the reader to explore its possibilities at some time.

6. The worksheet of Figure 3.26(a) contains lighting failure occurrences for different types of system failure, as indicated in row 3, over an 84-month period designated in cell B1. The failures are tabulated for urban and rural areas within three regions. Row and column totals for the failures appear in row 14 and column F, respectively. The average number of lights for the reporting period was 2160 (cell B2). We computed the probability of a lighting failure for a three-month

	A	B	C	D	E	F
1	Reporting period, mo.	84				
2	Ave. no. lights	2160				
3	Failure type	Line	Xfmr	Switch	Bulb	Row total
4	Urban area					
5	Region 1	65	234	111	325	735
6	Region 2	61	514	171	634	1380
7	Region 3	63	255	91	199	608
8	Urban totals	189	1003	373	1158	2723
9	Rural area					
10	Region 1	30	86	27	154	297
11	Region 2	42	170	102	460	774
12	Region 3	24	91	18	210	343
13	Rural totals	96	347	147	824	1414
14	Total failures	285	1350	520	1982	4137
15	Prob. failure (3 mo.)	0.004712	0.022321	0.008598	0.032771	
16	Prob. survival (3 mo.)	0.995288	0.977679	0.991402	0.967229	0.9330906

(a)

	A	B	C	D	E	F
1	Reporting period, mo.	84				
2	Ave. no. lights	2160				
3	Failure type	Line	Xfmr	Switch	Bulb	Row total
4	Urban area					
5	Region 1	65	234	111	325	735
6	Region 2	61	514	171	634	1380
7	Region 3	63	255	91	199	608
8	Urban totals	189	1003	373	1158	2723
9	Rural area					
10	Region 1	30	86	27	154	297
11	Region 2	42	170	102	460	774
12	Region 3	24	91	18	210	343
13	Rural totals	96	347	147	824	1414
14	Total failures	285	1350	520	1982	4137
15	Prob. failure (3 mo.)	0.00471	0.02232	0.0086	0.03277	
16	Prob. survival (3 mo.)	0.995288	0.977679	0.991402	0.967229	0.933091

(b)

Figure 3.26   (a) Worksheet for outlining and (b) its outlined display.

period in row 15 at the 50% confidence level from the sample data. Then, we computed the probability of survival for one bulb for a three-month period due to the different causes of failure (cell range B16 : E16) and for the system (cell F16). We will not explain this problem further but, instead, will refer to it while briefly discussing the outlining feature of version 3.0.

Outlining is a scheme for showing the hierarchical structure of computation in a worksheet organized as a table. It contributes no mathematical capability to Excel and it cannot be applied to a macro sheet to show program structure. Row and column hierarchy can be displayed, the hierarchy can be manipulated, and the worksheet contents can be selectively displayed and printed based on its hierarchy. The buttons related to outlining are indicated in Figure 3.23.

The worksheet prerequisites for creating a proper structure outline are that it must have backward only (or forward only) row and backward only (or forward only) column references and, if nested, must have levels that are completely nested. That is, formulas must refer to cells occurring in earlier (or later) rows and earlier (or later) columns only, and hierarchical levels must not partially overlap. The outline of our example is shown in Figure 3.26(b). It contains four levels of row hierarchy and two levels of column hierarchy. The outline buttons and symbols are displayed at the left and top edges of the figure.

Row 15 is at the topmost row hierarchy level. Its formulas refer to values in row 14. Row 14 formulas refer to values in rows 8 and 13 and thus it forms the second level in the row hierarchy. Rows 8 and 13 are at the third row hierarchy level. Their formulas each reach up only three rows for values from cells containing no formulas. The outlining symbols at the left side of Figure 3.26(b) show this structure. There is only one column hierarchy level. The formulas in column F reach left for values from cells containing no formulas.

We create an outline with the **Formula Outline** command of Figure 3.18(a) and its dialog box of Figure 3.27, or by clicking the *Promote* tool bar button. Thereafter, we can use the tool bar buttons for working with the outline. The *Promote* and *Demote* buttons are for changing rows or columns to different levels. The *Show outline symbols* button is for making the outlining symbols visible [as shown in Figure 3.26(b)] or hidden. The *Select visible cells* button is for selecting just visible cells for purposes such as charting or copying. There are also key combinations and menu dialog boxes for some of these operations. The squares with numbers are row and column level display buttons. Squares with a plus or minus sign are row and column expand or collapse buttons, respectively. Clicking on these buttons performs display or hide actions specific to outline levels.

Since outlining does not provide new calculation capability, we choose not to discuss it further, but do encourage the reader to explore its possibilities at some time.

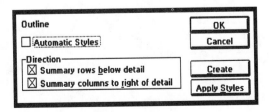

Figure 3.27 Formula Outline dialog box.

PROBLEMS

Write spreadsheet programs using built-in mathematical functions and named variables to solve the following problems:

3.1 Solve the following formula for β given that $a = 3$, $b = -2.9$, $k = 2$, $x = 4.6$, and $\theta = 35$ deg

$$\beta = \frac{x^2 - \dfrac{1}{1.25 + \dfrac{1}{x}}}{k^3 \sin\left(\theta + \dfrac{\pi}{1.5}\right)} + \frac{.7^{k+1}\sqrt{a + 12}\,\cos^2(2\theta^2)}{\left(\dfrac{a}{8} + \left|\dfrac{kx}{1 + b}\right|\right)^{.3}}$$

$$ans = 6.49328888$$

3.2 Solve the following formula for γ given that $x = 1.4$, $\theta = 2.6$ rad, $a = -1.8$, and $n = 3$.

$$\gamma = \frac{x^3 + \dfrac{\sqrt{14 + x^2}}{2.1 \sin(\theta + \pi)}}{(7.2 - a)^{1.6}\sqrt{x + \dfrac{a}{4 + a^2}}} - x^3\left|\sqrt{\dfrac{x}{1.5} + \dfrac{28}{a^n x^2}} - x^{n+2}\right|\cos\left(\dfrac{\theta^2}{a + 1}\right)$$

$$ans = 4.216735094$$

3.3 Solve the following formula for y given that $a = 1.2$ and $x = -0.2$.

$$y = \frac{e^{5x^2}}{\cos(x + \sqrt{a})} - \left|x - \dfrac{0.1}{a^2}\right| \ln\left(\dfrac{1}{a} + \dfrac{1}{|x|}\right) - \frac{1}{a + \dfrac{3x}{a^2 + \dfrac{5x}{a^3}}}$$

$$ans = -0.508068819$$

3.4 Solve the following formula for w given that $x = 3.7$ and $a = 2.4$.

$$w = \frac{e^{\left(\frac{x}{\sqrt{2}}\right)}\cos\left(\sqrt{\dfrac{x}{2}} + \dfrac{\pi}{8}\right)}{\sqrt{2\pi x} + x^{x+1}e^{-x}} - \frac{\pi}{2}\tan|x| + \frac{2a^2}{3(\sqrt{x^2 - a^2})^3}$$

$$ans = -0.960441549$$

3.5 Solve the following formula for t given that $a = 3.4$, $b = 4.3$, $\alpha = 37$ deg, $\beta = 26$ deg, $r = 1.8$, $w = 9.5$, and $x = 4.1$.

$$t = \frac{\sqrt{a^2 + b^2 - 2ab\cos\beta}}{\ln\left(b + \dfrac{36.8r}{\cos\alpha}\right) - |x + w\sin\beta|} + x^{x+1}\left(r^2 + \dfrac{a - b}{w - \sqrt{x}}\right)^{-2.8}$$

$$ans = 54.66072655$$

3.6 Solve the following formula for x given that $a = .65$, $b = .23$, $c = 4.7$, $n = 2.5$, $y = 5.4$, $z = .89$, $\alpha = 1.6$, and $\theta = .55$ rad.

$$x = \frac{y^{n+1}\sqrt{\alpha + \dfrac{30.5}{c}} - \dfrac{1}{a + b}}{(\cos^3 z + \sqrt{z^3 - b^2 \sin \theta})^3}$$

$$ans = 843.0660917$$

3.7 Solve the following formula for t given that $a = -2.7$, $b = -1.2$, $x = 5.6$, $y = -6.2$, and $\theta = .16$ rad.

$$t = \frac{(a - b)^3 \sqrt{3x + 48.5}}{\left(\dfrac{2}{a} + \dfrac{3}{x}\right) + \sin(\theta + \pi)} - \frac{x\left(\dfrac{2}{a} + \dfrac{3}{y}\right)\cos(\theta + \pi)}{(a - b)^2 \sqrt{x + y^2 - 4}}$$

$$ans = 75.26684495$$

CHAPTER **4**

Arrays

Engineering computations are often made on information stored in data structures known as arrays. Special techniques for working with such data, which need not be numerical, are needed to simplify and expedite the computations. We also need access to functions that perform familiar operations on these data. In this chapter, we explore the spreadsheet techniques for working with this data structure. Apart from the scalar values we worked with in Chapters 2 and 3, this chapter introduces the only other data structure in Excel. Upon completing this chapter, we will have substantially expanded the scope of problems that we can solve via spreadsheet programs.

4.1 INTRODUCTION

Mathematical formulations are often simplified through the symbolism of subscripted variables. Subscripting is a notational concept implying order. For example, we may identify a point in three-dimensional space through its coordinate values as (x_1, y_1, z_1), or (x_2, y_2, z_2), or, in general, as (x_i, y_i, z_i), where the subscript i assumes integer values. This means that the triplet of scalar variables having the same subscript value is associated with the same point, and that point is now uniquely identified. Subscripts are also used in equations. For example, the recursive relationship

$$y_n = ay_{n-1} + bx_n$$

is interpreted as meaning that the nth value of y is obtained by multiplying the $(n-1)$st value of y by a and adding this to the product of b and the nth value of x.

If we required the eighth value of *y,* we must use the seventh value of *y* and the eighth value of *x* in the computation.

The subscript notation is usually applied to suggest a family relationship among its members; that is, the members share common characteristics. However, this is not a requirement for the use of subscripts. When used in computer languages, subscripting implies a particular data structure. In Excel, this structure is a one- or two-dimensional array, or table. A one-dimensional array can be visualized as a single column (or row) of cells whereby each row (or column) of the array contains only one cell. The use of double-subscript notation, such as x_{ij}, implies a two-dimensional array for which the first subscript refers to a row and the second to a column. In Excel this is a rectangular array of cells. Three-dimensional arrays (not available in Excel) have three subscripts, which refer to rows, columns, and layers. In the work of this text, an *array* is a data structure in which information is located in cells, each of which is associated with a particular set of numbers called *indices.*

4.2 DEFINING ARRAYS

An array in a spreadsheet context is a rectangular area of cells. This is a natural geometric representation based on the structure of the worksheet. We may have single row or single column oriented arrays, square, or rectangular arrays. Various arrays are shown in Figure 4.1, where they each have been assigned a name, such as ARR3, and where their corresponding cell range is shown, for example, C3 : D6.

We may choose to assign symbolic names to an array or to use a cell range reference. To assign a name to an array, we select the cells in the usual manner, then invoke the **Formula Define Name** command, or we can name row or column

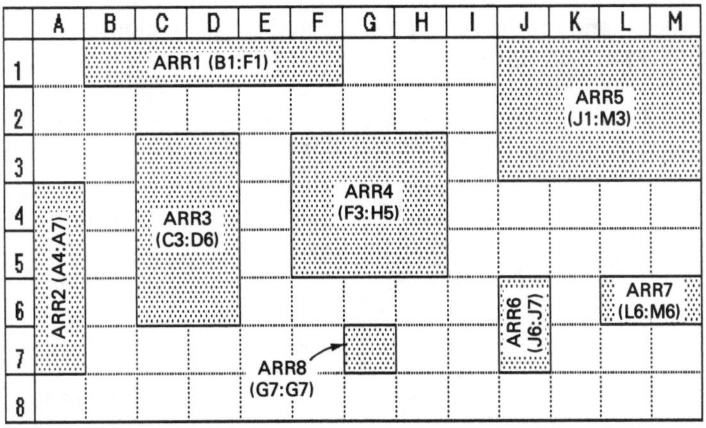

Figure 4.1   Examples of arrays.

array ranges with the **Formula Create Names** command. An array may also be referenced without a name by using its cell range, which is the reference operator (the colon, ":") placed between coordinate references of opposite corner cells as shown in Figure 4.1. The reference operator, as well as an array name, produces one reference to all cells in the range. Values may be entered into the cells of a values-only array either before or after it is named. Spreadsheet arrays share the characteristics that the range of cells (a) share a common name, when named, and that (b) they share a common formula. Because of these characteristics, Excel prohibits certain editing operations on arrays. For example, one cannot (a) insert cells to increase an array range, (b) delete cells to reduce an array range, (c) clear or move only a portion of an array, or (d) change the contents of only a portion of an array.

Having defined an array as discussed above, we can now reference the array in formulas. We may also use arrays without defining them. These are called array constants and are described in the following section.

4.3 MATHEMATICS WITH ARRAYS

We will illustrate array techniques in Excel, but first we must learn to construct array constants and formulas and become familiar with array functions.

4.3.1 Array Constants

In Excel, we can perform array mathematics without defining arrays. For this purpose, we use array constants directly in formulas. This is analogous to using scalar constants in simple formulas. Array constants are constructed as arrays whose elements are constants. To fit the requirement of expressing a formula uniquely on a single line, we follow the Excel rules that require (a) the array constant be enclosed within braces { }, (b) the elements of a row be separated by commas, and (c) the rows be separated by semicolons. Here are some examples of Excel array constants:

Mathematics	Dimensions	Excel
$\begin{bmatrix} 1 & 0 & 0 \\ 0 & 1 & 0 \\ 0 & 0 & 1 \end{bmatrix}$	3×3	{1,0,0;0,1,0;0,0,1}
$\begin{bmatrix} 9 & 8 & 1 & 4 \end{bmatrix}$	1×4	{9,8,1,4}
$\begin{bmatrix} 4 \\ 3 \\ 7 \end{bmatrix}$	3×1	{4;3;7}
$\begin{bmatrix} 2 & 0 & 6 \\ 0 & 4 & 4 \end{bmatrix}$	2×3	{2,0,6;0,4,4}
$\begin{bmatrix} 5 \end{bmatrix}$	1×1	{5}

Although matrices are shown in the Mathematics column in the previous table, the examples do not have to be subject to matrix operations to be used in Excel, as we show later. When entered directly into formulas, the array constants are typed with the braces, commas, and semicolons. Only integer numerical array elements are illustrated above. However, the elements can be numbers (integers or floating point), logical values, text, or error values. We will illustrate their use in the next section.

4.3.2 Array Formulas

We now describe how to construct an array formula. Because the formula will contain array references, the results obtained from using the basic arithmetic operators in the formula require special interpretation. We illustrate only compatible operands in the following table:

Operation	Result
$\{a_1,a_2,a_3\} \pm \{b_1,b_2,b_3\}$	$\{(a_1 \pm b_1), (a_2 \pm b_2), (a_3 \pm b_3)\}$
$\{a_1,a_2,a_3\} \overset{*}{/} \{b_1,b_2,b_3\}$	$\{(a_1 \overset{*}{/} b_1), (a_2 \overset{*}{/} b_2), (a_3 \overset{*}{/} b_3)\}$
$\{a_1,a_2,a_3\} \hat{}\ x$	$\{(a_1)\hat{}x, (a_2)\hat{}x, (a_3)\hat{}x\}$

We see that the operator affects corresponding elements of the operands as for matrix addition and subtraction. But we have element-by-element multiplication and division for corresponding elements of the arrays, quite unlike that for matrices. Exponentiation operates on a single-element basis, also unlike that for matrices. Therefore, multiplication, division, and exponentiation with the operators does not produce matrix arithmetic results. We show later that array functions must be used for this purpose. Here are some numerical examples:

Formula	Result
$\{=\{3,0,4\}+\{9,6,0\}\}$	$\{12,6,4\}$
$\{=\{5,3;1,4\}*\{2,9;7,4\}\}$	$\{10,27;7,16\}$
$\{=\{8,2,2;1,6,3\}\hat{}2\}$	$\{64,4,4;1,36,9\}$

The dimensions of the arrays in a formula should be the same for all arrays. Although Excel expands array constants to match the dimensions required of an operation, it does not do this for cell references. Because we advocate dimensional uniformity throughout a formula, we will not discuss this expansion further.

Because there is likely to be a difference in computed results from array formulas than when the same references are used in ordinary formulas, we must remember to enter the formula properly. Upon selecting the array range to correspond with the dimension of the result, then constructing the formula in the formula bar, we press CTRL+SHIFT+ENTER (keyboard) or press CTRL+SHIFT and click on the enter box (mouse) to enter the array formula. At this time, Excel encloses the formula within braces and stores it in the array range. The same formula appears in each cell of the array range. The outer braces for the examples in the Formula column of the above table were added by Excel. Suitable result array ranges for the examples of the above table could be A1 : C1, A1 : B2, and A1 : C2, respectively. If the formula bar is activated because a cell within the array range is selected, the array formula appears in the formula bar without the braces. Complete array formulas can be seen in the cells when the **Formulas** toggle is chosen in the **Options Display** command.

4.3.3 Functions

Array arguments may be used with most of the functions that appear in Table 3.1. The following examples illustrate array use with functions.

Function	Formula	Result
SQRT	{=SQRT({7,12,3}+{9,13,33})}	{4,5,6}
COS	{=COS({a,b,c})}	{cos a,cos b,cos c}
EXP	{=EXP({2,−4,3.6})}	{e^2,e^{-4},$e^{3.6}$}
SUM	{=SUM({a,b,c}*{d,e,f})}	$a*d+b*e+c*f$
AVERAGE	{=AVERAGE({−5,12,6,−2,11})}	4.4

When used with arrays, functions may return single values (e.g., SUM, AVERAGE) or arrays (e.g., SQRT, COS, EXP), depending on the function. The variables shown in the Formula column above are included only to show how the result is computed. Array constants must have numerical values. The basic operators may be used in combination with functions and functions may be nested as described in Chapter 3, for example, {=SQRT({a,b,c,d})+ABS({f,g,h,i}))}. The

TABLE 4.1   EXCEL MATRIX FUNCTIONS

Name	Algebraic notation	Symbol	Comments
Multiplication	**AB**	MMULT(**A**,**B**)	**A** premultiplies **B**. Array dimensions must be compatible.
Inverse	$\mathbf{A}^{-1}$	MINVERSE(**A**)	Result is the inverse of the square matrix **A**.
Transpose	$\mathbf{A}^{\mathrm{T}}$	TRANSPOSE(**A**)	Result is the transpose of matrix **A**.
Determinant	|**A**|	MDETERM(**A**)	**A** must be square.

SUM function combined with the multiplication operator as illustrated above implements the vector dot operator, for example, $\mathbf{a \cdot b} = a_1 b_1 + a_2 b_2 + a_3 b_3$.

Special functions are provided in Excel that perform matrix computations when operating on arrays of compatible dimensions. This set of functions is shown in Table 4.1. Two other Excel functions useful in array work are

COLUMNS(m)   Returns a single value, the number of columns in array m.

ROWS(m)   Returns a single value, the number of rows in array m.

4.3.4 Examples

The three examples below show how arrays can be used in Excel. The first example illustrates array use with basic operators and functions, the second uses matrix functions only, while the third demonstrates more array manipulation with matrix functions.

Example 4.1

The three electrical point charges Q_1, Q_2, and Q_3 are fixed in the positions shown in Figure 4.2, while Q_4, shown at the center of the symmetrical layout, is free to move due to the electrostatic force on it. From its present position, we will determine numerically the path that Q_4 will follow, given that it moves slowly so that momentum effects can be ignored.

Charge Q_4 is subject to the force

$$\mathbf{F}_4 = \sum_{i=1}^{3} \frac{Q_i Q_4 \mathbf{R}_{i4}}{4\pi\varepsilon_o |\mathbf{R}_{i4}|}$$

where

$$\mathbf{R}_{i4} = \text{direction vector from } Q_i \text{ to } Q_4$$

$$\varepsilon_o = \text{permittivity of free space}$$

Because we are interested only in the direction of the force and will reduce $\mathbf{F}_4$ to a unit vector, we will not include $4\pi\varepsilon_o$ and Q_4 in the computation, since they are common to each term of the equation. Our plan is to incrementally move Q_4 in the direction of the resultant force, then recompute the new force on it after the incremental move, and to continue iteratively in this manner, thus determining points on its path as shown by the dashed curve on Figure 4.2.

Symmetry of the figure places the charges at the following (x,y) locations (dimensions in meters):

$$Q_1: (0, \sqrt{3}/2)$$

$$Q_2: (.5, 0)$$

$$Q_3: (-.5, 0)$$

$$Q_4: (0, 1/2\sqrt{3})$$

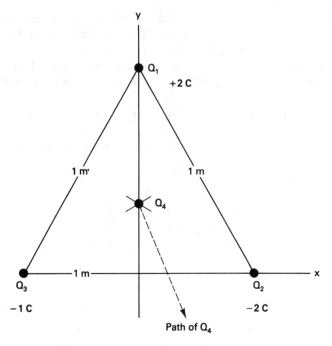

Figure 4.2 Point charge geometry for Example 4.1.

An Excel solution is shown in Figure 4.3, where variables used in the worksheet listings are defined as follows:

qa	B1	loc_qa	E1 : F1
qb	B2	loc_qb	E2 : F2
qc	B3	loc_qc	E3 : F3
qd	B4	loc_qd	E4 : F4
Rad	B6 : C6	Force	B10 : C10
Rbd	B7 : C7	Delta_d	B12 : C12
Rcd	B8 : C8	loc_qd'	B14 : C14

In the cell range A1 : B4, we defined the charges with names not in conflict with cell references. We replaced subscripts 1, 2, 3, and 4 with a, b, c, and d, respectively. Starting locations of the charges are defined in the cell range D1 : F4 of Figure 4.3(a), where we defined the (x,y) pairs as arrays with the names shown using the **Formula Create Names** command. The numerical values were placed in columns E and F of that range, with formulas used to compute the square root. We also copied into cells E6 : F6 of Figure 4.3(a) the starting location of Q_4 using the **Edit Copy** and **Edit Paste Special Values** commands. The normalized direction vectors are defined as array formulas in cell range A6 : C8 of Figure 4.3(b), where we again used the

Formula Create Names command. These values are used in the resultant force equation of cells named Force in B10:C10. Now that we know the direction of the resultant force, we reduce it to a unit vector in the cells named Delta_d in B12:C12. We used the **Formula Create Names** command for Force and Delta_d also, both of which have array formulas. We then move Q_4 to a new position 1 cm, considered to be a small amount, in the direction of the resultant force (see loc_qd' cells B14:C14).

The program was run with the starting values for the charge locations. This led to a value for loc_gd', the new location of Q_4. We then copied this value to the save area, shown shaded as cell range E6:F14, and to loc_qd for a new computation. This iterative process was continued to produce the values shown in the save area, which lie on the dashed curve of Figure 4.2.

We did not need matrix functions for this example. The basic operators and the SQRT and SUM functions calculate on the basis of associated array elements, which is sufficient for this example.

	A	B	C	D	E	F
1	qa	2		loc_qa	0	0.866025404
2	qb	-2		loc_qb	0.5	0
3	qc	-1		loc_qc	-0.5	0
4	qd	1		loc_qd	0.019215378	0.211017107
5						
6	Rad	0.019215378	-0.655008297		0	0.288675135
7	Rbd	-0.480784622	0.211017107		0.002401922	0.278967881
8	Rcd	0.519215378	0.211017107		0.004803845	0.269260628
9					0.007205767	0.259553374
10	Force	0.480784622	-1.943067915		0.009607689	0.249846121
11					0.012009612	0.240138867
12	Delta_d	0.240192231	-0.970725343		0.014411534	0.230431614
13					0.016813456	0.220724361
14	loc_qd'	0.021617301	0.201309854		0.019215378	0.211017107

(a)

	A	B	C
1	qa	2	
2	qb	-2	
3	qc	-1	
4	qd	1	
5			
6	Rad	=loc_qd-loc_qa	=loc_qd-loc_qa
7	Rbd	=loc_qd-loc_qb	=loc_qd-loc_qb
8	Rcd	=loc_qd-loc_qc	=loc_qd-loc_qc
9			
10	Force	=qd*(qa*Rad+qb*Rbd+qc*Rcd)	=qd*(qa*Rad+qb*Rbd+qc*Rcd)
11			
12	Delta_d	=Force/SQRT(SUM(Force^2))	=Force/SQRT(SUM(Force^2))
13			
14	loc_qd'	=loc_qd+Delta_d*0.01	=loc_qd+Delta_d*0.01

(b)

Figure 4.3 Worksheets for Example 4.1 in (a) values mode and (b) formulas mode.

Example 4.2

We show the straightforward application of matrix functions in this example by making the following computations.

(a) Figure 4.4 shows computations of $\mathbf{A}^T$, $\mathbf{A}^{-1}$, and $\text{adj}\mathbf{A} = |\mathbf{A}|\mathbf{A}^{-1}$ for the following matrix.

$$\mathbf{A} = \begin{bmatrix} 1 & 0 & -1 \\ 1 & 2 & 1 \\ 0 & 1 & 2 \end{bmatrix}$$

Matrix $\mathbf{A}$ is entered in B1:D3 and named Amat as shown in Figure 4.4(a). $\mathbf{A}^T$ is computed in B5:D7 with the formulas of Figure 4.4(b), $\mathbf{A}^{-1}$ is computed in B9:D11 and named AmatInv, and $\text{adj}\mathbf{A}$ is computed in B13:D15 by the product of $|\mathbf{A}|$ and the result computed for $\mathbf{A}^{-1}$. Entries for columns C and D of the computed matrices are not shown in Figure 4.4(b) since their entries are identical to those of the corresponding rows of column B.

(b) The probability transition matrix $[P]$ for a Markov process is given below. The matrix entries, which are probability values that sum to 1 for each row, are interpreted as follows: If the process is in state s_i (row i), the probability of transitioning to state s_j (column j) is given by the matrix entry p_{ij}. For example, the probability of transitioning from state s_2 to state s_3 is 0.15. The matrix is for a hypothetical unreliable system that periodically self-tests and attempts self-repair at that time if necessary. Restoration time is gradual and can extend over several periods of self-testing. Return to a fully operational status is possible except when the system becomes totally inoperative.

Given the initial vector of states $= [P^{(0)}] = [1 \quad 0 \quad 0 \quad 0]$ and the relationship $[P^{(r)} = [P^{(0)}][P]^r$, where $[P^{(r)}]$ is the row probability vector of the process reaching different states from all possible given initial states in r periods of self-test, compute $[P^{(3)}]$.

$$[P] = \begin{array}{c} \\ s_1 \\ s_2 \\ s_3 \\ s_4 \end{array} \begin{array}{cccc} s_1 & s_2 & s_3 & s_4 \\ \begin{bmatrix} .95 & .04 & 0 & .01 \\ .2 & .6 & .15 & .05 \\ .1 & .2 & .6 & .1 \\ 0 & 0 & 0 & 1 \end{bmatrix} \end{array}$$

The initial state vector B17:E17 is named Pinit and the transition matrix B19:E22 is Pmat. The required computation is made in two steps. First $[P]^2$ is computed in B24:E27 and named PmatSq. Then, $[P^{(3)}]$ is computed in B29:E29 by the formula $[P^{(0)}][P][P]^2$. Columns C, D, and E for these matrices are not shown in Figure 4.4(b) since their formula entries are identical to those of the corresponding rows of column B. The result in B29:E29 of Figure 4.4(a) shows that, for example, the probability of having a fully operational state for the given initial vector of states is 0.877975 after three periods of self-testing and attempted repair.

(a) Values mode

	A	B	C	D	E	F
1						
2	Amat	1	0	-1		
3		1	2	1		
4		0	1	2		
5						
6	AmatTran	1	1	0		
7		0	2	1		
8		-1	1	2		
9						
10	AmatInv	1.5	-0.5	1		
11		-1	1	-1		
12		0.5	-0.5	1		
13						
14	AdjAmat	3	-1	2		
15		-2	2	-2		
16		1	-1	2		
17	Pinit	1	0	0	0	
18						
19	Pmat	0.95	0.04	0	0.01	
20		0.2	0.6	0.15	0.05	
21		0.1	0.2	0.6	0.1	
22		0	0	0	1	
23						
24	PmatSq	0.9105	0.062	0.006	0.0215	
25		0.325	0.398	0.18	0.097	
26		0.195	0.244	0.39	0.171	
27		0	0	0	1	
28						
29	[P^(3)]	0.877975	0.07482	0.0129	0.034305	
30						

(b) Formulas mode

	A	B
1		
2	Amat	1
3		1
4		0
5		
6	AmatTran	=TRANSPOSE(Amat)
7		=TRANSPOSE(Amat)
8		=TRANSPOSE(Amat)
9		
10	AmatInv	=MINVERSE(Amat)
11		=MINVERSE(Amat)
12		=MINVERSE(Amat)
13		
14	AdjAmat	=MDETERM(Amat)*AmatInv
15		=MDETERM(Amat)*AmatInv
16		=MDETERM(Amat)*AmatInv
17	Pinit	1
18		
19	Pmat	0.95
20		0.2
21		0.1
22		0
23		
24	PmatSq	=MMULT(Pmat,Pmat)
25		=MMULT(Pmat,Pmat)
26		=MMULT(Pmat,Pmat)
27		=MMULT(Pmat,Pmat)
28		
29	[P^(3)]	=MMULT(Pinit,MMULT(Pmat,PmatSq))
30		

Figure 4.4 Example 4.2 worksheet in (a) values mode, and (b) formulas mode (columns C, D, and E not shown).

117

Example 4.3

A strain gage transducer converts mechanical displacement into an electrical
voltage change. The electrical system for one type of gage operates on the principle
that resistive wires under varying tension produce varying resistive values. Four
such wires in a mechanical structure can be connected in a bridge circuit as shown in
Figure 4.5. The degree of unbalance of the bridge network depends on various
mechanical and electrical factors that we will not discuss. The physical phenomena
are often far removed from the electrical recording circuitry, so we include connecting wire resistance, R_ℓ, in each line to the bridge circuit. We assume that all bridge
arm resistances are the same, R. Because applying a physical stimulus for calibration purposes after installation is often impractical, we unbalance the bridge "in-
place" by shunting one of its arms with a calibrating resistor, R_c, to simulate a
resistance change due to a known stimulus. R_c is then disconnected during normal
operation.

To simplify our work, we will omit the two line resistances in the input voltage
wires and work with the circuit of Figure 4.6. We numbered the circuit nodes
(square boxes) and indicated current direction through the resistors with arrows.

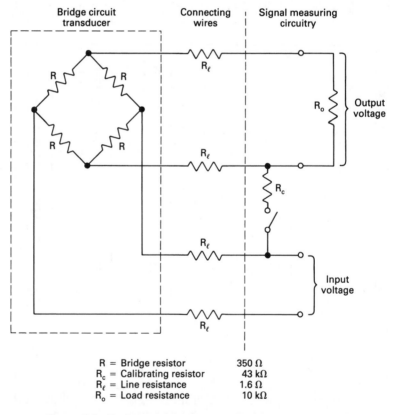

R = Bridge resistor	350 Ω
R_c = Calibrating resistor	43 kΩ
R_ℓ = Line resistance	1.6 Ω
R_o = Load resistance	10 kΩ

Figure 4.5   Strain gage transducer circuit with connecting wires.

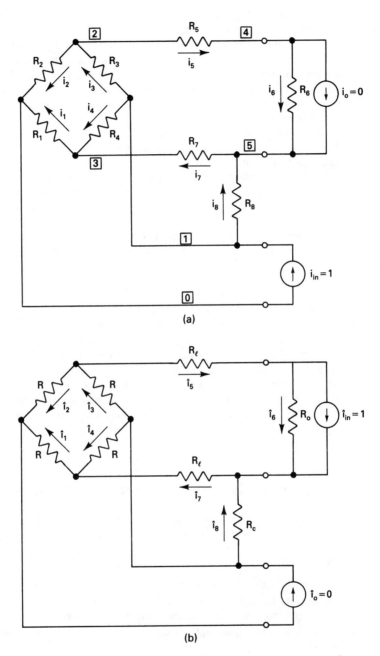

Figure 4.6   (a) Given network N and (b) its adjoint network $\hat{N}$.

The zero node is the voltage reference node for all other node voltages. We also uniquely numbered each resistor.

We will calculate the sensitivity factors for the output voltage with respect to each resistor value by the adjoint network method. The sensitivity factors reveal how the output varies with small changes in the element values. The adjoint network method predicts local behavior accurately, since it yields the exact partial derivatives. We state here only the equations needed for the computation.

Figure 4.6(a) shows current source forcing functions $I_{in} = 1$ and $i_o = 0$ connected to the input and output terminals, respectively, of the network labeled N. Figure 4.6(b) shows network $\hat{N}$ with a current source forcing function $\hat{i}_{in} = 1$ connected to the output terminals and with current source $\hat{i}_o = 0$ connected to the input terminals. The zero-valued sources do not affect the operation of the circuit but provide a convenient branch across which to measure the response to the forcing function. The adjoint network method of calculating sensitivities denotes the connection of Figure 4.6(b) to be the adjoint network of the one shown in Figure 4.6(a). It is labeled network $\hat{N}$. The choice of current source values and connections in the derivation of this method leads to an unnormalized sensitivity calculation as follows:

$$S_{R_k}^{v_o} = \frac{\Delta v_o}{\Delta R_k} = -i_k \hat{i}_k$$

Thus, to obtain the unnormalized sensitivities, we merely calculate the currents in the two networks under the conditions of Figure 4.6 and multiply them pairwise. The symbol v_o denotes the output voltage, while R_k denotes one of the resistances for which the sensitivity calculation is made. The derivation of the adjoint network solution is based on Tellegen's theorem, which relates to an interesting relationship between the branch voltages and currents when two networks, original network N and perturbed network $\hat{N}$, possess the same topology. For details of the method see Calahan [1] or Director [2]. The normalized sensitivities can be calculated from

$$S_{R_k}^{v_o} = \frac{R_k}{v_o} \frac{\Delta v_o}{\Delta R_k} = -\frac{R_k}{v_o} i_k \hat{i}_k$$

The unnormalized sensitivities can be calculated as follows:

1. Write the network node equations and compute the node matrix N for use in the matrix equation $\mathbf{Nv} = \mathbf{b}$, where $\mathbf{v}$ is the node voltage vector and $\mathbf{b}$ is the right-hand side vector (currents) for the network of Figure 4.6(a).
2. Find the inverse of N and solve for the node voltage vector, $\mathbf{v} = \mathbf{N}^{-1}\mathbf{b}$.
3. Compute the element currents and save them for the sensitivity calculation.
4. Set up the adjoint network matrix equation right-hand side vector for Figure 4.6(b) and repeat steps 2 and 3 using this vector.
5. Compute the unnormalized sensitivity factors using the current values from step 3.

The node equations and network matrix equation for our calculations are as follows [the node numbers are the boxed numbers of Figure 4.6(a)]:

node 1: $\dfrac{1}{R_c}(v_1 - v_5) + \dfrac{1}{R}(v_1 - v_2) + \dfrac{1}{R}(v_1 - v_3) = i_{in}$

node 2: $\dfrac{1}{R}(v_2 - v_1) + \dfrac{1}{R}v_2 + \dfrac{1}{R_\ell}(v_2 - v_4) = 0$

node 3: $\dfrac{1}{R_\ell}(v_3 - v_5) + \dfrac{1}{R}(v_3 - v_1) + \dfrac{1}{R}v_3 = 0$

node 4: $\dfrac{1}{R_\ell}(v_4 - v_2) + \dfrac{1}{R_o}(v_4 - v_5) = 0$

node 5: $\dfrac{1}{R_o}(v_5 - v_4) + \dfrac{1}{R_c}(v_5 - v_1) + \dfrac{1}{R_\ell}(v_5 - v_3) = 0$

$$
\begin{bmatrix}
\dfrac{2}{R} + \dfrac{1}{R_c} & -\dfrac{1}{R} & -\dfrac{1}{R} & 0 & -\dfrac{1}{R_c} \\[2ex]
-\dfrac{1}{R} & \dfrac{2}{R} + \dfrac{1}{R_\ell} & 0 & -\dfrac{1}{R_\ell} & 0 \\[2ex]
-\dfrac{1}{R} & 0 & \dfrac{2}{R} + \dfrac{1}{R_\ell} & 0 & -\dfrac{1}{R_\ell} \\[2ex]
0 & -\dfrac{1}{R_\ell} & 0 & \dfrac{1}{R_\ell} + \dfrac{1}{R_o} & -\dfrac{1}{R_o} \\[2ex]
-\dfrac{1}{R_c} & 0 & -\dfrac{1}{R_\ell} & -\dfrac{1}{R_o} & \dfrac{1}{R_o} + \dfrac{1}{R_\ell} + \dfrac{1}{R_c}
\end{bmatrix}
\begin{bmatrix} v_1 \\[2ex] v_2 \\[2ex] v_3 \\[2ex] v_4 \\[2ex] v_5 \end{bmatrix}
=
\begin{bmatrix} i_{in} \\[2ex] 0 \\[2ex] 0 \\[2ex] 0 \\[2ex] 0 \end{bmatrix}
$$

The element currents are defined in the direction of the arrows in Figure 4.6(a). The equations for these currents are

$$i_1 = \dfrac{-v_3}{R} \qquad i_3 = \dfrac{v_1 - v_2}{R} \qquad i_5 = \dfrac{v_2 - v_4}{R_\ell} \qquad i_7 = \dfrac{v_5 - v_3}{R_\ell}$$

$$i_2 = \dfrac{v_2}{R} \qquad i_4 = \dfrac{v_1 - v_3}{R} \qquad i_6 = \dfrac{v_4 - v_5}{R_o} \qquad i_8 = \dfrac{v_1 - v_5}{R_c}$$

Excel solutions appear in Figure 4.7(a) (a solution with the calibrating resistor R_c switched out of the circuit) and Figure 4.7(b) (R_c switched into the circuit). Figure 4.7(c) shows the formulas. The conductance values of the four resistor values were computed in cells A2:D2 for use in the matrix. R_c is given the value 43,000 ohms when switched into the circuit and 10^{15} ohms when switched out, an approximation to an open circuit. Their locations are named with the **Formula Create Names Top Row** toggle. Variables used in the worksheet listings of Figure 4.7 are defined as follows:

GRr	A2
GRc	B2
GRl	C2
GRo	D2

We deliberately used unnamed cell references to show their use in the matrix equations of Figure 4.7(c).

Node network N and adjoint network $\hat{N}$ are identical and appear in cells E2 : I6, with the inverse in E8 : I12. Note the array formula in the corresponding cells of Figure 4.7(c), part 2.

The right-hand side vectors are entered in A5 : A9 (node network) and C5 : C9 (adjoint network), with the matrix multiplications appearing in B5 : B9 and D5 : D9, respectively. Individually, these results are then transferred with the **Edit Copy** and **Edit Paste Special Values** commands to the node voltage temporary storage area, cell range F14 : F18. These node voltages are then used in the element current calculations of cell range B11 : B18. The resultant currents, cell ranges C11 : C18 (node network) and D11 : D18 (adjoint network) are then used in the unnormalized sensitivity formula of cell range B21 : B28. The designations in cell range A21 : A28 are text.

The uncalibrated circuit element sensitivities were calculated to help verify the worksheet computations. Symmetry of the bridge circuit, when unstressed, should yield identical numerical results for each resistor R, except for sign, and they are identical. In sensitivity calculations, a plus sign denotes an in-phase change of the network function with respect to the parameter, while a minus sign denotes an out-of-phase change. Our principal concern is with the connection of R_c. Calibration current will produce an added voltage drop as it flows through one of the connecting wires, thus causing an incorrect measured calibration value. An alternative is to

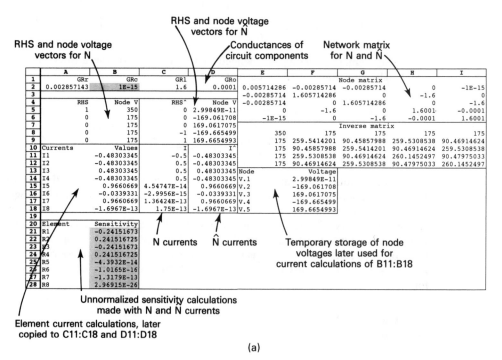

(a)

Figure 4.7 (a) Sensitivity calculations with calibration resistor R_c switched out of the circuit.

Table (spreadsheet grid, columns A–I, rows 1–28):

#	A	B	C	D	E	F	G	H	I
1	GRr	GRc	GR1	GRo			Node matrix		
2	0.00285714143	2.32558E-05	1.6	0.0001	0.005737542	-0.00285714	-0.00285714	0	-2.3256E-05
3					-0.00285714	1.605714286	0	-1.6	0
4	RHS	Node V	RHS^	Node V	-0.00285714	-1.6	1.605714286	0	-1.6
5	1	349.2920736	0	0.686346803	-2.3256E-05	0	-1.6	1.6001	-0.0001
6	0	174.6580479	0	-168.730179	0	0	0 *(Inverse matrix)*	-0.0001	1.600123256
7	0	175.3419521	0	168.7301791	349.2920736	174.6580479	175.3419521	174.6580908	175.3444376
8	0	174.6580908	-1	-169.334012	174.6580479	259.3762458	90.62375421	259.3657002	90.635211
9	0	175.3444376	1	169.3315612	175.3419521	90.62375421	259.3762458	90.63429984	259.3644789
10	Currents	Values	I	I^	174.6580908	259.3657002	90.63429984	259.9801168	90.6461043
11	I1	-0.48208623	-0.50097701	-0.48208623	175.3444376	90.635211	259.3644789	90.6461043	259.9776655
12	I2	-0.48208623	0.499022994	-0.48208623	Node	Voltage			
13	I3	0.484047217	0.498954359	0.484047217	V.1	0.686346803			
14	I4	-0.48012524	0.497000347	-0.48012524	V.2	-168.730179			
15	I5	0.96133443	-6.8635E-05	0.96133443	V.3	168.7301791			
16	I6	-0.03386656	-6.8635E-05	-0.03386656	V.4	-169.334012			
17	I7	0.962211461	0.003976659	0.962211461	V.5	169.3315612			
18	I8	-0.00392198	0.004045294	-0.00392198					
19									
20	Element	Sensitivity							
21	R1	-0.24151411							
22	R2	0.240572112							
23	R3	-0.24151747							
24	R4	0.238622408							
25	R5	6.63103E-05							
26	R6	-2.3244E-06							
27	R7	-0.00382639							
28	R8	1.58656E-05							

(b)

Figure 4.7 (b) Sensitivity calculations with the calibration resistor R_c switched into the circuit.

123

	A	B	C	D
1	GRr	GRc	GR1	GRo
2	=1/350	0.0000000000001	1.6	=1/10000
3				
4	RHS	Node V	RHS^	Node V
5	1	=MMULT(E8:I12,A5:A9)	0	=MMULT(E8:I12,C5:C9)
6	0	=MMULT(E8:I12,A5:A9)	0	=MMULT(E8:I12,C5:C9)
7	0	=MMULT(E8:I12,A5:A9)	0	=MMULT(E8:I12,C5:C9)
8	0	=MMULT(E8:I12,A5:A9)	-1	=MMULT(E8:I12,C5:C9)
9	0	=MMULT(E8:I12,A5:A9)	1	=MMULT(E8:I12,C5:C9)
10	Currents	Values	I	I^
11	I1	=-V.3*GRr	-0.50000000000000013	-0.483033450066363
12	I2	=V.2*GRr	0.4999999999999928	-0.483033450066362
13	I3	=(V.1-V.2)*GRr	0.4999999999999955	0.483033450066447
14	I4	=(V.1-V.3)*GRr	0.4999999999999987	-0.483033450066277
15	I5	=(V.2-V.4)*GR1	4.54747350886464E-14	0.966066900132864
16	I6	=(V.4-V.5)*GRo	-2.99564817396458E-15	-0.033933099867162
17	I7	=(V.5-V.3)*GR1	1.36424205265939E-13	0.966066900132637
18	I8	=(V.1-V.5)*GRc	1.74999999999954E-13	-1.6966549933578E-13
19				
20	Element	Sensitivity		
21	R1	=-C11:C18*D11:D18		
22	R2	=-C11:C18*D11:D18		
23	R3	=-C11:C18*D11:D18		
24	R4	=-C11:C18*D11:D18		
25	R5	=-C11:C18*D11:D18		
26	R6	=-C11:C18*D11:D18		
27	R7	=-C11:C18*D11:D18		
28	R8	=-C11:C18*D11:D18		

Figure 4.7 (c) Example 4.2 worksheet in formulas mode, part 1.

(c)

	E	F	G	H	I
1			Node matrix		
2	=2*GRr+GRc	=-GRr	=-GRr	0	=-GRc
3	=-GRr	=2*GRr+GRl	0	=-GRl	0
4	=-GRr	0	=2*GRr+GRl	0	=-GRl
5	0	=-GRl	0	=GRl+GRo	=-GRo
6	=-GRc	0	=-GRl	=-GRo	=GRo+GRl+GRc
7			Inverse matrix		
8	=MINVERSE(E2:I6)	=MINVERSE(E2:I6)	=MINVERSE(E2:I6)	=MINVERSE(E2:I6)	=MINVERSE(E2:I6)
9	=MINVERSE(E2:I6)	=MINVERSE(E2:I6)	=MINVERSE(E2:I6)	=MINVERSE(E2:I6)	=MINVERSE(E2:I6)
10	=MINVERSE(E2:I6)	=MINVERSE(E2:I6)	=MINVERSE(E2:I6)	=MINVERSE(E2:I6)	=MINVERSE(E2:I6)
11	=MINVERSE(E2:I6)	=MINVERSE(E2:I6)	=MINVERSE(E2:I6)	=MINVERSE(E2:I6)	=MINVERSE(E2:I6)
12	=MINVERSE(E2:I6)	=MINVERSE(E2:I6)	=MINVERSE(E2:I6)	=MINVERSE(E2:I6)	=MINVERSE(E2:I6)
13	Node	Voltage			
14	V.1	2.99849034490762E-11			
15	V.2	-169.061707523226			
16	V.3	169.061707523227			
17	V.4	-169.665499935809			
18	V.5	169.665499933581			
19					
20					
21					
22					
23					
24					
25					
26					
27					
28					

(c)

Figure 4.7 (c) Part 2.

125

connect R_c to the bridge with a fifth wire. Nevertheless, we should see an effect on the sensitivity value in the output due to the line resistance.

We see the expected difference by comparing the values in cell B27 in Figure 4.7(b) ($-.003826$, during calibration) with that of Figure 4.7(a) ($-1.31795E-13$, during operation). The calibration resistor also affects the sensitivities with respect to the measuring load resistance, cell B26.

The computations were readily made with the Excel basic operators and array functions and this example illustrates array computations on a small scale.

4.4 DEBUGGING

A sure way to quickly develop a functional worksheet is to never make arithmetical, logical, syntactical, or other errors while developing it. In the absence of such skill, however, it is wise to follow good worksheet programming procedures. In addition to remarks of previous chapters, we present the following suggestions when arrays are being used:

1. Observe the dimensionality requirements of matrix computations.

2. It is important to select a compatible cell range for multiple result operations; otherwise, automatic expansion of the result arrays occurs. Excel may not warn of the consequences when automatic expansion takes place. Furthermore, automatic expansion follows confusing and hard-to-remember rules so that, without extreme care, undesired results will eventually be produced. Use of this feature is contrary to good worksheet programming practices so we do not recommend its use.

3. Automatic expansion may also occur, even though the result array accommodates multiple values. In this case, array constants may be expanded with undesired results. An exception would be the use of a 1×1 array in multiplication or division operations in which its use functions as a scalar operating on individual array elements.

4. Enter array formulas properly by pressing CTRL+SHIFT before entering. Look for the brace-pair enclosing the entire formula.

5. Be careful not to omit the brace-pair in array constants, else the entry will be treated as a text constant because of the commas.

6. Select cell names carefully to avoid name conflicts. Names should not be the same as cell coordinate references or reserved words. This restriction is especially severe for electrical engineering work where schematic component reference designations almost always appear like cell coordinate references. A recommended solution is to use the special characters "." and "_" as part of the name. This tactic was used in Example 4.3.

7. Use the **Edit** commands to copy and paste cell contents to other parts of the worksheet. Never copy an entry by typing it. Numerical values are difficult

to proofread and numerical errors can propagate unnoticed throughout the worksheet. When pasting values, be sure to select the **Values** toggle in the **Paste Special** dialog box; otherwise, formulas will also be copied and cause undesired cell content changes.

8. Error values such a #N/A, #NUM!, #REF?, #VALUE!, and so on are often displayed immediately. When these values appear as one is entering a formula, several clues to the cause of the error should be evident; perhaps a cell name is incorrectly entered, maybe a cell has not yet been named, or the formula syntax may be incorrect. Such errors should be attended to immediately. This may require work in another part of the worksheet to name cells, define cell contents, and so on.

4.5 ABOUT VERSION 3.0

All worksheets of this chapter run under version 3.0 without change. We illustrate below the new function SUMPRODUCT, that applies to the material of this chapter, and the use of Solver with array formulas.

4.5.1 The SUMPRODUCT Function

The function SUMPRODUCT requires array arguments. Its format is

$$\text{SUMPRODUCT}(arg_1, arg_2, \ldots)$$

where the arg_i are arrays, all of the same dimensions. The function sums corresponding element products of all arguments and performs the same computation that we illustrated in Section 4.3.3 with the product of arrays within the SUM function, which we noted can be used to compute the vector dot product. The difference in use is that SUMPRODUCT does not have to be entered as an array formula as does the SUM function when used for the same purpose. Therefore, it is only a convenience function since we already have its capability within another function.

Example 4.4

In this example we use the SUMPRODUCT function to compute the coefficients of the equation

$$y = mx + b$$

by the linear least squares formulas

$$m = \frac{k\Sigma x_i y_i - \Sigma x_i \Sigma y_i}{k\Sigma x_i^2 - (\Sigma x_i)^2} \qquad b = \frac{\Sigma y_i - m\Sigma x_i}{k}$$

where k is the number of x-y pairs and each summation is over k. The SUMPRODUCT function will be used to compute the $\Sigma x_i y_i$ and Σx_i^2 terms.

	A	B
1	x(i)	y(i)
2	8.3	0.32
3	12.3	0.46
4	18.8	1.1
5	22.9	1.32
6	23.1	1.26
7	24	1.44
8	27.3	1.42
9	30	1.96
10	35.9	2.23
11	41.6	2.2
12		
13	k	10
14	sumx	244.2
15	sumy	13.71
16	sumxy	392.031
17	sumxsq	6872.3
18	m	0.0629668
19	b	-0.166649

(a)

	A	B
1	x(i)	y(i)
2	8.3	0.32
3	12.3	0.46
4	18.8	1.1
5	22.9	1.32
6	23.1	1.26
7	24	1.44
8	27.3	1.42
9	30	1.96
10	35.9	2.23
11	41.6	2.2
12		
13	k	=COUNT(Arr1)
14	sumx	=SUM(Arr1)
15	sumy	=SUM(Arr2)
16	sumxy	=SUMPRODUCT(Arr1,Arr2)
17	sumxsq	=SUMPRODUCT(Arr1,Arr1)
18	m	=(k*sumxy-sumx*sumy)/(k*sumxsq-sumx^2)
19	b	=(sumy-m*sumx)/k

(b)

Figure 4.8 Worksheet for Example 4.4 in (a) values mode and (b) formulas mode.

The worksheet is shown in Figure 4.8, where the arrays of x and y values were defined with the names Arr1 and Arr2, respectively. The variable names in rows 13 through 19 of Column A were assigned to their corresponding cells in column B. The worksheet formulas are a straightforward implementation of the least squares formulas given above. The Excel built-in functions that we used implicitly perform looping actions that conveniently save us programming effort. The results are in cells B18 and B19.

4.5.2 A Solver Application with Arrays

We introduced Solver in Section 3.6.2, where we applied it to single equations and performed optimization calculations. We now use it to solve a system of equations by matrix techniques.

Example 4.5.

The characteristic-value problem appears often in engineering closed-loop systems design. Given that the problem appears in the form

$$\mathbf{A}\mathbf{x} = \lambda\mathbf{x}$$

where $\mathbf{A}$ is a matrix of constants, $\mathbf{x}$ is a state vector, and λ is a constant. This equation can be written

$$(\mathbf{A} - \lambda\mathbf{I})\mathbf{x} = 0$$

where $\mathbf{I}$ is the unit matrix. It has a nontrivial solution if and only if

$$|\mathbf{A} - \lambda\mathbf{I}| = 0$$

This equation is called a *characteristic equation* because the closed-loop system response is characterized by the values of its roots, which are the closed-loop poles. When **A** is of order n, the characteristic equation which is an algebraic equation, is also of order n. When solved, it will yield n values for λ, called *characteristic values* or *eigenvalues*. For each characteristic value, there is a corresponding *characteristic vector*, or *eigenvector*, of the problem. The largest characteristic value is called the *dominant* characteristic number because of its role in shaping the response. We will solve for this value by an approximation method for the case where **A** is real and symmetric. The procedure is as follows:

1. Assume an initial vector, say $\mathbf{x}^{(1)} = [1,1, . . . ,1]^T$, with each element of unit value. Solve for $\mathbf{Ax}^{(1)} = \mathbf{y}^{(1)}$.
2. Normalize $\mathbf{y}^{(1)}$ to its largest value, k, such that $\mathbf{y}^{(1)} = k\mathbf{y}'^{(1)}$, where $\mathbf{y}'$ denotes the normalized vector.
3. Compare $\mathbf{y}'^{(1)}$ with $\mathbf{x}^{(1)}$. If they are equal, within some tolerance value, $k = \lambda_{max}$ is the dominant characteristic number and we are finished with our calculation. If the test fails, select a new vector, $\mathbf{x}^{(2)}$, to increase the value of k, and repeat the calculation of step 1. to get $\mathbf{y}^{(2)}$, continue with step 2., and make the above test again.

We will use Solver to select elements of $\mathbf{x}^{(i)}$ to maximize k. Our problem is entered in the worksheet of Figure 4.9(a) with formulas shown in Figure 4.9(b). Names for the matrices are created from row 1.

Matrix **y** is unnormalized. We search it for its maximum value in yimax and normalize it to get yprime. Our objective function is yimax and our constraints are $\mathbf{x} = \mathbf{y}'$ and $x_i \leq 1$ for all i. The Solver dialog box setup is shown in Figure 4.9(c). Solver chooses the x_i so as to increase yimax with each iteration. It ultimately finds λ_{max} and stops, with the values shown in Figure 4.9(d).

We also let Solver generate for us the Answer and Limit reports of Figures 4.10 and 4.11, respectively. Each report is displayed in a separate window. The variables' names are obtained from text to the left and above the cells. They are not the names defined in the worksheet for these cells.

The Answer report shows the original and final values of the objective function and the adjustable independent variables, and the constraint information. If the final value of the constraint cell equals its constraint value, its status is listed as *Binding*. If the constraint cell value satisfies the constraint but does not equal the constraint value, its status is listed as *Not Binding*. If the constraint was not met, its status would be listed as *Not Satisfied*. The slack value equals the constraint value minus the constraint cell value.

The Limit report shows the final values of the objective function and adjustable independent variables, and the limit value information on the adjustable cells. The lower and upper limit values for an adjustable cell are the smallest and largest values, respectively, that it will have when the other adjustable cells are fixed and the constraint is satisfied. The target result is the value of the objective

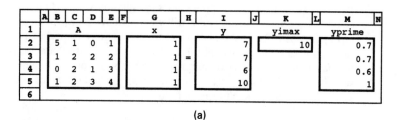

(a)

(b)

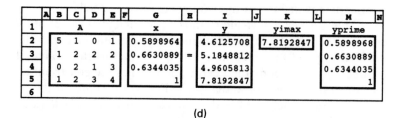

(c)

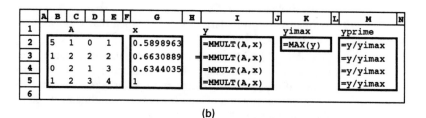

(d)

Figure 4.9 Worksheets and Solver dialog box for Example 4.5.

```
Excel  3.0  Answer Report
Worksheet: EX4P5.XLS
Report Created:   3/18/91 1:18 PM
```

Target Cell (Max)

Cell	Name	Original Value	Final Value
$K$2	yimax	10	7.819284714

Adjustable Cells

Cell	Name	Original Value	Final Value
$G$2	x	1	0.589896374
$G$3	x	1	0.663088906
$G$4	x	1	0.634403509

Constraints

Cell	Name	Cell Value	Formula	Status	Slack
$G$2	x	0.589896374	$G$2<=1	Not Binding	0.410103626
$G$2	x	0.589896374	$G$2=$M$2	Binding	-3.9347E-07
$G$3	x	0.663088906	$G$3<=1	Not Binding	0.336911094
$G$3	x	0.663088906	$G$3=$M$3	Binding	-3.2873E-08
$G$4	x	0.634403509	$G$4<=1	Not Binding	0.365596491
$G$4	x	0.634403509	$G$4=$M$4	Binding	-4.3794E-08
$G$5	x	1	$G$5=$M$5	Binding	0
$G$5	x	1	$G$5<=1	Binding	0

Figure 4.10 Answer report for Example 4.5.

```
Microsoft Excel  3.0  Limits Report
Worksheet: EX4P5.XLS
Report Created:   3/18/91 1:18 PM
```

Cell	Target Name	Value
$K$2	yimax	7.819284714

Cell	Adjustable Name	Value
$G$2	x	0.589896374
$G$3	x	0.663088906
$G$4	x	0.634403509

Lower Limit	Target Result
0.589896374	7.819284714
0.663088906	7.819284714
0.634403509	7.819284714

Upper Limit	Target Result
0.589896374	7.819284714
0.663088906	7.819284714
0.634403509	7.819284714

Figure 4.11 Limit report for Example 4.5.

function under these conditions. In our example, the limit values equal the final values.

REFERENCES

[1] Calahan, D. A., *Computer-Aided Network Design,* Revised Edition, New York: McGraw-Hill Book Co., 1972.

[2] Director, S. W., *Circuit Theory: A Computational Approach,* New York: John Wiley & Sons, 1975.

PROBLEMS

Use spreadsheet matrix functions and other operators as needed to solve the following:

4.1 Perform the following operations, if possible, using the given matrices.

    (a) $\mathbf{A}^T - \mathbf{B}$ **(c)** $\mathbf{B} - \mathbf{B}^T$ **(e)** $(\mathbf{A}^T)^T$

    (b) $2\mathbf{B} - \mathbf{C}^T$ **(d)** $(\mathbf{B} + 2\mathbf{C}^T)^T$

$$\mathbf{A} = \begin{bmatrix} 2 & 0 \\ 1 & 4 \\ 3 & 1 \end{bmatrix} \quad \mathbf{B} = \begin{bmatrix} 1 & -1 & 4 \\ 0 & 2 & 3 \end{bmatrix} \quad \mathbf{C} = \begin{bmatrix} 5 & -3 \\ 0 & 4 \\ 1 & 2 \end{bmatrix}$$

4.2 Determine the elements of $\mathbf{M}^T$ and $\mathbf{M}^{-1}$ for $\mathbf{M}$ and verify that $\mathbf{MM}^{-1} = \mathbf{I}$.

$$\mathbf{M} = \begin{bmatrix} 1 & 3 & 0 \\ 3 & 1 & 1 \\ 1 & 0 & -1 \end{bmatrix}$$

4.3 Determine the elements of $\mathbf{M}$ such that $\mathbf{XMY} = \mathbf{Z}$ when

$$\mathbf{X} = \begin{bmatrix} 3 & 1 & 2 \\ 0 & 1 & 1 \\ 1 & 0 & 2 \end{bmatrix} \quad \mathbf{Y} = \begin{bmatrix} 2 & 1 \\ 1 & 3 \end{bmatrix} \quad \mathbf{Z} = \begin{bmatrix} 2 & 1 \\ 1 & 2 \\ 2 & 1 \end{bmatrix}$$

4.4 Find the rank r of

$$\textbf{(a)} \quad \begin{vmatrix} 2 & -4 & 1 \\ 2 & 3 & 1 \\ 4 & -1 & 2 \end{vmatrix} \qquad \textbf{(b)} \quad \begin{vmatrix} 3 & 1 & -4 & 2 \\ 5 & 0 & -2 & 1 \\ 1 & 1 & -3 & 0 \\ -2 & 1 & -2 & 1 \end{vmatrix}$$

4.5 Determine the dimension of the vector space generated by each of the following sets of vectors:

    (a) {1,0,1}, {2,1,0}, {0,3,2}

    (b) {3,2,1}, {0,4,2}, {1,0,0}, {0,3,0}

    (c) {2,1,2}, {4,0,0}, {0,2,2}

4.6   Which of the following sets in R^4 are linearly independent over R?
   (a)   {(0,1,1,0), (0,1,0,1), (1,0,1,0), (1,0,0,1)}
   (b)   {(0,0,1,1), (1,0,1,0), (0,1,1,0), (1,1,1,1)}
   (c)   {(1,0,1,1), (1,1,1,−1), (2,1,2,2), (0,0,0,1)}

4.7   From the relationship

$$\mathbf{a} \cdot \mathbf{b} = |\mathbf{a}||\mathbf{b}| \cos \theta$$

   compute $\cos \theta$ for the vectors $\mathbf{u} = \{1,0,1\}$ and $\mathbf{v} = \{1,1,1\}$.

4.8   Use matrix methods to solve the following system of equations for a, b, c, and d, and
   to check the solution.

$$a + b + c + d = 1$$

$$a + 3b + 6c + 10d = 26$$

$$a + 4b + 10c + 20d = 47$$

$$a + 2b + 3c + 4d = 11$$

4.9   Computer graphics systems often use a homogeneous coordinate system whereby an
   n-component vector is represented by an $n + 1$ component vector. The transformation matrix, increased in size from $n \times n$ to $(n + 1) \times (n + 1)$, is applied to a two-
   dimensional application as follows:

$$[x' \quad y' \quad 1] = [x \quad y \quad 1] \begin{bmatrix} a & b & p \\ c & d & q \\ m & n & s \end{bmatrix}$$

   where x' and y' are the transformed values of the two-dimensional vector whose
   components are x and y; a, b, c, and d produce scaling, shearing, and rotation; m and
   n produce translation in the x and y directions, respectively; p and q produce projection; and s is an overall scale factor. The transformation matrix is no longer restricted
   to performing linear transformations. For positive rotation in the counterclockwise

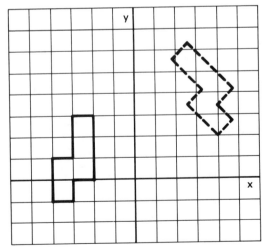

Figure P4.9

direction we have the elements $a = \cos\theta$, $b = \sin\theta$, $c = -\sin\theta$, and $d = \cos\theta$. For no scaling $s = 1$, and for no projection $p = 0$ and $q = 0$. Relative translation distances are given by the values of m and n in the geometrical units of the application. Determine the elements of the transformation matrix (or matrices) to transform Figure P4.9 from its present location to the dotted location. Remember that rotation, a linear transformation, is about the origin. It will be necessary to translate to the origin, then rotate the figure, then translate to the new location. Verify the elements of the transformation matrix (or matrices) by reading from the figure the coordinates of the corners (the grid squares are 1 unit on a side), transforming them, and drawing the new figure.

CHAPTER 5

Logic, Decisions, and Iteration

Spreadsheet programs are not limited to numerical computation. We can work with text and logical data types also. In this chapter, we introduce computation with the logical data type. This will enable us to work with a new class of engineering problems. It also provides us the opportunity to discuss how to make decisions in our formulas to control the outcome of a computation. This capability will be expanded upon in the chapters on macros to overcome the limitations of this feature that we are about to discover.

Finally, we discuss the iteration capability of the spreadsheet program. This feature allows us to control the number of iterations and permits an implied looping capability. The combination of new features introduced in this chapter will allow us to apply a spreadsheet program to an enlarged class of problems.

5.1 DATA TYPE LOGICAL

It is not surprising that numeric data types dominate in engineering applications, since engineering activities usually require calculation to produce the desired result. However, some applications suggest that nonnumeric techniques be applied. For these applications, the data type of choice is termed *logical*. It refers to a limited range of values as used in propositional calculus. We now describe this data type as used in Excel.

5.1.1 True/False Assertions

A simple sentence that may be pronounced to be true or false is regarded as a proposition. For example, the sentence "Wyoming and Nebraska are adjacent states" is a true proposition, whereas "eight is greater than thirteen" is a false proposition. We may assign a variable to each statement which may take on a truth value of true or false. We can mathematically manipulate the variables and arrive at truth values. We need not restrict ourselves to simple positive statements as given above but may choose to use negative statements such as "four is not more than twenty" or compound statements such as "the airport is closed and the buses are not running."

A variable that can acquire only two distinct values as described above is called a *logic variable*. Its logic values may be denoted by the symbol pairs true/false, high/low, 0/1, on/off, and the like. Although 0 and 1 are frequently treated as numbers, they have essentially no quantitative meaning in propositional calculus. Nonnumeric symbols are often used to stress the formal rather than quantitative meaning.

In Excel, the logical values TRUE and FALSE are logical constants, which also have the numerical equivalents 1 and 0, respectively. These values may be assigned by the names TRUE or FALSE, by the functions TRUE( ) or FALSE( ) (neither of which require an argument), by the constants 1 or 0, or by an expression whose outcome is true or false. The names are reserved words and need not be enclosed in quotation marks. The values are illustrated in the paragraphs to follow.

5.1.2 Logical Expressions and Functions

In Chapter 2, we identified the right-hand side of a formula as an arithmetic expression because it was an assembly of numerical variables, functions, constants, and operators. We will now discuss how to prepare logical expressions for formulas.

Recall that a formula in a cell causes a value to be computed for that cell, which can then be retrieved through its cell reference. Were this formula to compute a logical value, the cell value would be logical, TRUE or FALSE. Because variables are not declared to be of a certain type, a cell will hold a value type dependent on the outcome of its formula. Thus, to give it a logical value, we must prepare a logical expression for the formula.

Logical expressions, when literally formed into simple sentences, express a proposition. This usually requires that the expression contain a comparative relationship among numerical expressions, a logical association among logical variables, or some combination of the two. Table 5.1 contains examples of logical expressions. Formulas 1 and 2 in the table contain comparative expressions. These expressions contain numerical expressions bound by comparison opera-

TABLE 5.1 EXAMPLES OF LOGICAL EXPRESSIONS

Formula	Type of expression
1. =area>3*wfn	comparative
2. =ABS(6−a_4)<=700	comparative
3. =true	logical (simple)
4. =AND(u.7a,u.1c,u.12c)	logical (simple)
5. =OR(m4.hi,b3_A=jtal)	logical (simple)
6. =OR(NOT(switch),AND(relay1,relay2))	logical (compound)

tors. Table 5.2 shows the comparison operators of Excel, which are binary operators (requiring two operands) whereby the first operand is compared to the second operand in the sense of the operator. Formula 1 of Table 5.1 uses the ''greater than'' operator while formula 2 uses the ''equal to or less than'' operator. The outcome of the comparison is a logical value, TRUE or FALSE, depending on the numeric values for the variables. This outcome then becomes the value for the containing cell.

Formula 3 of Table 5.1 is an assignment of the logical constant TRUE to the cell. Formulas 4, 5, and 6 contain logical functions. The functions are defined in Table 5.3. Formula 4 is the intersection of the three logical arguments u.7a, u.1c, and u.12c. The function value is TRUE if and only if all three arguments are true. Formula 5 is the union of two logical arguments. Its second argument is a comparison expression that yields a logical value when evaluated. The function value is FALSE if and only if both arguments are false. Formula 6 is a compound logical expression that mathematically has the form =switch ∪ (relay 1 ∩ relay 2). The parentheses are redundant in this mathematical formula, since they do not alter the evaluation from the hierarchy shown in Table 5.3. The hierarchical priority is applied at the lowest level (within the innermost parentheses, or under a single complement bar) and is progressively moved upward as the expression is reduced by combining within the parentheses or under a common complement bar. Here is an example showing the application of the hierarchy rules. The letters are the names of logical variables which must have logical values assigned

TABLE 5.2 COMPARISON OPERATORS

Symbol	Meaning
=	Equal
<>	Not equal
<	Less than
>	Greater than
<=	Equal to or less than
>=	Equal to or greater than

TABLE 5.3 EXCEL LOGICAL FUNCTIONS

Operation	Priority	Symbol, with operands	Function	Comments*			
Complement	1	$\overline{A}$	NOT(arg)	One-variable truth table		A	A
						F	T
						T	F
Intersection	2	A∩B	AND(arg_1, . . . ,arg_n)	Two-variable truth table	A	B	A∩B
					F	F	F
					F	T	F
					T	F	F
					T	T	T
Union	3	A∪B	OR(arg_1, . . . ,arg_n)	Two-variable truth table	A	B	A∪B
					F	F	F
					F	T	T
					T	F	T
					T	T	T

* All function arguments must be logical expressions.

to them for the reduction to take place. The W_i indicate intermediate evaluation results.

$$
\begin{aligned}
\text{value} &= \overline{A \cap (B \cup \overline{C} \cap D) \cup E \cap \overline{F} \cup G} \\
&= \overline{A \cap (B \cup W_1 \cap D) \cup E \cap \overline{W_2}} \\
&= \overline{A \cap (B \cup \overline{W_3}) \cup E \cap W_4} \\
&= \overline{A \cap (\overline{W_5}) \cup W_6} \\
&= \overline{\overline{W_7} \cup W_6} \\
&= W_8 \cup W_6 \\
&= W_9 \qquad \text{(evaluation completed)}
\end{aligned}
$$

5.1.3 Examples

The following two examples illustrate logical expression computation in Excel. The first example shows how the logical expression can be conveniently developed from a logic formula. The second example illustrates the development of a logical expression from a logic diagram.

Example 5.1

We are given the logic formula

$$W = \overline{A} + (B \cdot C + D) \cdot (\overline{A} + D)$$

where A, B, C, D, and W are all logical variables and where we have replaced the symbols ∪ and ∩ with + and ·, respectively. The change in symbols is to conform with their appearance in engineering work. The logical complement is denoted by the overhead bar. We will prepare the worksheet solution.

The logic formula is of compound form. The parentheses, which are not redundant, require us to view the expression in nested form. Because of the way that the logical functions are defined, we must "look ahead" while constructing the expression because of the required ordering of the arguments. To simplify this process, we propose to first represent the expression in prefix (forward Polish) notation. It is now expressed in infix notation. Both of these notations differ from the reverse Polish notation (RPN) used in some hand calculators. The following construction shows the transformation from infix notation to prefix notation:

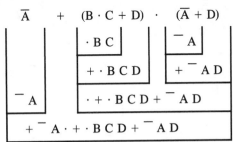

The bottom line above is the prefix notation. We can write the Excel formula directly from it. However, to show this development and association with the Excel functions, we first substitute the functions for the logical operators and get

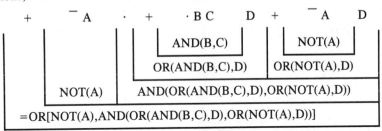

It is left to the reader to associate the parentheses with the vertical separation lines in the construction. With logic reduction techniques, the original expression can be simplified to $W = \overline{A} + D$. The formulas implemented in Excel and the results are shown in Figure 5.1. We chose not to use variable names in order to explicitly identify the cells involved with the computation. Because we have 4 variables in the expression, there are 16 possible combinations to enter in the formulas. We show all 16 of the input combinations (A2:D17) and the results from both formulas (E2:F17). To use the program, we entered truth values in cells A2:D2 for variables A, B, C, and D, since those cells are referenced in the formula of B18. The contents of B18 also appear in E2. The simplified expression is computed in cell F2. The text of cell F1 shows $\overline{A}$ as A', where the apostrophe is often used in the literature to designate complementation. The table is constructed by entering truth values for the variables, which trigger the computations, then saving the values by copying them to

(a)

	A	B	C	D	E	F
1	A	B	C	D	W	A'+D
2	FALSE	FALSE	FALSE	FALSE	TRUE	TRUE
3	FALSE	FALSE	FALSE	TRUE	TRUE	TRUE
4	FALSE	FALSE	TRUE	FALSE	TRUE	TRUE
5	FALSE	FALSE	TRUE	TRUE	TRUE	TRUE
6	FALSE	TRUE	FALSE	FALSE	TRUE	TRUE
7	FALSE	TRUE	FALSE	TRUE	TRUE	TRUE
8	FALSE	TRUE	TRUE	FALSE	TRUE	TRUE
9	FALSE	TRUE	TRUE	TRUE	TRUE	TRUE
10	TRUE	FALSE	FALSE	FALSE	FALSE	FALSE
11	TRUE	FALSE	FALSE	TRUE	TRUE	TRUE
12	TRUE	FALSE	TRUE	FALSE	FALSE	FALSE
13	TRUE	FALSE	TRUE	TRUE	FALSE	TRUE
14	TRUE	TRUE	FALSE	FALSE	FALSE	FALSE
15	TRUE	TRUE	FALSE	TRUE	TRUE	FALSE
16	TRUE	TRUE	TRUE	FALSE	FALSE	FALSE
17	TRUE	TRUE	TRUE	TRUE	TRUE	TRUE
18	W	TRUE				

(b)

	A	B	C	D	E	F
1	A	B	C	D	W	A'+D
2	FALSE	FALSE	FALSE	FALSE	=B18	=OR(NOT(A2),D2)
3	FALSE	FALSE	FALSE	TRUE	TRUE	TRUE
4	FALSE	FALSE	TRUE	FALSE	TRUE	TRUE
5	FALSE	FALSE	TRUE	TRUE	TRUE	TRUE
6	FALSE	TRUE	FALSE	FALSE	TRUE	TRUE
7	FALSE	TRUE	FALSE	TRUE	TRUE	TRUE
8	FALSE	TRUE	TRUE	FALSE	TRUE	TRUE
9	FALSE	TRUE	TRUE	TRUE	TRUE	TRUE
10	TRUE	FALSE	FALSE	FALSE	FALSE	FALSE
11	TRUE	FALSE	FALSE	TRUE	TRUE	TRUE
12	TRUE	FALSE	TRUE	FALSE	FALSE	FALSE
13	TRUE	FALSE	TRUE	TRUE	FALSE	TRUE
14	TRUE	TRUE	FALSE	FALSE	FALSE	FALSE
15	TRUE	TRUE	FALSE	TRUE	TRUE	FALSE
16	TRUE	TRUE	TRUE	FALSE	FALSE	FALSE
17	TRUE	TRUE	TRUE	TRUE	TRUE	TRUE
18	W	=OR(NOT(A2),AND(OR(AND(B2,C2),D2),OR(NOT(A2),D2)))				

Figure 5.1 Worksheet for Example 5.1 in (a) values mode and (b) formulas mode.

a row in the range A3 : F17. The last calculations remain in row 2. The results verify the equivalence of the two expressions.

Example 5.2

Figure 5.2 is a logic diagram of standard logic symbols. Marked on the diagram are the logical expressions at various nodes of the logic circuit, including the output at the far right. The circuit inputs are the variables A, B, and C. Like Example 5.1, this circuit can also be simplified. The equivalent expressions are given as F_1 and F_2 at the output. F_1 is the output without reduction, and F_2 is the simplified expression.

The Excel worksheet for this example is shown in Figure 5.3(a). We chose not to use variable names for the reason given in Example 5.1. The inputs, A2 : C2, are assigned the eight combinations of true/false values one at a time. F_1 (column D) and F_2 (column E) are computed in D2 : E2 and saved with the inputs in A3 : E9. The last calculations remain in row 2. The formulas for each expression of Figure 5.2 are entered in B10 : B19 as shown in Figure 5.3(b). Complementation is shown in column A with the apostrophe mark, an often-used symbol for this purpose. The values saved in A3 : E9 were copied from A2 : E2 with the **Edit Copy** and **Edit Paste Special Values** commands. A comparison of the values in columns D and E shows that F_1 and F_2 are equivalent.

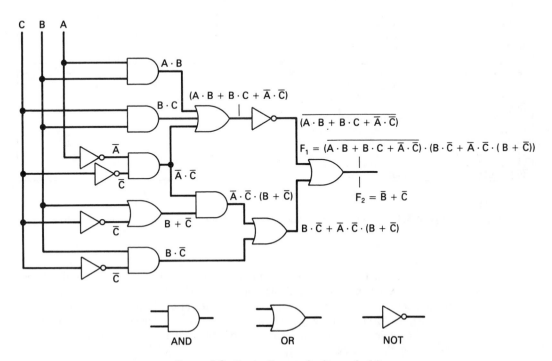

Figure 5.2 Logic diagram for Example 5.2.

	A	B	C	D	E
1	A	B	C	Result	B'+C'
2	FALSE	FALSE	FALSE	TRUE	TRUE
3	FALSE	FALSE	TRUE	TRUE	TRUE
4	FALSE	TRUE	FALSE	TRUE	TRUE
5	FALSE	TRUE	TRUE	FALSE	FALSE
6	TRUE	FALSE	FALSE	TRUE	TRUE
7	TRUE	FALSE	TRUE	TRUE	TRUE
8	TRUE	TRUE	FALSE	TRUE	TRUE
9	TRUE	TRUE	TRUE	FALSE	FALSE
10	A.B		FALSE		
11	B.C		FALSE		
12	A'.C'		TRUE		
13	B+C'		TRUE		
14	B.C'		FALSE		
15	A.B+B.C+A'.C'		TRUE		
16	A'.C'.(B+C')		TRUE		
17	(A.B+B.C+A'.C')'		FALSE		
18	B.C'+A'.C'.(B+C')		TRUE		
19	Result		TRUE		

(a)

	A	B	C	D	E
1	A	B	C	Result	B'+C'
2	FALSE	FALSE	FALSE	=OR(B17,B18)	=OR(NOT(B2),NOT(C2))
3	FALSE	FALSE	TRUE	TRUE	TRUE
4	FALSE	TRUE	FALSE	TRUE	TRUE
5	FALSE	TRUE	TRUE	FALSE	FALSE
6	TRUE	FALSE	FALSE	TRUE	TRUE
7	TRUE	FALSE	TRUE	TRUE	TRUE
8	TRUE	TRUE	FALSE	TRUE	TRUE
9	TRUE	TRUE	TRUE	FALSE	FALSE
10	A.B	=AND(A2,B2)			
11	B.C	=AND(B2,C2)			
12	A'.C'	=AND(NOT(A2),NOT(C2))			
13	B+C'	=OR(B2,NOT(C2))			
14	B.C'	=AND(B2,NOT(C2))			
15	A.B+B.C+A'.C'	=OR(B10,B11,B12)			
16	A'.C'.(B+C')	=AND(B12,B13)			
17	(A.B+B.C+A'.C')'	=NOT(B15)			
18	B.C'+A'.C'.(B+C')	=OR(B14,AND(B12,B13))			
19	Result	=OR(B17,B18)			

(b)

Figure 5.3 Worksheet for Example 5.2 in (a) values mode and (b) formulas mode.

We chose to use the logic variables of Figure 5.2 as text in row 1 and column A10: A18 rather than creating names from them to avoid the Excel restrictions on naming cells. Note the cell coordinate references in the formulas of Figure 5.3(b). Entering the formulas directly from the diagram is the preferred way and is a simple task. We retain one-to-one correspondence between the diagram and the worksheet, thus aiding the debugging effort.

5.2 DECISION MAKING

Thus far, we structured our problems so that computational paths were predetermined. We made all decisions a priori and prepared formulas to reflect this external control of computation. We used the computer for its great computational capability, progressing from simple computations to more complex ones. Now, we are about to use the computer to dynamically control the computations it must make. This controlling capability is available in most computer languages, but for spreadsheets, we must interpret its application somewhat differently. We now discuss the IF function.

5.2.1 IF—Conditional Assignment Function

The logical expressions introduced above imply that propositions have been formulated and their outcomes, either true or false, will be known at the time they are evaluated. We will now learn how, in Excel, to take advantage of such simple outcomes to dynamically control the assignment of values to a cell.

The IF function has the following syntax:

$$IF\ (logical\text{-}expression,\ true\text{-}value,\ false\text{-}value)$$

where

logical-expression = any expression yielding a logical outcome when evaluated.

true-value = the value to be assigned the function when *logical-expression* is true.

false-value = the value to be assigned the function when *logical-expression* is false.

Because conditions are specified in *logical-expression,* this function is also known as a conditional assignment function.

The IF function used in the worksheet has certain argument restrictions that are not present when it is used in a macro. It also operates differently than IF statements used in programming languages. The function produces a value for its containing cell. Therefore, it cannot cause transfer of control to another part of the worksheet. Furthermore, such transfer of control is contrary to the worksheet execution scheme whereby calculation is done on a need basis and is sequenced on a precedence basis.

The *true-value* and *false-value* arguments can be of any data type: logic, text, error value, or numeric. If numeric, the value may be derived from a formula as the argument. The argument may also be another IF function, which leads to the condition called nesting. Nesting may be seven levels deep in Excel.

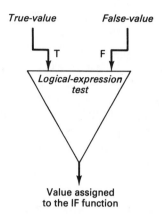

The IF function in the worksheet represents data flow, not control flow. For this reason, we must consider the events contributing to the argument values when preparing *logical-expression,* since the outcome, the value of the containing cell, will probably be used in subsequent calculations. Because there are no standard symbols representing data flow, we propose above our own for the IF function. In the next paragraph, we propose alternate symbols.

The two inputs of the triangular-shaped symbol represent *true-value* and *false-value,* one of which will be assigned as the value of the IF function. The IF function does not represent a branching process, it represents a selection process.

5.2.2 Data Flow Decision Structures

Decisions made for the examples presented thus far were made external to the worksheet. We purposely structured the problems to avoid discussing the IF function earlier than we thought necessary. Now, we will use the IF function to make decisions for us. We know that multiple decisions must often be made while solving a problem, and we know that the decision often rests on values obtained while computations are in progress. In discussing complex computational structures, we will continue our practice of discussing preferred ways to organize our worksheet to maintain the following characteristics:

1. It must be easily understood.
2. It must allow for a reduction in debugging iterations.
3. It must exhibit forward data flow.

The data flow diagram of the IF function shown in the preceding section appears contrary to the control flow of IF statements in programming languages. But we must remember that in worksheets, we are concerned with data flow, not program control flow. In Chapters 2, 3, and 4, our task was trivial, since we had only one path of data flow and since it was in the forward direction. Hereafter, we will construct a data flow diagram when it is useful in preparing the worksheet. It has advantages much like a programming flowchart does. It helps us to review the logic of our computational effort and to "see" the big picture, it indirectly contributes to our understanding of the problem by forcing us to organize our work, it expedites the debugging effort by forcing the logic to be correct, it helps document our work, and it imparts an organized appearance to the problem solution we have developed. For these reasons, we also try to maintain forward data flow in the worksheet (left to right and top to bottom). This is the worksheet counterpart of structured techniques for writing computer programs.

In the absence of data flow diagram symbol standards, any convenient set of symbols can be used to express the worksheet data flow. Here are other symbols suggested for the IF function:

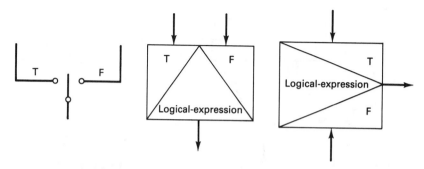

The IF function structure implies an inverted computation. Rather than deciding what is to be done, it decides what value to use that has already been computed. Consequently, the work to compute values is obscured by the simple decision that ensues. The data flow diagram does not reveal this effort either. But we can appreciate the ease in preparing the worksheet after giving much thought to the data flow. Here are two examples.

For a given x, a value for y is to be computed from the following waveform, where y is constant for $x < 0$ and $x \geq b$, is derived from $\sin x$ in the interval $0 \leq x < a$, and has a linear value for $a \leq x < b$.

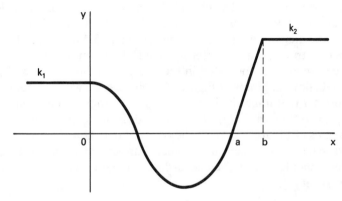

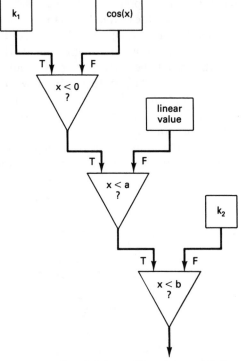

= IF(x < b, IF(x < a, IF(x < 0, k₁,cos(x)), linear value), k₂)

Figure 5.4 Proposed IF structure for the waveform example.

One solution is to use the nested IF structure of Figure 5.4, where the corresponding Excel formula is also shown. The diagram was constructed to follow the comparative "less than" operator. It flows from left to right and top to bottom. Or we may choose to use the structure of Figure 5.5, which uses the comparative "equal to or greater than" operator. Although its flow is not from left to right, its Excel implementation appears easier to understand than the one given for Figure 5.4. The nested IF functions work only if the logical expressions are mutually exclusive in the string. Should a series of separate IF functions be used, the diagram analogous to that of Figure 5.4 might be drawn as in Figure 5.6. This construction makes intermediate IF function results available via its containing cell reference, indicated in the figure with dashed lines. We should compare the data flow diagrams of Figures 5.4 through 5.6 with the control flow diagrams of Figure 5.7 that might be implemented in a programming language. The preferred diagram is Figure 5.7(a). It is more difficult to prepare a worksheet from the diagrams of Figure 5.7, since they are not data flow diagrams. One would have to work backward to determine what data should be made available and in what order it should be retrieved according to the precedence sequencing scheme of the worksheet.

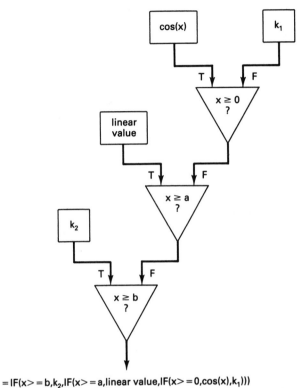

$$= IF(x> = b, k_2, IF(x> = a, linear\ value, IF(x> = 0, cos(x), k_1)))$$

Figure 5.5 Second IF structure for the waveform example.

We might assemble more complex structures such as shown in the skeleton diagram of Figure 5.8, where we used the switch symbol for the IF function. This symbol certainly reveals the data flow clearly, but it is necessary to place *logical-expression* as a caption adjacent to the switches where the boxes are drawn.

As a second example, we will convert the control flowchart of Figure 5.9 to data flow diagrams with the symbols not yet used. The figure shows command flow for solving the quadratic equation $ax^2 + bx + c = 0$ via the quadratic formula

$$x_1, x_2 = \frac{-b \pm \sqrt{b^2 - 4ac}}{2a}$$

Two proposed data flow diagrams are sketched in Figure 5.10. Because two numerical values might be calculated, we show dotted lines to two IF functions that assign values to x_1 and x_2. The outcome of the formula $=(b*b-4*a*c)<0$ is either true or false. This value is then tested in both diagrams before the assignments. Note that we chose not to test for zero or to test for $a = 0$, which would give problems in division. It should be apparent that when multiple values must be obtained via the IF functions, data flow diagramming becomes awkward.

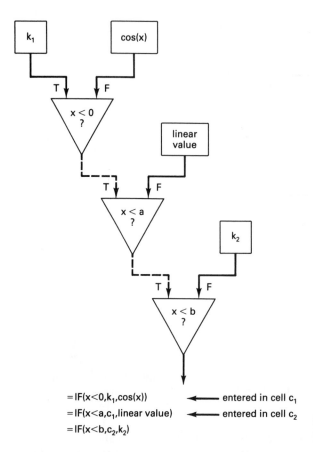

$= IF(x<0,k_1,cos(x))$ ◄─────── entered in cell c_1

$= IF(x<a,c_1,linear\ value)$ ◄─────── entered in cell c_2

$= IF(x<b,c_2,k_2)$

Figure 5.6 Separate IF functions for the structure of Figure 5.4.

5.2.3 Examples

The following two examples illustrate decision making in the worksheet. Data flow diagrams are included to develop the logic of the computations. The first example uses the comparative operators, while the second example uses both the comparative and logical operators.

Example 5.3

Figure 5.11 shows an angular assignment based on the signed values of the right triangle positioned in the coordinate system as shown. We will compute the proper angle through a series of IF functions and value assignments. Should angle values in quadrants other than the first and fourth be desired, we would normally use the ATAN2 function. But since we define the angle in the third quadrant differently, we will not use that function now.

A control flowchart is shown in Figure 5.12. From it we can prepare a data flow diagram. We choose to use the switch symbol for the IF function and develop

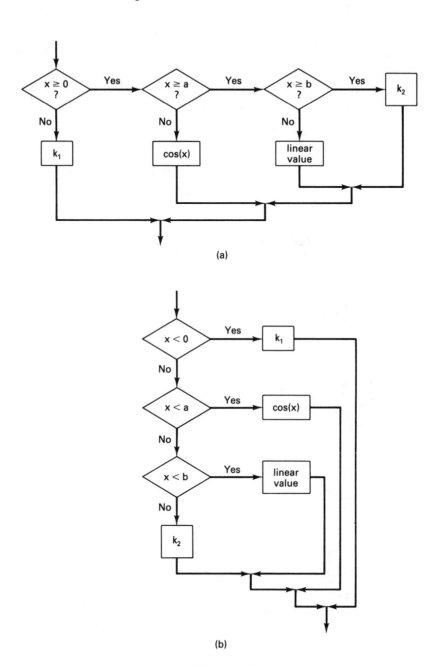

(a)

(b)

Figure 5.7 Control flow diagrams for the waveform example.

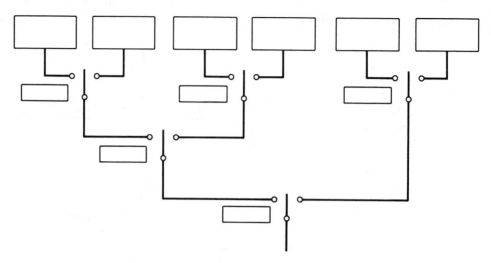

Figure 5.8 Complex data flow skeleton diagram.

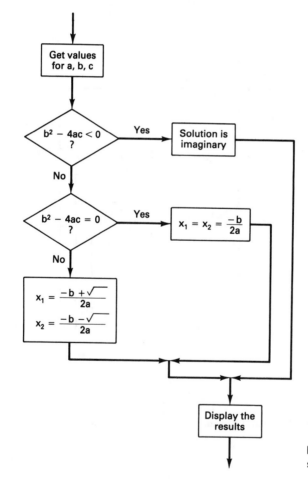

Figure 5.9 Control flowchart for solving the quadratic formula.

Get values
for a, b, c

$b^2 - 4ac < 0$
?

Yes

Solution is
imaginary

No

$b^2 - 4ac = 0$
?

Yes

$x_1 = x_2 = \dfrac{-b}{2a}$

No

$x_1 = \dfrac{-b + \sqrt{}}{2a}$

$x_2 = \dfrac{-b - \sqrt{}}{2a}$

Display the
results

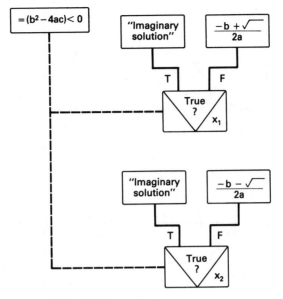

Temp = B*B $-$ 4*A*C

W = Temp$<$0

X1 = IF(W,"Imaginary solution",($-$B+SQRT(Temp))/(2*A))

X2 = IF(W,"Imaginary solution",($-$B$-$SQRT(Temp))/(2*A))

(a)

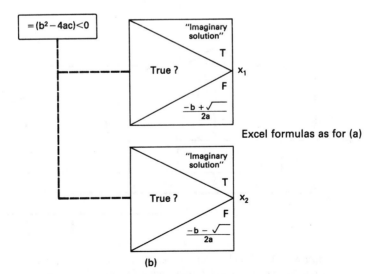

Excel formulas as for (a)

(b)

Figure 5.10   Data flow diagrams for the quadratic formula example.

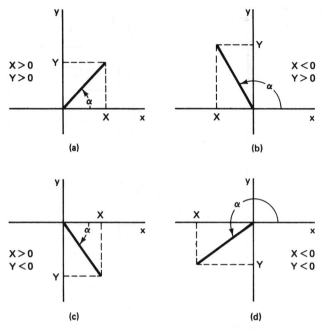

Figure 5.11 Determining the quadrant of an angle given the opposite and adjacent sides of a right triangle as signed quantities. Irvin H. Kral, *Numerical Control Programming In APT,* © 1986, p. 105. Reprinted by permission of Prentice Hall, Inc., Englewood Cliffs, New Jersey.

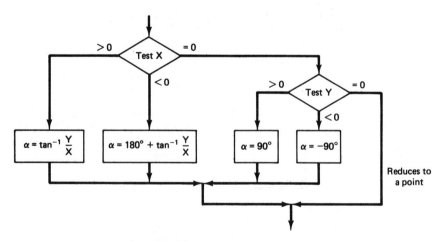

Figure 5.12 Flowchart for placing the angle in the correct quadrant. Irvin H. Kral, *Numerical Control Programming In APT,* © 1986, p. 105. Reprinted by permission of Prentice Hall, Inc., Englewood Cliffs, New Jersey.

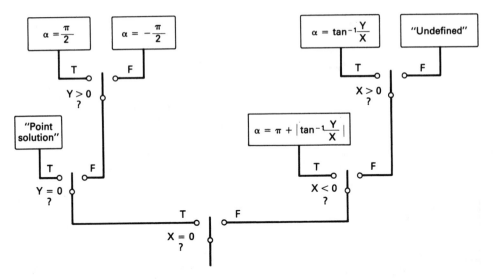

Figure 5.13 Data flow diagram for Example 5.3.

the diagram of Figure 5.13. Note that we consider the possibility of zero x and y values. The worksheet solution appears in Figure 5.14. The variables for this worksheet are defined as follows:

X	A2
Y	B2
Temp1	B9
Temp2	B10
Alpha	B11

Numerous x and y values were substituted into the input variable locations A2:B2 for the computations. These values and the result were then copied to the storage area A3:C8 with the **Edit Copy** and **Edit Paste Special Values** commands. The last set of values remains in row 2. All paths of the data flow diagram were verified with the values used.

Example 5.4

We will simulate the operation of a simplified factory water supply system to illustrate decision making with logical variables. The diagram of Figure 5.15 shows pumps P1 and P2 supplying water to process operations controlled by valves A, B, and C. G is a pressure gage, SPK is a valve supplying the factory fire sprinkler system, and SO is a shut-off valve to the process operations. The requirements of the system are:

1. P1 is to be turned on if one or more of valves A, B, and C are open.
2. P2 is to be turned on if P1 is on and G shows that the line pressure has dropped below 230 psi.

	A	B	C
1	X	Y	Alpha
2	2	3	0.982793723
3	-2	3	2.15879893
4	4	-5	-0.896055385
5	-4	-5	4.037648038
6	0	0	Point solution
7	0	7	1.570796327
8	0	-8	-1.570796327
9	Temp1	1.570796327	
10	Temp2	0.982793723	
11	Alpha	0.982793723	

(a)

	A	B	C
1	X	Y	Alpha
2	2	3	=Alpha
3	-2	3	2.15879893034246
4	4	-5	-0.896055384571344
5	-4	-5	4.03764803816113
6	0	0	Point solution
7	0	7	1.57079632679489
8	0	-8	-1.57079632679489
9	Temp1	=IF(Y=0,"Point solution",IF(Y>0,PI()/2,-PI()/2))	
10	Temp2	=IF(X<0,PI()+ATAN(Y/X),IF(X>0,ATAN(Y/X),"Undefined"))	
11	Alpha	=IF(X=0,Temp1,Temp2)	

(b)

Figure 5.14 Worksheet solution for Example 5.3 in (a) values mode and (b) formulas mode.

3. SPK automatically opens if a fire occurs.
4. Both P1 and P2 are to be turned on if SPK is open.
5. SO is to be closed if and only if SPK is open and G shows that the line pressure has dropped below 230 psi.
6. Both P1 and P2 are to be turned off if A, B, and C are closed and if SPK is not open.

If this water system were computer controlled, inputs to the computer would be the gage pressure and the open or closed status of valves A, B, C, and SPK. The

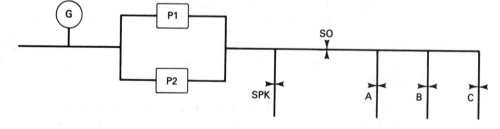

Figure 5.15 Diagram for the water supply system of Example 5.4.

computer could be programmed to periodically sample these parameters and control the pumps and valve SO. Optionally, the system could operate under interrupt control whereby a change in the status of the valves would cause branching to some appropriate program segment for further processing.

Figure 5.16 is a control flowchart that helps us verify the logic of the control operations. Instead of converting the flowchart to a data flow diagram, we choose to develop simplified logic equations for control of the pumps and shut-off valve. Then we can write the control formulas. By inspection, we have these equations from the flowchart:

$$P1(on) = (A + B + C) \cdot \overline{SPK} + SPK$$

$$= (A + B + C) + SPK$$

$$P2(on) = G < 230 \cdot (A + B + C) \cdot \overline{SPK} + SPK$$

$$= G < 230 \cdot (A + B + C) + SPK$$

$$SO(open) = \overline{SPK} + \overline{G < 230}$$

$$= \overline{SPK \cdot G < 230}$$

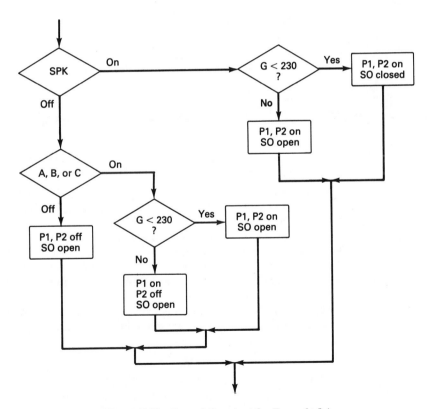

Figure 5.16 Control flowchart for Example 5.4.

	A	B	C	D	E	F	G	H	I	J
1	VAL	FALSE	Inputs					Outputs		
2	VBL	FALSE	Gage	Spklr	V_A	V_B	V_C	P_1	P_2	S_o
3	VCL	FALSE	237	Open				On	On	Open
4			250		Open			On	Off	Open
5	Spklr_Test	TRUE	261				Open	On	Off	Open
6	Gage_Test	FALSE	230				Open	On	Off	Open
7	VABC	FALSE	225			Open	Open	On	On	Open
8			223			Open		On	On	Open
9	Pump1	On	235	Open		Open		On	On	Open
10	Pump2	On	229	Open		Open		On	On	Closed
11	Shut_Off	Open	248	Open		Open		On	On	Open
12			253			Open		On	Off	Open
13			249		Open	Open	Open	On	Off	Open
14			222		Open	Open	Open	On	On	Open
15			241					Off	Off	Open
16			229					Off	Off	Open
17			228	Open				On	On	Closed
18			237	Open				On	On	Open

(a)

	A	B
1	VAL	=IF(V_A="Open",TRUE,FALSE)
2	VBL	=IF(V_B="Open",TRUE,FALSE)
3	VCL	=IF(V_C="Open",TRUE,FALSE)
4		
5	Spklr_Test	=IF(Spklr="Open",TRUE,FALSE)
6	Gage_Test	=IF(Gage<230,TRUE,FALSE)
7	VABC	=NOT(AND(NOT(VAL),NOT(VBL),NOT(VCL)))
8		
9	Pump1	=IF(OR(Spklr_Test,VABC),"On","Off")
10	Pump2	=IF(OR(Spklr_Test,AND(Gage_Test,VABC)),"On","Off")
11	Shut_Off	=IF(AND(Spklr_Test,Gage_Test),"Closed","Open")

(b)

Figure 5.17 Worksheet for Example 5.4 in (a) values mode and (b) formulas mode.

We chose to simplify the expressions through logic manipulation, although we could have used a Karnaugh map. We also applied DeMorgan's theorem to simplify the expression for SO.

When the expressions for P1 and P2 are true, we will turn the respective pumps on. When the expression for SO is true, we want to open the valve. We can perform logical inversion, the NOT function, in the IF function by interchanging the values for *true-value* and *false-value*. Therefore, we do not need to include the NOT function in *logical-expression*.

The Excel implementation of this example is given in Figure 5.17. Variable names, created from text for reference in the formulas are as follows:

V_A	E3	Gage	C3
V_B	F3	Spklr	D3
V_C	G3	Spklr_Test	B5
VAL	B1	Gage_Test	B6

VBL	B2	Pump1	B9
VCL	B3	Pump2	B10
VABC	B7	Shut_Off	B11

Various combinations of input values were entered in row C3 : G3. The results from B9 : B11 were placed in row H3 : J3 by formulas not shown in the figure. The values from row C3 : J3 were then saved in the rows of C4 : J18. All logic paths are verified with the data used. **Edit Copy** and **Edit Paste Special Values** were used to save the input and output values.

5.3 ITERATION

The iteration feature of Excel is a form of looping in which the bounds are determined by the dependency relationships of the loop variables, the circular references. We illustrate the capability with examples that require iteration counts and/or convergence conditions. The limitations of this feature are made prominent, and suggestions for including this feature in a worksheet are discussed.

5.3.1 Looping with Circular References

A series representation for the natural logarithm (base e) of a number x is

$$\ln x = \frac{x - 1}{x} + \frac{(x - 1)^2}{2x^2} + \frac{(x - 1)^3}{3x^3} + \cdots \qquad x \geq \frac{1}{2}$$

The number of terms of the series that must be computed is governed by accuracy considerations. This number cannot be infinite, of course, but may be predetermined and fixed or made variable with the number determined by convergence criteria as the computation proceeds. We outline a procedure for computing a fixed number of terms n for the logarithm of x in the control flowchart of Figure 5.18. Of course, the value of x must be equal to or greater than 1/2. We realize that the LN function will compute the value for us so that we would never

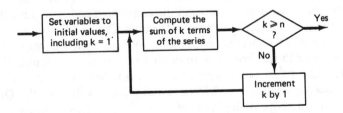

Figure 5.18 Flowchart for computing the logarithm of a number by a series. Irvin H. Kral, *Numerical Control Programming In APT,* © 1986, p. 112. Reprinted by permission of Prentice Hall, Inc., Englewood Cliffs, New Jersey.

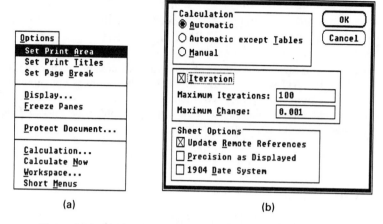

(a)   (b)

Figure 5.19   (a) Options menu and (b) the Calculation dialog box.

bother to do this work. However, we are illustrating a point that leads us to developing looping procedures, and this example serves that purpose.

The flowchart shows that we will initialize some variables before entering the loop, an important one being k, which is our loop counter. The loop structure is recognized by the backward flow of control when the decision-block outcome requires more iterations for the calculation. Each time through the loop we will have computed another term of the series and added it to a running sum of the terms thus far computed. The last time through the loop, when $k = n$, our partial sum will be the logarithm value. One Excel solution is as follows:

	A	B
1	x	(enter constant)
2	term	$=(x-1)/x$
3	k	$=k+1$
4	sum	$=\text{sum}+\text{term}^{k}/k$

We have circular references in rows 3 and 4 of this solution, where formula cell references are to the name of the containing cell, assuming the cells are named with the left column used in the **Formula Create Names** command. We deliberately inserted the circular references. Were they to be inadvertently inserted, we would have to remove them in order to continue developing the solution. However, Excel allows circular references provided we are in the iteration mode.

Before continuing with the solution, let us discuss the **Options Calculation** command and its dialog box of Figure 5.19. This command is used to select between manual and automatic worksheet computation and to select and set up the iteration mode.

Manual and automatic computation.   The **Calculation** selection box contains three toggles. We will discuss only the **Automatic** and **Manual** toggles.

Automatic

This is the default mode of operation. Whenever there is a change in a cell value that affects other cells, the worksheet is recomputed on a precedence basis. When many changes are made in the worksheet, many recalculations ensue. This is advantageous while developing a modest-size worksheet, since values can be checked as progress is made and errors can be quickly identified and corrected while working with the cells at fault. But recalculation is a disadvantage when the worksheet is large, since recalculation takes time and slows the development process.

Manual

This mode of operation defers calculation of the worksheet until the **Options Calculate Now** command is executed. It allows work to be done on the worksheet without the distraction of continually changing values rippling through the worksheet. However, it will also obscure the origin of some errors, since they will not be apparent during cell entry and modification. Manual operation is useful for iterative calculations, since computation does not begin until one is ready for it. An iterative calculation runs to completion once begun manually.

Iteration.   The **Iteration** box contains the iteration on/off toggle and two value-entry iteration control parameters.

Maximum Iterations

This value is a count of the maximum number of iterations to execute each time the **Iteration** toggle is on and the **OK** button is selected. Its default value is 100. It is a loop control parameter whose value is inaccessible by the user for use in the cells. The actual number of iterations executed is determined by this parameter in conjunction with the **Maximum Change** parameter value, as shown in Figure 5.20. It controls the number of iterations under divergence conditions when the **Maximum Change** parameter is ineffective.

Maximum Change

When greater than zero, **Maximum Change** is a convergence test value that is applied to each circular reference in the worksheet after each iteration calculation. In effect, it causes a difference computation and a comparison to be made as follows:

$$|previous\text{-}value - current\text{-}value| < \textbf{Maximum Change value?}$$

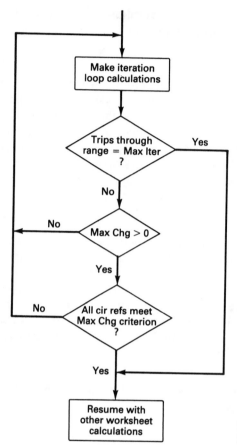

Figure 5.20 Control logic of the iteration feature.

When the result is true for all circular references, iteration stops if the iteration count is less than the value of **Maximum Iterations**. If **Maximum Change** is set to zero, the number of iterations is controlled by **Maximum Iterations**. A negative value for **Maximum Change** is not allowed. Figure 5.20 shows how this parameter controls the iterations.

We return to the discussion of our series computation example. We toggle **Iteration** on and then enter 5 for the **Maximum Iterations** count and leave the **Maximum Change** value as is. This means that **Maximum Iterations** count will control the number of iterations, since the change in the circular reference variable k will always be 1, a value that is larger than 0.001, the default value of **Maximum Change**. Now we choose **OK**. Excel then sets the cells with circular references to zero and proceeds with the calculations, since we are in **Automatic** mode. The worksheet solution is shown in Figure 5.21. Five iterations were made (note the value of k), and the logarithm value appears in cell B4. This

	A	B
1	x	1.4
2	term	=(x-1)/x
3	k	=k+1
4	sum	=sum+term^k/k
5	ln(x)	=LN(x)

(a)

	A	B
1	x	1.4
2	term	0.285714286
3	k	5
4	sum	0.336351917
5	ln(x)	0.336472237

(b)

Figure 5.21 Worksheet for computing the natural logarithm in (a) formulas mode and (b) values mode.

approximate value should be compared with the contents of cell B5, which was computed with the LN function. This series converges rapidly.

The flowchart of Figure 5.18 implies that the IF function should be used for the decision. After all, we did use it many times in prior sections of this chapter, so why not use it here for the same purposes as the dialog box values? However, we learned that we cannot branch to other formulas with it, at least not in the worksheet. So, for this example, we must use the iteration feature.

A flowchart for our Excel implementation really looks like that of Figure 5.22. In Figure 5.21, rows 1 and 2 initialize variables, and rows 3 and 4 compute values. The modification and testing are included in the iteration feature. Modification occurs to some unnamed internal variable after which it is then tested, and if the limit in the **Maximum Iterations** box is reached, iteration stops. We might wonder about the calculation of the sum. It is being formed with each trip through the calculations. At some time, its updated and prior values will differ by no more than the entry in the **Maximum Change** box, at which time it is a candidate to cause iteration to cease. Excel considers the entries in both boxes, however, and we have already noted that the value of k will never be less than 0.001. Therefore, **Maximum Iterations** control the loop computations of our example.

Observe that data flow is always forward during iteration. This is our preferred flow direction, so the flowchart of Figure 5.22 is a preferred loop structure.

5.3.2 Examples

In the first example, we illustrate loop termination on convergence criteria for the magnet design problem of Chapter 3. Then, we discuss a binary counter example that demonstrates some of the internal workings of the Excel iteration feature.

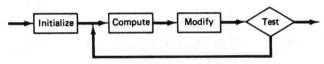

Figure 5.22 Loop structure used for the logarithm example. Irvin H. Kral, *Numerical Control Programming In APT,* © 1986, p. 113. Reprinted by permission of Prentice Hall, Inc., Englewood Cliffs, New Jersey.

Example 5.5

This is a rework of Example 3.4, the magnet design problem. Recall that we were concerned about the calculation of the leakage flux factor σ. We solved that problem with a manually controlled self-consistent calculation for its value, after which we then had the design solution. A worksheet self-consistent solution produced a circular reference which we avoided by manually reentering the computed value for σ as a new trial value. This continued until we were satisfied with the converging values.

In this example, we will allow the circular reference for σ and use the iteration process to obtain the solution. We show the formulas in Figure 5.23(a). The new value for σ, called σ', is computed in cell B23. This value is to be substituted for σ in the formula for A_m in cell B12. We named cell B23 Sigmap, for σ', and entered the name in B12. Sigma, cell B10, is not used in the calculation. Recall that Excel will set circular references to zero before iterating. This is a suitable starting value for σ, since the zero will not propagate as a perpetual value for σ. Upon starting the iteration, and because we remained on **Automatic** so iteration would begin when we chose **OK**, the solution quickly converged to the values shown in Figure 5.23(b) with **Maximum Change** and **Maximum Iterations** set to the values .00001 and 100, respectively.

	A	B
1	Hg	2000
2	Lg	0.25
3	rf	1.2
4	Hd	515
5	Lm	=Hg*Lg*rf/Hd
6	Bg	2000
7	h	1
8	w	1
9	Ag	=h*w
10	sigma	3.5
11	Bd	10200
12	Am	=Bg*Ag*Sigmap/Bd
13	t	=Am/w
14	a	=(Lm-Lg)/2
15	b	3
16	cc	=Lm
17	d	0.35
18	Ua	=2*(w+h)
19	Ub	=2*(w+d)
20	Uc	=2*(w+t)
21	sig1	=1.7*Ua*a/(a+Lg)
22	sig2	=1.4*b*SQRT(Ub/cc)+0.67*Uc
23	sigma'	=1+Lg/Ag*(sig1+sig2)

(a)

	A	B
1	Hg	2000
2	Lg	0.25
3	rf	1.2
4	Hd	515
5	Lm	1.165048544
6	Bg	2000
7	h	1
8	w	1
9	Ag	1
10	sigma	3.5
11	Bd	10200
12	Am	0.846330323
13	t	0.846330323
14	a	0.457524272
15	b	3
16	cc	1.165048544
17	d	0.35
18	Ua	4
19	Ub	2.7
20	Uc	3.692660647
21	sig1	4.397255575
22	sig2	8.867884319
23	sigma'	4.316284974

(b)

Figure 5.23 Worksheet for Example 5.5 in (a) formulas mode and (b) values mode.

Example 5.6

In this example, we illustrate logical variables in circular reference contexts and the effects of iterating them. Table 5.4 is a state table for a 3-bit binary up counter that counts in the natural binary number order. The left portion of the table shows the binary values for each bit in each of the eight states that the counter can occupy. Bit C is the most significant bit (MSB), while bit A is the least significant bit (LSB). The right portion of the table shows the corresponding next state values. When the counter is in state 0, the next count will take it to state 1, the following count to state 2, and so on until, from state 7, we wraparound to state 0 and begin the cycle again.

First, from the state table, we prepare the Karnaugh maps for bits B and C of the counter and write the simplified logic expressions as shown in Table 5.4. The logic equation for bit A is obvious. The superscripts denote state number.

We chose to use the engineering symbols for AND, OR, and NOT as described for Example 5.1. These formulas apply to a clocked system in which the counter bit values change simultaneously with their next state values depending on the current state. To illustrate how Excel handles circular references, we implement two versions of these equations as shown in Figure 5.24. The first version, cells B2:B4 of

TABLE 5.4 STATE TABLE FOR A BINARY UP COUNTER

State	Iteration n			Iteration $n + 1$		
	C	B	A	C	B	A
0	0	0	0	0	0	1
1	0	0	1	0	1	0
2	0	1	0	0	1	1
3	0	1	1	1	0	0
4	1	0	0	1	0	1
5	1	0	1	1	1	0
6	1	1	0	1	1	1
7	1	1	1	0	0	0

$$A^{n+1} = \overline{A}^n \text{ (by inspection)}$$

$$B^{n+1} = (\overline{A} \cdot B + A \cdot \overline{B})^n$$

$$C^{n+1} = (\overline{A} \cdot C + \overline{B} \cdot C + A \cdot B \cdot \overline{C})^n$$

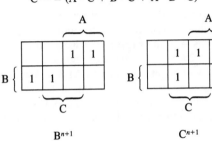

B^{n+1} C^{n+1}

	A	B
1	iteration	=iteration+1
2	lsb	=NOT(lsb)
3	middle	=OR(AND(NOT(lsb),middle),AND(lsb,NOT(middle)))
4	msb	=OR(AND(NOT(lsb),msb),AND(NOT(middle),msb),AND(lsb,middle,NOT(msb)))
5	cc	=OR(AND(NOT(aa),cc),AND(NOT(bb),cc),AND(aa,bb,NOT(cc)))
6	bb	=OR(AND(NOT(aa),bb),AND(aa,NOT(bb)))
7	aa	=NOT(aa)

(a)

	A	B
1	iteration	0
2	lsb	0
3	middle	0
4	msb	0
5	cc	0
6	bb	0
7	aa	0

(b)

	A	B
1	iteration	1
2	lsb	TRUE
3	middle	TRUE
4	msb	TRUE
5	cc	TRUE
6	bb	TRUE
7	aa	TRUE

(c)

	A	B
1	iteration	2
2	lsb	FALSE
3	middle	TRUE
4	msb	TRUE
5	cc	FALSE
6	bb	FALSE
7	aa	FALSE

(d)

	A	B
1	iteration	3
2	lsb	TRUE
3	middle	FALSE
4	msb	TRUE
5	cc	FALSE
6	bb	FALSE
7	aa	TRUE

(e)

	A	B
1	iteration	4
2	lsb	FALSE
3	middle	FALSE
4	msb	TRUE
5	cc	FALSE
6	bb	TRUE
7	aa	FALSE

(f)

	A	B
1	iteration	5
2	lsb	TRUE
3	middle	TRUE
4	msb	FALSE
5	cc	FALSE
6	bb	TRUE
7	aa	TRUE

(g)

Figure 5.24 Worksheet for Example 5.6 in (a) formulas mode and (b) through (g) values mode.

Figure 5.24(a), has the formulas for bits A, B, and C placed in row order with the corresponding cells named lsb, middle, and msb. Naming is via the **Formula Create Names** command applied to the left column. The second version, cells B5:B7 of Figure 5.24(a), has the formulas for bits C, B, and A placed in row order with their corresponding cells named cc, bb, and aa. We see that each cell has a circular reference. To keep the worksheet results in order, we count the iterations in B1, another circular reference. We will manually step through the iterations, with **Maximum Iterations** = 1 and **Maximum Change** at its default value.

Figure 5.24(b) is the starting condition. We see zeros in all cells of column B. These values will be interpreted as FALSE. When we invoke the **Options Calculate Now** command, or press key F9, the first iteration produces the output of Figure 5.24(c). Although our starting state shows state zero, this first iteration takes us to state 7, a seemingly reverse counter. The next command, iteration 2, takes us to

TABLE 5.5 WALK-THROUGH FOR BITS B2:B4 OF FIGURE 5.24

Iteration	Current values C	B	A	Formula computation	Updated values C	B	A
1	0	0	0	$= \bar{A} = \bar{0} = 1$	0	0	1
	0	0	1	$= \bar{A} \cdot B + A \cdot \bar{B} = \bar{1} \cdot 0 + 1 \cdot \bar{0} = 1$	0	1	1
	0	1	1	$= \bar{A} \cdot C + \bar{B} \cdot C + A \cdot B \cdot \bar{C} = \bar{1} \cdot 0 + \bar{1} \cdot 0 + 1 \cdot 1 \cdot \bar{0} = 1$	1	1	1
				End of first iteration, we are in state 7 [Figure 5.24(c)]			
2	1	1	1	$= \bar{A} = \bar{1} = 0$	1	1	0
	1	1	0	$= \bar{A} \cdot B + A \cdot \bar{B} = \bar{0} \cdot 1 + 0 \cdot \bar{1} = 1$	1	1	0
	1	1	0	$= \bar{A} \cdot C + \bar{B} \cdot C + A \cdot B \cdot \bar{C} = \bar{0} \cdot 1 + \bar{1} \cdot 1 + 0 \cdot 1 \cdot \bar{1} = 1$	1	1	0
				End of second iteration, we are in state 6 [Figure 5.24(d)]			
3	1	1	0	$= \bar{A} = \bar{0} = 1$	1	1	1
	1	1	1	$= \bar{A} \cdot B + A \cdot \bar{B} = \bar{1} \cdot 1 + 1 \cdot \bar{1} = 0$	1	0	1
	1	0	1	$= \bar{A} \cdot C + \bar{B} \cdot C + A \cdot B \cdot \bar{C} = \bar{1} \cdot 1 + \bar{0} \cdot 1 + 1 \cdot 0 \cdot \bar{1} = 1$	1	0	1
				End of third iteration, we are in state 5 [Figure 5.24(e)]			
4	1	0	1	$= \bar{A} = \bar{1} = 0$	1	0	0
	1	0	0	$= \bar{A} \cdot B + A \cdot \bar{B} = \bar{0} \cdot 0 + 0 \cdot \bar{0} = 0$	1	0	0
	1	0	0	$= \bar{A} \cdot C + \bar{B} \cdot C + A \cdot B \cdot \bar{C} = \bar{0} \cdot 1 + \bar{0} \cdot 1 + 0 \cdot 0 \cdot \bar{1} = 1$	1	0	0
				End of fourth iteration, we are in state 4 [Figure 5.24(f)]			
5	1	0	0	$= \bar{A} = \bar{0} = 1$	1	0	1
	1	0	1	$= \bar{A} \cdot B + A \cdot \bar{B} = \bar{1} \cdot 0 + 1 \cdot \bar{0} = 1$	1	1	1
	1	1	1	$= \bar{A} \cdot C + \bar{B} \cdot C + A \cdot B \cdot \bar{C} = \bar{1} \cdot 1 + \bar{1} \cdot 1 + 1 \cdot 1 \cdot \bar{1} = 0$	0	1	1
				End of fifth iteration, we are in state 3 [Figure 5.24(g)]			

state 6 for B2:B4 and to state 0 for B5:B7 as shown in Figure 5.24(d). Another command, iteration 3, takes us to state 5 for B2:B4 and to state 1 for B5:B7 as shown in Figure 5.24(e). Iterations 4 and 5 are shown in Figures 5.24(f) and (g), respectively.

To understand what is happening, we must remember that value assignment is made immediately upon calculation. The new values are then used for the cell references until again changed. Table 5.5 shows the walk-through values for the bits calculated with the formulas of B2:B4. The ordering causes the counter to count downward. We arranged the formulas to calculate from the least significant bit to the most significant bit as calculation would proceed downward in the worksheet. Normally, worksheet calculation order is dependency based, but since we are now operating in an iterative mode, calculation is left-to-right within rows that are computed from top-to-bottom in the worksheet. See the Box titled Dependents, Precedents, and Calculation Order on page 166. Calculation is correct, our statement ordering is incorrect.

Walk-through Table 5.6 illustrates the calculations for the formulas of B5:B7. We mentioned that we reversed the sequence of calculations from the formulas in the range B2:B4, where now bits C, B, and A are arranged in that order as one reads downward through the cells. Upon getting to state 7 during the first iteration, the ordering causes the counter to count upward thereafter.

TABLE 5.6   WALK-THROUGH FOR BITS B5:B7 OF FIGURE 5.24

Iteration	Current values C	B	A	Formula computation	Updated values C	B	A
1	0	0	0	$= \bar{A} \cdot C + \bar{B} \cdot C + A \cdot B \cdot \bar{C} = \bar{0} \cdot 0 + \bar{0} \cdot 0 + 0 \cdot 0 \cdot \bar{0} = 0$	0	0	0
	0	0	0	$= \bar{A} \cdot B + A \cdot \bar{B} = \bar{0} \cdot 0 + 0 \cdot \bar{0} = 0$	0	0	0
	0	0	0	$= \bar{A} = \bar{0} = 1$	0	0	1
				End of first iteration, we are in state 1 [Figure 5.24(c)]			
2	0	0	1	$= \bar{A} \cdot C + \bar{B} \cdot C + A \cdot B \cdot \bar{C} = \bar{1} \cdot 0 + \bar{0} \cdot 0 + 1 \cdot 0 \cdot \bar{0} = 0$	0	0	1
	0	0	1	$= \bar{A} \cdot B + A \cdot \bar{B} = \bar{1} \cdot 0 + 1 \cdot \bar{0} = 1$	0	1	1
	0	1	1	$= \bar{A} = \bar{1} = 0$	0	1	0
				End of second iteration, we are in state 2 [Figure 5.24(d)]			
3	0	1	0	$= \bar{A} \cdot C + \bar{B} \cdot C + A \cdot B \cdot \bar{C} = \bar{0} \cdot 0 + \bar{1} \cdot 0 + 0 \cdot 1 \cdot \bar{0} = 0$	0	1	0
	0	1	0	$= \bar{A} \cdot B + A \cdot \bar{B} = \bar{0} \cdot 1 + 0 \cdot \bar{1} = 1$	0	1	0
	0	1	0	$= \bar{A} = \bar{0} = 1$	0	1	1
				End of third iteration, we are in state 3 [Figure 5.24(e)]			
4	0	1	1	$= \bar{A} \cdot C + \bar{B} \cdot C + A \cdot B \cdot \bar{C} = \bar{1} \cdot 0 + \bar{1} \cdot 0 + 1 \cdot 1 \cdot \bar{0} = 1$	1	1	1
	1	1	1	$= \bar{A} \cdot B + A \cdot \bar{B} = \bar{1} \cdot 1 + 1 \cdot \bar{1} = 0$	1	0	1
	1	0	1	$= \bar{A} = \bar{1} = 0$	1	0	0
				End of fourth iteration, we are in state 4 [Figure 5.24(f)]			
5	1	0	0	$= \bar{A} \cdot C + \bar{B} \cdot C + A \cdot B \cdot \bar{C} = \bar{0} \cdot 1 + \bar{0} \cdot 1 + 0 \cdot 0 \cdot \bar{1} = 1$	1	0	0
	1	0	0	$= \bar{A} \cdot B + A \cdot \bar{B} = \bar{0} \cdot 0 + 0 \cdot \bar{0} = 0$	1	0	0
	1	0	0	$= \bar{A} = \bar{0} = 1$	1	0	1
				End of fifth iteration, we are in state 5 [Figure 5.24(g)]			

DEPENDENTS, PRECEDENTS, AND CALCULATION ORDER

The order in which Excel makes computations is context dependent. It may be dependency based or it may be an ordered scan. The ordering has implications on the numerical outcome and on the speed of computation. The following definitions are pertinent to this concept:

1. With respect to a reference cell α (also called an active cell), a *dependent cell* of α is a cell whose value depends on the value of α. If α is referenced within the dependent cell (a first level reference), the dependent cell is a *direct dependent*. If the value of the dependent cell depends on another cell whose value depends on the value of α (referenced at least two levels away), the dependent cell is an *indirect dependent*.

2. With respect to a reference cell α (also called an active cell), a *precedent cell* to α is a cell whose value is used to compute the value of α. If the precedent cell is referenced within α (a first level reference), the precedent cell is a *direct precedent*. If the precedent cell is referenced at least two levels away, the precedent cell is an *indirect precedent*.

Example (Data flow diagram for column A only):

	A	B
1	2	=A3+B2
2	5	=A1+A2
3	-4	=A2+B1+B2
4	=A1+A2	=A1+B1
5	=A3+A4	
6	=A2+A5+A4	
7	=A1+A5	

Worksheet formulas

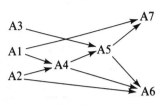

Data flow

```
      Cell:  A4
   Formula:  =A1+A2
Precedents:  A1:A2
Dependents:  A5:A6
      Note:
```

Sample Info window

Active cell	Precedents Direct	Precedents Indirect	Dependents Direct	Dependents Indirect
A1	—	—	A4,A7	A5,A6,A7
A2	—	—	A4,A6	A5,A6,A7
A3	—	—	A5	A6,A7
A4	A1,A2	—	A5,A6	A7
A5	A3,A4	A1,A2	A6,A7	—
A6	A2,A4,A5	A1,A2,A3,A4	—	—
A7	A1,A5	A1,A2,A3,A4	—	—

Calculation Order:

1. *Worksheet context* (*no circular references*). A list of dependent cells for each cell is maintained by Excel. A change in the value of a cell causes recalculation of the worksheet on a dependency basis with rippling of recalculated values throughout the worksheet when in **Options Calculation Automatic** mode. When in **Options Calculation Manual** mode, the **Options Calculate Now** command initiates worksheet recalculation on a dependency basis.

Example (Pertains to columns A and B of the worksheet above):

Cell changed	Order of calculation
A1	B2 − A4 − B1 − B3 − A5 − A6 − A7 − B4
A2	B2 − B1 − B3 − A4 − B4 − A5 − A7 − A6
A3	A5 − B2 − A6 − A7 − B1 − B4 − B3

2. *Worksheet context* (*with circular references*). With **Options Calculation Iteration** turned on, Excel updates the worksheet once during a scan made from left-to-right within rows made in a top-to-bottom direction. The dependency relations are used to skip computations only. There is no look-ahead, it is a first level computation only.

3. *Macro context.* Excel executes the macro from top-to-bottom, with the actual path subject to branching, jumps, and calls to other macros. The calculations are not based on dependency.

5.4 DEBUGGING

Not only must we strive to make our worksheet understandable, but we must adopt a strategy for handling problem complexity. This is necessary because problem complexity introduces worksheet complexity via the data handling structures introduced in this chapter. An attitude stressing organization must be adopted. For this purpose, we propose the following guidelines:

1. Simplify the problem for worksheet design purposes. Do not incorporate all the bells and whistles in the first design. Expand the worksheet to include all problem features through several design iterations.

2. Not all worksheets need be written for general-purpose application. The utility of a worksheet may be limited, thus justifying a modest straightforward approach to worksheet development.

3. Prepare the worksheet in manageable segments. The problem generally suggests partitions that may be added as development progresses. This guideline is derived from the often-stated observation that a limited number of things, typically seven or less, can be kept mentally organized in short-term memory (human) at one time.

Here are other guidelines derived from the logical and IF material of this chapter.

1. Use logical expressions whenever possible to limit choices, and thus reduce the possibility of error, and to speed up the calculations.

2. Use the preferred data flow structures, with consequent worksheet layout, to maintain an organized worksheet appearance.

3. Do not use the "equal" comparative operator in *logical-expression* of the IF function except when working with whole numbers. Use "equal to or greater than" or "equal to or less than" comparative operators with numbers containing fractional parts which, in the computer, can seldom be expected to be equal to each other.

4. Be aware of the IF function limitations in the main worksheet. This function

returns values of any type and fits into a data flow structure, not into a control flow structure.

5. If circular references are developed but not intended, clear them up immediately.

The iteration feature presents new problems to contend with. The looping action often camouflages important clues when problems exist. One must work carefully to understand the iteration action and to interpret the results. Here are suggestions for developing worksheets that use iteration.

1. Remember that iteration execution is based on dependency. Structure the worksheet to show clearly these dependencies in order to easily follow and hand check, if necessary, the sequence of computation.

2. Reset circular references to zero for testing purposes in order to have a known starting state. Iteration is cumulative with restarts, a condition not usually desired during development.

3. Single step through the iterations manually to observe the computational action. Identify the patterns displayed with normally operating computations. Check numerical values of the dependent cells, especially the circular references.

4. When nested loops are used, check out the loops individually, beginning with the innermost loop. Add subsequent loops progressing outward only when proper operation is obtained with the inner loops.

5. Save important cell values from one iteration to the next to have documented evidence for analysis. Do not rely on your memory to recall these values later. These intermediate results become important when complex problems must be debugged. They can always be cleared from the worksheet later.

6. Occasionally, it is useful to restart and continue iterating from the current state rather than to reset to zero. Look for unexpected values as clues to the nature of the problem.

7. Do not iterate more than necessary. If the stopping criteria is **Maximum Change**, also set **Maximum Iterations** to a value that allows ample time for convergence. If there are errors in the worksheet, there may be no convergence, in which case **Maximum Iterations** will terminate the computations without running longer than necessary.

5.5 ABOUT VERSION 3.0

All worksheets of this chapter run under version 3.0 without change. No new Excel features were added to affect logical and relational expressions, the conditional IF assignment function in the worksheet, or iteration. However, we can apply Solver to problems using iteration, as the following example shows.

Example 5.7

We will rework the magnet design problem of Example 3.4 with Solver. Recall that a trial value for the design parameter σ (leakage flux factor) was initially entered, then replaced by copying a refined value of it into its starting location after each iteration. That starting worksheet, Figure 3.8(a), is repeated as Figure 5.25(a). The worksheet in formulas mode is shown in Figure 3.7(d). The starting value of σ is entered in cell B11. Its effect is propagated into a refined value, σ', in cell B27, where it is available for another iteration starting value. With Solver, we establish constraints and let it do the work. The Solver dialog box of Figure 5.25(b) for this example shows that we did not specify an objective function, in which case the **Max** button becomes ineffective, but did ask that σ, cell B11, be varied to meet the constraints, namely, $\sigma \geq 0$ and $\sigma = \sigma'$. The Solver results are shown in Figure 5.25(c). They should be compared with those of Figure 3.8(b). Iterations for Example 3.4 were terminated through visual judgment.

Solver may converge to a solution very slowly, and thus run a long time, or not at all for some problems. For these problems it might be useful to examine intermediate results of its progress for debugging and testing purposes. We can interrupt its progress by turning on the **Show Iteration Results** box in the Solver **Options** dialog box of Figure 3.22. Then, during the run, Solver will occasionally pause and display the dialog box of Figure 5.26. During this time we can examine the values that Solver calculated for cells we believe provide insight into progress of the calculation and decide to continue or cancel the run. When using this option, first position the worksheet so that the key cells are visible since it cannot be activated and manipulated during the pause. If you cancel the run, you are asked whether to update the worksheet with the intermediate results or to restore the original independent variables values.

Settings of the **Formula Solver** dialog box of Figure 3.19 are automatically saved with the document when it is closed and reloaded with that document when it is opened. The save/load feature is used when different combinations of entries in the dialog box are to be retained and reused. Each of these combinations is called a *model* in Solver parlance. Models are developed during experimentation and differ from each other in some combination of objective function, independent variables, and constraints. Only the objective function, independent variables, and constraints entries are saved. Follow this procedure to save a model:

1. Select a cell range on the document of size $n + 2$, where n is the number of constraints. This will be the model save area.

2. Click on the **Save Model** button of the **Formula Solver Options** dialog box of Figure 3.22. The model is saved as formulas. The first cell of the range contains the objective function, the second the independent variables, and the remainder the constraints.

Figure 5.25 (a) Beginning worksheet, (b) Solver dialog box, and (c) final values for Example 5.7.

(a)

	A	B
1	Hg	2000
2	Lg	0.25
3	rf	1.2
4	Hd	515
5	Lm	1.165048544
6		
7	Bg	2000
8	h	1
9	w	1
10	Ag	1
11	sigma	3.5
12	Bd	10200
13	Am	0.68627451
14		
15	t	0.68627451
16		
17	a	0.457524272
18	b	3
19	cc	1.165048544
20	d	0.35
21	Ua	4
22	Ub	2.7
23	Uc	3.37254902
24		
25	sig1	4.397255575
26	sig2	8.653409529
27	sigma'	4.262666276

(b)

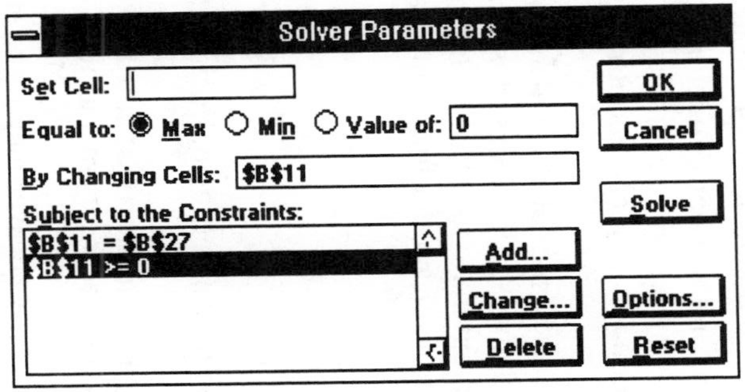

Solver Parameters

Set Cell:
Equal to: ● Max ○ Min ○ Value of: 0
By Changing Cells: $B$11

Subject to the Constraints:
$B$11 = $B$27
$B$11 >= 0

Add...
Change...
Delete

OK
Cancel
Solve
Options...
Reset

(c)

	A	B
1	Hg	2000
2	Lg	0.25
3	rf	1.2
4	Hd	515
5	Lm	1.165048544
6		
7	Bg	2000
8	h	1
9	w	1
10	Ag	1
11	sigma	4.31628996
12	Bd	10200
13	Am	0.846330391
14		
15	t	0.846330391
16		
17	a	0.457524272
18	b	3
19	cc	1.165048544
20	d	0.35
21	Ua	4
22	Ub	2.7
23	Uc	3.692660783
24		
25	sig1	4.397255575
26	sig2	8.867884411
27	sigma'	4.31628996

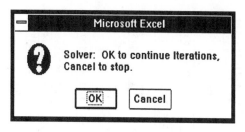

Figure 5.26 Show Iteration Results dialog box.

Follow this procedure to load a model:

1. Select the cell range of the desired model on the relevant document.
2. Click on the **Load Model** button of the **Formula Solver Options** dialog box. That model will be displayed in the **Formula Solver** dialog box after you respond to a query about resetting the previous dialog box.

Because a model is saved as formulas, its cells change value as their underlying data changes, regardless of which model may be in operation. The models on the document may be edited as any other cell would be. It is wise to add comment cells about each model for identification and information purposes.

PROBLEMS

Use the spreadsheet logic, decision, and iterative features to solve the following problems:

5.1 Integrated circuits (ICs) cost $1.05 each, or $10.25 a dozen, or $110 a gross (144). Write a spreadsheet program to calculate the price of IC purchases. For example, 13 ICs would cost $11.30 ($10.25 + $1.05). The sales clerk is kind-hearted and warns customers whenever they make unwise purchases. For example, a purchase of 11 ICs costs more than a dozen of them. Fix the program so it outputs a warning message in addition to the quantity being purchased whenever a customer selects an unwise purchase. Input various quantity values to test all logic paths of the program.

5.2 Write a spreadsheet program that determines a whole number, say n, such that, when compared with two other numbers, n^2 is equal to or greater than the smaller number and n^3 is equal to or less than the greater number. Write the program to also identify which of the two numbers is the smaller for comparison purposes. Note that no such whole number may exist, in which case output a message to this effect.

5.3 Write a spreadsheet program that computes the coins for change under the following circumstances:
   (a) $1.00 is the maximum purchase.
   (b) A dollar bill is always presented as payment.
   (c) The minimum number of coins is given as change.
   (d) Only pennies, nickles, dimes, and quarters are given in change.

5.4 Engineers wanting a loan for computer equipment must supply to the loan company a record of (a) their annual salary, (b) years employed on same job, (c) years residence in same location, and (d) monthly rental or mortgage payment. The company accepts a loan application automatically if the salary is $30,000 or more annually, if residence or employment tenure is 3 years or more, and if rent or mortgage payments are not greater than one weeks' pay, but rejects it otherwise. Write a spreadsheet program that requires as input the four values noted above and that determines whether a loan application shall be approved (display CREDIT APPROVED) or rejected (display CREDIT REJECTED). Run the program with as many values as needed to test all paths of the program.

5.5 An engineer spends $2000 a month advertising a finite-element program that she developed. Sales are running at 200 copies a month yielding about $300 profit per copy. From this, she must subtract another $10,000 as fixed operating costs which are independent of the volume of sales. An advertising agency informs her that each time she doubles the amount spent on advertising, the volume of sales will increase by 20%. Write a spreadsheet program that iteratively computes the amount spent on advertising, the number of sales made, and the net profit. Begin with the current status and successively double the amount spent on advertising until the net profit no longer increases but begins to decrease. Determine what amount should be spent on advertising, the corresponding sales volume, and the total profit.

5.6 Compute the value of the following series using the spreadsheet iterative feature. Terminate the computation whenever two consecutive computed values for y differ by no more than some small value, say ε, but in no case are more than m terms to be computed, including the constant term. Let $n = 2$, $x = 1.5$, and $\varepsilon = .000001$. Select an appropriate value for m.

$$y = 1 - nx + \frac{n(n + 1)x^2}{2!} - \frac{n(n + 1)(n + 2)x^3}{3!} + \cdots$$

5.7 Compute the value of the following series using the spreadsheet iterative feature. Compute as many terms as necessary to obtain a value for y that differs by no more than some small value, say ε, from its preceding calculated value. Let $x = -1.6$ and $\varepsilon = .000001$. Also, count the number of iterations in a variable called n.

$$y = x - \left(1 + \frac{1}{2}\right)x^2 + \left(1 + \frac{1}{2} + \frac{1}{3}\right)x^3 - \left(1 + \frac{1}{2} + \frac{1}{3} + \frac{1}{4}\right)x^4 + \cdots$$

5.8 The formula for computing the binomial probability is

$$p_b(r) = \frac{n!}{r!(n - r)!} p^r q^{n-r} = \frac{n(n - 1)(n - 2) \cdots (n - r + 1)}{r!} p^r q^{n-r}$$

This indicates the probability of r successes in n trials, where the probability of a success is p on any trial, and $q = 1 - p$. As an example, this could be used to compute the probability of producing r defective units in a run of n units on a machine that has a record of $100p$ percent defectives.

Write a spreadsheet program that requires input values for r, n, and p, and that computes the probability according to the rightmost expression above. Use values of $r = 7$, $n = 25$, and $p = 0.13$.

CHAPTER 6

Preparing Graphs

Thus far, our concern over computing has overshadowed any desire to prepare graphs of our data. Since engineers make graphs for many reasons, we must have the capability to graph our data from the spreadsheet program. Because we want to easily construct the graph of our choice, we look for and concentrate on the features that we need. Excel offers us a wide variety of capabilities, but as we will discover, the provisions of the program leave some voids for engineers' applications.

In this chapter, we first review some facts about graphing and identify the types of graphs most used in engineering. We then learn about the Excel graphing window (they call it a chart window) and the basics for its use. Because we must have data to plot, we then discuss how to use certain Excel features to easily and quickly generate some of the data for us. Since the standard spreadsheet graph formats seldom satisfy all our graphing needs, we then discuss the graph customizing features. This latter presentation enables us to put fine touches on our graphs.

6.1 INTRODUCTION

Numerical data collected by engineers is often presented in table, or matrix, form as we discussed in Chapter 4. It can also be presented graphically in the form of graphs and charts. We distinguish between graphs and charts as follows:

A *chart* presents numerical relations on a comparative basis. A *graph* presents a functional relation between the independent and dependent variables.

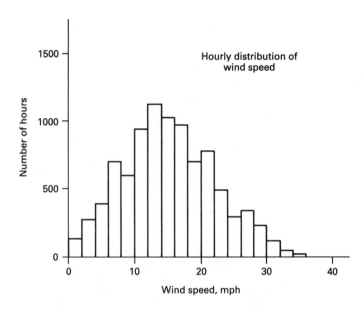

Figure 6.1 Vertically oriented bar chart.

Spreadsheet programs generally do not distinguish between the two as we do. Instead, more in line with their business orientation, they use the term chart. We prefer the engineering nomenclature. Examples of charts include the bar chart (Figure 6.1), the pie chart (Figure 6.2), and pictorial charts (Figure 6.3). Examples of graphs include continuous line plots (perhaps of straight line segments) on linear-linear coordinate scales (Figure 6.4), on semi-logarithmic coordinate scales (Figure 6.5), on logarithmic-logarithmic coordinate scales (Figure 6.6),

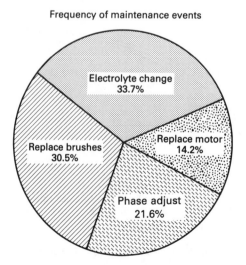

Figure 6.2 Pie chart.

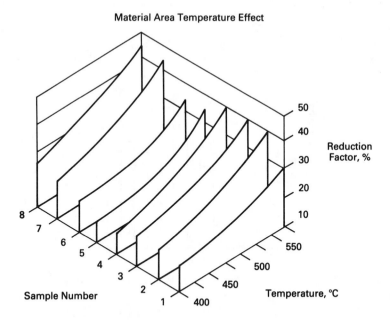

Figure 6.3 Pictorial chart.

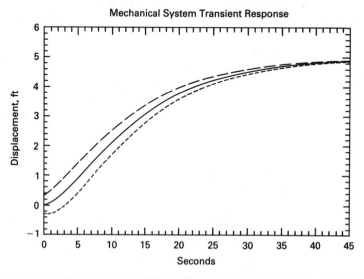

Figure 6.4 Graph on linear-linear coordinate axes.

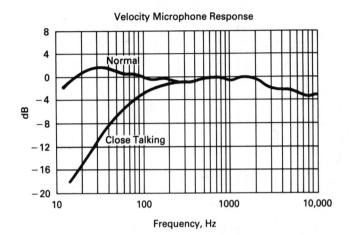

Velocity Microphone Response

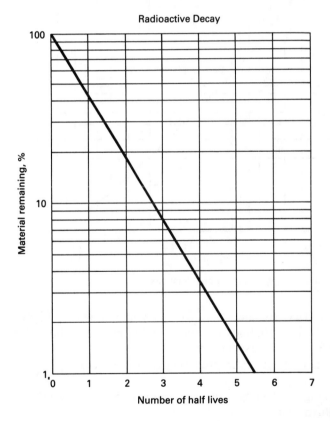

Radioactive Decay

Figure 6.5 Semi-logarithmic graphs.

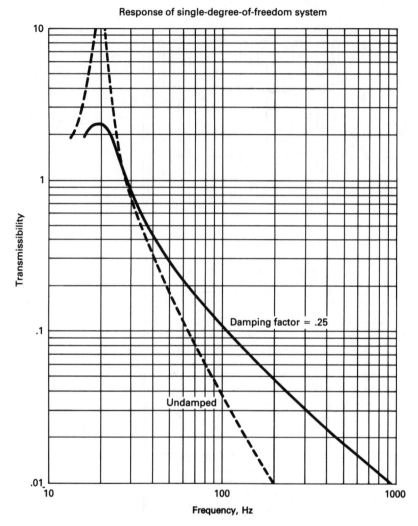

Response of single-degree-of-freedom system

Figure 6.6 Graph on log-log coordinate axes.

and on various other types of coordinate scales (one example shown in Figure 6.7). Excel does not have built-in routines to construct the pictorial and polar presentations of Figures 6.3 and 6.7, respectively.

Here are some important objectives in preparing graphs of data.

1. To save time in analyzing the data by causing attention to be focused only on the concepts being illustrated.
2. To gain the attention of the reader for the purpose of generating reader motivation.

3. To efficiently display the data, with verbal descriptions used only to highlight principal concepts.
4. To permit the study of the data for anomalies and correlations.
5. To show past, present, and future trend possibilities.
6. To suggest new ideas of interpretation for further consideration.

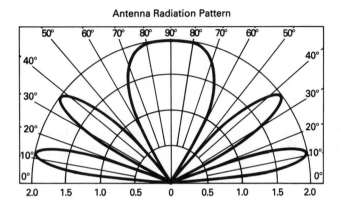

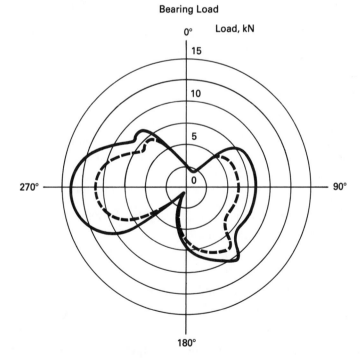

Figure 6.7   Polar charts.

Whether or not we achieve all of our objectives, we do realize many of the following advantages in graphically structuring our data.

1. Easily understanding the data.
2. Readily summarizing the results.
3. Rapidly creating a visual impression.
4. Easily interpreting the data.
5. Simplifying complex ideas.
6. Easily detecting computational or measurement errors.

Graphically portraying information is not without its risks, however. Graphs may contain errors, and they may be unknowingly misleading for the following reasons:

1. There may be errors in data collection and measurement.
2. Trivial data and outliers may appear on the graph.
3. The graph may be cluttered and contain excessive detail (e.g., too many curves, multiple curves too similar, high gridline density, etc.).
4. The type of graph may be inappropriate for the concepts being illustrated.
5. Improper coordinate scales may have been adopted (e.g., linear-linear, semi-logarithmic, or logarithmic-logarithmic).
6. Terms may be ill-defined or lack definition (e.g., axes titles, dimensional units, curve identification, etc.).

6.2 THE EXCEL CHART

Making a graph with Excel is aided by the automated construction procedures within the program. Unfortunately, not all automatically produced graphs are of the desired form. Therefore, some touch-up, or customization, is often required to produce the finished product.

We follow this procedure to construct a graph:

1. Prepare the data in table form in the worksheet.
2. Select the data to be plotted.
3. Choose **File New Chart OK**.
4. Customize the graph if necessary.
5. If desired, save the graph with the **Save As** command (default file extension is .XLC) and/or print it.

Before constructing a graph, let us first become familiar with the Chart window and its menu bar as shown in Figure 6.8. This is the view after entering the window and constructing a graph with the data shown in the worksheet. The

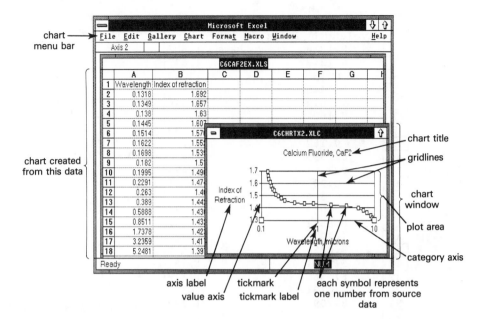

Figure 6.8 Chart window.

data is a table of index of refraction versus wavelength for calcium fluoride and is shown in Figure 6.9. Excel automatically forms a default bar chart from the data, if possible. In Excel, this form of the bar chart is called a column chart. Should that not be desired by the user, other standard chart formats can be chosen for display of the data. We will illustrate this later.

The chart window of Figure 6.8 is the active window. When sized smaller than the default, which is full window size, we can see part of the worksheet window, now inactive. A chart window contains the *chart,* within which we have the *plot area,* the *chart title,* the *axes labels,* the *category axis* (abscissa, or x-axis), the *value axis* (ordinate, or y-axis), axes *tickmarks, tickmark labels,* the *legend,* and the graphical representation of the values.

The menu bar of Figure 6.8 pertains to the chart window, now the active window. Some of its entries resemble those of the worksheet menu bar. Should the worksheet be selected, the chart becomes inactive and the worksheet menu bar reappears. To activate the chart again, click in the chart window. It automatically becomes the active window and the chart menu bar reappears.

We begin the following example by somewhat blindly accepting default values for initially displaying data in graphic form. This gives us a chance to explain various Excel chart commands as we extricate ourselves from an uncomfortable predicament.

The column chart of Figure 6.10 was formed from our data. We first selected the data of the worksheet, including the column headings, then invoked the

	A	B
1	Wavelength	Index of refraction
2	0.1318	1.692
3	0.1349	1.657
4	0.138	1.63
5	0.1445	1.607
6	0.1514	1.576
7	0.1622	1.552
8	0.1698	1.539
9	0.182	1.51
10	0.1995	1.496
11	0.2291	1.474
12	0.263	1.46
13	0.389	1.442
14	0.5888	1.436
15	0.8511	1.432
16	1.7378	1.423
17	3.2359	1.417
18	5.2481	1.397
19	6.4565	1.379
20	7.4131	1.358
21	8.7096	1.332
22	9.3325	1.317

Figure 6.9 Worksheet data for the example of Section 6.2.

File New command, which displayed the dialog box of Figure 2.5(b). In the dialog box, we toggled **Chart** on and chose **OK**. This produced the default column chart of Figure 6.10. We see that one set of bars represents the wavelength, the other the index of refraction. This is clearly not what we want. We want a line graph with wavelength as abscissa and index of refraction as ordinate, on an appropriate

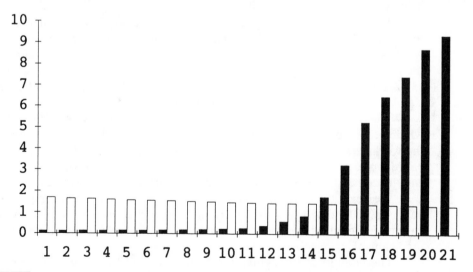

Figure 6.10 Column chart constructed from the data of Figure 6.9.

set of axes, of course. Several predefined chart formats are available in Excel through the **Gallery** command. We will now discuss some entries of this menu and then proceed with developing the graph of our choice.

The Gallery Command .   This command is used to produce selections of chart formats, called a *gallery,* in dialog boxes. The type of chart is chosen from the **Gallery** menu of Figure 6.11(a). The resulting gallery contains commonly used formats for that chart type as shown in Figures 6.11(b) through 6.11(h). To select a format, click on the numbered box of the desired format, then choose **OK**. A check mark appears adjacent to the choice in the menu to show the current format of the chart. Figure 6.11(a) shows this to be a scatter chart. The **Next** and **Previous** buttons allow one to step through the chart types of the **Gallery** menu without retreating to the menu. **Next** will display the gallery for the chart type following the current selection, the next one downward in the **Gallery** menu, while **Previous** will advance upward in the menu for the same purpose. In the order in which the types appear in the menu, here are some words on each chart type available. The numbers in parentheses are keyed to the charts of the respective gallery.

Area

> This type of chart emphasizes the area under the curve. The area between the curves is usually shaded to emphasize each variable represented. The areas between the curves have no significance. One can choose an area chart that is (1) simple, (2) normalized to 100% area, or that has (3) drop lines, (4) gridlines, or (5) areas labeled by values.

Bar

> This type of chart shows the data displayed as horizontal bars. It is easily understood by nontechnical readers. One can choose a bar chart that (1) is simple, has (2) varied patterns, (3) stacked bars, or (4) overlapped bars, (5) is normalized to 100% or has (6) vertical gridlines or (7) bars labeled by values.

Column

> This type of chart shows the data displayed as vertical bars. Apart from having vertical bars and an eighth member of the gallery, a step chart with no space between bars, the column chart is a close relative to the bar chart.

Line

> This type of chart, which we prefer to call a graph, shows data plotted with or without symbols, called markers, at the data point locations and with or without line segments connecting the points. Its scales are usually linear but may be logarithmic. It is used to display discrete or continuous data. One can choose from among the formats with (1) lines and symbols, (2) lines only, (3) markers only, (4) horizontal gridlines added, (5) horizontal and

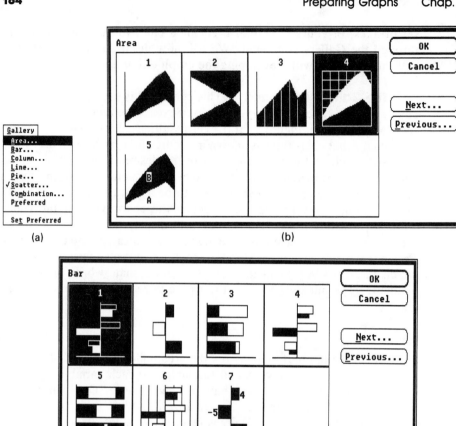

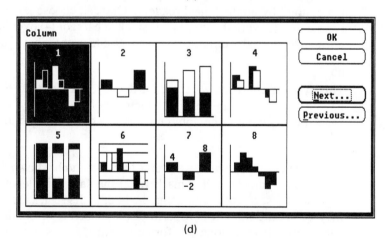

Figure 6.11　Gallery menu and the selection of galleries.

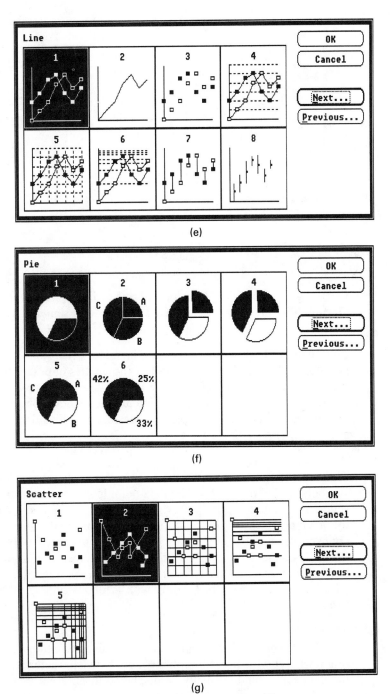

(e)

(f)

(g)

Figure 6.11 Continued

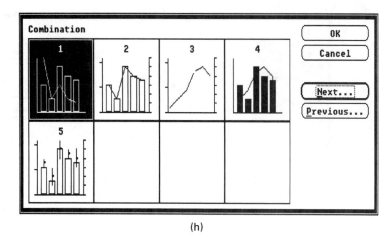

(h)

Figure 6.11 Continued

vertical gridlines added, (6) a logarithmic ordinate scale and gridlines added, (7) high-low lines, or (8) high, low, and close designations.

Pie

This type of chart presents the data in sectored circular form. The sectors are often called wedges. It is used to show parts in percentage form, where the entire circle is understood to be 100%. One can choose the pie chart that (1) is simple or that has (2) patterned and labeled sectors, (3) its first sector exploded, (4) all sectors exploded, (5) sectors labeled by category, or (6) sectors labeled as percentages.

Scatter

This type of chart, which we prefer to call a graph, shows data plotted with symbols, called markers, at the data point locations and with or without line segments connecting the points. It is similar to the line chart but provides for a greater variety of built-in axes proportional calibrations. One can choose from among the formats that show symbols (1) only on linear-linear axes, (2) connected by lines on linear-linear axes, (3) only with gridlines on linear-linear axes, (4) only with gridlines on the logarithmic ordinate and with a linear abscissa, or (5) only with gridlines on logarithmic-logarithmic axes.

Combination

This is an overlay of two chart types. It is used to compare data of different origin whereby the presentation is to retain the characteristics. Individually, the data sets would normally be displayed in different graphical form. One can choose from among formats that include (1) column with line overlay, (2) column with line overlay having an independent scale, (3) line with line overlay having an independent scale, (4) area with column overlay, or (5) bar with line overlay.

Returning to our example, and rejecting the column chart, it seems logical that we should now reformat it as a line graph with the **Gallery** command. So, choosing **Gallery Line** and format 2 shown in Figure 6.11(e), Excel reformats the graph to look as shown in Figure 6.12. Again, this is not what we want. It is obvious that Excel is not using the wavelength column of data for the abscissa. We now digress to learn how Excel constructs its charts. Area, bar, column, line, and pie charts are treated differently from scatter charts.

For plotting purposes, Excel groups data values by categories. Thus, it must choose these categories from the table of data. We illustrate this grouping in Figure 6.13(a), where we assumed that each row is a category. The figure shows that there are two values for each of the six categories, with the values coming from the two columns. Each column of values is referred to as a *data series*. Thus, for Figure 6.9, we would have two data series to plot.

The categories of Figure 6.13(a) do not connote any relationship to each other beyond that they each contain two values from the same two series. Identification is sequential by row with no inference of numerical differences between adjacent categories. Thus, for plotting purposes, each category can be allocated the same amount of space on a chart. That is, there can be uniformly spaced categories regardless of the meaning of each category, as indicated in Figure 6.13(b). Such is the case for categories derived for area, bar, column, line, and pie charts. The series values, however, will be plotted according to the relative numerical differences between series data points in order to infer a continuous origin rather than a discrete one. For a scatter chart, however, the category values are

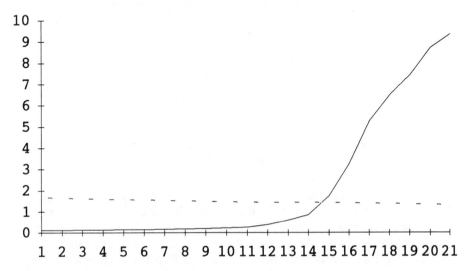

Figure 6.12 Column chart of Figure 6.10 reformatted as a line graph.

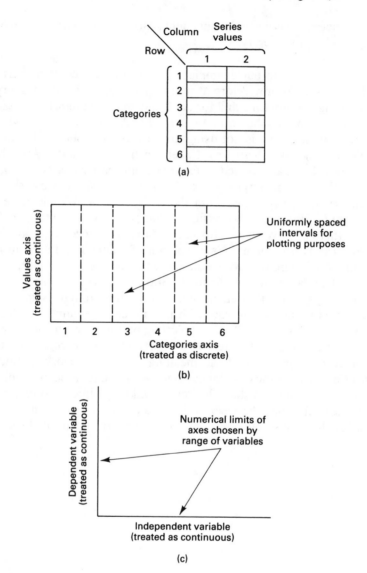

Figure 6.13 (a) Representation of categories, (b) area, bar, column, and line charts (pie chart on circular axes), and (c) a scatter chart.

not axis labels but are treated as if they are values to be placed on a continuous scale as shown in Figure 6.13(c). Thus, they are treated the same as the series values. In effect, we have two continuous numerical scales on which to locate the data point to plot. As a result, we need at least two series to plot.

We now relate the above to the way Excel selects default category names. These names can be plotted as axes tick mark labels. Figure 6.14 shows the

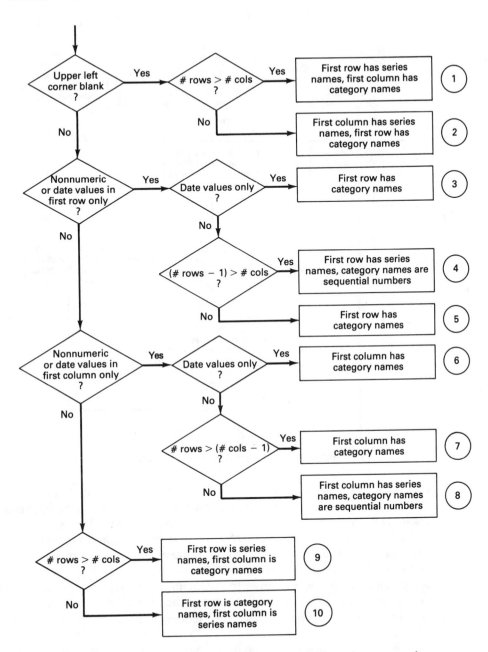

Figure 6.14 Area, bar, column, line, and pie chart series and category assignment.

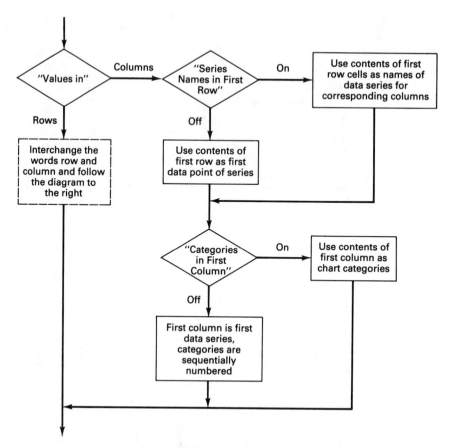

Figure 6.15 Scatter chart series and category assignment.

procedure for area, bar, column, line, and pie charts, while Figure 6.15 shows
similar details for the scatter chart. Figure 6.14 shows that Excel first keys on the
contents of the upper left corner cell of the area selected. If it is blank, category
and series names are obtained from the first row and first column, with actual
assignment made according to the ratio of number of rows to number of columns
as shown in the figure. If the upper left corner cell is not blank, category names
are obtained from the first row, first column, or neither, depending on whether
nonnumeric or date values are included in the respective row or column. Under
certain conditions, category names are sequential numbers, beginning with number one.

Figure 6.15 shows how the user controls scatter chart configuration via the
chart window **Edit Paste Special** dialog box. This dialog box differs from its
worksheet counterpart, as can be seen by comparing Figure 6.16(c) with Figure
3.4(e). The choices of this box allow the user to determine the assignment of data
from the selected cells to the axes of the chart. The procedure is to select and **Edit**

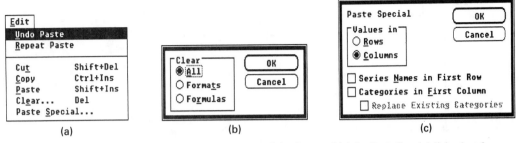

Figure 6.16   (a) Edit menu, (b) the Clear dialog box, and (c) the Paste Special dialog box for charts.

Copy the worksheet data, activate the window for a new chart, or for an existing one, and execute the **Edit Paste Special** command. First, the **Values in** box must be set to **Rows** or **Columns**. Depending on this choice, the **Series Names in First _____** and **Categories in First _____** are completed with **Row** or **Column** as appropriate. These boxes may be toggled on or off to reflect the desires of the user and the structure of the selected table of data. The net result is that the scatter chart can be configured with the desired category axis, names of series, and data point identification.

Again returning to our example and applying what we learned above, we can now explain what was happening to our abortive efforts to get the graph we wanted, and we can proceed to prepare it properly. First, Figure 6.10 was formed according to the **Column** chart format. The table we selected led us through the chart of Figure 6.14 to the box numbered ④. We reformatted the display as a line chart in Figure 6.12 but could not affect the appearance, since the line chart is determined in the same manner as the column chart. If we now try a scatter chart selection from the gallery, we will obtain Figure 6.17. Again, this is not what we want. We realize that we did not follow the procedure of Figure 6.15 to get a scatter chart with the proper axes. Finally, by following that procedure, we get Figure 6.18. But this is another column chart because that is the default type for a new chart. To get this figure, we selected the data range A1:B22 of Figure 6.9, then **Edit Copy**, and then **File New Chart**. On the blank chart window that appeared, we then executed **Edit Paste Special** and set up the dialog box as follows:

> **Values in** *Columns*
> **Series Names in First** *Row*
> **Categories in First** *Column*

We chose **OK** and saw the chart of Figure 6.18. This is not a scatter chart, but we notice that the x-axis labels are the abscissa values for the x-coordinates of their corresponding y-coordinate values. Therefore, we must be on the right track. Now, if we choose **Gallery Scatter**, we will get the scatter chart of Figure 6.19. We still do not have a logarithmic x-axis. However, we can easily obtain one, but we will include that topic later when we discuss how to customize graphs.

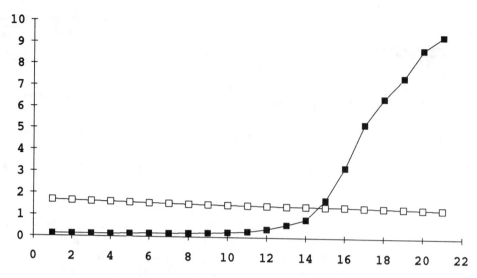

Figure 6.17   Figure 6.12 reformatted as a scatter chart.

In review, here are the steps for displaying a scatter chart.

1. In the worksheet, select the data table to plot.
2. Perform the **Edit Copy** command.
3. Choose **File New Chart**. A blank chart window will appear.
4. Perform the **Edit Paste Special** command of the chart window. Complete the dialog box for the desired display and choose **OK**.
5. The default column chart appears. Perform the **Gallery Scatter** command to display the scatter chart formats available. Select the format desired and choose **OK**.

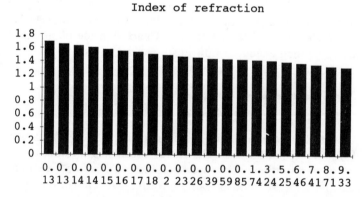

Figure 6.18   Data of Figure 6.9 displayed as a default column chart after being prepared according to the procedure of Figure 6.15.

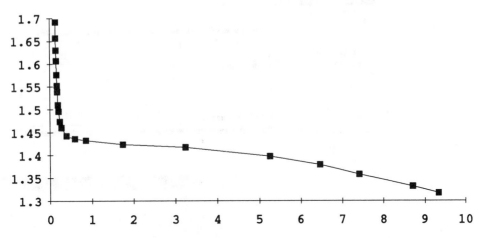

Figure 6.19 Scatter chart from the data of Figure 6.9.

Instead of beginning with the default column chart, as we described above, we could change the default with the **Gallery Set Preferred** command shown in Figure 6.11(a) in order to begin with another chart format of our choice.

Discontinuous cell ranges can be plotted by pasting them into the chart individually. The cell range that contains the category labels must be plotted first. It is also possible to plot curves containing data breaks, as we illustrate in Example 11.2.

Now that we have prepared one chart, we should be aware of the following factors at work while displaying it.

1. The underlying values are used to display chart data. So, even though integers may appear on the worksheet, the plot could be based on non-integer values.

2. The axes' tickmark values are based on the worksheet data formats. Therefore, the **Format Number** command should be applied to the worksheet to affect the chart appearance.

3. When the worksheet and its chart are both open, new worksheet values cause immediate updating of the chart.

6.3 GENERATING DATA TO PLOT

The material of preceding chapters shows us how to calculate a succession of data values that we may choose to plot. Of course, we could always manually enter the point coordinates as we did in the example above. In either case, we usually

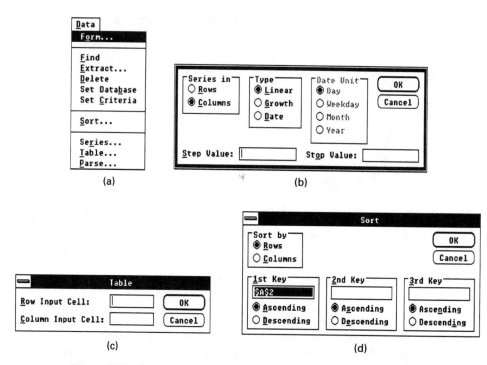

Figure 6.20 Data menu and dialog boxes useful in preparing data to plot.

have some starting point for the independent variable value after which we proceed to compute a value for the dependent variable and for succeeding data points. Since we need a succession of values, we could use certain spreadsheet functions to help us generate them. We could also use other computational aids to help us rapidly produce the values. In this section, we discuss ways to prepare tables of values to plot.

The Excel features we now describe are invoked from the worksheet **Data** menu shown in Figure 6.20(a). We will not discuss the commands of this menu that are for database manipulation.

6.3.1 The Data Series Command

The **Data Series** command, and its associated dialog box of Figure 6.20(b), is used to generate a table of numbers or dates. The tables can be row- or column-oriented. The values of the series are computed according to the following formulas:

$$\text{Linear: } value_{n+1} = value_n + step\ value$$

$$\text{Growth: } value_{n+1} = value_n * step\ value$$

where

$$value_1 = \text{value in first cell.}$$

The subscripts refer to relative cell numbers in the table. $Value_1$ must be supplied as the starting value in the first cell of the row- or column-oriented table. *Step value* may be negative. To generate the series of numbers, series in this context is not the same as chart data series discussed in Section 6.2; one must first select the table, then execute the command **Data Series**, set the toggles in the **Series in** (determines the direction to fill the table) and **Type** (determines arithmetic or geometric progression or by date) boxes, enter the **Step Value** (see formulas above) and the **Stop Value**, then choose **OK**. The table will be automatically filled, or partially filled if **Stop Value** is reached first. This table can be used as a source of values for the independent variable.

Example 6.1

We will calculate the frequencies of the chromatic scale according to the system of equal temperament in the octave containing 440 Hz, musical note A, with the **Data Series** command. Because the starting frequency of this octave, corresponding to C, is not an integer quantity, we begin our series with 220 Hz, the musical note A in the next lower octave, and generate it to cover the octave of interest. We will compute a geometric series for which the factor is $2^{\frac{1}{12}}$. Since we cannot enter formulas in the **Step Value** box of the **Data Series** dialog box, we must calculate the factor beforehand. This we do in cell B1 of Figure 6.21 (formula not shown). The starting value, 220 Hz, is entered in cell B3 and a large value is entered for **Stop Value** to ensure that all desired values are computed. We select the range B3:B17, choose **Data Series**, complete the dialog box by toggling **Columns** and **Growth** on, enter the factor in the **Step Value** box, enter the large value, say 20, in the **Stop Value** box, and then choose **OK**. The desired frequency values are computed as shown in cells B4:B17 of Figure 6.21.

	A	B
1	Factor	1.059463094
2	Note	Freq, Hz
3	A	220
4	A#	233.0818798
5	B	246.9416486
6	C	261.6255621
7	C#	277.1826264
8	D	293.6647619
9	D#	311.126976
10	E	329.6275474
11	F	349.2282199
12	F#	369.994409
13	G	391.9954199
14	G#	415.3046788
15	A	439.9999783
16	A#	466.1637366
17	B	493.8832728

Figure 6.21 Worksheet for Example 6.1.

6.3.2 The Data Table Command

The **Data Table** command and its associated window shown in Figure 6.20(c) are used to create a table of values from user-supplied formulas. The command operates with a table of values for the independent variable, which could have been generated with the **Data Series** command, and causes at least one other table to be filled with values computed via formulas that have, as their precedent, the independent variable. The table may be row- or column-oriented as shown in Figure 6.22, where the components of the tables are further defined. The **Data Table** command is useful in producing output values without manually changing an input value location. It may also be used with iteratively derived values. To use this command, one must first select the table of input values, the header formulas, and the output area, choose **Data Table**, enter the row or column first input cell location, and then choose **OK**. Execution causes the table values to be computed and entered into the table.

Example 6.2

We will compute the acoustic pressure displacement of the audio frequencies computed in Example 6.1 for a pressure variation of 28 N/m². This is the maximum pressure variation that the ear can tolerate. The formula is

$$\text{displacement (m)} = \frac{P}{2\pi f \rho v}$$

where P = sound pressure variation = 28 N/m² (assumed)

f = sound wave frequency, Hz

ρ = density of air = 1.22 kg/m³ (assumed)

v = velocity of sound = 331 m/sec (assumed)

We expect to compute a table of displacements with the **Data Table** command.

Figure 6.23(a) shows the completed worksheet while Figure 6.23(b) shows the formulas. We took the desired columns of data from Example 6.1, added the rows of variable definitions and the formulas, and arranged the worksheet for the calculation. Our input cell is B1, which references cell B16, the 440 Hz frequency. Any frequency in the range B7:B18 could have been chosen for this computation. The data table is set up in cell range C6:C18. The table formula, =*Displacement* in cell C6, references the computation in cell B5 that refers to the input cell. Thus, our dependency relationship is complete. We first selected the range B6:C20, then chose **Data Table**, clicked on **Column Input Cell**, selected cell B1 (or we could have entered its name, Frequency), then chose **OK**. The computations were made with the values appearing in cell range C7:C18. Note how small the displacement really is for sounds of such a high pressure variation.

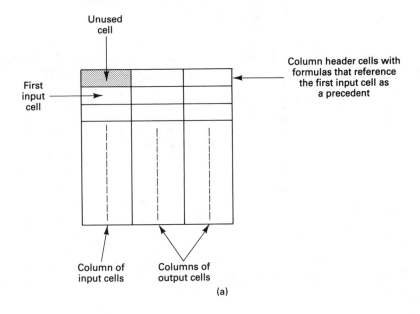

Unused
cell

Column header cells with
formulas that reference
the first input cell as
a precedent

First
input
cell

Column of
input cells

Columns of
output cells

(a)

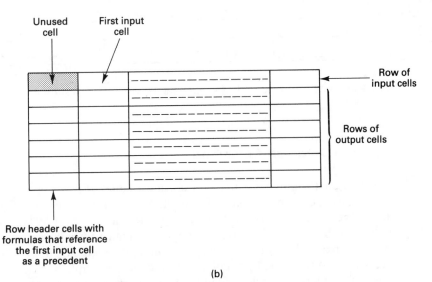

Unused
cell

First input
cell

Row of
input cells

Rows of
output cells

Row header cells with
formulas that reference
the first input cell
as a precedent

(b)

Figure 6.22   Data Table layouts shown in (a) column orientation and (b) row
orientation.

	A	B	C
1	Frequency	439.9999783	Hz
2	Max_pressure	28	nt/m^2
3	Velocity	331	m/sec
4	Rho	1.22	kg/m^3
5	Displacement	2.50806E-05	m
6	Note	Freq, Hz	2.50806E-05
7	C	261.6255621	4.21803E-05
8	C#	277.1826264	3.98129E-05
9	D	293.6647619	3.75784E-05
10	D#	311.126976	3.54693E-05
11	E	329.6275474	3.34786E-05
12	F	349.2282199	3.15996E-05
13	F#	369.994409	2.9826E-05
14	G	391.9954199	2.8152E-05
15	G#	415.3046788	2.6572E-05
16	A	439.9999783	2.50806E-05
17	A#	466.1637366	2.36729E-05
18	B	493.8832728	2.23443E-05

(a)

	A	B	C
1	Frequency	=B16	Hz
2	Max_pressure	28	nt/m^2
3	Velocity	331	m/sec
4	Rho	1.22	kg/m^3
5	Displacement	=Max_pressure/(2*PI()*Frequency*Rho*Velocity)	m
6	Note	Freq, Hz	=Displacement
7	C	261.625562071123	=TABLE(,B1)
8	C#	277.182626414859	=TABLE(,B1)

(b)

Figure 6.23 Worksheet for Example 6.2 in (a) values mode and (b) formulas mode.

6.3.3 The Data Sort Command

The **Data Sort** command is used for sorting a table. It is set up and executed via the window of Figure 6.20(d). To use this command, one must first select the table to be sorted, choose **Data Sort**, toggle the desired **Sort by** button, enter into the **1st Key** box any cell reference from the column/row being sorted as the key to sort on, toggle the corresponding **Ascending/Descending** button, then choose **OK**. When sorting multiple column/row tables, multiple sort keys may be entered. These keys act independently of each other and are used to break "ties" in higher priority key sorts. The **1st Key**, **2nd Key**, and **3rd Key** selections are the priority assignments of the columns/rows on which sorting is based. Should it be desired not to retain the results of a sort operation, it can be undone with the **Edit Undo** command.

Example 6.3

We will use the **Data Sort** command on the results of Example 5.4. The input and output are shown in Figure 6.24(a) just as we constructed it in the example. However, we did copy just values and column headings, not formulas, into the cell range shown. Now, we will sort the table on the gage pressure, column A, in de-

	A	B	C	D	E	F	G	H
1			Inputs				Outputs	
2	Gage	Spklr	V_A	V_B	V_C	P_1	P_2	S_o
3	237	Open				On	On	Open
4	250		Open			On	Off	Open
5	261				Open	On	Off	Open
6	230				Open	On	Off	Open
7	225			Open	Open	On	On	Open
8	223			Open		On	On	Open
9	235	Open		Open		On	On	Open
10	229	Open		Open		On	On	Closed
11	248	Open		Open		On	On	Open
12	253			Open		On	Off	Open
13	249		Open	Open	Open	On	Off	Open
14	222		Open	Open	Open	On	On	Open
15	241					Off	Off	Open
16	229					Off	Off	Open
17	228	Open				On	On	Closed

(a)

	A	B	C	D	E	F	G	H
1			Inputs				Outputs	
2	Gage	Spklr	V_A	V_B	V_C	P_1	P_2	S_o
3	261				Open	On	Off	Open
4	253			Open		On	Off	Open
5	250		Open			On	Off	Open
6	249		Open	Open	Open	On	Off	Open
7	248	Open		Open		On	On	Open
8	241					Off	Off	Open
9	237	Open				On	On	Open
10	235	Open		Open		On	On	Open
11	230				Open	On	Off	Open
12	229	Open		Open		On	On	Closed
13	229					Off	Off	Open
14	228	Open				On	On	Closed
15	225			Open	Open	On	On	Open
16	223			Open		On	On	Open
17	222		Open	Open	Open	On	On	Open

(b)

Figure 6.24 Worksheet of Example 6.3 in (a) original form and (b) sorted by gage pressure in descending order.

scending order. We select the range A3:H17, being sure not to include the column headings, and execute the **Data Sort** command to get the dialog box of Figure 6.20(d). We set the **Sort by** toggle to **Rows**, toggle the **Descending** button on in the **1st Key** box, enter any cell from the range A3:A17 in the **1st Key** entry box, then choose **OK**. The result is Figure 6.24(b).

Had we more equal gage pressure values, we probably would have entered a **2nd Key**. For this example, it would have been the status of the sprinkler, the second column. Remember that the sort process also sorts on alphabetic characters. The first character of the valve status, either O for open or blank for closed, would be used to sort on. In ascending or descending order, blanks are always sorted last.

6.3.4 Curve-Fitting Functions

Experimental data often does not follow a curve with an analytical representation. But there are ways to fit curves to data, and we look for such routines in spreadsheet programs to help us with our data analysis effort. In Excel, we have the functions of Table 6.1 to perform linear and exponential regression calculations on sets of data. The equations produced by the functions are as follows:

$$y = m_1 x_1 + m_2 x_2 + \ldots + m_k x_k + b \qquad \text{(linear)}$$

$$y = b m_1^x m_2^x \ldots m_k^x \qquad\qquad\qquad \text{(exponential)}$$

Functions LINEST and LOGEST each return the coefficients for the linear and exponential best fits, respectively, while TREND and GROWTH each return an array of ordinate values along the curve for the linear and exponential best fits, respectively. These values are all returned in horizontal arrays.

Example 6.4

　　We have experimental data in the cell range B2:E8 of the worksheet in Figure 6.25(a). It represents the results of testing piston ring designs (types 1, 2, and 3) for frictional force under pressure, actually differential pressure Δp, which is the difference in pressure across cell rings in the piston. We expect the frictional force to follow a near linear relationship, so we will fit a linear equation to the data for each ring design using a least squares function. In this case it is the TREND function because we want data points to plot on the same graph as the experimental data values.

　　Our first act is to set up for the least squares computation. The TREND function uses the experimental x and y values, and x values for which the function is to return y values on the regression line. The x values for the line computations are entered for Min and Max in B9 and B10, respectively. TREND functions are entered for each dependent variable (column) of Figure 6.25(b) so that the regression lines for each set of data may be calculated. They are entered in rows 9 and 10 as arrays. For example, for the type 1 piston design the experimental y and x data values, the first and second TREND arguments, are in the ranges C2:C8 and B2:B8, respectively. The third TREND argument, the abscissa values for which we want the corresponding ordinate values, is the range B9:B10. The result, an array, appears in the range

(a)

	A	B	C	D	E
1		Delta p	Type 1	Type 2	Type 3
2		0	0.1	6.7	2.1
3		0.46	2.3	12.3	7.1
4		1.13	3.6	19.4	12.8
5		1.54	5.5	26.2	17.9
6		2.06	7.8	31.3	22
7		2.49	9.3	36.7	24.8
8		3.03	10.1	42.4	31.1
9	Min	0	0.309664351	6.784369717	2.523726675
10	Max	3	10.54281548	42.50129184	30.57244188

(a)

(b)

	A	B	C	D	E
1		Delta p	Type 1	Type 2	Type 3
2		0	0.1	6.7	2.1
3		0.46	2.3	12.3	7.1
4		1.13	3.6	19.4	12.8
5		1.54	5.5	26.2	17.9
6		2.06	7.8	31.3	22
7		2.49	9.3	36.7	24.8
8		3.03	10.1	42.4	31.1
9	Min	0	=TREND(C2:C8,B2:B8,B9:B10)	=TREND(D2:D8,B2:B8,B9:B10)	=TREND(E2:E8,B2:B8,B9:B10)
10	Max	3	=TREND(C2:C8,B2:B8,B9:B10)	=TREND(D2:D8,B2:B8,B9:B10)	=TREND(E2:E8,B2:B8,B9:B10)

(b)

Figure 6.25 Worksheet for Example 6.4 in (a) values mode and (b) formulas mode.

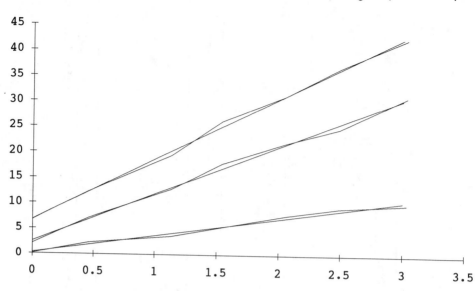

Figure 6.26   Plot of the results for Example 6.4.

C9:C10. Similarly for the other types of piston design. The result, when plotted as a scatter chart, is shown in Figure 6.26. The least squares fit lines and experimental data curves are both plotted for each piston type. There is not much variation of the experimental data from a straight line.

TABLE 6.1   CURVE-FITTING FUNCTIONS

Type	Name	Input arrays (ordered arguments)	Output arrays (function value)	Comment
Exponential	GROWTH	$(\{y_i\},\{x_i\},\{x_n\})$	$\{y_n\}$	Returns ordinate values on the curve for the corresponding $\{x_n\}$.
Exponential	LOGEST	$(\{y_i\},\{x_i\})$	$\{m_1,m_2, \ldots , b\}$	Returns coefficients of the least squares fit exponential equation.
Linear	TREND	$(\{y_i\},\{x_i\},\{x_n\})$	$\{y_n\}$	Returns ordinate values on the curve for the corresponding $\{x_n\}$.
Linear	LINEST	$(\{y_i\},\{x_i\})$	$\{m_1,m_2, \ldots , b\}$	Returns coefficients of the least squares fit linear equation.

Input arrays above can be:
  Cell range   e.g., C6:C20
  Variable name   e.g., Stress
  Constants   e.g., {7,4.2,12,8.6,10.4}

6.4 CUSTOMIZING THE GRAPH

The default graph should meet the minimum requirements for displaying the data. However, other uses of the graph may create a need to tailor it for a different appearance. We now discuss various commands in Excel that are available for this purpose. Because we must almost always first select the object or text that we wish to modify, here are the directions for making selections on a chart or graph.

Keyboard: By pressing one of the arrow keys, one automatically makes the first selection. Thereafter, pressing the keys causes selection as follows:
↑ Select the first item in the next class.
↓ Select the last item in the previous class.
→ Select the next item in the current class.
← Select the previous item in the current class.

Mouse: Move the cursor to the object or text desired, then click on it.

A selection is obvious because the object or text is delineated by an imaginary box outline of eight small black or white filled selection squares placed at the corners and in the middle of each side of the box, as shown in Figure 6.27. The next command or action will affect the selected object or text. The color of the squares is interpreted as follows:

Black: The object or text can be formatted with menu commands and moved or sized directly with the keyboard or mouse.

White: The object or text may be formatted or realigned with menu commands but cannot be moved or sized directly.

A discussion of customizing possibilities follows.

6.4.1 Adding/Deleting/Changing/Formatting Objects

Except for the overlay chart, the following objects must first be selected for customization action.

(a)   (b)

Figure 6.27   Selection indication on a graph for (a) attached text and (b) unattached text.

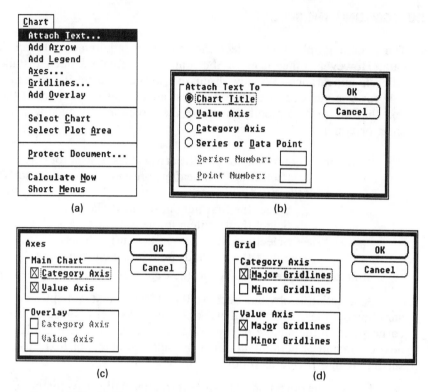

Figure 6.28   (a) Chart menu and dialog boxes for (b) Attach Text, (c) Axes, and (d) Gridlines commands.

Chart background

The **Chart Select Chart** command of Figure 6.28(a) selects the entire chart in the active window. Its background may be formatted with the **Format Patterns** command of Figure 6.29(a) whereby, via the dialog box of Figure 6.30(a), its border may be specified for style, color, weight, and automatic/invisible/shadow display, and its area may be specified for the type of pattern, foreground and background color, and automatic/invisible display. The **Format Font** command dialog box of Figure 6.29(b) allows changes to be made to all text in the chart.

Plot area

The **Chart Select Plot Area** command of Figure 6.28(a) selects the region bounded by and including the axes. It may be formatted with the **Format Patterns** command of Figure 6.29(a) whereby, via the dialog box of Figure 6.30(a), its border may be specified for style, color, weight, and automatic/invisible display, and its area may be specified for the type of pattern, foreground and background color, and automatic/invisible display.

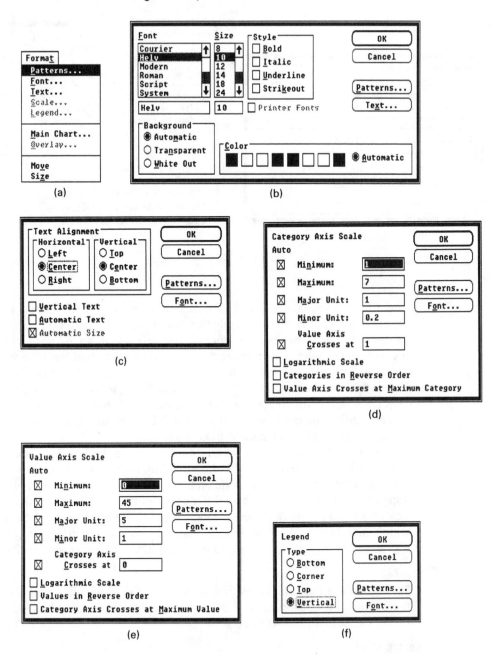

Figure 6.29   (a) Format menu and dialog boxes for (b) Font, (c) Text, (d) and (e) Scale, (f) Legend, (g) Main Chart, and (h) Overlay commands.

(g)

(h)

Figure 6.29   Continued

Axes

The **Chart Axes** command of Figure 6.28(a) produces the dialog box of Figure 6.28(c). It is used to toggle the x- and y-axis labels on (visible) or off (invisible). The **Overlay** box appears there only if an overlay chart is present. After being selected, each axis may be formatted with the **Format Patterns** command of Figure 6.29(a) whereby, via a dialog box similar to Figure 6.30(b), the axis line may be specified for style, color, and weight, the major and minor tickmarks on that axis may be turned on or off, and the corresponding tickmark labels may be turned off, positioned at either end of the graph border, or positioned next to the axis.

Certain attributes of the axes are specified via the **Format Scale** dialog boxes of Figure 6.29(d) or 6.29(e), depending on which axis was selected. Entries in these boxes also depend on the type of chart. One may control the appearance of the axes, such as the number of intervals between the x-axis tickmarks and tickmark labels, the location of the axes crossing, the order in which each axis is to be sequenced, and the axis scale limits. One can also toggle on, or off, the axis scale to be logarithmic, or linear, respectively.

Tickmarks

Tickmarks are customized by first selecting the desired axis, then invoking the **Format Patterns** command of Figure 6.29(a). The dialog box selection choices described for Axes above appear.

Tickmark labels

Tickmark labels are customized by first selecting the desired axis, then invoking the **Format Patterns** command of Figure 6.29(a). The dialog box selection choices described for Axes above appear.

Gridlines

The **Chart Gridlines** command of Figure 6.28(a) produces the dialog box of
Figure 6.28(d). It is used to toggle the major and minor gridlines on (add, or
make visible) or off (delete, or make invisible). When any one gridline of a
type is selected and the **Format Patterns** command of Figure 6.29(a) is invoked, a dialog box similar to Figure 6.30(b) permits that type of gridline to
be specified for style, color, weight, or automatic display.

Plotting symbols (markers)

The plotting symbols, and their connecting line, are a consequence of the
data being plotted. Excel derives a data series that specifies the particulars
for plotting the curve. When the curve, or its symbol, is selected, the series
appears in the formula bar. It may then be edited in the same manner as for
formulas. Before editing a data series, the user must be thoroughly familiar
with its meaning and construction. As an alternative, the **Format Patterns**
command of Figure 6.29(a) may be invoked, at which time the dialog box of
Figure 6.30(b) permits the plotted line style, color, and weight to be specified, and toggled for automatic/invisible display. Also, the symbols may be
specified for style, foreground and background color combinations, and toggled for automatic/invisible display.

Legend

A legend may be added via the **Chart Add Legend** command of Figure
6.28(a). For multiple series, the series headings become the legend. Upon
being added, it may then be deleted via the altered command, which now
reads **Chart Delete Legend**. It is a toggle command. The **Format Legend**
command produces the dialog box of Figure 6.29(f), which allows placement
and alignment of the legend on the chart background. When the legend is
selected, and the **Format Patterns** command of Figure 6.29(a) is invoked, a
dialog box similar to Figure 6.30(a) permits the border to be specified for
style, color, weight, or automatic/invisible/shadow display. Also, the legend area can be specified for pattern, foreground and background color, or
automatic/invisible display.

Arrows

Arrows may be added to the chart to point to certain features for annotation. The arrows are added via the **Chart Add Arrow** command of Figure
6.28(a). When arrows have been added, a **Chart Delete Arrow** command
becomes available for removing them, after being selected, of course. Upon
selection, the arrow is delineated with black boxes, which means it may be
moved and sized with the mouse by first clicking on it, then dragging for
placement. Either end of it may be moved individually, or the arrow in its
entirety may be moved while parallel to its original orientation. The arrow

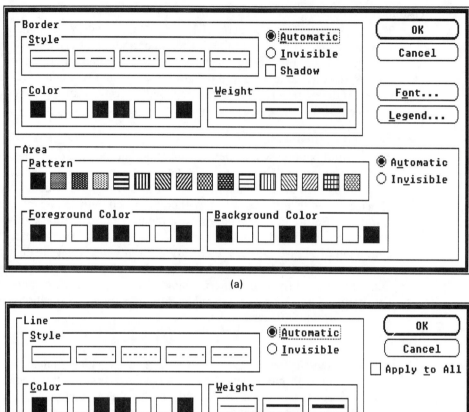

(a)

(b)

Figure 6.30 Typical dialog boxes displayed by the Format Patterns command.

may be sized with the keyboard arrow keys after invoking the **Format Size** command. When an arrow is selected and the **Format Patterns** command of Figure 6.29(a) is invoked, a dialog box similar to Figure 6.30(b) permits the arrow shaft to be specified for style, color, and weight, and the arrow head specified for style, width, and length.

Overlay chart

> If a chart has been produced with a single curve, an overlay may be added with the **Chart Add Overlay** command of Figure 6.28(a). This command becomes a **Chart Delete Overlay** if a combination chart is active. It may also be formatted via the dialog box of Figure 6.29(h) produced by the **Format Overlay** command.

Main chart

> The **Format Main Chart** command of Figure 6.29(a) allows one to choose the chart type and format according to the choices of the dialog box in Figure 6.29(g). In effect, one determines the chart appearance in a manner different from the galley format. The **Format** choices of the box depend on the **Type** chosen.

Move

> Certain chart objects can be individually moved within the chart confines with the **Format Move** command of Figure 6.29(a). The procedure is to first select the object, execute **Format Move**, and then move the object with either the keyboard or mouse. This command differs from the window **Control Move** command which is used to move the entire window.

Size

> Certain chart objects can be individually sized with the **Format Size** command of Figure 6.29(a). The procedure is to first select the object, execute **Format Size**, and then resize the object with either the keyboard or mouse. This command differs from the window **Control Size** command which is used to resize the entire window.

6.4.2 Adding/Deleting/Changing/Formatting Text

Text can be made to appear at many locations on a chart. It is often part of an object, in which case it is called *attached text,* or it can be disassociated with objects, in which case it is called *unattached text.* The axes labels are attached text, since they move with and are sized with the axes to which they are attached. Notes added to the chart are unattached text, since they are not coupled to any object and are manipulated as if they were objects themselves. The following commands apply to chart text.

Chart Attach Text

> This command produces the dialog box of Figure 6.28(b). It allows one to enter attached text to the title, axes, data series, or data points. When the selection is toggled and the **OK** button chosen, Excel attaches the text, selects it, and displays it in the formula bar. Initially, there is default text for some of the accessible objects. For the title it is ''Title'', for the x-axis, ''X'', and for the y-axis, ''Y''. However, for a single data series table, its

heading becomes the chart title. The selection squares surround the attached text as previously explained in connection with Figure 6.27. This
text appears in the formula bar and can be edited. As new text is entered, it,
too, appears there as does existing text that was selected. All such text may
be edited or deleted in the usual manner.

Format Text

This command produces the dialog box of Figure 6.29(c). It allows one to
specify text alignment and orientation, and to restore original text if later
modified. The text must first be selected, the **Format Text** command executed, the dialog box choices entered, and **OK** chosen. Some of the options
are context sensitive, so the actual dialog box may differ from that of Figure
6.29(c).

Format Font

This command produces the dialog box of Figure 6.29(b). It allows one to
change part or all text fonts in the chart, depending on the extent of the
selection. The font may be specified as well as the size and style of the
characters. If the **Printer Fonts** box is toggled on, the font list contains the
font names available via the printer driver. Otherwise, the fonts pertain to
screen display. The background within the selected text area is controlled
via the **Background Automatic/Transparent/White Out** buttons. The text
color on the screen may also be specified.

6.4.3 Using Edit Commands with Charts

We have discussed most of the **Edit** menu commands in connection with worksheet development activities. Some of the commands also apply to charts. We
now briefly discuss the commands and note how they apply to charts. The **Edit**
menu is shown in Figure 6.16.

Edit Undo

This command applies to all chart **Edit** menu commands and will undo the
last such command executed.

Edit Cut

This command cuts only selected characters in the formula bar. It will not
work with other selected parts of a chart.

Edit Copy

This command allows one to copy any part, or all, of a chart. For this
purpose, it works as we discussed for a worksheet, namely, it requires
follow-on with **Edit Paste** or **Edit Paste Special** to complete the copy.

Edit Paste

This command completes the action of the **Edit Copy** command by inserting into the active chart the part(s) being copied from another chart. It also causes to be placed, at the insertion point of the formula bar, the copied contents of another chart's formula bar.

Edit Clear

This command causes to be cleared from the chart portions of its entities as determined by those selected and the choice toggled in the dialog box of Figure 6.16(b). **Edit Clear All** clears the chart format and all data series, **Edit Clear Formats** resets the chart format to its default format, and **Edit Clear Formulas** clears all data series but does not affect the chart format.

Edit Paste Special

This command completes a chart operation begun with the **Edit Copy** command. Choices must be made in the ensuing dialog box of Figure 6.16(c). The copy operation may have been begun in a worksheet or a chart. If begun in a worksheet, a new chart series is produced from the copied data. It can have numeric values as series names or category labels. If begun in a chart, the data series being copied is added to the active chart. This command differs from **Edit Paste** by allowing selective copying through dialog box choices. We used this command for the example in Section 6.2

6.4.4 Examples

It took us a long time to develop the graph of Figure 6.19 because we were explaining chart development in Excel along the way. Even then, we did not really finish the job, since the graph could be improved. We also left the graph of Figure 6.26 unfinished so that we could customize it in this section. The following examples illustrate graph customization techniques.

Example 6.5

Our index of refraction data of Figure 6.9 should really be plotted with a logarithmic abscissa, since frequency and wavelength data usually spans a wide range and can be expanded and compressed at both ends on a logarithmic scale, thus better revealing characteristics of the data. A logarithmic ordinate is a standard Excel scatter chart gallery choice, but that type of display is not at all suited for this kind of data, which must be plotted with wavelength as abscissa. However, from Figure 6.29(d), produced in a scatter chart context, we see that the categories scale dialog box allows us to toggle on, or off, a logarithmic axis. So, we should be able to format the graph as we wish. Here is what can be done to produce the graph of Figure 6.31.

1. Execute **Format Scale**. In the dialog box of Figure 6.29(d), toggle the **Logarithmic Scale** text box on and choose **OK**. This changes the graph abscissa to a two-decade logarithmic scale from 0.1 to 10 with the ordinate crossing at 1.

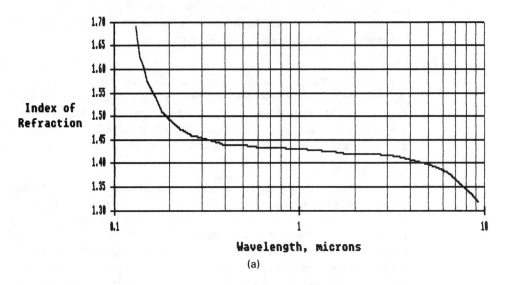

(a)

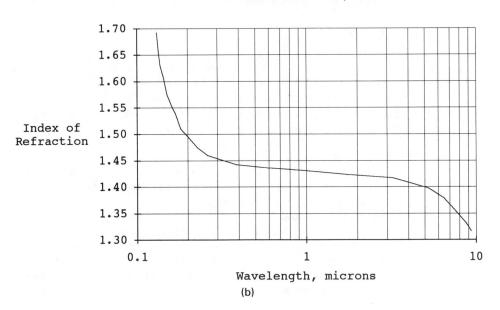

(b)

Figure 6.31 Edited graph of Example 6.5 when printed by (a) 24-pin dot matrix and (b) laser printers.

2. Execute **Format Scale**. In the dialog box of Figure 6.29(d), enter 0.1 in the **Value Axis Crosses at** text box and choose **OK**. The value axis is now displayed at the left edge of the graph as shown in Figure 6.31.

3. Execute **Chart Gridlines**. In the dialog box of Figure 6.28(d) toggle the **Category Axis Minor Gridlines** text box on and choose **OK**. The grid structure is now as shown in Figure 6.31.

4. Select the title "Index of refraction" shown in Figure 6.19. It is now surrounded by the attached text selection squares of Figure 6.27(a), and it also appears in the formula bar. Delete it from the formula bar, type in "Calcium Fluoride, CaF2" (without the quotation marks, of course), and choose the Enter box. The title appears on the graph as shown in Figure 6.31.

5. Execute **Chart Attach Text**. In the dialog box of Figure 6.28(b), toggle on the **Value Axis** button and choose **OK**. The default text of "X" appears in the formula bar. Delete it and type in "Index of Refraction" for the new value axis label and choose the Enter box.

6. Repeat step 5 for the **Category Axis** button but type in "Wavelength, microns". The axes labels now appear as shown in Figure 6.31.

7. The format of the value axis of Figure 6.19 was determined by Excel. Needless to say, it would be preferred that an equal number of decimal places be used for each tickmark. We can force this condition by formatting the data in the "Index of refraction" column of Figure 6.9, since that format will be used for the value axis also. Therefore, activate the worksheet, select only the values in column B, execute **Format Number**, select a format suitable for this data (we chose 0.00), and choose **OK**. The value axis now appears as shown in Figure 6.31.

8. Text fonts can be formatted via the **Format Font** command after first selecting the target text. One can effect a global font change by executing the **Chart Select Chart** command, then applying the **Format Font** command. The screen presentation is affected by font changes but so also may the printed output. If the **Printer Fonts** check box of Figure 6.29(b) is on, one may choose from the fonts available for the printer chosen by the **File Printer Setup** command. Some experimentation with fonts produced the graphs of Figure 6.31. Printer limitations do not always allow one to get the desired presentation.

Example 6.6

The piston rings test data of Example 6.4 is plotted as a scatter chart in Figure 6.26. Linear scales are appropriate for this type of data, so we leave the axes alone. We even anticipated a linear relationship and plotted the best fitting straight lines calculated with the TREND function. Even the scale markings are satisfactory. However, we will add a title, label the axes, and identify the curves. The following must be done to produce the graph of Figure 6.32.

1. Execute **Chart Attach Text**. In the dialog box of Figure 6.28(b) toggle on the **Chart Title** button and choose **OK**. The default text of "Title" appears in the formula bar. Delete it and type in "Piston Rings Force Test" for the new title and choose the Enter box.

Piston Rings Force Test

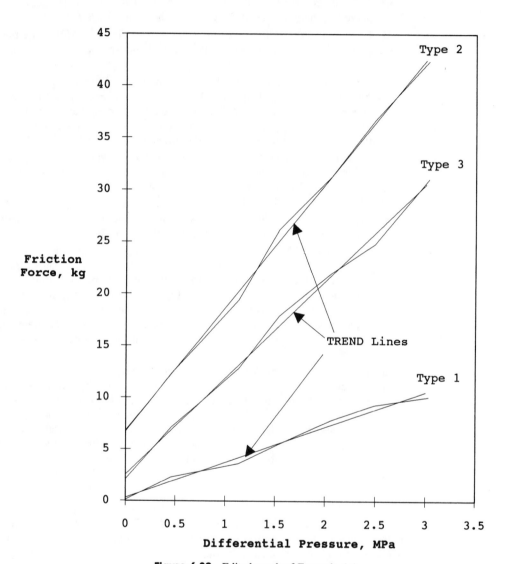

Figure 6.32   Edited graph of Example 6.6.

2. Repeat step 1 for the **Value Axis** button, but type in "Friction Force, kg", and for the **Category Axis** button, type in "Differential Pressure, MPa".

3. Add the type of piston force test as unattached text to the curves. Do this by first making sure that no text is selected, type the text to be added, say "Type 2", then choose the Enter box. The text will appear in the middle of the

chart. It must be moved to its desired location with the **Format Move** command (keyboard) or by dragging it (mouse) to the desired location.

4. Repeat step 3 for the curves to be labeled "Type 3" and "Type 1".

5. Add the trend lines to the chart. First, activate the worksheet containing the data (Figure 6.25), select the data (B9 : E10), and execute **Edit Copy**. Now, activate the chart, execute **Edit Paste Special**, toggle the **Values in Columns** button and the **Series Names in First Column** text box on, then choose **OK**. The trend lines are now added to the curve as shown in Figure 6.32.

6. Add "TREND Lines" as unattached text and position it such that arrows can be added from it to each of the three trend lines.

7. Execute the **Chart Add Arrow** command to place an arrow on the chart. Reposition it so that its head touches a trend line and its tail is near the "TREND Lines" text. Repeat this step for each arrow as shown in Figure 6.32.

8. Turn off the curve markers by first selecting any curve, executing the **Format Patterns** command, setting the **Marker** button to **Invisible**, setting the **Apply to All** text box on, then choosing **OK**. Markers for all curves will now be invisible.

9. Set each curve to be black and of the default line style and weight by first selecting any curve, executing the **Format Patterns** command, setting **Line Color** to black, setting the **Apply to All** text box on, then choosing **OK**. All curves now look alike as shown in Figure 6.32.

10. Place a border around the plot area by first executing **Chart Select Plot Area**, setting the **Border Color** to black, accepting the default solid line **Style**, selecting the heaviest line **Weight**, then choosing **OK**.

11. If we had the print capability, we could set the text fonts as follows. Execute **Chart Select Chart**, execute **Format Font** [see Figure 6.29(b)], set **Font** to Helvetica, **Size** to 10 points, and choose **OK**. This would set all chart characteristics to the same font. Then, we could select the title, execute **Format Font**, set **Font** to Helvetica, **Size** to 24 points, and choose **OK**. And we could select, individually, the axes labels, execute **Format Font**, set **Font** to Helvetica, **Size** to 14, **Style** to Bold, and choose **OK**.

All conditions for the graph to look like Figure 6.32 have now been set. Unfortunately, the display does not look like the printed copy because we do not have a "what you see is what you get" (wysiwyg) presentation on the screen. For the moment, let's believe that the customization is what we want and go on to the next section to learn how to visually verify the graph before printing it.

6.5 PRINTING GRAPHS

The procedure for printing graphs does not differ much from that for printing worksheets as we discussed in Section 2.4. We must set up the printer and the page, and then issue the print command. Figure 6.33(a) is the **File** menu, which is

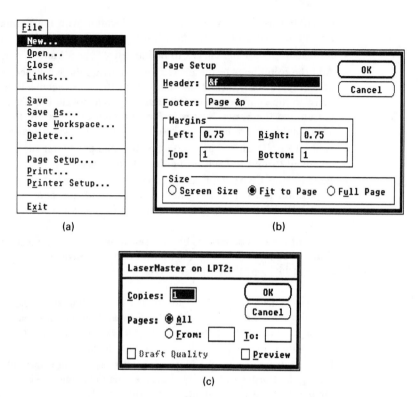

Figure 6.33 (a) File drop-down menu and the dialog boxes for the (b) Page Setup and (c) Print commands for charts.

the same for charts as for worksheets. The **Printer Setup** command leads to the same dialog boxes as shown in Figures 2.10(b) and 2.10(c). Their discussion is not repeated here.

The **Page Setup** command of Figure 6.33(a) leads to the dialog box of Figure 6.33(b). It differs from the dialog box for worksheets by offering the **Size** button choices at the bottom of the box instead of having the headings and gridlines check boxes. **Screen Size** means to print the chart the same size as displayed on the screen, **Fit to Page** adjusts the size according to the limiting dimension of the sheet but keeps the aspect ratio the same (Figure 6.31 was printed in this manner), while **Full Page** causes both chart dimensions to be adjusted to fill the sheet regardless of the aspect ratio (Figure 6.32 was printed in this manner).

The **Print** command of Figure 6.33(a) leads to the dialog box of Figure 6.33(c). It differs from the dialog box for worksheets by not having the **Print Sheet**, **Notes**, or **Both** buttons. They are not needed for a chart, of course. We can preview the printed chart by toggling on the **Preview** text box in the same manner as for a worksheet. The discussion of this feature is found in Section 2.4. It is useful for displaying a chart prior to printing it. We used it with the chart of

Figure 6.32 because we had unattached text and printed the graph with the **Size Full Page** button. Some realignment of graph features was inevitable because of the aspect readjustment and because our screen did not present a "what you see is what you get" view. What appeared to be severe text scaling problems on the screen while developing the figure for Example 6.6 really turned out to be a nice-looking graph. Several iterations between adjustment of the graph in the chart window and viewing it in preview mode were required for that example before printing took place.

6.6 ABOUT VERSION 3.0

All worksheets and charts of this chapter run under version 3.0 without change. New capability is described in the sections that follow. First, we will discuss the new features that directly affect the material of this chapter.

At the beginning of this chapter we had a difficult time displaying a scatter chart because the default chart values did not directly display one and the procedures to follow were not intuitively satisfying. Although we could set up a more appropriate preferred default chart, we usually are more interested in performing actions that produce engineering results than in setting up software to run more conveniently. Occasional computer users seldom care about software flexibility for custom setups. However awkward the Excel chart system was to use, some enhancements have simplified our job.

Even Excel appeared confused about the type of chart to display when the selected data suggested that alternative chart types were possible. Now, in version 3.0, it asks for user help in deciding the issue via dialog box response. We are merely providing guidance for Exel to follow the paths of Figures 6.14 and 6.15. Whenever the selected data presents ambiguity of interpretation for display, the dialog box of Figure 6.34 is displayed. The data of Figure 6.9 causes it to be displayed after we execute the **File New Chart** command from the worksheet. By choosing the **X-Values for XY-chart** button followed by **OK**, we will get a scatter chart. A graph similar to the embedded one of Figure 6.41 will be displayed in a chart window, which is the first choice from the **Gallery Scatter** display. When this chart is compared with the one of Figure 6.19 we see that only the ordinate range is different.

We can now format and move single data points. To format the marker, first select it (press CTRL, then single click), then execute the **Format Patterns** command, or go directly to the **Format Patterns** dialog box by pressing CTRL and

Figure 6.34 Chart data interpretation dialog box.

double-clicking the marker. We can also move a single marker. Make sure the worksheet of data is open, select the marker (press CTRL, then single click), and then click on it and drag it to its new location, which will be an ordinate change only. The cell value for that marker will be changed on the worksheet to its newly determined value. However, if the marker being moved was computed in the worksheet by a formula, Excel will activate the worksheet and invoke the **Formula Goal Seek** command discussed in Section 3.6.1 to compute the corresponding independent variable value. The user is prompted by the dialog box of Figure 3.18(b) to make the **By changing cell** box entry for this purpose.

The least squares curve fitting functions we discussed in Section 6.3.4 and presented in Table 6.1 now each have additional optional arguments. The new third argument for LINEST and LOGEST and the new fourth argument for TREND and GROWTH is a logical value that when TRUE, or omitted, causes calculation to proceed according to the formulas of Section 6.3.4 and when FALSE, to calculate the linear best fit with $b = 0$ and the exponential best fit with $b = 1$. The new fourth argument for LINEST and LOGEST is a logical value that when TRUE causes additional regression statistics to be returned (standard error values for the coefficients and constant; coefficient of determination; standard error for y estimate; F statistic; degrees of freedom; regression sum of squares; and residual sum of squares) and when FALSE, or omitted, suppresses return of these statistics.

Numerous menus and dialog boxes in this chapter have been changed slightly. Some changes to note are:

1. The **Format Font** dialog box of Figure 6.29(b) now includes a **Sample** box that shows characters chosen from the **Font** list box.
2. The **Format Text** dialog box of Figure 6.29(c) now contains text orientation check boxes.
3. The **Format Patterns** command produces context sensitive dialog boxes that are completely different from those of Figure 6.30. The replacement ones of Figure 6.35 are displayed when the axis, curve, and title are selected.
4. The **Chart Edit Series** command is new and provided for the convenience of those who add, delete, or change data series.
5. The **Chart Color Palette** command is new and provided for the convenience of those who customize the colors of their chart window.

6.6.1 The 3-D Chart

A limited three-dimensional display capability is included in version 3.0. Only four chart types are available (area, column, line, and pie) and only one axis can be numerically continuously variable (the value axis). Figure 6.36 shows the axes designation for the 3-D charts and the positive angular designations of the view-

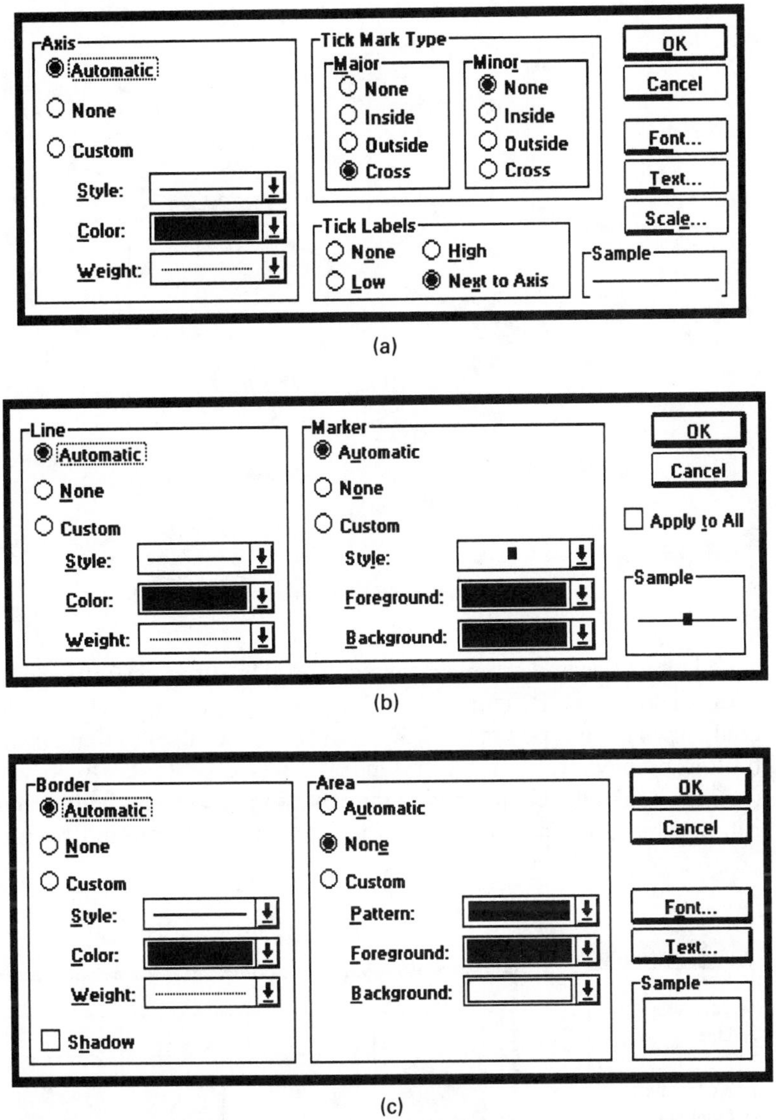

(a)

(b)

(c)

Figure 6.35   Chart Format Patterns dialog boxes for (a) axis, (b) curve, and (c) title selections.

point relative to the axes. The 3-D chart gallery choices are shown in Figure 6.37. We cannot plot a scatter chart in 3-D form.

To plot a 3-D chart, we must have a table arranged with a category axis (x-axis) and a data series axis (y-axis), and have values within the table (z-axis). The worksheet of Figure 6.38(a) will produce the chart of Figure 6.38(b). We

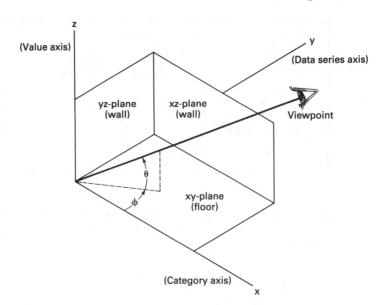

Figure 6.36 3-D chart axes designation.

added axis titles and arranged the viewpoint location via entries of the **Format 3-D View** dialog box of Figure 6.39. Angle θ of Figure 6.36 was set to $+25°$ (which could have been typed in the **Elevation** box or scrolled to that angle with the arrow buttons immediately above this box), angle ϕ of Figure 6.36 was set to $-140°$ (which could have been typed in the **Rotation** box or scrolled to that angle with the rotation buttons immediately to the right of this box), and the perspective ratio

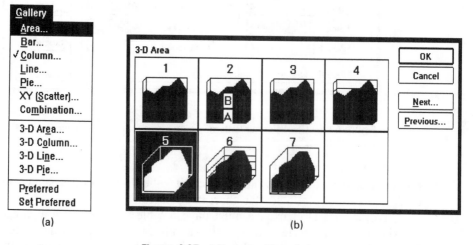

(a)   (b)

Figure 6.37 3-D chart gallery choices.

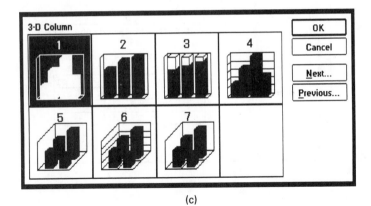

(c)

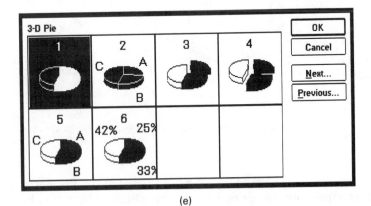

(d)

(e)

Figure 6.37 Continued

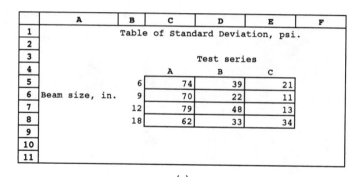

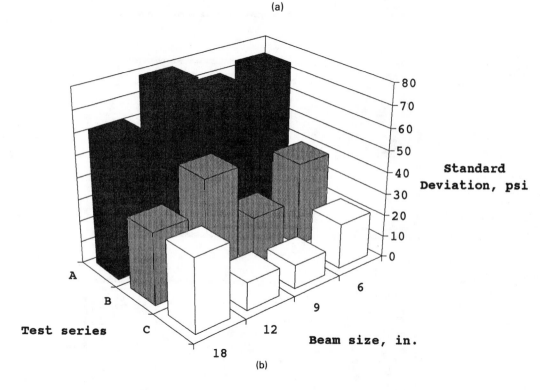

Figure 6.38 (a) Worksheet data and (b) its 3-D column chart.

was set to 30 (which could have been typed in the **Perspective** box or scrolled to that value with the arrow buttons immediately above that box). When the **Right Angle Axes** check box is on, the perspective effect is turned off. The **Height** percentage factor controls the ratio of the z-axis wall height to the x-axis length. The 100% value means that they are equal in length.

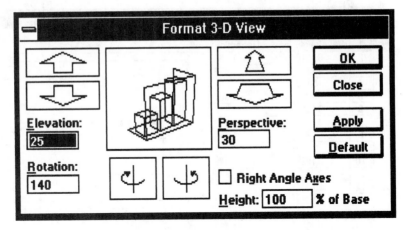

Figure 6.39 Format 3-D View dialog box.

6.6.2 The Tool Bar

In this section we comment on the tool bar buttons labeled in Figure 6.40. They are all related to charts or graphic objects.

1. The *Chart tool* button of Figure 6.40 is used to embed a new chart on the worksheet or macro sheet. The chart is formed from the data selected on the corresponding document. Figure 6.41 was formed with this feature. The procedure for creating an embedded chart is as follows:

1. Select the data to be charted, including the column or row labels, in the same manner as for a chart window.
2. Click the *Chart tool* button. The cursor changes to a cross-hair symbol for drawing a rectangular box.

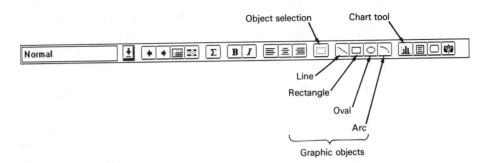

Figure 6.40 Excel tool bar.

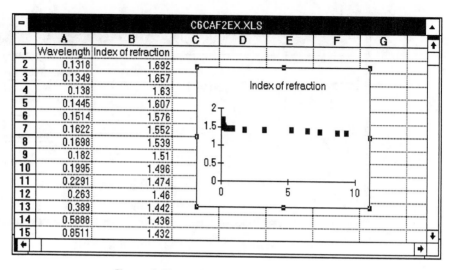

Figure 6.41 Worksheet with embedded chart.

3. Position the cross-hair cursor to the location for one corner of the embedded chart's box outline. Press the mouse button and drag it to shape and size the ensuing box, which will become the chart rectangle. Pressing SHIFT during this operation will generate a square box; pressing CTRL will align the box to the cell grid. When the mouse button is released, the chart is displayed within the rectangle in the preferred format and remains selected. If necessary, Excel will display the dialog box of Figure 6.34 for a response to help choose the chart format.

Figure 6.41 is a screen copy of the embedded chart. The black squares, or handles, surrounding the rectangle indicate that it is selected. Now, it can be sized by dragging a handle on the side or corner while observing the dotted outline of its new dimensions. Pressing SHIFT while dragging a corner handle will keep the rectangle proportioned; pressing CTRL while dragging will align the rectangle to the cell grid. The rectangle can be moved to a new location by dragging it there after first clicking on its border with an arrow cursor. If not already selected, it becomes selected upon doing this. The following are characteristics of an embedded chart:

1. The embedded chart will be updated whenever the worksheet data is updated.

2. An embedded chart can be edited upon opening it in its own window. It is opened by double clicking it and edited as if it were a separate document, as we discussed earlier in this chapter. For this purpose, the worksheet menu bar changes to a chart menu bar.

3. The embedded chart, upon being opened in its own window, can be saved as

a separate document. If it is closed without being saved, the embedded chart and all changes made to it will be closed with the worksheet.

4. An embedded chart can be removed from the worksheet after clicking on it (to select it) and executing the **Edit Clear** command, or by pressing the BACKSPACE or DELETE key.

   2. The *Line, Rectangle, Oval, Arc,* and *Object selection* buttons of Figure 6.40 are used to create and work with graphic objects for supplementing the worksheet or macro sheet information. The objects may be used as documentation aids, as custom buttons for starting macros, as a picture chart marker, or as otherwise desired by the user. It is not intended to be a general purpose engineering graphics system and would not serve that purpose well. Therefore, we will not further discuss this feature.

PROBLEMS

6.1 Plot the following spreadsheet data of temperature profiles as (a) a vertical bar chart, (b) a horizontal bar chart, (c) a line graph, and (d) an area chart.

	Profile		
Section	A	B	C
1	420	400	175
2	550	560	180
3	605	700	200
4	685	780	500
5	730	820	725
6	790	830	830
7	815	825	830
8	820	810	830

6.2 Plot the following vent experimental data as a linear-linear scatter chart.

	Vent flow rate (cfm)		
Wind speed (mph)	Design A	Design B	Design C
0	0	0	0
10	280	370	590
20	540	710	1060
25	675	800	1210
30	805	1100	1615
35	1050	1300	1750
40	1100	1405	2030
45	1150	1380	2000

6.3 Experimental induction heater data for two steel specimens are given below. Plot these data as a semi-logarithmic graph with frequency, the abscissa, as the logarithmic axis.

Frequency (kHz)	Heat penetration (mils)	
	Sample A	Sample B
20	100	48
80	50	22
300	27	12
1000	16	6
5000	5.5	2.8

6.4 The evolution of a company's product shows power consumption per product decreasing according to the following average data. Plot these data as a semi-logarithmic graph with power, the ordinate, as the logarithmic axis.

Year	Avg. Power (watts)
1960	243
1967	112
1975	36
1981	12
1988	4.6
2000	1.7 (est)

6.5 Plot the following experimental data of battery cell discharge time at 20°C as a log-log graph.

Time (hrs)	Discharge current (Amps)		
	5 AH	15 AH	30 AH
.02	40		
.05		60	
.1	12		98
.3	5	15	48
1	1.9	5.6	18.5
3	.76	2.2	7.8
10	.24	.83	2.6
30	.11	.32	1.05
50		.18	.56
100			.28

6.6 Using the spreadsheet data generation capability, compute a table of data to plot for the serpentine equation given as

$$y = \frac{b^2 x}{a^2 + x^2}$$

Let $a = 3$, $b = 6$, and $-15 \leq x \leq 15$. Plot the curve as a scatter chart.

6.7 Repeat Problem 6.6 for the epitrochoid given by the parametric equations

$$\left. \begin{array}{l} x = m \cos t - h \cos\frac{m}{b} t \\[2mm] y = m \sin t - h \sin\frac{m}{b} t \end{array} \right\} \quad -\pi \leq t \leq \pi$$

where (x,y) defines a point on the curve. Vary t throughout the range given and let $m = 18$, $b = 2$, and $h = 5$. Plot the curve as a scatter chart.

6.8 Given the table of experimental data below, compute the least squares linear equation to fit the data. Plot the experimental data and the linear equation.

Offset, in.	Strength, k-lbs/sq in.
.602	0.1
.567	0.1
.611	0.1
.587	0.3
.553	0.9
.498	1.8
.560	1.8
.471	3.2
.525	4.5
.496	6.5
.430	8.2
.399	10.9
.441	4.9
.466	5.6
.557	3.9
.583	1.2
.586	0.6
.549	3.5
.537	0.0
.541	4.7
.480	6.8
.357	10.5

6.9 Creep-strength test data of a material under temperature are given below. Compute the least squares nonlinear equation to fit the data (stress as a function of temperature). Plot the experimental data and the nonlinear equation.

Temperature, °F	Stress, lb/sq in.
980	6560
1040	4820
1180	1470
1250	900
1400	280

6.10 Display the data of Problem 6.1 as a line chart. Use the spreadsheet formatting capability to experiment with the title, axes labeling, axes value number formatting, marker display, and line texture. Experiment with the formatting for display and line printer output.

6.11 Repeat Problem 6.10 for the display of Problem 6.2.

6.12 Repeat Problem 6.10 for the display of Problem 6.3.

6.13 Repeat Problem 6.10 for the display of Problem 6.4.

6.14 Repeat Problem 6.10 for the display of Problem 6.5.

6.15 Display the data of Problem 6.2 as a multiple curve line graph. Use the spreadsheet formatting capability to add free text, arrows, and a legend. Experiment with the formatting for display and line printer output.

CHAPTER 7

Function Macros

Spreadsheet program users should be grateful that various built-in functions are provided for them. However, for numerous reasons, some desired functions will not be available, so users must develop their own workarounds in the worksheet to achieve the enhanced capability. We are about to discover that the macro feature will enable us to conveniently develop custom functions. Until now, we became aware of limitations of spreadsheet programs, in our case with Excel, that caused us much grief when developing an algorithm for the worksheet. For example, we found that structures for conditional branching limited our ability to develop complex worksheets, and the iteration feature applied only to a narrow class of looping constructs. The Excel macro feature overcomes some of these limitations so that now we can produce logical and control structures within macros that are somewhat comparable to those of conventional computer programming languages. Thus, our ability to use the spreadsheet program will be greatly enhanced through use of the macro feature.

In this chapter, we describe the concept of a custom function macro, introduce its structure, and describe its use. We also describe new decision and looping features, available only within a macro in Excel, and expand our use of arrays. Debugging procedures unique to macros are also introduced.

7.1 THE CONCEPT OF A MACRO

Situations arise in which it would be convenient if certain worksheet statements were collected together and defined in a manner such that they could be referenced as a group via a symbolic name. The idea is that the group of statements be written once, assigned a symbolic name and, thereafter, be referred to as a group by name wherever required in the worksheet. This implies that certain statement sequences occur often in the worksheet, either identically or with great similarity, or, as we will see, for various other important reasons. The feature that permits the above to be realized is known as a *macro*.

Macro is the term used for a group of statements that have been combined according to established rules in such a way that they may be collectively referenced by name. The macro is thus a worksheet module, now called a *macro sheet module,* which possesses the characteristic for independently defining a segment of worksheet statements. This concept is used in many programming languages. In Excel we have the following types of macros:

Command macro

This macro is composed of commands that collectively perform the equivalent of a custom command. This assemblage of commands must be assigned a name and sequenced to carry out the desired action. It is invoked by its name and is called a command macro because of its resemblance to the built-in Excel commands. A command macro might construct a particular type of graph from selected cells and format it in a special way.

Function macro

This macro is composed of statements that collectively perform the equivalent of a custom function. This assemblage of commands must be assigned a name, sequenced to carry out the desired calculations, and return a value. It is invoked in the same manner as the built-in worksheet functions of Excel, hence its name function macro. A function macro might be written to integrate according to Simpson's rule a function represented by an array of values.

Subroutine macro

This is a macro that is started by another macro. It can be either a command macro or a function macro. Its name, followed by a pair of parentheses within which may appear a list of arguments, must appear as a reference (location of a cell or a group of cells) in the starting macro. A complex worksheet solution typically starts a macro, called a control macro, that starts a series of hierarchically arranged subroutines to perform the task.

Use of a macro in a worksheet solution is suggested by the following situations:

1. Sequences of identical, or quite similar, statements are executed more than once at separate places in the worksheet program. A macro could replace these sequences of statements.

2. A sequence of similar statements is required in different worksheets and

would normally be separately prepared for each worksheet. A macro could be used with more than one worksheet.

3. A worksheet program is so complex and extensive that it would be advantageous to partition it into logical sections for individual preparation and checkout, perhaps even by different persons. Several macros could be prepared individually, then combined to form the program.

A macro is developed in a macro sheet, which is first opened via the **File New Macro** worksheet command dialog box. Thereafter, it is opened by name via the **File Open** command dialog box. This sheet is then the active sheet within which the macro is developed in a manner analogous to that of a worksheet. Within the confines of the Excel program, we now can work with the worksheet, chart window, macro sheet, or any combination of these work spaces as our problem requires.

The worksheet program and macros can be hierarchically structured in a variety of ways, depending on the needs of the problem and the scope of the macros. Some possible structural organizations are shown in skeleton form in Figure 7.1. We may have multiple macros on one macro sheet, and not necessarily use all of them in our problem, and we may have multiple macro sheets open and in use with one worksheet problem. Our collection of macro sheets and multiple macros per sheet constitutes our "library."

The structures of Figure 7.1 are drawn such that sequential execution through the worksheet is implied. We know that Excel calculates worksheets on a dependency basis and that sequential execution may not occur. However, the macros are executed sequentially. Consequently, we take advantage of this fact to organize the macro statements according to the algorithm to be programmed. We must be constantly aware of this dual execution paradigm to avoid unnecessarily complicating the development and debugging effort through oversight. The sequential execution connotes control flow rather than the data flow we are now used to in worksheet development. This means we can follow the principles of program development, such as we apply to computer programming languages.

Figure 7.1 shows that macros can be used a multiple number of times with the same worksheet, one macro may invoke the execution of another (the subroutine macro defined above), and multiple macros can be used by a single macro.

Basic principles of using macros require that the macro sheets be opened along with the worksheet using them. This is no different than requiring a worksheet to be open in order to construct a graph of its data. Because macros may be buried deep within the program's organizational structure, it is easy to overlook some of them before beginning worksheet execution. Consequently, an organized approach to developing the solution with macros is needed. We discuss this effort also as macro development procedures are introduced.

In Chapter 3, we learned that many built-in functions are available in Excel. We now find that many built-in macro functions are also available for our use. We will introduce many of them as our development of the material progresses.

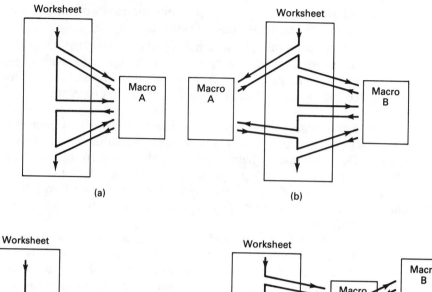

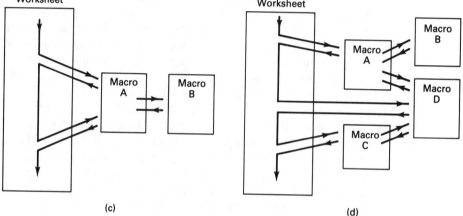

Figure 7.1   Skeleton worksheet and macro structures. Irvin H. Kral, *Numerical Control Programming In APT*, © 1986, p. 329. Reprinted by permission of Prentice Hall, Inc., Englewood Cliffs, New Jersey.

However, since there are so many of these functions, some of which perform equivalent actions, it remains for the user to become acquainted with them and use those most appropriate for the application.

7.2 DEFINITION AND USE OF SIMPLE MACROS

The function macro was defined in Section 7.1. It is used for calculation purposes and fits in well with engineering applications of the spreadsheet program. In this section, we will learn to prepare and use simple function macros. We arbitrarily define a *simple macro* as being one with a single computational path, that is, no branching or looping, and passing few values into and out of the macro.

7.2.1 Structure of the Macro

The structure of a function macro is shown in Figure 7.2. The required parts of a function macro are its name, the formulas, and the RETURN function. Optional parts are the ARGUMENT and RESULT functions. The name assigned to the function is the first statement of the function and is constructed in the same manner as names for cells, as we first learned in Chapter 3. The name must be by itself on a separate line.

Values passed to the macro require an ARGUMENT function for each value, now called an *argument*. The macro is executed in statement order within the column as written in the macro. This is in contrast to calculation of a worksheet, where formulas are calculated according to a dependency relationship regardless of which column they are in (see Dependents, Precedents, and Calculation Order Box on page 166). Therefore, sequencing of macro statements must be predetermined to compute the desired values. As we will see, sequencing allows the representation of procedural algorithms. Output from the macro is via the RETURN function. A sample macro is shown in Figure 7.3. The major parts of the macro are easily identified in column A (its name in row 1, arguments in rows 2 through 6, formulas in rows 7, 8, and 9, and the RETURN function in row 10). Column B contains comments.

We now discuss the macro functions mentioned above.

Argument.   The format of the first form of this function is:

ARGUMENT(*name* [,*type-code*])

where

name = name assigned to the argument value being brought into the macro.

type-code = data type of *name* (default is number, text, or logical).

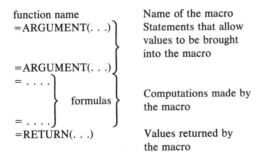

Figure 7.2   Structure of a macro.

	A	B
1	Shield.Cov	Braided shield coverage
2	=ARGUMENT("OD")	OD under shield, inches
3	=ARGUMENT("Strand.Dia")	Dia of one strand, inches
4	=ARGUMENT("Picks")	Picks per inch
5	=ARGUMENT("Carriers")	Number of carriers
6	=ARGUMENT("Ends")	No. ends per carrier
7	=ATAN(2*PI()*(OD+2*Strand.Dia)*Picks/Carriers)	Braid angle
8	=Ends*Picks*Strand.Dia/SIN(A7)	Intermediate value
9	=(2*A8-A8^2)*100	Shield coverage,%
10	=RETURN(A9)	

Figure 7.3 Sample Excel macro.

Punctuation shown is required. This function is required only if arguments are to be passed to the macro. One argument function is required for each argument. There is a one-to-one correspondence between the left-to-right ordering of arguments in the macro call argument list and the top-to-bottom ordering of the ARGUMENT functions in the macro. Excel allows up to 13 arguments. *Type-code* is used for specifying the data type of *name* according to the code shown in Table 7.1. Some combining of types is possible by adding type codes, but reference and array type-codes may not be combined. The type-code for the default value is 7, the sum of number, text, and logical.

The format of the second form of this function is

$$\text{ARGUMENT}([name][,[type\text{-}code][,cell\text{-}ref]])$$

where

name = the name given to the cell entered as *cell-ref*.

type-code = data type of *name* (default is number, text, or logical).

cell-ref = the cell on the macro sheet into which the argument value is to be placed.

Punctuation shown is required. Because all entries of this function are optional and position dependent, omitted entries must be indicated with consecutive commas. This form of the function differs from the first form by the presence of

TABLE 7.1 TYPE-CODE
INTERPRETATION

Type-code	Value type
1	number
2	text
4	logical
8	reference
16	error
64	array

cell-ref, which also changes the meaning of *name.* In Excel, this happens to be one of only two ways to name cells in a macro.

Return.   The format of this function is

$$RETURN([value])$$

where *value* is the reference of the value being returned via the name of the function. It can be a cell name (see the second form of the ARGUMENT function above), *name* as given in the first form of the ARGUMENT function, a constant, text, or logical value, or a cell coordinate reference. This function is used to end the macro and return control to the worksheet or macro that called it and, if required, to return a value.

Result.   The format of this command is:

$$RESULT(type\text{-}code)$$

where *type-code* is given a value as shown in Table 7.1. This is an optional function that is used to specify the data type of the function's return value. When omitted, the default value for the data type is number, text, or logical (*type-code* = 7).

7.2.2 Writing the Macro

In the preceding section, we introduced the types of statements needed to construct a simple macro. We now describe a problem for which we will assemble a macro.

The formulas of this example compute the shielding percentage coverage of metal braid over an insulated conductor. Braids are formed by weaving carriers composed of fine strands of wire, called ends, over the insulation (Figure 7.4). As the cable is pulled through the braiding machine, the carriers are interlaced at an angle called the braid angle. Several carriers are used at one time and, because of

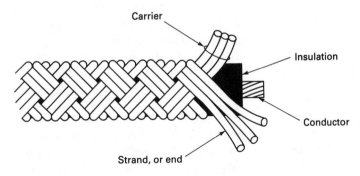

Figure 7.4   Shielded cable for the example of Section 7.2.2.

the angle, are weaved at a linear density along the cable called picks per unit distance.

The formulas for calculating the shielding percentage coverage are

$$\tan \alpha = \frac{2\pi(D + 2d)P}{c}$$

$$F = \frac{NPd}{\sin \alpha}$$

$$K = 100(2F - F^2)$$

where

D = outside diameter of insulation under shield, in

d = diameter of carrier end (one strand), in

P = picks per inch

c = number of carriers

α = braid angle

N = ends per carrier

K = percentage of coverage

The percentage coverage is affected by the number of carriers, the number of ends per carrier, the diameter of the end, and the picks per inch. Audio frequency cables have a coverage of 75% to 85%, while cables for high-frequency applications usually require coverage from 85% to 95% to reduce interference.

We will pass several values to the macro but return only one value, the percentage coverage. The basic macro structure is shown in Figure 7.2. For our example, the figure shows everything we need to include in our macro except our formulas. Remembering that the statements of the macro are executed sequentially, all we need do is establish the sequence of calculation. From the description of the problem, it is obvious that we should first compute the angle α, then the intermediate value F, and then the percentage coverage K. We will need to use the worksheet pi, sin, and arctangent functions.

We must first open a new macro sheet. We execute **File New,** then select **Macro Sheet** in the resulting dialog box, then choose **OK** [Figures 2.5(a) and (b)]. A blank macro sheet fills the screen. Once we develop our macro and save it (default file extension is .XLM), we access it thereafter with the **File Open** command, select the desired macro sheet name from the list of files shown in the resulting dialog box, then choose **OK** [Figures 2.5(a) and (c)].

The procedure for entering statements into a macro sheet is nearly identical to that for preparing a worksheet. We first select a cell, then type its contents in the formula bar. Assuming we have planned our macro thoroughly, we continue in this manner until the macro is complete. Because our example macro is so simple, we will enter the statements in column A and we will place comments in column B.

In cell A1, we enter the name of the macro, Shield.Cov (Figure 7.3). From the formulas, we see that values for the variables D, d, P, c, and N must be passed to the macro. So, we enter five ARGUMENT functions into the macro (cells A2 through A6). We use the first form of the function and make up names that convey their purpose in the formulas. The names, which are text, must be enclosed in quotation marks, otherwise Excel believes them to be cell names. Because ARGUMENT is a macro function, we must first enter the equal sign into the cell.

We now enter the formulas, again beginning each of them with an equal sign as we did in the worksheet. The three formulas are entered in cells A7, A8, and A9. They will be executed sequentially. We used the argument names, constants, the worksheet functions PI, SIN, and ATAN, and cell coordinate references. Finally, in cell A10, we enter the RETURN function, with cell A9 as its argument, since that cell will contain the percentage coverage. We have just finished entering the macro as it looks in Figure 7.3.

On the screen we see formulas in the cells instead of values as when we make entries in worksheets. This is because the default display mode for macro sheets is to show formulas. We can show values by executing the **Option Display** command, toggling the **Formulas** box off, then choosing **OK.**

When writing function macros, one makes various decisions that affect its use, such as the order in which arguments must be passed to the macro, the data type of the arguments and return values, and implementing, or excluding, special cases in the formulas. Such facts are readily identified in simple macros, but we must document complex ones more thoroughly. Short comments are included in column B of our example and these should be sufficient. Later, when we include complex control structures, we will have to resort to various techniques for documenting our work. Remember that development of a macro requires careful planning to avoid rework, incorrect results, and various errors. Layout of the macro is also important. Planning and organizing cannot be over-emphasized. We are now ready to use our macro.

7.2.3 Using the Macro

Above, we prepared a function macro that we will now use. Since function macros are used in Excel as any ordinary worksheet function, all we must now do is write a worksheet program that uses it. For the moment, we will make just one calculation with the macro to illustrate its use. Our macro computes the percent coverage of a braid over an insulated conductor or cable.

We must construct a formula that uses our macro. This means that we must also determine the numerical values for the arguments. Since the worksheet normally displays values, we should be able to see the result directly if we use just the macro in a formula, since the macro's return value is what we are after. For one solution, Figure 7.5 shows the results and Figure 7.6 the formulas. In both figures, part (a) is the worksheet program and part (b) is the macro.

A worksheet program using a built-in function refers to the function by its name followed by a set of parentheses within which, optionally, may appear arguments. The function macro reference differs from the worksheet function reference in that the function macro name must be preceded by the name of the macro sheet on which the function macro appears followed by an exclamation mark. This applies only if the macro sheet is open, otherwise the complete path name to the macro must be included. Its general format is as follows:

$$macro\text{-}sheet!macro\text{-}name(arg_1, arg_2, ..., arg_k)$$

where

$macro\text{-}name$ = the name of the macro

$macro\text{-}sheet$ = the name of the macro sheet in which $macro\text{-}name$ is stored

arg_i = the argument values to be passed to the macro

The exclamation mark and the parentheses are required. Arguments, if any, must be delimited by commas. The arguments must be placed in order from left to right according to the ordering of the corresponding ARGUMENT statements of the macro. For our example, we defined the names in rows 2 through 6 of column A of Figure 7.5(a) with the **Formula Create Names** command in order to name the corresponding cells in column B. We then used them as arguments to the macro in row 7 of Figure 7.6(a) in the order of the ARGUMENT functions in rows 2 through 6 of Figure 7.6(b).

The macro name can be conveniently inserted via the **Formula Paste Function** command. User-defined function macros for all open macro sheets are placed at the end of the list of functions in the dialog box. One merely scrolls to the end of the list, selects the desired macro, then chooses **OK**. Since one is

	A	B
1		Braided Shield Coverage
2	OD	0.375
3	StrD	0.0075
4	Picks	15
5	Carriers	16
6	N	6
7	Coverage,%	93.03978789

(a)

	A	B
1	Shield.Cov	Braided shield coverage
2	TRUE	OD under shield, inches
3	TRUE	Dia of one strand, inches
4	TRUE	Picks per inch
5	TRUE	Number of carriers
6	TRUE	No. ends per carrier
7	1.160237657	Braid angle
8	0.736177861	Intermediate value
9	93.03978789	Shield coverage,%
10	TRUE	

(b)

Figure 7.5   Shielded cable example in values mode where (a) is the worksheet and (b) is the macro.

	A	B
1		Braided Shield Coverage
2	OD	0.375
3	StrD	0.0075
4	Picks	15
5	Carriers	16
6	N	6
7	Coverage,%	='C7P2EXA.XLM'!Shield.Cov(OD,StrD,Picks,Carriers,N)

(a)

	A	B
1	Shield.Cov	Braided shield coverage
2	=ARGUMENT("OD")	OD under shield, inches
3	=ARGUMENT("Strand.Dia")	Dia of one strand, inches
4	=ARGUMENT("Picks")	Picks per inch
5	=ARGUMENT("Carriers")	Number of carriers
6	=ARGUMENT("Ends")	No. ends per carrier
7	=ATAN(2*PI()*(OD+2*Strand.Dia)*Picks/Carriers)	Braid angle
8	=Ends*Picks*Strand.Dia/SIN(A7)	Intermediate value
9	=(2*A8-A8^2)*100	Shield coverage,%
10	=RETURN(A9)	

(b)

Figure 7.6 Shielded cable example in formulas mode where (a) is the worksheet and (b) is the macro.

working in the formula bar while doing this, it is then conveniently accessible for insertion of the arguments.

With the function macro completed, its macro sheet open, and the worksheet program complete, Excel makes the calculations and displays the results. We see our solution in cell B7 of Figure 7.5(a), the value being about 93.04%. Both the worksheet and the macro have two display modes; values and formulas. Figures 7.5 and 7.6 show them both for our example.

Alternate ways for passing arguments are shown in Figure 7.7, where only the worksheet program is shown. We entered some numerical values directly as arguments. For one use of the function, row 9 of Figure 7.7(b), we substituted some numerical values for the variables in the argument list of the macro named Shield.Cov, while in another, row 11, we shortened the argument list to correspond with a rewritten macro named Shield.Cov1 shown in rows 12 through 18 of Figure 7.8. In the latter case, we were able to use the arguments from macro Shield.Cov because the two macros are on the same macro sheet. Since Shield.-Cov was used first, its arguments still have values from the first two references to it and are available to Shield.Cov1 because the same argument names are used in that macro. The argument names are available throughout the macro sheet. We do not recommend sharing arguments in this manner, since it makes the macro calls order dependent and since it is subject to errors through modification of the macros.

	A	B
1		Braided Shield Coverage
2	OD	0.375
3	StrD	0.0075
4	Picks	15
5	Carriers	16
6	N	6
7	Coverage,%	93.03978789
8		Use same macro, insert constants for arguments.
9	Coverage,%	93.03978789
10		Modify macro, use global variables.
11	Coverage,%	93.03978789

(a)

	A	B
1		Braided Shield Coverage
2	OD	0.375
3	StrD	0.0075
4	Picks	15
5	Carriers	16
6	N	6
7	Coverage,%	='C7P2EXB.XLM'!Shield.Cov(OD,StrD,Picks,Carriers,N)
8		Use same macro, insert constants for arguments.
9	Coverage,%	='C7P2EXB.XLM'!Shield.Cov(OD,StrD,15,16,6)
10		Modify macro, use global variables.
11	Coverage,%	='C7P2EXB.XLM'!Shield.Cov1(StrD,N)

(b)

Figure 7.7 Worksheet program for the shielded cable example showing alternate ways for passing arguments to the macro. (a) Values mode and (b) formulas mode.

	A	B	C
1		Shield.Cov	Braided shield coverage
2		=ARGUMENT("OD")	OD under shield, inches
3		=ARGUMENT("Strand.Dia")	Dia of one strand, inches
4		=ARGUMENT("Picks")	Picks per inch
5		=ARGUMENT("Carriers")	Number of carriers
6		=ARGUMENT("Ends")	No. ends per carrier
7		=ATAN(2*PI()*(OD+2*Strand.Dia)*Picks/Carriers)	Braid angle
8		=Ends*Picks*Strand.Dia/SIN(B7)	Intermediate value
9		=(2*B8-B8^2)*100	Shield coverage,%
10		=RETURN(B9)	
11		Modify Shield.Cov macro for global variables.	
12		Shield.Cov1	Braided shield coverage
13		=ARGUMENT("Strand.Dia")	Dia of one strand, inches
14		=ARGUMENT("Ends")	No. ends per carrier
15	Alpha	=ATAN(2*PI()*(OD+2*Strand.Dia)*Picks/Carriers)	Braid angle
16	F	=Ends*Picks*Strand.Dia/SIN(Alpha)	Intermediate value
17	Coverage	=(2*F-F^2)*100	Shield coverage,%
18		=RETURN(Coverage)	

Figure 7.8 Shielded cable macros used by the worksheet of Figure 7.7.

7.2.4 Variables and Arrays in Macros

Because arrays of data are used often in engineering work, we consider them separately in macros along with the use of other variables. Thus far, we passed to macros, and returned from them, only simple variables. The argument list was simply constructed; we only had to order the variables according to the ARGU-MENT statement ordering of the macro. We also had to include a simple variable in the macro RETURN function. We begin this section by discussing the return of arrays from macros.

To properly return array values, we must first declare the type of returned value with the RESULT function, which we defined in Section 7.2.1. Thus far, we have accepted the default returned value as type number, logical, or text, with Excel automatically determining the type, so we did not use the RESULT function. To return an array, we would place the =RESULT(64) statement in our macro, usually before or after the ARGUMENT statements or just before the RETURN statement. Of course, we must include an array name, or other array reference, as the argument of the RETURN function.

Storage must be set aside in the calling routine for the array values being returned. Since the function macro returns one value, and in this case it is part of an array, the cell using the function must be part of the receiving array. Because the function returns only one value for the cell that it occupies, it will have to be replicated for the other cells of the array to return the remainder of the values. This is done in the manner described in Chapter 4. We first select the cells of the array, type into the formula bar the statement using the function, and enter it with the CTRL+SHIFT+ENTER key combination. Braces will enclose the statement, and it will be entered into each cell of the array. Of course, the dimensions of the transmitting and receiving arrays must be compatible to accommodate all the data.

We will have the problem of entering values into the cells of an array, whether or not they are returned from a macro. While the values for a constant array are entered directly via the keyboard and those involved with matrix operations are placed where needed during calculation, arbitrary placement of values into array cells and retrieval of values from them must be done with the macro functions SET.VALUE, INDEX, or SET.NAME. These functions are defined in Tables 7.2 and 7.3. Before we present the meaningful examples, we first illustrate the SET.VALUE and INDEX functions in isolated context as follows:

1. =SET.VALUE(Alpha,J)

    This formula causes the value of variable J to be placed in the cell named Alpha.

2. =INDEX(MatA,I,J)

    The cell containing this formula will contain the value in the Ith row and Jth column of array MatA.

TABLE 7.2 FUNCTIONS USEFUL FOR STORING VALUES

Macro function	Arguments	Purpose
SET.VALUE(*reference,value*)	*reference*: cell reference on the macro sheet into which *value* is to be placed. *value*: the value, or values, to be entered into the cell, or cells, of *reference*.	To store values during macro execution. Often used for loop initialization purposes and for convenient access to common data storage areas on a macro sheet. Cannot be used to replace a formula that may already occupy *reference*.
SET.NAME(*name*[,*value*])	*name*: a name in text form to refer to *value*. *value*: the value, or values, to be referred to by *name;* if a reference, *value* refers to that reference.	To assign a name to a value, or values (in the case of arrays), during macro execution.
DEREF(*reference*)	*reference*: cell reference on the macro sheet from which a value, or values (in the case of arrays), is to be obtained.	To obtain the value of the cells in *reference*. Used in functions whose cell reference arguments do not automatically return values, such as SET.NAME.

3. =SET.VALUE(INDEX(BLB,kk,1),35)

   The cell in row kk and column 1 of array BLB will be set to the value 35.

4. =SET.VALUE(Beta,INDEX(Fctn,m,n))

   The value in row m and column n of array Fctn will be placed in the cell named Beta.

The DEREF function returns values of references and is used with certain functions that do not automatically return values from references.

Example 7.1

   In this example, we illustrate the return of an array from a function macro. We also manipulate individual elements of an array.

   The input impedance to the electrical network of Figure 7.9 will be complex-valued for AC signals because of the reactive components. Therefore, computations of the impedance involve complex numbers, whereby we have a real part and an imaginary part. We will use phasor techniques to illustrate array-handling procedures.

TABLE 7.3 FUNCTIONS FOR ARRAY LOOKUP

Macro function	Arguments	Purpose
INDEX(*reference,row,column*[,*range-num*])	*reference*: reference to one or more cell ranges. *range-num*: an integer designating a particular range of a multiple cell range given in *reference;* the first range is 1, the second 2, and so on; when this argument is omitted, its default value of 1 is assumed. *row*: an integer designating a particular row within that range of *reference* designated by *range-num*. *column*: an integer designating a particular column within that range of *reference* designated by *range-num*.	To return the reference to a cell or cell range within *reference* as determined by the values given for *range-num*, *row*, and *column*. The special case for *row*, or *column*, being 0, causes the reference for the entire *column*, or *row*, being returned, respectively. When *row* or *column* do not point to an element within *reference*, a value of #REF! is returned.
INDEX(*array,row,column*)	*array*: an array entered as a constant. *row*: an integer designating a particular row of *array*. *column*: an integer designating a particular column of *array*.	To return the value of the (*row,column*) element of *array*. When *row*, or *column*, is given as 0, the entire *column*, or *row*, of values is returned, respectively. When *row* or *column* do not point to an element of *array*, a value of #REF! is returned.

Since there are no complex number arithmetic operators in Excel, we will write them in macro form to implement the following operations (j is the engineering symbol for $\sqrt{-1}$):

Addition: $(a + jb) + (c + jd) = (a + c) + j(b + d)$

Subtraction: $(a + jb) - (c + jd) = (a - c) + j(b - d)$

Multiplication: $(a + jb)*(c + jd) = (ac - bd) + j(bc + ad)$

Division: $\dfrac{(a + jb)}{(c + jd)} = \dfrac{(ac + bd) + j(bc - ad)}{c^2 + d^2}$

Our procedure is to compute the circuit impedances according to the equations shown in Figure 7.9. The desired result is a value for Z_{in}.

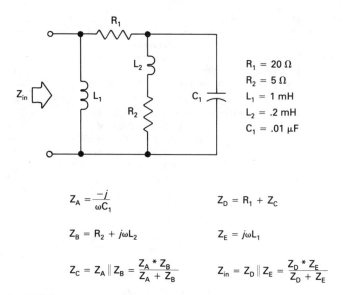

$$Z_A = \frac{-j}{\omega C_1} \qquad\qquad Z_D = R_1 + Z_C$$

$$Z_B = R_2 + j\omega L_2 \qquad\qquad Z_E = j\omega L_1$$

$$Z_C = Z_A \,\|\, Z_B = \frac{Z_A * Z_B}{Z_A + Z_B} \qquad Z_{in} = Z_D \,\|\, Z_E = \frac{Z_D * Z_E}{Z_D + Z_E}$$

Figure 7.9   Circuit diagram and impedance equations for Example 7.1.

We will write a macro for each complex operation, then use them in another macro that computes the circuit input impedance. Our worksheet program will be used for entering the frequency and for calling the circuit input impedance macro. The input impedance will be returned to the worksheet program as a complex number. The macro call structure of our program will be as shown in Figure 7.10. We

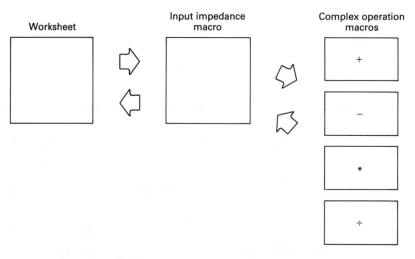

Figure 7.10   Macro call structure for Example 7.1.

may not need all the complex operation macros for this example. The names of our macros are

Cmplx.add   (complex addition)

Cmplx.sub   (complex subtraction)

Cmplx.mult   (complex multiplication)

Cmplx.div   (complex division)

Circuit.z   (circuit impedance calculation)

The complex number operators are all contained on the macro sheet of Figure 7.11, the circuit impedance calculation macro is shown in Figure 7.12, and the worksheet program is in Figure 7.13.

Each complex number operator macro requires the real and imaginary components of each complex number. Thus, there are four arguments to each of the macros shown in Figure 7.11. Because we are returning an array containing the real and imaginary parts of the result, we must declare the returned value as an array with the RESULT function using code number 64. We use an array named Cmplx, with elements named Real and Imag, in the macro sheet for temporary storage for all macros on the sheet. This is array A39:B39 of Figure 7.11. Each macro uses the names in the ARGUMENT functions as variables in the formulas for its complex operation. The real and imaginary values are stored into their respective parts of array Cmplx with the SET.VALUE function.

The circuit impedance calculations of Figure 7.12 use the complex number operator macros to compute the value of paralleled impedances $Z_A\|Z_B$ and $Z_D\|Z_E$ in rows 15 through 17 and 23 through 25. Because the macros return an array of values in adjacent cells of the same row, we must enter the macro call statements in adjacent cells of the same row as array formulas with CTRL+SHIFT+ENTER. Since we use these array element values in subsequent computations, we also name them to easily identify the real and imaginary components (note the .R and .I suffixes to arrays ZA, ZB, etc.). The real and imaginary parts of impedances Z_A, Z_B, Z_D, and Z_E are computed individually, while the parts for impedances Z_C, returned in array ZAPB, and ZCKT, the network impedance, are automatically computed in the macros and returned together in array form.

The worksheet program of Figure 7.13(b) shows the call to macro Circuit.Z with the argument Freq (frequency, Hz), which is passed to the macro and used to compute $\omega = 2\pi f$ as required for the reactance calculation. Because the Circuit.Z macro is specific to the circuit of Figure 7.9, we assign component values to variables in rows 4 through 8 of its macro, Figure 7.12, to avoid passing so many arguments. Passing the frequency as an argument is appropriate because we usually use it as the variable for studies in frequency response, network stability, and so on.

When the worksheet program is run, by entering a value for Freq, computations proceed automatically until the network impedance value is returned. These values are visible in the macro call array location of Figure 7.13(a) because the default value of the worksheet is to display values, rather than formulas, and because the figure is shown in the default display mode. The network impedance is 34.828 + j305.539 ohms as we see from cells B3:C3. We see in Figure 7.11 that the final value

	A	B
1		Cmplx.add
2		=RESULT(64)
3		=ARGUMENT("ARA")
4		=ARGUMENT("AIA")
5		=ARGUMENT("BRA")
6		=ARGUMENT("BIA")
7		=SET.VALUE(Real,ARA+BRA)
8		=SET.VALUE(Imag,AIA+BIA)
9		=RETURN(Cmplx)
10		Cmplx.sub
11		=RESULT(64)
12		=ARGUMENT("ARS")
13		=ARGUMENT("AIS")
14		=ARGUMENT("BRS")
15		=ARGUMENT("BIS")
16		=SET.VALUE(Real,ARS-BRS)
17		=SET.VALUE(Imag,AIS-BIS)
18		=RETURN(Cmplx)
19		Cmplx.mult
20		=RESULT(64)
21		=ARGUMENT("ARM")
22		=ARGUMENT("AIM")
23		=ARGUMENT("BRM")
24		=ARGUMENT("BIM")
25		=SET.VALUE(Real,ARM*BRM-AIM*BIM)
26		=SET.VALUE(Imag,AIM*BRM+ARM*BIM)
27		=RETURN(Cmplx)
28		Cmplx.div
29		=RESULT(64)
30		=ARGUMENT("ARD")
31		=ARGUMENT("AID")
32		=ARGUMENT("BRD")
33		=ARGUMENT("BID")
34	Denom	=BRD^2+BID^2
35		=SET.VALUE(Real,(ARD*BRD+AID*BID)/Denom)
36		=SET.VALUE(Imag,(AID*BRD-ARD*BID)/Denom)
37		=RETURN(Cmplx)
38	Real	Imag
39	34.8282429624	305.53873609037

Figure 7.11   Macros for the elementary complex number operations.

in work array Cmplx is also the network impedance value, which it should be since the last computation to make use of it was the Cmplx.div call of cells B25:C25 of Figure 7.12.

Example 7.2

This example is a rework of Example 7.1 with array arguments to the complex number operator macros. Instead of passing four arguments to each macro, with the values representing the real and imaginary parts of two complex numbers, we will pass to each macro two array arguments of two cells each. These arrays will each

	A	B	C
1		Circuit.Z	
2		=RESULT(64)	
3		=ARGUMENT("Freq")	
4	R.1	20	Ohms
5	R.2	5	Ohms
6	L.1	0.001	Henrys
7	L.2	0.0002	Henrys
8	C.1	0.00000001	Farads
9	Omega	=2*PI()*Freq	Radians
10	ZA.R	=0	ZA real
11	ZA.I	=-1/(Omega*C.1)	ZA imaginary
12	ZB.R	=R.2	ZB real
13	ZB.I	=Omega*L.2	ZB imaginary
14		Compute ZA in parallel with ZB.	
15	ZCN	=CMPLX.XLM!Cmplx.mult(ZA.R,ZA.I,ZB.R,ZB.I)	=CMPLX.XLM!Cmplx.mult(ZA.R,ZA.I,ZB.R,ZB.I)
16	ZCD	=CMPLX.XLM!Cmplx.add(ZA.R,ZA.I,ZB.R,ZB.I)	=CMPLX.XLM!Cmplx.add(ZA.R,ZA.I,ZB.R,ZB.I)
17	ZAPB	=CMPLX.XLM!Cmplx.div(ZCN.R,ZCN.I,ZCD.R,ZCD.I)	=CMPLX.XLM!Cmplx.div(ZCN.R,ZCN.I,ZCD.R,ZCD.I)
18	ZD.R	=R.1+ZAPB.R	ZD real
19	ZD.I	=ZAPB.I	ZD imaginary
20	ZE.R	=0	ZE real
21	ZE.I	=Omega*L.1	ZE imaginary
22		Compute ZD in parallel with ZE.	
23	ZIN	=CMPLX.XLM!Cmplx.mult(ZD.R,ZD.I,ZE.R,ZE.I)	=CMPLX.XLM!Cmplx.mult(ZD.R,ZD.I,ZE.R,ZE.I)
24	ZID	=CMPLX.XLM!Cmplx.add(ZD.R,ZD.I,ZE.R,ZE.I)	=CMPLX.XLM!Cmplx.add(ZD.R,ZD.I,ZE.R,ZE.I)
25	ZCKT	=CMPLX.XLM!Cmplx.div(ZIN.R,ZIN.I,ZID.R,ZID.I)	=CMPLX.XLM!Cmplx.div(ZIN.R,ZIN.I,ZID.R,ZID.I)
26		=RETURN(ZCKT)	

Figure 7.12 Circuit impedance calculation macro of Example 7.1.

	A	B	C
1		Network input impedance	
2	Freq	100000	
3	Zin	34.82824296	305.5387361

(a)

	A	B	C
1		Network input impedance	
2	Freq	=100000	
3	Zin	=CIRCUITZ.XLM!Circuit.Z(Freq)	=CIRCUITZ.XLM!Circuit.Z(Freq)

(b)

Figure 7.13 Worksheet of Example 7.1 in (a) values mode and (b) formulas mode.

contain the real and imaginary parts of the respective complex numbers used in the calculation. The complex number operator macros are shown in Figure 7.14 while the circuit impedance calculation macro is shown in Figure 7.15. The corresponding worksheet program is not shown but is identical to that for Example 7.1 except that the macro call is to Circuit.zar instead of to Circuit.Z.

	A	B	C
1		Cmplx.mult	
2		=RESULT(64)	
3		=ARGUMENT("ABM",64)	
4		=ARGUMENT("CDM",64)	
5	Real.M	=ABM*CDM*{1,-1}	=ABM*CDM*{1,-1}
6		=SET.VALUE(Real,SUM(Real.M))	
7		=Inter.chg(CDM)	=Inter.chg(CDM)
8	Imag.M	=ABM*Ary	=ABM*Ary
9		=SET.VALUE(Imag,SUM(Imag.M))	
10		=RETURN(Cmplx)	
11		Cmplx.div	
12		=RESULT(64)	
13		=ARGUMENT("AB",64)	
14		=ARGUMENT("CD",64)	
15	Den.sq	=CD^2	=CD^2
16	Denom	=SUM(Den.sq)	
17	Real.D	=AB*CD	=AB*CD
18		=SET.VALUE(Real,SUM(Real.D)/Denom)	
19		=Inter.chg(AB)	=Inter.chg(AB)
20	Imag.D	=Ary*CD*{1,-1}	=Ary*CD*{1,-1}
21		=SET.VALUE(Imag,SUM(Imag.D)/Denom)	
22		=RETURN(Cmplx)	
23		Inter.chg	
24		=RESULT(64)	
25		=ARGUMENT("In.ar",64)	
26		=SET.VALUE(Ary.R,INDEX(In.ar,1,2))	
27		=SET.VALUE(Ary.I,INDEX(In.ar,1,1))	
28		=RETURN(Ary)	
29	Cmplx	34.8282429624355	305.53873609037
30	Ary	81965.5531591748	-364852.893325399

(a)

Figure 7.14 Multiplication and division macros of Example 7.2 in (a) formulas mode and (b) values mode.

	A	B	C
1		Cmplx.mult	
2		TRUE	
3		TRUE	
4		TRUE	
5	Real.M	0	-364852.8933
6		TRUE	
7		628.3185307	0
8	Imag.M	81965.55316	0
9		TRUE	
10		TRUE	
11		Cmplx.div	
12		TRUE	
13		TRUE	
14		TRUE	
15	Den.sq	17017.78418	1461680.868
16	Denom	1478698.652	
17	Real.D	-47595873.37	99096349.3
18		TRUE	
19		81965.55316	-364852.8933
20	Imag.D	10692589.15	441107128.1
21		TRUE	
22		TRUE	
23		Inter.chg	
24		TRUE	
25		TRUE	
26		TRUE	
27		TRUE	
28		TRUE	
29	Cmplx	34.82824296	305.5387361
30	Ary	81965.55316	-364852.8933

Figure 7.14 (continued)

(b)

The Excel addition and subtraction arithmetic operators perform element-by-element addition and subtraction operations on arrays also. Since these operations directly correspond with their complex number counterparts, we need not write macros for them. However, we do need new macros for the multiplication and division complex number operators. These macros are shown in Figure 7.14(a). We find it easier to interchange real and imaginary parts of a complex number for the imaginary part during multiplication (to get $bc + ad$) and for the imaginary part during division (to get $bc - ad$). The macro for this purpose is called Inter.chg, and it also requires an array argument as shown in Figure 7.14(a).

Two data-storage arrays are used for the macros of Figure 7.14(a). One of them, Cmplx in B29:C29, is the array of returning values. The other, Ary in B30:C30, is for temporary storage of the interchanged values.

We name the arguments to each macro for convenience and declare them as arrays with type-code = 64 (see Table 7.1). We must declare the returning value as type array in the RESULT function with type-code = 64.

The real part of the product is computed in the formulas of rows 5 and 6 of Figure 7.14(a). The formula =ABM*CDM*{1,−1} performs the following calculation:

$$(a + jb)*(c + jd)*\{1,-1\} = \{a*c*1,\ b*d*(-1)\}$$

	A	B	C
1		Circuit.zar	
2		=RESULT(64)	
3		=ARGUMENT("Freq")	
4	R.1	20	
5	R.2	5	
6	L.1	0.001	
7	L.2	0.0002	
8	C.1	0.00000001	
9	Omega	=2*PI()*Freq	
10		=SET.VALUE(ZAR,0)	
11		=SET.VALUE(ZAI,-1/(Omega*C.1))	
12		=SET.VALUE(ZBR,R.2)	
13		=SET.VALUE(ZBI,Omega*L.2)	
14		Compute ZA in parallel with ZB.	
15	ZCN	=CMPLXAR.XLM!Cmplx.mult(ZA,ZB)	=CMPLXAR.XLM!Cmplx.mult(ZA,ZB)
16	ZC	=CMPLXAR.XLM!Cmplx.div(ZCN,ZA+ZB)	=CMPLXAR.XLM!Cmplx.div(ZCN,ZA+ZB)
17		=SET.VALUE(ZDR,R.1+ZCR)	
18		=SET.VALUE(ZDI,ZCI)	
19		=SET.VALUE(ZER,0)	
20		=SET.VALUE(ZEI,Omega*L.1)	
21		Compute ZD in parallel with ZE.	
22	ZCKTN	=CMPLXAR.XLM!Cmplx.mult(ZD,ZE)	=CMPLXAR.XLM!Cmplx.mult(ZD,ZE)
23	ZCKT	=CMPLXAR.XLM!Cmplx.div(ZCKTN,ZD+ZE)	=CMPLXAR.XLM!Cmplx.div(ZCKTN,ZD+ZE)
24		=RETURN(ZCKT)	
25	ZA	0	-159.154943091895
26	ZB	5	125.663706143591
27	ZD	130.452229485441	580.681414741172
28	ZE	0	628.318530717958

(a)

	A	B	C
1		Circuit.zar	
2		TRUE	
3		TRUE	
4	R.1	20	
5	R.2	5	
6	L.1	0.001	
7	L.2	0.0002	
8	C.1	0.00000001	
9	Omega	628318.5307	
10		TRUE	
11		TRUE	
12		TRUE	
13		TRUE	
14		Compute ZA in parallel with ZB.	
15	ZCN	20000	-795.7747155
16	ZC	110.4522295	580.6814147
17		FALSE	
18		FALSE	
19		TRUE	
20		TRUE	
21		Compute ZD in parallel with ZE.	
22	ZCKTN	-364852.8933	81965.55316
23	ZCKT	34.82824296	305.5387361
24		TRUE	
25	ZA	0	-159.1549431
26	ZB	5	125.6637061
27	ZD	130.4522295	580.6814147
28	ZE	0	628.3185307

(b)

Figure 7.15 Circuit impedance calculation macro of Example 7.2 in (a) formulas mode and (b) values mode.

By summing the elements of this calculation, we get $ac - bd$, the value of the real part of the complex number product (see discussion for Example 7.1).

If we now interchange the real and imaginary parts for array CDM, we transform $c + jd$ into $d + jc$. Then, with the formula of row 8 of Figure 7.14(a), =ABM*Ary, we perform the calculation:

$$(a + jb)*(d + jc) = \{a*d, b*c\}$$

which, when the array elements are summed, gives $ad + bc$, the value for the imaginary part of the complex number product. The real and imaginary values are stored in array Cmplx with the SET.VALUE function for return to the calling macro.

The Inter.chg macro merely takes the imaginary part of the input array, called In.ar, and stores it in Ary.R, the real part of array Ary (see row 26). The real part of the input array is stored in the imaginary part of Ary in a similar manner in row 27.

The Cmplx.div macro carries out computations similar to those described above to effect the division defined in Example 7.1.

The circuit impedances are handled in array form in macro Circuit.zar of Figure 7.15(a). Impedances Z_A, Z_B, Z_D, and Z_E, stored in arrays of the same names (rows 25 through 28), are computed in rows 10 through 13 and 17 through 20. Impedance $Z_C = Z_A*Z_B/(Z_A + Z_B)$ is computed in two steps (numerator in row 15 and quotient in row 16). A similar computation is performed in rows 22 and 23 for the network impedance = $Z_D*Z_E/(Z_D + Z_E)$.

The values shown in arrays Cmplx.Ary, ZA, ZB, ZD, and ZE are the last values stored in those locations because the network impedance calculation was completed. Figures 7.14(b) and 7.15(b) show the macros in their values display mode. These numbers are useful in checking accuracy of the computations. The network impedance in array ZCKT, row 23, is identical to the value computed in Example 7.1.

7.3 MACRO CONTROL STRUCTURES

We now abandon the designation of a simple macro and permit macro construction of arbitrary complexity. This means that various control structures will be allowed that were not permitted in a worksheet. Specifically, we will discuss the conditional and unconditional branching possibilities, and the looping and repetition constructs. Most of our discussion now applies to macros only, else we would have discussed the features earlier in a worksheet context.

7.3.1 Selection of Alternatives

The IF statement introduced in Chapter 5 allowed us to make decisions in the worksheet. We had to abide by data flow restrictions, so the statement was, at times, inconvenient to apply. We always obtained a value from its application. In a macro, however, we can use the GOTO function, which is an unconditional transfer of control statement, in the IF to effect conditional branching to other parts of the macro. Normally, the macro statements are executed sequentially, but now the GOTO function will allow us to jump forward or backward in the macro, a feature useful in constructing loops, as we will discuss in Section 7.3.2. In this section, we concentrate on the branching capabilities in Excel macros.

The IF statement, in conjunction with the GOTO function, is used to effect conditional branching. To branch to another part of the macro requires us to use the GOTO function with a cell reference to which flow of control is to be transferred. The GOTO function can not be used in a worksheet. The format of this function is

GOTO(*cell-ref*)

where *cell-ref* is the cell to which transfer of control is to take place. It may be a macro-sheet cell reference or a label. A *label* is text entered in a cell and then defined as a name with the **Formula Define Name** or **Formula Create Names** commands. It is constructed in the same manner as are variable names.

Since in a macro, we think in terms of flow of control, rather than data flow, we will also use the decision symbol normally used for programming language flowchart construction. It is as follows:

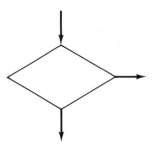

This symbol is used only when branching is intended (when the GOTO function is used for at least one of the selections in the IF statement); otherwise, the data flow symbol introduced in Chapter 5 should be used. There is one entry to the IF symbol and two exits, corresponding to the true and false outcomes. It is not necessary that the input and output arrows be attached to the corners of the symbol shown above. They may enter and leave the symbol at those corners most convenient for drawing the flowchart.

We emphasize, again, the need to maintain forward flow in the flowchart, except for loops. One possible flowchart is shown in skeleton form in Figure 7.16. Generally, we draw the flowchart to follow the right arrow for a true outcome and the downward arrow for a false outcome. For Figure 7.16, the two paths eventually merge. The structure of this flowchart would appear in the macro as in Figure 7.17. Branching to label-2 with a GOTO(label-2) function is not necessary when the GOTO is replaced with, say, a computing statement. Then, normal sequential flow would take us to statements B anyway when the IF

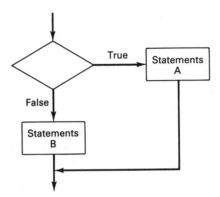

Figure 7.16 Skeleton flowchart with conditional transfer of control paths.

outcome is false. However, we need the GOTO at the end of statements B in order to bypass statements A. For forward flow, the preferred arrangement of the statements on the macro sheet would correspond with that shown in Figure 7.17. Other possible decision skeleton flowcharts are shown in Figures 7.18 and 7.19 together with diagrams showing the linear placement of statements in the macro.

The GOTO statement is an unconditional transfer of control command that makes the IF function a conditional branching function in a macro. It can also be used in a macro with the CHOOSE function, in which case it converts that function into another unconditional branching function based on a selection process. The format of the CHOOSE function is

$$\text{CHOOSE}(index, value\text{-}1, \ldots, value\text{-}n)$$

where

$index$ = integer, where $1 \leq index \leq n$.

$value\text{-}i$ = value to be assigned to the function; in a macro it can be another function, including the GOTO function.

Because we are now concerned with macro flow of control, we will discuss the CHOOSE function with GOTO functions for the $value\text{-}i$ arguments. In this case, the CHOOSE function can be diagrammed by the following flowchart symbol.

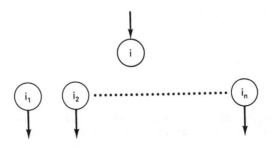

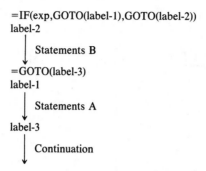

```
=IF(exp,GOTO(label-1),GOTO(label-2))
label-2
    │
    ↓  Statements B
=GOTO(label-3)
label-1
    │
    ↓  Statements A
label-3
    │
    ↓  Continuation
```

Figure 7.17 Linear placement of statements to effect the structure of Figure 7.16.

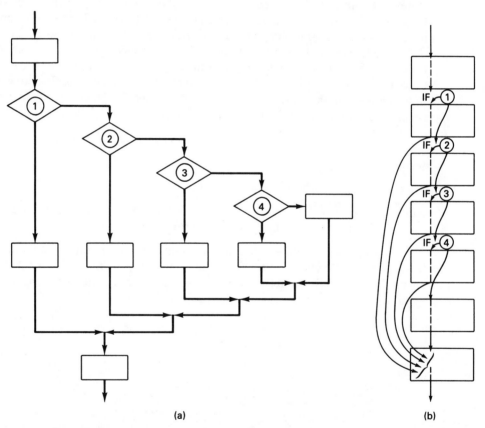

(a)   (b)

Figure 7.18 (a) Skeleton flowchart with multiple decision symbols and (b) linear placement of the statements as would occur in a macro.

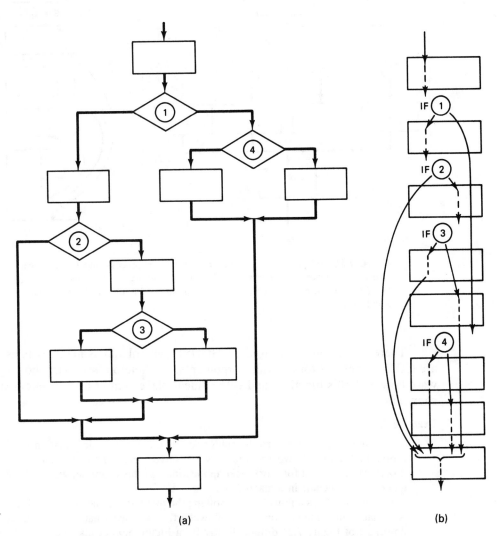

Figure 7.19   (a) Another skeleton flowchart with multiple alternatives and (b) its linear placement of macro statements. Irvin H. Kral, *Numerical Control Programming In APT,* © 1986, p. 124. Reprinted by permission of Prentice Hall, Inc., Englewood Cliffs, New Jersey.

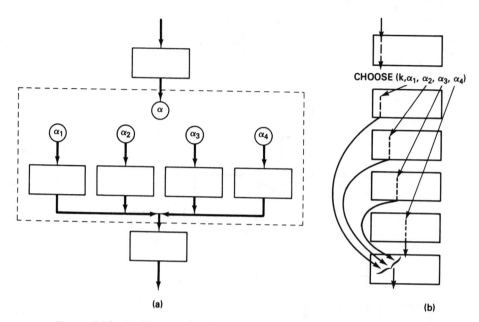

Figure 7.20 (a) Skeleton flowchart of a selection process and (b) its linear placement of macro statements. Irvin H. Kral, *Numerical Control Programming In APT,* © 1986, p. 123. Reprinted by permission of Prentice Hall, Inc., Englewood Cliffs, New Jersey.

There is only one entry to the CHOOSE symbol and as many exits as there are GOTO functions for the value arguments. A skeleton flowchart showing forward flow with this function, and with a linear placement of macro statements, is shown in Figure 7.20.

Example 7.3

Figure 5.9 is a control flowchart to solve the quadratic equation for its two roots. In Chapter 5, we showed how to convert part of the flowchart to a data flowchart equivalent for worksheet application. In this example, we will implement its control flowchart in a macro.

Figure 7.21 is a flowchart for solving the quadratic equation, while Figure 7.22 is a macro implementation of this flowchart. The macro name is Quad.eqn. The flowchart of Figure 7.21 differs slightly from Figure 5.9 because we wanted to simplify the macro. We did this by structuring the IF so that we needed to branch to only one label, the one corresponding to the true conditional outcome. By omitting the false conditional statement, flow control is to the next sequential statement by default when the outcome is false. This eliminates the need for another GOTO statement in the IF statement and another label, thus simplifying the macro. This is a preferred structure when writing in a programming language, since it simplifies the program. We advocate simplicity, but not at the expense of clarity. Fewer labels do lead to clarity because of more appropriate macro organization.

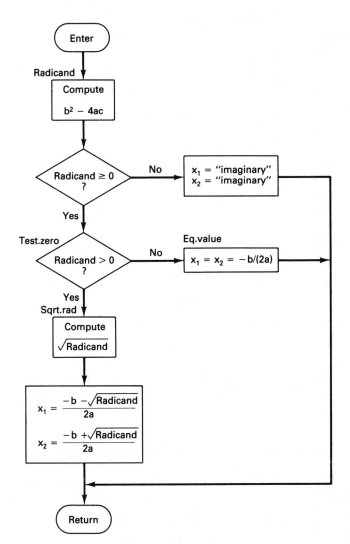

Figure 7.21 Flowchart for the solution of the quadratic equation in Example 7.3.

Figure 7.22 is the first macro we have prepared that contains labels. A *label* is nothing more than a name for a cell and is no different from a variable name other than that we intend to reference it for control flow purposes. Our macro is written for control flow down column B. Therefore, we used the names in column A for assignment to the adjacent cells in column B. We used Test.zero, Sqrt.rad, and End as labels. It so happens that Sqrt.rad is also used as the name of a variable that appears in the formulas of rows 17 and 18.

We defined X1X2 as an array, A21:B21, with elements X.1 and X.2 for individual reference. This array is a work space within the macro and is referenced in the RETURN statement to return the results to the calling program.

	A	B
1		Quad.eqn
2		=RESULT(64)
3		=ARGUMENT("AI")
4		=ARGUMENT("BI")
5		=ARGUMENT("CI")
6	Radicand	=BI*BI-4*AI*CI
7		=IF(Radicand>=0,GOTO(Test.zero))
8		=SET.VALUE(X.1,"Imaginary")
9		=SET.VALUE(X.2,"Imaginary")
10		=GOTO(End)
11	Test.zero	=IF(Radicand>0,GOTO(Sqrt.rad))
12	Eq.value	=-BI/(2*AI)
13		=SET.VALUE(X.1,Eq.value)
14		=SET.VALUE(X.2,Eq.value)
15		=GOTO(End)
16	Sqrt.rad	=SQRT(Radicand)
17		=SET.VALUE(X.1,(-BI-Sqrt.rad)/(2*AI))
18		=SET.VALUE(X.2,(-BI+Sqrt.rad)/(2*AI))
19	End	=RETURN(X1X2)
20	X.1	X.2
21	Imaginary	Imaginary

Figure 7.22   Macro implementation of the flowchart of Figure 7.21.

The worksheet program that uses macro Quad.eqn is shown in Figure 7.23. The macro is called in cells D3:E3, since it returns an array of values. Three sets of values for A.1, B.1, and C.1 (the arguments, obtained from A3:C5) exercise all paths of the macro. Some of the results are copied into rows D4:E5 for retention.

Example 7.4

In Example 5.3, we computed angles based on the sides of a right triangle positioned on a coordinate system (see Figure 5.11). We also provided a control flowchart in Figure 5.12 as a candidate solution algorithm. However, in Figure 5.12, we show decision blocks with output paths based on three conditions (>0, <0, and $=0$). Excel has no such multiple branching IF function. Therefore, we will prepare a new control flowchart and rework the problem as a macro.

Figure 7.24 is a candidate flowchart for our problem. From it, we can determine exactly the condition that causes a given formula to be used for calculating the angle. We expect to implement our algorithm to reduce the number of labels and to simplify the layout in order to avoid using more GOTOs than necessary. Our macro implementation appears in Figure 7.25.

Our philosophy of minimizing the use of labels for branching purposes causes us to place the IF statements in consecutive cells so that, for false conditions, we drop through to the next IF statement without having to label that statement for branching purposes. The last IF statement in the chain allows us to assign "Undefined" to α when $x = y = 0$. When an IF condition is true, we branch to the appropriate computational statement, execute it, then branch to the label End. We placed the labels in column A of the macro for visibility. Since our statement execution flows downward in column B, we used the **Formula Create Names** command to

(a)

	A	B	C	D	E
1		Quadratic Equation Roots			
2	A.1	B.1	C.1	X.1	X.2
3	3	-2	6	Imaginary	Imaginary
4	1	8	16	-4	-4
5	2	4	-30	-5	3

(b)

	A	B	C	D	E
1		Quadra			
2	A.1	B.1	C.1	X.1	X.2
3	3	-2	6	=QUADEQN.XLM!Quad.eqn(A.1,B.1,C.1)	=QUADEQN.XLM!Quad.eqn(A.1,B.1,C.1)
4	1	8	16	-4	-4
5	2	4	-30	-5	3

Figure 7.23 Worksheet program that uses the macro of Figure 7.22. (a) Values mode and (b) formulas mode.

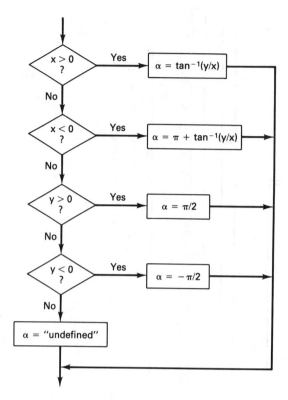

Figure 7.24   Macro flowchart for Example 7.4.

	A	B	C
1		Angle.rad	
2		=ARGUMENT("Xcoord")	
3		=ARGUMENT("Ycoord")	
4		=IF(Xcoord>0,GOTO(xGT0))	
5		=IF(Xcoord<0,GOTO(xLT0))	
6		=IF(Ycoord>0,GOTO(yGT0))	
7		=IF(Ycoord<0,GOTO(yLT0))	
8		=SET.VALUE(Alpha,"Undefined")	Origin of coordinate system.
9		=GOTO(End)	
10	xGT0	=SET.VALUE(Alpha,ATAN(Ycoord/Xcoord))	Angle in 1st or 4th quadrant.
11		=GOTO(End)	
12	xLT0	=SET.VALUE(Alpha,PI()+ATAN(Ycoord/Xcoord))	Angle in 2nd or 3rd quadrant.
13		=GOTO(End)	
14	yGT0	=SET.VALUE(Alpha,PI()/2)	Angle is 90 degrees.
15		=GOTO(End)	
16	yLT0	=SET.VALUE(Alpha,-PI()/2)	Angle is -90 degrees.
17	End	=RETURN(Alpha)	
18	Alpha	0.982793723247329	Work area.

Figure 7.25   Macro implementation of the flowchart of Figure 7.24.

	A	B	C
1	Xcoord	Ycoord	Result
2	2	3	0.982793723
3	-2	3	2.15879893
4	4	-5	-0.896055385
5	-4	-5	4.037648038
6	0	0	Undefined
7	0	7	1.570796327
8	0	-8	-1.570796327

(a)

	A	B	C
1	Xcoord	Ycoord	Result
2	2	3	=ANGLE1.XLM!Angle.rad(Xcoord,Ycoord)
3	-2	3	2.15879893034246
4	4	-5	-0.896055384571344
5	-4	-5	4.03764803816113
6	0	0	Undefined
7	0	7	1.57079632679489
8	0	-8	-1.57079632679489

(b)

Figure 7.26   Worksheet program that uses the macro of Figure 7.25 in (a) values mode and (b) formulas mode.

name the cells in column B to which we can branch. We chose to save our computed value in the variable named Alpha (B18).

The worksheet program that uses this macro is shown in Figure 7.26. The result for each set of *x* and *y* coordinates named in A2 and B2 appears in C2. These values are then copied to a following row for retention and a new set of coordinate values entered for another computation. The macro computed results of this figure are identical with those of Example 5.3 in Figure 5.14(a).

Should we prefer to place the statements for computing the angle immediately following their respective IF statement, we must structure the flowchart as shown in Figure 7.27. A macro solution for it appears in Figure 7.28. The desire to avoid extra labels leads to a negative logic structure which can introduce errors of interpretation. For this reason, this structure is not recommended. The results are correct as can be seen from the worksheet program of Figure 7.29.

7.3.2 Looping

Because we could not branch to other parts of a worksheet with the IF statement, we also could not construct our own loops. Of course, we had the iteration feature available for this purpose, but much of the time we prefer to keep control of our computations so other ways of forming loops are desired. In this section, we consider the use of the IF statement in a macro for this purpose, since, via the

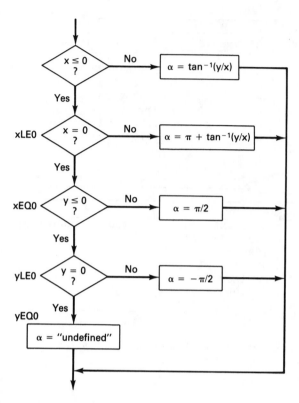

Figure 7.27 Another macro flowchart for Example 7.4.

	A	B	C
1		Angle.rad	
2		=ARGUMENT("Xcoord")	
3		=ARGUMENT("Ycoord")	
4		=IF(Xcoord<=0,GOTO(xLE0))	
5		=SET.VALUE(Alpha,ATAN(Ycoord/Xcoord))	Angle in 1st or 4th quadrant.
6		=GOTO(End)	
7	xLE0	=IF(Xcoord=0,GOTO(xEQ0))	
8		=SET.VALUE(Alpha,PI()+ATAN(Ycoord/Xcoord))	Angle in 2nd or 3rd quadrant.
9		=GOTO(End)	
10	xEQ0	=IF(Ycoord<=0,GOTO(yLE0))	
11		=SET.VALUE(Alpha,PI()/2)	Angle is 90 degrees.
12		=GOTO(End)	
13	yLE0	=IF(Ycoord=0,GOTO(yEQ0))	
14		=SET.VALUE(Alpha,-PI()/2)	Angle is -90 degrees.
15		=GOTO(End)	
16	yEQ0	=SET.VALUE(Alpha,"Undefined")	Origin of coordinate system.
17	End	=RETURN(Alpha)	
18	Alpha	0.982793723247329	Work area.

Figure 7.28 Macro implementation of the flowchart of Figure 7.27.

	A	B	C
1	Xcoord	Ycoord	Result
2	2	3	0.982793723
3	-2	3	2.15879893
4	4	-5	-0.896055385
5	-4	-5	4.037648038
6	0	0	Undefined
7	0	7	1.570796327
8	0	-8	-1.570796327

(a)

	A	B	C
1	Xcoord	Ycoord	Result
2	2	3	=ANGLE2.XLM!Angle.rad(Xcoord,Ycoord)
3	-2	3	2.15879893034246
4	4	-5	-0.896055384571344
5	-4	-5	4.03764803816113
6	0	0	Undefined
7	0	7	1.57079632679489
8	0	-8	-1.57079632679489

(b)

Figure 7.29   Worksheet program that uses the macro of Figure 7.28 in (a) values mode and (b) formulas mode.

GOTO statement, we can branch backward in the sequentially executed statements of the macro.

In Chapter 5, we discussed iteration at length and prepared flowcharts to illustrate the control aspects of this feature. We only needed to discuss one loop structure for iteration control because its functioning nature was built into the Excel program and we could not alter it. We are referring to the arrangement of the four parts of a loop as shown in Figure 5.22. We are not now constrained in this manner, so we will discuss other ways to construct loops.

The four parts of a loop may be arranged in any permutation that is logical, such as the ones shown in Figure 7.30. Still other permutations are possible. However, we stress forward flow in the macro and this applies to loop structures as well. Consequently, our preferred loop structure is the one of Figure 7.31(a), where the linear placement of its statements is shown in Figure 7.31(b). One backward branch is required and no statements are bypassed. This diagram should be compared with Figure 7.32, where bypassing of statements results in a macro more difficult to understand and debug. Loop structures with unorthodox exit locations, such as the one shown in Figure 7.33, cause awkward program organization and should be avoided.

Multiple loops are often required. Such loops may be cascaded (in series form) or nested as shown in Figure 7.34, where two cascaded loops are nested

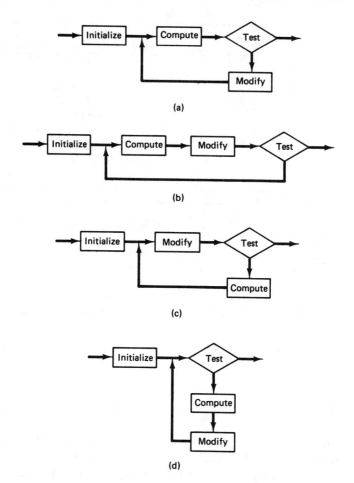

Figure 7.30 Some loop structures. Irvin H. Kral, *Numerical Control Programming In APT,* © 1986, p. 113. Reprinted by permission of Prentice Hall, Inc., Englewood Cliffs, New Jersey.

within another loop. Such loop structures require initialization of the inner loops for each pass through the range of the outer loop. The high-frequency loops are the inner ones, those most often executed, while the lowest-frequency loop is the outer one.

Complex loop structures that reuse code for multiple loops, that often overlap, and that reenter a loop at other than its normal entry point are shown in Figure 7.35. These complicated loop structures should be avoided for reasons already given.

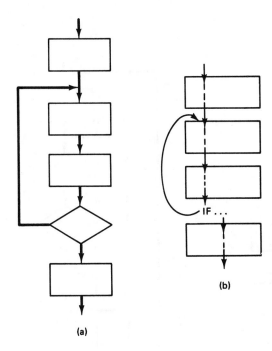

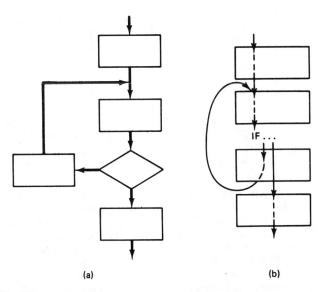

(a)

(b)

Figure 7.31 (a) Preferred loop structure and (b) its linear placement of macro statements. Irvin H. Kral, *Numerical Control Programming In APT,* © 1986, p. 125. Reprinted by permission of Prentice Hall, Inc., Englewood Cliffs, New Jersey.

(a)

(b)

Figure 7.32 (a) Alternative loop structure and (b) its linear placement of macro statements showing statement bypassing. Irvin H. Kral, *Numerical Control Programming In APT,* © 1986, p. 126. Reprinted by permission of Prentice Hall, Inc., Englewood Cliffs, New Jersey.

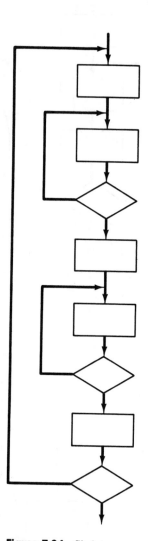

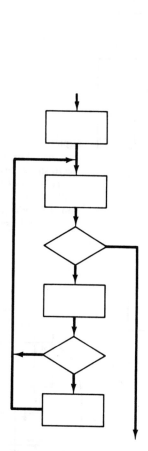

Figure 7.33 Loop
structure with an
unorthodox exit. Irvin H.
Kral, *Numerical Control
Programming In APT,* ©
1986, p. 126. Reprinted by
permission of Prentice
Hall, Inc., Englewood
Cliffs, New Jersey.

Figure 7.34 Skeleton
diagram showing cascaded
and nested loops. Irvin H.
Kral, *Numerical Control
Programming In APT,* ©
1986, p. 127. Reprinted by
permission of Prentice
Hall, Inc., Englewood
Cliffs, New Jersey.

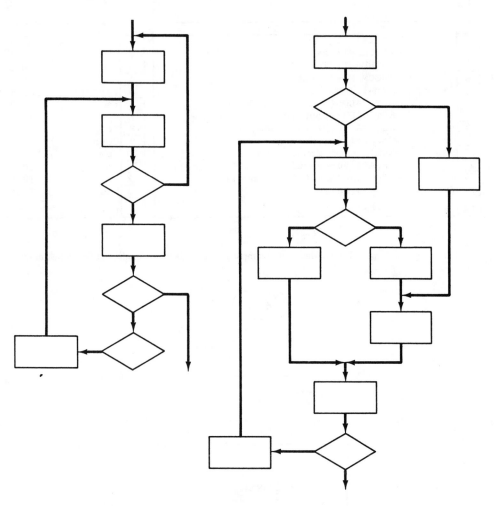

Figure 7.35 Two skeleton diagrams showing complicated loop structures that are to be avoided. Irvin H. Kral, *Numerical Control Programming In APT,* © 1986, p. 128. Reprinted by permission of Prentice Hall, Inc., Englewood Cliffs, New Jèrsey.

Example 7.5

In Section 5.3.1, we demonstrated the iteration feature by computing the natural logarithm via its series representation. We now use that same example to illustrate computation with loops in a macro. The series representation for the natural logarithm (base e) of a number x is

$$\ln x = \frac{x - 1}{x} + \frac{(x - 1)^2}{2x^2} + \frac{(x - 1)^3}{3x^3} + \cdots \qquad x \geq \frac{1}{2}$$

	A	B
1		Natural.log
2		=ARGUMENT("xx")
3		=ARGUMENT("Tol")
4		=ARGUMENT("Limit")
5	Factor	=(xx-1)/xx
6		=SET.VALUE(Sum,0)
7		=SET.VALUE(Count,0)
8	Loop	=SET.VALUE(Partial,Sum)
9	Count	=Count+1
10	Sum	=Sum+Factor^Count/Count
11		=IF(ABS(Sum-Partial)<Tol,GOTO(End))
12		=IF(Count<Limit,GOTO(Loop))
13	End	=RETURN(Sum)
14	Partial	0.336464785746001

(a)

	A	B
1		Natural.log
2		TRUE
3		TRUE
4		TRUE
5	Factor	0.285714286
6		TRUE
7		TRUE
8	Loop	TRUE
9	Count	8
10	Sum	0.336470337
11		TRUE
12		TRUE
13	End	TRUE
14	Partial	0.336464786

(b)

Figure 7.36   Macro of Example 7.5 in (a) formulas mode and (b) values mode.

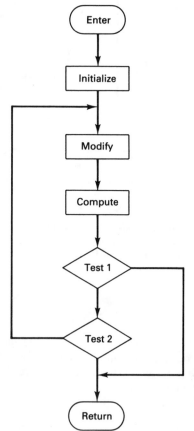

Figure 7.37   Loop structure of Example 7.5.

Our macro for this example is shown in Figure 7.36(a). It does not exactly follow our preferred loop structure of Figure 7.31 because we inserted in it a second exit condition. We first want to exit the macro when convergence is obtained. Since, in many problems, convergence may never be obtained, we also want to stop the looping action when a predetermined number of loop passes have been made. The first condition is tested in row 11, the second in row 12. Our loop structure is shown in Figure 7.37. It is a nonpreferred loop organization that we discuss further in Example 7.6.

We bring into the macro of Figure 7.36 as arguments in rows 2, 3, and 4 the value of x (the number for which we want the natural logarithm), the convergence tolerance value, and a value that will limit the number of passes that we can make through the loop. Initialization is performed in rows 5, 6, and 7. Variable references pertain to the column B cells in rows where names are shown in column A. Loop modification is done in rows 8 and 9, while computation is performed in row 10. We use the permutation of the parts of a loop shown in Figure 7.37.

Our convergence test is made in row 11 based on the value of argument Tol, which received the value 0.00001 from the worksheet program of Figure 7.38(a). Were this computation not to converge in "Limit" number of passes through the loop, we would exit the loop at row 12. We passed to the macro a value of 20 for the Limit argument. Convergence took place in eight iterations as shown in row 9 of Figure 7.36(b), so the limit check was redundant. We verify that our convergence criterion was met by comparing the computed values for the last two computations, rows 14 (previous) and 10 (current) of Figure 7.36(b). The value returned by the function macro, row 5 of Figure 7.38(b), agrees to the fifth decimal place with the worksheet natural logarithm function, row 6 of Figure 7.38.

	A	B
1	Test of	
2	x	1.4
3	Limit	20
4	Tol	0.00001
5	Sum	=NATLOG.XLM!Natural.log(x,Tol,Limit)
6	ln(x)	=LN(x)

(a)

	A	B
1	Test of natural.log macro.	
2	x	1.4
3	Limit	20
4	Tol	0.00001
5	Sum	0.336470337
6	ln(x)	0.336472237

(b)

Figure 7.38 Worksheet program of Example 7.5 in (a) formulas mode and (b) values mode.

Example 7.6

We further illustrate the looping concept by reworking the magnet design problem of Example 3.4. The macro flowchart we will follow is shown in Figure 7.39. Because much data is needed for this problem, we will pass it to the macro in an array, then reference the values via individual variables.

Our macro is shown in Figure 7.40. Rows 3 through 6 contain the loop to separate the input data into individual values. We define an array Work (B39:B51 of Figure 7.41) into which we transfer the values for later reference individually. The names in column A of rows A39:A51 are defined for the column B cells. Our loop is set up and executed in the manner previously illustrated. Because we know that 13 values will be brought into array Work, we use this constant in the test statement of the loop (row 6 of Figure 7.40).

The magnet design computations, initialization in rows 7 through 14, loop in rows 15 through 26 of Figure 7.40, reference the simple variables of array Work. The loop follows our preferred loop structure. The magnet design computations follow those used in Example 3.4.

The principal computation of this problem requires a self-consistent computation for σ, the leakage flux factor. Therefore, in row 27, we compare its current value (variable Sigmap, σ', in row 26) with its previous iteration value (variable Sigma, σ, in row 37 of Figure 7.41) to determine whether the two values are within our acceptance tolerance (variable Tol in row 50). If they are, we intend to exit the macro. Otherwise, we will iterate until we do converge or until we have exceeded a predetermined maximum number of iterations (variable Limit in row 51 of Figure 7.41).

According to the flowchart, we compute a value for Gamma (row 29) that will determine the path through the conditional test of the CHOOSE function in row 30. Variables Alpha and Beta are assigned values that help determine the value of Gamma. They are initialized to zero in rows 8 and 9. If we fail both the convergence and limit tests, Alpha and Beta are still zero and Gamma is assigned the value 1. The CHOOSE function then causes loopback to Loop, row 15, for another iteration of calculation. When Alpha only is set (row 27), we exit the macro after placing the message of row 31 in location Msg (row 38). When Beta only is set (row 28), we do the same thing with the message of row 33. When both Alpha and Beta are set, we place the message of row 35 in Msg. The manipulation of Alpha and Beta in this manner allows us to follow our preferred loop structure. The CHOOSE function is important in this respect. Remember that in Example 7.5 we temporarily accepted a nonstandard loop structure so that later (now) we could show how to modify it to conform with our accepted practice. Although we did not return the value of Msg to the worksheet, we can always find its value in the macro to determine under what condition the macro was exited. It is useful more for debugging and checkout purposes than for routine operation.

The worksheet program of Figure 7.42 uses the macro. Our input data is in array InData (B3:B15). A change in any one of these values automatically causes another computation to be made. The final value of σ (cell B2) should be compared with the result of Example 3.4.

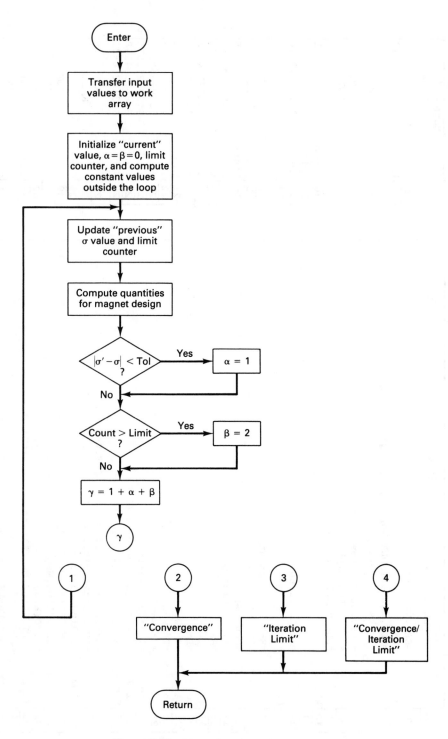

Figure 7.39 Macro flowchart of Example 7.6.

(a)

	A	B
1		Magnet
2		=ARGUMENT("Temp",64)
3		=SET.VALUE(k,0)
4	k	=k+1
5		=SET.VALUE(INDEX(Work,k,1),INDEX(Temp,k,1))
6		=IF(k<13,GOTO(k))
7		=SET.VALUE(Sigmap,Sig)
8		=SET.VALUE(Alpha,0)
9		=SET.VALUE(Beta,0)
10	Alpha	1
11	Beta	0
12	Lm	=Hg*Lg*rf/Hd
13	Ag	=h*w
14		=SET.VALUE(Count,0)
15	Loop	=SET.VALUE(Sigma,Sigmap)
16	Count	=Count+1
17	Am	=Bg*Ag*Sigmap/Bd
18	t	=Am/w
19	a	=(Lm-Lg)/2
20	cc	=Lm
21	Ua	=2*(w+h)
22	Ub	=2*(w+d)
23	Uc	=2*(w+t)
24	sig1	=1.7*Ua*a/(a+Ig)
25	sig2	=1.4*b*SQRT(Ub/cc)+0.67*Uc
26	Sigmap	=1+Lg/Ag*(sig1+sig2)
27		=IF(ABS(Sigmap-Sigma)<Tol,SET.VALUE(Alpha,1))
28		=IF(Count>Limit,SET.VALUE(Beta,2))
29	Gamma	=1+Alpha+Beta
30		=CHOOSE(Gamma,GOTO(Loop),GOTO(Cnvrg),GOTO(Iter),GOTO(CvItr))
31	Cnvrg	=SET.VALUE(Msg,"Convergence")
32		=GOTO(End)
33	Iter	=SET.VALUE(Msg,"Iteration Limit")
34		=GOTO(End)
35	CvItr	=SET.VALUE(Msg,"Convergence/Iteration Limit")
36	End	=RETURN(Sigmap)

(b)

	A	B
1		Magnet
2		TRUE
3		TRUE
4	k	13
5		TRUE
6		FALSE
7		TRUE
8		TRUE
9		TRUE
10	Alpha	1
11	Beta	0
12	Lm	1.165048544
13	Ag	1
14		TRUE
15	Loop	TRUE
16	Count	6
17	Am	0.846330196
18	t	0.846330196
19	a	0.457524272
20	cc	1.165048544
21	Ua	4
22	Ub	2.7
23	Uc	3.692660391
24	sig1	4.397255575
25	sig2	8.867884148
26	Sigmap	4.316284931
27		TRUE
28		FALSE
29	Gamma	2
30		TRUE
31	Cnvrg	TRUE
32		TRUE
33	Iter	TRUE
34		TRUE
35	CvItr	TRUE
36	End	TRUE

Figure 7.40 Macro of Example 7.6 in (a) formulas mode and (b) values mode.

272

	A	B
37	Sigma	4.316283998
38	Msg	Convergence
39	Sig	3.5
40	Hg	2000
41	Hd	515
42	Bg	2000
43	Bd	10200
44	rf	1.2
45	Lg	0.25
46	h	1
47	w	1
48	b	3
49	d	0.35
50	Tol	0.00001
51	Limit	10

Figure 7.41 Macro data storage area of Example 7.6.

7.3.3 Repetition

We have already illustrated repetition, or looping, in worksheets with the iteration feature (Chapter 5) and in macros with the IF-GOTO combination (Section 7.3.2). As a convenience feature, Excel has other looping constructs incorporated in its statement repertoire. These constructs, the FOR-NEXT and WHILE-NEXT statement pairs, automate certain parts of the loop structure. No new capability is realized over that discussed in Section 7.3.2, but these built-in features impose a structured programming methodology on the user and thus help avoid some problems with macro organization. The FOR-NEXT and WHILE-NEXT statement pairs, along with the BREAK function, can be used only in macros. The NEXT and BREAK functions are always used with an empty set of parentheses.

	A	B
1	Magnet Design	
2	Sigma	=MAGNET.XLM!Magnet(InData)
3	InitSig	3.5
4	Hg	2000
5	Hd	515
6	Bg	2000
7	Bd	10200
8	rf	1.2
9	Lg	0.25
10	h	1
11	w	1
12	b	3
13	d	0.35
14	Tol	0.00001
15	Limit	10

(a)

	A	B
1	Magnet Design	
2	Sigma	4.316284931
3	InitSig	3.5
4	Hg	2000
5	Hd	515
6	Bg	2000
7	Bd	10200
8	rf	1.2
9	Lg	0.25
10	h	1
11	w	1
12	b	3
13	d	0.35
14	Tol	0.00001
15	Limit	10

(b)

Figure 7.42 Worksheet of Example 7.6 in (a) formulas mode and (b) values mode.

     The control diagram for the FOR-NEXT statement pair is shown in Figure 7.43. The various parts of the loop being implemented are marked in the figure. Note that our preferred loop structure is not followed. However, since the FOR statement alone incorporates the initialize, test, and modify actions, the use of this single statement removes our objection to the structure. Because the organization and forward flow of statement execution recommendations we make are for the benefit of the user, behind-the-scenes nonconformance is irrelevant.

     The syntax of the FOR statement is as follows.

$$FOR(count, init\text{-}val, final\text{-}val, increment)$$

where

       count = variable used to keep track of the number of iterations

     init-val = the initial value for *count*

   final-val = the final value for *count*

increment = the amount by which *count* is incremented, or stepped, each time through the range of the FOR-NEXT pair. When omitted, its value is 1 (default).

     Statements of the FOR-NEXT structure are organized as follows:

```
=FOR(. . .)
```

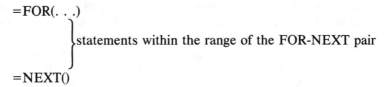

         statements within the range of the FOR-NEXT pair

```
=NEXT()
```

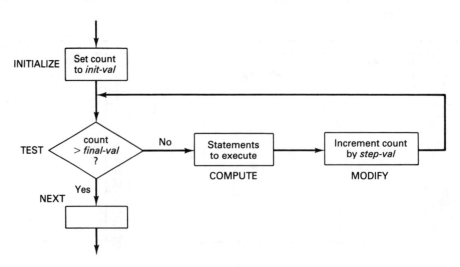

Figure 7.43 FOR-NEXT control diagram.

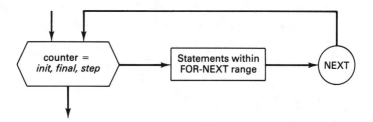

Figure 7.44 FOR-NEXT flowchart symbol.

The user must prepare the FOR statement and the computational statements within the FOR-NEXT range. A suitable FOR-NEXT flowchart symbol is shown in Figure 7.44.

Often, it is desired to exit the FOR-NEXT range prior to normal completion of the loop. In these cases, we exit the loop prematurely, but properly, with the BREAK function. The function has no arguments, so it must appear with an empty pair of parentheses. It is often used in an alternative path of the IF statement or CHOOSE function. Figure 7.45 shows its use in a skeleton flowchart.

The syntax of the WHILE statement is as follows:

$$\text{WHILE}(logical\text{-}exp)$$

where *logical-exp* is an assemblage of operands and operators that collectively form a logical expression; that is, one whose outcome is true or false. Here are two examples of the WHILE statement.

$$=\text{WHILE}(\text{Alpha}-\text{Theta}<\text{Delta})$$

$$=\text{WHILE}(\text{AND}(\text{Clk},\text{Enable}))$$

In the first example, the WHILE statement executes until Alpha−Theta is equal to or greater than Delta. In the second example, execution continues until Clk or Enable, or both, are false. Statements of the WHILE-NEXT structure are organized as follows:

=WHILE(. . .)

⎫
⎬ statements within the range of the WHILE-NEXT pair
⎭

=NEXT()

The flowchart of the WHILE-NEXT pair is shown in Figure 7.46. Looping through the WHILE-NEXT range is performed automatically as long as *logical-exp* is true. When it becomes false, macro execution continues with the first statement following NEXT. The variables of *logical-exp* must be initialized beforehand, and some change in the expression must occur within the WHILE-NEXT range to eventually make it false, or else the loop will not be exited. A

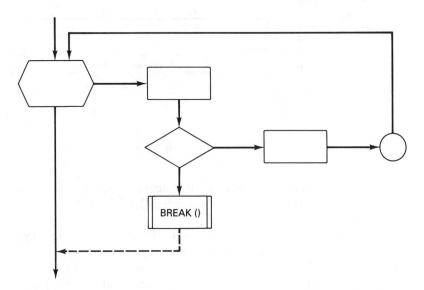

Figure 7.45   Skeleton diagram showing the BREAK function with the FOR-NEXT structure.

premature exit from the WHILE-NEXT loop may occur with the BREAK function as described for the FOR-NEXT pair. A diagram showing how it could be effected is shown in Figure 7.47.

FOR-NEXT and WHILE-NEXT statement pairs may be nested as needed. Some possible nesting skeleton diagrams are shown in Figure 7.48.

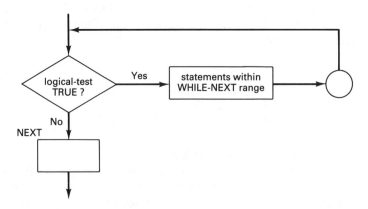

Figure 7.46   WHILE-NEXT control diagram and flowchart symbol.

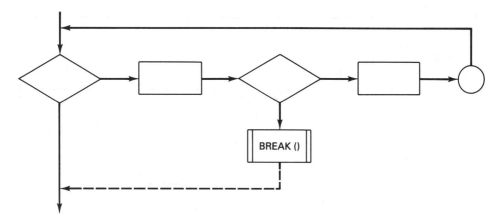

Figure 7.47   Skeleton diagram showing the BREAK function with the WHILE-NEXT structure.

Example 7.7

In this example, we rework the magnet design problem of Example 7.6 to illustrate the FOR-NEXT and WHILE-NEXT constructs. Because we tested for convergence of the leakage flux factor σ, we can now use the WHILE-NEXT construct for this purpose. The logical-expression of the WHILE statement will be the absolute value of the difference in σ values from one iteration to the next, just as it was the condition of the IF statement in Example 7.6. Also, because we bring in a known number of arguments, we will use the FOR-NEXT construct to store them in the Work array for individual reference.

Our macro is shown in Figure 7.49. The FOR-NEXT construct is in rows 3, 4, and 5. The WHILE-NEXT construct is in rows 10 through 24. We added the iteration limit check in the IF statement of row 23 to avoid unlimited looping. The BREAK function will take us out of the WHILE-NEXT loop if Count exceeds Limit. As before, we return the last value of σ', called Sigmap.

Figure 7.50(a) shows the worksheet program. The value of σ in this figure agrees with that computed in Example 7.6 (Figure 7.42). Figure 7.51 shows the work area of the macro.

Example 7.8

In this example, we illustrate nested FOR-NEXT constructs and more array manipulation. We will prepare a macro to compute the convolution between the input signal and the system's unit-impulse response for a discrete-time, linear, time-invariant system.

A discrete-time system meeting the above requirements performs an operation, $R[x(n)]$, on an input signal, $x(n)$, to produce an output signal, $y(n)$, as shown in Figure 7.52. A broad class of digital signal processors meets these requirements and is completely characterized by its unit-impulse response, $h(n) = R[\delta(n)]$. Given such

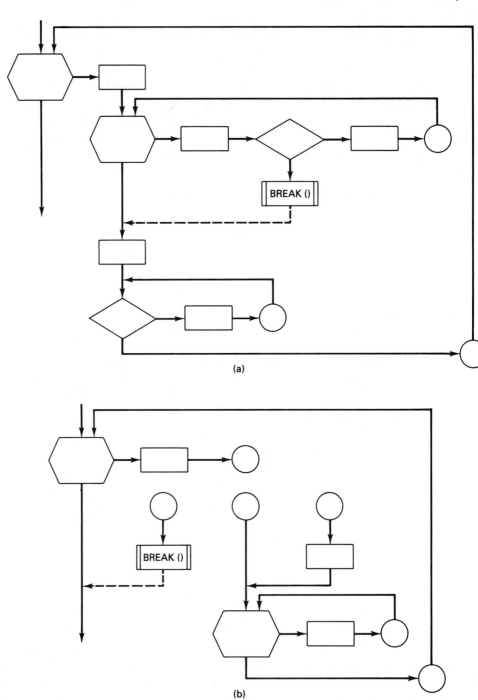

(a)

(b)

Figure 7.48 Skeleton diagrams showing nested loops.

	A	B
1		Magnet
2		=ARGUMENT("Temp",64)
3		=FOR("k",1,13,1)
4		=SET.VALUE(INDEX(Work,k,1),INDEX(Temp,k,1))
5		=NEXT()
6		=SET.VALUE(Count,0)
7		=SET.VALUE(Sigmap,Sig)
8	Lm	=Hg*Lg*rf/Hd
9	Ag	=h*w
10		=WHILE(ABS(Sigmap-Sigma)>Tol)
11	Count	=Count+1
12		=SET.VALUE(Sigma,Sigmap)
13	Am	=Bg*Ag*Sigmap/Bd
14	t	=Am/w
15	a	=(Lm-Lg)/2
16	cc	=Lm
17	Ua	=2*(w+h)
18	Ub	=2*(w+d)
19	Uc	=2*(w+t)
20	sig1	=1.7*Ua*a/(a+Lg)
21	sig2	=1.4*b*SQRT(Ub/cc)+0.67*Uc
22	Sigmap	=1+Lg/Ag*(sig1+sig2)
23		=IF(Count>Limit,BREAK())
24		=NEXT()
25		=RETURN(Sigmap)

(a)

	A	B
1		Magnet
2		TRUE
3		TRUE
4		TRUE
5		TRUE
6		TRUE
7		TRUE
8	Lm	1.165048544
9	Ag	1
10		TRUE
11	Count	6
12		TRUE
13	Am	0.846330196
14	t	0.846330196
15	a	0.457524272
16	cc	1.165048544
17	Ua	4
18	Ub	2.7
19	Uc	3.692660391
20	sig1	4.397255575
21	sig2	8.867884148
22	Sigmap	4.316284931
23		FALSE
24		TRUE
25		TRUE

(b)

Figure 7.49   Macro of Example 7.7 in (a) formulas mode and (b) values mode.

	A	B
1	Magnet Design	
2	Sigma	=MAGWHILE.XLM!Magnet(InData)
3	InitSig	3.5
4	Hg	2000
5	Hd	515
6	Bg	2000
7	Bd	10200
8	rf	1.2
9	Lg	0.25
10	h	1
11	w	1
12	b	3
13	d	0.35
14	Tol	0.00001
15	Limit	10

(a)

	A	B
1	Magnet Design	
2	Sigma	4.316284931
3	InitSig	3.5
4	Hg	2000
5	Hd	515
6	Bg	2000
7	Bd	10200
8	rf	1.2
9	Lg	0.25
10	h	1
11	w	1
12	b	3
13	d	0.35
14	Tol	0.00001
15	Limit	10

(b)

Figure 7.50   Worksheet program of Example 7.7 in (a) formulas mode and (b) values mode.

	A	B
26	Sigma	4.316283998
27	Sig	3.5
28	Hg	2000
29	Hd	515
30	Bg	2000
31	Bd	10200
32	rf	1.2
33	Lg	0.25
34	h	1
35	w	1
36	b	3
37	d	0.35
38	Tol	0.00001
39	Limit	10

Figure 7.51 Work area for the macro of Figure 7.49.

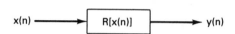

Figure 7.52 System diagram of Example 7.8.

a response, the output of the system for any input is given by

$$y(n) = R[x(n)] = \sum_{k=-\infty}^{\infty} x(k)h(n - k)$$

or

$$y(n) = \sum_{k=-\infty}^{\infty} h(k)x(n - k)$$

Both of these equations are the convolution operation we mentioned above. Convolution is illustrated in Figure 7.53. It is performed by transposing (reversing the order of) and shifting $h(n)$ along the n axis of $x(n)$. For each alignment, beginning at the left end of $x(n)$, the products of corresponding values of $x(n)$ and transposed $h(n)$ are summed to form $y(n)$ for that value of n. Subsequent shifting, multiplying, and summing until all subsequent sums are zero produces $y(n)$, as shown in Figure 7.53. In principle, we have summed from $-\infty$ to $+\infty$ since values not shown are zero. This is the output of the system when $x(n)$ is applied to the input given that the unit-impulse response is as shown. We will now perform this operation via an Excel macro. If the lengths of sequences x and h are l and m, respectively, the length of the output sequence is $l + m - 1$, which, for our example, is $11 + 5 - 1 = 15$.

Our macro is shown in Figure 7.54. Arguments to it are the arrays X.in, for which the first element is the number of values for $x(n)$, and H.in, for which the first element is the number of values for $h(n)$. These two arrays are transferred to work arrays X and H, which begin in row 28 of Figure 7.55, with the FOR-NEXT loops of rows 5 through 8, for $h(n)$, and rows 9 through 15, for $x(n)$, of Figure 7.54. We also transpose the values for $h(n)$ as we store them in the H array. The number of values for X and H are stored in row 26 of Figure 7.55 and named NumX and NumH, respectively. We chose to expand the array for $x(n)$ and initialize to zero those locations not occupied by nonzero values for $x(n)$. This was for convenience in making the multiplication and in illustrating that we can branch to different columns

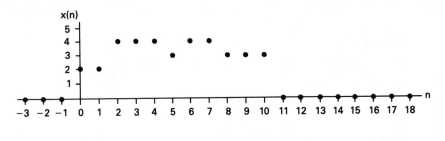

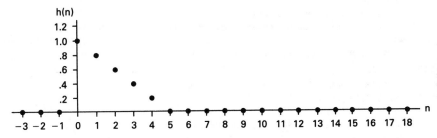

$$\boxed{2 \mid 2 \mid 4 \mid 4 \mid 4 \mid 3 \mid 4 \mid 4 \mid 3 \mid 3 \mid 3}$$

$h(0-k)$ $\boxed{.2 \mid .4 \mid .6 \mid .8 \mid 1}$ → $y(0) = (2)(1) = \boxed{2}$

$h(1-k)$ $\boxed{.2 \mid .4 \mid .6 \mid .8 \mid 1}$ → $y(1) = (2)(.8) + (2)(1) = \boxed{3.6}$

$h(2-k)$ $\boxed{.2 \mid .4 \mid .6 \mid .8 \mid 1}$ → $y(2) = (2)(.6) + (2)(.8) + (4)(1) = \boxed{6.8}$

$h(13-k)$ $\boxed{.2 \mid .4 \mid .6 \mid .8 \mid 1}$ → $y(13) = (3)(.2) + (3)(.4) = \boxed{1.8}$

$h(14-k)$ $\boxed{.2 \mid .4 \mid .6 \mid .8 \mid 1}$ → $y(14) = (3)(.2) = \boxed{.6}$

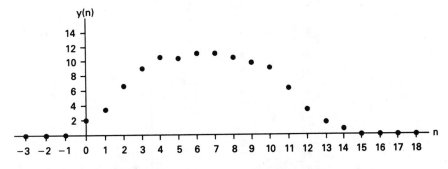

Figure 7.53 Convolution operation of Example 7.8.

	A	B	C
1		Convolve	
2		=RESULT(64)	
3		=ARGUMENT("X.in",64)	
4		=ARGUMENT("H.in",64)	
5		=SET.VALUE(NumH,INDEX(H.in,1,1))	
6		=FOR("I",1,NumH,1)	
7		=SET.VALUE(INDEX(H,NumH-I+1,1),INDEX(H.in,I+1,1))	
8		=NEXT()	
9		=SET.VALUE(NumX,INDEX(X.in,1,1))	
10		=SET.VALUE(J,1)	
11		=FOR("I",1,2*NumH+NumX-2,1)	
12		=IF(OR(I<NumH,I>NumH-1+NumX),GOTO(ZeroX))	ZeroX
13	J	=J+1	=SET.VALUE(INDEX(X,I,1),0)
14		=SET.VALUE(INDEX(X,I,1),INDEX(X.in,J,1))	=GOTO(Nxt)
15	Nxt	=NEXT()	
16		=FOR("K",NumH,2*NumH+NumX-2,1)	
17		=SET.VALUE(Sum,0)	
18		=FOR("I",1,NumH,1)	
19	Sum	=Sum+INDEX(H,I,1)*INDEX(X,K-NumH+I,1)	
20		=NEXT()	
21	Len	=K-NumH+1	
22		=SET.VALUE(INDEX(Convol,Len,1),Sum)	
23		=NEXT()	
24		=RETURN(Convol)	

Figure 7.54 Macro of Example 7.8.

	A	B	C
25	NumH	NumX	
26	5	11	
27	H	X	Convol
28	0.2	0	2
29	0.4	0	3.6
30	0.6	0	6.8
31	0.8	0	9.2
32	1	2	10.8
33		2	10.6
34		4	11.2
35		4	11.4
36		4	10.6
37		3	10
38		4	9.6
39		4	6.2
40		3	3.6
41		3	1.8
42		3	0.6
43		0	
44		0	
45		0	
46		0	
47		0	
48		0	

Figure 7.55 Work area for the macro of Figure 7.54.

	A	B	C
1	X	H	Convolution
2	11	5	=CONVOLVE.XLM!Convolve(X,H)
3	2	1	=CONVOLVE.XLM!Convolve(X,H)
4	2	0.8	=CONVOLVE.XLM!Convolve(X,H)
5	4	0.6	=CONVOLVE.XLM!Convolve(X,H)
6	4	0.4	=CONVOLVE.XLM!Convolve(X,H)
7	4	0.2	=CONVOLVE.XLM!Convolve(X,H)
8	3	0	=CONVOLVE.XLM!Convolve(X,H)
9	4		=CONVOLVE.XLM!Convolve(X,H)
10	4		=CONVOLVE.XLM!Convolve(X,H)
11	3		=CONVOLVE.XLM!Convolve(X,H)
12	3		=CONVOLVE.XLM!Convolve(X,H)
13	3		=CONVOLVE.XLM!Convolve(X,H)
14			=CONVOLVE.XLM!Convolve(X,H)
15			=CONVOLVE.XLM!Convolve(X,H)
16			=CONVOLVE.XLM!Convolve(X,H)
17			=CONVOLVE.XLM!Convolve(X,H)
18			=CONVOLVE.XLM!Convolve(X,H)

(a)

	A	B	C
1	X	H	Convolution
2	11	5	2
3	2	1	3.6
4	2	0.8	6.8
5	4	0.6	9.2
6	4	0.4	10.8
7	4	0.2	10.6
8	3	0	11.2
9	4		11.4
10	4		10.6
11	3		10
12	3		9.6
13	3		6.2
14			3.6
15			1.8
16			0.6
17			0
18			0

(b)

Figure 7.56   Worksheet of Example 7.8 in (a) formulas mode and (b) values mode.

and resume calculation there (see locations C12:C14 of Figure 7.54). We then multiply all $h(n)$ locations by as many values of $x(n)$, even though some may have zero values. Our macro is not intended to be a general purpose convolution routine but is to demonstrate some Excel features. The macro can easily be modified to avoid the multiplications by zero.

The convolution sums are stored in array Convol (C28:C42) of Figure 7.55. The values hand calculated in Figure 7.53 can be found in this array, which is returned to the worksheet, and can be seen in C2:C16 of Figure 7.56(b). We made the receiving array larger than was required for this set of data.

The convolution calculation is made in the nested loops of rows 16 through 23 of the macro (Figure 7.54). We step k, the index of the convolution formulas above, in the outer loop while i, the index of the inner loop, is used for the multiplication of corresponding values of $x(n)$ and $h(n)$.

7.4 DEVELOPMENT AND DEBUGGING

Good worksheet development habits can help avoid many problems that interfere with making the calculations intended. We have stated this many times for worksheet development, but it also applies to macro development. Because we now can have several interacting macros, each with potentially complicated control structures, our testing and debugging effort can be much more involved.

One must carefully develop the macros and the worksheet with which they will be used. We recommend preparing a flowchart for planning purposes to be sure the logic is correct before beginning any code development. Analyze the problem and partition it into logical segments. Keep the partitions small and simple so development can proceed in increments. Remember that all variables in a macro sheet are accessible by all macros in that sheet, as are the argument names, but they are not available to the worksheet or other macro sheets unless they are passed or returned as arguments.

Document all assumptions, the algorithms of each macro, the data work areas, and variable name assignments for ready reference during checkout. Upon entering the macro statements, save the macro to avoid loss (destruction) in case there are problems in carrying out highly interactive and complex calculations. The objective is to be able to quickly recover and continue checkout if all does not go well.

Anticipate mistakes. Proofread statements before entry. Enter function names via the **Formula Paste Function** command to avoid misspelling them. If typing built-in function names, use lower case letters and, after the formula is entered, check to see if the names are converted to capital letters, signifying that Excel has recognized them and has accepted the statement.

Prepare hand calculations of intermediate results to check certain formulas for accuracy and to check stored values. Decide on a standard set of test data for this purpose to avoid the extra work of additional verification. Use the **Options Display Formulas** command to see values stored in formula locations; make print-outs of intermediate results and annotate them for positive recognition of context.

When having trouble with a macro, activate the step command. This is done by inserting the STEP() function into the macro at a location just before the statements to be stepped through. During execution, this command causes a dialog box to appear (Figure 7.57) that shows the statement to be executed the next time the **Step** button of the dialog box is chosen. To see the result of this step, you open two windows, one showing the macro in formulas mode, the other with it in values mode. The windows can be sized and moved to convenient locations. The dialog box can also be moved out of the way. Normal execution can be resumed by selecting the **Continue** button. Execution can be stopped with the **Halt** button.

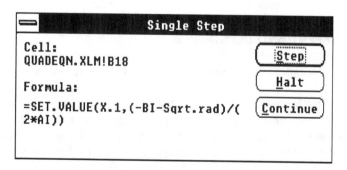

Figure 7.57   Dialog box displayed by the STEP function.

Figure 7.58 Dialog box displayed when a macro is interrupted with the ESC key.

A macro can always be stopped with the ESC key. The dialog box of Figure 7.58 then appears which allows one to stop execution, to single step through the macro, or to continue execution. There is a problem of synchronizing the halting action with an exact statement location in the macro. Therefore, if one believes stepping will be necessary, it is better to use the STEP() function described above.

The built-in functions of Table 7.4 are useful during development and debugging activities. If more extensive review of results or if incremental progress only is to be made, the HALT() function can be inserted to stop further execution of the macro. At this time, intermediate values may be inspected for confirmation of proper macro operation. The HALT function can then be reinserted elsewhere for a repeat of this action during further checkout attempts. The RETURN function can also be used in this manner during checkout.

Convergence tests often have the possibility of never ending program execution, especially during checkout. An alternate exit based on a loop iteration limit test should be used to avoid this possibility. We used this scheme in Examples 7.5, 7.6, and 7.7. Upon program checkout and verification, and if the algorithm is known to always converge, you can remove this alternate exit code to simplify and speed up the program. Remember that a convergence test is often used in the WHILE-NEXT structure.

TABLE 7.4   EXCEL MACRO FUNCTIONS FOR DEVELOPMENT PURPOSES

Function	Meaning
HALT()	Stops the macro.
BEEP([*integer*])	When executed, it sounds the tone corresponding to $1 \leq integer \leq 4$ (default value = 1). The tone frequency is hardware dependent. The beep is used to attract attention and can be used as a signal to indicate program paths being executed.
MESSAGE(*logical-exp*[,*text*])	When *logical-exp* is TRUE, *text* is displayed in the message area of the status bar. If *text* is " ", the status bar is cleared of any message. When *logical-exp* is FALSE, the status bar is cleared of any message and returned to normal display of command help messages. If the last message is not cleared, it remains displayed until Excel is exited.

Loop limit tests should always be thoroughly checked out. When the loop must execute *n* times, incorrect programming may cause it to really execute 0, 1, $n - 1$, $n + 1$, or ∞ number of times.

7.5 ABOUT VERSION 3.0

All worksheets of this chapter run under version 3.0 without change. Several new macro functions have been added, few macro functions have been changed slightly, and modifications have been made to several dialog boxes. Some changes to note are:

1. The IF function we introduced in Chapter 5, and discussed again in this chapter, is now referred to as Form 1. Another IF function, referred to as Form 2, has been added that has just one argument. To accomplish the branching control action with the Form 2 IF function, statements to be executed for true or false outcomes upon evaluation of the argument are determined by placement of the ELSE.IF, ELSE, and END.IF functions to delineate the span of control in a structured programming manner. These four new functions are described in Table 7.5 and illustrated in Figure 7.59. We reworked Example 7.4 to use these new

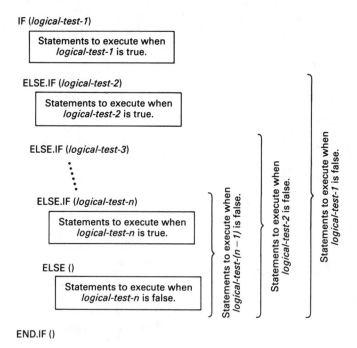

Figure 7.59 Structure of the Form 2 IF function.

TABLE 7.5   SOME VERSION 3.0 MACRO FUNCTIONS

Macro function	Arguments		Purpose
IF(*logical-test*) (FORM 2, macro sheet only)	*logical-test:*	an expression that yields a logical result (TRUE or FALSE), such as from a relational or logical expression, or from a logical value returning function. If TRUE, all statements between the IF and the next ELSE.IF, ELSE, or END.IF function are executed; if FALSE, control is transferred to the next ELSE.IF, ELSE, or END.IF function.	To control which statements of a macro are to be executed.
ELSE.IF(*logical-test*)	*logical-test:*	an expression that yields a logical result (TRUE or FALSE), such as from a relational or logical expression, or from a logical value returning function. If TRUE, all statements between the ELSE.IF and the next ELSE.IF, ELSE, or END.IF function are executed; if FALSE, control is transferred to the next ELSE.IF, ELSE, or END.IF function.	To control which statements of a macro are to be executed based on multiple conditions when the outcome of the preceding Form 2 IF and associated ELSE.IF statements are all FALSE.
ELSE()	None.		To designate which statements are to be executed when the outcome of the preceding Form 2 IF and associated ELSE.IF statements are all FALSE.
END.IF()	None.		Ends the statements within the control span of the preceding Form 2 IF statement and its associated ELSE.IF and ELSE statements.

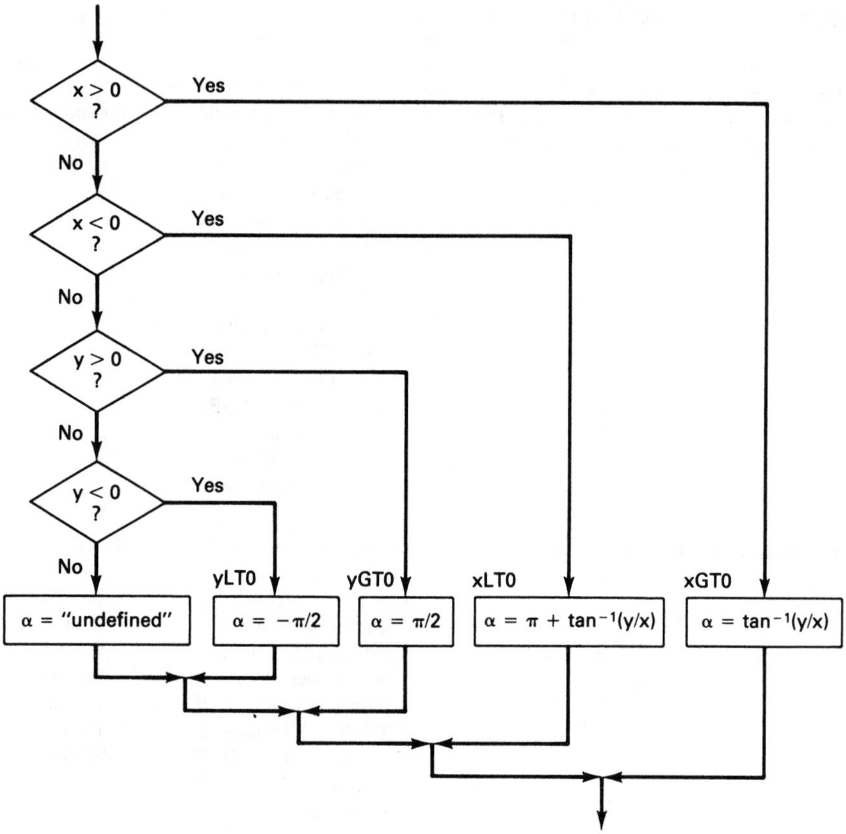

Figure 7.60   Structured flowchart for Example 7.4.

functions. The END.IF function is always paired with the Form 2 IF function. The ELSE.IF and ELSE functions are used as needed to implement the logical control flow desired. A revised flowchart, comparable to Figure 7.24, is shown in Figure 7.60. It should be compared with the structured flowcharts of Figures 7.18 and 7.19. The corresponding macro and worksheet programs are given in Figure 7.61. The labels of column A in Figure 7.61(a) are retained from Figure 7.25 for association purposes only. They do not define cell names. The data for Example 7.4 was rerun with this macro and, of course, the results given in Figure 7.61(b) are the same as in Figure 7.26. In Figure 7.61(a) we added spaces after the equal sign in rows 5, 7, 9, 11, and 13 for indentation purposes. This is a new feature with version 3.0.

2. The HALT function we show in Table 7.4 now contains an optional argument for use with macros that run automatically whenever a document is opened or closed. When the argument is omitted the HALT function operates as we described. We do not discuss automatic opening and closing of documents.

	A	B	C
1		Angle.rad	
2		=ARGUMENT("Xcoord")	
3		=ARGUMENT("Ycoord")	
4		=IF(Xcoord>0)	
5	xGT0	= SET.VALUE(Alpha,ATAN(Ycoord/Xcoord))	Angle in 1st or 4th quadrant.
6		=ELSE.IF(Xcoord<0)	
7	xLT0	= SET.VALUE(Alpha,PI()+ATAN(Ycoord/Xcoord))	Angle in 2nd or 3rd quadrant.
8		=ELSE.IF(Ycoord>0)	
9	yGT0	= SET.VALUE(Alpha,PI()/2)	Angle is 90 degrees.
10		=ELSE.IF(Ycoord<0)	
11	yLT0	= SET.VALUE(Alpha,-PI()/2)	Angle is -90 degrees.
12		=ELSE()	
13		= SET.VALUE(Alpha,"Undefined")	Origin of coordinate system.
14		=END.IF()	
15		=RETURN(Alpha)	
16	Alpha	0.982793723247329	Work area.

(a)

	A	B	C
1	Xcoord	Ycoord	Result
2	2	3	=ANGLE3.XLM!Angle.rad(Xcoord,Ycoord)
3	-2	3	2.15879893034246
4	4	-5	-0.896055384571344
5	-4	-5	4.03764803816114
6	0	0	Undefined
7	0	7	1.5707963267949
8	0	-8	-1.5707963267949

(b)

Figure 7.61   (a) Macro sheet and (b) worksheet for revised Example 7.4.

3. The STEP function dialog box of Figure 7.57 now contains the **Evaluate** button of Figure 7.62(a). When it is chosen, the formula of the dialog box is evaluated and displayed as in Figure 7.62(b). These figures were obtained from the macro of Figure 7.22 after the STEP function was added at its beginning.

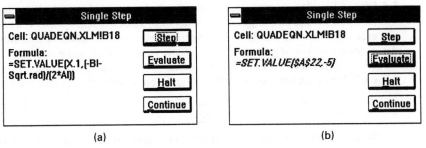

(a)   (b)

Figure 7.62   (a) Revised STEP dialog box and (b) the result of choosing the Evaluate button.

4. The Macro Error dialog box that is displayed whenever Excel detects an error in a running macro now contains a **GOTO** button that, when chosen, stops the macro, activates the macro sheet, and selects the cell that was in error. Its purpose is to help speed up the debugging process.

PROBLEMS

7.1 Given the following expansion (valid for $y^2 < x^2$)

$$(x + y)^n = x^n + nx^{n-1}y + \frac{n(n-1)}{2!} x^{n-2}y^2 + \frac{n(n-1)(n-2)}{3!} x^{n-3}y^3 + \cdots$$

Write a function macro containing loops to compute the $n + 1$ terms for the value of $(x + y)^n$ according to the series expansion. Provide for an arbitrary integer value of n. Perform the series computation using the values $x = 2.5$, $y = 1.25$, and $n = 5$. Also, compute the value of $(x + y)^n$ directly in a cell to check your result.

7.2 The function

$$y = \frac{b^2 x}{a^2 + x^2}$$

is an odd function for a symmetrical range of x about the origin. It was computed in Problem 6.6 with the data generation feature. Only half of it need be computed; the remainder copied in reverse order with a sign change. Write a function macro to compute a table of y values for $a = 3$, $b = 6$, and $-15 \le x \le 15$.

7.3 Write a function macro to compute the vector cross product $\mathbf{a} \times \mathbf{b}$ for three-component vectors. Pass the component values for $\mathbf{a}$ and $\mathbf{b}$ through the argument list and return the result via an array as the value of the function. Test your macro with representative vectors that avoid special case values.

7.4 Write a function macro to scan a one-dimension array of length n to determine how many times three consecutive elements of the array have values that are all positive (zero is neither positive or negative). Overlapping sequences of three elements are to be counted. Return the number of sequences counted as the function value.

7.5 Write a function macro to scan a one-dimension array of integer elements to determine how many times two adjacent elements have values that are both even (zero is considered to be an even number). Overlapping sequences of adjacent elements meeting the requirement are to be counted. The array length n shall be an argument to the macro, while the number counted shall be returned as the value of the function. For example, the value of the function is 4 after scanning an array containing the following numbers:

1	10	0	−5	6	6	−12	7	9	16	−11	0	4	3

7.6 Write a function macro that determines if a given square array of size n is a particular magic square. This magic square is to be classified as such if and only if the elements of each row, column, and main diagonal sum to the same value. Here is an example of a 3×3 magic square where the sum is 15.

$$
\begin{array}{ccc}
8 & 1 & 6 \\
3 & 5 & 7 \\
4 & 9 & 2
\end{array}
$$

7.7 Write a function macro that checks a two-dimension square array to determine whether it is in tridiagonal form (all elements are zero except those on the principal diagonal and its two adjacent diagonals, provided that none of these three diagonals contains all zeros). The following is such an array:

$$
\begin{array}{ccccccc}
x & x & 0 & 0 & 0 & 0 & 0 \\
x & x & x & 0 & 0 & 0 & 0 \\
0 & x & x & x & 0 & 0 & 0 \\
0 & 0 & x & x & x & 0 & 0 \\
0 & 0 & 0 & x & x & x & 0 \\
0 & 0 & 0 & 0 & x & x & x \\
0 & 0 & 0 & 0 & 0 & x & x
\end{array}
$$

7.8 The following rectangular array of integer numbers (the elements are also called the binomial coefficients) appears in a variety of applications and is known as Pascal's triangle:

$$
\begin{array}{cccccc}
1 & 1 & 0 & 0 & 0 & . \\
1 & 2 & 1 & 0 & 0 & . \\
1 & 3 & 3 & 1 & 0 & . \\
1 & 4 & 6 & 4 & 1 & . \\
 & . & . & . & . & .
\end{array}
$$

Except for the boundary elements, which are all 1s, the principal feature of the array of interest to us is that each element is the sum of two elements of the preceding row. For example, the (3,2) element is the sum of the (2,1) and (2,2) elements, and the (4,4) element is the sum of the (3,3) and (3,4) elements. Write a function macro that computes all elements of a Pascal's triangle of size n, where n is passed to the function macro as an argument.

CHAPTER 8

Command Macros,
Menus, and Dialog Boxes

The function macros of Chapter 7 gave us an increment of much greater capability from Excel than we obtained from any previous chapter. We can do so much more within a macro than within a worksheet that now it seems as if all the prior material was just preparation for learning macros. Even then, we limited our discussion to functions for making computations. In Excel, we can also prepare macros that appear as commands, actually as custom commands. But why would we want to learn to write our own commands? Don't we expect Excel to contain all the commands we need to use the product? Aren't we more interested in preparing the application than in extending the system? Well, we most certainly are, but we will reveal in this chapter that preparing custom commands, dialog boxes, and menus to complement the spreadsheet application will impart a synergistic quality to the application that no set of built-in capabilities can match.

We are not interested in customizing for the sake of being different. We want to add quality, convenience, and capability that reflect the engineering attributes prominent in our other work. We want to "complete" the job of applying a product designed for one area of application to our area—engineering.

8.1 INTRODUCTION

We defined the Excel macros in Section 7.1 and thoroughly discussed function macros in that chapter. Now, we will discuss command macros in some detail. We repeat the definition of a command macro from Section 7.1.

This macro is composed of commands that collectively perform the equivalent of a custom command. This assemblage of commands must be assigned a name and sequenced to carry out the desired action. It is invoked by its name and is called a command macro because of its resemblance to the built-in Excel commands.

Although there can be hybrid macros, which are combinations of function and command macros, we limit our discussion now to command macros. What we learned about function macro call structures, and discussed in Section 7.1 and illustrated in Figure 7.1, applies also to command macros. So we will not repeat any of that discussion but instead consider the unique characteristics of command macros.

Since command macros are intended to carry out actions rather than computations, we do not pass arguments to them. Command macros use no arguments, and they return no values. Therefore, the RETURN function in a command macro is used only with a set of empty parentheses. This does not mean that we do not work with values in a command macro. We can still manipulate values via calls to function macros, via calls to command-equivalent or action-equivalent functions, and we can compute within a command macro.

Here are some ways that command macros can be used for engineering applications.

1. Opening and closing files. Some applications may use multiple worksheets and macro sheets. To save time and to be sure that all documents are opened or closed, a command macro can be written to consolidate the commands and activate them by one user command.

2. Performing often-needed tasks. These tasks may be for chart preparation, text formatting, data preparation for presentation, work area preparation (initialization), and so on. Most such tasks require that short sequences of similar commands be executed.

3. Interacting with the user. Custom menus and dialog boxes can be created to allow the user to respond to program requests for data entry or other action for on-the-fly decision making. These macros offer a less imposing interface for inexperienced users of the program.

4. Scheduling for periodic execution. Command macros can be programmed to run at a predetermined time. This may be for the purpose of processing data that must be entered according to a schedule. The data could be derived from continuing experiments, and the macro could input the data and initiate computations on it for experiment control purposes, for data logging purposes, for report preparation, and the like.

5. Running other applications. Under a windows environment that permits Excel to communicate with other applications, macros can cause other applications to run, and they can move data between applications.

TABLE 8.1 MACRO FUNCTION CLASSIFICATIONS

Classification	Description
Command-equivalent function	A function that performs an action that corresponds to a menu command.
Dialog box function	A command-equivalent function that displays the dialog box corresponding to the command.
Action-equivalent function	A function that performs an action that is not performed by a menu command.
Customizing function	A function that performs an action that can only be performed by a macro.
Control function	A function that alters the sequential flow of macro execution.
Value returning function	A function that returns a value that can be used in the macro.

An enormous number of macro functions are available in Excel for use in command macros. Macro functions are classified in the Excel macro reference manual according to whether or not they perform an action. Action here is broadly defined to mean performing an operation that affects the view in at least one of the windows for the worksheet program. When no action is performed, we cannot see the effects, which usually are values being returned or macro-execution control being altered because of, say, branching. The macro-function classifications are shown in Table 8.1.

In Tables 8.2 through 8.7 we list the Excel names of some of the macro functions for the classifications of Table 8.1. We are already familiar with all the functions of Table 8.6. Because an action-macro function name is similar to its menu counterpart, it is not difficult to identify the action that will be performed by the function. Because the tables contain function names only, they are to be used to quickly narrow the list of possible functions to the few believed available for the purpose desired. The Excel macro reference manual should be consulted for the complete list and for descriptions of the macro functions. As we progress through the material of this chapter, we will describe only those macro functions that are used in our examples.

While the command macros we write will not have arguments, the macro commands for the most part require them. We show in Figure 8.1 an example

TABLE 8.2 EXCEL COMMAND-EQUIVALENT FUNCTIONS

Purpose	Function names	
Formula preparation	APPLY.NAMES	FORMULA.GOTO
	CREATE.NAMES	FORMULA.REPLACE
	DEFINE.NAME	LIST.NAMES
	DELETE.NAME	NOTE
	FORMULA.FIND	SELECT.SPECIAL

TABLE 8.2 (Continued)

Purpose	Function names	
Chart preparation	ADD.ARROW ATTACH.TEXT AXES DELETE.ARROW	GRIDLINES LEGEND SELECT.CHART SELECT.PLOT.AREA
Gallery selection	COMBINATION GALLERY.AREA GALLERY.BAR GALLERY.COLUMN GALLERY.LINE	GALLERY.PIE GALLERY.SCATTER PREFERRED SET.PREFERRED
Formatting	ALIGNMENT BORDER COLUMN.WIDTH FORMAT.FONT FORMAT.LEGEND FORMAT.MOVE FORMAT.NUMBER FORMAT.SIZE	FORMAT.TEXT JUSTIFY MAIN.CHART OVERLAY PATTERNS REPLACE.FONT ROW.HEIGHT SCALE
Editing	CLEAR COPY COPY.CHART COPY.PICTURE CUT EDIT.DELETE FILL.DOWN	FILL.LEFT FILL.RIGHT FILL.UP INSERT PASTE PASTE.SPECIAL UNDO
File management	CLOSE CLOSE.ALL FILE.CLOSE FILE.DELETE NEW OPEN PAGE.SETUP	PRINT PRINTER.SETUP QUIT SAVE SAVE.AS SAVE.WORKSPACE
Macro control	RUN	
Information	DISPLAY	
Options selection	CALCULATE.DOCUMENT CALCULATE.NOW CALCULATION DISPLAY PRECISION	REMOVE.PAGE.BREAK SET.PAGE.BREAK SET.PRINT.AREA SET.PRINT.TITLES WORKSPACE
Database management	DATA.DELETE DATA.FIND DATA.FIND.NEXT DATA.FIND.PREV DATA.FORM DATA.SERIES	EXTRACT PARSE SET.CRITERIA SET.DATABASE SORT TABLE
Window control	ACTIVATE ARRANGE.ALL HIDE	NEW.WINDOW SHOW.INFO UNHIDE

TABLE 8.3 EXCEL DIALOG BOX FUNCTIONS

Purpose	Function names	
Formula preparation	APPLY.NAMES CREATE.NAMES DEFINE.NAME	FORMULA.FIND FORMULA.GOTO FORMULA.REPLACE
Chart preparation	AXES ATTACH.TEXT	FORMAT.LEGEND GRIDLINES
Gallery selection	COMBINATION GALLERY.AREA GALLERY.BAR GALLERY.COLUMN	GALLERY.LINE GALLERY.PIE GALLERY.SCATTER
Formatting	ALIGNMENT BORDER COLUMN.WIDTH FORMAT.FONT FORMAT.MOVE	FORMAT.NUMBER FORMAT.SIZE FORMAT.TEXT ROW.HEIGHT
Editing	CLEAR EDIT.DELETE	INSERT PASTE.SPECIAL
File management	FILE.DELETE NEW OPEN PAGE.SETUP	PRINT PRINTER.SETUP SAVE.AS SAVE.WORKSPACE
Macro control	RUN	
Options selection	CALCULATION DISPLAY	WORKSPACE
Database management	DATA.DELETE DATA.SERIES EXTRACT	SORT TABLE

TABLE 8.4 EXCEL ACTION EQUIVALENT FUNCTIONS

Purpose	Function names	
Formula preparation	FORMULA FORMULA.ARRAY	FORMULA.FILL
Cell selection	FORMULA.FIND.NEXT FORMULA.FIND.PREV SELECT	SELECT.END SELECT.LAST.CELL SHOW.ACTIVE.CELL
Database management	DATA.FIND.NEXT DATA.FIND.PREVIOUS	
Window management	ACTIVATE ACTIVATE.NEXT ACTIVATE.PREV APP.ACTIVATE HLINE HPAGE	HSCROLL SPLIT VLINE VPAGE VSCROLL
Miscellaneous	A1.R1C1 DELETE.FORMAT	DIRECTORY STYLE

TABLE 8.5   EXCEL CUSTOMIZING FUNCTIONS

Purpose	Function names	
Display input dialog boxes	ALERT DIALOG.BOX	DISABLE.INPUT INPUT
Display messages	BEEP CANCEL.KEY ECHO ERROR	HELP MESSAGE WAIT
Create custom menus and dialog boxes	ADD.BAR ADD.COMMAND ADD.MENU CHECK.COMMAND DELETE.BAR DELETE.COMMAND DELETE.MENU	ENABLE.COMMAND GET.BAR RENAME.COMMAND SET.NAME SET.VALUE SHOW.BAR STEP
Access text files	FCLOSE FOPEN FPOS FREAD	FREADLN FSIZE FWRITE FWRITELN
Start other macros and applications	APP.ACTIVATE CALL EXEC EXECUTE INITIATE ON.DATA ON.KEY	ON.TIME ON.WINDOW POKE REGISTER REQUEST SEND.KEYS TERMINATE

TABLE 8.6   EXCEL CONTROL FUNCTIONS

Purpose	Function names
Direct flow of control	BREAK GOTO HALT IF RETURN
Loop control	FOR NEXT WHILE
Define arguments and data types	ARGUMENT RESULT

TABLE 8.7 EXCEL VALUE RETURNING FUNCTIONS

Associated entity	Function names	
Cell	ABSREF	GET.FORMULA
	ACTIVE.CELL	OFFSET
	CALLER	RELREF
	DEREF	SELECTION
	GET.CELL	
Chart	GET.CHART.ITEM	
Document	DOCUMENTS	
	GET.DOCUMENT	
	LINKS	
File	FILES	
Menu	GET.BAR	
Name	GET.DEF	
	GET.NAME	
	NAMES	
Note	GET.NOTE	
Text	REFTEXT	
	TEXTREF	
Window	GET.WINDOW	
	WINDOWS	
Workspace	GET.WORKSPACE	

command macro to reveal the similarity of it to the functions we wrote in Chapter 7. Our example macro activates the window named "Magwhile.xlm", the macro window of Example 7.7, and toggles it between formulas and values modes. We use it to expedite these actions during debugging operations. The macro has a name (Display.mode, in row 1), some comments (rows 2, 3, and 4), some macro functions for toggling the mode (rows 5 and 6), and the return function (row 7). We will explain this macro in Section 8.2.

	A
1	Display.mode
2	Toggles the activated window between "values"
3	and "formulas" mode.
4	Shortcut key = "m"
5	=ACTIVATE("Magwhile.xlm")
6	=IF(GET.WINDOW(8),DISPLAY(FALSE),DISPLAY(TRUE))
7	=RETURN()

Figure 8.1 Example command macro.

8.2 PREPARING AND USING COMMAND MACROS

We begin this section by describing how to write and run a command macro. Then, we will describe a semi-automated way to prepare it. We use examples to illustrate both methods.

8.2.1 Writing and Running Command Macros

The procedure for writing a command macro differs little from that for writing a function macro. We first plan the logic of the macro, determine the sequence for carrying out the tasks to be performed, write the statements as formulas, then test the macro. Let us prepare the macro of Figure 8.1.

Our task is to write a sequence of statements that allows us to toggle the display of the function macro for Example 7.7 between formulas and values modes for checkout purposes. Manually, we know what to do. We activate the macro sheet, select **Options Display**, toggle the **Formulas** box, then choose **OK**. We will let the command macro do all these steps once we invoke it.

A glance at Table 8.1 shows that we should be able to find most of our statements in the command-equivalent list of functions. From Table 8.2, we see an ACTIVATE command under Window control, and we see a DISPLAY command under Options selection. From the macro reference manual, we discover the real meaning of these commands. We show their syntax in Table 8.8. The only problem we have is that the DISPLAY macro function sets the mode to Formulas (with first argument TRUE) or Values (with first argument FALSE) but only with a predetermined argument. Since we want to use only one macro to toggle the display mode, we must look for a way to conditionally choose the mode. This means we need the current display mode status. From Table 8.1, we decide that a value returning function may be what we need and, from Table 8.7, we believe that the GET.WINDOW macro function may be suitable. It is described in Table 8.8.

The GET.WINDOW macro function uses two arguments. The value returned by the function depends on *info-code,* the first argument. We see that when this argument is set to 8, the value returned depends on whether formulas are displayed (value returned is TRUE) or values are displayed (value returned is FALSE). The information returned pertains to the window specified as the optional second argument. We will accept the default value for it, which is the window we made active with the ACTIVATE function. Now, the plan is to test the display mode, then change it to the opposite mode. We can do all of this in one IF statement.

When we assemble our statements as shown in rows 5, 6, and 7 of Figure 8.1, we need only name the macro to complete it. We enter the name "Display.mode" in row 1 and add a few comments. To declare this name as a command macro name, we must select it (cell A1), execute **Formula Define Name** [Figure 8.2(a)], visually verify that Excel proposed "Display.mode" in the **Name** box of the

TABLE 8.8   SYNTAX OF SELECTED EXCEL MACRO FUNCTIONS

Activate a pane in a window

ACTIVATE([*window-name*][, *pane-num*])

window-name = The name in text form of the window to be activated (name to be enclosed within quotation marks).

panel-num = Integer code for window panel to be activated: 1 = top left (if split vertically and horizontally), top (if split horizontally only), left (if split vertically only), entire (if not split); 2 = top right (if split vertically and horizontally), right (if split vertically only); 3 = bottom left (if split vertically and horizontally), bottom (if split horizontally only); 4 = bottom right.

Execute Options Display

DISPLAY([*formula*][,[*gridline*][,[*heading*][,[*zero*][,*color*]]]])

formula = Formulas check box toggle (TRUE = on, FALSE = off).

gridline = Gridlines check box toggle (TRUE = on, FALSE = off).

heading = Row & Column Headings check box toggle (TRUE = on, FALSE = off).

zero = Zero Values check box toggle (TRUE = on, FALSE = off).

color = Color selection integer (0 = Automatic (default), 1-8 color in order displayed in dialog box).

Note: Arguments are position sensitive; omitted arguments must be delimited by commas.

Return information about a window

GET.WINDOW(*info-code*[,*window-name*])

info-code = Value returned as follows:

     1 = Name of document in *window-name* as text.

     2 = Number of *window-name* window.

     3 = X distance (in points) from left edge of screen to left edge of window.

     4 = Y distance (in points) from top edge of screen to top edge of window.

     5 = Width of window in points.

     6 = Height of window in points.

     7 = Window hidden (TRUE), or not (FALSE).

     8 = Formulas displayed (TRUE), or not (FALSE).

     9 = Gridlines displayed (TRUE), or not (FALSE).

     10 = Row and column headings displayed (TRUE), or not (FALSE).

     11 = Zeros displayed (TRUE), or not (FALSE).

     12 = A number from 0 to 8 denoting the color of gridlines and headings.

     13 ⎫
       . ⎬ = Pane information, not described here.
       .
     17 ⎭

window-name = Name of window (of text value) about which the information is requested; default is active window.

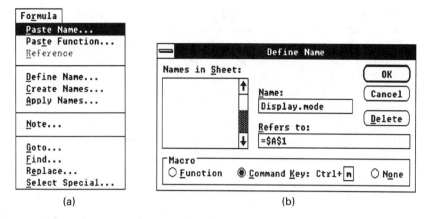

Figure 8.2   (a) Formula drop-down menu and (b) Define Name dialog box.

dialog box [Figure 8.2(b)], choose **Command** as the **Macro** type, and, optionally, type a one-letter key in the **Key: Ctrl+** text box (we chose lower case ''m''), then choose **OK** to complete the command. We have now named our command macro ''Display.mode'' and given it the shortcut key ''m'' by which we may activate it from the keyboard with CTRL+m. We are now ready to try out the macro.

To try out our macro, we must first open the worksheet and function macro sheets for Example 7.7. Then, to run our command macro, we can type CTRL+m, or execute **Macro Run** [Figure 8.3(a)], scroll the list of macro names in

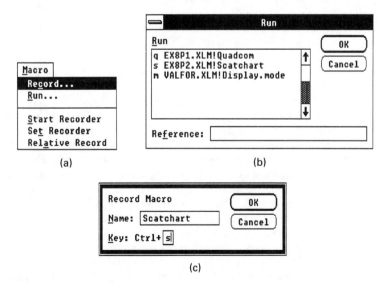

Figure 8.3   (a) Macro drop-down menu, (b) Run dialog box, and (c) Record dialog box.

the **Run** list of the dialog box [Figure 8.3(b)] until we find the one we want, select the macro name (in this case VALFOR.XLM!Display.mode), then choose **OK**. Consecutive executions of our command macro will toggle the function macro window between formulas and values modes. We can verify this visually.

The shortcut key is case sensitive; we chose lower case ''m'' for Magwhile. Unless we enter the shortcut key as a comment in the command macro, as we did on line 4 of Figure 8.1, there is a good chance that eventually we will forget it. In that case, if we locate the macro name in the **Macro Run** dialog box, we will see the shortcut key listed in front of the macro name [Figure 8.3(b)]. When multiple macros have the same shortcut key, Excel will run the one first listed in the dialog box.

Example 8.1

In this example we will modify a function macro to be a command macro. We will illustrate functions that allow us to input data to a macro, to display messages by a macro, and to interact with the macro. We will rework the quadratic equation solving macro of Example 7.3. Recall that we passed three coefficients to the macro and returned two root values (Figure 7.22). The descriptions in Table 8.1 suggest that we look at action-equivalent functions (Table 8.4) and customizing functions (Table 8.5). From Table 8.5, we are encouraged to consider dialog boxes for input and output purposes.

Before discussing the macro, let us look at some Excel functions for interacting with a macro. In Table 8.9, we define the functions INPUT and ALERT. Both of these functions display a dialog box. The INPUT macro function allows us to enter information into a running macro. We are able to display a prompt of our choice, to declare the type of data to be input, and to enter the information. Only one element of information can be input for each INPUT function. Because we require values for three quadratic equation coefficients, we will have to use three INPUT functions.

The ALERT macro function displays a message of our choice and waits for a response before continuing program execution. We can select from among three styles of dialog box. We will use the ALERT function to display the roots of the polynomial.

Figure 8.4 shows our command macro, which we named Quadcom and assigned the shortcut key ''q''. We replaced the RESULT and ARGUMENT statements of the original macro with three INPUT statements like the one of Figure 8.5(a). The message of each INPUT statement prompts for one of the coefficients a, b, or c, which are to be numbers. We also assigned to these locations the names AI, BI, and CI for use as variables during subsequent calculations (rows 5, 6, and 7 of Figure 8.4), and we inserted an ALERT statement for displaying the values of the roots [Figure 8.5(b)]. This statement was formed by concatenating the root identification text with the root numerical values (row 21). The ''&'' symbol is the concatenation operator. This dialog box is displayed until the **OK** button is selected.

To allow us to compute roots for more than one quadratic equation, we inserted a GOTO statement in the macro to return us to the beginning of the macro—provided the outcome of the IF statement in row 23 is true. To make the choice, we used an ALERT function in row 22 to display our message interpretation [Figure 8.5(c)]. The *type-code* of the ALERT dialog box displays the **OK** and **Cancel** buttons

TABLE 8.9   SYNTAX OF EXCEL INPUT AND ALERT FUNCTIONS

Input information via a dialog box

INPUT(*message,data-type*[,[*box-title*][,[*default-entry*][,[*x-pos*][,*y-pos*]]]])

message = Text displayed for use of the dialog box.

data-type = Type of data to be entered:

        0 = formula   8 = reference

        1 = number   16 = error

        2 = text   64 = array

        4 = logical

box-title = Name of the dialog box.

default-entry = The entry displayed in the edit box for input as the default value when OK is selected and no overriding value is input.

x-pos = The number of points the dialog box is displaced from center in the *x*-direction.

y-pos = The number of points the dialog box is displaced from center in the *y*-direction.

Notes: 1. The input value must be typed in the edit box when the dialog box is displayed, the default value must be accepted, or the dialog box canceled.

          2. Arguments are position sensitive; omitted arguments must be delimited by commas.

Display a message and wait for operator response

ALERT(*message,type-code*)

message = The text to be displayed in the dialog box.

type-code = Type of dialog box to be displayed:

        1 = Accept (OK) or deny (Cancel) a choice.

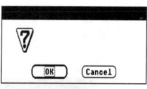

        2 = Confirm (OK) receipt of message.

        3 = Confirm (OK) receipt of error message.

Note: The function returns a value of TRUE for OK and FALSE for Cancel.

	A	B
1		Quadcom
2		Command macro - shortcut key = "q"
3		Inputs: coefficients a, b, and c.
4		Outputs: Roots X1 and X2.
5	AI	=INPUT("Type coefficient a:",1)
6	BI	=INPUT("Type coefficient b:",1)
7	CI	=INPUT("Type coefficient c:",1)
8	Radicand	=BI*BI-4*AI*CI
9		=IF(Radicand>=0,GOTO(Test.zero))
10		=SET.VALUE(X.1,"Imaginary")
11		=SET.VALUE(X.2,"Imaginary")
12		=GOTO(End)
13	Test.zero	=IF(Radicand>0,GOTO(Sqrt.rad))
14	Eq.value	=-BI/(2*AI)
15		=SET.VALUE(X.1,Eq.value)
16		=SET.VALUE(X.2,Eq.value)
17		=GOTO(End)
18	Sqrt.rad	=SQRT(Radicand)
19		=SET.VALUE(X.1,(-BI-Sqrt.rad)/(2*AI))
20		=SET.VALUE(X.2,(-BI+Sqrt.rad)/(2*AI))
21	End	=ALERT("X1 = "&X.1&", X2 = "&X.2,2)
22	Repeat	=ALERT("Solve another equation? OK=Yes, Cancel=No",1)
23		=IF(Repeat,GOTO(AI))
24		=RETURN()
25	X.1	X.2
26	-5	3

Figure 8.4 Function macro of Figure 7.22 converted to a command macro for Example 8.1.

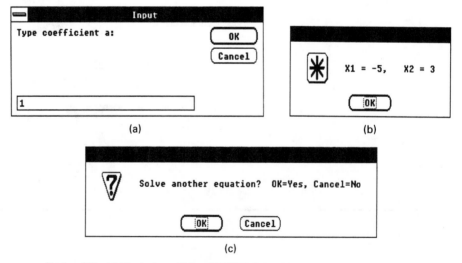

(a)

(b)

(c)

Figure 8.5 (a) Typical coefficient INPUT dialog box, (b) root values ALERT dialog box, and (c) repeat ALERT dialog box of Example 8.1.

so that the outcome will be either TRUE or FALSE, respectively. The IF statement tests this outcome in row 23 via variable Repeat.

We used the set of macro test values shown in Figure 7.23. The residual values in row 26 of Figure 8.4 are the roots for one set of values in the test set.

8.2.2 Recording and Editing Command Macros

In the previous section, we described how to manually prepare command macros. We have the greatest flexibility possible when manually preparing them, and in many instances, this is the only way to make the macro do what we want it to do. We will demonstrate this later in this section. Meanwhile, we will describe how to prepare some command macros automatically via the macro record feature.

When we speak of recording a command macro in Excel, we refer to using a feature that records our commands in a macro sheet. The procedure is simply to turn on the recorder, execute the commands to be recorded, then stop the recorder. We cannot record function macros this way, since they do not perform actions. Recording can be useful even for parts of a command macro, since we can edit the macro to change, delete, or add other commands that complete or correct it. We can even record part of a macro into an existing macro. If we make errors, we can correct the macro or begin over. Advantages in recording a macro are that we do not have to decide which commands from the macro reference manual we will use, nor do we have to worry about the command syntax, since the recording feature takes care of these details.

The straightforward way to record a new macro is as follows:

1. Execute **Macro Record** [Figure 8.3(a)].
2. Enter the name of the macro into the **Name** text box of the dialog box [Figure 8.3(c)]. If desired, type a shortcut key into the **Key: Ctrl+** text box; and choose **OK**. A new macro sheet is opened behind other open sheets, unless a command macro sheet is already open, in which case the new macro will be recorded in the existing sheet.
3. Execute **Start Recorder** [Figure 8.3(a)]. The menu will toggle to **Stop Recorder,** which will be the command visible in the menu when next called up.
4. Perform the actions to be recorded.
5. Execute **Macro Stop Recorder** [see step 3].

The RETURN function is automatically recorded as the last statement of the macro. The macro sheet can now be brought to the top and sight checked for accuracy. It can be edited for changes, as described below, or executed as described in Section 8.2.1.

A recorded macro may require editing because (a) there are errors in it, since the wrong command may have been entered unknowingly, (b) some statements need rearrangement for efficiency purposes, (c) there is redundancy in it; for example the **Edit Undo** command causes an UNDO function to be recorded along with the command to be undone, both of which should be removed, or (d) some operations cannot be performed during the recording operation and must be manually added, the IF function of Figure 8.1, for example. A command macro sheet is edited in the same manner as any other Excel sheet. Commands may be added, deleted, or modified in any way with which the user is familiar.

We are not limited to recording a macro on a new macro sheet each time we use the recorder. We can select a cell range on an existing macro sheet before recording to indicate placement of the commands on the sheet. In Excel, this cell range is called the *recorder range*. With it, the procedure to follow in recording a macro is as follows:

1. Open an existing macro sheet.
2. Select the recorder range and execute **Macro Set Recorder** [Figure 8.3(a)].
3. Activate the document on which you will perform the commands to be recorded.
4. Execute **Macro Start Recorder** [Figure 8.3(a)]; the status bar will show "Recording".
5. Perform the commands to be recorded.
6. Execute **Macro Stop Recorder** (command replaced **Start Recorder** in step 4).

Because we may use the above procedure to extend or modify a macro, we may not enjoy the luxury of having an unlimited amount of recorder range into which our commands are to be placed. Most restrictions of this procedure are implied by the flowchart of Figure 8.6. Selecting a recorder range should be made with respect to these restrictions. To avoid premature termination of the recording operation, one should make sure that the first cell of the range is either blank or contains the RETURN command. The recorder will record over the RETURN statement but stops when it encounters a statement of any other kind. If the first cell of the range is not blank or does not contain the RETURN command, there should be blank cells at the end of the range or the recorder will stop and issue the message "Recorder range full." By adding blank lines within a macro, one can use the recorder to insert commands in the blank cells as part of a macro modification procedure.

A range spanning several contiguous columns is considered continuous for recording purposes. However, to execute the commands sequentially, Excel inserts the GOTO command at the end of each column within the range to transfer control to the beginning of the range in the next adjacent column as shown in Figure 8.7. A range cannot be formed from multiple cell selections.

The **Relative Record** command of the Macro main menu of Figure 8.3(a) is used to set the cell reference recording mode to relative. When selected, this command toggles to **Absolute Record** so that when next selected the cell refer-

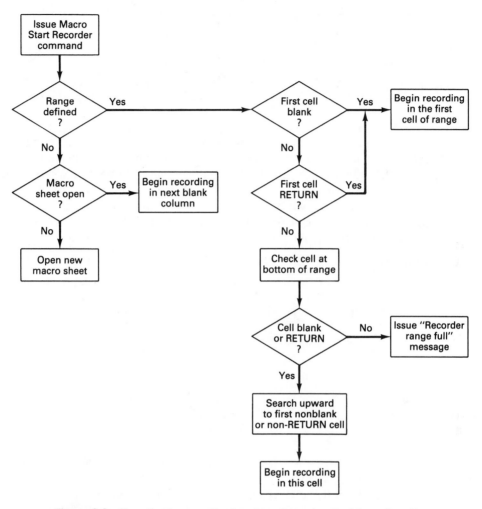

Figure 8.6 Choosing the recording location when using the Macro Start Recorder command.

ences will be recorded in absolute mode. This command may be toggled during a recording session.

At times, it may be useful to watch the macro being recorded. All we need do is make the macro sheet visible at all times. This means we should size and position both the worksheet being worked on and the macro sheet so both are visible during the entire session. The recording action can then be watched as the recording session takes place in the usual manner.

We can record a segmented series of commands during one macro recording session by alternately using the **Macro Start Recorder** and **Macro Stop Recorder** commands, provided we do not use **Macro Set Recorder** after beginning the ses-

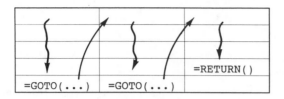

Figure 8.7 Macro recording over a range of contiguous columns.

sion. We record in the usual manner between the Start-Stop commands. No recording takes place between the Stop-Start commands. Thus, during this latter interval, actions not to be recorded can take place. Recording will be continuous within the recorder range. The RETURN command arising from a **Macro Stop Recorder** command will be overwritten with a different command once another **Macro Start Recorder** command is issued. Only after the **Macro Set Recorder** command is issued will a new recorder range have to be defined.

Example 8.2

In this example, we will record a command macro to display a scatter chart as we did in Chapter 6. Upon activating the worksheet window, and after selecting the data range in the worksheet, we follow this procedure:

1. Execute **Edit Copy**.
2. Execute **File New Chart** (get blank window).
3. Execute **Edit Paste Special**.
   a. Select **Values in Columns**.
   b. Select **Series Names in First Row**.
   c. Select **Categories in First Column**.
   d. Choose **OK** (get a column chart).
4. Execute **Gallery Scatter**, select the second chart format, and choose **OK** (get a scatter chart).
5. Select the category axis and execute **Format Scale**.
   a. Toggle on the **Logarithmic Scale** check box.
   b. Set **Value Axis Crosses at** to 0.1.
   c. Choose **OK**.
6. Execute **Chart Gridlines**.
   a. Toggle **Value Axis major gridlines** on.
   b. Toggle **Category axis minor gridlines** on.
   c. Choose **OK**.

First, we activate the worksheet with the data to plot. We will use the index of refraction data of Figure 6.9. We also apply the **Format Number** 0.00 selection to the category values to ensure decimal point alignment. Then, we open a new macro sheet and enter the name of the command macro (row 1 of Figure 8.8). We define this name as a command macro name with the **Define Name** command, assign it the

	A
1	Scatchart
2	Command macro: shortcut key = "s".
3	Construct scatter chart.
4	=COPY()
5	=NEW(2)
6	=PASTE.SPECIAL(2,TRUE,TRUE,FALSE)
7	=GALLERY.SCATTER(2,TRUE)
8	=SELECT("Axis 2")
9	=SCALE(TRUE,TRUE,TRUE,TRUE,0.1,TRUE,FALSE,FALSE)
10	=GRIDLINES(FALSE,TRUE,FALSE,FALSE)
11	=GRIDLINES(FALSE,TRUE,TRUE,FALSE)
12	=RETURN()

Figure 8.8 Command macro of Example 8.2.

shortcut key "s", and enter some comments to this effect. Now we are ready to record the macro.

We must first set the recorder with the **Macro Set Recorder** command. Then, we activate the worksheet and select the data that we will plot. Now, we execute **Macro Start Recorder** and perform the procedure given above. When we finish the procedure, the chart of Figure 8.9 will appear on the screen as the active window (compare with Figure 6.31). Then we stop the recorder with the **Macro Stop Recorder** command. This inserts the RETURN function in our macro as shown in Figure 8.8. We can now also edit the chart for the proper title and axes' labels.

The recorder inserts rather terse versions of the commands into the macro. We can always look up the arguments in the macro reference manual and, if necessary, edit them to change the procedure slightly. This is not necessary for our example.

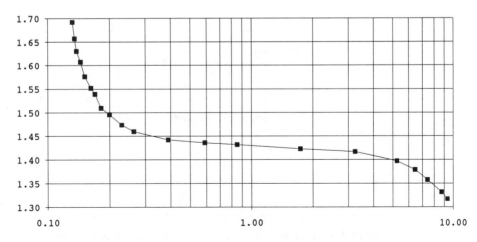

Figure 8.9 Chart prepared with the command macro of Figure 8.8.

8.3 CUSTOM DIALOG BOXES AND MENUS

We now can write our own commands. This is important, not because it may allow us to make a trivial improvement over something that is supplied with Excel but because we can develop truly new capability that others may find difficult or impossible to develop. Were it not possible in macros to make decisions, to iterate calculations, and to access and affect Excel internal variables, we would not have the opportunity to extend our capability via this spreadsheet program. In this section, we will learn to apply our customizing capability to dialog boxes and menus.

8.3.1 The Custom Dialog Box

Excel custom dialog boxes are user-prepared dialog boxes that can fulfill various needs for data entry, command execution, or convenience of interaction for control purposes. The procedure for preparing and using a custom dialog box follows these basic ideas.

1. The dialog box is to be displayed in an Excel window in the same manner as dialog boxes for Excel built-in commands. It is to appear because of a user-invoked command or via a macro-executed command. Eventually, the user must decide on the size and position of the box within the window as shown in Figure 8.10.

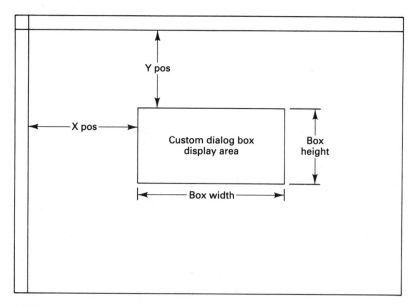

Figure 8.10 Parameters for specifying a custom dialog box within an Excel window.

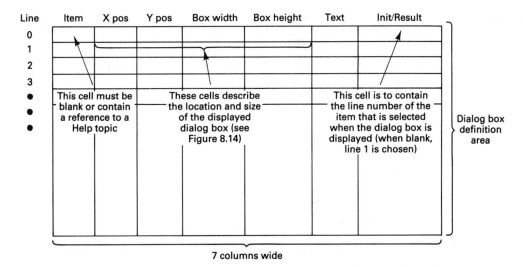

Figure 8.11 Table construction for specifying the features of a custom dialog box.

2. The contents and physical features of a custom dialog box must be specified by the user in table form as shown in Figure 8.11. The table must be seven columns wide and have as many rows as required by the number and types of elements used in describing the box appearance. The first row, line 0 of the table, specifies the size and location of the box as mentioned in step 1 above. The elements that complete the table have item numbers unique to the type of element used, as described in Tables 8.10 through 8.14.

3. The custom dialog box is displayed by executing the DIALOG.BOX function of Table 8.15, which requires as its only argument a reference to the definition table mentioned in step 2 above.

TABLE 8.10 CUSTOM DIALOG BOX OK/CANCEL ELEMENTS

Item number	Description	Example
1	OK button with thick border. It contains text from the Text column and is the default OK button for the ENTER key. It closes the dialog box, enters the dialog box data into the Init/Result column, and returns control to the macro.	
2	Cancel button with thin border. It contains text from the Text column. It closes the dialog box and returns control to the macro.	
3	OK button with thin border. It is like item 1 except it is not the default button for the ENTER key.	
4	Cancel button with thick border. It is like item 2 but is the default cancel button for the ENTER key.	

TABLE 8.11 CUSTOM DIALOG BOX TEXT ELEMENTS

Item number	Description	Example
5	Fixed text, from the Text column, for general purpose labeling.	`Solve another equation?`
20	Directory text that displays the name of the current directory, which is obtained from the system. It does not change after the dialog box is displayed.	`C:\BOOK\EXCEL`

4. Communication between the user and the macro using the dialog box is via entries placed in the Init/Result column of the dialog box table upon return from the DIALOG.BOX function (Figure 8.11). These entries may be tested, used in computations, stored in a database, or otherwise acted upon for the purpose desired. This means that the macro calling the DIALOG.BOX function must contain additional statements that process the data of the dialog box table.

To help decide whether to consider a custom dialog box, here is a list of characteristics that are unique to it.

1. One value of type text, integer, number, formula, or reference may be entered per entry box element (types 6 through 10 of Table 8.12).
2. Initial values may be specified for entry box elements, option buttons, or linked lists.
3. Lists of items may be displayed for selection.

TABLE 8.12 CUSTOM DIALOG BOX ENTRY BOX ELEMENTS

Item number	Description	Example
6	Text box: for entry of text. Optional initial value is obtained from the Init/Result column.	`A text box`
7	Integer box: for entry of integers in the range $-32765 \leq n \leq 32767$. Optional initial value is obtained from the Init/Result column.	`428`
8	Number box: for entry of real or integer numbers. Optional initial value is obtained from the Init/Result column.	`6.28E6`
9	Formula box: for entry of formulas only. Optional initial value is obtained from the Init/Result column. References must be entered in R1C1-style or as variable names but are displayed in the style set for the workspace.	`=PI()*radius^2`
10	Reference box: for entry of cell reference. Optional initial value is obtained from the Init/Result column.	`$C$11:$E$23`

TABLE 8.13   CUSTOM DIALOG BOX OPTION BUTTON AND CHECK BOX ELEMENTS

Item number	Description	Example
11	Option button group designator. Must precede each group of option buttons (item 12). Only one button can be selected in each group. The Init/Result column will contain the number of the option button of this group that was selected. The buttons of the group are numbered sequentially (1,2, . .) as they are listed in the group. If no buttons were selected, #N/A appears in the Init/Result column. There is no graphical symbol for this item.	
12	Option button, with text obtained from the Text column.	◯ <u>M</u>acro Sheet
13	Check box, with text obtained from the Text column. Optional initial value is obtained from the Init/Result column (TRUE = on, FALSE = off, #N/A = grey). The final box status is the value in the Init/Result column.	☐ <u>W</u>ide Carriage
14	Group box for enclosing elements for visual grouping purposes. The text, which is optional, is obtained from the Text column. When used without text and made long and narrow, this box will appear as a line that can be vertically or horizontally oriented.	┌Button Type────┐

4. A choice may be selected from among a group of option buttons.

5. Check boxes with text may be displayed and toggled on or off.

6. Enter/cancel buttons with custom text may be included.

Assuming that a list of requirements suggests use of a custom dialog box, one must first choose the customizing element, or elements, that most appropriately satisfies each requirement. This demands thorough familiarity with the types of elements available and their intended use. All elements available are detailed in Tables 8.10 through 8.14. Here is a brief description of these elements.

1. At least one of the elements of Table 8.10 must be used to end a dialog box entry session. When selected, each of these elements returns control to the macro that called the DIALOG.BOX function. More than one of these elements can be used in a given dialog box and each element may contain customizing text.

2. The text elements of Table 8.11 may be used to enhance understanding of parts of the dialog box. They are usually used with the entry box elements for annotation purposes.

3. The entry box elements of Table 8.12 allow user entry of information. As many entry box elements as needed may be used in a dialog box. Initial values may be assigned to each element. Data type error checking accounts

TABLE 8.14   CUSTOM DIALOG BOX LIST BOX ELEMENTS

Item number	Description	Example
15	List box for displaying names of items. It can be scrolled. The names are obtained from the range of cells given in R1C1-style, or as a range name, in the Text column. The Init/Result column will contain the list item that was selected. The items of the list are numbered sequentially (1,2, . .) beginning with the first item. A default selection can be specified in the Init/Result column ($n = n$th item of the list, blank = first item, #N/A = none selected).	Triangle Quadrilateral Rhombus Circle Regular polygon Ellipse Parabola
16	Linked list box. Like item 15 but must be preceded by a text box (item 6). When an item is selected from the list box, it then appears in the text box.	Circle Regular polygon Ellipse Parabola Hyperbola Cone Sphere
17	Icon. The character displayed is determined by the number entered in the Text column (1 = ?, 2 = *, 3 = !).	
18	Linked file list box for listing files in a directory. It must precede the drive and directory list box (item 19) and must follow a text box (item 6). The text box is used to screen file names that will appear in the linked file list box.	C6CAF2EX.XLS C6CHRTX1.XLC C6CHRTX2.XLC C6CHRTX3.XLC C6TEXTEX.XLS C7P2EX.XLM C7P2EX.XLS
19	Linked drive and directory list box for listing drives and directories on the system. It must follow a linked file list box. If followed immediately by text (item 5), the text displayed is the name of the current drive and directory and is updated if the drive or directory is changed. The directory can be changed by entering the new directory path in the text box that precedes the linked file list box.	[..] [-A-] [-C-] [-D-]

for the assortment of entry box elements available. These elements usually require an associated text box for annotation purposes.

4. The option button elements of Table 8.13 allow only one choice to be made from a group of buttons. As many buttons may be used in a group as required by the application. An initial choice can be specified.

5. The check box with text element, item 13 of Table 8.13, allows an active box to be toggled on or off. As many text boxes may be used in a dialog box as needed for the application. An initial state may be specified and the box may be greyed to designate an inactive box.

TABLE 8.15 THE DIALOG.BOX FUNCTION

Display a custom dialog box

> DIALOG.BOX*(table-ref*
>
> *table-ref* = The cell reference of the dialog box definition area as shown in Figure 8.11.
>
> Notes: 1. If an OK button is chosen, values entered are placed in *table-ref* and the line number of the activated button is returned as the value of the function. The lines (rows) of the definition table are assumed numbered as shown in Figure 8.11.
>
>   2. If a cancel button is chosen, FALSE is returned as the value of the function.
>
>   3. If the definition table is in error, #VALUE! is returned as the value of the function.

6. The list box elements of Table 8.14 allow the names of items to be displayed, and scrolled if necessary. A name may be selected and possibly made to appear in a text box.

7. The icon element of Table 8.14 is often used to designate the condition state of a dialog box. It is useful for providing visual identification of a dialog box with additional information.

A thorough understanding of the functional relationships between the elements in the context of the application, an ability to visually manipulate the elements in their geometric representation for size and location purposes within the confines of the dialog box, and an ability to create text and label information that is both compact and unambiguous are necessary requisites for layout of the dialog box. Unless one chooses to let Excel make the dialog box layout, careful planning is required to achieve a satisfactory custom layout of the elements in the box. The basic idea is to specify the location of the elements by the size and location of their containment boxes as defined in Figure 8.12. These values will eventually be entered in the definition table of Figure 8.11.

Physical dimensions and location of each containment box are in units related to the size of one character in the system font. Horizontally, the unit is one eighth the width of a character, vertically it is one twelfth the height of a character. A box must be specified for all elements except the option box group, item number 11 of Table 8.13, even though it may be invisible when the dialog box is displayed.

It is convenient to use cross-section paper for planning the dialog box physical appearance. The grid squares should be designated as one character size and should be large enough to allow hand printing of characters within the square. Because the characters will be displayed in a uniform size, attention should be directed more at spacing considerations, since that is under direct user control.

Assuming that, based on the requirements for the box, one has determined the type of elements to be used in the box, the next task is to locate these elements

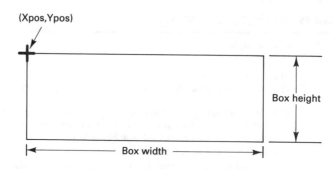

(Xpos,Ypos) = coordinate reference location of the delimiting box for the item (visible or invisible) measured from the left and top edges of the dialog box.

Xpos = horizontal screen unit (1/8th the width of one character in the system font).

Ypos = vertical screen unit (1/12th the height of one character in the system font).

Figure 8.12 Element containment box.

within the confines of the proposed dialog box. For this purpose, it may be more convenient to first sketch the design on a sheet of plain paper. After several iterations of redesign in this manner, the preferred composite of text and boxes should be more accurately transferred to the cross-section paper for size and location purposes.

We begin our layout on the cross-section paper by working in left-to-right and top-to-bottom directions beginning in the upper left corner of the dialog box. Whenever text is a required part of the element, it should be entered on the paper first, with only one character per grid square. This action will help determine the width and height of the containment box for the text. The entry box elements of Table 8.12 should be sized only after sample contents are lettered in the box location on the sheet. The containment box size should then be determined after allowing for the largest width, in characters, of the entry. As the elements are entered on the cross-section paper, they should be labeled with their item number for quick reference when transferring the information to the table. Also, characters to be underlined for keyboard item selection should be noted.

After all elements have been positioned on the cross-section paper, including optional elements such as text for labels, labeled and unlabeled group boxes, and group boxes sized as vertical or horizontal lines, the coordinate reference location (Xpos, Ypos) and the width and height of each element containment box should be determined. Since we chose to use a grid square for one character size, we need merely apply the horizontal and vertical scale factors to the squares for sizing purposes (8 units horizontally and 12 units vertically). The four values thus computed for each containment box should then be written on the cross-section paper for later transfer to the dialog box definition table.

When the above work is finished, the information should be transferred to the Excel sheet and the dialog box definition table completed. This means typing in all the item numbers, dimensions, text (be sure to precede the character to be underlined with the ampersand, &), and initialization values. After sight-checking all the entries for accuracy, name the table with the **Formula Define Name** command, enter this name as the argument to the DIALOG.BOX function, and write a simple command macro to display the dialog box. Make corrections to the table entries and redisplay the box as often as needed until the box appears satisfactory.

Now that we have described in detail the work needed to prepare a custom dialog box, it is only fair to say that we could have let Excel do some of the layout work for us. Should any of the entries in the X pos and/or Y pos columns be omitted (left blank), Excel will position the corresponding element to avoid interference with other elements. Similarly, should any of the entries in the Box width and/or Box height columns be omitted (left blank), Excel will size the corresponding element containment box to accommodate its contents. A vertically oriented dialog box will be formed when a substantial number of the above entries are omitted. It is not necessary that we accept the resulting layout. We could enter values in some, or all, of the blank cells to modify the layout for our requirements.

Example 8.3

In our quadratic equation solving routine of Example 8.1, we used the INPUT and ALERT functions to enter the coefficients and to display the results, respectively. The macro of Figure 8.4 was the result. We will now replace those functions with custom dialog boxes. One dialog box will replace the INPUT functions (we will enter the three coefficients in this box), while another one will replace the ALERT functions (we will display the roots and provide the choice of solving more equations or exiting the macro in this box).

Since the coefficient-entry dialog box is conceptually simple and since we already envisioned the box layout, we will skip the trial layout step and enter the proposed layout on cross-section paper. The first, and only, attempt is shown in Figure 8.13, where each grid square represents one character and where reference coordinates and size are estimated for each containment box. These values

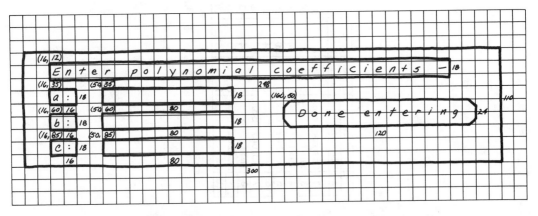

Figure 8.13 Proposed layout of the dialog box of Example 8.3.

	A	B	C	D	E	F	G	H
1	Element	Item	X pos	Y pos	Box width	Box height	Text	Init/Result
2	Dialog box		0	0	300	130		
3	Text	5	20	10	248	18	Enter polynomial coefficients -	
4	Text	5	14	35	16	18	&a:	
5	Number box	8	50	35	80	18		2
6	Text	5	14	65	16	18	&b:	
7	Number box	8	50	65	80	18		4
8	Text	5	14	95	16	18	&c:	
9	Number box	8	50	95	80	18		-30
10	OK	1	162	40	120	24	Done entering	

Figure 8.14 Input dialog box definition table of Example 8.3.

318

are entered into the definition table (B2 : H10 of Figure 8.14) and the table named "Coef.box". The macro is then modified by deleting the three rows of INPUT functions and inserting the DIALOG.BOX function with its definition table reference (row 15 of Figure 8.15). We will debug this dialog box before making changes for the output dialog box.

The coefficient values that we enter will be placed in cells H5, H7 and H9 of Figure 8.14 when we choose the OK button, now labeled "Done entering". We must reference these values in our macro calculations. To avoid many macro changes, we will name these locations AI, BI, and CI for the coefficients a, b, and c, respectively, to correspond with the variables of the original macro. After naming the DIALOG.BOX cell "Box" (row 15 of Figure 8.15) and changing the last IF statement accordingly, we are ready to try out the modified macro.

We enter CTRL+q (the shortcut key) and run the macro. The dialog box appears and we enter a set of coefficient values. We also inspect the box layout and decide to make minor changes in containment box locations. We choose "Done entering" and exit the macro as before, but not until we check the numerical value of the roots for accuracy. After a few iterations of minor containment box positioning and sizing and running the macro, the final values of Figure 8.14 are accepted. These should be compared with those first estimated as shown in Figure 8.13. The dialog box that we see on the screen is shown in Figure 8.16(a).

We follow the above procedure to develop the output dialog box. It is shown in Figure 8.16(b), while its definition table appears in Figure 8.17. We eliminate the temporary root storage locations X.1 and X.2 of Figure 8.4 and, instead, assign these names to cells G36 and G38, respectively. These are the initial values for the corresponding text boxes that will display the root values. The reason we are using text

	A	B
11		Quadcom
12		Command macro - shortcut key = "q"
13		Inputs: coefficients a, b, and c.
14		Outputs: Roots X1 and X2.
15	Box	=DIALOG.BOX(Coef.box)
16	Radicand	=BI*BI-4*AI*CI
17		=IF(Radicand>=0,GOTO(Test.zero))
18		=SET.VALUE(X.1,"Imaginary")
19		=SET.VALUE(X.2,"Imaginary")
20		=GOTO(End)
21	Test.zero	=IF(Radicand>0,GOTO(Sqrt.rad))
22	Eq.value	=-BI/(2*AI)
23		=SET.VALUE(X.1,Eq.value)
24		=SET.VALUE(X.2,Eq.value)
25		=GOTO(End)
26	Sqrt.rad	=SQRT(Radicand)
27		=SET.VALUE(X.1,(-BI-Sqrt.rad)/(2*AI))
28		=SET.VALUE(X.2,(-BI+Sqrt.rad)/(2*AI))
29	End	=DIALOG.BOX(Output.box)
30		=IF(End=8,GOTO(Box))
31		=RETURN()

Figure 8.15 Macro of Example 8.3.

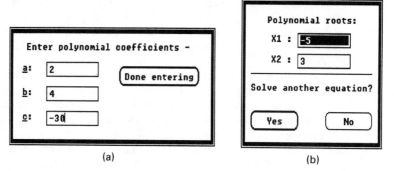

(a)   (b)

Figure 8.16 Custom dialog boxes of Example 8.3: (a) input box and (b) output box.

boxes is to accommodate the "Imaginary" message when the radicand is negative. Text in the Init/Result column will not be displayed by the entry box elements of Table 8.12, so we place the values to be displayed in the Text column. We incorporate an OK button named "Yes" and a cancel button named "No." By testing the value of B29 in row 30 of Figure 8.15, we determine whether to loop back and compute roots for another polynomial. If the value returned by the DIALOG.BOX function is 8, for row 41 (line 8) of Figure 8.17, the outcome of the comparison operation of the IF statement in row 30 of Figure 8.15 is TRUE, and we branch back to label Box in row 15 and prompt for another set of coefficients. When we select the "No" button, FALSE is returned as the value of the DIALOG.BOX function (see Table 8.15), and we drop through the IF statement to the RETURN statement to end the macro.

The values in the Init/Result column of Figure 8.14 and in the Text column of Figure 8.17 are for the same polynomial (a = 2, b = 4, c = −30, X1 = −5, X2 = 3).

8.3.2 The Dialog Editor

Introduction. The Dialog Editor is an application program for graphically preparing custom dialog boxes. It is a convenience feature that is useful but that adds no capability over that described in Section 8.3.1. However, we suggest

	A	B	C	D	E	F	G	H
32	Element	Item	X pos	Y pos	Box width	Box height	Text	Init/Result
33	Dialog box		0	0	200	168		
34	Text	5	32	12	136	18		
35	Text	5	38	35	40	18	Polynomial roots:	
36	Text box	5	78	35	80	18	X1 :	
37	Text	5	38	60	40	18	−5	
38	Text box	5	78	60	80	18	X2 :	
39	Group box	14	8	85	184	2	3	
40	Text	5	8	95	184	18		
41	OK	1	8	130	72	24	Solve another equation?	
42	Cancel	2	120	130	72	24	Yes	
							No	

Figure 8.17 Output dialog box definition table of Example 8.3.

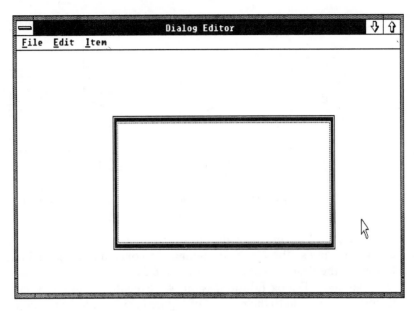

Figure 8.18 Dialog Editor window.

using it to quickly construct a dialog box graphically and to conveniently evaluate different dialog box layouts.

We can perform in the Dialog Editor all the tasks described in Section 8.3.1. We can place the entities of Tables 8.10 through 8.14 in a dialog box and we can move, resize, and delete them. For these purposes, we work in the Dialog Editor window of Figure 8.18. Upon completing the dialog box, we transfer to the macro sheet its definition table for use with the DIALOG.BOX function as described in Section 8.3.1. We described the definition table in connection with Figure 8.11.

Because the Dialog Editor is an application program, we use Clipboard to communicate between it and the macro sheet with **Edit Copy** and **Edit Paste** operations. Whenever we create a dialog box in the Dialog Editor, we must then transfer the definition table to the macro sheet as shown in Figure 8.19. We can also copy an existing dialog box from a macro sheet to the Dialog Editor for modification as shown in Figure 8.20. Eventually, we can return the modified copy to the macro sheet.

Beginning and ending a Dialog Editor session.   To create a new dialog box, we first enter the Dialog Editor by executing the Excel window **Control Run** command. This brings up the **Run Application** dialog box of Figure 8.21 from which we select **Dialog Editor** and choose **OK**. The Dialog Editor window of Figure 8.18 appears, in which a blank dialog box is produced and selected. That dialog box can then be developed into the final product, or it may be replaced by an existing dialog box pasted into the window with the **Edit Paste** command of

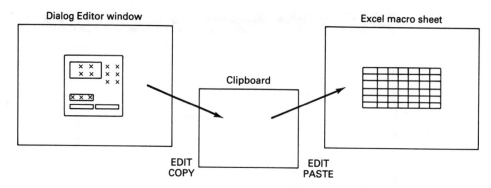

Figure 8.19 Copying a custom dialog box to a macro sheet.

Figure 8.22. If at any time during dialog box development we prefer to begin anew, we can use the **File New** command to open a new dialog box. We are now following the dashed line path of Figure 8.21.

To end a Dialog Editor session, we execute the **File Exit** command and, if necessary, respond to the prompt of Figure 8.23 if we have not copied our custom dialog box to Clipboard.

Dialog Editor procedures.   The purpose of working with the Dialog Editor is to construct a graphical image of a custom dialog box from which a definition table can be extracted. From Section 8.3.1, we know that much planning and attention to details are required to achieve the desired result. The Dialog Editor simplifies this task somewhat but finishing work is still needed to complete the task. We now introduce procedures that ease the graphical construction effort.

The procedures of Tables 8.16 and 8.17 describe how to use the **Item** and **Edit** menu commands for placing and adjusting various entities in the dialog box. The **Item** menu of Figure 8.24(a) contains the types of entities that can be placed in a dialog box. These entities are all described in detail in Tables 8.10 through 8.14.

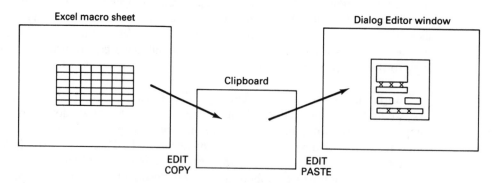

Figure 8.20 Changing an existing custom dialog box.

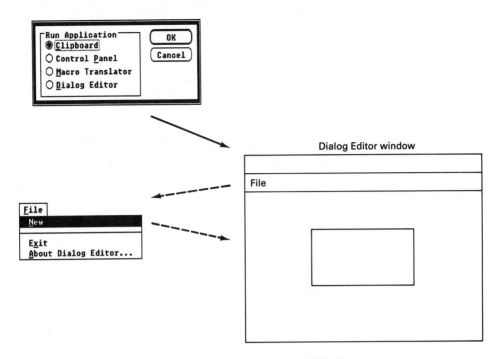

Figure 8.21   Creating a custom dialog box.

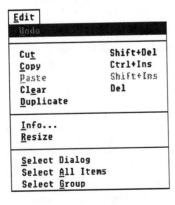

Figure 8.22   Dialog Editor Edit menu.

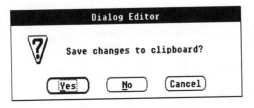

Figure 8.23   Dialog Editor output prompt.

TABLE 8.16   DIALOG EDITOR PROCEDURES

Selecting

  Single items, groups, and the dialog box:
  - Keyboard—TAB until the desired item is selected.
  - Mouse—Click the desired item.
  - Consider using **Edit** menu commands.

  Multiple items:
  - Keyboard—TAB to select the first item, CTRL+TAB to the second item desired (SHIFT+CTRL+TAB to reverse the direction), and CTRL+SPACEBAR to select the second item. Repeat the last two steps for each subsequent item to be selected.
  - Mouse—Click each item while holding down the SHIFT key.

Typing text

  During initial placement:
  Type the new text while the item is still selected.

  During second and subsequent selection:
  1. Select the item, type new text to be added to end of existing text. Press BACKSPACE to remove existing text one letter at a time from right to left.
  2. Select the item, execute **Edit Info**, type the text in the text box or modify it as when working in the formula bar.
  3. With the mouse, double-click the item to display the **Edit Info** dialog box, then type the text in the Text box.

Adding entities

  Button: Execute the **Item Button** command and select the desired button from the **Button Type** group box of Figure 8.24(b). Toggle the **Default** box to the desired value and choose **OK**. The button is added to the dialog box and automatically selected. The text may be changed as described above or in the **Edit Info** dialog box.

  Text: Execute the **Item Text** command. The word "Text" is added to the dialog box and automatically selected. The text may be changed as described above or in the **Edit Info** dialog box.

  Edit Box: Execute the **Item Edit Box** command, select the desired **Edit Type** box from the dialog box of Figure 8.24(c), and choose **OK**. The box is added to the dialog box and automatically selected.

  List Box: Execute the **Item List Box** command, select the desired **List Box Type** from the dialog box of Figure 8.24(d), and choose **OK**. The box is added to the dialog box and automatically selected. The **Standard** list box contains a vertical scroll bar for scrolling a list of items, the **Linked** list box is linked with an edit box that displays the item selected in the scrolling linked list box, and the **Linked File/Directory** button produces two scrolling list boxes, one of which is linked to an edit box that displays the item selected, and, if the **Tracking Text** box is toggled on, a text box is produced that displays the selection in the other list box.

  Icon: Execute the **Item Icon** command, select the desired button from the **Icon** group box of Figure 8.24(e), and choose **OK**. The icon is added to the dialog box and automatically selected. It can be resized if the **Width** and **Height** auto check boxes of its **Edit Info** dialog box are off.

TABLE 8.16   (Continued)

Deleting entities

    Single items:

        Select the item to delete and execute **Edit Clear** or press DELETE.

    Multiple items:

        • Keyboard—Select the items to delete as described under ''Selecting'' and execute **Edit Clear** or press DELETE.

        • Mouse—Select the items to delete as described under ''Selecting'' and execute **Edit Clear** or Press DELETE.

        Note: The dialog box cannot be deleted with the **Edit Clear** command. **Edit Clear** applied to a selected dialog box deletes all items in the box.

Moving entities

Entity	Keyboard	Mouse
Item	Select the item, position it with the arrow keys, use CTRL+arrow key for precise positioning, press ENTER.	Select the item and drag it to the desired location. Hold down the SHIFT key while dragging to cause vertical or horizontal movement only, depending on the direction of the initial drag.
Dialog box	Execute **Edit Select Dialog** and position the box with the arrow keys, then press ENTER.	Click in the box not on an item and drag it to the desired location.

Cancel a move by pressing ESCAPE before pressing ENTER or releasing the mouse button.

Resizing entities

Entity	Keyboard	Mouse
Item	Select the item, use SHIFT+arrow key to change its size ($\rightarrow$ or $\downarrow$ increases the size; $\leftarrow$ or $\uparrow$ decreases the size), then press ENTER.	Select the item and drag a side or corner of the item to the desired size.
Dialog box	Execute **Edit Select Dialog**, use SHIFT+arrow key to change the size (arrow keys as defined for Item), then press ENTER.	Click in the box not on an item and drag a side or corner of the box to the desired size.

We use the **Item** menu commands, and their associated dialog boxes, to place an entity in our custom dialog box. Thereafter, we use the procedures of Tables 8.16 and 8.17 to position and size the entities and to enter text wherever necessary. For these purposes, we can also use the **Edit Info** command dialog box (Figure 8.25). We see that its entries correspond to the last 6 of the 7 columns of the definition table. Whereas graphically we can position and size the entities, we really do not know their coordinate and size values until we see them in the **X**, **Y**, **Width**, and **Height** boxes of the **Info** dialog box. The **Auto** check boxes are used for Dialog Editor determined position and size (box checked), or for manual

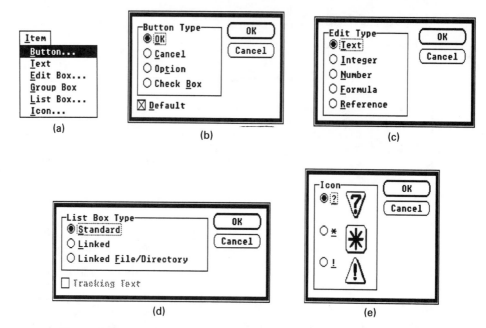

Figure 8.24 (a) Item drop-down menu and dialog boxes for the (b) Button, (c) Edit Box, (d) List Box, and (e) Icon commands.

entry of these values (box unchecked). The **Text** and **Init/Result** boxes are for entry of the values to complete the row of the definition table.

Some commands of the **Edit** menu of Figure 8.22 are special to the Dialog Editor. The **Clear** command deletes the selected item(s) from the dialog box (except the dialog box itself), the **Duplicate** command causes another copy of the selected entity to be reproduced immediately below the selected one, and the

TABLE 8.17 PROCEDURES FOR WORKING WITH GROUPS

Adding a group box

    Execute the **Item Group Box** command to create a group box within the dialog box. It is automatically selected, at which time its text may be changed in the **Edit Info** dialog box or as described in Table 8.16.

Creating a group

    Add a group box to the dialog box as described above. Then, add items to the group by choosing them from the **Item** menu according to the procedures of Table 8.16.

Changing a group

    Edit, move, or resize individual items in a group according to the procedures of Table 8.16. Execute the **Edit Select Group** command, after first selecting an item in the group, and move, resize, or clear the group as if all its members were a single item.

```
┌─────────────────────────────────────────────┐
│ Dialog Info              ☐ Resettable        │
│                                              │
│              X: [156]  ☐ Auto   ╭─────────╮  │
│              Y: [87]   ☐ Auto   │   OK    │  │
│          Width: [205]  ☐ Auto   ╰─────────╯  │
│         Height: [101]  ☐ Auto   ( Cancel )   │
│           Text: [                  ]         │
│    Init/Result: [                  ]         │
│        Comment: [                  ]         │
└─────────────────────────────────────────────┘
```

Figure 8.25   Edit Info dialog box.

Resize command automatically adjusts the size of the selected item(s) to provide reasonable clearance for the contents. **Select Dialog** selects the dialog box and its contents, **Select all Items** selects all items within the dialog box, while **Select Group** selects all items within the group selected when the command is executed. This latter command is useful when following the procedures of Table 8.17.

Example 8.4

In this example, we will use the Dialog Editor to prepare a new output dialog box for Example 8.3. The current output dialog box is shown in Figure 8.16(b). Our new dialog box will contain an echo of the input coefficients, the root values, and revised wording of the next solution and exit routine buttons. The result will be the dialog box of Figure 8.26.

We will prepare our new dialog box beginning with the blank dialog box that appears when we first enter the Dialog Editor. Our plan is to prepare the dialog box from top to bottom as shown in Figure 8.26. Therefore, we first use the **Item Group Box** command to place the box with its text "Input coefficients" in the dialog box. We use the group box only for appearance. It will need resizing. The text and number boxes are then placed as shown in the figure. We remember that the root display boxes of Example 8.3 were text boxes in order to display the word "Imagi-

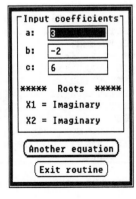

Figure 8.26   Output dialog box of Example 8.4.

	A	B	C	D	E	F	G	H
35	Element	Item	X pos	Y pos	Box width	Box height	Text	Init/Result
36	Dialog box		0	0	176	207		
37	Group box	14	8	1	160	148	Input coefficients	
38	Text	5	12	88	153		***** Roots *****	
39	Number box	8	55	19	90	18		3
40	Number box	8	55	40	90	18		-2
41	Number box	8	55	61	90	18		6
42	Text	5	20	20	16	18	a:	
43	Text	5	20	41	16	18	b:	
44	Text	5	20	62	16	18	c:	
45	Text box	5	60	107	95	18	Imaginary	
46	Text box	5	60	126	95	18	Imaginary	
47	OK	1	16	156	144		Another equation	
48	Cancel	2	32	182	112		Exit routine	
49	Text	5	20	107	40	18	X1 =	
50	Text	5	20	127	40	18	X2 =	

Figure 8.27   Dialog definition table for Figure 8.26.

nary'' when required. Believing that more than one equation will be solved whenever the macro using this dialog box is executed, we use a default OK button labeled ''Another equation''. We then add a cancel button labeled ''Exit routine''.

Much moving and resizing of the entities was needed to achieve the layout of Figure 8.26. Precise positioning for alignment and uniformity was finally accom-

	A	B
11		Quadcom
12		Command macro - shortcut key = "q"
13		Inputs: coefficients a, b, and c.
14		Outputs: Roots X1 and X2.
15	Box	=DIALOG.BOX(Coef.box)
16	Radicand	=BI*BI-4*AI*CI
17		=IF(Radicand>=0,GOTO(Test.zero))
18		=SET.VALUE(X.1,"Imaginary")
19		=SET.VALUE(X.2,"Imaginary")
20		=GOTO(End)
21	Test.zero	=IF(Radicand>0,GOTO(Sqrt.rad))
22	Eq.value	=-BI/(2*AI)
23		=SET.VALUE(X.1,Eq.value)
24		=SET.VALUE(X.2,Eq.value)
25		=GOTO(End)
26	Sqrt.rad	=SQRT(Radicand)
27		=SET.VALUE(X.1,(-BI-Sqrt.rad)/(2*AI))
28		=SET.VALUE(X.2,(-BI+Sqrt.rad)/(2*AI))
29	End	=SET.VALUE(AI.out,AI)
30		=SET.VALUE(BI.out,BI)
31		=SET.VALUE(CI.out,CI)
32	Exit	=DIALOG.BOX(Output.box)
33		=IF(Exit=11,GOTO(Box))
34		=RETURN()

Figure 8.28   Macro of Example 8.4.

plished with the **Edit Info** command. The **Auto** check box was turned on for some dimensions of several entities.

The custom dialog box was pasted into the macro sheet of Example 8.3, replacing the existing output dialog box definition table. It is shown in Figure 8.27. The macro was modified as shown in Figure 8.28 to accommodate the new output dialog box. We added rows 29, 30, and 31 to echo the input values, gave cells H39, H40, and H41 of Figure 8.27 the names AI.out, BI.out, and CI.out, respectively, to accommodate the echoed values, relocated the End label, relabeled the DIALOG.BOX call statement to Exit, and entered the new line number in the IF statement of row 33. We also had to give cells G45 and G46 of Figure 8.27 the names X.1 and X.2, respectively.

It is very important that the macro be run through all test values to check out the dialog box. Testing of the macro required refinement of layout, which was done by changing some definition table entries manually. The definition table of Figure 8.27 shows blank entries for the box height in rows 38, 47, and 48. The blank cells were pasted in from the Dialog Editor and result from having the **Auto** check box on for these entries. One must also inspect the definition table for rows that describe hidden entities, such as text boxes without text. These can be removed manually.

8.3.3 The Custom Menu

The custom menu feature of Excel allows us to prepare our own menus. This is really only a convenience feature, since we already are able to do everything the custom menu would do. But there are times when the custom menu is useful. For example, we can place the names of our command macros in a custom menu and execute them more conveniently. Also, we avoid the problems of remembering their names, since they would be displayed for us to merely recognize. We can create our own computational sequences and select them from a menu. This is most useful when there are involved sequences and for persons less familiar with what is to be done. It is also preferred when demos are to be run automatically and often. Or, we may wish to reorganize the menu layouts for preferential reasons.

The Excel menu bar structure is shown in Figure 8.29. It consists of a menu bar in which menu names appear, beginning from the left end, that are internally referred to by their numerical position in the bar. The Help menu is always in the far rightmost position as shown. The menu bars are numbered. Six built-in menu bars, numbered from 1 through 6, are provided, four of which are shown in Figure 8.30. The other two are short menu versions of Figures 8.30(a) and 8.30(b). The user may add 15 custom menu bars to the system. They will be numbered consecutively as they are added, continuing from the built-in bar numbers. Only one menu bar is displayed at any time. It is the active bar.

Upon selecting a menu name, a drop-down menu of command names appears as shown in Figure 8.29. When one of these command names is selected, that command is automatically executed. A command name in the menu may be greyed (not selectable) or may have a check mark placed next to it. We have seen

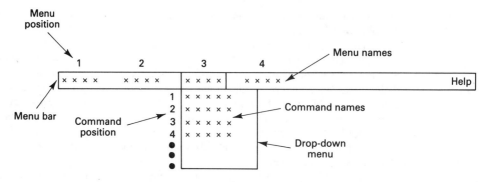

Figure 8.29   Excel menu bar structure.

check marks in the Window menu where they were used to indicate the active window. The meaning of a check mark inserted by the user is not limited to this interpretation.

Several macro functions are available in Excel to help us develop custom menus. These functions, described in Tables 8.18 through 8.20, allow us to do the following:

1. Create new menu bars or delete user-created menu bars.
2. Add or delete built-in or user-created menus from menu bars.
3. Add or delete built-in or user-created commands from menus.

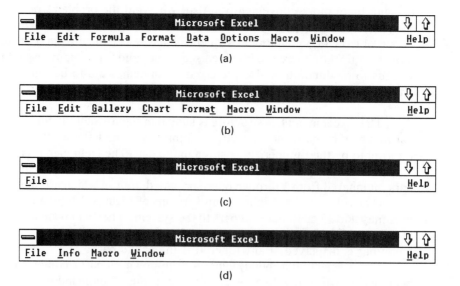

Figure 8.30   Excel built-in menu bars: (a) Worksheet and macro sheet (bar ID = 1), (b) chart (bar ID = 2), (c) nil (bar ID = 3), and (d) info (bar ID = 4).

TABLE 8.18 MENU BAR MACRO FUNCTIONS

Create an empty menu bar	
ADD.BAR()	Creates a new custom menu bar. The bar ID number is returned as the function value. The new bar is not displayed. The Excel limit is 15 custom menu bars. When the limit will be exceeded, the function returns #VALUE!.
Delete a specific menu bar	
DELETE.BAR(*bar-ID*)	Deletes the custom menu bar numbered *bar-ID*, an integer, which cannot be the currently displayed menu bar.
Get the number of the active menu bar	
GET.BAR()	The active menu bar ID number is returned as the function value.
Display a specific menu bar	
SHOW.BAR([*bar-ID*])	Displays the menu bar numbered *bar-ID*, which may be either a built-in or custom menu bar. If a custom menu bar is displayed, the automatic menu bar switching to accompany different types of documents is disabled. If *bar-ID* for a built-in menu bar is selected, the corresponding sheet or window must be active. If *bar-ID* is omitted, the menu bar corresponding to the active window is displayed.

TABLE 8.19 MENU ADD/DELETE MACRO FUNCTIONS

Add a menu to a menu bar
ADD.MENU(*bar-ID*,*menu-ref*)
bar-ID = The number of the menu bar to which a menu is to be added. It may be an Excel built-in menu bar or the number of a bar added by the ADD.BAR function.
menu-ref = The name of the cell area in which the menu to be added is described.
Note: If the menu was added to *bar-ID*, it is placed immediately to the right of the existing menus on the bar and the function returns the position number for the new menu.
Delete a menu from a menu bar
DELETE.MENU(*bar-ID*,*menu-pos*)
bar-ID = The number of the menu bar from which a menu is to be deleted. It may be an Excel built-in menu bar or the number of a bar added by the ADD.BAR function.
menu-pos = The number of a menu, or the name of a menu as text, that is to be deleted from menu bar numbered *bar-ID*.
Note: Upon deletion, *menu-pos* values for all menus to the right of the deleted one are decreased by 1. If *menu-pos* does not exist in *bar-ID*, #VALUE! is returned as the function value.

TABLE 8.20 MENU COMMAND MACRO FUNCTIONS

> Add command(s) to a menu of a specific menu bar

> ADD.COMMAND(*bar-ID*,*menu-pos*,*menu-ref*)
>
> *bar-ID* = The number of the menu bar to which commands are to be added to a menu. It may be an Excel built-in menu bar or the number of a bar added by the ADD.BAR function.
>
> *menu-pos* = The number of a menu, or the name of a menu as text, to which the commands are to be added.
>
> *menu-ref* = The name of the cell area in which the commands to be added are described.
>
> *Note:* The function returns the position number in *menu-pos* at which the first command from *menu-ref* was added.

> Delete a command from a menu of a specific menu bar

> DELETE.COMMAND(*bar-ID*,*menu-pos*,*cmd-pos*)
>
> *bar-ID* = The number of the menu bar from which a command is to be deleted. It may be an Excel built-in menu bar or the number of a bar added by the ADD.BAR function.
>
> *menu-pos* = The number of a menu, or the name of a menu as text, from which a command is to be deleted.
>
> *cmd-pos* = The position number, or title as text, of the command to be deleted.
>
> *Note:* Upon deletion, *cmd-pos* values for all commands below the deleted one are decreased by 1. If *cmd-pos* does not exist in *menu-pos*, #VALUE! is returned as the function value.

> Add or remove a check mark beside a command

> CHECK.COMMAND(*bar-ID*,*menu-pos*,*cmd-pos*,*mark*)
>
> *bar-ID* = The number of the menu bar for which a command is to be marked. It may be an Excel built-in menu bar or the number of a bar added by the ADD.BAR function.
>
> *menu-pos* = The number of a menu, or the name of a menu as text, in which a command is to be marked.
>
> *cmd-pos* = The position number, or title as text, of the command to be marked.
>
> *mark* = When TRUE, a check mark is placed next to the command; when FALSE, the check mark is removed.
>
> *Note:* Excel may add or remove check marks set on built-in commands by this function.

> Enable or disable a command

> ENABLE.COMMAND(*bar-ID*,*menu-pos*,*cmd-pos*,*flag*)
>
> *bar-ID* = The number of the menu bar for which the enable flag for a command is to be set. It may be an Excel built-in menu bar or the number of a bar added by the ADD.BAR function.
>
> *menu-pos* = The number of a menu, or the name of a menu as text, in which the enable flag for a command is to be set.
>
> *cmd-pos* = The position number, or title as text, of the command whose enable flag is to be set.
>
> *flag* = When TRUE (enabled), the command can be selected (black color); when FALSE (disabled), it cannot be selected (grey color).
>
> *Note:* If the specified command does not exist, or is a built-in command, #VALUE! is returned as the function value.

> Rename a command

> RENAME.COMMAND(*bar-ID*,*menu-pos*,*cmd-pos*,*new-name*)
>
> *bar-ID* = The number of the menu bar for which a command is to be renamed. It may be an Excel built-in menu bar or the number of a bar added by the ADD.BAR function.
>
> *menu-pos* = The number of a menu, or the name of a menu as text, in which a command is to be renamed.
>
> *cmd-pos* = The position number, or title as text, of the command to be renamed.
>
> *new-name* = The new name of the command, as text.
>
> *Note:* If the specified command does not exist, #VALUE! is returned as the function value. Excel may rename built-in commands renamed by this function.

4. Rename and add or remove check marks from built-in or user-created commands.

5. Set or reset the grey tone of user-created commands.

To develop a custom menu, we must write a command macro using the macro functions of Tables 8.18 through 8.20 so as to construct the menu bar with its menu names and the drop-down menus with their lists of commands. For each command in a menu, we must prepare its corresponding command macro that will be executed whenever we select the command from the menu.

Assuming we have commands in mind that we want to place in menus, we have a choice in how to accomplish this. We could (1) develop an entirely new custom menu with its own menu bar, (2) add the commands to menus of a built-in menu bar, or (3) use a combination of these schemes. The procedures to follow are similar for these alternatives. We will describe in detail the first alternative and then indicate the procedural change for the second alternative. Here is the procedure (also see Figure 8.31).

1. Write a macro for each custom command to be added to a menu. Be sure to thoroughly check out the commands.

2. Prepare the cell area for each menu as shown in Figure 8.32. Each such area defines the menu content and contains lists of the corresponding commands, status bar messages, and help topic references.

3. Open a new or existing macro sheet on which this procedure will be entered.

4. Enter on the macro sheet the ADD.BAR function to create a custom menu bar. Name the cell in which the bar ID (identification number) is returned for reference in the functions to follow.

5. Enter on the macro sheet as many ADD.MENU functions as required to form the custom menu. Use the bar ID cell reference of step 4 and the menu cell area references of step 2.

6. Enter the SHOW.BAR function, the RETURN function, and name this custom menu macro in the usual manner.

7. Try out the custom menu macro. If necessary, correct errors and make changes until the custom menu meets with approval.

The above procedure, when performed without errors, will create the menu bar and menus and, because of the SHOW.BAR function of step 6, will display it. Since there can be only one menu bar visible in a window, it will be necessary to prepare another command macro to return the screen to its original display after the custom menu is no longer required. For this purpose, use only the SHOW.BAR function with the bar ID of the previous menu bar number.

During the development phase, one must be careful not to create too many menu bars. Each time the above procedure is run, another menu bar is created. Eventually, the limit of 15 bars will be reached. One must then delete some of

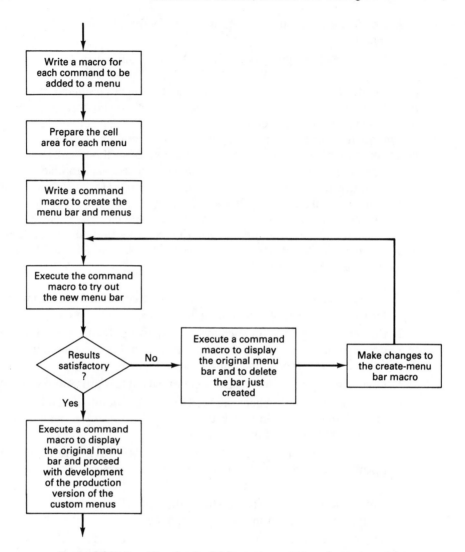

Figure 8.31 Procedure for developing custom menus and a new menu bar.

these bars to make room for new ones. This is done in another command macro with the DELETE.BAR function referencing the bar ID of the menu bar to be deleted. The bar ID can be determined by displaying the command macro sheet in values mode and reading the bar ID number from the cell that contains the ADD.BAR function.

To augment a built-in menu, one must use the ADD.MENU and/or ADD.COMMAND functions of Tables 8.19 and 8.20 in conjunction with the cell areas for any new menus. Changes can be made by modifying the cell areas and/or using the remainder of the functions in the tables.

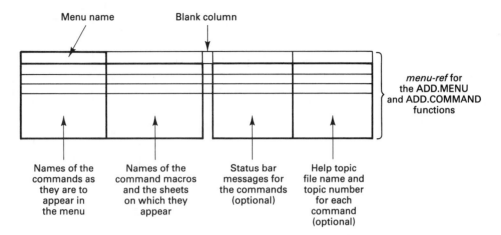

Figure 8.32   Cell area for a menu.

Example 8.5

In this example, we will create a new menu bar, add to it a custom menu of commands, and add a command to a built-in menu.

Thus far, in this chapter, we prepared three command macros as described in Examples 8.1, 8.2, and 8.3. We will add these commands to our custom menu as well as provide a way to return to a built-in menu bar. We will invoke our custom menu bar with the command "Custom" that we will add to the Macro menu of the built-in worksheet menu bar (bar 1) as shown in Figure 8.33(a) and prepare a new menu bar (bar 7) with its menu as shown in Figure 8.33(b).

The ADD.COMMAND function of Table 8.20 shows that we need only specify the bar ID, the menu position, and the reference at which the table describing the

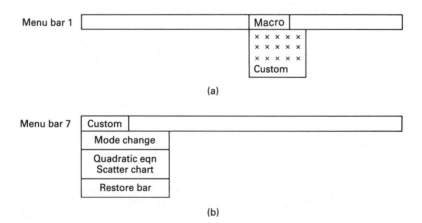

Figure 8.33   (a) Proposed built-in menu modification for Example 8.5, and (b) custom menu bar and menu for Example 8.5.

	A	B	C	D	E
1		Custom.menu			
2		Shortcut key = "u"			
3	Bar.ID	=ADD.BAR()			
4		=ADD.MENU(Bar.ID,A19:E25)			
5		=SHOW.BAR(Bar.ID)			
6		=RETURN()			
7		Restore.bar			
8		Shortcut key = "r"			
9		=SHOW.BAR()			
10		=RETURN()			
11		Del.bar			
12		Shortcut key = "b"			
13		=DELETE.BAR(Bar.ID)			
14		=RETURN()			
15		Sho.bar			
16		Shortcut key = "o"			
17		=SHOW.BAR(Bar.ID)			
18		=RETURN()			
19	&Custom	VALFOR.XLM!Display.mode			
20	&Mode change			Dialog box interaction	
21	-				
22	&Quadratic eqn	EX8P3.XLM!Quadcom			
23	&Scatter chart	EX8P2.XLM!Scatchart			
24	-				
25	&Restore bar	EX8P5.XLM!Restore.bar			
26		Add.cmd			
27		Shortcut key = "a"			
28		=ADD.COMMAND(1,7,A30:E30)			
29		=RETURN()			
30	&Custom	EX8P5.XLM!Sho.bar			

Figure 8.34 Macro of Example 8.5.

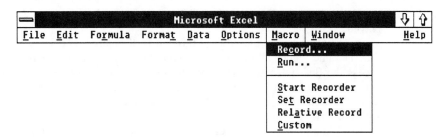

Figure 8.35   Modified Macro menu of Example 8.5.

command is found in order to add a command to an existing menu. Since we want to add the command to the Macro menu (position 7) of the worksheet menu bar (bar ID = 1), we prepare the command macro as shown in Figure 8.34, rows 26 through 29. The table describing the command is in row 30, where we see that the command name will be "Custom" and, when invoked, it will call the command macro named "Sho.bar", which is shown in rows 15 through 18 of the figure. Because we have the macro for creating the menu bar on the same sheet as this macro, we use the variable Bar.ID to reference it in the SHOW.BAR function. After we run this macro and take a look at the Macro menu, we see our command added to the bottom of the menu as shown in Figure 8.35.

Next, we must prepare the cell area for our Custom menu. We open the macro sheets for the three commands we will place in the menu. In column A of figure 8.34, we enter the name of our menu (row 19) and the names of the commands as we want them to appear in the menu (rows 20 through 25). The hyphens in rows 21 and 24 will cause dividing lines to be placed in their respective positions of the menu. In column B, we enter the names of the macro sheets with the macro names, separated by the exclamation mark. For the moment, we leave the other columns blank.

To generate the menu bar, we use the command macro in rows 1 through 6 of Figure 8.34. The bar number will be entered in cell B3 (named Bar.ID) when we run the macro. The information in the cell area of A19:E25 causes the menu to appear as shown in Figure 8.36. When we select "Restore bar", the command macro in rows 7 through 10 of Figure 8.34 executes and causes the displayed menu bar to conform with the type of active window currently displayed. If we had just executed the "Quadratic eqn" command, the active window would be a macro sheet so menu bar 1 would be displayed. If we had just executed the "Scatter chart" command, the

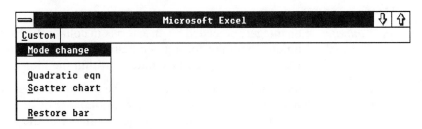

Figure 8.36   Custom menu bar and menu of Example 8.5.

active window would be the chart the macro creates so menu bar 2 would be displayed.

The Del.bar macro in rows 11 through 14 of Figure 8.34 deletes the menu bar of Bar.ID value. Since all our custom menu macros are on one macro sheet, they all access the Bar.ID variable. During our menu development effort, we may wish to delete the last menu bar and make changes for the next iteration of development. Since the number of the bar will still be available in Bar.ID, we would delete that bar with the Del.bar command macro. Otherwise, the menu bars will accumulate until we reach the limit of 15. We do not execute the Del.bar function from our custom menu because we cannot delete an active menu bar.

Figure 8.34 shows a status bar message in column D of row 22. We added it to try out this feature. Unfortunately, the way the Quadcom macro works this message is caused to be displayed for only an instant of time. To really be useful, execution must linger within the macro for enough time to allow us to read the message.

8.4 PROVIDING CUSTOM HELP INFORMATION

Because we now can customize our spreadsheet application to a considerable degree, we most surely will not have appropriate built-in help information to accompany it. Help may be needed to understand something about our custom dialog box, it may be needed to learn more about our custom menu commands, or it may be needed while running an application macro or worksheet that contains some involved concept. In this section, we will describe how to make help-information available to Excel users under each of the above circumstances.

The concept of providing custom-help information is based on preparing help topics in a file according to established procedures and then referencing them via the file name and the topic identifying number. We are not limited to using just one file for this purpose, and we have no stringent file organization rules to follow that would cause help-file maintenance to become burdensome.

A help file is composed of a succession of help entries. Each entry is a help topic that is composed of at least two lines as follows:

topic-number comment

help-message

where

topic-number = an integer, preceded by an asterisk in column 1, that represents a unique identifier for a given help message. The integers do not have to be assigned in sequence within the file.

comment = an optional short comment for the benefit of those who read the help file. It is separated from *topic-number* by at least one space and occupies no more than the remainder of the first line of the help topic entry.

help-message = the message to be displayed as the help topic. It begins on the second line of the entry and may occupy as many succeeding lines as is required to hold the message. There are no special delimiting characters for it.

The help file entries can be prepared in a text editor. The file, saved under a name that will be referenced in a custom dialog box, custom menu, or HELP function, can contain help topics for unrelated applications. When used in the context for which it is intended, the complete reference is constructed as follows:

file-name! topic-integer

where

file-name = the name of the file and, if necessary, its path name.

topic-integer = the *topic-number* assigned to the help topic in *file-name*.

Figure 8.37 is a help file containing 7 help topics. The topics are in ascending topic number order because they can be visually located rapidly by number in a file containing many entries. This is in keeping with our philosophy of simplicity of organization and convenience in utilization. We also want to avoid duplication of topic number assignment. Sequential searching of the file will retrieve the first of identically numbered topics only. Here are examples for using custom-help information in the three contexts referred to at the beginning of this section.

Example 8.6

The meaning of dialog box entries is often not obvious to beginning users, so help information should be provided. Because the need for such help is usually not realized until the dialog box is displayed, help information should be available when the dialog box appears. We provide this help by including a file reference to its access in the dialog box definition area (upper left cell of Figure 8.11). This reference follows the format described above. The user can display the selected help information in its own window by pressing the F1 key.

We prepared help information for both dialog boxes of Example 8.3 by adding two help topics to our help file, named USER.HLP. These topics, numbered 32 for the coefficient entry dialog box and 33 for the root display dialog box, are shown in Figure 8.37, which is a listing of the USER.HLP file. The dialog box definition areas are shown in Figure 8.38, where reference to these topics appears in the Item column of line 0 for each dialog box. In operation, press F1 when the dialog box is displayed, read the topic when it is displayed in the help window, then execute **Close** in the help window control menu (upper left corner) to return to the dialog box. Figure 8.39 shows the help window for the root display dialog box.

Example 8.7

In Example 8.1, we communicated with the Quadcom macro via INPUT and ALERT dialog boxes as shown in the macro of Figure 8.4. It may be useful to provide help information for this type of macro also. We are displaying dialog boxes, but since we did not construct them, there is no opportunity for us to specify a help

*32 Quadcom input dialog box (Example 8.6).
The coefficients a, b, and c relate to the
polynomial a*x^2 + b*x + c = 0. Coefficient
a must not be zero. This condition is not
checked for in the macro. The last coefficient
values entered are displayed as the initial
values.

*33 Quadcom output dialog box (Example 8.6).
Numerical values for the two real roots only
are displayed. Imaginary roots are indicated
with the word "Imaginary" appearing in the
root value boxes. To go back and solve another
quadratic equation, select Yes. To quit the
macro, select No.

*45 Quadcom (Example 8.7).
This routine solves a quadratic equation for
its two real roots. Coefficients a, b, and c
of the polynomial a*x^2 + b*x + c = 0 are
prompted for one at a time via INPUT dialog
boxes. The roots are displayed in an ALERT
dialog box, which is followed by another ALERT
box that prompts for a return to the beginning
of the routine to solve another equation or to
quit the routine.

*50 Quadcom (Example 8.8).
This command starts the macro for solving a
quadratic equation. Its input, via dialog
box, requires the coefficients a, b, and c of
the polynomial a*x^2 + b*x + c = 0. Its
output, via dialog box, are the roots of the
equation. The macro is written to allow
repeated calculations on additional equations.

*57 Restore.bar (Example 8.8).
This command starts the macro that returns
the menu bar from its custom appearance to
the menu bar consistent with the type of
active window.

*66 Display.mode (Example 8.8).
This command starts the macro that changes
the active window display from its current
display mode to the opposite mode.

*70 Scatchart (Example 8.8).
This command starts the macro that displays
the selected data of the active window in
scatter chart form. The chart window is
the active window when the macro finishes.

Figure 8.37 Sample help file.

	A	B	C	D	E	F	G	H
1	Element	Item	X pos	Y pos	Box width	Box height	Text	Init/Result
2	Dialog box	USER.HLP!32	0	0	300	130		
3	Text	5	20	10	248	18	Enter polynomial coefficients -	
4	Text	5	14	35	16	18	&a:	
5	Number box	8	50	35	80	18		2
6	Text	5	14	65	16	18	&b:	
7	Number box	8	50	65	80	18		4
8	Text	5	14	95	16	18	&c:	
9	Number box	8	50	95	80	18		-30
10	OK	1	162	40	120	24	Done entering	

(a)

	A	B	C	D	E	F	G	H
32	Element	Item	X pos	Y pos	Box width	Box height	Text	Init/Result
33	Dialog box	USER.HLP!33	0	0	200	168		
34	Text	5	32	12	136	18	Polynomial roots:	
35	Text	5	38	35	40	18	X1 :	
36	Text box	5	78	35	80	18	-5	
37	Text	5	38	60	40	18	X2 :	
38	Text box	5	78	60	80	18	3	
39	Group box	14	8	85	184	2		
40	Text	5	8	95	184	18	Solve another equation?	
41	OK	1	8	130	72	24	Yes	
42	Cancel	2	120	130	72	24	No	

(b)

Figure 8.38 Dialog box definition areas of Example 8.6: (a) Coefficient entry, and (b) root display.

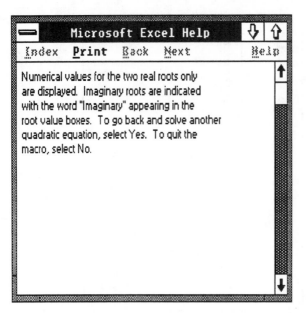

Figure 8.39 Help window for the root display dialog box of Example 8.6.

file for use with them. However, we can set up the macro to query the user for the need to display help information. We do this with another ALERT box and the HELP function of Table 8.21. The plan is to invoke this function with the topic number and file name should the user so indicate. We need two additional statements to do this (rows 5 and 6 of Figure 8.40). Our choice of ALERT box type displays the **OK** and **Cancel** buttons. When **OK** is chosen, the ALERT function is true (the cell is named Hlp), and we execute the true argument of the IF statement. Otherwise, we drop through and immediately begin prompting for the coefficients. The help topic for this example also appears in Figure 8.37. Our help ALERT box is displayed outside the loop for consecutive polynomial root calculations.

Example 8.8

Explanation of custom menus is often needed by persons unfamiliar with the commands. This is made available in a help file accessed in a manner similar to that described for Example 8.7. Since we are working with custom menus, and they are defined by the entries of their cell area, we include in the cell area a reference to the help topic being provided for each command. These references are the help-file names and topic numbers as described above. They are entered in column 5 of the menu definition area of Figure 8.32. The help-file references for our custom menu of Example 8.5 are shown in Figure 8.41, which is Figure 8.34 with the help-file references added to column E of the menu definition area for each command we used in that example, and with an additional macro that is for the Help command we added to our custom menu.

We cannot use the help-file references in the menu definition area as conveniently as we did the reference in the dialog box definition area. The fifth column of the menu definition area serves more as a storage location for the file references from which we retrieve the contents. However, with the HELP function, we should be able to access any file reference we choose.

	A	B
1		Quadcom
2		Command macro - shortcut key = "q"
3		Inputs: coefficients a, b, and c.
4		Outputs: Roots X1 and X2.
5	Hlp	=ALERT("Help info",1)
6		=IF(Hlp,HELP("USER.HLP!45"))
7	AI	=INPUT("Type coefficient a:",1)
8	BI	=INPUT("Type coefficient b:",1)
9	CI	=INPUT("Type coefficient c:",1)
10	Radicand	=BI*BI-4*AI*CI
11		=IF(Radicand>=0,GOTO(Test.zero))
12		=SET.VALUE(X.1,"Imaginary")
13		=SET.VALUE(X.2,"Imaginary")
14		=GOTO(End)
15	Test.zero	=IF(Radicand>0,GOTO(Sqrt.rad))
16	Eq.value	=-BI/(2*AI)
17		=SET.VALUE(X.1,Eq.value)
18		=SET.VALUE(X.2,Eq.value)
19		=GOTO(End)
20	Sqrt.rad	=SQRT(Radicand)
21		=SET.VALUE(X.1,(-BI-Sqrt.rad)/(2*AI))
22		=SET.VALUE(X.2,(-BI+Sqrt.rad)/(2*AI))
23	End	=ALERT("X1 = "&X.1&", X2 = "&X.2,2)
24	Repeat	=ALERT("Solve another equation? OK=Yes, Cancel=No",1)
25		=IF(Repeat,GOTO(AI))
26		=RETURN()
27	X.1	X.2
28	-1	1

Figure 8.40   Macro of Example 8.7.

For this example, we will add a command called "Help" to our custom menu (rows 26 and 27 of Figure 8.41). This command will display a dialog box whose definition area is shown in Figure 8.42. The name of each custom command appears there as a button box of a group in rows 47 through 50. We will then select one of these buttons for the command for which we want help. This dialog box is shown in Figure 8.43.

We added macro "User.help" to use our new dialog box. It is in rows 33 through 42 of Figure 8.41. The DIALOG.BOX function of this macro returns the line number (line 7) of the box definition area for the **OK** button that was selected in the

TABLE 8.21   THE HELP TOPIC FUNCTION

Display a help topic
HELP(*help-ref*)   *help-ref* = The help file name and topic number in the form *file-name!topic-number*. It must be in the form of text and normally would be enclosed within quotation marks. If it is omitted, the function causes the Excel Help index to be displayed.

	A	B	C	D	E
1		Custom.menu			
2		Shortcut key = "u"			
3	Bar.ID	=ADD.BAR()			
4		=ADD.MENU(Bar.ID,A19:E27)			
5		=SHOW.BAR(Bar.ID)			
6		=RETURN()			
7		Restore.bar			
8		Shortcut key = "r"			
9		=SHOW.BAR()			
10		=RETURN()			
11		Del.bar			
12		Shortcut key = "b"			
13		=DELETE.BAR(Bar.ID)			
14		=RETURN()			
15		Sho.bar			
16		Shortcut key = "o"			
17		=SHOW.BAR(Bar.ID)			
18		=RETURN()			
19	&Custom				
20	&Mode change	VALFOR.XLM!Display.mode			USER.HLP!66
21	-				
22	&Quadratic eqn	EX8P3.XLM!Quadcom		Dialog box interaction	USER.HLP!50
23	&Scatter chart	EX8P2.XLM!Scatchart			USER.HLP!70
24	-				
25	&Restore bar	EX8P8.XLM!Restore.bar			USER.HLP!57
26	-				
27	&Help...	EX8P8.XLM!User.help			
28		Add.cmd			
29		Shortcut key = "a"			
30		=ADD.COMMAND(1,7,A32:E32)			
31		=RETURN()			
32	&Custom	EX8P8.XLM!Sho.bar			
33		User.help			
34		Shortcut key = "h"			
35	Box	=DIALOG.BOX(B44:H52)			
36		=IF(Box<>7,GOTO(Ret))			
37		=IF(Val=1,HELP(E20))			
38		=IF(Val=2,HELP(E22))			
39		=IF(Val=3,HELP(E23))			
40		=IF(Val=4,HELP(E25))			
41		=GOTO(Box)			
42	Ret	=RETURN()			

Figure 8.41 Macro of Example 8.8.

dialog box, or indicates FALSE if we selected a **Cancel** button. Choosing this button means that we want a help topic for one of the commands. Otherwise, we want to exit the Help command.

When DIALOG.BOX returns a 7, we check the group button Init/Result column for the number of the button that was selected. In cell H46 of Figure 8.42,

	A	B	C	D	E	F	G	H
	Element	Item	X pos	Y pos	Box width	Box height	Text	Init/Result
43								
44	Dialog box		0	0	232	144		
45	Text	5	16	12	200	18	Custom command help info:	
46	Button group	11						1
47	Button 1	12	8	36	128	18	Mode change	
48	Button 2	12	8	60	128	18	Quadratic eqn	
49	Button 3	12	8	84	128	18	Scatter chart	
50	Button 4	12	8	108	128	18	Restore bar	
51	OK	1	160	48	64	24	OK	
52	Cancel	2	160	90	64	24	Return	

Figure 8.42 Definition area for the dialog box of Example 8.8.

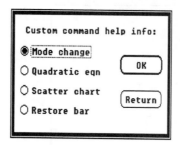

Figure 8.43   Dialog box of Example 8.8.

also given the name Val, we see that a 1 was returned, which means that the "Mode change" command was chosen. The series of IF statements in rows 37 through 40 of Figure 8.41 determine which command was selected and call the HELP function with the cell location of the menu definition area in which the corresponding help file reference appears. This causes the Help information box to appear, at which time our command help message can be read.

8.5 DEVELOPMENT AND DEBUGGING

Many of the macro development principles we stated in Section 7.4 apply to the macros of this chapter. We cannot overstress the importance of developing good work habits and employing them in all aspects of spreadsheet work. Because the command macros of this chapter are somewhat different from those of Chapter 7, we will make these additional recommendations for their development and debugging.

Since command macros carry out actions, many of which will be visible, their checkout is somewhat simplified since we can see the action. If the action is too rapid, step through the macro to provide time for analysis and verification of the operation. Use established and comprehensive data for macro checkout. Whenever possible, use data from other problems, since the result is now known and since slight differences in results will be easily recognized. We are addressing those macros that compute as part of their operation. We used this technique in Example 8.2, which displayed the scatter chart. Because we already knew the result from our chart work of Chapter 6, we were concentrating our effort on macro development rather than on chart development in this chapter.

Whenever possible, use the macro record feature of Excel. Many mistakes can be avoided because we do not have to remember exact function syntax to use the feature. Editing actions can always be used to clean up the record to produce the final macro. Be sure to make copies of complex macros before beginning the testing effort, since it is easy to unintentionally destroy one's work. Much time can be lost while having to reconstruct a macro no longer available.

Incremental progress is as important while developing command macros as it was for function macros. Insert RETURN functions at key locations in the macro so intermediate results are readily observable as checkout progresses.

These RETURN functions can be removed individually as incremental progress is made. Switching display modes between values and formulas should be done often to obtain the intermediate results. Don't forget—an ungraceful exit can always be made by using the escape key, although it may have to be pressed several times to truly abort the execution.

Because custom dialog boxes are self-contained entities, they are also relatively easy to check out. Usually, they will require some changes for refinement of the display. Write a separate macro to display the box and check out each element of the box before declaring the box ready for production use. Switching the display mode is useful for this effort also. The physical appearance of the dialog box can be quickly arrived at by using the Dialog Editor described in Section 8.3.2. As a variation on arriving at a layout, let Excel perform the entire layout as discussed in Section 8.3.1, then make changes to its proposed layout. When the box contains few elements, the single column orientation of the box entries of an Excel constructed box may be satisfactory. It would also save time that can usually be better spent developing the remainder of the macro.

Take special care in developing custom menus, especially before deleting built-in commands. They cannot be reinserted without exiting and reentering Excel. Much work can be lost while doing this if intermediate work saving actions are not taken. Be sure that the proper windows are active, that the required documents are available, and that other macro and worksheet requirements are met to ensure uninterrupted menu construction during checkout. Custom menu work often involves access to multiple macros and worksheets. These must be available when needed. Organized work habits are essential for custom menu checkout.

8.6 ABOUT VERSION 3.0

Version 3.0 additions and changes to material of this chapter eliminate some deficiencies in features already discussed and add new capability. Principal matters of interest are discussed in the following sections.

8.6.1 Update for Command Macro Development

Numerous new macro functions have been added to Excel version 3.0. Corresponding updates to Tables 8.2 through 8.7 appear in Table 8.22. Examples 8.1 and 8.2 run under version 3.0 without change.

The FOR.CELL and GOAL.SEEK functions should be considered for engineering work. They are described in Table 8.23. The FOR.CELL command does not bring us new capability, but it is convenient to use since it automates a nested FOR loop. GOAL.SEEK allows the goal seek routine to be called from a macro. We discussed goal seeking in Section 3.6.1. Both functions can be used only in command macros.

TABLE 8.22 VERSION 3.0 UPDATES TO TABLES 8.2 THROUGH 8.7

Table number	Function purpose	Additional function names		
8.2	Formula preparation	GOAL.SEEK		
	Chart preparation	EDIT.SERIES	OUTLINE	
	Gallery selection	GALLERY.3D.AREA GALLERY.3D.COLUMN	GALLERY.3D.LINE	GALLERY.3D.PIE
	Formatting	APPLY.STYLE BRING.TO.FRONT DEFINE.STYLE DELETE.STYLE	FORMAT.MAIN FORMAT.OVERLAY GROUP MERGE.STYLES	PLACEMENT SEND.TO.BACK UNGROUP VIEW.3D
	Editing	EDIT.REPEAT		PASTE.PICTURE
	File management	PRINT.PREVIEW	FILL.WORKGROUP	
	Macro control	ASSIGN.TO.OBJECT		
	Options selection	COLOR.PALETTE	EDIT.COLOR	STANDARD.FONT
	Database management	CONSOLIDATE	SET.EXTRACT	
	Window control	WORKGROUP		
8.3	Formula preparation	GOAL.SEEK	SELECT.SPECIAL	
	Gallery selection	GALLERY.3D.AREA GALLERY.3D.COLUMN	GALLERY.3D.LINE	GALLERY.3D.PIE
	Formatting	APPLY.STYLE DEFINE.STYLE	PATTERNS SCALE	VIEW.3D
	File management	SAVE.NEW.OBJECT		
	Macro control	ASSIGN.TO.OBJECT		
	Options selection	COLOR.PALETTE	EDIT.COLOR	
	Database management	CONSOLIDATE	PARSE	
	Other	DEMOTE	PROMOTE	
8.4	Formula preparation	FORMULA.CONVERT		
	Miscellaneous	CREATE.OBJECT DEMOTE DUPLICATE	HIDE.OBJECT PROMOTE SET.UPDATE.STATUS	SHOW.DETAIL SHOW.LEVELS TEXT.BOX
8.5	Create custom menus and dialog boxes	VOLATILE		
	Start other macros and applications	CUSTOM.REPEAT CUSTOM.UNDO	ON.RECALC	UNREGISTER
8.6	Direct flow of control	ELSE	ELSE.IF	END.IF
	Loop control	FOR.CELL		
8.7	Other	GET.OBJECT	LAST.ERROR	

TABLE 8.23 THE FOR.CELL AND GOAL.SEEK MACRO FUNCTIONS

Macro function	Arguments		Purpose
FOR.CELL(cell-name[,[cell-range] [,skip-blanks]])			To perform the instructions within the FOR.CELL-NEXT pair in a looping manner on each cell within a selected range. The cells are operated on from left to right within a range and in range order for multiple range selections.
	cell-name:	the name in text form that Excel is to use for the cell currently being operated on. It refers to a new cell during each pass through the FOR.CELL-NEXT range.	
	cell-range:	the cell range, within which is cell-name, that the FOR.CELL-NEXT instructions are to operate on. When omitted, it is the current selection.	
	skip-blanks:	a logical flag indicating, when TRUE, to skip blank cells in cell-range and, when FALSE or omitted, to operate on all cells in the range.	
GOAL.SEEK(formula-cell, goal,variable-cell)			To perform the function of the Formula Goal Seek command. It determines the value of the independent variable in a formula to yield a target value for the formula.
	formula-cell:	the worksheet cell containing the formula to be solved for the independent variable value that yields goal as the formula value.	
	goal:	the numerical value of the formula in formula-cell to be used to inversely solve for the independent variable value of variable-cell.	
	variable-cell:	the independent variable cell that is to be varied to reach the goal value.	

The FOR.CELL command implements a FOR.CELL-NEXT looping structure. It is always paired with a NEXT statement. Between these statements is the range of statements to be operated on in a looping manner. The FOR.CELL-NEXT loop operates very much like a FOR-NEXT loop except that it operates on a single cell within its cell range for each pass through the loop until all cells within its range have been operated on. The cell range may be rectangular or it may be a multiple selection. When rectangular, all cells within a row are operated on in a left-to-right manner before following rows are operated on. Hence the inference of implementing a nested loop structure.

Example 8.9

The worksheet of Figure 8.44 contains temperature and pressure data (columns A and B) acquired during an experiment. They are in units of ohms and volts that must be converted to °C and psi, respectively, as shown in columns D and E with the formulas

$$T(°C) = \frac{1}{\frac{1}{\beta} \ln\left(\frac{R}{R_o} + \frac{1}{T_o}\right)}$$

where

R = resistance at measured temperature, ohms

R_o = resistance at reference temperature T_o, ohms

T_o = reference temperature, °K

β = conversion constant

and

$$p(\text{psi}) = \alpha e^{\delta v}$$

where

v = measured voltage, volts

α = conversion constant

δ = conversion constant

	A	B	C	D	E
1	Resistance, ohms	Voltage, volts		Temperature, deg C	Pressure, psi
2	5800	0		273.6331271	4.3
3	2000	1.6		295.1288461	5.644124106
4	800	4.45		316.5280261	9.162462942
5	180	7.3		358.8906303	14.87400447
6	55	11.8		401.613156	31.96415193
7	21	14.7		444.591538	52.33236549
8	10	18.2		484.5498261	94.88019806
9	6	20		516.5116259	128.8456302

Figure 8.44 Worksheet for Example 8.9.

	A
1	Unit.Conv
2	Command macro: shortcut key = "u".
3	Demonstrate FOR.CELL function.
4	=FOR.CELL("k")
5	=IF(GET.CELL(3,k)=4)
6	= FORMULA(1/((1/4000)*LN(k/6000)+1/273),k)
7	=ELSE()
8	= FORMULA(4.3*EXP(0.17*k),k)
9	=END.IF()
10	=NEXT()
11	=RETURN()

Figure 8.45   Macro for Example 8.9.

The numerical values for the sensors used in the experiment are:

$$T_o = 273°K$$

$$R_o = 6000 \text{ ohms}$$

$$\beta = 4000$$

$$\alpha = 4.3$$

$$\delta = 0.17$$

The command macro for the conversion of units is given in Figure 8.45. The GET.CELL function in row 5 is used to determine if we are in the first column of the table (column D, with a numerical value of 4) which contains the temperature resistance values. If it is not the first column, then it must be the second column, since we have only a two-column table, which contains the pressure voltage values. To make the calculations we activate the worksheet, copy the experiment data from A2:B9 to D2:E9 so before and after results will be available, select the data of range D2:E9, then enter the macro shortcut key. The result is in D2:E9 of Figure 8.44.

8.6.2 Update for Custom Dialog Box Development

New dialog box items were added, some old items were changed slightly, and a new operation mode of the dialog box was included. Following is a discussion of matters that affect a custom dialog box.

1. Example 8.3 did not produce an output dialog box exactly as shown in Figure 8.16(b). We can no longer produce a horizontal, or vertical, line with a group box (item 14) because Excel automatically changes its minimum vertical dimension to 12 units. Instead of the line, we get a narrow rectangle. Also, we did not get "equation?" as part of the query message. Increasing the box width to 187 (Figure 8.17, cell E40) then caused the entire message to be visible. Since dimensions are given in terms of character height and width, the font also affects the display.

TABLE 8.24   NEW CUSTOM DIALOG BOX ITEMS

Item number	Description	Example
21	Drop-down list box for displaying names of items. It can be scrolled. The names are obtained from the range of cells given in R1C1-style, or as a range name, in the Text column. The length of the displayed drop-down list is given in the Box Height column. The Init/Result column will contain the list item that was selected. The items of the list are numbered sequentially (1,2,..) beginning with the first item. A default selection can be specified in the Init/Result column ($n = n$th item of the list, blank = 1st item, #N/A = none selected).	Rate of climb / True airspeed / Altimeter / Rate of climb / Compass / Accelerometer / Tachometer
22	Drop-down combination edit/list box. Similar to item 21 but must be preceded by a text edit box (item 6). The entry of the text edit box can be edited before the drop-down list is displayed. Except for the following, the Init/Result entry is interpreted as for item 21. If #N/A is given as the default Init/Result entry, the initial value is taken from the accompanying text edit box. If text not in the list is typed in the drop-down list box, it is returned in the Init/Result column of the accompanying text edit box.	True airspeed / Directional gyro / Attitude gyro / Turn coordinator / True airspeed / Altimeter

2. The two new dialog box items of Table 8.24 were added to the list box elements of Table 8.14. They provide user developed drop-down menu choices with scroll capability.

3. The entry box elements of Table 8.12 are now referred to as edit boxes (text edit box, etc.). They can each be made multi-line in length with the Box Height entry value in screen units. When their length allows, a scroll bar is included. Entries to an edit box wrap around to a multi-line appearance as governed by the Box Width value.

4. The item 15 list box of Table 8.14 can now be made into a multiple selection list box whereby, by pressing SHIFT, multiple entries can be selected from the list by clicking on them. To accomplish this, its Init/Result column must contain a valid name that refers to a single number or a one-dimensional array of numbers that correspond to the order in which the list of items is displayed. After items are selected from the list and the dialog box is closed, this array contains, in ascending order, the numbers of the entries chosen.

5. A custom dialog box can be named by entering a title in the Text column of line 0 of the dialog box table (see Figure 8.11). When the dialog box is displayed, its title appears in the title bar, which can be selected and the dialog box dragged across the screen for repositioning.

6. The initial selection of an item when the dialog box is first displayed can be specified by entering its line number in the Init/Result column of line 0.

7. A *dynamic* dialog box can be created. This is a dialog box that causes interruption of its processing yet remains displayed. Interruption is caused by selecting a dialog box item that is designated as a *trigger*. While the dialog box remains displayed, control is returned to the macro that caused it to be displayed in the first place. This macro is expected to alter the dialog box definition table and to display its altered version, hence the term dynamic. Eventually, the dialog box can be exited in the usual manner. Not only must the dialog box definition table be prepared for its first display, but its display macro must be written to process it for redisplay according to the interpretation assigned to the trigger. Recall that we can read from and write to cells of a dialog box definition table as we can to any cell of the macro sheet. A dialog box not to be redisplayed can be removed from the screen with the function DIALOG.BOX(FALSE).

Items that can be designated as triggers include the OK/cancel elements (items 1 through 4), the option buttons and check box (items 11 through 13), the list box and linked list box (items 15 and 16), the linked file list box and linked drive and directory list box (items 18 and 19), and the drop-down list box (item 21). For this purpose, we add 100 to the number in the Item column of the dialog box definition table line containing the trigger. Many of the Excel system dialog boxes are dynamic. Often, they cause items to be dimmed or brightened. To dim an item, add 200 to its number in the Item column.

8.6.3 Update on the Dialog Editor

Few changes were made to the Dialog Editor. With it we can produce the dialog box of Example 8.4 with no change in our procedure. Primary changes in version 3.0 relate to the dynamic dialog box and the new items of Table 8.24. Some changes to note are:

1. The **List Box Type** selections of the **Item List Box** dialog box of Figure 8.24(d) now include the Dropdown and Combination Dropdown elements of Table 8.24.
2. The **Edit Info** dialog box of Figure 8.25 now contains **Dimmed** and **Trigger** check boxes for use with dynamic dialog boxes, which we discussed in Section 8.6.2.
3. There is now no indication that the dialog box displayed on entry to the Dialog Editor is selected since the dotted selection outline is no longer visible, and it can no longer be repositioned by dragging as we described in the procedure of Table 8.16. However, we can select the dialog box at any time by clicking within it while not on an item within the box.

4. The edit boxes cannot be made multiline with the mouse during placement in the dialog box. Instead, one must place the item, display its **Info** box, switch off the **Width Auto** or **Height Auto** check box as described, exit the **Info** box, then use the mouse for edit box sizing.

5. The group box (item 14) must be greater than zero in height or an error message appears. Also, if made less than 12 units in height, it will be automatically sized to 12 units. This means that no longer can a single horizontal or vertical line be placed in a dialog box.

6. The icons of Figure 8.24(e) now are of slightly different shapes.

8.6.4 Update for Custom Menu Development

Minor changes, or argument value interpretations, have been made to some commands of Tables 8.19 and 8.20. It is easier now to work with built-in commands. Example 8.5 runs under version 3.0 without change. Some differences to note are:

1. Deleted built-in commands can be restored to their original menus with the ADD.COMMAND function by using the command name for the *menu-pos* argument (see Table 8.20). Deleted custom commands cannot be restored in this manner.

2. Deleted built-in menus can be restored to their original menu bars with the ADD.MENU function by using the menu name for the *menu-ref* argument (see Table 8.19). However, custom or add-in commands of that menu will be lost.

3. A built-in or custom menu can be renamed with the RENAME.COMMAND function when the *cmd-pos* argument is set to 0, and it may be disabled with the ENABLE.COMMAND function when the *cmd-pos* argument is set to 0 (see Table 8.20).

4. The ADD.MENU and ADD.COMMAND functions now have an optional argument for specifying the position where the new menu or command is to appear.

5. The list of most recently opened files in the **File** menu or the list of open windows in the **Window** menu can be deleted with the DELETE.COMMAND function when the *cmd-pos* argument is set to "File List" or "Window List", respectively (see Table 8.20).

8.6.5 Update on Custom Help Development

The help file format we discussed in Section 8.4 is not used directly by Excel version 3.0. Consequently, Examples 8.6 through 8.8 each caused an error message to be displayed in the help window indicating this incompatibility. Excel version 3.0 now uses the Windows 3.0 help facility. All help files in text format must first be converted to a Windows Help-file format with a utility program supplied by Microsoft Corporation. This program, called helpconv, can be run from the DOS prompt or from the Windows Program Manager. Although there are optional parameters for the conversion program command, we choose not to describe them here. We run the helpconv program as follows:

helpconv   *helpfile*

where *helpfile* is the name of the help file, in text format, to be converted to the new format. The converted file will have the same name as *helpfile* while the text file will now have its original name but with a .BAK extension. Actually, two utility programs are involved. The first program, helpconv, converts the text file to an intermediate text file while the second program, hc, which is automatically called from helpconv, compiles the intermediate text file into the Help-file format. For our examples, with text file USER.HLP as *helpfile,* this conversion will create a new USER.HLP file in the Help-file format and change the name of our text file to USER.BAK. With the converted help file. Examples 8.6 through 8.8 run properly under version 3.0.

8.6.6 The Macro Debugger

Macro Debugger, an add-in macro for debugging a macro, is supplied with version 3.0. We run this macro so that it, in turn, can run and control the command macro we are to debug. Control, in this sense, means that with *tracepoints,* we can enter different macro operating modes at selected points within our macro for single stepping, formula evaluation, or halting operation purposes, and with *breakpoints,* we can direct it at selected points within our macro to cause our macro to temporarily pause and, optionally, to have specified variable values displayed for analysis purposes. The tracepoints and breakpoints are both called *debug points*. When we have debugged our macro we exit Macro Debugger.

To run Macro Debugger we first use the **File Open** command to open its file DEBUG.XLA, which is in the LIBRARY subdirectory of the Excel version 3.0 installation directory. This also causes the **Debug** command to appear in the **Macro** menu. To start a debugging session we activate the command macro sheet to be debugged and execute the **Macro Debug** command, which runs Macro Debugger causing the menu bar of Figure 8.46 to appear. The dropdown menus of these new commands are shown in Figures 8.47 and 8.48. Following are operational characteristics of Macro Debugger:

1. The macro being debugged will pause at cells designated as tracepoints and display a dialog box similar to the one of Figure 8.49(a) and enter single-step mode.
2. The macro being debugged will pause at cells designated as breakpoints and display a dialog box similar to the one of Figure 8.49(b), from which we

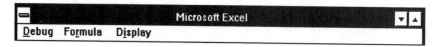

Figure 8.46   Macro Debugger menu bar.

control further macro operation and from which we read values for our chosen variables.

3. The cell protection status of the macro being debugged is changed during the debugging session, with all cells locked and unhidden at the end of the session. Therefore, document protection must be off when beginning the session so Macro Debugger can operate properly.

We now must set up the conditions for debugging our macro. The procedure is to first specify breakpoints, tracepoints, and variables to be displayed with the **Debug** menu **Set Breakpoint**, **Set Trace Point**, and **Breakpoint Output** commands, respectively. Then, when we run our macro from the **Debug Run** command dialog box of Figure 8.47(b), it stops at each debug point as it is reached and displays its associated dialog box of Figure 8.49. We use the displayed information to analyze the performance of our macro, making changes in our debug point settings

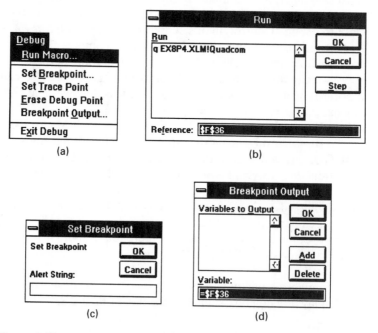

Figure 8.47   (a) Debug menu and dialog boxes for the (b) Run Macro, (c) Set Breakpoint, and (d) Breakpoint Output commands for Macro Debugger.

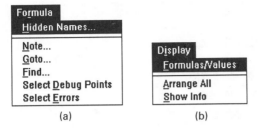

Figure 8.48 Macro Debugger
(a) Formula and (b) Display menus.

and variable choices as needed, and rerun the macro until we have it debugged. We set tracepoints and breakpoints as follows:

1. Select the cell in which to insert a debug point.
2. Execute the **Debug Set Trace Point** or **Debug Set Breakpoint** command as desired. For the latter, a message may be entered in the dialog box of Figure 8.47(c) to be displayed whenever the breakpoint is reached.

We designate variables to be displayed at breakpoints as follows:

1. Execute the **Debug Breakpoint Output** command to obtain the dialog box of Figure 8.47(d).
2. Enter the variable name, or reference, and choose **OK** to add it to the display list.
3. Select the variable in the list and choose **Delete** to remove it from the list.

Figure 8.50 shows several debug points in the macro of Figure 8.28 for Example 8.4. Commands of the **Formula** and **Display** menus of Figure 8.48 are used to help with the debugging activity by displaying information, searching for cells, switching the macro sheet display mode, and arranging the windows. Except for the cells containing the debug points, we can edit our macro sheet between debugging runs within the macro debugger as usual. We end a macro debugging session by executing the **Debug Exit Debug** command of Figure 8.47(a).

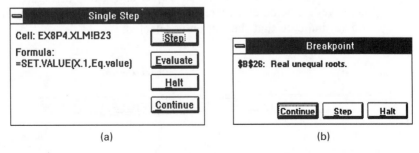

(a)   (b)

Figure 8.49 Macro Debugger (a) tracepoint and (b) breakpoint dialog boxes.

	A	B
14		Outputs: Roots X1 and X2.
15	Box	=DIALOG.BOX(Coef.box)
16	Radicand	=BI*BI-4*AI*CI
17		=IF(Radicand>=0,GOTO(Test.zero))
18		=SET.VALUE(X.1,"Imaginary")
19		=SET.VALUE(X.2,"Imaginary")
20		=GOTO(End)
21	Test.zero	=IF(Radicand>0,GOTO(Sqrt.rad))
22	Eq.value	=-BI/(2*AI)
23		=SET.VALUE(X.1,Eq.value)
24		=SET.VALUE(X.2,Eq.value)
25		=GOTO(End)
26	Sqrt.rad	=SQRT(Radicand)
27		=SET.VALUE(X.1,(-BI-Sqrt.rad)/(2*AI))
28		=SET.VALUE(X.2,(-BI+Sqrt.rad)/(2*AI))
29	End	=SET.VALUE(AI.out,AI)

Figure 8.50 Macro sheet with debug points preceding cells B16, B22, and B26.

8.6.7 The Tool Bar

We can assign a command macro to a button and run it by clicking on the button with the mouse. We use the tool bar *Button tool* to create a button, which is a graphical object resembling the OK and cancel buttons of a dialog box. We do this as follows:

1. Open the macro sheet containing the command macro to be assigned to the button and activate the window on which the button is to be placed.
2. Click on the *Button tool* labeled in Figure 8.51. The cursor changes to a cross hair symbol for drawing a rectangular button.
3. Position the cross hair cursor to the location for one corner of the command button. Press the mouse button and drag to shape and size the ensuing box, which will become the button. Pressing SHIFT during this operation will generate a square button; pressing CTRL will align the button to the cell grid. When the mouse button is released, the button will resemble the one of Figure 8.52(a) and the **Assign to Object** dialog box of Figure 8.52(b) will be displayed. The black squares, or handles, surrounding the button of Figure 8.52(a) indicate that the button is selected.

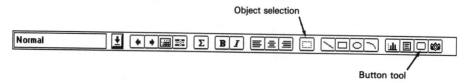

Object selection

Button tool

Figure 8.51 Excel tool bar.

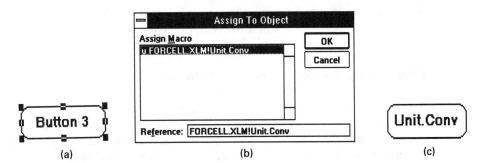

Figure 8.52   (a) Command button with selection handles created by the button tool, (b) the Assign to Object dialog box, and (c) new text for the command button.

4. The command macros on the open macro sheets will be listed in the **Assign to Object** dialog box. Select one of them, or type its name in the **Reference:** box, then choose **OK**. The macro name is now assigned to the button.

5. While the button is still selected, a new name for it can be typed in at this time, as was done in Figure 8.52(c).

The button of Figure 8.52(c) was created on the worksheet of Example 8.9 in Figure 8.44. To use it with that example, we activate the worksheet and copy the input data from A2:B9 to D2:E9. While this latter range is still selected, we click on our command button and watch the information in the selected range change. Of course, we can still run the macro with its shortcut key or from the **Macro Run** dialog box.

We can customize the command button by resizing it, by changing its shape, or by altering its text or text font. We do these things upon selecting the button, which is done as follows:

1. Activate the document containing the command button.

2. Click on the *Object selection* button shown in Figure 8.51.

3. Place the mouse cursor at the location of a corner which will begin a rectangle that will enclose the button to be selected. Press the mouse button and drag to shape and size the rectangular area over the command button, then release it. The handles will appear indicating that the button is selected.

With the command button selected, the **Format Text** and **Format Font** commands can be used to alter the button text in the usual manner. Also, when the button is selected, it can be deleted with the **Edit Clear** command or by pressing the BACKSPACE or DELETE key. The button can be sized by dragging a handle, on the side or corner, while observing the dotted outline of its new dimensions. Pressing SHIFT while dragging a corner handle will keep the button proportioned; pressing CTRL while dragging will align the button frame to the cell grid. The button can be moved to a new location by dragging it there after first clicking on its border with an arrow cursor. The button must be selected for this latter operation.

8.6.8 A Solver Application Using Macros

We can use Solver in an automated manner with the macros supplied with it. These macros, shown in Table 8.25, allow us to set up and use the dialog boxes of Figures 3.19, 3.20, and 3.22. Thus, we can conveniently and rapidly use Solver for similar problems that we must solve frequently. The following example demonstrates use of these macros.

TABLE 8.25 SOLVER MACRO FUNCTIONS

Reset the Formula Solver dialog box

SOLVER.RESET()	Initializes Solver by removing all user entered values and restoring Solver controls to their default values. It requires no arguments and is equivalent to choosing the RESET button.

Enter options in the Formula Solver dialog box

SOLVER.OK([*objcell*],[*maxmin*],[*valueof*],*adjcells*)

    objcell = The cell name or reference containing the objective function on the active worksheet.

    maxmin = The type of optimization entered as an integer as follows: Max = 1, Min = 2, and Value of = 3.

    valueof = A numeric value to which *objcell* is to be optimized when *maxmin* = 3.

    adjcells = The independent variables, entered by cell name or reference, to be adjusted during optimization.

Add a constraint to the current Formula Solver dialog box

SOLVER.ADD(*leftside*,*relation*,*rightside*)

    leftside = A cell name or reference, or range of cells, that is the left-hand side of the constraint expression.

    relation = The relational operator entered as an integer as follows: 1 means <=, 2 means =, and 3 means >=.

    rightside = A number, cell name or reference, range of cells, or a formula as text, that is the right-hand side of the constraint expression.

Change the right-hand side only of a constraint

SOLVER.CHANGE(*leftside*,*relation*,*rightside*)

    leftside = Must match the left-hand side of the constraint to be changed.

    relation = Must match the relational operator of the constraint to be changed.

    rightside = A number, cell name or reference, range of cells, or a formula as text, that will replace the right-hand side of the constraint to be changed.

TABLE 8.25 (Continued)

Delete a constraint from the current Formula Solver dialog box

SOLVER.DELETE(*leftside,relation,rightside*)
    leftside = Must match the left-hand side of the constraint to be deleted.
    relation = Must match the relational operator of the constraint to be deleted.
    rightside = Not used.

Begin a Solver run

SOLVER.SOLVE([*finish-box*][,*macro-name*])   Performs the function of the Solve button in the Formula Solver dialog box.
    finish-box = When FALSE, or omitted, displays the standard Solver completion dialog box; when TRUE returns an integer stopping condition code without displaying anything.
    macro-name = The name of a macro to be called when the Show Iterations Results check box is on in the Solver Options dialog box.

Control ending activities of a Solver run

SOLVER.FINISH([*keep-values*][,*report-arg*])
    keep-values = When 1, or omitted, saves the final solution values for the independent variables; when 2, discards the final solution values and restores the independent variables to their former values.
    report-arg = An array argument that when {1} creates the Answer report, when {2} creates the Limit report, and when {1,2} creates both reports.
    Note: SOLVER.FINISH must be used after the SOLVER.SOLVE macro call when the *finish-box* argument of that macro is TRUE.

Specify options of the Solver Options dialog box

SOLVER.OPTIONS(*time,iter,prec,linear,stepiter,est,deriv,search*)
    time = A positive number for the Max Time box.
    iter = A positive integer for the Iterations box.
    prec = A number n for the Precision box where $0 < n < 1$.
    linear = When TRUE, turns on the Assume Linear Model check box; when FALSE, turns it off.
    stepiter = When TRUE, turns on the Show Iteration Results check box; when FALSE, turns it off.
    est = Flag to set the Estimates option as follows: 1 = Tangent, 2 = Quadratic.
    deriv = Flag to set the Derivatives option as follows: 1 = Forward, 2 = Central.
    search = Flag to set the Search option as follows: 1 = Newton, 2 = Conjugate.

To save a model to the worksheet

SOLVER.SAVE(*save-range*)   Performs the function of the Save Model button in the Solver Options dialog box.
    save-range = The cell range on the active worksheet to contain the model being saved.

To load a model from the worksheet

SOLVER.LOAD(*model-range*)   Performs the function of the Load Model button in the Solver Options dialog box.
    model-range = The cell range on the active worksheet that contains a saved model.

Example 8.10

Figure 8.53 shows two intersecting geometric objects given by these equations:

$$\frac{x^2}{12} + \frac{y^2}{8} + \frac{z^2}{20} = 1 \quad \text{ellipsoid}$$

$$y = e^x - 2 \quad \text{exponential cylinder}$$

Mentally, with trial values, we easily determine that the objects intersect. The figure shows that portion of the ellipsoid removed which is above the xy-plane and on our side of the exponential cylinder. We will obtain the curve of intersection above the xy-plane, not analytically, but numerically. We also will compute the maximum height of that curve.

We stated earlier that it is essential to give Solver as much help as possible to increase its probability of a successful run. For this example, we can narrow its search range because the intersecting curve is of finite extent, and we can determine its extremities. Therefore, we will let Solver calculate the intersection curve points on the xy-plane and use them for restricting the search for the maximum. Our objective function will be z^2 and the independent variable will be x. Maximizing z^2 is the same as maximizing z since we are working above the xy-plane where z is positive. Thus, Solver will avoid computing the square root, a potential source of difficulty in obtaining a useful solution because of possible negative radicands.

The formulas of our worksheet are shown in Figure 8.54. The cells of row 3 were given the names in row 2. The complete worksheet, with data storage areas,

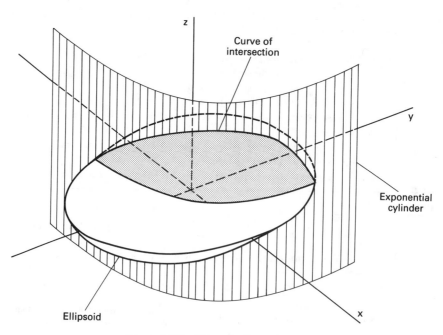

Figure 8.53 Object for Example 8.10.

	A	B	C	D
1		Computations		
2	x	y	z	zsq
3		=EXP(x)-2	=SQRT(zsq)	=(1920-160*x^2-240*y^2)/96

Figure 8.54   Worksheet formulas for Example 8.10.

appears in Figure 8.55(a). The plan is to compute the coordinates of each point in cells named x, y, and z, then transfer these values to the array named CurvPt (rows 8 through 18), except for the maximum point which will be transferred to row 5.

Our macro is shown in Figure 8.56. Comments appear in the text boxes. Upon initializing variables to worksheet row numbers and the number of intervals on the intersecting curve in rows 2 through 5, we then initialize Solver with the SOLVER-.RESET macro. This removes all user entered values and restores Solver controls to their default values. We then enter the objective function and independent variable with SOLVER.OK and the constraints to find the intersecting point in the left half plane with the SOLVER.ADD macros. We did not write our macro general purpose in order to keep it short for clarity, so we must enter numerical values specific to this problem. We know the maximum range over which x can possibly vary since it is determined by the size of the ellipsoid. We used $-4 < x < 4$ for this range. We also gave Solver help by entering $x = -4$ as the starting point, since this value will head us towards the solution. The SOLVER.SOLVE macro initiates the computation. We instructed it to save the values found, which are in row 3 of the worksheet. SOLVER.FINISH ends this part of the run. The call to the Move.val function in row 13 places our coordinates in the first row of Curv.Pt (row 8) on the worksheet.

	A	B	C	D
1		Computations		
2	x	y	z	zsq
3			-1	4.1833001	17.5
4		Maximum point		
5				
6		Curve values		
7	x	y	z	
8				
9				
10				
11				
12				
13				
14				
15				
16				
17				
18				

(a)

	A	B	C	D
1		Computations		
2	x	y	z	zsq
3	1.1082168	1.0289524	3.9123184	15.306235
4		Maximum point		
5	0.5786953	-0.21629	4.3960095	
6		Curve values		
7	x	y	z	
8	-2.542216	-1.921308	0.0005556	
9	-2.136612	-1.881946	1.8807388	
10	-1.731009	-1.822894	2.5881761	
11	-1.325405	-1.734305	3.0907341	
12	-0.919801	-1.601402	3.4898027	
13	-0.514198	-1.40202	3.8269028	
14	-0.108594	-1.102906	4.1157434	
15	0.2970095	-0.654172	4.3339501	
16	0.7026132	0.0190219	4.3790775	
17	1.1082168	1.0289524	3.9123184	
18	1.5138205	2.5440581	0.0008135	

(b)

Figure 8.55   Worksheet for Example 8.10 (a) before the run, and (b) after the run.

	A	B
1		Intersect
2	FirstRow	8
3	Intvrls	10
4	LastRow	=FirstRow+Intvrls
5	MaxRow	5
6		=SOLVER.RESET()
7		=SOLVER.OK(!$D$3,3,0,!$A$3)
8		=SOLVER.ADD(!$A$3,1,0)
9		=SOLVER.ADD(!$A$3,3,-4)
10		=FORMULA(-4,INDEX(!CurrPt,1,1))
11		=SOLVER.SOLVE(TRUE)
12		=SOLVER.FINISH()
13		=Move.val(FirstRow)
14		=SOLVER.CHANGE(!$A$3,1,4)
15		=SOLVER.CHANGE(!$A$3,3,0)
16		=FORMULA(4,INDEX(!CurrPt,1,1))
17		=SOLVER.SOLVE(TRUE)
18		=SOLVER.FINISH()
19		=Move.val(LastRow)
20		=SOLVER.CHANGE(!$A$3,1,INDEX(!CurvPt,Intvrls+1,1))
21		=SOLVER.CHANGE(!$A$3,3,INDEX(!CurvPt,1,1))
22		=FORMULA((INDEX(!CurvPt,1,1)+INDEX(!CurvPt,Intvrls+1,1))/2,INDEX(!CurrPt,1,1))
23		=SOLVER.OK(!$D$3,1,,!$A$3)
24		=SOLVER.SOLVE(TRUE)
25		=SOLVER.FINISH()
26		=Move.val(MaxRow)
27		=SET.VALUE(Xval,INDEX(!CurvPt,1,1))
28	Interval	=(INDEX(!CurvPt,Intvrls+1,1)-Xval)/Intvrls
29		=FOR("m",1,Intvrls-1)
30	Xval	=Xval+Interval
31		=FORMULA(Xval,INDEX(!CurrPt,1,1))
32		=Move.val(FirstRow+m)
33		=NEXT()
34		=RETURN()
35		Move.val
36		=ARGUMENT("row")
37		=FORMULA(INDEX(!CurrPt,1,1),"R"&row&"C1")
38		=FORMULA(INDEX(!CurrPt,1,2),"R"&row&"C2")
39		=FORMULA(INDEX(!CurrPt,1,3),"R"&row&"C3")
40		=RETURN()

Rows 7 through 13: Compute left half plane curve intersection point and save it as first point in array.

Rows 14 through 19: Compute right half plane curve intersection point and save it as last point in array.

Rows 20 through 26: Compute maximum value point on intersection curve.

Rows 27 through 33: Compute intermediate points on intersection curve.

Move.val: Function to move points from computation area to curve values array.

Figure 8.56 Macro for Example 8.10.

Rows 14 through 19 solve for and save the intersecting point in the right half plane and place it in the last row (as determined by the number of intervals to be computed) of array Curv.Pt. We used the SOLVER.CHANGE macro to change the constraints. The starting value of $x = 4$ heads us towards the solution. We now have the extreme points of our intersecting curve. Before computing the interior points, we find the maximum point on the curve in rows 20 through 26. We use the minimum and maximum values found above as constraints; we use their average value as the initial x value; and we change the **Formula Solver** dialog box for a maximum computation.

We need not use Solver to compute the interior points of the curve since we now know the extreme points. The FOR-NEXT loop is used for this purpose. We rely on the fact that the worksheet is automatically recomputed whenever a precedent value is changed. In our case x is the precedent cell. We step along equal intervals of x in the FOR-NEXT loop. Each time the new value is stored in the worksheet with the statement of row 31, a new worksheet computation ensues. The coordinates for this new point are then stored in the proper row of Curv.Pt by the statement in row 32. The worksheet after the run appears in Figure 8.55(b).

8.6.9 Other New Features

1. A *template* for a worksheet, macro sheet, or chart, is a partially completed document that serves as a pattern for preparing another similar document. It may contain formulas, styles for formatting, text, macros, chart structures, etc., for the purpose of giving the user a head start toward preparing a custom document. Some templates solve problems and may require modification for problem specification, some provide a basic structure with supporting macros and chart formats, some provide the basics of a form that can be varied for specific use, some provide reports from supporting documents, and so on. Templates are created to save time and effort and to allow consistency of output.

The template feature allows virtually any document created to be declared a template. The functional difference between a template and any other Excel document is that a template, when opened, is merely supplied in copied form, the original is not opened for use in the usual manner and, thus, not subject to alteration. The copy may be altered as desired, provided that protection features permit this. We now illustrate the preparation of a template that solves a single variable equation for a minimum value within a specified independent variable interval. The template is to provide the structure for performing the optimization (minimization). The user is expected to supply the equation, the constraint interval, and accuracy tolerance.

We will develop a form like the one in Figure 8.57. The entry blocks above the Compute button are for user constraint, accuracy tolerance, and objective function entry. The blocks below the button display solution results. We will use a strategy called the *Fibonacci search* method, which is suitable for optimizing a nonlinear unimodal function. A multimodal function is best solved with this strategy by using multiple starting points. The user must supply the lower and upper values of the independent variable constraint interval, the desired accuracy, and $F(x)$, which is the objective function with x as the independent variable. Figure 8.57 shows that $F(x) = 49x/(x^2 + 9)$ in the interval $-10 \le x \le 0$ is to be optimized so that its value is within .0001 times the constraint interval. Optimization results appear below the Compute button.

We developed our template on a macro sheet. The output form of Figure 8.57, shown in values mode, was prepared in columns A through F, the macros in columns G through I, and an array of Fibonacci numbers stored in column J. The

Fibonacci Single Variable Constrained Optimization

Inputs: Lower constraint   Upper constraint

                        -10   0

Desired accuracy (fraction of constraint interval):   0.0001

Objective function = F(x) =   49*x/(x^2+9)

Compute

Results: -3.000182715   <=   x   <=   -3.001096291

                  -8.166666652   <=   y   <=   -8.166666122

                With accuracy: 9.13576E-05

Figure 8.57   Form displayed by a macro template.

macros in formulas mode and array are shown in Figure 8.58. We prepared text box comments with the tool bar as described in Section 3.6.3. The command macro is run by clicking on the Compute button which was prepared with the tool bar *Button tool* as described in Section 8.6.7. The spreadsheet interpretive mode allows us to use character manipulation for formula construction. User objective function entry, which is the right-hand side of the equation only, is operated on by the statement of cell H58 which concatenates it with the equal sign and enters it in cell H59. Were the user to enter the equal sign with the right-hand side in the objective function box of Figure 8.57, we would see only its numerical result since the macro sheet is run in values mode. By entering only the right-hand side, we are entering text and no evaluation is done on it.

The procedure for creating a template in Excel is as follows:

1. Prepare the document to be used as a template.
2. Save it with the **File Save As** command. In its dialog box, set the directory as desired and type in the file name either by itself or with an .XLT extension, choose the **Options** button to get another dialog box within which select the **Template** option in its **File Format** list box and choose **OK** to close the **Options** dialog box.
3. Choose **OK** to close the **File Save As** dialog box.

To use the template, first open it with the **File Open** command. A copy of it is displayed which can be modified, permissions allowing. There are no differences in display of the copied template from the version that was saved. That is, no cells can be flagged for special handling when the template document is first displayed. Figure 8.57 shows our template when first displayed, since the macro was saved as a template just after running the problem shown there. The template document, the one with the .XLT extension, can be edited after being opened with SHIFT+**OK** in the **File Open** dialog box. It can be deleted in the usual manner for deleting files.

Not all features of the template may be functional in the copy. For example, the Fibonacci macro did not run with the Compute button until it was reassigned to the button with the **Macro Assign to Object** command, after first being selected with the tool bar *Selection tool*. Setting permissions and hiding cells with the document protection feature may also lead to undesired results. This points out the need to fully test out the copy before releasing the template for general use.

A final word on using the Fibonacci macro of Figure 8.58. It is designed to minimize a function. But, as with most optimization routines, it can be used to maximize a function by minimizing the negative of the function. For example, the serpentine function $f(x) = b^2 x/(x^2 + a^2)$ of our example also has a maximum value. Not only is the function value zero at the origin, but it also asymptotically approaches zero at the extreme points. We found its minimum value in the third quadrant by the chosen constraint interval. Noting that it is an odd function, it also has a maximum value in the first quadrant. With our routine, this is found by setting the constraint interval with positive values and entering the objective function as $(-49*x/(x^2 + 9))$. The outer parentheses are needed to permit its recognition as text, otherwise Excel will enter it with an equal sign. We can also use Solver for problems of this type.

2. A macro or custom function can be made to appear as if it were part of Excel, in which case it is called an *add-in macro*. The procedure for creating an add-in macro is simple, but we choose not to describe this feature.

3. Functions written in a traditional programming language, such as FORTRAN or C, can be placed in a dynamic-link library. This is an operation external to Excel. Then, when functions in the dynamic-link library are made known to Excel with the REGISTER macro function listed in Table 8.5, they can be pasted into a worksheet or macro sheet when selected from the list in the **Formula Paste** command dialog box. We also choose not to describe this feature.

PROBLEMS

8.1   Rework Problem 5.2 with INPUT and ALERT functions for input and output of the function.

8.2   Rework Problem 7.3 with INPUT and ALERT functions for input and output of the function.

8.3   Prepare custom dialog boxes for the input and output interface of Problem 5.2.

	G	H	I	J
1	Fibonacci			Fibo
2	Fibonacci single variable constrained optimization.		Variables on form:	1
3		=FORMULA("",Xmin)		1
4		=FORMULA("",Xmax)	InLow C4	2
5		=FORMULA("",Ymin)	InHigh E4	3
6		=FORMULA("",Ymax)	Accuracy E6	5
7		=FORMULA("",ActAcy)	ObjFctn D8	8
8	Xlow	=InLow	Xmin C12	13
9	Xhigh	=InHigh	Xmax E12	21
10	Interval	=Xhigh-Xlow	Ymin C14	34
11	tol	=Accuracy	Ymax E14	55
12		=IF(Accuracy>=0.5,SET.VALUE(tol,0.001))	ActAcy D16	89
13	Invtol	=1/tol		144
14		=SET.VALUE(INDEX(Fibo,1),1)		233
15		=SET.VALUE(INDEX(Fibo,2),1)		377
16		=SET.VALUE(INDEX(Fibo,3),2)	other variables:	610
17		=FOR("k",4,60)	Fibo J2:J61	987
18	Fibok	= INDEX(Fibo,k-1)+INDEX(Fibo,k-2)		1597
19		= SET.VALUE(INDEX(Fibo,k),Fibok)	Names in column G are	2584
20		= IF(Fibok>=Invtol,BREAK())	assigned to corresponding	4181
21		=NEXT()	cells of column H.	6765
22	kk	=k		10946
23	DX	=Interval		
24	dxF	=INDEX(Fibo,kk-2)*DX/INDEX(Fibo,kk)		
25	XP	=Xlow+dxF		
26	YP	=Fctn(XP)		
27	XM	=Xhigh-dxF		
28	YM	=Fctn(XM)		

Annotations (column H):
- Rows 3–4: Blank out Results boxes.
- Rows 16–17: Compute Fibonacci numbers.
- Rows 24–26: Compute starting values.

(a)

Figure 8.58 (a) First part of the Fibonacci macro and part of the Fibonacci numbers array and (b) the remainder of the Fibonacci macro and the function macro for computing the objective function value.

	G	H	I
29		=FOR("m",kk-1,3,-1)	
30		= IF(YM>YP,,GOTO(I31))	ELSE
31		= SET.VALUE(Xhigh,xhigh-dxF)	= SET.VALUE(Xlow,Xlow+dxF)
32		= SET.VALUE(DX,Xhigh-Xlow)	= SET.VALUE(DX,Xhigh-Xlow)
33		= SET.VALUE(dxF,INDEX(Fibo,m-2)*DX/INDEX(Fibo,m))	= SET.VALUE(dxF,INDEX(Fibo,m-2)*DX/INDEX(Fibo,m))
34		= SET.VALUE(XM,XP)	= SET.VALUE(XP,XM)
35		= SET.VALUE(YM,Fctn(XM))	= SET.VALUE(YP,Fctn(XP))
36		= SET.VALUE(XP,Xlow+dxF)	= SET.VALUE(XM,xhigh-dxF)
37		= SET.VALUE(YP,Fctn(XP))	= SET.VALUE(YM,Fctn(XM))
38	Cont	END IF	= GOTO(Cont)
39		=NEXT()	Above is interval reduction search.
40	YLast	=Fctn(1.001*XP)	
41		=SET.VALUE(Xmin,XP)	
42		=SET.VALUE(Ymin,YP)	
43		=IF(YLast>YP)	
44	Ylow	= Fctn(Xlow)	on left we place values in Results boxes.
45		= SET.VALUE(Xmax,Xlow)	
46		= SET.VALUE(Ymax,Ylow)	
47		=ELSE()	
48	Yhigh	= Fctn(Xhigh)	
49		= SET.VALUE(Xmax,Xhigh)	
50		= SET.VALUE(Ymax,Yhigh)	
51		=END.IF()	
52	RealAcy	=(XP-Xlow)/Interval	
53		=SET.VALUE(ActAcy,RealAcy)	
54		=RETURN()	
55			
56	Fctn		
57		=ARGUMENT("x")	construction of the
58		=FORMULA("="&objFctn,Fofx)	objective function for use above.
59	Fofx	=49*x/(x^2+9)	
60		=RETURN(Fofx)	

(b)

Figure 8.58 (Continued)

8.4   Prepare custom dialog boxes for the input and output interface of Problem 7.3.

8.5   A one-dimension array contains data values that are either zero or positive. The first element of the array contains the number of data values in the array. It is known that many of the values in the array are zero.

       To conserve memory space, write a command macro to compress the array by eliminating two or more consecutive zeros and replace them with a single integer whose value is the number of zeros being replaced. To distinguish this number from positive data values, make it negative so that its sign acts as an indicator that a specified number of zeroes have been eliminated. A single zero between nonzero data values is not to be replaced. The contents of the first element of the array is to be updated upon completion of compression. The following illustrates the process:

	Before:	Number of data values which follow	After:	
	13		9	
	0		−2	
	0		41	
	41		0	
	0		6	
	6		98	
	98		−3	
	0		81	
	0		280	
	0		−2	
	81			
	280			
	0			
	0			

       Use command macros to select and delete the cells with zeros and to compress the array. Refer to the examples of Sections 11.1.2, 11.1.3, 11.2.2, and 11.4.1 for clues to using command macros for this purpose.

8.6   Rework Problem 6.7 as a command macro by enhancing it with the commands to automatically display the curve as a scatter chart upon computing the values. Use the Macro Record command in conjunction with manually executed chart display commands to obtain a reasonable set of commands to incorporate in your macro. Edit them as required to complete the macro.

8.7   Numerous trials are often required while developing macros to plot curves. Consequently, the chart sheet must be cleared of the residual display features as preparation for the next debugging attempt. Write a macro that, when executed, clears the chart sheet and prepares it for the next attempt so that debugging can be expedited with fewer manual commands. This macro would have been useful while working Problem 8.6.

8.8   Prepare a custom menu to conveniently execute various of your command macros. If necessary, rewrite as command macros the macros from the problem set of Chapter 7 to have several for placement in the menu. Add custom-help messages for the menu entries.

CHAPTER 9

The Database

We have emphasized making computations with engineering data. In practice, these data may be collected from experiments, they may be engineering design computations, they may be product specifications and characteristics, they may be production statistics, or they may be any of the information associated with the running of an engineering organization. Usually, a common characteristic of data from such sources is the large amount that must be processed. Although we can store the information in a file and proceed to process it from there with normal editing techniques, we often find it more convenient and efficient to store it in a special structure called a database and to process it with a set of commands specially designed to perform the operations on the data that are usually required, such as searching and extracting.

In this chapter, we will learn about the database management capability of Excel and illustrate its features on engineering data. We will learn to construct search criteria and to customize a form that allows convenient database access, and we will learn to use the built-in database management commands. Finally, we will learn how to prepare macros that manipulate the database with Excel functions and macros.

9.1 INTRODUCTION

In a traditional sense, a computer database is a collection of data structured in a way that storage, retrieval, and modification of its contents can be easily performed. For these purposes, it is usually accessed by a set of routines that make

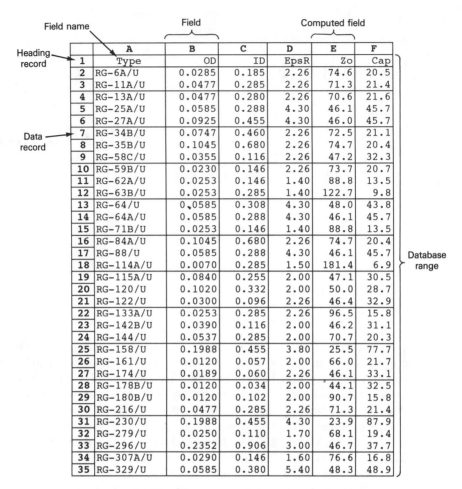

Figure 9.1 Elements of an Excel database.

the database structure transparent to the user. The principal characteristic of these routines is the convenience they afford the user in adding, deleting, modifying, searching, and computing entities of the database. We are about to learn the Excel database feature. It so happens that we must know its structure to use it properly. In that sense, it is a limited implementation of a general purpose database.

An Excel database is a rectangular area of the worksheet that is limited to the maximum size of a worksheet. A small database is shown in Figure 9.1. The rectangular area confines us to organizing the data in that fashion. From the figure, we deduce that the information within the database is recognized by the column headings and that each row of the database is self-contained with respect to its information. Thus, the data of each row represents a complete database entry, and all rows have similar kinds of information organized in the same manner. Each row is called a *record*. It is apparent that the rectangular organization should allow easy access to the database. This is indeed the case. We will explain later how to search the database for information specified as criteria. During the search, we may extract or delete records, or parts of records, we may perform calculations on the contents of selected records, or we may modify the contents of selected records. We may also perform functions on the database, such as sorting and computing, that we already can perform on arrays.

Excel provides certain functions and macros that allow us to manipulate the contents of a database. We can also invoke certain commands that work for us directly, that is, without us having to write a macro for this purpose. We introduce these commands, functions, and macros as we need them in the sections that follow.

9.2 CREATING A DATABASE

In previous chapters, we were able to conveniently manage all the data that we needed for a problem or that was created by a worksheet or macro. We did almost no planning beyond that needed for the immediate problem. Had we much data to contend with, we surely would have spent more time in selecting the data needed and in organizing the way it was to be stored. The need for a database implies possession of more than a superficial quantity of data. It also means that some characteristics of the data are of interest, either associated with individual data entries or statistically derived from the entire set of data. Therefore, we must make sure that we have placed into our database the data that will yield the results we expect after processing it and that we have organized it for ease of manipulation in seeking those results. We must consider various factors for this purpose before we begin creating the database. We discuss this topic first, after which we discuss details of setting up the database.

There has to be some reason for having our data in a database, or else we could just place it in a file. Before organizing the storage structure, we must know, or anticipate, the possible needs for the data and how the needs can be satisfied. We should obtain answers to such questions as: Will we query the database? Extract from it? Will we add or delete entries often? Must it be ordered according to certain keywords? Will it be reordered according to different keywords? Will we make computations on the entries? What kinds of computations will be made? Are they statistical and based on parts of or on the entire database? Are they unique to each entry? Will the results of auxiliary computations also be stored in the database? Will certain entries require modification at times? Must text be accurately spelled? Will the operations we make on text be case sensitive? What will be the consequences of errors in the data? How much data do we really need to keep in the database?

Getting answers to questions as above is important to us for at least two reasons. First, it causes us to thoroughly understand what we will do with the data and, second, it causes us to critically assess the data items to place into the database. We do not want to waste time and effort collecting the wrong data, nor do we want to collect insufficient data. We now consider the subdivisions of data in our database.

We learned in Section 9.1 that our database is a collection of records, each record being a row in the rectangular area of our database. A record is the major subdivision of our database. It contains all the information for one entry of our database. A record is subdivided into fields, whereby a *field* is an element of data comprising the record. It is the minimum subdivision of an Excel database. Each column of the database is a field; thus all records contain the same fields for a given database. Each field is identified by a name, called a *field name,* in the top row of the database. This row is not a data record but merely a heading record. A field may contain raw information for a record or it may contain computed data, in which case it is called a *computed field*. Formulas have to be prepared for computed fields. Figure 9.1 identifies the above terms for our database.

The utility of a database is determined by partitioning the data of a record into fields, since this is the minimum amount of data that may be accessed in a record. It also implicitly determines the nature of the operations that may be made on the data of a record. Answers to the questions we posed above help determine the fields into which the data of a record will be placed. The fields must be logically and precisely determined before any data is placed into a database. It is usually difficult to combine several fields into one, or to separate one field into several, after a database is constructed. Here are some suggestions for organizing and naming the fields of a record.

1. Identify the parts of a record that will be used to search on, sort on, or compute with. They will be placed into separate fields for convenient access.

2. Determine the computed values that must be stored in a record and kept in separate fields.

3. Assign field names to each field. These names must be text constants for proper recognition by the database commands. Derive names whose length is consistent with the amount of data within the field to keep columns narrow and thus with more of the database visible at one time. Names for use in formulas should be short and constructed according to the rules for defining variable names.

Here are suggestions for organizing and constructing the database proper.

1. Determine the order of the fields in the record. Assign them to columns in a left-to-right manner according to interfield associations. Unique record identifiers are placed first (e.g., part numbers, serial numbers, stock num-

bers, etc.), followed by descriptions (e.g., part names and qualifiers, company names and addresses, etc.), attributes (e.g., ratings, size, color, dimensions, unit cost, etc.), and computed values (e.g., totals, derived quantities, etc.).

2. Mentally assign a rectangular area for the database. It is convenient, but not necessary, that it begin with the very first row of the worksheet. Be sure that enough rows and columns are available for the expected number of records and fields to be entered into the database. If the length of the database will vary with use, allow for at least one blank row at the end to avoid redefining the database yet to allow Excel to automatically expand the range as entries are added.

3. Space can be assigned for multiple databases on the same worksheet, although only one at a time can be defined as a database.

4. Enter the field names into the heading record of the database and size the columns for the expected length of the entries.

5. Manually enter the data records in the rows below the heading record. As data are entered, keep in mind the eventual use of the database. Data in fields to be searched should not be preceded or followed by extra spaces, which might affect the outcome. Fields may be left blank if there is no data for it in a given record. There are alternate ways to get the data into the database, as we will describe later.

6. Enter the appropriate formulas into the first data records. Use field names as variables (but first define them with the **Formula Create Names** command) and use constants, functions, and other variables on the worksheet as needed. Then, **Edit Copy** each formula and **Edit Paste** it into the fields of the remainder of the records.

7. If the database is to be extensive or if complicated operations are to be performed on it, initially limit the number of records entered to those required for testing and debugging purposes. Changes may have to be made in the database organization and a small database is preferred for this purpose.

8. Consider formatting of entries in the data records (standard and custom formats for numbers and text, font and alignment formats). Limit the formatting to be the same for entire fields at a time. Field names should be formatted separately from data fields.

Example 9.1

We will prepare a database of coaxial cable characteristics. The result is shown in Figure 9.1. The construction of a coaxial cable is shown in Figure 9.2. We are generally interested in the cable type number, characteristic impedance (Z_o), capacitance (C), attenuation (α), velocity of propagation (V_p), cutoff frequency (f_{co}), time delay (t_d), and physical size. To illustrate Excel database layout, we will limit our interests to the cable type, characteristic impedance, capacitance, and size, to the extent it affects Z_o and C. Formulas for Z_o and C are given in Figure 9.2, for

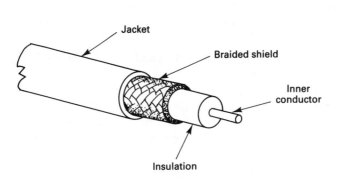

$$\text{Characteristic impedance} = Z_o = \frac{138}{\sqrt{\epsilon_R}} \ell og_{10}(D/d) \quad \text{ohms}$$

$$\text{Capacitance} = C = \frac{7.354\epsilon_R}{\ell og_{10}(D/d)} \quad \text{pF/ft}$$

where ϵ_R = relative dielectric constant of insulation
         D = inner diameter of shield
         d = diameter of inner conductor (same units as D)

Figure 9.2 Coaxial cable construction and formulas for its characteristic impedance and capacitance.

which we need the outer diameter of the inner conductor (d), the inner diameter of the shield (D), and the relative dielectric constant of the insulation (ε_R).

Our heading record will contain, in order, names for the cable type, the outer diameter of the inner conductor, the inner diameter of the shield, the insulation relative dielectric constant, the characteristic impedance, and the capacitance. Tables of coaxial cable characteristics usually contain values for Z_o and C, but we will compute these values to illustrate computed fields. Construction characteristics for RG type cable are readily available, so we enter the type and diameter values into the first three fields using normal editing procedures. Because the insulation type is also given, we determine the relative dielectric constant from material characteristics and enter the values in the fourth field. The characteristic impedance and capacitance are computed for the fifth and sixth fields, respectively. Formulas for part of the database are shown in Figure 9.3.

	E	F
1	Zo	Cap
2	=138/SQRT(EpsR)*LOG(ID/OD)	=7.354*EpsR/LOG(ID/OD)
3	=138/SQRT(EpsR)*LOG(ID/OD)	=7.354*EpsR/LOG(ID/OD)
4	=138/SQRT(EpsR)*LOG(ID/OD)	=7.354*EpsR/LOG(ID/OD)
5	=138/SQRT(EpsR)*LOG(ID/OD)	=7.354*EpsR/LOG(ID/OD)

Figure 9.3 Some rows of the formulas of the database of Figure 9.1.

We chose the field names of Figure 9.1 because they convey the purpose of the field values, because they are unique (we cannot use *D* and *d* for the two diameters since they have the same meaning to Excel), and because they do not interfere with reserved names of Excel. The variables for the formulas were defined with the **Formula Create Names** command. The formulas were copied into the other records using editing commands.

After preparing the database, or a limited version of it, as suggested above, we now define it as follows.

1. Select the cells of the database range (the header record, the data records, and the trailing blank rows, if any).
2. Execute the **Data Set Database** command of Figure 9.4(a). Excel defines the selected area as the database range and assigns it the name "Database". This name is reassigned to another database if we choose to define another one.

We have just created a database. Perhaps we are ready to use it immediately, but we may also want to make changes to it, such as correcting errors, or

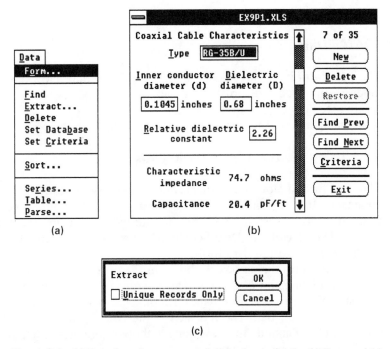

(a)   (b)

(c)

Figure 9.4   (a) Data drop-down menu and dialog boxes for the (b) Form and (c) Extract commands.

deleting from or adding to its contents. So, before proceeding to the next section to describe how to use it, we first discuss some editing procedures.

Because we edit a database in the same manner as we do a worksheet, we have to learn some techniques for doing it so as not to invalidate some of what we have already done. Of chief concern is the need to maintain the range and to include in this range all new records we add to the database. The reason we recommended adding blank records at the end of the range was to permit inserting new records without having to redefine the range. If we do not have a blank record as the last record and we add a new record to the end of the database with the **Edit Insert** command, we must then redefine the database to include the new record. An extra blank record at the end would have caused the new record to be inserted before this last blank record, and the database would have automatically been redefined. By having the last record blank, we can delete records, or we can sort the database without invalidating the range, since Excel automatically retains the range.

Whenever we invalidate the database range, we must again select our range and execute the **Data Set Database** command to reestablish it. We can follow this latter procedure to establish a new database on the same worksheet. The name ''Database'' is merely reassigned to the new database. Thus, we can maintain multiple databases on the same worksheet and merely redefine them as needed to process from the desired one.

9.3 THE DATA FORM

The data form is a convenience feature of Excel that allows us to add, delete, modify, and inspect records of a database and to perform a search operation to locate specific records. In this section, we learn to use an Excel constructed data form dialog box and to construct a custom data form dialog box.

9.3.1 Using the Data Form Dialog Box

The data form dialog box is displayed in response to executing the **Data Form** command. It is a simplified method for accessing individual records of a database. It is not a substitute for but an alternative to using the **Data Find**, **Data Extract**, **Data Delete**, or **Data Set Criteria** commands of Figure 9.4(a). We cannot extract records with a data form.

A data form dialog box is shown in Figure 9.4(b). It is displayed when the **Data Form** command is chosen. This customized dialog box is for use with the database of Figure 9.1. The data form dialog box is separated into two parts by the vertical scroll bar: The left side is the data form itself; the right side is a selection of commands for traversing and operating on the database from which the data form was constructed.

The data form entries are derived from the database header record and from the values of a data record to which the dialog box is directed to display. Along the left edge of the dialog box are the header record field names. Next to these names are the values from a data record, in this case record 7 of Figure 9.1. The record number whose values are displayed in the data form is shown in the upper right corner of the dialog box. This number changes as one scrolls through the database. The values that are boxed in were placed in the database when it was created. These values, and hence those in the database fields, may be edited via the data form. The values that are not boxed in are obtained from computed fields and may not be edited via the data form.

Along the right edge of the dialog box is a column of command buttons. These are chosen as needed to edit, add, delete, or search data records, as we explain below. Table 9.1 shows keyboard and mouse procedures for traversing the data form dialog box and moving within the database. We learned to work within a dialog box in Section 8.3.1, so we will not repeat that discussion here.

TABLE 9.1 WORKING WITHIN THE DATA FORM

Operation	Mouse	Keyboard
Select a field	Click in text box of desired field	ALT+key of field name underlined letter
Move to same field in next record	Click ↓ in scroll bar	↓ key
Move to same field in previous record	Click ↑ in scroll bar	↑ key
Move to same field 10 records forward	Click scroll bar below scroll box	PAGE DOWN
Move to same field 10 records back	Click scroll bar above scroll box	PAGE UP
Move to last record	Drag scroll box to bottom of scroll bar	CTRL+PAGE DOWN
Move to first record	Drag scroll box to top of scroll bar	CTRL+PAGE UP
Move to next field in record	——	TAB
Move to previous field in record	——	SHIFT+TAB
Move to first field in next record	——	ENTER
Move to first field in previous record	——	SHIFT+ENTER
Move and edit within a field	Click at desired position of insertion bar	HOME, ←, →, END
Choose a command button	Click on desired command button	ALT+key of button underlined letter

However, here are particulars for using the data form dialog box, especially the commands.

1. Editing records: Only data within a text box can be edited. The procedures of Table 9.1 apply for selecting the desired records and fields. Data within the text box is edited as for ordinary dialog boxes. When all changes are made for a given record, they are entered into the record by scrolling to the next record to be edited or by choosing the **Exit** button to exit the data form. Changes to a record can be canceled by choosing the **Restore** button, provided this is done *before* scrolling to another record.

2. Adding a new record to the database: A new blank record is added to the end of the database when there is room for it, or else a "Can't extend database" message is displayed if the **New** button is chosen or by scrolling past the last record of the database. In this case, all the data form text boxes are blank. Entries can be made as described in Table 9.1. If computed fields are used, their formulas are copied to the new record. Be sure to first define the fields by selecting their columns to ensure that sufficient rows are included to allow the computations to be made, or else the #VALUE entry will appear in the computed field. The new record is placed in the database by scrolling to another record or by exiting the data form.

3. Deleting a record from the database: A database record is deleted by first scrolling to the record, then choosing the **Delete** button. Confirmation of the deletion is requested. The deleted record cannot be restored by choosing the **Restore** button. The records following the deleted record are moved up one row.

4. Searching for specific data: The procedure to search the database for records satisfying some search criteria is as follows:

- Choose the **Criteria** button. This button is then renamed **Form** so that one can return to the regular form dialog box by choosing the button again. Also, the **Delete** button is renamed **Clear** so that all existing criteria can be quickly cleared, and the position indicator changes to "Criteria" to show that the dialog box is in the search mode.
- Set up the search criteria in the text boxes (see below).
- Perform the search. Choose the **Find Next** button to search forward and display the next record meeting the criteria or choose the **Find Prev** button to search backward and display the previous record meeting the criteria.

The search performs a simple matching operation, comparing the entries in the fields of a record, including computed fields, against the criteria that were entered in the text boxes of the corresponding fields of the dialog box. When a match is found, that record is displayed in the dialog box. Multiple criteria may be specified for a search, in which case all criteria must be satisfied for a match. Criteria are constructed as follows:

- By typing in the text boxes the text, numbers, or logical values to be searched for. Capitalization is ignored during the search. Also, see wildcard below.

    Examples:

Form	matches	form, Form, and formation (when at beginning of field)
1234	matches	1234, 1234.00, and $1,234.00
RG-13	matches	Type field for cables RG-13A/U and RG-133A/U in Figure 9.1

- By typing a comparison operator with the number to be searched for. The comparison operators are shown in Table 5.2, which is repeated here as Table 9.2. Compound expressions cannot be formed since logical operators are not available for this purpose. Multiple comparison operators are not permitted in a single text box.

    Examples:

=300	matches	300.0, 300, and $300.00
<=25	matches	any number equal to or less than 25, including all negative numbers
>14.5	matches	all positive numbers greater than 14.5
<.1	matches	ID field for cables RG-122/U, RG-161/U, RG-174/U, and RG-178B/U in Figure 9.1

- By typing the wildcard characters asterisk (*) or question mark (?) for unspecified characters. The asterisk will match all characters in its posi-

TABLE 9.2 COMPARISON OPERATORS

Symbol	Meaning
=	Equal
<>	Not equal
<	Less than
>	Greater than
<=	Equal to or less than
>=	Equal to or greater than

tion in the target text, while the question mark will match only one character in its position in the target text. To find an actual asterisk or question mark, precede it with the tilde (~). All comparison criteria text strings are followed by an implicit asterisk.

Examples:

?ain	matches	gain, pain, rain, and vain when at the beginning of the field
*ain	matches	gain, pain, rain, and vain anywhere in the field
*t*expansion	matches	thermal expansion and temperature expansion anywhere in the field

9.3.2 Constructing a Custom Data Form Dialog Box

We discussed thoroughly the construction of custom dialog boxes in Section 8.3. Those were dialog boxes for general application wherever we felt they were needed. One such application we suggested was data entry. But that is one application for the data form dialog box also. We will find that there is little difference in purpose between the dialog boxes as we discussed them in Section 8.3 and the data form dialog box. We will concentrate on the database application of the dialog box now, however.

We affect only the side left of the scroll bar of the data form dialog box with our customizing talent. That is where the display unique to our database appears. Figure 9.5 shows two variations of the data form for the database of Figure 9.1. We now explain how to prepare such custom dialog boxes.

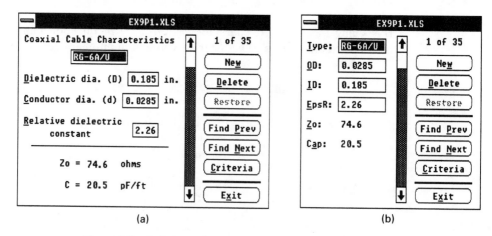

(a)   (b)

Figure 9.5 Variations of the data form for the database of Figure 9.1.

The data form dialog box entries we specify are limited to element types 5 through 10 as described in Tables 8.11 and 8.12. These are the fixed text and entry boxes. As was done in Section 8.3, we will prepare a table (a table definition area) describing how the dialog box is to look. Two tables that we prepared before appear in Figures 8.14 and 8.17. The table for the data form dialog box will resemble the tables of these figures. The principal differences are that we have a limited number of element types to work with and that we must define the table as "Data_Form". Before, we were allowed to define the table definition area of Figure 8.11 with a name of our choosing, which was then used in the DIALOG.BOX function of Table 8.15. The fixed name Data_Form means that we can have only one data form table defined at a time. Of course, we will be able to switch to other tables merely by redefining the Data_Form name. When we execute the **Data Form** command, Excel looks first for a table we defined as Data_Form. If it is found, that is the table used for the data form dialog box. Otherwise, Excel will construct a dialog box for us just as it did to produce the one shown in Figure 9.5(b).

In Section 8.3.1, we discussed in detail the construction of the table definition area. We described its columns and rows (Figure 8.11) and the element containment box (Figure 8.12). We even recommended a procedure for trial layout of the dialog box, which was based on the use of cross-section paper (see Figure 8.13). In Section 8.3.2, we discussed the Dialog Editor and its use in preparing dialog boxes. We will not repeat those discussions here, but they apply

First row to be blank

Area within heavy outline to be named Data_Form.

	O	P	Q	R	S	T	U	V
1	Element	Item	X pos	Y pos	Box width	Box height	Text	Init/Result
2								
3	Text	5	8	6	232	18	Coaxial Cable Characteristics	
4	Text box	6	80	26	88	18		Type
5	Text	5	8	54	152	18	&Dielectric dia. (D)	
6	Number box	8	168	52	48	18		ID
7	Text	5	224	54	24	18	in.	
8	Text	5	8	80	144	18	&Conductor dia. (d)	
9	Number box	8	160	78	56	18		OD
10	Text	5	224	80	24	18	in.	
11	Text	5	8	106	152	18	&Relative dielectric	
12	Text	5	48	122	64	18	constant	
13	Number box	8	176	114	40	18		EpsR
14	Text	5	20	133	212	18		
15	Text	5	64	158	32	18	Zo =	
16	Number box	8	102	156	48	18		Zo
17	Text	5	158	158	32	18	ohms	
18	Text	5	72	184	24	18	C =	
19	Number box	8	102	182	48	18		Cap
20	Text	5	158	184	40	18	pF/ft	

Fixed text (5) or entry box (6-10)

(x, y) location with respect to upper left corner of dialog box

Size of containment box

Text to be displayed in the dialog box

The name of the database field corresponding to each entry box

Figure 9.6   Table definition area for the dialog box of Figure 9.5(a).

directly to the data form dialog box. The reader is encouraged to study Section 8.3.1 before proceeding with the remainder of this discussion.

The table definition area for the data form dialog box of Figure 9.5(a) appears in Figure 9.6. Notice that all columns of the first row (line 0) are blank and do not contain data that specifies the size and location of the dialog box. We labeled the column headings with the same names as in Figure 8.11 to emphasize the nearly identical meaning of the entries. The single difference is that, for the data form, the Init/Result column contains the name of the database field corresponding to each text box. The **Data Form** command interprets these names as locations from which to obtain the values for display in the entry boxes.

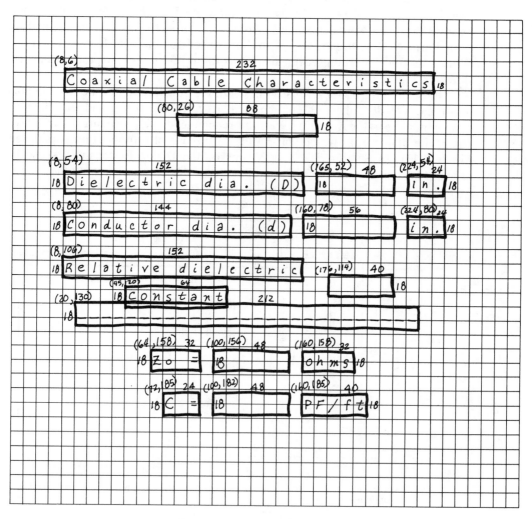

Figure 9.7 Trial data form for Figure 9.5(a).

Our trial data form dialog box is shown in Figure 9.7. This is the cross-section paper layout that we recommend as a first step in developing the dialog box. The table of Figure 9.6 includes the values of the final version after minor adjustments in position and size of the containment boxes have been made. We used just three different types of elements.

9.4 SEARCHING A DATABASE

The **Data Form** command that we described in Section 9.3.1 is useful for adding, deleting, and finding records in our database. However, its search capability is limited. We can set up only simple criteria, the form finds only one record for each **Find Next** or **Find Prev** command, and we cannot extract and group elsewhere the records that meet our criteria. Therefore, we now discuss alternative ways to search our database with the built-in commands of Excel.

The commands that we will discuss in this section are **Data Find** (it finds one matched record at a time but does not copy them to an extract area), **Data Extract** (it finds and copies matched records to an extract area), and **Data Delete** (it deletes permanently from the database the matched records). These commands all have the characteristics of being easily executed and being capable of working with complex search criteria. Our job is to prepare the search criteria, define the criteria range and possibly an extract range, and then invoke the desired command. The procedures for using the commands are simple. First, we must learn to prepare the search criteria and criteria range.

The *criteria range* is a rectangular area on the same worksheet as the database. It consists of one row for criteria names followed by additional rows that contain the criteria. The criteria, similar to that for the data form, are placed in cells of criteria rows which follow the row containing criteria names. There must be at least one criteria row and as many columns as needed to contain the criteria names (one name per column). Figure 9.8 shows a criteria range with two criteria rows and three criteria names. Before we can use the criteria range in a search, we must define it. First, we select all cells of the range, then execute the **Data Set**

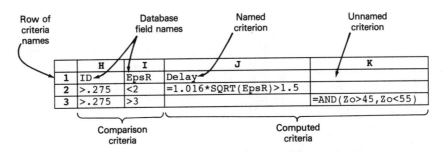

Figure 9.8 Database search criteria range.

Criteria command. Excel names the range "Criteria". As for the database, we can redefine the criteria range to suit our search needs by maintaining multiple criteria ranges on our worksheet.

The criteria can be constructed as fragments of comparison expressions, in which case it is called *comparison criteria,* or it can be constructed in formula form, in which case it is called *computed criteria.* The purpose in constructing both types of criteria is the same, namely, to find records for which the contents of at least one field satisfies the conditions specified as the criteria. The conditions may be simple matching or comparing operations, mathematical relationships, or some combination of these conditions. Criteria placed into the cells of the criteria range are constructed as follows.

1. Matching criteria: Type into the cells under the criteria names the text, numbers, or logical values to be searched for. Capitalization is ignored during the search. Use the wildcard characters asterisk (*) and question mark (?) for unspecified characters in text. The asterisk matches all characters in its position in the target text, while the question mark matches only one character in its position in the target text. To find an actual asterisk or question mark, precede it with the tilde (~). All comparison criteria text strings are followed by an implicit asterisk. For this reason, any match occurs only at the beginning of the target text unless the comparison text is preceded by the asterisk, in which case matches may be found anywhere in the target text. To match a text value exactly, construct it as text in a formula of the form ="=text", where *text* is the string of characters to be matched. The matched record will contain *text* as the only characters in the searched field. The above is actually the "equal to" comparison operation.

Example: We can search the database of Figure 9.1 with either criterion of Figure 9.9(a) to find the coaxial cables of Figure 9.9(b). The left criterion uses a wildcard to accept all characters preceding the −6 in the field Type, while the right criterion searches for RG-6 beginning in the first character position of the field. In both cases, we find all coaxial cables whose number begins with 6. The wildcard following the 6 of the criteria ensures that we find single- and double-digit numbers.

	H			H
1	Type		1	Type
2	*-6*/		2	RG-6*/U

(a)

	H	I	J	K	L	M
6	Type	ID	OD	EpsR	Zo	Cap
7	RG-6A/U	0.185	0.0285	2.26	74.6	20.5
8	RG-62A/U	0.146	0.0253	1.40	88.8	13.5
9	RG-63B/U	0.285	0.0253	1.40	122.7	9.8
10	RG-64/U	0.308	0.0585	4.30	48.0	43.8
11	RG-64A/U	0.288	0.0585	4.30	46.1	45.7

(b)

Figure 9.9 (a) Two examples of matching criterion and (b) the records extracted from the database of Figure 9.1.

	J
1	Zo
2	<40

(a)

	H	I	J	K	L	M
6	Type	ID	OD	EpsR	Zo	Cap
7	RG–158/U	0.455	0.1988	3.80	25.5	77.7
8	RG–230/U	0.455	0.1988	4.30	23.9	87.9

(b)

Figure 9.10 (a) Comparison criterion example and (b) the records extracted from the database of Figure 9.1.

2. Comparison criteria: Type into the cells under the criteria names the comparison operator followed by the comparing value. The comparison operators are shown in Table 9.2. In effect, one prepares a modified form of the comparison expression where the first operand is implied and is the field name while the remainder of the expression is entered in the cell. An exception is the "equal to" operator, which must be prepared as a formula as follows:

$$=``=text"$$

where *text* is the value to be matched. Compound criteria are prepared as discussed in paragraph (4) below.

Example: The comparison criterion of Figure 9.10(a) will find all coaxial cables in the database of Figure 9.1 with $Z_o < 40$ ohms. The two cables of Figure 9.10(b) match the criterion.

3. Computed criteria: A computed criterion is a formula that is entered in a field of the criteria range that is not a field of the database. This field may be named or unnamed. The formula may compute a logical, numerical, text, or error value, but it is interpreted as TRUE or FALSE for search purposes. If TRUE, a match has occurred. If the numerical result of a formula is zero, it is interpreted as FALSE; otherwise, it is TRUE. If the result of a formula is text or an error value, it is interpreted as FALSE. Logical formulas return either TRUE or FALSE as their value.

A formula may contain field names as variables (when defined as such), constants, cell references, variables outside the database, and functions. All criteria are applied to the record being tested, with the field names interpreted to apply to the first record of the database. When cell references are entered in the formulas, they, too, would be for the first record. Should it be required to refer to a field in a record other than the one being tested, the cell reference is chosen from a record above, or below, the first record.

Example: The computed criterion of Figure 9.11(a) will find all coaxial cables in the database of Figure 9.1 whose time delay = $1.016 \sqrt{\varepsilon_R}$ is less than 1.25. The cables of Figure 9.11(b) match the criterion. We named the criterion "Delay" although it was not necessary to do so. Naming helps us remember the reason for preparing the criterion. The criterion is constructed as a formula that yields TRUE or FALSE.

	M
1	Delay
2	=1.016*SQRT(EpsR)<1.25

(a)

	H	I	J	K	L	M
6	Type	ID	OD	EpsR	Zo	Cap
7	RG-62A/U	0.146	0.0253	1.40	88.8	13.5
8	RG-63B/U	0.285	0.0253	1.40	122.7	9.8
9	RG-71B/U	0.146	0.0253	1.40	88.8	13.5
10	RG-114A/U	0.285	0.0070	1.50	181.4	6.9

(b)

Figure 9.11 (a) Computed criterion example and (b) the records extracted from the database of Figure 9.1.

4. Combined criteria: A criterion is placed in a single cell of the criteria range. But more than one criterion may be entered in the criteria range for a search operation, in which case the criteria are applied simultaneously during the search. Also, there may be more than one row of criteria in the criteria range. The question that now arises is how to interpret the criteria that are being combined.

The structure of the criteria range possesses an implicit combining order of logical operations, as shown in Figure 9.12. All criteria of a given row are connected by an implicit logical AND function. The logical results of all rows are connected by implicit logical OR functions. A blank cell is considered to have the logical value TRUE. Therefore, blank cells do not affect the search outcome unless all cells of a row in the criteria range are blank, in which case all records match the criteria.

Examples: The combined criteria of Figure 9.13(a) illustrate the implicit AND. It will find all cables in the database of Figure 9.1 that have a shield ID greater than 0.3 in. and that have $70 < Z_o < 75$ ohms. The three cables of Figure 9.13(b) match the criteria.

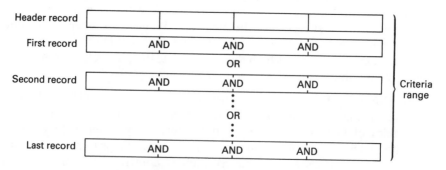

Figure 9.12 Implicit ordering of combined criteria.

	K	L
1	ID	Range
2	>.3	=AND(Zo>70,Zo<75)

(a)

	H	I	J	K	L	M
6	Type	ID	OD	EpsR	Zo	Cap
7	RG-34B/U	0.460	0.0747	2.26	72.5	21.1
8	RG-35B/U	0.680	0.1045	2.26	74.7	20.4
9	RG-84A/U	0.680	0.1045	2.26	74.7	20.4

(b)

Figure 9.13 (a) Combined criterion illustrating the implicit AND and (b) the records of Figure 9.1 extracted with it.

The combined criteria of Figure 9.14(a) illustrate the implicit AND and the implicit OR. It will find all cables in the database of Figure 9.1 that have a shield ID greater than 0.275 in. and that have $\varepsilon_R < 2$ or $\varepsilon_R > 3$. The cables of Figure 9.14(b) match the criteria. The combined criteria of Figure 9.15 illustrate the implicit AND by using two columns with the same field name. It will find all cables in the database of Figure 9.1 with $70 < Z_o < 75$ ohms. The combined criteria of Figure 9.8 applied to the database of Figure 9.1 will find all coaxial cables whose shield inside diameter is greater than 0.275 in. and (a) have ε_R less than 2 and a time delay greater than 1.5 or (b) have ε_R greater than 3 and $45 < Z_o < 55$ ohms. The cables of Figure 9.16 match the criteria.

With the description of the criteria specification complete, we now proceed to the discussion of the Excel built-in search commands.

1. Data Find: The purpose of this command, shown in Figure 9.4(a), is to find and select records in the database. For this purpose, one must define the

	H	I
1	ID	EpsR
2	>.275	<2
3	>.275	>3

(a)

	H	I	J	K	L	M
6	Type	ID	OD	EpsR	Zo	Cap
7	RG-25A/U	0.288	0.0585	4.30	46.1	45.7
8	RG-27A/U	0.455	0.0925	4.30	46.0	45.7
9	RG-63B/U	0.285	0.0253	1.40	122.7	9.8
10	RG-64/U	0.308	0.0585	4.30	48.0	43.8
11	RG-64A/U	0.288	0.0585	4.30	46.1	45.7
12	RG-88/U	0.288	0.0585	4.30	46.1	45.7
13	RG-114A/U	0.285	0.0070	1.50	181.4	6.9
14	RG-158/U	0.455	0.1988	3.80	25.5	77.7
15	RG-230/U	0.455	0.1988	4.30	23.9	87.9
16	RG-329/U	0.380	0.0585	5.40	48.3	48.9

(b)

Figure 9.14 (a) Combined criteria illustrating the implicit AND and OR and (b) the records of Figure 9.1 extracted with it.

	J	K
1	Zo	Zo
2	>70	<75

Figure 9.15 Another combined criteria illustrating the implicit AND.

criteria range as described above. Records that match the criteria will be selected one at a time according to the manner in which the database is scrolled. No extracting of records is done.

Beginning the search

- Choose **Data Find**.
- If the active cell is outside the database, the search is downward beginning from the first record unless the SHIFT key is held down when the **Data Find** command is executed, in which case the search is upward beginning from the last record.
- The search stops at the first record that matches the criteria. This record is then selected, and the scroll bars become diagonally striped.
- If the active cell is inside the database, the search begins from that point, and the next matching record is selected.
- If there are no matching records in the database, an alert box with the message "No match" is displayed.
- The **Data Find** command changes to **Data Exit Find** in the menu.

Continuing the search

- Follow the procedures of Table 9.3 to scroll within the database with the mouse or keyboard. Scrolling is not continuous; it is discrete and depends on finding matching records.

	H	I	J	K	L	M
6	Type	ID	OD	EpsR	Zo	Cap
7	RG-25A/U	0.288	0.0585	4.30	46.1	45.7
8	RG-27A/U	0.455	0.0925	4.30	46.0	45.7
9	RG-64/U	0.308	0.0585	4.30	48.0	43.8
10	RG-64A/U	0.288	0.0585	4.30	46.1	45.7
11	RG-88/U	0.288	0.0585	4.30	46.1	45.7
12	RG-329/U	0.380	0.0585	5.40	48.3	48.9

Figure 9.16 Records of Figure 9.1 extracted with the combined criteria of Figure 9.8.

TABLE 9.3 SCROLLING IN DATA FIND

Operation	Mouse	Keyboard
Find next matching record	Click scroll bar down arrow	↓ key
Find previous matching record	Click scroll bar up arrow	↑ key
Find next matching record at least one screen down	Click below scroll box	PAGE DOWN
Find previous matching record at least one screen up	Click above scroll box	PAGE UP
Find record nearest arbitrary scroll box location	Drag scroll box in desired direction	———

- Upon finding the last matching record in the database, in either search direction, further efforts to scroll cause no movement or other indication of action. The last selected record remains selected.

Editing matched records

- Cells of the matched records may be selected and edited in the usual manner. However, this action causes the **Data Find** command to be terminated (note that the scroll bars return to their normal pattern). It must again be executed to resume the search from the current record.

Ending the search

- Choose **Data Exit Find,** choose another command, select a cell outside the database, edit the contents of a cell, or press ESC.

2. Data Extract: The purpose of this command, and its dialog box of Figure 9.4(c), is to find matching records of the database and copy values from them to an area of the worksheet known as the *extract range*. For this purpose, one must define a criteria range, as described above, and create an extract range.

Creating an extract range

- Determine the fields to be extracted. Type the field names into adjacent cells of a row exactly as they appear in the database heading row. This will be the heading row of the extract range.
- If all fields of the database need not be extracted, enter only the desired field names in the extract heading row. They need not be in the same order as they appear in the database.

- The rows below the extract heading row will contain the information from the extracted records. Be sure there is sufficient space below this heading row to hold the anticipated number of extracted records.
- Select the cells of the extract range heading row and, if desired, cells below the heading row that will hold the copied values. This is the extract range. If the heading row only is selected, Excel will clear all cells below the heading to the bottom of the worksheet, then copy the extracted fields into these rows. If the heading row and a range below the heading are selected, Excel will clear this range and then copy the extracted records into the rows. Should there be more extracted records than rows, an alert box with the message "Extract range is full" is displayed and no more records are extracted.

The procedure to extract records from a database is as follows:

- Define the criteria range and create the extract range.
- Choose **Data Extract**. The dialog box of Figure 9.4(c) appears. The **Unique Records Only** check box is to be turned off if all records matching the criteria are to be extracted. It is to be turned on to not extract matched records with extracted fields that are identical to those of a record already extracted. In this latter case, matching records with different values in fields not in the extract range will not be extracted.
- Choose the **OK** button of the dialog box. Clearing of the value cells of the extract range and copying of matched record values into the extract range are the only visible evidence that the extract operation took place.

3. Data Delete: The purpose of this command [Figure 9.4(a)] is to delete records from the database that match the search criteria. Follow this procedure.

- Define the criteria range.
- Choose **Data Delete**. An alert box appears with the message "Matching records will be deleted permanently". This means that the action cannot be reversed with any other command.
- Choose **OK** to delete matching records or **Cancel** to terminate the command. If records are deleted, the remaining records are shifted upward to close all gaps in the database. The remainder of the worksheet is unaffected by this shifting operation.

It is possible that records will be deleted unintentionally with this command. To avoid this happening, we recommend that the delete search criteria first be run with the **Data Extract** command. The extracted records should then be inspected to verify, or not, that the desired records will be deleted with the specified criteria. Alternative preventive ways may be to first search for the records with the **Data Find** command or to work with a copy of the database.

9.5 DATABASE FUNCTIONS AND MACROS

We find few built-in functions and macros associated with the Excel database feature because it is not as extensive as the computational features. The functions and macros available are shown in Tables 9.4 and 9.5, respectively. We will comment on their use in this section.

The numeric functions of Table 9.4 operate on values in a field of records of the database that meet matching criteria. Therefore, they perform their own search operations. The functions compute simple arithmetic and statistical quantities common to data stored in databases. The syntax for all functions is as follows:

$$\textit{function-name (db-ref, field, criteria-ref)}$$

where

$\textit{function-name}$ = name of the function as given in Table 9.4.

$db\text{-}ref$ = range reference or name given to the database range, usually Database.

$\textit{field}$ = the field whose value the function is to operate on. It is text and must be enclosed within quotation marks. This field is optional for some functions.

$\textit{criteria-ref}$ = range reference or name given to the criteria range, usually Criteria.

The macro functions of Table 9.5 are equivalent to the commands described in Sections 9.3 and 9.4. They are used in the same manner as we described other such functions in Chapter 8. Because they apply to databases, they expect to find a database and criteria range defined as Database and Criteria, respectively. An extract range must be selected before beginning an extract search. We have the flexibility with macro functions that we have with individual commands, including the ability to step through the database forward and backward while searching.

Example 9.2

The purpose of this example is to illustrate the use of database functions and macros. We will find matching mechanical parts with a sliding fit as shown in Figure 9.17(a). The male part has two different size pins that must slide into the female part. Assume that we have uniquely identified male and female parts in stock with measured dimensions DiaA, DiaB, and Space as shown in Figure 9.17(b). We will write a macro to find all female parts that accommodate each male part.

Figure 9.18 is a diagram of our plan. We will begin with a database of female parts and a table of male parts. The parts will have been generated earlier on a macro sheet, sorted, and copied to the worksheet where we have the database. We will describe their generation later. A partial listing of the female and male parts on the

TABLE 9.4 EXCEL DATABASE FUNCTIONS

Function	Description
DAVERAGE (*db-ref*, *field*, *criteria-ref*)	Computes the average of the values in the *field* of the records in database *db-ref* that meet the criteria in the range *criteria-ref*.
DCOUNT (*db-ref*, [*field*], *criteria-ref*)	Counts the number of records in database *db-ref* that meet the criteria in the range *criteria-ref* and that have numbers in the *field* of those records. If *field* is omitted, the function counts all records that meet the search criteria.
DCOUNTA (*db-ref*, [*field*], *criteria-ref*)	Counts the number of nonblank cells in the *field* of the records in database *db-ref* that meet the criteria in the range *criteria-ref*. If *field* is omitted, the function counts all nonblank records that meet the search criteria.
DMAX (*db-ref*, *field*, *criteria-ref*)	Determines the algebraically largest value in the *field* of records in database *db-ref* that meet the criteria in the range *criteria-ref*.
DMIN (*db-ref*, *field*, *criteria-ref*)	Determines the algebraically smallest value in the *field* of records in database *db-ref* that meet the criteria in the range *criteria-ref*.
DPRODUCT (*db-ref*, *field*, *criteria-ref*)	Determines the product of all values in the *field* of the records in database *db-ref* that meet the criteria in the range *criteria-ref*.
DSTDEV (*db-ref*, *field*, *criteria-ref*)	Computes the nonbiased or n-1 standard deviation of a population based on the values in the *field* of the records in database *db-ref* that meet the criteria in the range *criteria-ref*.
DSTDEVP (*db-ref*, *field*, *criteria-ref*)	Computes the biased or n standard deviation of a population based on the values in the *field* of the records in database *db-ref* that meet the criteria in the range *criteria-ref*.
DSUM (*db-ref*, *field*, *criteria-ref*)	Computes the sum of the values in the *field* of the records in database *db-ref* that meet the criteria in the range *criteria-ref*.
DVAR (*db-ref*, *field*, *criteria-ref*)	Computes an estimate of the variance of a sample of a population from the values in the *field* of the records in database *db-ref* that meet the criteria in the range *criteria-ref*.
DVARP (*db-ref*, *field*, *criteria-ref*)	Computes the variance of the entire population from the values in the *field* of the records in database *db-ref* that meet the criteria in the range *criteria-ref*. The assumption is that the database is the entire population.

TABLE 9.5 EXCEL DATABASE MACRO FUNCTIONS

Database command	Macro function
Data Set Database	SET.DATABASE( )
Data Set Criteria	SET.CRITERIA( )
Data Form	DATA.FORM( )
Data Find	DATA.FIND(*log-exp*)
	log-exp = TRUE for Data Find, FALSE for Data Exit Find
	DATA.FIND.NEXT( )
	Selects the next matching record of the database. If none, function value is FALSE.
	DATA.FIND.PREV( )
	Selects the previous matching record of the database. If none, function value is FALSE.
Data Extract	EXTRACT(*log-exp*)
	log-exp = TRUE (turns on Unique check box), FALSE (turns off Unique check box).
Data Delete	DATA.DELETE( )

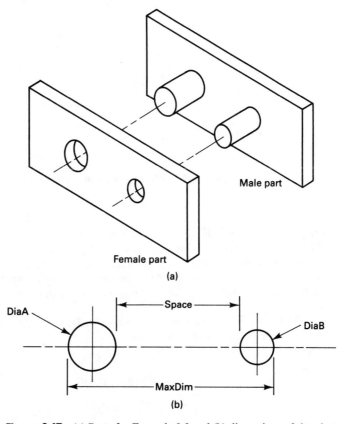

Figure 9.17 (a) Parts for Example 9.2 and (b) dimensions of the pins.

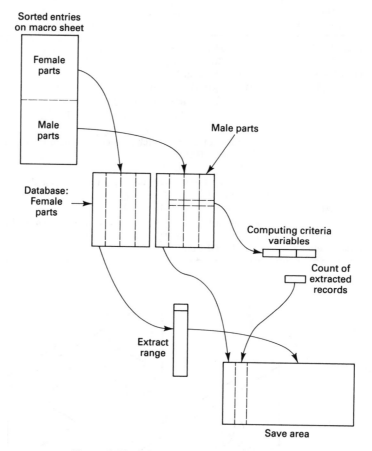

Figure 9.18   Data movement of Example 9.2.

worksheet is shown in Figure 9.19. The female parts begin with "F", the male ones with "M". Measured dimensions (inches) are shown in the table. We will use the dimensions of one male part and search the database for matching female parts. The part numbers of the female parts will be extracted, then transferred to a save area together with the male part number and a count of the female parts that meet the criteria.

The criteria to be met are [subscript f for female parts, m for male parts with variables as defined in Figure 9.17(b)]:

$$\text{DiaA}_f > \text{DiaA}_m$$

$$\text{DiaB}_f > \text{DiaB}_m$$

$$\text{Space}_f < \text{Space}_m$$

$$\text{MaxDim}_f > \text{MaxDim}_m$$

	A	B	C	D	E	F	G	H	I
1	Part	DiaAF	SpaceF	DiaBF		Part	DiaAM	SpaceM	DiaBM
2	F1	0.753	1.999	0.498		M1	0.737	1.995	0.491
3	F2	0.743	1.995	0.498		M2	0.740	2.005	0.492
4	F3	0.754	1.997	0.500		M3	0.738	2.004	0.492
5	F4	0.735	2.003	0.497		M4	0.744	2.002	0.496
6	F5	0.756	2.002	0.498		M5	0.740	2.000	0.481
7	F6	0.745	1.999	0.505		M6	0.750	1.999	0.488
8	F7	0.758	1.999	0.506		M7	0.741	2.006	0.485
9	F8	0.751	2.002	0.493		M8	0.732	2.005	0.491
10	F9	0.753	2.001	0.495		M9	0.743	1.995	0.485
11	F10	0.749	2.002	0.506		M10	0.741	1.996	0.486

Figure 9.19 Partial listing of the parts in the database of the worksheet of Example 9.2.

The criteria range formulas are shown in Figure 9.20 (range K1:N2). We used computed criteria exclusively. The male part dimensions are first copied to K4:M4. These locations are used in the computed criteria formulas as absolute references. The values of the female parts are referenced by their database field names.

Variables used in the macro listings of Figures 9.21 and 9.23 are defined as follows:

NoFind	G15	RNG2	B17	RNG6	B21
Rad	B9	RNG3	B18	S	B7
Rndary	B16:B21	RNG4	B19	Vr1	B5
RNG1	B16	RNG5	B20	Vr2	B6

Figure 9.21 shows the macro for searching the database and extracting the part numbers and count of matching parts. We used the macro record feature to record the commands for one manually directed operation, after which we edited the macro to incorporate iteration. We begin by activating the worksheet, since all our selections will be made on it. A FOR-NEXT loop will iterate through all the male parts. We had 60 of each part type. For each iteration, we do the following (row references for Figure 9.21):

1. For one male part, copy the measured dimensions to the computing criteria variable locations (rows 5 through 8).
2. Select the extract range cell, K6, and extract the female part numbers for parts that meet the criteria (rows 10 and 11).
3. Copy the transpose of the matching female part numbers from the extract range to the save area (rows 12 through 14).
4. Copy the male part number to the save area and place it in the same row as the matching female part numbers (rows 15 through 18).
5. Copy the count of matched parts, N4, to the save area and place it in the same row as the matching female part numbers (rows 19 through 22).

	K	L	M	N	O
1	A fit	Space	B fit	Max dim	
2	=DiaAF>$K$4	=SpaceF<$L$4	=DiaBF>$M$4	=DiaAF+SpaceF+DiaBF>$K$4+$L$4+$M$4	
3					
4	0.741	1.996	0.486	=DCOUNT(Database,,Criteria)	Match

Figure 9.20 Criteria range formulas (K1:N2), male part dimensions (K4:M4), and matching count function (N4) of the worksheet of Example 9.2.

	F	G
1		PartFit
2		Command macro - shortcut key = "p"
3		=ACTIVATE("EX9P2.XLS")
4		=FOR("m",2,11,1)
5		=SELECT("R"&m&"C7:R"&m&"C9")
6		=COPY()
7		=SELECT("R4C11:R4C13")
8		=PASTE.SPECIAL(3,1,FALSE,FALSE)
9		=IF(EX9P2.XLS!Match>0,,GOTO(NoFind))
10		=SELECT("R6C11")
11		=EXTRACT(TRUE)
12		=COPY()
13		=SELECT("R"&m+4&"C14")
14		=PASTE.SPECIAL(3,1,FALSE,TRUE)
15	NoFind	=SELECT("R"&m&"C6")
16		=COPY()
17		=SELECT("R"&m+4&"C13")
18		=PASTE.SPECIAL(3,1,FALSE,FALSE)
19		=SELECT("R4C14")
20		=COPY()
21		=SELECT("R"&m+4&"C14")
22		=PASTE.SPECIAL(3,1,FALSE,FALSE)
23		=NEXT()
24		=RETURN()

Annotations (right side):
- get three M part values and copy them to computing criteria variable locations (rows 5–8)
- jump if no matched parts (row 9)
- select extract range cell and extract F part numbers for matches (rows 10–11)
- copy matching F part numbers to save area (rows 12–14)
- get M part number and copy it to save area (rows 15–18)
- copy count of matched parts to save area (rows 19–22)

Figure 9.21   Macro of Example 9.2 that searches the database, extracts matching part numbers, and counts the matched parts.

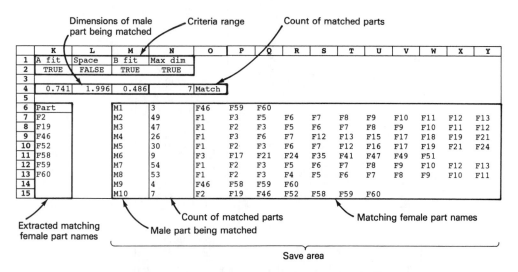

	K	L	M	N	O	P	Q	R	S	T	U	V	W	X	Y
1	A fit	Space	B fit	Max dim											
2	TRUE	FALSE	TRUE	TRUE											
3															
4	0.741	1.996	0.486	7	Match										
5															
6	Part		M1	3	F46	F59	F60								
7	F2		M2	49	F1	F3	F5	F6	F7	F8	F9	F10	F11	F12	F13
8	F19		M3	47	F1	F2	F3	F5	F6	F7	F8	F9	F10	F11	F12
9	F46		M4	26	F1	F3	F6	F7	F12	F13	F15	F17	F18	F19	F21
10	F52		M5	30	F1	F2	F3	F6	F7	F12	F16	F17	F19	F21	F24
11	F58		M6	9	F3	F17	F21	F24	F35	F41	F47	F49	F51		
12	F59		M7	54	F1	F2	F3	F5	F6	F7	F8	F9	F10	F12	F13
13	F60		M8	53	F1	F2	F3	F4	F5	F6	F7	F8	F9	F10	F11
14			M9	4	F46	F58	F59	F60							
15			M10	7	F2	F19	F46	F52	F58	F59	F60				

Labels (Figure 9.22):
- Dimensions of male part being matched
- Criteria range
- Count of matched parts
- Extracted matching female part names
- Count of matched parts
- Male part being matched
- Matching female part names
- Save area

Figure 9.22   Part of the worksheet of Example 9.2 in values mode.

	A	B	C	D
1		RNG()	MakeDB	
2		Shortcut key = "g"	Shortcut key = "b"	
3		Gaussian random number generator	Part dimensions generator	
4		=FOR("I",1,6,2)	=FOR("k",2,120,2)	
5	Vr1	=2*RAND()-1	**** Male parts ****	
6	Vr2	=2*RAND()-1	=RNG()	
7	S	=Vr1*Vr1+Vr2*Vr2	=SET.VALUE(INDEX(Tmp,k-1,1),"M"&(k/2))	
8		=IF(S>=1,GOTO(Vr1))	=SET.VALUE(INDEX(Tmp,k-1,2),0.74+RNG1*0.004)	
9	Rad	=SQRT(-2*LN(S)/S)	=SET.VALUE(INDEX(Tmp,k-1,3),2+RNG2*0.004)	
10		=SET.VALUE(INDEX(Rndary,I,1),Vr1*Rad)	=SET.VALUE(INDEX(Tmp,k-1,4),0.49+RNG3*0.004)	
11		=SET.VALUE(INDEX(Rndary,I+1,1),Vr2*Rad)	**** Female parts ****	
12		=NEXT()	=SET.VALUE(INDEX(Tmp,k,1),"F"&(k/2))	
13		=RETURN()	=SET.VALUE(INDEX(Tmp,k,2),0.75+RNG4*0.004)	
14			=SET.VALUE(INDEX(Tmp,k,3),2+RNG5*0.004)	
15		Rndary	=SET.VALUE(INDEX(Tmp,k,4),0.5+RNG6*0.004)	
16	RNG1	-0.569838066300174	=NEXT()	
17	RNG2	-1.63822088350221	=RETURN()	
18	RNG3	0.0242024427549405		
19	RNG4	-0.244083369738405		
20	RNG5	-1.91688704022361		
21	RNG6	-0.735363432819062		

Figure 9.23 Part dimensions macros of Example 9.2.

We used the EXTRACT macro (row 11 of Figure 9.21) and the DCOUNT function (cell N4 of Figure 9.20). The DCOUNT function, named Match by the cell to its right, returns a count of all records in the database that meet the criteria. We used Database and Criteria as names for the respective ranges. Omitting the field in the function causes it to count all nonblank records that meet the criteria. Two different female parts could have the same dimensions, and we want to count both of them. Whenever we perform step 1 of the procedure, we have new values for the criteria and thus, by the precedence rule, trigger a database search to return a value for function DCOUNT. Because we now know how many female parts matched the criteria, we can save the count in the save area for future use. If the count is zero, no parts matched, and we need not make another database search. For this purpose, we test the count in the IF statement of row 9 of Figure 9.21 and branch to label NoFind to skip the search. The count is saved in column N beginning with cell N6 as shown in Figure 9.22.

Figure 9.22 shows part of the worksheet in values mode. We searched all 60 female parts in the database for matches with each of the first 10 male parts (see row 4, Figure 9.21). The extract range (K6: K+) shows the results from the M10 search (7 parts matched). We always selected cell K6 for the extract range, which caused all cells in that column below K6 to be cleared before conducting the search. The extracted female part numbers were transposed and copied to the unnamed work area, part of which is shown in M6: Y15 (it extends further to the right). We can see the seven M10 matches copied to row 15 of the save area.

The two macros of Figure 9.23 generate the dimensions for the male and female parts. Macro MakeDB generates one male and one female part with each pass through the FOR-NEXT loop. It uses macro RNG, which uses the polar method described by Knuth [1] to compute two independent normally distributed variables for each call. The Excel RAND random number function is used in macro RNG. The six values computed by RNG are stored in array Rndary (B16: B21), whose individual elements are named RNG1 through RNG6. They are then adjusted for the mean and variance and transferred to the macro sheet array Tmp by MakeDB. Part of the result is shown in Figure 9.24. Tmp begins in row 23, is 4 columns wide, and is long enough to hold all the parts, in this case at least 120. The FOR-NEXT loop of MakeDB computes 60 male and 60 female parts. The data in

	A	B	C	D
23	M1	0.736776695723342	1.99458975808282	0.49117438793443
24	F1	0.752794258639541	1.99901267930366	0.497975730455117
25	M2	0.739986659172156	2.00499757403977	0.491697607670207
26	F2	0.743392727135317	1.9954367964277	0.497582130920081
27	M3	0.738088351852684	2.00383207147237	0.492010517011965
28	F3	0.754133174078054	1.99719408916878	0.500280967200862
29	M4	0.74363320911012	2.00245971300554	0.495715728923068
30	F4	0.735417310351213	2.00320534589018	0.497064230507112
31	M5	0.740361799458509	1.99968249073803	0.481444719895714
32	F5	0.7564030810955	2.00206368360908	0.497832118897744

Figure 9.24   Alternating rows of male and female part dimensions generated by the macros of Figure 9.23.

array Tmp of Figure 9.24 were then sorted and the values copied to the worksheet as shown in Figure 9.19, where they were also numerically formatted.

We have already illustrated the use of database functions and macros. This example could be worked further. We could develop an algorithm to pair off the male and female parts, now that we have all the information in the work area. We would then know whether any parts are unmatched. This example is really a simulation to determine the yield (number of paired parts) for given part tolerances. Based on the yield, we could tighten, or loosen, the tolerances for minimum cost. We are assuming that matching parts, a costly operation, has been accepted.

9.6 ABOUT VERSION 3.0

Very few changes were made to the database feature. Our examples for Chapter 9 run under version 3.0 without change. Some database feature changes to note are:

1. The **Set Extract** command was added to the **Data** menu of Figure 9.4(a). It functions in the same manner as do the **Set Database** and **Set Criteria** commands that we discussed in Sections 9.2 and 9.4, respectively. In this case, upon selecting a range of cells and executing the **Data Set Extract** command, we define a range with the name "Extract". Excel will use this range for the extract range instead of the currently selected cells. If we choose not to name an extract range with this command, our discussion of Section 9.4 applies without change.

2. The DGET database function is new and should be added to Table 9.4. Its format is

$$DGET(db\text{-}ref, field, criteria\text{-}ref)$$

It extracts a single record from database *db-ref* whenever the value in the *field* of the records meet the criteria in the range *criteria-ref*.

3. The SET.EXTRACT macro function is new and should be added to Table 9.5. It is the macro equivalent of the **Data Set Extract** command we described above and requires no arguments.

The Q+E database utility program is included with version 3.0 to allow access to a variety of external databases and for use with the Excel internal database. Q+E is used to access databases for retrieval, extraction, and modification of information. It, and a variety of database drivers, can be installed with, or later than, Excel version 3.0 and can be run standalone or from within Excel with the QE.XLA add-in macro. The add-in macro modifies the Excel **Data** menu by adding three new commands to it. The standard Excel database commands are also used with Q+E. Q+E maintains the SQL (Structured Query Language) SELECT statement for query purposes. Also, various Excel macros are available for controlling and exchanging information with Q+E. Because Q+E is a utility program which does not bring new computational capability to Excel, we choose not to discuss it further.

REFERENCES

[1] Knuth, D. E., *The Art of Computer Programming: Vol. 2, Seminumerical Algorithms,* Reading, MA: Addison-Wesley Pub. Co., 1969.

PROBLEMS

9.1 Develop a database of milling machine cutting speeds taken from the following table. Given the material to be milled, the depth of cut, the type of finish desired, and the tool diameter, compute, on extracted records, the tool rpm appropriate for the application.

	Cutting speed (fpm)—Tungsten carbide					
	Roughing				Finishing	
	Depth = 1/8 in.		Depth < 1/8 in.		Depth < 1/16 in.	
Material	min	max	min	max	min	max
Cast iron (soft)	195	270	270	315	315	360
Cast iron (medium)	120	220	220	265	265	300
Cast iron (hard)	90	170	170	205	205	255
Malleable iron	190	290	270	350	350	460
Cast steel	90	190	140	240	200	310
Low-carbon steel (soft)	150	240	170	260	200	360
Low-carbon steel (medium)	100	160	160	230	180	265
Low-carbon steel (hard)	70	110	110	160	160	220
Brass	280	420	340	525	390	650
Bronze	190	300	240	360	360	530
Aluminum	800	1250	1000	1600	1600	2200

9.2 Develop a database of temperature sensitive resistors taken from the following table. For design purposes, one usually must know the resistance at a specified temperature, or the resistance change for a temperature excursion. Calculations are made with this formula:

$$\frac{R}{R_o} = 0.4343\beta \left(\frac{1}{T} - \frac{1}{T_o}\right)$$

where R is the resistance at temperature T, and R_o is the resistance at the reference temperature T_o. Computations are made on extracted records.

Stock no.	Length	Dia.	Res. (25°C)	Temp. coef. (β)
12-43A	.35	.120	10	1100
12-44A	.35	.120	100	1500
12-45A	.35	.120	1000	1750
12-46A	.35	.120	10k	2000
12-47A	.35	.120	100k	2250
12-48A	.35	.120	1 Meg	2350
14-810	.55	.200	10	240
14-811	.55	.200	100	295
14-812	.55	.200	1000	370
14-813	.55	.200	10k	450
14-814	.55	.200	100k	510
14-815	.55	.200	1 Meg	550
18-K20	1.125	.400	10	3000
18-K21	1.125	.400	100	3700
18-K22	1.125	.400	1000	4500
18-K23	1.125	.400	10k	5000
18-K24	1.125	.400	100k	5400
18-K25	1.125	.400	1 Meg	5700

9.3 Develop a database of gear specifications taken from the following table. Among other requirements, gears are selected to satisfy a gearing ratio. Because gears have an integral number of teeth, techniques for solving equations that yield integer solutions are often used to determine the set of gears for this purpose. Develop an algorithm to help choose a set of gears for the arrangement shown in Figure P9.3 where the input and output shafts are collinear and the gearing ratio (G1/G2) (G3/G4) = .5.

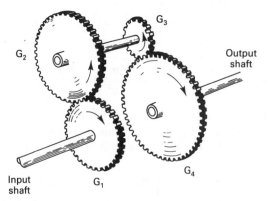

G_3

G_2

Output shaft

Input shaft G_1 G_4

Figure P9.3

Part no.	No. of teeth	Pitch dia.	Outside dia.
J32010	10	.313	.375
J32011	11	.344	.406
J32012	12	.375	.438
J32013	13	.406	.469
J32014	14	.438	.500
J32015	15	.469	.531
J32016	16	.500	.562
J32018	18	.562	.625
J32020	20	.625	.688
J32022	22	.688	.750
J32024	24	.750	.813
J32025	25	.781	.844
J32026	26	.813	.875
J32028	28	.875	.938
J32030	30	.938	1.000
J32032	32	1.000	1.062
J32036	36	1.125	1.188
J32040	40	1.250	1.313
J32044	44	1.375	1.438
J32048	48	1.500	1.562
J32050	50	1.562	1.625
J32052	52	1.625	1.688
J32056	56	1.750	1.812
J32060	60	1.875	1.938
J32064	64	2.000	2.062
J32070	70	2.188	2.250
J32072	72	2.250	2.312
J32075	75	2.344	2.406
J32080	80	2.500	2.562
J32088	88	2.750	2.812
J32090	90	2.812	2.875
J32096	96	3.000	3.062
J32100	100	3.125	3.188
J32108	108	3.375	3.438
J32112	112	3.500	3.562
J32120	120	3.750	3.812
J32128	128	4.000	4.062
J32132	132	4.125	4.188
J32144	144	4.500	4.562
J32156	156	4.875	4.938
J32160	160	5.000	5.062

9.4 Rework Problem 9.3 but offset the input/output shafts to no longer be collinear, that is, they are each a different distance from the idler shaft.

CHAPTER **10**

Linking, Importing,
and Exporting

Until now, we introduced certain concepts as they were needed and then presented only enough information to get us through the particular Excel topic. Many of those concepts could be applied in a broader context if they were somehow integrated into a functional system managed by Excel. Indeed, we are able to realize such a system and it gives us a synergistic effect that we find important for engineering applications of Excel. This concerns the intercommunication of information between Excel documents and non-Excel applications.

We now unify several Excel concepts via the linking, importing, and exporting features. First, we will review numerous topics so as to incorporate them later in a broader context. These include operating within the Windows environment, the Clipboard, the process of copying documents, and working with directories. Then, we introduce the linking of Excel documents and the exchange of information dynamically. We also show how we can import information from other applications to Excel documents and how we can export information from Excel documents to other applications. We will also learn to control other applications from Excel.

Because we can apply Excel to the most stringent applications, we assume that our Excel and operating environment are configured compatibly and supported by a complement of hardware components to realize the full potential of Excel.

10.1 INTRODUCTION

Thus far, our discussions on various Excel features were limited in scope so that we could explore them in depth. In particular, we minimized any discussion of the Excel window system, copying and pasting documents via Clipboard, and using a file directory system. Now we must apply them in a broader context, so further review is necessary. In this section, we will consolidate our views on these subjects to prepare ourselves for the principal subject matter of this chapter, namely, linking documents and importing and exporting data between Excel and other applications. The material of this section is an expansion of basic Excel concepts.

10.1.1 Excel Windows

We have not made a big issue over windows so far. We recognized the need to work within a particular window because that is the way Excel is organized. Consequently, we have been working extensively with worksheet, chart, and macro windows. But there are other Excel windows, some of which we have already mentioned, that are important to the proper use of Excel. We now briefly review the Excel window system in order to orient ourselves for its use later in the chapter. For the moment, we assume that we are using the Excel run-time version. Later we consider using Excel with the Microsoft® Windows program.

Each window of the Excel system is classified as either an *application window* or a *document window*. Application windows have menus and workspaces for documents of that application. Example windows are

- Excel window (Section 2.2.1 and below)
- Help (Section 8.4)
- Control panel (Section 3.4)
- Clipboard (below)

Document windows are the primary-user data, formula, and chart entry and display work areas. Example windows are:

- Worksheet (Section 2.2)
- Chart (Section 6.2)
- Macro (Section 7.1)
- Info (Section 3.4)

All of our work with Excel is done within the Excel window shown in Figure 10.1. It allows access to the File, Help, and Control menus. We discussed at length most commands of these menus. In this section, we will discuss only those menu commands pertinent to our goal of unifying the material of this chapter.

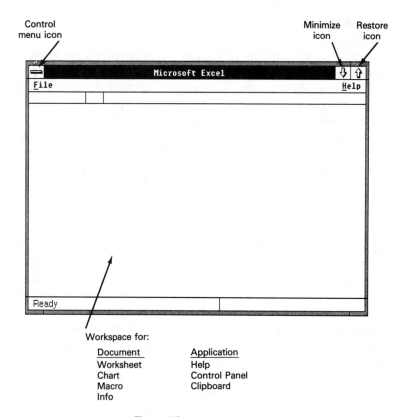

Figure 10.1 Excel window.

Organizing the workspace. We often find ourselves with too many windows open and, hence, have difficulty quickly finding the one we want to work on. Perhaps we even accidentally modify or close the wrong ones. It could be that our workspace is cluttered and in disarray, again causing errors to be made. It could be that we want to see parts of multiple windows simultaneously or, maybe, just put some windows temporarily out of sight to relieve the screen congestion. We can do much to help our cause by using some commands of the **Control** menu (Figure 10.2) and **Window** menu [Figure 10.3(a)].

The **Control** menu of Figure 10.2(a) applies to application windows, while that of Figure 10.2(b) applies to documents. We have already discussed the **Move, Size, Close**, and **Run** commands elsewhere. The **Move** and **Size** commands are useful in cleaning up the screen presentation and arranging our work for convenient reference. However, these commands do require experimentation on our part to achieve the desired screen appearance. Instead, we can execute the **Window Arrange All** command of Figure 10.3(a). Excel will arrange all open windows to fill the available workspace. The windows are automatically sized and moved with no unfilled spaces in the workspace, as shown in Figure 10.4. To

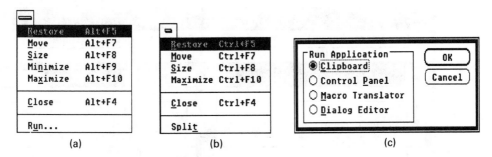

(a)   (b)   (c)

Figure 10.2   (a) Application window control menu, (b) document control menu, and (c) Run dialog box of the control menu of (a).

recover from this presentation, execute the **Control Maximize** command of any open window. All windows are returned to full size, each filling nearly the entire screen. The **Control Move** and **Size** commands can be used thereafter for arranging purposes.

Another way to clean up the work area is to temporarily put away as icons some currently unneeded application windows. This is done with the **Control Minimize** command of Figure 10.2(a). The minimized window is reduced to a very small figure and usually placed at the bottom of the screen. Individual icons can be identified because they are labeled with the name of the window. An icon can be restored to its window form with the **Control Restore** command. It reappears in its previous size and location. Documents cannot be reduced to icons, but documents as part of an application window being made into an icon are reduced with it. The documents are also restored when the application is restored.

Icons in the upper right corner of application windows as shown in Figure 10.1 can be used to minimize, maximize, and restore the windows. The restore icon shown there becomes a maximize icon with an upward directed arrow for document windows. Document windows do not have the minimize icon.

Cleanup of the work area can also be effected by hiding windows with the **Window Hide** command of Figure 10.3(a). This causes the active window to

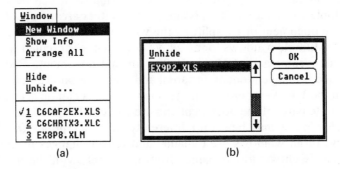

(a)   (b)

Figure 10.3   (a) Window drop-down menu and (b) Unhide dialog box.

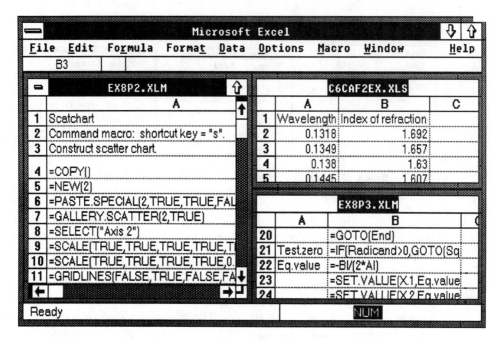

Figure 10.4   Window appearance after using the Window Arrange All command.

become invisible. The window is still open and its data is accessible from other documents. Macros on hidden macro sheets can also be run. This command is useful when windows are needed but do not have to be visible. They can always be made visible with the **Window Unhide** command of Figure 10.3(a). This command causes a dialog box to appear within which the names of all hidden windows appear, as shown in Figure 10.3(b). Select the desired window name, then **OK**. The window becomes visible.

Creating multiple views.   The inconvenience of having to scroll through a large document or application while working on it can be overcome by having multiple views into it. This is achieved by either creating another window into the active document or by splitting the window into panes.

Multiple windows for an active document are created with the **Window New Window** command of Figure 10.3(a) for that document. Each new window thus created is independent of its parent and is not the same as a new document opened with the **File New** command. All such windows can be scrolled independently to separate parts of the document and are useful when working on large documents. Each window may be set up differently with its **Options Display** command. The views of all windows are dynamic and reflect changes in the document as they occur. Each window is named from its parent, with the title bar containing the parent's name followed by ":*n*", where *n* is a sequence number.

A document may be split into panes with the **Control Split** command of Figure 10.2(b) or by moving the split bars to the desired window split location. No extra window is created, but the effect is almost the same. This scheme is used to observe two different parts of a document at the same time. Because the panes are dynamic, changes in one pane that affect the presentation in another one will be seen instantly. A window can be split into as many as four panes. Figure 10.5 shows a worksheet split horizontally. The views in the panes are synchronized while scrolling unless frozen. Scrolling directions for the various panes are shown in Figure 10.6. The top and/or left panes may be prevented from scrolling by executing the **Options Freeze Panes** command of Figure 10.7(a), which then toggles to the **Options Unfreeze Panes** command to allow scrolling to be resumed.

The **Control Split** command allows one to move a set of crosshairs with the mouse or keyboard. These crosshairs extend across the window dimensions. Their intersection is at the mouse position. Keyboard arrow keys move the split bars along the row and column title bars. By either method, the window may be split into two or four panes. Split bar home positions are at the left edge of the horizontal scroll bar and at the top edge of the vertical scroll bar of a window and its panes, as shown in Figures 10.4 and 10.5. These split bars can be moved with the mouse by a drag motion. The cursor shape is shown in the Box on page 25. The scrolled pane cannot overlap the rows or columns of a frozen pane.

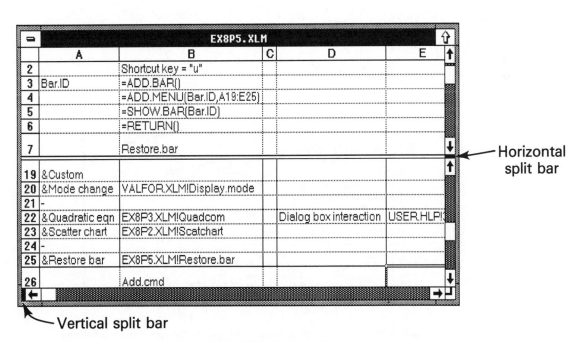

Figure 10.5 Window split horizontally.

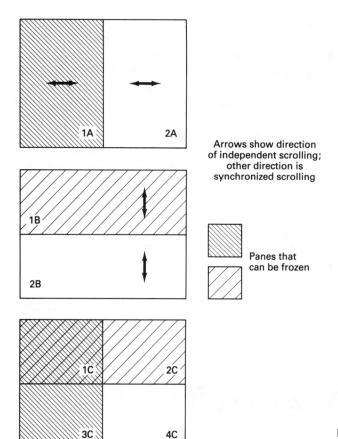

Arrows show direction
of independent scrolling;
other direction is
synchronized scrolling

Panes that
can be frozen

Figure 10.6 Scrolling direction for
window panes.

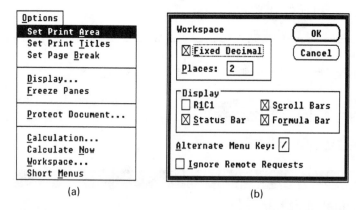

(a)   (b)

Figure 10.7 (a) Options drop-down menu and (b) Options Workspace dialog
box.

Saving the workspace.   We have discussed ways to organize and clean up the workspace. Sometimes we have many windows to work with on a given application, often we cannot finish our development work and must save it all temporarily, or we may have demos that use numerous windows that we otherwise would not need. All these tasks can be simplified by the techniques we described above. But these scenarios all have in common the management of multiple windows for a task. This often leads to problems of remembering which windows are associated with a given task, time lost in opening and closing the numerous windows, and time lost in arranging the workspace. One remedy for these problems is to save a list of all open documents and their layout for a given application. Then, when needed, this list can be referred to and all documents retrieved for continuation of work. In Excel, we do this with the **File Save Workspace** command of Figure 10.8 and the usual **File Open** command.

We must remember that the **File Save Workspace** command saves a list of all the documents open and their characteristics when the command is executed. The effects of this command extend to the moment one wants to exit Excel when it causes prompts for saving documents that have been changed. If responding Yes, that document will be saved. If it is a new document that has not yet been saved, responding Yes will cause it to be saved also. Responding No will cause the new document to be lost upon exiting Excel unless it is saved at that time. The **File Save Workspace** command produces the dialog box of Figure 10.8(b), in which one must enter a name under which the workspace is to be saved. The default file extension for a workspace name is .XLW. The documents of the workspace may all be opened together with the **File Open** command after selecting the name of the workspace file. They may also be opened separately in the usual manner. Subsequent **File Save Workspace** commands prompt for permission to replace the existing workspace file if being saved under the same name.

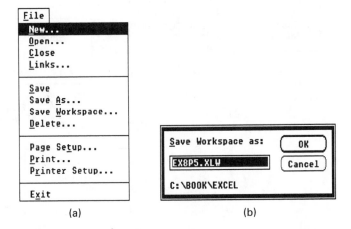

(a)   (b)

Figure 10.8   (a) File drop-down menu and (b) File Save Workspace dialog box.

The characteristics of the documents that get saved by the **File Save Workspace** command are those shown in the dialog box of the **Options Workspace** command of Figure 10.7(b).

10.1.2 Clipboard

The Excel Clipboard is a storage area with special access for transferring information into and out of it. It functions as temporary storage while moving information during copying operations. We mentioned its use for this purpose in Section 3.3. It will become important later in this chapter when we discuss importing and exporting.

Figure 10.9 shows the structural location of Clipboard with respect to Excel documents. It is an application, not a document. The Edit menu commands of Figure 10.9 affect the contents of Clipboard. Executing these commands automatically addresses Clipboard without further intervention by the user. The Edit menu is shown in Figure 10.10.

The **Edit Copy**, **Edit Copy Picture**, and **Edit Cut** commands require that an area first be selected in the source document. For the following discussion, the source and target documents may be the same document. Upon executing the desired command, the selected area is copied to Clipboard, overwriting its previous contents, if any. In the case of **Edit Cut**, no deletion from the source document takes place yet. The following selection in the target document identifies the area into which the contents of Clipboard will be placed. To retrieve Clipboard's contents, one must then execute the **Edit Paste** or **Edit Paste Special** command, at which time Clipboard's contents are copied into the selected area of the target document. The contents of Clipboard are unaffected by these last two

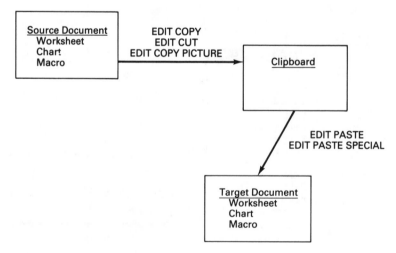

Figure 10.9   Structural location of Clipboard with respect to Excel documents.

(a)   (b)

Figure 10.10   Edit drop-down menu for (a) a worksheet and (b) a chart.

commands. If **Edit Cut** was executed, the source document selected area contents are removed. Figure 10.11 shows the Clipboard window and its contents. This view is obtained with the **Control Run** command, after which one selects **Clipboard** and **OK** in the dialog box of Figure 10.2(c).

Clipboard holds only the contents of the most recent **Edit Copy**, **Edit Copy Picture**, or **Edit Cut** command. There is no command to erase Clipboard of its

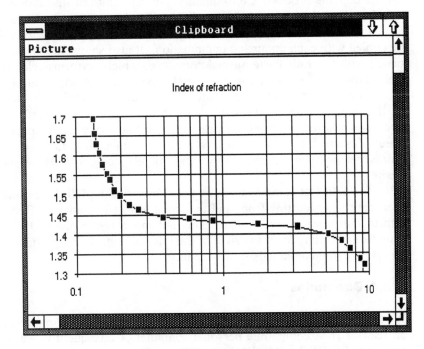

Figure 10.11   Clipboard window.

contents, and there is no way to edit or format its contents. We will use Clipboard for copying information between documents of the same application and for importing and exporting information between applications.

10.1.3 Document Copying

Given the review of some of Excel's basics above, we now take another look at copying documents, or parts of documents, among worksheets, macro sheets, and charts. The purpose in doing so is to consolidate our knowledge of this capability so that we have a unified view of the process. Later on in this chapter, we will discuss the copying of documents between applications, and we will not distinguish among the different types of documents for that purpose. We first discussed copying of worksheets, or parts thereof, to different parts of the same worksheet or to another one in Section 3.3. That discussion also applies to macro sheets and the interchange of information between worksheets and macro sheets. Then, in Sections 6.2 and 6.4.3, we discussed briefly the copying of charts, or parts thereof, to other charts.

We prepared Figure 10.9 to aid our discussion of how Clipboard is involved with the Excel copying process. Our use of source and target document nomenclature for this purpose emphasizes the almost transparent nature of the process with respect to type of document. We also see that very few commands are used for the copying process. Consequently, we can limit our discussion to the commands only and merely emphasize differences due to command uniqueness.

Figure 10.12 is more explicit with respect to the type of information that can be copied with each command combination. It also shows the dialog boxes associated with the **Edit Paste Special** command, which performs selective copying. This allows us to merge information from one document with that of another and thus not have to develop from scratch another document with all the information. In the case of worksheets and macro sheets, we can also perform arithmetic operations during the paste operation. We cannot copy from a chart to a worksheet or macro sheet. We do not really have to, since the data of a chart is in some worksheet or macro sheet, and we can merely copy from there should we so desire.

The **Edit Cut** command can be used only with the **Edit Paste** command, and then only when cutting from and pasting into like documents. Because the cut information goes into Clipboard does not mean that Clipboard's contents are transparent with respect to origin of the information. Excel prohibits such transfers by greying commands in the menu.

10.1.4 Directories

We are writing about the Excel program running under a disk operating system on an IBM or IBM compatible personal computer. Consequently, we will be using either the PC-DOS or MS-DOS operating system. These operating systems use a

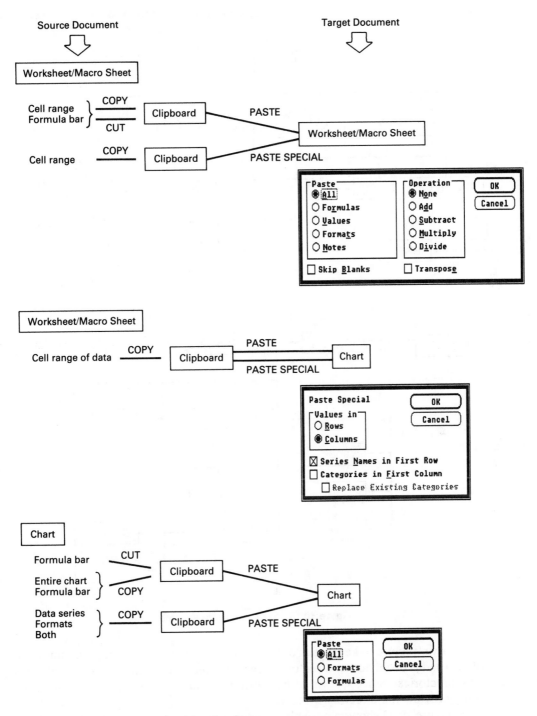

Figure 10.12 Command combinations for copying via Clipboard.

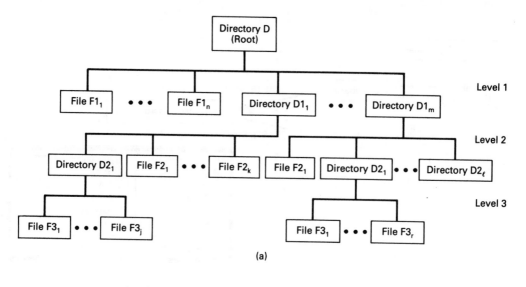

(a)

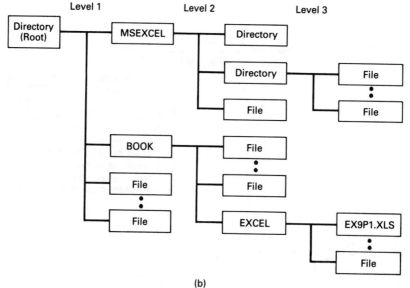

(b)

Figure 10.13 Skeleton directory systems.

directory structure to keep track of files on a disk drive. A directory contains lists of files and probably other directories, each of which can contain lists of more files and directories. Since we will discuss using files in different directories, we now briefly review the directory system.

Figure 10.13 shows a possible skeleton directory system drawn in two different ways. The directory system for each disk drive always has a main directory, or highest level directory, called a *root* directory. It is labeled as such in the hierarchy diagram of Figure 10.13. At the level of the root directory, we may have files and/or other directories. These other directories are now called *subdirectories*. Each subdirectory may lead to more lists of files and/or subdirectories. The composite of all such files and subdirectories for our disk drive is the *directory structure*. The structures of Figure 10.13 are also called *tree structures*. A directory structure is an organization of files and provides a means for specifying the location of a file. In Excel, we add files to a directory with the **File Save As** command. We cannot add a new subdirectory from Excel; we must do that while in the operating system.

We locate a file via its *pathname,* which is an arrangement of the disk drive name and names of subdirectories in descending hierarchical order from the root directory to the file. For example, the pathname leading to file EX9P1.XLS is

C:\BOOK\EXCEL\EX9P1.XLS

where C: is the disk drive in which the directories are stored, the first backslash is the root directory, and BOOK and EXCEL are subdirectories, each followed by a backslash. The file name with extension, if any, is always last. We do not usually operate at the root directory level. Instead, we change the directory to one more suited for the work we will be doing. Usually, this is a directory we have created for the application we are working on. This latter directory is called the *current*

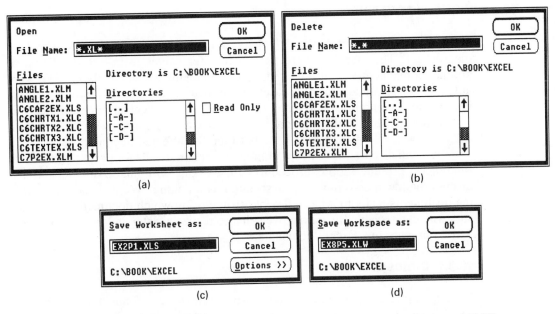

Figure 10.14   Dialog boxes for (a) File Open, (b) File Delete, (c) File Save As, and (d) File Save Workspace commands.

directory. While in this directory, we can access all the files we need without having to specify a full pathname provided, of course, that they are in this directory. The current directory is the one Excel accesses when we execute **File Open**, **File Delete**, **File Save As**, or **File Save Workspace** when we use the default pathname setting. We are referring to default settings for the dialog boxes of Figure 10.14.

The dialog boxes of Figure 10.14 are the means for specifying file names, path names, and directories in Excel. We always have the option of typing pathnames in the text box of each dialog box whenever we intend to specify a file, directory, or disk drive different from the default. Figure 10.15 is a flowchart of actions for using a dialog box in this manner. For the **File Open** and **File Delete** commands, we have the flexibility to select files and directories from the list boxes. We can traverse all paths of all directories in our system by following the actions indicated in the flowchart. Typing in the pathname allows us to access or save a file anywhere within the directory system. The **Directories** list box allows us to go up and down the hierarchy only one directory at a time. However, the dialog box does not disappear at these times, so we are not inconvenienced much by this action. Only after entering a file name and choosing **OK** does the dialog box disappear. We can change the current directory by selecting from the **Directories** list box, and we can also do so by typing in the text box the next subdirectory name or the doubleperiods.

10.2 LINKING DOCUMENTS

Very often we cannot have all values computed on the same worksheet or macrosheet. Thus far, we were able to transfer values from one document to another conveniently to fit the needs of the problems we were solving. We were able to do this manually in some cases, we used argument lists and returned arrays in the case of communication with macros, and we let Excel automatically do this for plotting graphs. In this section, we introduce a more formal way for automatically doing this by establishing links between the affected documents.

We will discuss the concept of linking, explain details for preparing external references, present various procedures for working with linked documents, and discuss the few macro functions associated with linking. We will show that linking documents leads to a more flexible structure by which documents communicate with each other. By linking, we will also realize a faster and more convenient way to prepare our Excel documents.

10.2.1 Concept

Linking in Excel is a scheme whereby two documents are connected together in a special way for the purpose of transferring information unilaterally from one document to the other. A link is a pathname that includes the name of the file

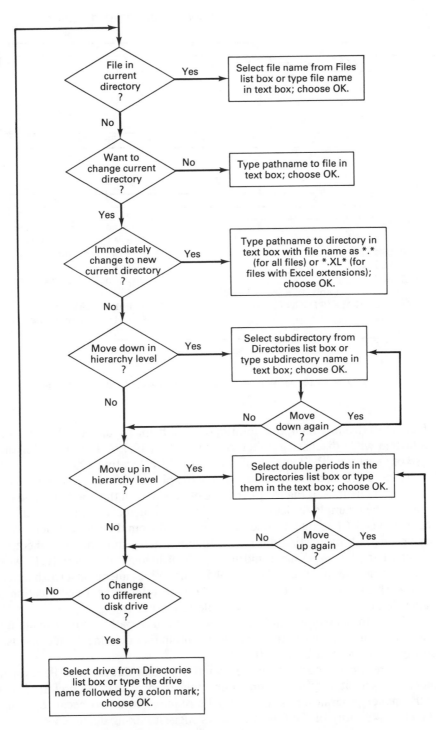

Figure 10.15 Flowchart for traversing the directory structure.

	A	B
1		Braided Shield Coverage
2	OD	0.375
3	StrD	0.0075
4	Picks	15
5	Carriers	16
6	N	6
7	Coverage,%	='C7P2EXA.XLM'!Shield.Cov(OD,StrD,Picks,Carriers,N)

(a)

	A	B
1	Shield.Cov	Braided shield coverage
2	=ARGUMENT("OD")	OD under shield, inches
3	=ARGUMENT("Strand.Dia")	Dia of one strand, inches
4	=ARGUMENT("Picks")	Picks per inch
5	=ARGUMENT("Carriers")	Number of carriers
6	=ARGUMENT("Ends")	No. ends per carrier
7	=ATAN(2*PI()*(OD+2*Strand.Dia)*Picks/Carriers)	Braid angle
8	=Ends*Picks*Strand.Dia/SIN(A7)	Intermediate value
9	=(2*A8-A8^2)*100	Shield coverage,%
10	=RETURN(A9)	

(b)

Figure 10.16 (a) Worksheet and (b) macro sheet to illustrate linking.

(document) from which the information is being obtained. We defined this pathname while discussing directories in Section 10.1.4. Linking is for the purpose of specifying the location of a value, not for locating a file.

Figures 10.16 and 10.17 show two examples of linking. The worksheet and macro sheet listings of Figure 10.16 were obtained from the braided shield calculations for the example of Section 7.2.3. The link connects worksheet cell B7 with the macro cell A1 so that a value can be returned from the macro Shield.Cov. We set up this link by pasting the macro function name into the worksheet via the formula bar. The worksheet and macro sheet listings of Figure 10.17 were obtained from Example 9.2 of Section 9.5. The link connects macro sheet cell G9 with worksheet cell N4. In this case, the path references a cell location by its name, Match, so that a value is available to the macro.

From the above examples, we see that a link path is partly made up of a document name and a cell reference from within that document. We discuss path construction more in Section 10.2.2.

There are various reasons for wanting to link documents. Perhaps it is a more convenient way to organize our application, it may be preferred to work with smaller program units, or it may be required to do so because of the way Excel works. Any of the following ways suggest linking documents.

	K	L	M	N	O
1	A fit	Space	B fit	Max dim	
2	=DiaAF>$K$4	=SpaceF<$L$4	=DiaBF>$M$4	=DiaAF+SpaceF+DiaBF>$K$4+$L$4+$M$4	
3					
4	0.741	1.996	0.486	=DCOUNT(Database,,Criteria)	Match

(a)

	F	G
1		PartFit
2		Command macro - shortcut key = "p"
3		=ACTIVATE("EX9P2.XLS")
4		=FOR("m",2,11,1)
5		=SELECT("R"&m&"C7:R"&m&"C9")
6		=COPY()
7		=SELECT("R4C11:R4C13")
8		=PASTE.SPECIAL(3,1,FALSE,FALSE)
9		=IF(EX9P2.XLS!Match>0,,GOTO(NoFind))
10		=SELECT("R6C11")
11		=EXTRACT(TRUE)
12		=COPY()
13		=SELECT("R"&m+4&"C14")
14		=PASTE.SPECIAL(3,1,FALSE,TRUE)
15	NoFind	=SELECT("R"&m&"C6")
16		=COPY()
17		=SELECT("R"&m+4&"C13")
18		=PASTE.SPECIAL(3,1,FALSE,FALSE)
19		=SELECT("R4C14")
20		=COPY()
21		=SELECT("R"&m+4&"C14")
22		=PASTE.SPECIAL(3,1,FALSE,FALSE)
23		=NEXT()
24		=RETURN()

(b)

Figure 10.17 (a) Another worksheet and (b) macro sheet to illustrate linking.

1. A combination of a database and macro requires a worksheet and macro sheet. The documents must be linked to use them together.

2. A library of macros on several macro sheets will require linking for macro access.

3. A large application could be partitioned into several documents, each performing separate computations whose results eventually must be merged to produce the final outcome. The documents must be linked for value transfer. The partitioning may be required for work assignment purposes, in which case development time and cost are distributed. Also, one large document need not be opened each time. Instead, several smaller documents that are each faster to open, edit, debug, and save would be worked on individually.

4. Several design documents may be required for a task, but not all data from each document need be forwarded as part of the task report. Only pertinent data need be extracted through linking to form the task report. This scheme allows development to proceed with full disclosure but yet not demand substantial editing or separate document preparation for reporting purposes.

5. A combination of a worksheet and chart requires linking for data series display, which is linked automatically, and for possible linked text.

The linking structure is determined by the hierarchy of documents that constitute the application. There may be multiple links between documents, there may be simple, complex, or some combination of these types of external references, and there may be links in both directories between pairs of documents. Figure 10.18 is a skeleton diagram of a possible linking structure.

10.2.2 External References

In order to link documents, we must refer to the particular cell or cell range, or their named versions, in a manner that identifies the document in which they appear. Since such a cell is external to the document in which its value is needed,

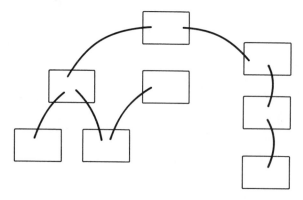

Figure 10.18 Skeleton diagram of a possible linking structure.

its reference is called an *external reference*. The document that contains the external reference is called a *dependent document,* because it depends on another document for the value, while the document that contains the value being referenced is called the *supporting document,* because it provides supporting data. These documents may be worksheets, macro sheets, charts, or some combination thereof, although special cases often are the rule for charts.

Figures 10.16 and 10.17 each contain an external reference. In Figure 10.16, the external reference in the worksheet (dependent document) is the name of the macro in the formula

$$=\text{'C7P2EXA.XLM'!Shield.Cov(OD,StrD,Picks,Carriers,N)}$$

external reference

It is interpreted to mean that the macro Shield.Cov is on the macro sheet (supporting document) named C7P2EXA.XLM. Because there is no additional path reference, the worksheet using the macro and the macro itself are probably in the same directory (see below). In Figure 10.17, the external reference appears in the macro sheet (dependent document) IF statement.

$$=\text{IF(EX9P2.XLS!Match>0,,GOTO(NoFind))}$$

external reference

It is interpreted to mean that the value for the relational expression is found in the cell named Match on worksheet EX9P2.XLS (cell N4 of the worksheet, which is the supporting document). The macro sheet and worksheet are also probably in the same directory.

The external references we just illustrated are constructed as follows:

path!immed-ref

where

    path = pathname to the document (file) in which the cell being referenced resides. If the document is open, *path* is the file name only.

immed-ref = name of the cell being referenced in the document of *path*. It may be a cell reference, cell range, or named cell or cell range.

External references for documents not in the same directory require the full pathname to the file, as discussed in Section 10.1.4. If the supporting document is open, the external reference in the dependent document shows only the file name part of the path. That is why, in the above examples, we stated that the supporting and dependent documents were probably in the same directory. Should the supporting document not be open, the full pathname is displayed as part of the external reference. The recommended way to enter the external reference is to use the **Formula Paste Name** command. This requires that the supporting docu-

TABLE 10.1   SIMPLE AND COMPLEX EXTERNAL REFERENCE FORMULAS

Formula	Type	Explanation
=COORD.XLS!$F$4	Simple	Absolute reference (cell)
=COORD.XLS!F4	Complex	Relative reference (cell)
=COORD.XLS!$D$6:$D$8	Simple	Absolute reference (range)
=RESPONSE.XLS!Phase	Simple	If Phase is cell, range, or constant
=RESPONSE.XLS!dB	Complex	If dB is formula like =20*LOG10(VR1/VR2)
=IF(EX9P2.XLS!Match>0,,GOTO(NoFind))	Complex	Formula is not only a path and cell, cell range, or name.
=MDETERM(EQN.XLS!$A$1:$D$4	Complex	Formula is not only a path and cell, cell range, or name.
=POLY.XLS!Width*POLY.XLS!Length	Complex	Formula is not only a path and cell, cell range, or name.

ment be open for the selection, but we can be assured that no errors in path entry will be made.

Special care is required in constructing formulas that contain external references so that they are automatically adjusted when cell locations change during editing operations and have automatically updated values without the supporting document being open. For these purposes, Excel distinguishes between simple and complex external reference formulas. A *simple external reference formula* is a formula containing only the path and (a) the cell or cell range as an absolute reference only, or (b) a name that refers only to a cell, cell range, or constant. A *complex external reference formula* is any arrangement of formula entities that does not satisfy the simple external reference formula definition. Examples of the two types of external references are shown in Table 10.1.

An unnamed cell or cell range in an external reference formula is not automatically adjusted when that cell or cell range in the supporting document is moved. This is, of course, contrary to what happens within the supporting document. Were the cell or cell range to be named, and this name used in the external reference formula, adjustment in the dependent document would be automatic. Consequently, it is recommended that named cells and cell ranges be used in all external reference formulas.

If a supporting document supplies a value only, that is, it does not also have to be executed, the supporting document does not have to be open for the dependent document to obtain the value for an external reference, provided that the external reference is in a simple external reference formula. This suggests that complex external reference formulas not be used in order to provide more memory for the working documents. Were the values to be obtained via complex external reference formulas, the supporting documents must be opened.

10.2.3 Linking Worksheets and Macro Sheets

In this section we discuss procedures for establishing links and for working with linked documents. Unless we are removing links, the objective is to keep the links connected. It is possible that we may inadvertently disturb links by working in the document, so we need procedures for minimizing this risk. We also need to formally present procedures for carrying out actions involving links that are deliberate, such as creating, redirecting, and removing them. The flowchart of Figure 10.19 presents concisely the procedures that we will discuss. In this section, we do not differentiate between worksheets and macro sheets; they are both referred to as documents.

Creating a link between documents. The following procedure applies when setting up a new link between documents. An alternative procedure is given immediately following it.

- Open the dependent and supporting documents to be linked.
- Activate the supporting document window.
- Select the cell or cell range whose values are to be referenced in the dependent document.
- Execute the **Edit Copy** command.
- Activate the dependent document window.
- Select the cell, or cell for a range, that will receive the external reference.
- Execute the **Edit Paste Link** command of Figure 10.10(a).

Excel automatically creates the link with the above procedure. It is a simple external reference formula with absolute references. One can also type the link into the formula bar by following the usual editing procedures. However, letting Excel do the linking prevents entry errors and is recommended. We also recommend the use of cell names rather than absolute references for the reasons given in Section 10.2.2. Names can be typed in the formula bar to replace the absolute reference inserted by the **Edit Paste Link** command. One cannot paste into the formula bar with the **Edit Paste Link** command. It is used to insert a simple external reference formula with an absolute reference into the selected cell.

Saving linked documents. The procedure for saving linked documents differs little from saving documents without links. However, we must be certain that we are saving current document names in the external references. Our procedure is altered slightly for the different circumstances that would prevent current document names to be saved. These differences are shown in the flowchart of Figure 10.19. From the figure, we see that we must save the supporting documents before saving the dependent document. Failure to do so causes the message "Save with references to unsaved documents?" to be displayed. In this case, choose **Cancel** and save the supporting documents first.

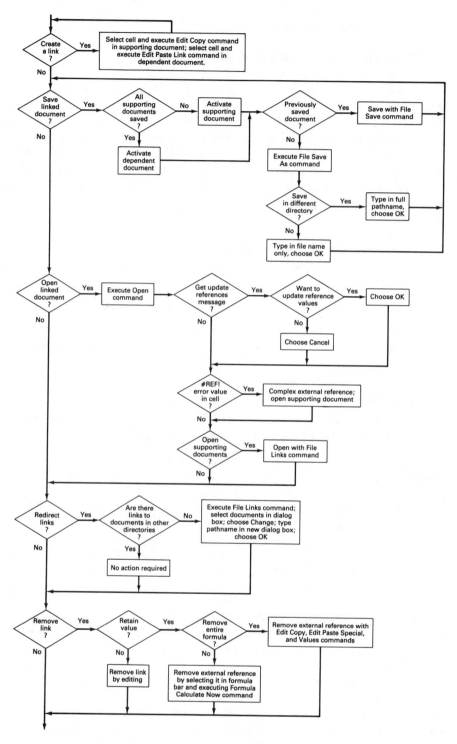

Figure 10.19 Procedure for linking worksheets and macro sheets.

Use the following procedure for saving changes in previously saved linked documents.

- Activate a supporting document window and execute the **File Save** command. Repeat this step for each supporting document.
- Activate the dependent document window and execute the **File Save** command.

Use the following procedure for saving new linked documents.

- Activate a supporting document window and (a) execute **File Save** for a previously saved document, or (b) execute **File Save As** for a new document, in which case type in a full pathname if saving in a different directory or type in the file name only if saving in the current directory. Choose **OK**.
- Activate the dependent document window and perform part (a) or (b) of the above step.

If at all possible, arrange the document structure such that the linked documents are in the same directory. This helps simplify the work of saving and opening linked documents and avoids problems with document maintenance.

Opening linked documents.   The procedure for opening linked documents is shown in Figure 10.19. Deciding on the exact commands to use depends on whether the supporting documents are open or even if they are to be opened. Even then, the choice of action to take depends on whether simple or complex external references are involved. Here is the procedure.

- Open the desired document with the **File Open** command.
- Did the "Update external references?" message appear? If not, there are no supporting documents or the supporting documents are already open, in which case proceed to the next step. If the message appeared, choose **OK** to update the contents of the external reference formula to the current value of the referenced cell, or choose **Cancel** to keep the last value in the external reference formula.
- Did #REF! appear in a cell? If not, proceed to the next step; otherwise, a complex external reference formula needs updating. This can be done only by opening the supporting document. Use the **File Links** command of Figure 10.20(b) for this purpose.
- Are other supporting documents to be opened? If so, open them with the **File Links** command.

Whenever a dependent document is opened before its supporting documents, the message "Update external references?" appears. A supporting docu-

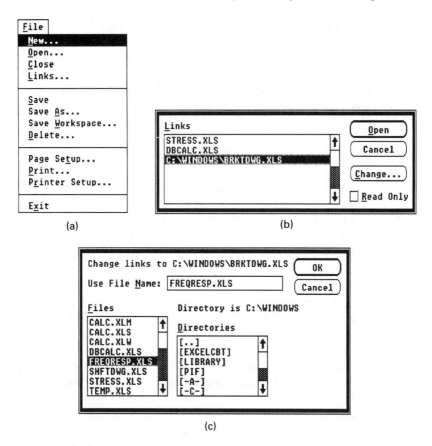

Figure 10.20   (a) File drop-down menu, (b) Links command dialog box, and (c) dialog box that appears when Change of the Links dialog box is executed.

ment could have had an externally referenced cell value changed since the dependent document last used it. This could happen when the supporting document is used as part of another system of computations. One must choose **OK** to update the dependent document simple external reference formulas with this new value, or choose **Cancel** to stay with the last value saved with the dependent document. If the dependent document has complex external reference formulas, the #REF! error value appears in those cells. In this case, the corresponding supporting documents must be opened.

The **File Links** command dialog box contains a **Links** list box that contains the names of the supporting documents for the active dependent document, as shown in Figure 10.20(b). This list may be consulted to determine the names of the supporting documents and it can be used to open any of these documents. It is a convenient reference when multiple supporting documents are used or when pathnames are difficult to remember or enter. The **Change** button of this dialog box is discussed below.

Multiple supporting documents with the same name but in different directories cannot all be open simultaneously. The ones not being used must be closed. Only one document of that name can be open at any time.

Redirecting links.   We have discussed creating, saving, and opening linked documents. For document structures that are not very involved, we should be able to manage our documents quite well, applying what we learned. However, for some reason, our links may become disconnected. This means that the external reference is no longer valid; that is, the supporting document cannot be found at the end of the given path. We usually discover this problem when the message "Can't find '*filename*'." is displayed. This is not usually as bad as it may first appear. Generally, we must reestablish the link to the document, which may now be located elsewhere or may now be known under a different name. Real problems arise when the document has been inadvertently deleted and cannot be relinked. The following are common reasons why we may have to redirect (reconnect) a link:

- A dependent or supporting document was moved to another directory without both linked documents being open at the time and without moving them with the **File Save As** command. This could have been caused by using DOS commands.
- A supporting document was renamed without its dependent document being open. This could also have been caused by using DOS commands.

The procedure for redirecting links for moved or renamed documents is shown in Figure 10.19 and is as follows.

- Open the dependent document that contains the links to be redirected.
- Execute the **File Links** command. The dialog box of Figure 10.20(b) appears. Select the documents in the **Links** list box for which you want to redirect links. The procedure for making multiple selections in this box was described earlier in this section. Choose the **Change** button.
- The dialog box of Figure 10.20(c) appears for a document that was selected. In the text box, type the document name and its pathname, whether for renaming or moving. Choose the **OK** button. Repeat this step for each document selected.

Removing links between documents.   Linked documents do not have to be permanently connected. It may be that a value is required from a special computation that must be performed only once, yet requires a substantial document for its computation. It may be a value that is obtained from a database and is unchanged after computation, such as a statistical quantity. In any case, links are to be removed from between documents. We present three procedures for removing links. In all cases, however, simple editing procedures will accomplish the same purpose.

• Removing a link but retaining a value for an entire external reference formula.
Select the cell with the external reference, execute **Edit Copy**, execute **Edit Paste Special**, choose **Values**, and choose **OK**.

Only the dependent document is involved and only the cell(s) containing the formula are affected by this procedure. The entire formula is removed and replaced by the value of the cell at that time.

• Removing a link but retaining a value for an external reference that is only part of the formula.
Select the cell with the external reference, select only the external reference in the formula bar, execute **Options Calculate Now**, and choose the enter box.

The selected part of the formula is replaced by the value of the external reference at the time the **Options Calculate Now** command is executed. The value becomes a part of the formula and the link is removed.

• Delete the external references with standard editing procedures. No values will automatically replace the deleted links.

For complex documents, verify that all links were removed as required. For this purpose, it is best to search for the exclamation mark with the **Formula Find** command and then visually confirm that remaining links, if any, were not to be removed, or remove missed ones by any of the above procedures.

10.2.4 Linking Charts

Links between charts and the documents containing data to plot are created automatically when a new chart is created from that data. However, we must be careful to avoid breaking links when moving or renaming documents to which the chart is linked. And we must also observe the supporting/dependent relationship between a chart and the documents from which it obtains the data to plot.

While the chart data is obtained from a series formula that is automatically constructed as described in Section 6.2, we have the option of editing the series in the formula bar if desired. We can also link attached and unattached text to a chart so that changes can be reflected in chart text as well as in its data. The links for this purpose are created and maintained as we discussed in Section 10.2.3. The only limitation is that the external reference must be to a single cell or a named single cell only. A range of cells or an array are not allowed as an external reference for this purpose.

TABLE 10.2 MACRO FUNCTIONS FOR LINKING

Function	Purpose
CHANGE.LINK(*old-link,new-link*)	To change the links to supporting documents for external references in the active document. The links will be changed from *old-link* to *new-link,* where both links must be the names of documents in the form of text.
LINKS([*dep-doc*])	To return the names of all supporting documents for a dependent document, where *dep-doc* must be the name of the dependent document in the form of text. If *dep-doc* is omitted, the dependent document is assumed to be the active document. The names of the supporting documents are returned as a horizontal array beginning in the cell where this function is located. The #N/A error value is returned when there are no external references.
OPEN.LINKS(*doc-1*[,...,*doc-n*][,*read-only*])	To open supporting documents linked to the active document. Each of the 14 possible documents *doc-i* will be opened in a read-only status when *read-only* is TRUE, corresponding to the Read Only check box of the File Links command being on, in which case you cannot change the opened documents. If it is FALSE, also the default condition when omitted, you can change the opened documents. The names of the documents *doc-i* must be in the form of text, or must be arrays or references that contain text. If any of the *doc-i* has external references to supporting documents, their external and remote references will be updated.

10.2.5 Macro Functions for Linking

The macro functions of Table 10.2 are used with linked documents. With these functions, we can dynamically change the documents from which we obtain values, determine all supporting documents for a dependent document, and open supporting documents.

10.3 IMPORTING AND EXPORTING INFORMATION

It is time for us to consider working with other applications while we use Excel. The connections between various Excel documents as discussed in Section 10.2 narrow the scope of our work to an Excel environment. Exceptions to this occur when we transfer information via Clipboard to other applications, but because such transfers are manually invoked, we dismiss them because they are not per-

TABLE 10.3 FILE FORMATS SUPPORTED BY EXCEL

Format	Extension
Microsoft Excel files	.XLS, .XLM, .XLC, .XLW
Text (tab delimited)	.TXT
Comma separated values	.CSV
Symbolic link	.SLK
Lotus 1-2-3 Version 1A	.WKS
Lotus 1-2-3 version 2.0	.WK1
Data interchange	.DIF
dBase II	.DBF
dBase III	.DBF

formed in an interactive dynamic integrated environment. Often we must transfer information from a non-Excel application to our document (a process called importing) and also from an Excel document to a non-Excel document (a process called exporting).

We will discuss these processes in this section in a real-time environment. Real time for this purpose means at once, as the information is available, and without manual intervention. Typical engineering contexts for this environment include the processing of data obtained from experiments run by another program, the integration of information prepared by multiple sources to generate up-to-the-minute reports and computations, and to control experiments dependent on interaction of various hardware and software processes.

10.3.1 Direct Access to Files

We can import and export data through direct access to files written by and for other applications. Excel supports certain formats that are common to other programs, as shown in Table 10.3. Reading and writing files in the supported formats is automatic with the **File Open** and **File Save As** commands, respectively.

To read supported formats, one merely selects the desired file in the **File Open** dialog box. It must have one of the file extensions shown in Table 10.3. To write a document in a supported format with the **File Save As** command one must select **Options** in its first dialog box [Figure 10.21(b)], toggle on the desired format in the **File Format** box of the second dialog box [Figure 10.21(c)], then choose **OK**.

Example 10.1

To illustrate the above scheme, we first export data with the .TXT format. Figure 6.9 shows the index of refraction data that we plotted in that chapter. To save this data in a .TXT file, we open the document, execute **File Save As**, select **Options** in its first dialog box, toggle on the **File Format Text** button in the second dialog box, then choose **OK**. We now have a text file. To import this data to a word processor, we first exit Excel. Then, we execute the word processor, in our case Microsoft Word, **Transfer Load** the above file into it, and print it. The result is shown in Figure 10.22.

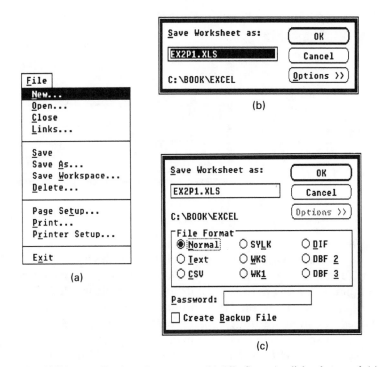

Figure 10.21 (a) File drop-down menu, (b) File Save As dialog box, and (c) dialog box produced by selecting Options of the dialog box in (b).

```
Wavelength      Index of refraction
0.1318      1.692
0.1349      1.657
0.138       1.63
0.1445      1.607
0.1514      1.576
0.1622      1.552
0.1698      1.539
0.182       1.51
0.1995      1.496
0.2291      1.474
0.263       1.46
0.389       1.442
0.5888      1.436
0.8511      1.432
1.7378      1.423
3.2359      1.417
5.2481      1.397
6.4565      1.379
7.4131      1.358
8.7096      1.332
9.3325      1.317
```

Figure 10.22 Printout of the text file transferred to Microsoft Word in Example 10.1.

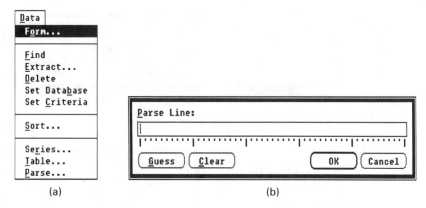

Figure 10.23 (a) Data drop-down menu and (b) Parse command dialog box.

Before importing a file to Excel, we first describe the **Data Parse** command. The function of this command is to separate the fields of each record into adjacent columns. For this purpose, the dialog box of Figure 10.23(b) is used to delineate the fields, which are then placed in the columns to the right of the column being parsed. Field delineation is via bracket symbols placed in chosen locations.

To use the **Data Parse** command, we must first select the range of cells to be parsed. The data to be parsed must be in one column only. We then execute the **Data Parse** command. The **Parse Line** of the dialog box of Figure 10.23(b) will contain the contents of the first cell of our selected range. We can choose to insert the brackets in the parse line through a manual editing process like that for the formula bar, or we can have Excel make its estimate of where the brackets should be placed. We do the latter by selecting the **Guess** button of the dialog box. Excel places brackets in the parse line as shown in Figure 10.24. We can now edit the parse line to make changes if desired. The **Clear** button deletes all brackets, after which we can reenter them as desired.

All cells of the selected range will be separated into fields at the brackets of the parse line. The column containing the unparsed data will become the first column of parsed data. Additional columns of parsed data appear to the immediate right of the column parsed. Data already in those columns will be overwritten by the parsed data. Depending on the location of the brackets with respect to the data in each cell, it is possible that fields of some cells may be separated at the wrong place. Should field separation be undesirable, the **Edit Undo Parse** com-

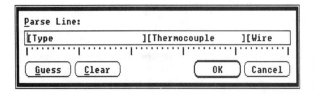

Figure 10.24 Parse dialog box showing placement of brackets with the Guess command.

mand should be executed immediately to return the data to a single column so that the brackets can be repositioned for another parsing attempt.

Example 10.2

We will now import the word processor text file of Figure 10.25(a) to Excel. It was saved unformatted in a .TXT file. In Excel, we execute the **File Open** command for a new worksheet, type in the dialog box our incoming .TXT file name, and choose **OK**. The result is shown in Figure 10.25(b), which shows all our data in one column of the worksheet. The printed output may appear different from that shown on the screen. The spacing of the words in each row may not be as uniform as shown in the figure. Each cell contains one record (line) of incoming data. Our task now is to separate the data into four columns. For this purpose, we use the **Data Parse** command of Figure 10.23(a).

```
Temperature Sensor Comparison
Type                    Thermocouple    Wire        Thermister
Max Temp, deg F         4200            2000        600
Sensitivity             Very low        Best        Good
Linearity               Excellent       Excellent   Poor
Long term stability     Excellent       Excellent   Poor to
moderate
Point sensing           Excellent       Poor        Excellent
Area sensing            Poor            Excellent   Poor
```

(a)

	A
1	Temperature Sensor Comparison
2	Type Thermocouple Wire Thermister
3	Max Temp, deg F 4200 2000 600
4	Sensitivity Very low Best Good
5	Linearity Excellent Excellent Poor
6	Long term stability Excellent Excellent Poor to moderate
7	Point sensing Excellent Poor Excellent
8	Area sensing Poor Excellent Poor

(b)

	A	B	C	D
1	Temperature Sensor Comparison			
2	Type	Thermocouple	Wire	Thermister
3	Max Temp, deg F	4200	2000	600
4	Sensitivity	Very low	Best	Good
5	Linearity	Excellent	Excellent	Poor
6	Long term stability	Excellent	Excellent	Poor to moderate
7	Point sensing	Excellent	Poor	Excellent
8	Area sensing	Poor	Excellent	Poor

(c)

Figure 10.25   (a) Word processor text file for Example 10.2, (b) file imported to Excel for parsing, and (c) parsed data.

Upon selecting the column of data (range A2:A8, we will leave the table title in row 1) and executing the **Data Parse** command, the data of cell A2 appears in the **Parse Line**. We select the **Guess** button to let Excel insert brackets in the parse line and manually readjust them according to our estimate of where we think they really should be. After we have done that, the parse line appears as shown in Figure 10.24. The contents of cell A2 is too long to appear in the dialog box. It must be scrolled to the left for the remainder to become visible. For this purpose, one places the cursor at the right end of the parse line and moves it to the right. If we compare the contents of the parse line of Figure 10.24 with the contents of cell A2, we should observe that the brackets between "Thermocouple" and "Wire" should be moved left and that the end bracket should be moved to the right to accommodate the "Poor to moderate" entry of cell A6. Upon making the adjustments and choosing **OK** in the dialog box, parsing takes place with the result shown in Figure 10.25(c). We will accept the results and perhaps touch them up with the **Format Alignment** command or through manual editing.

Example 10.3

Files generated with the .CSV extension offer opportunities for properly importing values to Excel. One file, characterized by comma separated values, is shown in Figure 10.26(a). Opening this file with the **File Open** command after typing in the file name with the .CSV extension produces the data layout of Figure 10.26(b). We see that the comma delimiters have caused a natural parsing of the data into columns. Were the .CSV file to be renamed with a .TXT extension and then opened, the result would be one column of values that would then have to be parsed. Parsing would be complicated because the values would not be conveniently

```
Temperature Sensor Comparison
Type,Thermocouple,Wire,Thermister
Max Temp  deg F,4200,2000,600
Sensitivity,Very low,Best,Good
Linearity,Excellent,Excellent,Poor
Long term stability,Excellent,Excellent,Poor to moderate
Point sensing,Excellent,Poor,Excellent
Area sensing,Poor,Excellent,Poor
```

(a)

	A	B	C	D
1	Temperature Sensor Comparison			
2	Type	Thermocouple	Wire	Thermister
3	Max Temp deg F	4200	2000	600
4	Sensitivity	Very low	Best	Good
5	Linearity	Excellent	Excellent	Poor
6	Long term stability	Excellent	Excellent	Poor to moderate
7	Point sensing	Excellent	Poor	Excellent
8	Area sensing	Poor	Excellent	Poor

(b)

Figure 10.26   (a) .CSV (comma separated values) file and (b) the file imported to an Excel worksheet.

separated as if they were tabulated. Strange effects may also be observed, such as missing commas.

10.3.2 Static Exchange

We now discuss information exchange between two documents, whereby one of them is in the Excel system and the other is an application that either runs within the Microsoft Windows system (it was written to operate within Windows) or is a standard application for Windows as defined by Microsoft (it was not written specifically for Windows). Our purpose is to present methods for exchanging information. Consequently, we do not discuss Windows except as the concept affects our purpose. The reader is referred to the Windows documentation for complete information on that program.

The basic procedure for exchanging information in the Windows system uses Clipboard. This is the same clipboard that we discussed in Section 10.1.2. We show its place in the system in Figure 10.27. Clipboard is directly accessible while in Windows by executing the CLIPBRD.EXE command from the MS-DOS Executive window. By opening Clipboard, we may inspect its contents. While in Excel, we run Clipboard via the Excel Control menu as discussed in connection with Figure 10.2. We can cut, copy, and paste to and from Clipboard in applications designed to work with Windows. The formats of the type of information supported by Clipboard to and from Excel are shown in Table 10.4. The Clipboard window itself is shown in Figure 10.11. The type of information on the clipboard is indicated in the box just below the menu bar as shown in the figure.

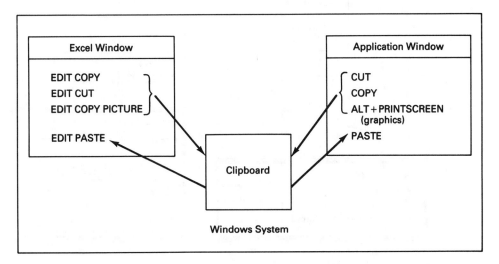

Figure 10.27 Relationship between Excel windows, Clipboard, and the Windows system.

TABLE 10.4 FORMATS SUPPORTED BY CLIPBOARD

Format	Clipboard type
Microsoft® Excel file	CF_BIFF
Text (tab delimited)	CF_TEXT
Formatted text	CF_RTF*
Comma separated values	CF_CSV
Symbolic link	CF_SYLK
Lotus 1-2-3 version 2.0	CF_WK1
Data interchange	CF_DIF
Picture	CF_METAFILEPICT*
Bitmap	CF_BITMAP*

* From Microsoft® Excel only

This is a clue to whether the information can be pasted to another application. Pasting will occur only if the other application accepts that type of information.

The procedures for transferring information to and from Clipboard within Excel are the same regardless of the type of application involved. These procedures are described in Section 10.1.2 and involve the **Edit Copy**, **Edit Cut**, **Edit**

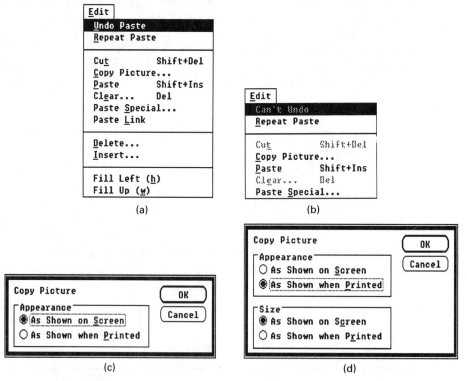

Figure 10.28 SHIFT-Edit drop-down menu for (a) a worksheet and (b) a chart and the Copy Picture command dialog boxes for (c) a worksheet and (d) a chart.

Paste, and **Edit Copy Picture** commands. The **Edit Copy Picture** command is used to copy a pictorial representation of the Excel selection into Clipboard. From there it can be pasted into an application. The command is invoked by holding down the SHIFT key and choosing the **Edit** menu. **Copy Picture** replaces the **Copy** command of the menu as shown in Figure 10.28(a) and 10.28(b). Choosing this command causes the dialog box of Figure 10.28(c) to appear when the selection is on a worksheet or that of Figure 10.28(d) when the selection is a chart. In both cases, the **Appearance** toggle allows the copy to appear as seen on the screen or as printed. In the latter case, the appearance depends on the kind of printer used for your Excel output. For a chart, the **Size** toggle controls the size of the copied picture, either the size of the window it is displayed in or as printed by the printer, in which case the actual size also depends on the shape of the window, the **Size** setting in the **File Page Setup** dialog box of Figure 6.33(b), and the kind of printer.

We must distinguish between applications designed to run under Windows and those running as standard applications because the procedures for exchanging information with them and Excel are different.

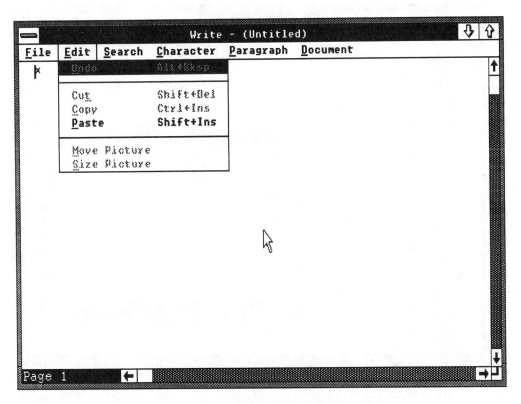

Figure 10.29   Write application window.

Exchanging data between Excel and applications designed to run under Microsoft Windows. Applications designed for Microsoft Windows run in their own window, which has a title bar and a menu bar. One such application is the Write word processor supplied with Windows. Its window is shown in Figure 10.29, where we see the **Cut, Copy**, and **Paste** commands of the **Edit** menu.

The procedure for transferring information from Excel to Write is no different than if we were to transfer it to another Excel document. Here are the steps.

- Activate the Write document to which the contents of Clipboard are to be transferred.
- Position the insertion marker at the desired location.
- Choose the **Edit Paste** command.

We illustrate the procedure by transferring the index of refraction data of Figure 6.9 from Excel to Write. The data are shown in Clipboard in Figure 10.30. We activate the Write document, position the insertion marker at the desired

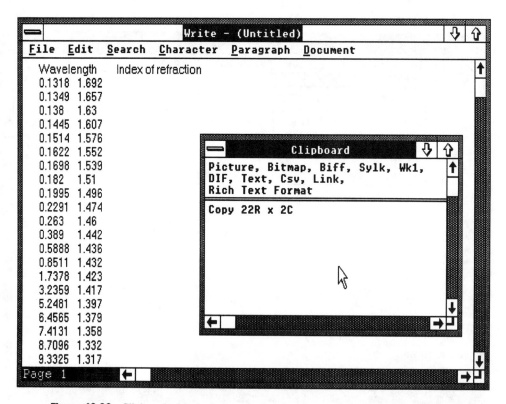

Figure 10.30 Clipboard with the index of refraction data copied to it and the Write window after its Edit Paste command is executed.

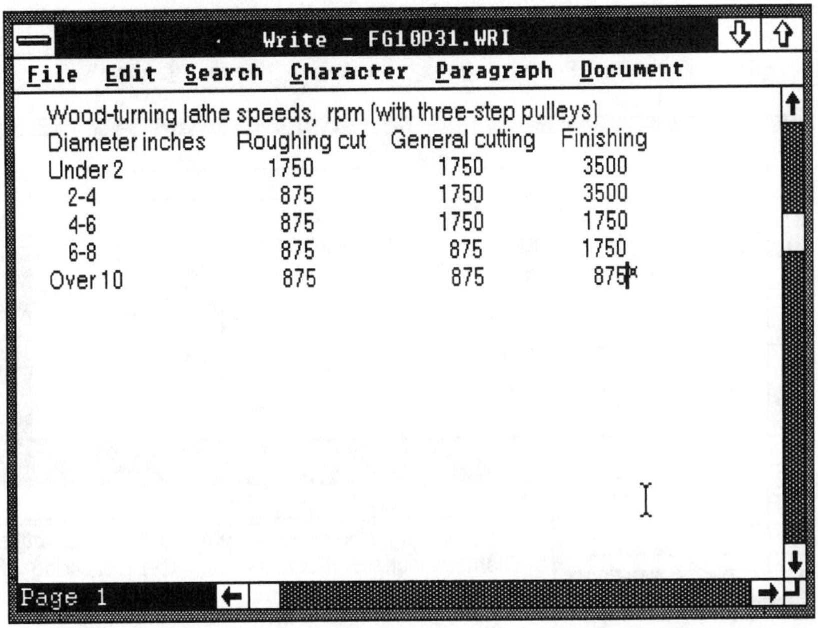

Figure 10.31   Write document with tabular data to be transferred to Excel.

location, and choose the **Edit** menu as shown in Figure 10.29. We then execute the **Edit Paste** command. The results of the data transfer are also shown in Figure 10.30.

The procedure for transferring information from Write to Excel is analogous to that we described above.

- Activate the Write document and select the information to be transferred.
- Choose the **Edit Copy** command and copy the information to Clipboard.
- Activate the Excel document to which the information is to be transferred and select the area into which the information will be placed.
- Choose the **Edit Paste** command to complete the transfer.

We now transfer text from Write to Excel. Figure 10.31 shows the Write document tabular data to be transferred. It is selected, then placed in Clipboard with the Write **Edit Copy** command. Then, we activate the Excel document and select the area into which we will paste the information. Upon choosing the Excel **Edit Paste** command, the information is transferred as shown in Figure 10.32, where the content of Clipboard is also shown.

Let us demonstrate the transfer of graphics from Excel to Write with the **Edit Copy Picture** command. The information selected is in the range A1:B13 of Figure 10.33. We execute the **Edit Copy Picture** command to copy the informa-

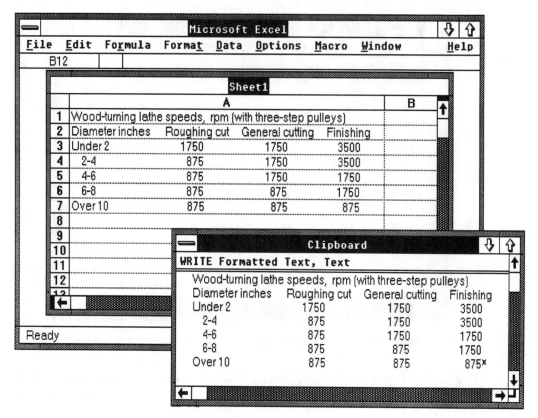

Figure 10.32 Excel document after transferring the Write tabular data of Figure 10.31 to it via Clipboard.

tion to Clipboard. The window of Figure 10.34 appears when we switch to the Windows MS-DOS Executive window and execute the **CLIPBRD.EXE** command. Now, after switching to the Write window, we position the insertion point to receive Clipboard's content and execute the **Edit Paste** command. The result is shown in Figure 10.35.

The names of the commands for an application written for Windows may differ from those we discussed above. Except for graphics, there should be no difference in transferred results. Some differences in graphics contents may be observed because of the way the graphics routines of the application program are written.

Exchanging data between Excel and standard applications.   Standard applications run in Windows may be written to display on the screen in a window or full-screen. Full-screen means that the entire screen is dedicated to the application. This does not mean that other applications cannot be run simultaneously;

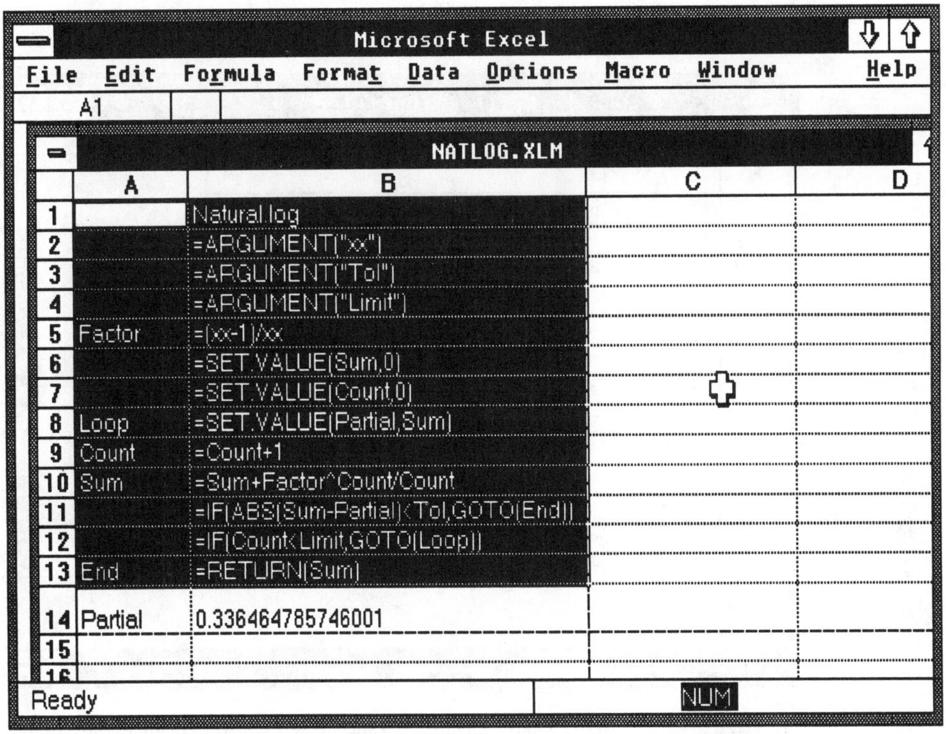

Microsoft Excel

File   Edit   Formula   Format   Data   Options   Macro   Window   Help

A1

NATLOG.XLM

	A	B	C	D
1		Natural.log		
2		=ARGUMENT("xx")		
3		=ARGUMENT("Tol")		
4		=ARGUMENT("Limit")		
5	Factor	=(xx-1)/xx		
6		=SET.VALUE(Sum,0)		
7		=SET.VALUE(Count,0)		
8	Loop	=SET.VALUE(Partial,Sum)		
9	Count	=Count+1		
10	Sum	=Sum+Factor^Count/Count		
11		=IF(ABS(Sum-Partial)<Tol,GOTO(End))		
12		=IF(Count<Limit,GOTO(Loop))		
13	End	=RETURN(Sum)		
14	Partial	0.336464785746001		
15				
16				

Ready   NUM

Figure 10.33   Range of information to be transferred with the Edit Copy Picture command from an Excel document to a Write document via Clipboard.

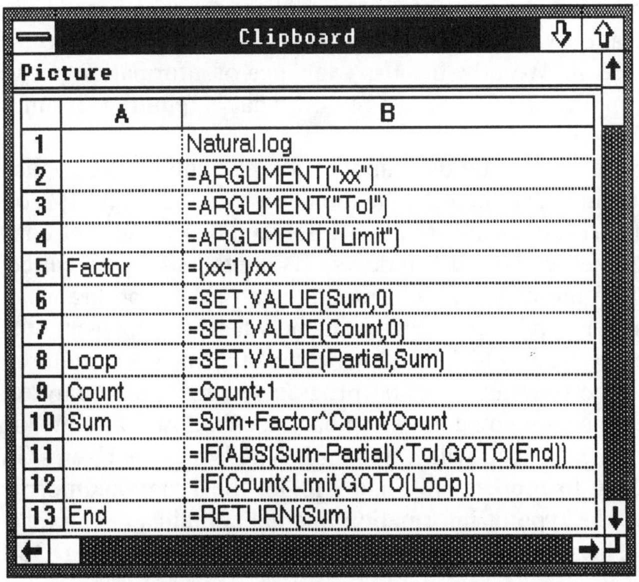

Clipboard

Picture

	A	B
1		Natural.log
2		=ARGUMENT("xx")
3		=ARGUMENT("Tol")
4		=ARGUMENT("Limit")
5	Factor	=(xx-1)/xx
6		=SET.VALUE(Sum,0)
7		=SET.VALUE(Count,0)
8	Loop	=SET.VALUE(Partial,Sum)
9	Count	=Count+1
10	Sum	=Sum+Factor^Count/Count
11		=IF(ABS(Sum-Partial)<Tol,GOTO(End))
12		=IF(Count<Limit,GOTO(Loop))
13	End	=RETURN(Sum)

Figure 10.34   Clipboard with data of Figure 10.33.

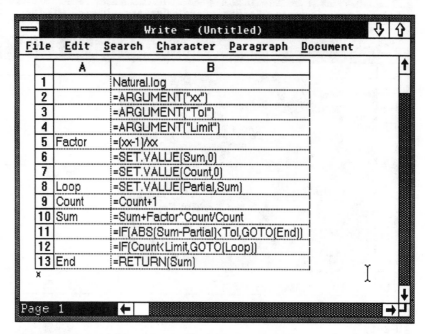

	A	B
1		Natural.log
2		=ARGUMENT("xx")
3		=ARGUMENT("Tol")
4		=ARGUMENT("Limit")
5	Factor	=(xx-1)/xx
6		=SET.VALUE(Sum,0)
7		=SET.VALUE(Count,0)
8	Loop	=SET.VALUE(Partial,Sum)
9	Count	=Count+1
10	Sum	=Sum+Factor^Count/Count
11		=IF(ABS(Sum-Partial)<Tol,GOTO(End))
12		=IF(Count<Limit,GOTO(Loop))
13	End	=RETURN(Sum)

Figure 10.35 Write window with the Edit Copy Picture data of Figure 10.33 pasted into it.

it just means that the standard application, when made visible, can be the only application visible at that time. Usually, graphics requirements force it to be run full-screen. We now discuss exchange of information between Excel and a standard application. First, we review what is required to run a standard application in Windows.

We start a standard application by running the application's PIF file, or by executing the application file (denoted by a .EXE, .COM, or .BAT file type). The PIF file (Program Information File) contains preset options that help the application run efficiently in Windows. Its contents may be edited with the PIF Editor. The PIF file contains information such as the program name, title, parameters (those typed after the program name when starting from outside Windows), initial directory from which it is to be run, the memory requirements, resources that cannot be shared with other programs (screen, keyboard, communications port), whether or not you can switch back to Windows, and the kind of information that may be exchanged with Clipboard. The Windows User's Guide describes this file and how to prepare it. Figure 10.36, the Program Information Editor window, shows the type of information this file contains.

The standard application is started from the MS-DOS Executive window as follows:

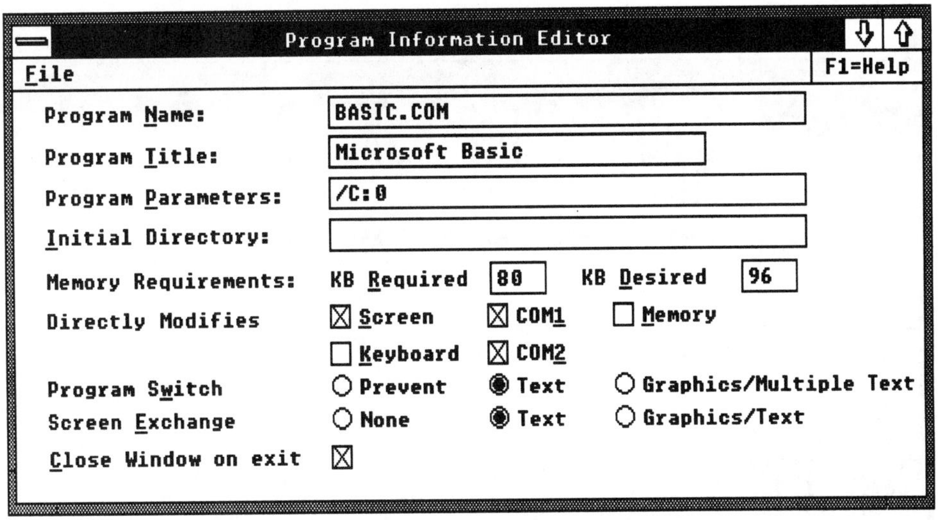

```
┌─────────────────────────────────────────────────────────────────────────┐
│  ▭                    Program Information Editor                    ⇩  ⇧  │
├─────────────────────────────────────────────────────────────────────────┤
│  File                                                             F1=Help │
│                                                                           │
│   Program Name:         ┌─────────────────────────────────────┐          │
│                         │ BASIC.COM                           │          │
│   Program Title:        ┌─────────────────────────────┐                  │
│                         │ Microsoft Basic             │                  │
│   Program Parameters:   ┌─────────────────────────────────────┐          │
│                         │ /C:0                                │          │
│   Initial Directory:    ┌─────────────────────────────────────┐          │
│                         │                                     │          │
│   Memory Requirements:  KB Required  ┌──┐   KB Desired  ┌──┐              │
│                                      │80│              │96│              │
│   Directly Modifies     ☒ Screen     ☒ COM1    ☐ Memory                  │
│                         ☐ Keyboard   ☒ COM2                              │
│   Program Switch        ○ Prevent    ◉ Text    ○ Graphics/Multiple Text   │
│   Screen Exchange       ○ None       ◉ Text    ○ Graphics/Text            │
│   Close Window on exit  ☒                                                │
│                                                                           │
└─────────────────────────────────────────────────────────────────────────┘
```

Figure 10.36   Program Information Editor window.

- Run the application's PIF file. Change to the directory that contains the PIF file. If this is not the application's directory, either copy the PIF file to that directory or place the directory name as a PATH variable in the AUTOEXEC.BAT file. Then, execute the application: keyboard—select the PIF file and press ENTER; mouse—double click the PIF file name.
- Execute the application file. Change to the directory that contains the application. Be sure the application's PIF file name is the same as the .EXE, .COM, or .BAT file, except for the file type of course. Then, execute the application: keyboard—select the application file name and press ENTER; mouse—double click the .EXE, .COM, or .BAT file name.

If the application is full-screen, Windows temporarily removes itself from the screen, and its applications, as well as other standard applications, suspend operation until the full-screen application is quit or shrunk to an icon.

For convenience in transferring information with the standard application, we prefer that it run in a window, even if it is full-screen because then a **Control** menu will probably become available. The **Control** menu will also allow us to switch between applications, something that usually must be done to effect an information transfer. If the application runs in a window, the **Control** menu will be evident. Windows adds the **Mark, Copy, Paste**, and **Scroll** commands to this menu, as can be seen in Figure 10.37(a). A full-screen application may also have a **Control** menu, which can be tested for by pressing ALT, then SPACEBAR. From Figure 10.37(a), we see that the **Control** menu commands allow us to switch

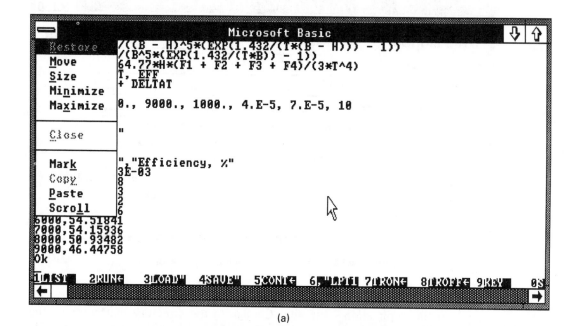

(a)

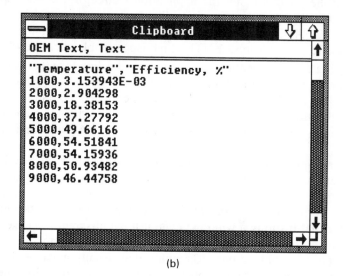

(b)

Figure 10.37 (a) An application, and its Control menu, designed to run under Windows and (b) its screen output copied into Clipboard.

between applications by reducing the window to an icon, thereby giving us access to a window that now becomes visible or can be made visible from its icon. With the added commands, one can copy to Clipboard from the application or can paste from Clipboard to the application. These commands are used as follows:

Mark

This command is used to select the information on the screen that is to be copied to Clipboard. When choosing **Control Mark**, a rectangular cursor appears in the upper left corner of the window. This cursor is moved with the arrow keys or the mouse to the beginning of the information to be selected. Then, with the keyboard, hold down the SHIFT key and use the arrow keys to select the desired information or, with the mouse, drag the cursor over the desired information to make the selection. This procedure is like selecting in Excel. Cancel the selection with the ESCAPE key or click the mouse outside the selection.

Copy

This command causes the selected information to be copied to Clipboard. Choose **Control Copy**.

Paste

This command causes information to be copied from Clipboard to the insertion point of the application. First, position the insertion point marker at the desired location in the application. Then, choose **Control Paste**. The information is pasted into the application and its effect should be seen immediately.

Selected parts of the screen are copied to and from Clipboard with the **Mark**, **Copy**, and **Paste** commands as described above. We copied the screen output of the BASIC program of Figure 10.37(a) with these commands. The resulting content of Clipboard is shown in Figure 10.37(b). We already know how to paste this information into Excel. Alternatively, we can copy the entire screen to Clipboard with the **ALT + PRINTSCREEN** command, after which it is available for pasting to other documents. At times, graphics screens cannot be copied in this manner because of improper PIF file settings, insufficient memory, or improperly written applications. If no transfer is possible, the response to **ALT + PRINTSCREEN** is a beep.

10.3.3 Dynamic Data Exchange

In Section 10.3.2, we exchanged information between applications and Excel through a manual intervention process. We called this a static exchange process. In this section, we will discuss means for dynamically exchanging the information. Once set up, we will not manually perform any of the operations to effect the transfer. Even more important, we will be able to program information exchange into our Excel worksheets and macros and into our applications. As in Section 10.3.2, we limit our discussion to information exchanges between Excel and other applications.

To dynamically exchange information, we must be operating within Microsoft Windows. The Excel program must be the version for the full Windows environment, and the application program must have been written to operate as a window under Windows. We will use a Windows feature called Dynamic Data Exchange (DDE).

DDE is a protocol for interprocess communication. It defines how two processes can send messages to each other and how they can exchange information in real time. We can use DDE in a document linking manner or with macros. While linking documents, we set up remote references, which are similar to the external references we used to link Excel documents in Section 10.2.

Remote references: Importing.   Figure 10.38 illustrates the operating environment, the relationship of the documents, the direction of information transfer, and the commands for creating links to initiate DDE requests from an Excel document. The concept of establishing a link to an application document is similar to linking Excel documents as discussed in Section 10.2. The central issue in using links for DDE requests is to prepare the remote reference formula. The remote reference format is as follows.

$$= \textit{app-name} \mid \textit{topic} \: ! \: \textit{item}$$

where the punctuation is required and

> *app-name* = name of the application as a legal Excel name or, if not a legal name, enclosed in quotation marks.

> *topic* = name of the application document to which the Excel document is to be linked. If not a legal Excel name, it must be enclosed in quotation marks.

> *item* = reference to a cell, cell range, value, or field of data in the document *topic*. Data resembling a cell reference must be enclosed in apostrophe marks.

Examples

$$='EXPT3' \mid 'FILTER' \: ! \: 'B7'$$

The application is named EXPT3, the document referred to is FILTER, and its *item*, whose name resembles an Excel cell reference, is B7.

$$=DATABASE \mid STRESS \: ! \: BRACKET$$

The application is named DATABASE, the document referred to is STRESS, and its *item* is the field of data named BRACKET.

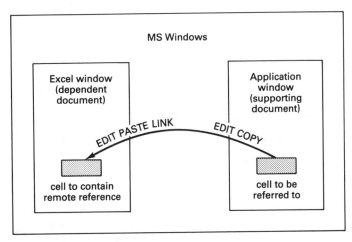

Figure 10.38   Linking for initiating DDE requests from an Excel document.

The remote reference is entered as a formula in a cell, or range of cells, in the Excel document, which is the dependent document. The application document is the supporting document. To create the link, Excel and the application must both be running under Windows. Then, follow this procedure.

- Activate the supporting document (application) window.
- Select the cell, cell range, value, or field of data to be referenced.
- Execute **Edit Copy** in the application window.
- Activate the dependent document (Excel) window.
- Select the cell or upper left corner of a range to contain the remote reference.
- Execute **Edit Paste Link** in the Excel window.

The remote reference formula should now be created. Should the **Edit Paste Link** command be greyed, a problem exists in establishing the link. Either the application does not support DDE or it cannot supply the information in a format that Excel accepts.

An alternative to the above procedure is to type the remote reference in the formula bar. An error message is displayed if problems similar to the above are encountered.

The dependent and supporting documents are often run at different times. Consequently, different data values may be offered by the supporting document each time the dependent document is opened. The choice now is whether to update the worksheet with a new set of values or whether to use the values last made available to it. The flowchart of Figure 10.39 shows the choices available via dialog box queries and the resultant values available to the worksheet. One

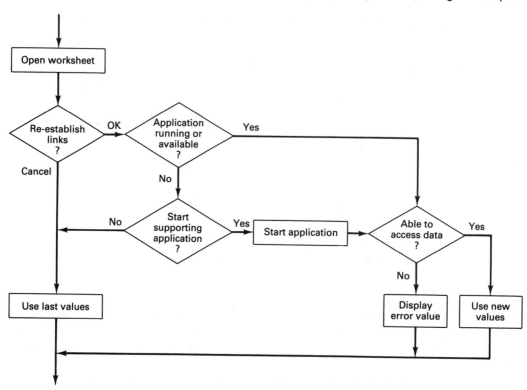

Figure 10.39   Flowchart for DDE updating of values for a newly opened linked document.

other possibility still exists. We may want to suspend continuous updating and use the last set of values obtained from the remote reference. We do this as follows:

- Activate the dependent document with the remote references.
- Execute **Options Calculation**.
- Toggle off the **Sheet Options Update Remote References** check box of the dialog box.
- Choose **OK**.

The dialog box is shown in Figure 10.40(b). Its action affects the dependent document only. We resume updating by toggling the check box to on.

Finally, links for remote references are removed as discussed earlier.

Remote references: Exporting.   Figure 10.41 illustrates the operating environment, the relationship of the documents, the direction of information transfer, and the commands for creating links to allow an Excel document to respond to a

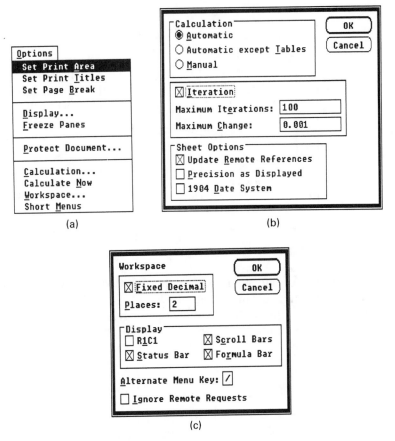

Figure 10.40 (a) Options drop-down menu and dialog boxes for its (b) Calculation and (c) Workspace commands.

DDE request from an application document. The application must have been written to communicate via the DDE protocol, and more specifically, it must have been written with knowledge of what Excel recognizes via DDE remote references.

The remote reference format we discussed earlier applies to the application document also. To export information from Excel, we must know the DDE specifics recognized by Excel. These are shown in Figure 10.42. From this figure, we see that the application name is "Excel" and that the topic must be either "System" or an Excel document name. When it is "System", the application will either be asking for information or be executing a command in Excel. The type of information being requested depends on the value of item. Table 10.5 gives the value returned for each item name recognized by Excel. The values are returned in CF_TEXT format (ASCII text). Values in a list are separated by tab characters.

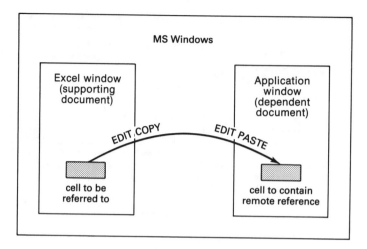

Figure 10.41 Exporting via DDE from Excel to an application.

The roles of dependent and supporting documents are now reversed from that of the section on importing above. Consequently, when constructing the remote reference in the application (dependent document) we must copy the *document-name* and *reference* from the supporting document, which is the active window of Excel.

$$\text{``Excel''} \mid \left\{ \begin{array}{l} \text{``System''!} \left\{ \begin{array}{l} \left\{ \begin{array}{l} \text{``SysItems''} \\ \text{``Topics''} \\ \text{``Status''} \\ \text{``Formats''} \\ \text{``Selection''} \end{array} \right\} \\ command \end{array} \right\} \\ document\text{-}name \text{ ! } reference \end{array} \right\}$$

command = Excel command equivalent macro function (equivalent to commands on menus) within brackets as a text value. It may be composed of concatenated commands, each within brackets. Arguments to the functions must be constants.

document-name = the file name, with extension, of any open Excel document as text.

reference = reference to a cell, cell range, value, or field of data in *document-name*. Data resembling a cell reference must be enclosed in apostrophe marks. For a chart, this value must be "Chart".

Figure 10.42 Excel DDE remote reference possibilities.

TABLE 10.5 EXCEL DDE REMOTE REFERENCE ITEM RETURN VALUES

Item	Value returned
"SysItems"	A list of all the items you can use with the "System" topic, i.e., SysItems, Topics, Status, etc.
"Topics"	A list of all currently open documents, including their full pathnames.
"Status"	"Ready" if Excel is ready to execute commands; "Busy" otherwise.
"Formats"	A list of all the Clipboard formats supported by Excel.
"Selection"	A list of the external references of all ranges currently selected in Excel. References are given in absolute R1C1 style.

To execute an Excel command, Figure 10.42 shows that we must construct a command-equivalent macro function as the item. The item can contain multiple commands, which are single commands concatenated to form the item. The general form of a multiple command item is as follows.

"[*command-1*][*command-2*] . . . [*command-n*]"

The item must be a text value with each macro function enclosed within brackets. Arguments to the functions must be constants, with references in R1C1 style in text form. Concatenated functions are executed in left-to-right order.

Examples:

"Excel" | "System" ! "[OPEN("C:\EXCEL\SURVEY.XLS")]"

This command causes Excel to open the file C:\EXCEL\SURVEY.XLS.

"Excel" | "System" ! "Formats"

The application is requesting a list of Clipboard formats supported by Excel. The values of the list are returned in CF_TEXT format separated by tab characters.

"Excel" | "FILTER.XLS" ! "D4 : D12"

The contents of the range D4 : D12 of the Excel document FILTER.XLS will be sent to the dependent document as an array.

"Excel" | "System" ! "[Run("R1C1")][BEEP( )]"

The macro beginning in location R1C1 of the active document is run, then a beep is sounded.

We are discussing communications between two programs that can be running simultaneously. As a result, DDE requests can occur at any time in an asyncronous manner and, perhaps, at unwanted times. Within Excel, via the **Options Workspace** dialog box, we can inhibit remote requests. Figure 10.40(c) shows the dialog box and the **Ignore Remote Requests** check box. This check box is important only when remote requests are used. When the box is turned on (checked), other applications are denied DDE access to the Excel documents. When it is turned off (unchecked), a DDE request by an application is recognized by Excel after the link has been established. An application can create a link only when this box is turned off. The **Edit Paste Links** command will only work with another application if the box is off.

Macros: Communicating with other applications.   The DDE remote reference procedures described above set up permanent data links between the documents. As a result, updates of the linked item are sent to the dependent application whenever the data associated with the item in the supporting application changes. Thus, we operate on a real-time basis. This data transfer process continues until the link is disconnected. Now, with macros, we will be able to establish DDE communications initiated on a demand basis. We still have one-way communications, however, but we will be able to use it selectively under full control of a macro program. We have not lost our ability to start another application, to execute commands in that application, and to send and receive information with that application.

We cannot conduct an exchange of information via DDE without the application supporting the protocol. This requires that the three-level hierarchy of *app-name, topic,* and *item* as described above be maintained. We will reference these levels as arguments in the macros written for DDE communication, so we must know what values are recognized for the levels by the application.

With macros, the primary means of communication is via message passing. This requires that a communication channel be established between the applications. In fact, we may have more than one channel connected between applications, there may be channels in both directions for simultaneous communication, and there may be more than the two applications involved. There may be arbitrarily complex DDE interconnection of documents, as shown in Figure 10.43.

Our general procedure involves using some or all of the macros described in Table 10.6 as follows.

• First, open a communications channel with the INITIATE macro function. Channels are shown in Figure 10.43 as lines with arrowheads. The INITIATE message is broadcast to all other applications to request that a conversation be initiated. Upon receiving this message, applications whose names match *app-name* and that support *topic* are expected to acknowledge the request. A channel is then said to be opened. Failure to open a channel

TABLE 10.6   DDE MACRO FUNCTIONS

Macro name (Argument list)	Description
INITIATE (*app-name, topic*)	This macro requests that a DDE channel be opened to the supporting application whose DDE name is *app-name*. Access is requested to *topic*, a logical data context whose form depends on the application and that often is a file name. If the request is successful, the number of the open channel is returned as the value of the function.
REQUEST (*channel-num, item*)	This macro requests that the information specified by *item* be sent to the dependent application by the supporting application connected to *channel-num*. Channel *channel-num* must have been opened by the INITIATE function. The form of *item* is determined by the supporting application. If the request is successful, the values returned are given as the value of the function in the form specified for *item*. Error values returned may be #VALUE! (invalid *channel-num*), #N/A (supporting application busy), #DIV/O! (supporting application timeout, canceled by ESCAPE key), and #REF! (REQUEST refused).
POKE (*channel-num, item, data-ref*)	This macro requests that the data of *data-ref* be sent to the item specified by *item* in the supporting application connected to *channel-num*. This is an unsolicited request. Channel *channel-num* must have been opened by the INITIATE function. The form of *data-ref* is an Excel reference to the document containing the data to send. The form of *item* is determined by the supporting application. Error values returned may be #VALUE! (invalid *channel-num*), #DIV/O! (supporting application time-out, canceled by ESCAPE key), and #REF! (POKE refused).
EXECUTE (*channel-num, command*)	This macro requests that the command or commands given in *command* be executed in the supporting application connected to *channel-num*. Channel *channel-num* must have been opened by the INITIATE function. The form of *command* is determined by the supporting application. If the request is successful, TRUE is returned as the value of the function. Error values returned may be #VALUE! (invalid *channel-num*), #N/A (supporting application busy), #DIV/O! (supporting application time-out, canceled by ESCAPE key), and #REF! (EXECUTE refused).
TERMINATE (*channel-num*)	This macro requests that the DDE channel given by *channel-num* be closed. Channel *channel-num* must have been opened by the INITIATE function. If the request is successful, TRUE is returned as the value of the function. Otherwise, the #VALUE! error value is returned.

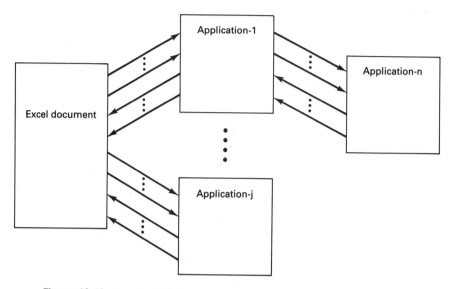

Figure 10.43   Possible DDE interconnection paths between documents and applications.

constitutes an error, which must be tested for with the ERROR macro function so that appropriate action can be taken.

- Engage in a conversation with some or all of the macro functions RE-
  QUEST, POKE, and EXECUTE. Each use of one of these macro functions
  transmits one message. As long as a channel is open, these macro functions
  may be used any number of times to fulfill the requirements of the program
  logic.

- Finally, terminate each channel of a conversation with the TERMINATE
  macro function before stopping the application. The INITIATE macro sets
  up a modal condition that can be countermanded only by the TERMINATE
  macro. Failure to close a channel may leave that application inaccessible via
  DDE, perhaps because there may be only one channel to the application. If
  any channels were not closed because of macro interruption, another macro
  should be run to close all channels.

10.4 CONTROLLING AN APPLICATION FROM EXCEL

We have discussed the preferred ways to communicate with an application from
Excel. The requirement placed on the application is that it be written to operate
under Windows and, perhaps, that it incorporate the DDE protocol. But applications do not always have to be written for DDE in order for us to take advantage of
their capability. We saw in Section 10.3.1 that often we can directly exchange

files, provided, of course, that the file formats are compatible. We can also use Clipboard, as long as the application runs under Windows. In this section, we discuss more ways, though limited in scope, to interact with other applications.

Starting a separate program under Windows.   We can use the EXEC macro function to start a program under Windows. The format of this statement is as follows:

$$EXEC\ (program[,window\text{-}type])$$

The name of the program, with pathname if necessary, is entered as text for *program*. It takes the same form as if it were entered in response to the **File Run** command in the Windows MS-DOS Executive. It can include any arguments and switches acceptable to the program to be started. If *program* is a file name only, the function causes the application to be started, with the file name as a parameter provided that the file name's extension corresponds to the requirements of the application. An integer for *window-type* determines how the window for the started program will appear: 1 (normal), 2 (minimized, default), or 3 (maximized).

If the EXEC function cannot start *program*, the #VALUE! error value is returned. Otherwise, the application is started and the Windows task ID is returned as the value of the function. This ID number distinguishes among the applications running and can be used with the INITIATE function to open a channel to an application as described in Section 10.3.3.

The macro of Figure 10.44(a) shows several examples of the EXEC function. In row 2, Excel is started and the worksheet EX3P4A.XLS is opened as a normal window. The file must be in the current directory or it cannot be opened. In row 3, we ask that Excel be started and to open the worksheet EX4P1.XXX as a minimized window. The file must be in the current directory. In row 4, we start Clipboard as a minimized window. Because the program is not in the current directory, we provide its full pathname. Figure 10.44(b) shows the task IDs for this run.

Remotely controlling an application.   We can perform one-way communication from Excel to an application running under Windows, given that it has already been started. We do this by making the application active, then sending a

	A
1	Exec.test
2	=EXEC("EX3P4A.XLS",1)
3	=EXEC("EXCEL.EXE EX4P1.XXX",2)
4	=EXEC("C:WINDOWSCLIPBRD.EXE",2)
5	=RETURN()

(a)

	A
1	Exec.test
2	1602
3	1722
4	1570
5	TRUE

(b)

Figure 10.44 Macro illustrating the EXEC function shown in (a) formulas mode and (b) values mode.

TABLE 10.7   APPLICATION CONTROL MENU EQUIVALENT COMMANDS

Macro function	Description
APP.ACTIVATE([*name*][,*wait-flag*])	This macro activates the application with *name* in its title bar. If *name* is omitted, Excel is activated. Activation occurs immediately when *wait-flag* is FALSE. It does not occur until Excel is activated when *wait-flag* is TRUE or omitted.
APP.MAXIMIZE( )	This macro is equivalent to the Control Maximize command for the application window and, if the active window is Excel, it maximizes the Excel application window.
APP.MINIMIZE( )	This macro is equivalent to the Control Minimize command for the application window and, if the active window is Excel, it minimizes the Excel application window.
APP.RESTORE( )	This macro is equivalent to the Control Restore command for the application window and, if the active window is Excel, it restores the Excel application window.
APP.MOVE(*x-coord*,*y-coord*)	This macro is equivalent to the Control Move command for the application window and, if the active window is Excel, it causes the window to be moved so that its left side is *x-coord* points from the left edge of the screen and its top side is *y-coord* points from the top edge of the screen. Points are measured in terms of character size whereby a character width is 8 points and its height is 12 points.
APP.SIZE(*x-dim*,*y-dim*)	This macro is equivalent to the Control Size command for the application window and, if the active window is Excel, it causes the window to be made *x-dim* points wide and *y-dim* points high. Points are measured as for APP.MOVE.

TABLE 10.8   KEYBOARD EQUIVALENT MACRO

Macro function	Description
SEND.KEYS(*key-text*[,*wait-flag*])	This macro sends *key-text*, a coded representation of keyboard characters, to the active application as a string of characters in text form. The objective is to send a character sequence to the application as if it were typed at the keyboard. If *wait-flag* is TRUE, Excel waits for the keys to be processed before resuming macro execution. If *wait-flag* is FALSE, the default value, Excel continues macro execution without waiting for the keys to be processed. Excel does not process keys while a macro is running so if the active application is Excel, *wait-flag* is always considered to be FALSE.

key sequence to it. The macros appropriate for this scheme are described in Tables 10.7 and 10.8. The basic procedure is to execute the APP.ACTIVATE function of Table 10.7 to make sure the application is activated, then send messages to it with the SEND.KEYS function of Table 10.8. The messages are constructed from the coded representation of keyboard characters shown in Table 10.9.

Scheduled starting conditions of macros.   The four macro functions of Table 10.10 allow us to set a condition under which our macro is to start running. The macro that is related to another application is ON.DATA, which starts our macro whenever the application sends new data to a document specified in the function. The other macros start running when some local condition arises.

TABLE 10.9   KEYBOARD KEY REPRESENTATIONS

Key classification	Code description			
Printing keys	No special coding. The characters are entered as typed.			
Nondisplaying keys	Key	Code	Key	Code
	BACKSPACE	{BACKSPACE}	PRTSC	{PRTSC}
		or {BS}	RIGHT	{RIGHT}
	BREAK	{BREAK}	TAB	{TAB}
	CAPSLOCK	{CAPSLOCK}	UP	{UP}
	CLEAR	{CLEAR}	F1	{F1}
	DELETE	{DELETE}	F2	{F2}
		or {DEL}	F3	{F3}
	DOWN	{DOWN}	F4	{F4}
	END	{END}	F5	{F5}
	ENTER	{ENTER}	F6	{F6}
		or ~ (tilde)	F7	{F7}
	ESCAPE	{ESCAPE}	F8	{F8}
		or {ESC}	F9	{F9}
	HELP	{HELP}	F10	{F10}
	HOME	{HOME}	F11	{F11}
	INSERT	{INSERT}	F12	{F12}
	LEFT	{LEFT}	F13	{F13}
	NUMLOCK	{NUMLOCK}	F14	{F14}
	PAGEDOWN	{PGDN}	F15	{F15}
	PAGEUP	{PGUP}	F16	{F16}
Key combinations (for held-down combining key, enclose combined key only in parentheses)	Combining key		Precede combined key with	
	SHIFT		+	
	CONTROL		^	
	ALT		%	
Repeating key sequences	{key number}			

TABLE 10.10   MACRO FUNCTIONS FOR RUNNING MACROS

Macro function	Description
Run a macro when new data is sent to a document	
ON.DATA(*document*[,*macro*])	Whenever a supporting application sends data to the dependent application given in text form as *document* (implying that the latter application contains at least one remote reference), the macro specified in R1C1 style in text form as *macro* starts running. If the received data causes recalculation in an Excel dependent application, the recalculation is performed before running the macro. ON.DATA controls a modal condition. Once this condition is activated, it can be turned off by omitting the *macro* argument.
Run a macro whenever a specified key is pressed	
ON.KEY(*key*[,*macro*])	Whenever the key, or key combination, given in text form as *key* is pressed, its response depends on the contents of *macro* as follows. When *macro* is a macro reference in R1C1 style in text form, the macro starts running. When *macro* is ′′′′ (empty text string) the key is ignored. When *macro* is omitted, the modal condition established by this function is canceled. The *key* codes are given in Table 10.9.
Run a macro at a specified time	
ON.TIME(*time*,*macro*[,[*tolerance*][,*insert-flag*]])	This macro depends on the value of *insert-flag* for its operation. If *insert-flag* is TRUE, or omitted, at time *time* the macro given by *macro* is executed. If *insert-flag* is FALSE, at time *time* all requests to run *macro* will be ignored. Other restrictions on running *macro* are: • If *time* is a serial number, macro *macro* is run every day at that time. • If the sheet containing *macro* is not in memory at time *time,* the request is ignored. • If at time *time* Excel is not in READY, COPY, CUT, or FIND mode, Excel waits no longer than a time determined by *tolerance* (a serial number) to run *macro*. If the wait time exceeds *tolerance* the request is canceled. The default value for *tolerance* is the maximum possible serial time. • For two or more identical ON.TIME macros, only the first one is executed; the others are ignored and return the value #N/A!.
Run a macro when a window is activated	
ON.WINDOW([*window*][,*macro*])	Whenever the window given by *window* is activated, the macro given by *macro* is executed. Both arguments must be in the form of text. If *window* is omitted, the macro given by *macro* is started whenever the window is activated, except for windows named in other ON.WINDOW macros. If *macro* is omitted, activating *window* no longer starts a macro.

Because we already know how to communicate with other applications from what was presented earlier in this chapter, we can now use our local conditions to indirectly control other applications also.

10.5 ABOUT VERSION 3.0

Much of this chapter does not concern Excel. Instead, it covers interfacing Excel with other products. We discussed Excels' use with Windows, Clipboard, and other applications, and learned about directories, linking various documents with those of Excel, and communicating with other applications. Some of the improvements we observed can be credited to Windows version 3.0, but Excel version 3.0 also brings improvements and new features that relate to the material of this chapter.

10.5.1 Improvements

Additions and changes related to the material above follow:

1. Changes to some dialog boxes discussed in this chapter make it easier for us to perform operations ancillary to our engineering calculations. The control menus of Figures 10.2(a) and 10.2(b) now permit more convenient switching to other applications and documents because of additional commands; the **File Save As** and **File Save Workspace** dialog boxes of Figures 10.14(c) and 10.14(d) now have a directory list box for convenience in specifying a path; the **File Links** dialog box of Figure 10.20(b) was redone as shown in Figure 10.45; the **File Save Worksheet Options** dialog box of Figure 10.21(c) was changed to the one of Figure 10.46; the **File Open** dialog box of Figure 10.14(a) now has a **Text** button that leads to the dialog box of Figure 10.47; and the **Options Calculation** dialog box of Figure 10.40(b) now has a **Save External Link Values** check box.

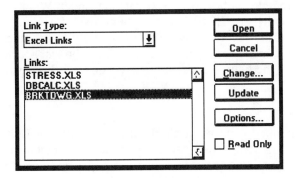

Figure 10.45   Version 3.0 File Links command dialog box.

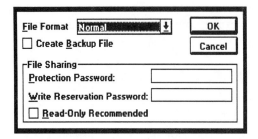
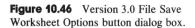
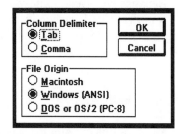

Figure 10.46 Version 3.0 File Save
Worksheet Options button dialog box.

Figure 10.47 File Open Text button
dialog box.

    2. New macro functions related to document linking are:

GET.LINK.INFO
SET.UPDATE.STATUS
UPDATE.LINK

All macro functions of Table 10.2 now have an additional argument. These
macros should all be reviewed carefully before being used in complex document
linking schemes.

    3. More file format choices are supported by Excel. However, some new
ones are variations of several now listed in Table 10.3 because of changes appearing in new software versions of other products. Our Examples 10.1 through 10.3
run under version 3.0 without change. A new macro function, PARSE, is command equivalent to the **Data Parse** command.

    4. We can easily start standard applications from Windows version 3.0, but
note that the PIF file window of Figure 10.36 was totally rearranged, and we can
access Clipboard from the Main window of Windows. Clipboard now supports a
format called NATIVE for embedded objects.

    5. Our discussion in Section 10.3.2 on screen copying for static exchange
via Clipboard is more credible with version 3.0 running under Windows 3.0.
Now, we merely press the PRINT SCREEN key, without the ALT key, to copy
information to Clipboard. Thereafter, we can paste it into any other document
that accepts this format. We made copies of the menus, dialog boxes, and screens
this way via Paintbrush for the figures used with our version 3.0 discussions.

10.5.2 The Tool Bar

We discussed copying unlinked pictures of charts and cells with the **Edit Copy
Picture** command in Section 10.3.2. Now, we can copy a linked picture of cells
from one worksheet or macro sheet to another worksheet or macro sheet with a

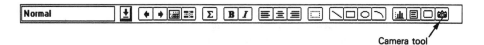

Camera tool

Figure 10.48 Excel tool bar.

tool bar button or with the **Edit Paste Picture Link** command. We do this as follows:

   1. Activate the worksheet or macro sheet that contains the cells to copy and select them.

   2. Click the *Camera tool* button labeled in Figure 10.48.

   3. Activate the worksheet or macro sheet onto which the copy is to be made.

   4. Select the cell where the camera copy of cells is to be pasted. Pasting occurs immediately upon cell selection.

    Figure 10.49 shows the worksheet information for the example of Section 6.6.1 pasted as a picture of cells onto another worksheet according to this procedure and still selected, as denoted by the black squares or handles, on the surrounding rectangle. The above procedure can also be performed with the keyboard and the **Edit Copy** and **Edit Paste Picture Link** commands.

    While selected, the picture can be sized by dragging a handle, on the side or corner, while observing the dotted outline of its new dimensions. Pressing SHIFT while dragging will keep the picture proportioned; pressing CTRL while dragging

	A	B	C	D	E	F	G	H
1								
2				Table of Standard Deviation, psi.				
3								
4					Test series			
5				A	B	C		
6			6	74	39	21		
7		Beam size, in.	9	70	22	11		
8			12	79	48	13		
9			18	62	33	34		
10								
11								
12								
13								
14								
15								
16								

Sheet1

Figure 10.49 Linked picture of cells.

will align the picture to the cell grid. The picture can be moved to a new location by dragging it there after first clicking on its border with an arrow cursor. If not already selected, it becomes selected upon doing this. The following are characteristics of a linked cell picture:

1. The linked cell picture will be updated whenever its opened source document changes.

2. A linked cell picture whose source document is not open can be updated by double clicking the linked picture, after which Excel automatically opens the source document and selects the source cell range, thus allowing updating to take place.

3. The link formula of a selected linked cell picture is displayed in the formula bar. It is subject to editing as we discussed such procedures in this chapter.

4. A selected linked cell picture can be removed from a document by executing the **Edit Clear** command or by pressing the BACKSPACE or DELETE key.

10.5.3 New Features

The following new features may involve material of this chapter but, since they provide no new calculation capability, they are not detailed here.

1. Data from several worksheets can be combined in another worksheet for summarization purposes with the *consolidation* feature. Arithmetic operations with functions like those used with databases are performed during consolidation. The **Data Consolidate** command of Figure 10.50(a), with its dialog box of Figure 10.50(b), is used for the procedure. One specifies the cell range for the consolidated information (the destination area) in the target document and the cell

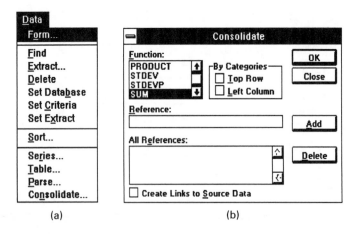

(a)   (b)

Figure 10.50   (a) Data menu and (b) its Consolidate command dialog box.

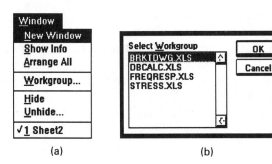

Figure 10.51 (a) Window menu and (b) its Workgroup command dialog box.

ranges of data to be consolidated (the source area) in each of the source documents; the arithmetic operation to be performed during consolidation; and whether links to the source data are to be created for updating purposes. All source documents must exist but do not have to be open during consolidation.

2. A *workgroup* is a collection of similar worksheets, macro sheets, or a combination thereof, defined to be a workgroup by the **Window Workgroup** command of Figure 10.51(a) with its dialog box of Figure 10.51(b). The workgroup documents share the common characteristic of being nearly alike, to the extent that operations performed on one of them, the active document, affect all of them in a like manner. This pertains to data entry and editing, document formatting, and file management. Actions performed on the selected cell locations of the active document are duplicated simultaneously in the corresponding cell locations of all documents of the workgroup. There can be only one workgroup defined at any time. It becomes undefined whenever another document of the workgroup is activated. Therefore, it is a temporary document relationship convenient for duplicating actions in multiple documents simultaneously. It facilitates identical multiple document preparation while a workgroup is defined without having to address individual documents for their share of similarity of action.

3. We introduced embedding of charts into worksheets in Section 6.6.2 and learned that we could start an application from the embedded object, in this case the Excel chart feature, complete with its own window and menu bar. But, this really is a special case of embedding whereby the source and target documents are within the same system. *Embedding* means to copy an object from a source application to a target application for the purpose of sharing information and to acquire the ability to edit the object and update the linked information from within the target application. Excel can be used with embedded objects obtained from other applications and can be used as the source of objects embedded into other applications.

Embedded objects are usually used when dynamic linking is not needed but when updating is desired. Both applications must support the embedding concept and the target application must have the capability for running the applications so that updating can occur. Documents containing embedded objects may require considerably more memory than otherwise needed because the embedded object brings to the target application the supporting document that contains the data used to create the object. An example embedded object could be a document with data collected from a program that monitors an experiment in real time. In this case the target application must be able to run the program also so that the embedded document could be updated.

Because we discuss only features built into Excel, and since it is not supplied with an external application that supports embedding, there is no need to discuss the embedding concept further.

CHAPTER **11**

Applications

We now provide several comprehensive examples that illustrate how Excel can be applied on a larger scale than presented in examples of prior chapters. The context is still tutorial. However, the examples have practical application even though they are not integrated into a production version of the spreadsheet.

Because Excel macros provide the most powerful capability of the spreadsheet, we use them exclusively in this chapter. We show how to convert programs from a scientific programming language, in our case FORTRAN, to Excel. We could have chosen to use Pascal, or another language, just as well. Since most engineers probably already have a personal library of their own programs in some programming language, they now will discover how to adapt their programs for spreadsheet use. With Excel macros, we also have the capability to control execution, much as with a scientific programming language.

In the first example, we apply Excel to solving a system of sparse matrix equations. We incorporate a routine that performs node renumbering to reduce the number of matrix "fills." The second example shows how to use Excel's chart capability for general plotting purposes. We implement one version of the hidden-line elimination algorithm. The third example uses a balanced binary tree structure as the basis for beginning the plane-sweep algorithm. Finally, we generate a polar coordinate grid, a graph format not included in Excel's gallery of chart formats.

11.1 SPARSE MATRIX TECHNIQUES

Systems of equations set up for solving engineering problems often result in matrices containing a large percentage of zero-valued off-diagonal elements. Such matrices are called *sparse*. They may contain from 5% to 50% nonzero entries and generally result from node analysis rather than from loop analysis formulation. Consequently, traditional solution techniques use more computer time and memory than necessary to solve such equations because operations add and multiply by zero and because memory is needed to store many zero values. Sparse matrix techniques have been developed that avoid storing the zero-valued elements and thus also avoid computing with them. The application described below applies Excel to one approach for solving sparse matrix problems.

Our approach is to incrementally describe one solution technique. We implement the algorithms on macro sheets but do not integrate the computations for a production version of the solution. This is done for expository purposes. We describe algorithms for:

1. Computing an array for sparse matrix storage.
2. Performing a symbolic LU decomposition for determining the matrix zero structure and for node renumbering purposes.
3. Preparing reordered arrays of the diagonal, lower triangular, and upper triangular nonzero entries for convenience in solving the equations.
4. Performing the numeric LU decomposition.
5. Performing the forward and back substitution to solve the equations.

11.1.1 Packed Matrix Storage

In this section, we are concerned with entering the raw data and storing it in the manner needed for manipulation by subsequent algorithms. Several data storage formats are in use for this purpose. Chang [3] proposed an efficient storage technique that was also used in the Yale sparse matrix package by Eisenstat et al. [5]. Berry [2] earlier described his storage structure in connection with a symbolic LU decomposition and node renumbering algorithm, which we implemented and describe in Section 11.1.2. We now describe entry and storage of data for use by this algorithm.

The requirement is to input the matrix element values and the row/column coordinates at which they are to be stored. A routine that prompts for each value and its coordinates would serve the purpose. For expository purposes, we will enter the values in an unpacked matrix, from which we will then extract the element values with their matrix coordinates. This will ordinarily not be done because of the matrix storage requirement, something that our sparse matrix approach is to avoid.

We will extract the element values from the matrix and store the relevant information in arrays as indicated in Figure 11.1. This is a packed format compati-

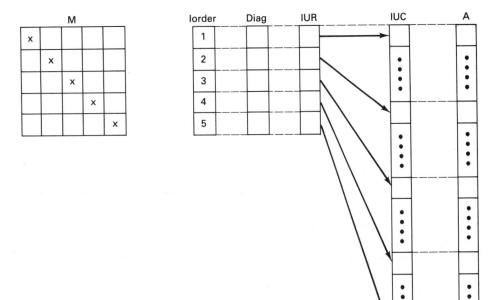

N = order of the matrix M.

A = array of nonzero off-diagonal elements packed in row order. The array size is determined by the sparsity of the original matrix. Its maximum size, for a nonsparse matrix, is $N(N-1)$.

Diag = array of the diagonal terms (size N).

Iorder = array containing the row order in which the equations are originally stored in the arrays (size N).

IUR = array of pointers to the starting location of the elements in A and IUC associated with each row (size $N + 1$).

IUC = array of column numbers of the entries in A (same size as A).

Node = array containing the elements of Iorder corresponding to row m, i.e., for m = Iorder(j), then j = Node(m) (size N).

Numoff = array indicating the number of nonzero off-diagonal elements in each row of A and IUC (size N).

Figure 11.1   Packed matrix storage structure and definition of variables.

ble with the symbolic LU decomposition routine of Section 11.1.2. The array packing is done according to the algorithm of Figure 11.2. Its macro is shown in Figure 11.3. In essence, we are scanning matrix M in row order and storing the diagonal elements in array Diag and nonzero off-diagonal elements in array A. We save the column numbers of the off-diagonal elements in IUC, for which the rows are delimited by the location points in IUR. Iorder contains the node order of the matrix while Node is its counterpart to locate the node given its row

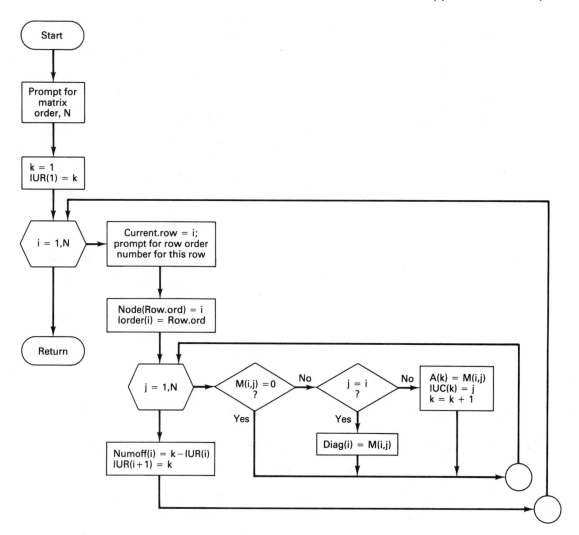

Figure 11.2   Flowchart for packing sparse matrix data.

number. Numoff contains the number of nonzero off-diagonal elements for each row of A. This is really redundant information, since it can be determined from IUR. However, Numoff is used for the symbolic LU decomposition, and its contents are easily determined now.

The macro of Figure 11.3 follows the flowchart of Figure 11.2 exactly. We prompt for the order N of the matrix with the INPUT statement (row 4) and use it to control the FOR-NEXT loops to process each row of the matrix. Because our matrix may be ordered differently from that given in matrix M, we prompt for the node number with a custom dialog box (row 9). Input.order is the dialog box area

	A	**B**
1		Compact.Array
2		Compacts an array for sparse matrix solution.
3		Shortcut key = "c"
4	N	=INPUT("Enter the matrix order:",1)
5	k	=1
6		=SET.VALUE(INDEX(IUR,1),k)
7		=FOR("i",1,N,1)
8		=SET.VALUE(Current.row,i)
9		=DIALOG.BOX(Input.order)
10		=SET.VALUE(INDEX(Node,Row.ord),i)
11		=SET.VALUE(INDEX(Iorder,i),Row.ord)
12		=FOR("j",1,N,1)
13		=IF(INDEX(M,i,j)=0,GOTO(Next.j))
14		=IF(j=i,GOTO(Set.diag))
15		=SET.VALUE(INDEX(A,k),INDEX(M,i,j))
16		=SET.VALUE(INDEX(IUC,k),j)
17		=SET.VALUE(k,k+1)
18		=GOTO(Next.j)
19	Set.diag	=SET.VALUE(INDEX(Diag,i),INDEX(M,i,j))
20	Next.j	=NEXT()
21		=SET.VALUE(INDEX(Numoff,i),k-INDEX(IUR,i))
22		=SET.VALUE(INDEX(IUR,i+1),k)
23		=NEXT()
24		=RETURN()

Figure 11.3   Macro for packing sparse matrix data.

not shown here. We display the row to be processed in the cell named Current.row and receive the response in the cell named Row.ord, both locations being in the dialog box area. Figure 11.4 shows the contents of array M before and after it was processed with this macro.

11.1.2 Symbolic LU Decomposition and Node Renumbering

Having entered our data and packed the arrays for storage conservation, we now proceed with preparations for solving the equations. We have accounted for the zeros in the original matrix and retained only nonzero matrix entries. We are about to determine the zero structure of the matrix so we can use it to our advantage for matrix decomposition later. We must be aware that nonzero elements may arise later where zero elements exist now. Because these nonzero elements will develop as we perform a numeric LU decomposition, they are called *fills*. In this section, we will perform a symbolic LU decomposition (we will not make matrix computations) during which time we will determine the location of any fills and allocate storage for them. It is to our advantage to reduce the number

	L	M	N	O	P
1	3	6	4	-3	0
2	5	1	-1	4	4
3	3	2	6	0	2
4	2	1	0	4	-1
5	0	-2	-1	1	2

(a)

	D	E	F	G	H	I	J
13	IUR	IUC	Iorder	Node	Numoff	Diag	A
14	1	2	1	1	3	3	6
15	4	3	2	2	4	1	4
16	8	4	3	3	3	6	-3
17	11	1	4	4	3	4	5
18	14	3	5	5	3	2	-1
19	17	4					4
20		5					4
21		1					3
22		2					2
23		5					2
24		1					2
25		2					1
26		5					-1
27		2					-2
28		3					-1
29		4					1

(b)

Figure 11.4 (a) Example matrix input to the packed storage macro and (b) its packed storage equivalent.

of fills so we will also rearrange the rows of the matrix, and hence also the columns (the nodes), to eliminate the possibility of creating fills, or at least to reduce their number.

The algorithm we will program is the one reported by Berry [2]. It was developed to solve equations that produce a *structurally symmetric* matrix, such as results from node analysis formulation. The matrix does not have to be *numerically symmetric*. The algorithm is simple to grasp in concept, but its implementation is difficult to follow because of the generous use of pointers, the dynamics of row reassignment, fill determination, and the bookkeeping operations required to maintain the state of progress of decomposition. For these reasons, we do not explain in detail the algorithm but, instead, refer the reader to Berry's paper.

Before describing our implementation of the algorithm, we will perform by hand a symbolic LU decomposition to gain insight into its operation, to understand the origin of fills, and to realize the benefits of row renumbering.

LU decomposition means that we can decompose (factor) a matrix **A** into the product of two matrices **L** and **U,** where **L** is a lower triangular matrix while **U** is an upper triangular matrix such that

$$\mathbf{LU} = \mathbf{A}$$

When used in a matrix equation of the form

$$\mathbf{Ax} = \mathbf{b}$$

we have

$$\mathbf{LUx} = \mathbf{b}$$

We gain certain advantages in solving the system of equations represented by this latter matrix equation and will discuss them later. There are variations in representing the **L** and **U** matrices. We adopt that used by Berry. Our matrices appear as follows, for a fourth-order matrix.

$$
\begin{bmatrix}
1 & 0 & 0 & 0 \\
\ell_{21} & 1 & 0 & 0 \\
\ell_{31} & \ell_{32} & 1 & 0 \\
\ell_{41} & \ell_{42} & \ell_{43} & 1
\end{bmatrix}
\begin{bmatrix}
u_{11} & u_{12} & u_{13} & u_{14} \\
0 & u_{22} & u_{23} & u_{24} \\
0 & 0 & u_{33} & u_{34} \\
0 & 0 & 0 & u_{44}
\end{bmatrix}
=
\begin{bmatrix}
a_{11} & a_{12} & a_{13} & a_{14} \\
a_{21} & a_{22} & a_{23} & a_{24} \\
a_{31} & a_{32} & a_{33} & a_{34} \\
a_{41} & a_{42} & a_{43} & a_{44}
\end{bmatrix}
$$

We begin the LU decomposition by multiplying the first row of **L** by each column of **U** and equating the resulting elements with those of **A**. We get

$$u_{11} = a_{11}$$

$$u_{12} = a_{12}$$

$$u_{13} = a_{13}$$

$$u_{14} = a_{14}$$

Similarly, by multiplying each row of **L** by the first column of **U**, we have

$$
\left.
\begin{aligned}
\ell_{21}u_{11} &= a_{21} \\
\ell_{31}u_{11} &= a_{31} \\
\ell_{41}u_{11} &= a_{41}
\end{aligned}
\right\}
\blacktriangleright
\left\{
\begin{aligned}
\ell_{21} &= a_{21}/u_{11} \\
\ell_{31} &= a_{31}/u_{11} \\
\ell_{41} &= a_{41}/u_{11}
\end{aligned}
\right.
$$

Because we know that each element of the diagonal of **L** is 1, we need not store these values. Instead, we will store the **L** and **U** values in the **A** matrix by replacing the corresponding a_{ij} with the ℓ_{ij} or u_{ij} just computed. Thus far, we have determined the row and column values boxed off in the following matrix.

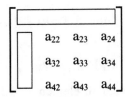

Continuing similarly to the above, we obtain the following:

$$\left.\begin{array}{l}\ell_{21}u_{12} + u_{22} = a_{22}\\ \ell_{21}u_{13} + u_{23} = a_{23}\\ \ell_{21}u_{14} + u_{24} = a_{24}\end{array}\right\} \blacktriangleright \left\{\begin{array}{l}u_{22} = a_{22} - \ell_{21}u_{12}\\ u_{23} = a_{23} - \ell_{21}u_{13}\\ u_{24} = a_{24} - \ell_{21}u_{14}\end{array}\right.$$

and

$$\left.\begin{array}{l}\ell_{31}u_{12} + \ell_{32}u_{22} = a_{32}\\ \ell_{41}u_{12} + \ell_{42}u_{22} = a_{42}\end{array}\right\} \blacktriangleright \left\{\begin{array}{l}\ell_{32} = \dfrac{a_{32} - \ell_{31}u_{12}}{u_{22}}\\[2ex] \ell_{42} = \dfrac{a_{42} - \ell_{41}u_{12}}{u_{22}}\end{array}\right.$$

The row and column values determined so far as as follows:

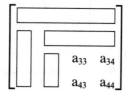

Continuing in this manner gives

$$\left.\begin{array}{l}\ell_{31}u_{13} + \ell_{32}u_{23} + u_{33} = a_{33}\\ \ell_{31}u_{14} + \ell_{32}u_{24} + u_{34} = a_{34}\end{array}\right\} \blacktriangleright \left\{\begin{array}{l}u_{33} = a_{33} - \ell_{31}u_{13} - \ell_{32}u_{23}\\ u_{34} = a_{34} - \ell_{31}u_{14} - \ell_{32}u_{24}\end{array}\right.$$

and

$$\ell_{41}u_{13} + \ell_{42}u_{23} + \ell_{43}u_{33} = a_{43} \blacktriangleright \ell_{43} = \dfrac{a_{43} - \ell_{41}u_{13} - \ell_{42}u_{23}}{u_{33}}$$

so that we now have

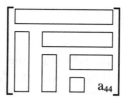

Finally,

$$\ell_{41}u_{14} + \ell_{42}u_{24} + \ell_{43}u_{34} + u_{44} = a_{44}$$

from which

$$u_{44} = a_{44} - \ell_{41}u_{14} - \ell_{42}u_{24} - \ell_{43}u_{34}$$

Now we have determined all elements of the **L** and **U** matrices.

$$
\begin{bmatrix} \end{bmatrix} = \begin{bmatrix} u_{11} & u_{12} & u_{13} & u_{14} \\ \ell_{21} & u_{22} & u_{23} & u_{24} \\ \ell_{31} & \ell_{32} & u_{33} & u_{34} \\ \ell_{41} & \ell_{42} & \ell_{43} & u_{44} \end{bmatrix}
$$

We note these characteristics of the calculations just made.

1. To determine each new ℓ_{ij} and u_{ij} value, we use only the corresponding value of a_{ij} and values of **L** and **U** elements already calculated.
2. Each ℓ_{ij} is determined by dividing a combination of terms by u_{jj}.
3. The calculations for succeeding ℓ_{ij} and u_{ij} elements require the subtraction of additional **L** and **U** element products as calculation proceeds into the submatrices.

It is worthwhile to consider the expression for ℓ_{43}, for example. That equation is

$$
\ell_{43} = \frac{a_{43} - \ell_{41}u_{13} - \ell_{42}u_{23}}{u_{33}}
$$

$$
= \frac{1}{u_{33}}(a_{43} - \ell_{41}u_{13} - \ell_{42}u_{23})
$$

$$
= \frac{1}{u_{33}}(a'_{43} - \ell_{42}u_{23})
$$

$$
= \frac{1}{u_{33}}(a''_{43})
$$

where we made the substitutions

$$
a'_{43} = a_{43} - \ell_{41}u_{13}
$$

$$
a''_{43} = a'_{43} - \ell_{42}u_{23}
$$

Had we subtracted the $\ell_{ij}u_{jk}$ products from all elements of each submatrix before computing a new row and column, we would have formed partial sums for each element as we progressed through the calculations. The sample calculation above shows that we would have formed a'_{43} while working on the 3×3 submatrix before computing the second row and second column and we would have formed a''_{43} while working on the 2×2 submatrix before computing the third row and third column. This technique for computing the new elements incrementally has programming advantages. The decomposition algorithm applied to the sparse matrix is a variation of the method described by Doolittle [4]. It is shown as an algorithm in Figure 11.5 and programmed in the solution algorithm of Section 11.1.3. We will illustrate the algorithm with a hand computation in that section. This algo-

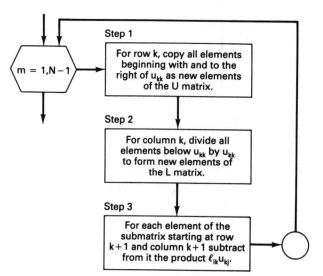

Figure 11.5 LU decomposition algorithm.

rithm is mentioned now because we can show from it how fills are created; that is one of the reasons for the topic of this section.

Let us consider the following matrix, where the x's represent nonzero elements.

$$\begin{bmatrix} x & x & 0 & 0 \\ x & x & 0 & x \\ 0 & x & x & 0 \\ 0 & x & 0 & x \end{bmatrix} \blacktriangleright \begin{bmatrix} x & x & 0 & 0 \\ x & x & \textcircled{x} & x \\ 0 & x & x & \textcircled{x} \\ 0 & x & \textcircled{x} & x \end{bmatrix}$$

According to the algorithm of Figure 11.5, the zeros in row 1 and column 1 cannot be filled in. However, for the 3×3 submatrix, only element $a'_{23} = a_{23} - \ell_{21}u_{13} = 0 - \ell_{21}u_{13}$ is subject to fill-in. Since one of the two product factors happens to be zero, we will not have a fill-in for that element. Because it is much more work to determine this condition, and costly of time, we establish that if either of the factors is nonzero, fill-in will occur and we must provide storage space for it. For the 2×2 submatrix, elements $a''_{34} = a'_{34} - \ell_{32}u_{24} = 0 - \ell_{32}u_{24}$ and $a''_{43} = a'_{43} - \ell_{42}u_{23}$ are subject to fill-in and we must provide storage for them also. Element a''_{43} is subject to fill-in because a'_{23} could, in general, be filled in. We show the fill-ins as $\textcircled{x}$ in the matrix on the right. Because of the assumption we made above about possible individual product factors being zero, we note that the right-hand matrix is now symmetric. It is structurally symmetric but not numerically symmetric.

It is implicit that our matrix has no zero elements on the principal diagonal. This is our second assumption. Consequently, should any node renumbering take place, we must also renumber the rows accordingly to keep the diagonal element of that row on the diagonal. We do not select new pivots with this algorithm. The purpose in renumbering nodes is to arrange the matrix such that the fewest possible fills are created.

Because we did not compute new element values and because we did establish the matrix structure by allocating storage for fills, we have just created the *zero structure* symbolically.

Berry's algorithm appears in flowchart form in his paper [2]. We show a greatly simplified version of it in Figure 11.6. Figures 11.7, 11.8, and 11.9 are the parts of our macro that implement Parts I, II, and III, respectively. Figures 11.10 and 11.11 show the renumbering and fill insertion subroutines, respectively. Renumber is called from three different cells of the macro, rows 18, 52, and 58, while Insertfill is called from one cell only, row 47. Execution stops when the Halt function is reached in row 105 of Renumber. We used the variables of Berry's flowchart for correlation purposes.

Before-and-after contents of the arrays for our example data are shown in Figure 11.12. Arrays Ifill and ITA are work arrays. We copied data from the macro sheet of Section 11.1.1 to arrays of Figure 11.12(a) from which some arrays were then copied to their respective arrays of Figure 11.12(b) before execution began. Remember, we started with the matrix of Figure 11.4(a), which was re-

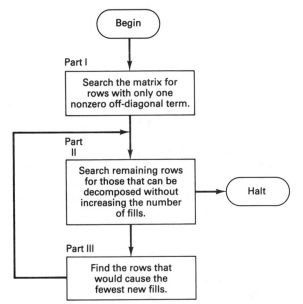

Figure 11.6 Simplified flowchart of Berry's algorithm. Adapted with permission from R. D. Berry, "An optimal ordering of electronic circuit equations for a sparse matrix solution, *IEEE Trans. Cir. Th.,* vol. CT-18, no. 1, January 1971, pp. 40–50. © 1971 IEEE.

	A	B
1		Decompose
2		LU decomposition and node renumbering.
3		Shortcut key = "d"
4	N	=INPUT("Enter the matrix order:",1)
5	IC	=0
6	ICS	=0
7	ICT	=0
8	Inserts	=0
9	IR	=0
10	IRO	=0
11	IRT	=0
12	Itest	=0
13	J	=0
14	K	=0
15	Load	=1
16		=FOR("ii",1,N,1)
17		=SET.VALUE(IR,INDEX(Iorder,ii))
18		=IF(INDEX(Numoff,IR)<=1,Renumber())
19		=NEXT()

Figure 11.7 Part I of the symbolic decomposition macro.

packed for our use as shown in Figure 11.4(b). The macro of this section merely renumbered nodes [compare array Iorder in Figures 11.4(b) and 11.12(b)] and inserted fills [note the data in rows 12 and 15 of array A in Figure 11.12(b)]. If we now rewrite the matrix in its traditional form, we have the following:

$$
\begin{bmatrix}
3 & 4 & -3 & 6 & 0 \\
3 & 6 & 0 & 2 & 2 \\
2 & 0 & 4 & 1 & -1 \\
5 & -1 & 4 & 1 & 4 \\
0 & -1 & 1 & -2 & 2
\end{bmatrix}
$$

where the boxed-off zeros are subject to fill-in.

We did not start out with a very sparse matrix. However, the node renumbering of Berry's algorithm applied to small sparse matrices usually generated no fills, a fact certainly in its favor, so we settled on the above example to generate fills.

11.1.3 Solving the Equations

Output from the symbolic LU decomposition macro is a symmetric matrix with possibly fills and possibly renumbered nodes. For convenience in writing the numeric LU decomposition and the forward-back substitution macros, and for

	A	B
20	PartII	
21	Loaded	=0
22		=SET.VALUE(IRO,Load)
23	Continue1	=SET.VALUE(IR,INDEX(Iorder,IRO))
24		=SET.VALUE(INDEX(Ifill,IRO),0)
25		=SET.VALUE(ICS,INDEX(IUR,IR+1)-1)
26		=SET.VALUE(ICT,INDEX(IUR,IR))
27	NUM	=0
28	Loop1	=SET.VALUE(IC,INDEX(IUC,ICT))
29		=IF(INDEX(Node,IC)<Load,GOTO(next.ICT))
30		=SET.VALUE(NUM,NUM+1)
31		=SET.VALUE(INDEX(ITA,NUM),IC)
32	next.ICT	=SET.VALUE(ICT,ICT+1)
33		=IF(ICT>ICS,,GOTO(Loop1))
34	I	=0
35	Continue2	=SET.VALUE(I,I+1)
36		=SET.VALUE(J,I+1)
37		=IF(J>NUM,GOTO(Continue5))
38	Continue3	=SET.VALUE(IRT,INDEX(ITA,I))
39		=SET.VALUE(IC,INDEX(ITA,J))
40		=SET.VALUE(ICS,INDEX(IUR,IRT+1)-1)
41		=SET.VALUE(ICT,INDEX(IUR,IRT))
42	Loop2	=IF(IC=INDEX(IUC,ICT),GOTO(Continue4))
43		=SET.VALUE(ICT,ICT+1)
44		=IF(ICT>ICS,,GOTO(Loop2))
45		=SET.VALUE(INDEX(Ifill,IRO),INDEX(Ifill,IRO)+1)
46		=IF(Inserts=1,,GOTO(Continue4))
47		=Insertfill()
48	Continue4	=IF(J=NUM,GOTO(Continue2))
49		=SET.VALUE(J,J+1)
50		=GOTO(Continue3)
51	Continue5	=IF(Inserts=1,,GOTO(Continue6))
52		=Renumber()
53		=SET.VALUE(Loaded,0)
54		=SET.VALUE(Inserts,0)
55		=GOTO(PartII) ·
56	Continue6	=IF(INDEX(Ifill,IRO)=0,,GOTO(Continue7))
57		=SET.VALUE(Loaded,1)
58		=Renumber()
59	Continue7	=SET.VALUE(IRO,IRO+1)
60		=IF(IRO>N,,GOTO(Continue1))
61		=IF(Loaded=0,,GOTO(PartII))

Figure 11.8   Part II of the symbolic decomposition macro.

	A	B
62	PartIII	=SET.VALUE(J,Load)
63	Continue8	=SET.VALUE(Itest,INDEX(Iorder,J))
64		=SET.VALUE(K,J+1)
65	Continue9	=IF(INDEX(Ifill,K)<INDEX(Ifill,J),,GOTO(Continue10))
66		=SET.VALUE(IR,INDEX(Iorder,K))
67		=SET.VALUE(INDEX(Iorder,K),Itest)
68		=SET.VALUE(INDEX(Iorder,J),IR)
69		=SET.VALUE(INDEX(Node,IR),J)
70		=SET.VALUE(INDEX(Node,Itest),K)
71		=SET.VALUE(Itest,IR)
72		=SET.VALUE(IR,INDEX(Ifill,K))
73		=SET.VALUE(INDEX(Ifill,K),INDEX(Ifill,J))
74		=SET.VALUE(INDEX(Ifill,J),IR)
75	Continue10	=SET.VALUE(K,K+1)
76		=IF(K>N,,GOTO(Continue9))
77		=IF(INDEX(Ifill,Load)=INDEX(Ifill,J),,GOTO(Continue11))
78		=SET.VALUE(J,J+1)
79		=IF(J>=N,,GOTO(Continue8))
80	Continue11	=SET.VALUE(Itest,INDEX(Iorder,Load))
81		=SET.VALUE(K,Load+1)
82	Continue12	=IF(K>J-1,,GOTO(Continue13))
83		=SET.VALUE(Inserts,1)
84		=GOTO(PartII)
85	Continue13	=SET.VALUE(IR,INDEX(Iorder,K))
86		=IF(INDEX(Numoff,IR)<=INDEX(Numoff,Itest),GOTO(Continue14))
87		=SET.VALUE(INDEX(Iorder,K),Itest)
88		=SET.VALUE(INDEX(Iorder,Load),IR)
89		=SET.VALUE(INDEX(Node,IR),Load)
90		=SET.VALUE(INDEX(Node,Itest),K)
91		=SET.VALUE(Itest,IR)
92	Continue14	=SET.VALUE(K,K+1)
93		=GOTO(Continue12)

Figure 11.9 Part III of the symbolic decomposition macro.

	A	B
94		Renumber
95	LoadIR	=0
96	Numfil	=0
97	Label1	=IF(INDEX(Node,IR)<Load,GOTO(Label4))
98	Itemp	=INDEX(Iorder,Load)
99	IROT	=INDEX(Node,IR)
100		=SET.VALUE(INDEX(Iorder,Load),IR)
101		=SET.VALUE(INDEX(Node,IR),Load)
102		=SET.VALUE(INDEX(Iorder,IROT),Itemp)
103		=SET.VALUE(INDEX(Node,Itemp),IROT)
104		=SET.VALUE(Load,Load+1)
105		=IF(Load>=N,HALT())
106		=SET.VALUE(ICS,INDEX(IUR,IR+1)-1)
107		=SET.VALUE(ICT,INDEX(IUR,IR))
108	Label2	=SET.VALUE(IR,INDEX(IUC,ICT))
109		=IF(INDEX(Node,IR)<Load,GOTO(Label3))
110		=SET.VALUE(INDEX(Numoff,IR),INDEX(Numoff,IR)-1)
111		=IF(INDEX(Numoff,IR)>1,GOTO(Label3))
112		=SET.VALUE(Numfil,Numfil+1)
113		=SET.VALUE(INDEX(ITA,Numfil),IR)
114	Label3	=SET.VALUE(ICT,ICT+1)
115		=IF(ICT>ICS,,GOTO(Label2))
116	Label4	=SET.VALUE(LoadIR,LoadIR+1)
117		=IF(LoadIR>Numfil,RETURN())
118		=SET.VALUE(IR,INDEX(ITA,LoadIR))
119		=GOTO(Label1)

Figure 11.10 Row renumbering function.

	A	B
120		Insertfill
121	KK	=0
122	Idown	=0
123		=SET.VALUE(Idown,INDEX(IUR,N+1)-INDEX(IUR,IRT+1))
124	L	=0
125		=SET.VALUE(KK,INDEX(IUR,N+1)-Idown)
126		=SELECT(INDEX(IUC,KK))
127		=INSERT(2)
128		=SET.VALUE(INDEX(Numoff,IRT),INDEX(Numoff,IRT)+1)
129		=SET.VALUE(INDEX(IUC,KK),IC)
130		=SELECT(INDEX(A,KK))
131		=INSERT(2)
132		=SET.VALUE(INDEX(A,KK),0)
133		=SET.VALUE(L,IRT)
134	Ins2	=SET.VALUE(L,L+1)
135		=SET.VALUE(INDEX(IUR,L),INDEX(IUR,L)+1)
136		=IF(L>N,,GOTO(Ins2))
137		=SET.VALUE(Idown,INDEX(IUR,N+1)-INDEX(IUR,IC+1))
138		=SET.VALUE(KK,INDEX(IUR,N+1)-Idown-1)
139		=SELECT(INDEX(IUC,KK))
140		=INSERT(2)
141		=SET.VALUE(INDEX(Numoff,IC),INDEX(Numoff,IC)+1)
142		=SET.VALUE(INDEX(IUC,KK),IRT)
143		=SELECT(INDEX(A,KK))
144		=INSERT(2)
145		=SET.VALUE(INDEX(A,KK),0)
146		=SET.VALUE(L,IC)
147	Ins4	=SET.VALUE(L,L+1)
148		=SET.VALUE(INDEX(IUR,L),INDEX(IUR,L)+1)
149		=IF(L>N,,GOTO(Ins4))
150		=RETURN()

Figure 11.11 Fill insertion function.

expository purposes, we will first rearrange the matrix entries and their pointers. The flowchart of Figure 11.13 for this purpose is implemented by the macro of Figure 11.14. There is no matrix computation in this routine, just pointer and data storage rearrangement. The operations are sequential whereby, first, we reorder the Diag, IUC, and A arrays according to the renumbered nodes. Then, because references to columns within a row are not necessarily in order, we use the Excel Sort function to order them properly so that we can compute according to the algorithm described in Section 11.1.2. Finally, we form IUR and prepare the Upack and Lpack arrays. Data before and after being processed by this macro are shown in Figure 11.15.

We will now work with data in the Diag (diagonal), Lpack (lower triangular), and Upack (upper triangular) arrays instead of in the Diag and A arrays only.

	N	O	P	Q	R	S	T
1	IUR-O	IUC-O	Iorder-O	Node-O	Numoff-O	Diag-O	A-O
2	1	2	1	1	3	3	6
3	4	3	2	2	4	1	4
4	8	4	3	3	3	6	-3
5	11	1	4	4	3	4	5
6	14	3	5	5	3	2	-1
7	17	4					4
8		5					4
9		1					3
10		2					2
11		5					2
12		1					2
13		2					1
14		5					-1
15		2					-2
16		3					-1
17		4					1

(a)

	D	E	F	G	H	I	J	K	L
1	IUR	IUC	Iorder	Node	Numoff	Ifill	ITA	ODiag	A
2	1	2	1	1	3	1	2	3	6
3	4	3	3	4	1	0	5	1	4
4	8	4	4	2	3	0	4	6	-3
5	12	1	2	3	2	1	5	4	5
6	16	3	5	5	1	2		2	-1
7	19	4							4
8		5							4
9		1							3
10		2							2
11		5							2
12		4							0
13		1							2
14		2							1
15		3							0
16		5							-1
17		2							-2
18		3							-1
19		4							1

(b)

Figure 11.12 Example data for symbolic LU decomposition and row renumbering computations: (a) Before execution and (b) after execution.

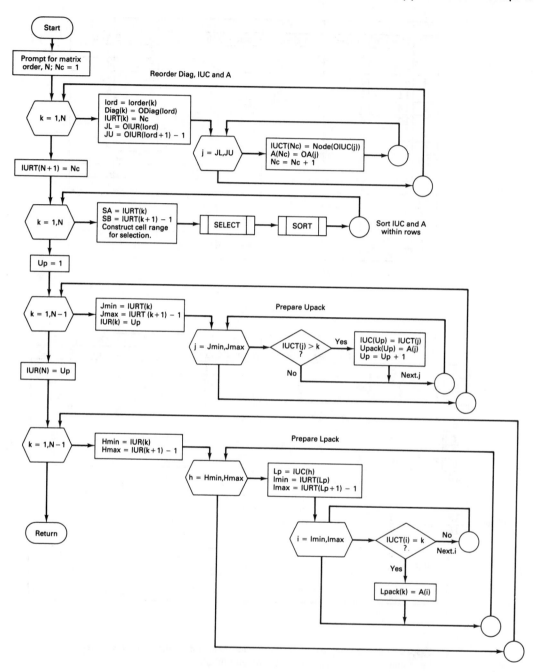

Figure 11.13 Flowchart for rearranging the matrix entries and their pointers.

	A	B
1		LUpack
2		Prepare reordered Diag, Upack, and Lpack arrays.
3		Shortcut key = "L"
4	N	=INPUT("Enter the matrix order:",1)
5	Nc	=1
6		=FOR("k",1,N,1)
7	Iord	=INDEX(Iorder,k)
8		=SET.VALUE(INDEX(Diag,k),INDEX(ODiag,Iord))
9		=SET.VALUE(INDEX(IURT,k),Nc)
10	JL	=INDEX(OIUR,Iord)
11	JU	=INDEX(OIUR,Iord+1)-1
12		=FOR("j",JL,JU,1)
13		=SET.VALUE(INDEX(IUCT,Nc),INDEX(Node,INDEX(OIUC,j)))
14		=SET.VALUE(INDEX(A,Nc),INDEX(OA,j))
15		=SET.VALUE(Nc,Nc+1)
16		=NEXT()
17		=NEXT()
18		=SET.VALUE(INDEX(IURT,N+1),Nc)
19		=FOR("k",1,N,1)
20	SA	=INDEX(IURT,k)
21	SB	=INDEX(IURT,k+1)-1
22		=SET.NAME("ColA",COLUMN(IUCT))
23		=SET.NAME("ColB",COLUMN(A))
24		=SET.NAME("RowA",DEREF(SA)+1)
25		=SET.NAME("RowB",DEREF(SB)+1)
26		=SELECT("R"&RowA&"C"&ColA&":R"&RowB&"C"&ColB)
27		=SORT(1,"IUCT",1)
28		=NEXT()
29	Up	=1
30		=FOR("k",1,N-1,1)
31	Jmin	=INDEX(IURT,k)
32	Jmax	=INDEX(IURT,k+1)-1
33		=SET.VALUE(INDEX(IUR,k),Up)
34		=FOR("j",Jmin,Jmax,1)
35		=IF(INDEX(IUCT,j)>k,,GOTO(Next.j))
36		=SET.VALUE(INDEX(IUC,Up),INDEX(IUCT,j))
37		=SET.VALUE(INDEX(Upack,Up),INDEX(A,j))
38		=SET.VALUE(Up,Up+1)
39	Next.j	=NEXT()
40		=NEXT()
41		=SET.VALUE(INDEX(IUR,N),Up)
42		=FOR("k",1,N-1)
43	Hmin	=INDEX(IUR,k)
44	Hmax	=INDEX(IUR,k+1)-1
45		=FOR("h",Hmin,Hmax,1)
46	Lp	=INDEX(IUC,h)
47	Imin	=INDEX(IURT,Lp)
48	Imax	=INDEX(IURT,Lp+1)-1
49		=FOR("i",Imin,Imax,1)
50		=IF(INDEX(IUCT,i)<>k,GOTO(Next.i))
51		=SET.VALUE(INDEX(Lpack,h),INDEX(A,i))
52		=BREAK()
53	Next.i	=NEXT()
54		=NEXT()
55		=NEXT()
56		=RETURN()

Figure 11.14 Macro implementing the flowchart of Figure 11.13.

	M	N	O	P	Q	R
1	OIUR	OIUC	Iorder	Node	ODiag	OA
2	1	2	1	1	3	6
3	4	3	3	4	1	4
4	8	4	4	2	6	-3
5	12	1	2	3	4	5
6	16	3	5	5	2	-1
7	19	4				4
8		5				4
9		1				3
10		2				2
11		5				2
12		4				0
13		1				2
14		2				1
15		3				0
16		5				-1
17		2				-2
18		3				-1
19		4				1

(a)

	D	E	F	G	H	I	J	K
1	IUR	IUC	Diag	Lpack	Upack	IURT	IUCT	A
2	1	2	3	3	4	1	2	4
3	4	3	6	2	-3	4	3	-3
4	7	4	4	5	6	8	4	6
5	9	3	1	0	0	12	1	3
6	10	4	2	-1	2	16	3	0
7		5		-1	2	19	4	2
8		4		4	1		5	2
9		5		1	-1		1	2
10		5		-2	4		2	0
11							4	1
12							5	-1
13							1	5
14							2	-1
15							3	4
16							5	4
17							2	-1
18							3	1
19							4	-2

(b)

Figure 11.15 (a) Before and (b) after data are rearranged with the macro of Figure 11.14.

Pointers in arrays IUR and IUC have the same meaning as before except that now, because of matrix symmetry, IUC entries apply to both the rows of Upack and the columns of Lpack. Node renumbering was accounted for during the repacking.

The LU decomposition algorithm was presented in flowchart form in Figure 11.5. It is shown in detail for numeric LU decomposition in Figure 11.16. The arrays being operated on are those produced by the macro of Figure 11.14. The numeric LU decomposition macro is shown in Figure 11.17 with example output in Figure 11.18. Since we are performing an in-place decomposition, there is no need for the copying operation of Step 1 of the flowchart of Figure 11.5. The FOR-NEXT loop of rows 15, 16, and 17 in Figure 11.17 performs the column division by the diagonal element of Step 2 in Figure 11.5. The subtraction of the row/column product term, Step 3 in Figure 11.5, is performed by the nested FOR-NEXT loops of rows 18 through 38 of Figure 11.17.

As promised in Section 11.1.2, here is a manual computation of numeric LU decomposition.

Given:

$$\begin{bmatrix} 3 & 4 & -3 & 6 & 0 \\ 3 & 6 & 0 & 2 & 2 \\ 2 & 0 & 4 & 1 & -1 \\ 5 & -1 & 4 & 1 & 4 \\ 0 & -1 & 1 & -2 & 2 \end{bmatrix}$$

where the boxed off zeros will be replaced by fills.

Pass 1:   Steps 1 and 2   Step 3

$$\begin{bmatrix} 3 & 4 & -3 & 6 & 0 \\ 1 & 6 & 0 & 2 & 2 \\ \frac{2}{3} & 0 & 4 & 1 & -1 \\ \frac{5}{3} & -1 & 4 & 1 & 4 \\ 0 & -1 & 1 & -2 & 2 \end{bmatrix} \blacktriangleright \begin{bmatrix} 3 & 4 & -3 & 6 & 0 \\ 1 & 2 & 3 & -4 & 2 \\ \frac{2}{3} & -\frac{8}{3} & 6 & -3 & -1 \\ \frac{5}{3} & -\frac{23}{3} & 9 & -9 & 4 \\ 0 & -1 & 1 & -2 & 2 \end{bmatrix}$$

Pass 2:   Steps 1 and 2   Step 3

$$\begin{bmatrix} 3 & 4 & -3 & 6 & 0 \\ 1 & 2 & 3 & -4 & 2 \\ \frac{2}{3} & -\frac{4}{3} & 6 & -3 & -1 \\ \frac{5}{3} & -\frac{23}{6} & 9 & -9 & 4 \\ 0 & -\frac{1}{2} & 1 & -2 & 2 \end{bmatrix} \blacktriangleright \begin{bmatrix} 3 & 4 & -3 & 6 & 0 \\ 1 & 2 & 3 & -4 & 2 \\ \frac{2}{3} & -\frac{4}{3} & 10 & -\frac{25}{3} & \frac{5}{3} \\ \frac{5}{3} & -\frac{23}{6} & \frac{41}{2} & -\frac{73}{3} & \frac{35}{3} \\ 0 & -\frac{1}{2} & \frac{5}{2} & -4 & 3 \end{bmatrix}$$

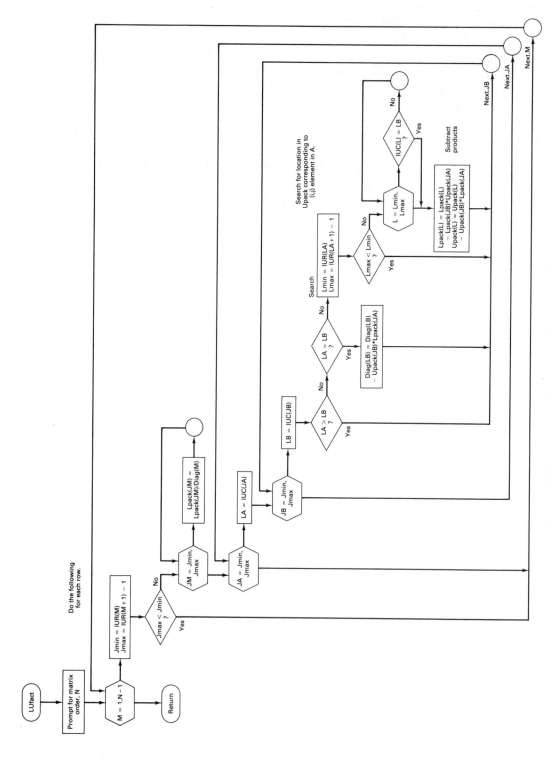

Figure 11.16 Flowchart for numeric LU decomposition.

	A	B
1		LUfact
2		Performs the LU decomposition
3		Shortcut key = "f"
4	N	=INPUT("Enter the matrix order:",1)
5	Jmin	=0
6	Jmax	=0
7	Lmin	=0
8	Lmax	=0
9	LA	=0
10	LB	=0
11		=FOR("M",1,N-1,1)
12		=SET.VALUE(Jmin,INDEX(IUR,M))
13		=SET.VALUE(Jmax,INDEX(IUR,M+1)-1)
14		=IF(Jmax<Jmin,GOTO(Next.M))
15		=FOR("JM",Jmin,Jmax,1)
16		=SET.VALUE(INDEX(Lpack,JM),INDEX(Lpack,JM)/INDEX(Diag,M))
17		=NEXT()
18		=FOR("JA",Jmin,Jmax,1)
19		=SET.VALUE(LA,INDEX(IUC,JA))
20		=FOR("JB",Jmin,Jmax,1)
21		=SET.VALUE(LB,INDEX(IUC,JB))
22		=IF(LA>LB,GOTO(Next.JB))
23		=IF(LA=LB,,GOTO(Search))
24	Partial1	=INDEX(Upack,JB)*INDEX(Lpack,JA)
25		=SET.VALUE(INDEX(Diag,LB),INDEX(Diag,LB)-Partial1)
26		=GOTO(Next.JB)
27	Search	=SET.VALUE(Lmin,INDEX(IUR,LA))
28		=SET.VALUE(Lmax,INDEX(IUR,LA+1)-1)
29		=IF(Lmax<Lmin,GOTO(Next.JB))
30		=FOR("L",Lmin,Lmax,1)
31		=IF(INDEX(IUC,L)=LB,BREAK())
32		=NEXT()
33	Partial2	=INDEX(Lpack,JB)*INDEX(Upack,JA)
34		=SET.VALUE(INDEX(Lpack,L),INDEX(Lpack,L)-Partial2)
35	Partial3	=INDEX(Upack,JB)*INDEX(Lpack,JA)
36		=SET.VALUE(INDEX(Upack,L),INDEX(Upack,L)-Partial3)
37	Next.JB	=NEXT()
38	Next.JA	=NEXT()
39	Next.M	=NEXT()
40		=RETURN()

Figure 11.17 Numeric LU decomposition macro.

Pass 3:   Steps 1 and 2   Step 3

$$
\begin{bmatrix}
3 & 4 & -3 & 6 & 0 \\
1 & 2 & 3 & -4 & 2 \\
\frac{2}{3} & -\frac{4}{3} & 10 & -\frac{25}{3} & \frac{5}{3} \\
\frac{5}{3} & -\frac{23}{6} & \frac{41}{20} & -\frac{73}{3} & \frac{35}{3} \\
0 & -\frac{1}{2} & \frac{1}{4} & -4 & 3
\end{bmatrix}
\blacktriangleright
\begin{bmatrix}
3 & 4 & -3 & 6 & 0 \\
1 & 2 & 3 & -4 & 2 \\
\frac{2}{3} & -\frac{4}{3} & 10 & -\frac{25}{3} & \frac{5}{3} \\
\frac{5}{3} & -\frac{23}{6} & \frac{41}{20} & -\frac{87}{12} & \frac{99}{12} \\
0 & -\frac{1}{2} & \frac{1}{4} & \frac{23}{12} & \frac{31}{12}
\end{bmatrix}
$$

Pass 4:   Steps 1 and 2   Step 3

$$
\begin{bmatrix}
3 & 4 & -3 & 6 & 0 \\
1 & 2 & 3 & -4 & 2 \\
\frac{2}{3} & -\frac{4}{3} & 10 & -\frac{25}{3} & \frac{5}{3} \\
\frac{5}{3} & -\frac{23}{6} & \frac{41}{20} & -\frac{87}{12} & \frac{99}{12} \\
0 & -\frac{1}{2} & \frac{1}{4} & \frac{23}{87} & \frac{31}{12}
\end{bmatrix}
\blacktriangleright
\begin{bmatrix}
3 & 4 & -3 & 6 & 0 \\
1 & 2 & 3 & -4 & 2 \\
\frac{2}{3} & -\frac{4}{3} & 10 & -\frac{25}{3} & \frac{5}{3} \\
\frac{5}{3} & -\frac{23}{6} & \frac{41}{20} & -\frac{87}{12} & \frac{99}{12} \\
0 & -\frac{1}{2} & \frac{1}{4} & \frac{23}{87} & \frac{35}{87}
\end{bmatrix}
$$

The **L** and **U** matrices of our example are now determined.

Our matrix **A** is numerically decomposed into the Lpack, Upack, and Diag arrays of Figure 11.18. We are ready to solve the set of equations for the unknowns given a right-hand-side vector. First, let us review how this will be done via a forward and back substitution technique.

This is the matrix equation we are to solve.

$$\mathbf{Ax} = \mathbf{LUx} = \mathbf{L(Ux)} = \mathbf{Ly} = \mathbf{b}$$

We will first solve **Ly** = **b** for **y**. Then, we will solve **Ux** = **y** for **x**. For a fourth-order system, we have

$$
\mathbf{Ly} =
\begin{bmatrix}
1 & 0 & 0 & 0 \\
\ell_{21} & 1 & 0 & 0 \\
\ell_{31} & \ell_{32} & 1 & 0 \\
\ell_{41} & \ell_{42} & \ell_{43} & 1
\end{bmatrix}
\begin{bmatrix}
y_1 \\ y_2 \\ y_3 \\ y_4
\end{bmatrix}
= \mathbf{b} =
\begin{bmatrix}
b_1 \\ b_2 \\ b_3 \\ b_4
\end{bmatrix}
$$

where the b_i's must be ordered according to the renumbered nodes. We can immediately write

$$y_1 = b_1$$

$$y_2 = b_2 - \ell_{21}y_1$$

$$y_3 = b_3 - \ell_{31}y_1 - \ell_{32}y_2$$

$$y_4 = b_4 - \ell_{41}y_1 - \ell_{42}y_2 - \ell_{43}y_3$$

	D	E	F	G	H
1	IUR	IUC	Diag	Lpack	Upack
2	1	2	3	1	4
3	4	3	2	0.6666666666	-3
4	7	4	10	1.6666666666	6
5	9	3	-7.25	-1.333333333	3
6	10	4	0.4022988505	-3.833333333	-4
7		5		-0.5	2
8		4		2.05	-8.333333333
9		5		0.25	1.6666666666
10		5		0.2643678160	8.25

Figure 11.18 Results from the numeric LU decomposition macro of Figure 11.17.

We have just performed the forward substitution step and now have numerical values for the y_i's. We can solve for the x_i's from the following:

$$\mathbf{Ux} = \begin{bmatrix} u_{11} & u_{12} & u_{13} & u_{14} \\ 0 & u_{22} & u_{23} & u_{24} \\ 0 & 0 & u_{33} & u_{34} \\ 0 & 0 & 0 & u_{44} \end{bmatrix} \begin{bmatrix} x_1 \\ x_2 \\ x_3 \\ x_4 \end{bmatrix} = \mathbf{y} = \begin{bmatrix} y_1 \\ y_2 \\ y_3 \\ y_4 \end{bmatrix}$$

We see that

$$x_4 = \frac{y_4}{u_{44}}$$

$$x_3 = \frac{y_3 - u_{34}x_4}{u_{33}}$$

$$x_2 = \frac{y_2 - u_{23}x_3 - u_{24}x_4}{u_{22}}$$

$$x_1 = \frac{y_1 - u_{12}x_2 - u_{13}x_3 - u_{14}x_4}{u_{11}}$$

The back substitution step is finished and there are numerical values for our solution, the x_i's. Of course, we must now relate these numerical values to the originally numbered nodes.

The flowchart for performing the forward and back substitution is shown in Figure 11.19; its macro is in Figure 11.20. Data used for this macro is in Figure 11.21(a) with the final result, in array B, seen in Figure 11.21(b). We leave it to the reader to reconcile the results with the original nodes.

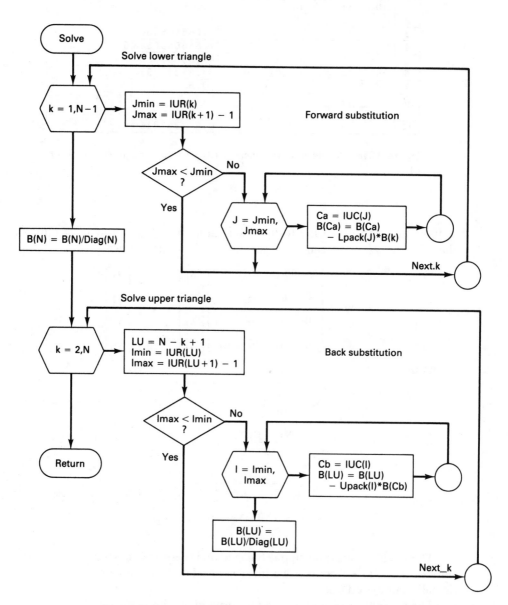

Figure 11.19 Flowchart for performing the forward and back substitution.

	A	B
1		Solve
2		Performs the forward and back substitution.
3		Shortcut key = "s"
4	N	=INPUT("Enter the matrix order:",1)
5		=FOR("k",1,N-1,1)
6	Jmin	=INDEX(IUR,k)
7	Jmax	=INDEX(IUR,k+1)-1
8		=IF(Jmax<Jmin,GOTO(Next.k))
9		=FOR("J",Jmin,Jmax,1)
10	Ca	=INDEX(IUC,J)
11	Tmp1	=INDEX(Lpack,J)*INDEX(B,k)
12		=SET.VALUE(INDEX(B,Ca),INDEX(B,Ca)-Tmp1)
13		=NEXT()
14	Next.k	=NEXT()
15		=SET.VALUE(INDEX(B,N),INDEX(B,N)/INDEX(Diag,N))
16		=FOR("k",2,N,1)
17	LU	=N-k+1
18	Imin	=INDEX(IUR,LU)
19	Imax	=INDEX(IUR,LU+1)-1
20		=IF(Imax<Imin,GOTO(Next_k))
21		=FOR("I",Imin,Imax,1)
22	Cb	=INDEX(IUC,I)
23	Tmp2	=INDEX(Upack,I)*INDEX(B,Cb)
24		=SET.VALUE(INDEX(B,LU),INDEX(B,LU)-Tmp2)
25		=NEXT()
26		=SET.VALUE(INDEX(B,LU),INDEX(B,LU)/INDEX(Diag,LU))
27	Next_k	=NEXT()
28		=RETURN()

Figure 11.20   Macro for Figure 11.19.

11.1.4 Discussion

This completes our presentation of the Excel implementation of a sparse matrix routine. We did not associate the computed values with the original vector of unknowns, but this is a trivial task anyway. We did not set out to construct an integrated routine, but the five macros we developed well illustrate the manipulation of sparse matrices.

We deliberately partitioned the task into easily identifiable segments to point out the following important characteristics of the LU solution scheme and use of the zero structure computation.

1. Many problems require multiple calculations of the system of equations because of different values for components that affect the matrix nonzero en-

	D	E	F	G	H	I
1	IUR	IUC	Diag	Lpack	Upack	B
2	1	2	3	1	4	2
3	4	3	2	0.6666666666	-3	1
4	7	4	10	1.6666666666	6	-3
5	9	3	-7.25	-1.333333333	3	0
6	10	4	0.4022988505	-3.833333333	-4	0
7		5		-0.5	2	
8		4		2.05	-8.333333333	
9		5		0.25	1.6666666666	
10		5		0.2643678160	8.25	

(a)

	D	E	F	G	H	I
1	IUR	IUC	Diag	Lpack	Upack	B
2	1	2	3	1	4	2.0171428571
3	4	3	2	0.6666666666	-3	-0.177142857
4	7	4	10	1.6666666666	6	-1.582857142
5	9	3	-7.25	-1.333333333	3	-1.348571428
6	10	4	0.4022988505	-3.833333333	-4	-0.645714285
7		5		-0.5	2	
8		4		2.05	-8.333333333	
9		5		0.25	1.6666666666	
10		5		0.2643678160	8.25	

(b)

Figure 11.21 (a) Data prior to performing the forward and back substitution and (b) the final result.

tries. Consequently, the matrix zero structure does not change and does not have to be recomputed for each solution. New values for the A matrix must be computed and the solution continued as described in Section 11.1.3. This situation occurs when computing the frequency response of a system that contains frequency dependent components. It can also occur when making a transient analysis on a system that contains nonlinear components whose values are computed by a linearization scheme for use in iterative computations to achieve convergence.

2. Many problems require multiple calculations of the same system but subject to different forcing functions. In these cases, only the right-hand side of the matrix equation changes. Therefore, only the forward and back substitution steps need be repeated on the LU matrices already determined.

Our Excel implementation shows the correspondence between it and the implementation of the algorithm in traditional computer languages. Berry's algorithm was published in flowchart form that incorporated FORTRAN statements. We find it awkward to use the SET.VALUE function to store values and INDEX functions for array referencing and cannot help but be concerned about the extra time used to evaluate them. But, since Excel operates in an interpretive mode, we should not expect as much performance as from a compiled program.

We could have spent more time exploiting the features of Excel. An obvious adaptation occurred in subroutine Insertfill of the symbolic LU decomposition macro in Section 11.1.2 where we used a cell select and cell insert scheme for entering fill locations instead of moving array values down in a loop to make room for the fill. However, execution time would have been shorter if we had inserted the fills in the traditional way of array manipulation.

It would also be wise to check for errors and include error messages, especially in those routines that work directly with the input data.

11.2 HIDDEN-LINE ELIMINATION PLOTTING

Plotted surfaces of experimental or computed values are often required. No Excel chart format addresses this need. But because the scatter chart format allows us to plot x-y pairs, we should be able to use it for general plotting purposes. A common surface graph appears as if a cargo net, or mesh, were shaped to form the surface. A variation on this method uses two-dimensional curves displaced in the depth direction to achieve a similar effect. It is this variation that we implement in macro form in Excel to demonstrate the possibilities of using Excel for general graphics purposes.

11.2.1 The Algorithm

We implement most of the algorithm given in FORTRAN as ACM Algorithm 420 by Williamson [13]. Since, in this example, we are more interested in demonstrating curve plotting possibilities with Excel, we omit plotting a title, a border, and the axes. Limitations or inconveniences of Excel cause us, at times, to modify Williamson's algorithm. Because most of what we have done follows his algorithm, we do not show a detailed flowchart of the resulting macro. Instead, we have prepared the functional flowchart shown in Figure 11.22. Block labels of the figure correspond with those of macro Hide.curve of Figure 11.23.

The idea of the algorithm is to plot the foreground curve first. It is also saved to become the current visual maximum (or minimum) function. Then, by stepping subsequent curves for lateral displacement and to simulate depth, we determine the portions of each curve that exceed the current visual maximum (or minimum) function and plot those segments only. Continuing in this manner ultimately produces the plot, which has hidden-lines eliminated and that has a three-dimensional appearance, as shown in Figure 11.24. This is the closed loop step response of a second-order system given by

$$y(\zeta,t) = 1 - \frac{1}{\sqrt{1-\zeta^2}}\, e^{-\zeta\omega t} \sin(\omega_n\sqrt{1-\zeta^2}\, t + \psi)$$

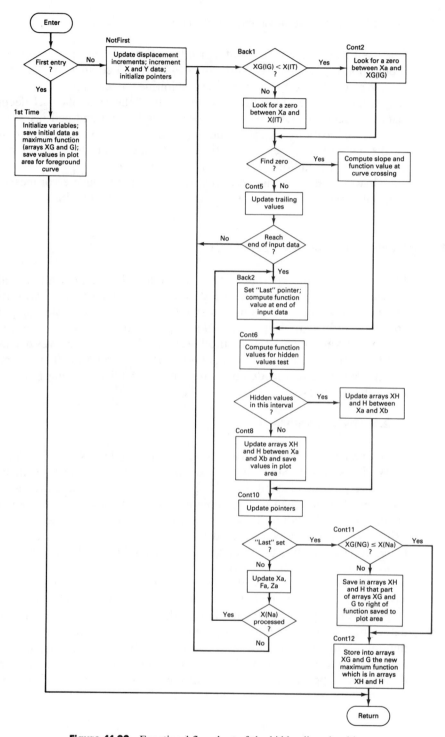

Figure 11.22 Functional flowchart of the hidden-line algorithm.

	A	**B**
1		Hide.curve
2		Hidden line elimination macro (Hugh Williamson).
3		=ARGUMENT("Na")
4		=ARGUMENT("NFNS")
5		=ARGUMENT("DXIN")
6		=ARGUMENT("DYIN")
7		=ARGUMENT("Sign")
8		=ARGUMENT("First")
9		=IF(First>0,GOTO(NotFirst))
10	YZ	=INDEX(Y,1)-DYIN
11	1stTime	=FOR("j",1,Na,1)
12		=SET.VALUE(INDEX(XG,j+2),INDEX(X,j))
13		=SET.VALUE(INDEX(G,j+2),Sign*INDEX(Y,j))
14		=NEXT()
15	EPS	=0.000001
16	NG	=Na+4
17		=SET.VALUE(INDEX(XG,1),-(NFNS-1)*DXIN-ABS(INDEX(XG,3))-1)
18		=SET.VALUE(INDEX(XG,2),INDEX(XG,3)-EPS)
19		=SET.VALUE(INDEX(XG,Na+3),INDEX(XG,Na+2)+EPS)
20		=IF(Sign<0,SET.VALUE(YZ,INDEX(Y,1)+DYIN))
21		=SET.VALUE(INDEX(G,1),YZ)
22		=SET.VALUE(INDEX(G,2),YZ)
23		=SET.VALUE(INDEX(G,Na+3),YZ)
24		=SET.VALUE(INDEX(G,NG),YZ)
25		=Pdata(X,Y,1,Na,1)
26	DXKK	=0
27	DYKK	=0
28		=RETURN()
29	NotFirst	=SET.VALUE(INDEX(XG,NG),INDEX(X,Na))
30		=SET.VALUE(DXKK,DXKK+DXIN)
31		=SET.VALUE(DYKK,DYKK+DYIN)
32		=FOR("j",1,Na,1)
33		=SET.VALUE(INDEX(X,j),INDEX(X,j)-DXKK)
34		=SET.VALUE(INDEX(Y,j),Sign*(INDEX(Y,j)+DYKK))
35		=NEXT()
36	JJ	=T.Lookup(INDEX(X,1),XG,1)
37		=FOR("j",1,JJ,1)
38		=SET.VALUE(INDEX(XH,j),INDEX(XG,j))
39		=SET.VALUE(INDEX(H,j),INDEX(G,j))
40		=NEXT()

Figure 11.23   Hidden-line elimination macro.

	A	B
41	IG	=JJ+1
42		=SET.VALUE(INDEX(XH,IG),INDEX(X,1))
43	Temp1	=Fctn(INDEX(X,1),INDEX(XG,JJ),INDEX(G,JJ),INDEX(XG,IG),INDEX(G,IG))
44		=SET.VALUE(INDEX(H,IG),Temp1)
45	IndexG	=JJ
46	IndexT	=1
47	Za	=INDEX(X,1)
48	Fa	=INDEX(H,IG)-INDEX(Y,1)
49	IT	=2
50		=SET.VALUE(JJ,IG)
51		=IF(INDEX(H,IG)>=INDEX(Y,1),GOTO(Cont1))
52		=SET.VALUE(JJ,IG+1)
53		=SET.VALUE(INDEX(XH,JJ),Za+EPS)
54		=SET.VALUE(INDEX(H,JJ),INDEX(Y,1))
55	Cont1	
56	Last	=0
57	Xa	=Za
58	Back1	=IF(INDEX(XG,IG)<INDEX(X,IT),GOTO(Cont2))
59	Iwhich	=0
60	Xb	=INDEX(X,IT)
61	Temp2	=Fctn(Xb,INDEX(XG,IG-1),INDEX(G,IG-1),INDEX(XG,IG),INDEX(G,IG))
62	Fb	=Temp2-INDEX(Y,IT)
63		=SET.VALUE(IT,IT+1)
64		=GOTO(Cont3)
65	Cont2	=SET.VALUE(Iwhich,1)
66		=SET.VALUE(Xb,INDEX(XG,IG))
67	Temp3	=Fctn(Xb,INDEX(X,IT-1),INDEX(Y,IT-1),INDEX(X,IT),INDEX(Y,IT))
68		=SET.VALUE(Fb,INDEX(G,IG)-Temp3)
69		=SET.VALUE(IG,IG+1)
70	Cont3	=IF(Fa*Fb>0,GOTO(Cont5))
71		=IF(Fa=Fb,GOTO(Cont5))
72	Slope	=(Fb-Fa)/(Xb-Xa)
73	JG	=IG-1-Iwhich
74	JT	=IT-2+Iwhich
75		=IF(ABS(Slope)>0.000001,GOTO(Cont4))
76	Zb	=Xb
77		=GOTO(Cont6)
78	Cont4	=SET.VALUE(Zb,Xa-Fa/Slope)
79		=GOTO(Cont6)
80	Cont5	=SET.VALUE(Xa,Xb)
81		=SET.VALUE(Fa,Fb)
82		=IF(IT<=Na,GOTO(Back1))

Figure 11.23   (Continued)

	A	B
83	Back2	=SET.VALUE(Last,1)
84		=SET.VALUE(Zb,INDEX(X,Na))
85		=SET.VALUE(JG,T.Lookup(Zb,XG,IndexG))
86		=SET.VALUE(JG,IndexG+JG-1)
87		=SET.VALUE(JT,Na-1)
88	Cont6	
89	ZZ	=0.99*Za+0.01*Zb
90	Kt	=T.Lookup(ZZ,X,IndexT)
91	Kg	=T.Lookup(ZZ,XG,IndexG)
92	Temp4	=Fctn(ZZ,INDEX(X,Kt),INDEX(Y,Kt),INDEX(X,Kt+1),INDEX(Y,Kt+1))
93	Temp5	=Fctn(ZZ,INDEX(XG,Kg),INDEX(G,Kg),INDEX(XG,Kg+1),INDEX(G,Kg+1))
94		=IF(Temp4>Temp5,GOTO(Cont8))
95		=IF(IndexG=JG,GOTO(Cont7))
96		=FOR("i",IndexG+1,JG,1)
97		=SET.VALUE(JJ,JJ+1)
98		=SET.VALUE(INDEX(XH,JJ),INDEX(XG,i))
99		=SET.VALUE(INDEX(H,JJ),INDEX(G,i))
100		=NEXT()
101	Cont7	=SET.VALUE(JJ,JJ+1)
102		=SET.VALUE(INDEX(XH,JJ),Zb)
103	Temp6	=Fctn(Zb,INDEX(XG,JG),INDEX(G,JG),INDEX(XG,JG+1),INDEX(G,JG+1))
104		=SET.VALUE(INDEX(H,JJ),Temp6)
105		=GOTO(Cont10)
106	Cont8	
107	Ngraph	=JT-IndexT+2
108	Nb	=JJ
109		=IF(Ngraph=2,GOTO(Cont9))
110		=FOR("i",IndexT+1,JT,1)
111		=SET.VALUE(JJ,JJ+1)
112		=SET.VALUE(INDEX(XH,JJ),INDEX(X,i))
113		=SET.VALUE(INDEX(H,JJ),INDEX(Y,i))
114		=NEXT()
115	Cont9	=SET.VALUE(JJ,JJ+1)
116		=SET.VALUE(INDEX(XH,JJ),Zb)
117	Temp7	=Fctn(Zb,INDEX(X,JT),INDEX(Y,JT),INDEX(X,JT+1),INDEX(Y,JT+1))
118		=SET.VALUE(INDEX(H,JJ),Temp7)
119		=Pdata(XH,H,Nb,Ngraph,Sign)
120	Cont10	=SET.VALUE(IndexT,JT)
121		=SET.VALUE(IndexG,JG)
122		=IF(Last=1,GOTO(Cont11))
123		=SET.VALUE(Xa,Xb)
124		=SET.VALUE(Fa,Fb)
125		=SET.VALUE(Za,Zb)
126		=IF(IT<=Na,GOTO(Back1),GOTO(Back2))

Figure 11.23   (Continued)

	A	B
127	Cont11	=IF(INDEX(XG,NG)<=INDEX(XG,NG-1),SET.VALUE(NG,NG-1))
128		=IF(INDEX(XG,NG)<=INDEX(X,Na),GOTO(Cont12))
129		=SET.VALUE(INDEX(XH,JJ+1),INDEX(XH,JJ)+EPS)
130		=SET.VALUE(JJ,JJ+1)
131	Temp8	=INDEX(X,Na)
132	Temp9	=Fctn(Temp8,INDEX(XG,JG),INDEX(G,JG),INDEX(XG,JG+1),INDEX(G,JG+1))
133		=SET.VALUE(INDEX(H,JJ),Temp9)
134		=FOR("j",JG+1,NG,1)
135		=SET.VALUE(JJ,JJ+1)
136		=SET.VALUE(INDEX(XH,JJ),INDEX(XG,j))
137		=SET.VALUE(INDEX(H,JJ),INDEX(G,j))
138		=NEXT()
139	Cont12	=SET.VALUE(NG,JJ+2)
140		=FOR("i",1,JJ,1)
141		=SET.VALUE(INDEX(G,i),INDEX(H,i))
142		=SET.VALUE(INDEX(XG,i),INDEX(XH,i))
143		=NEXT()
144		=SET.VALUE(INDEX(XG,JJ+1),INDEX(XG,JJ)+EPS)
145		=SET.VALUE(INDEX(G,JJ+1),DYKK)
146		=IF(Sign<0,SET.VALUE(INDEX(G,JJ+1),YZ+DYKK))
147		=SET.VALUE(INDEX(G,NG),INDEX(G,JJ+1))
148		=RETURN()

Figure 11.23   (Continued)

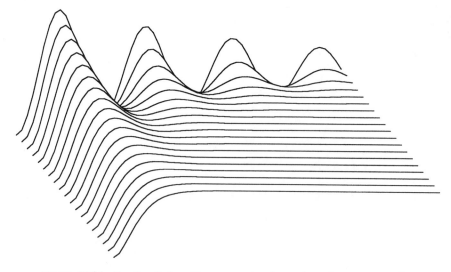

Figure 11.24   Family of closed-loop second-order system step responses for $.05 < \zeta < .95$.

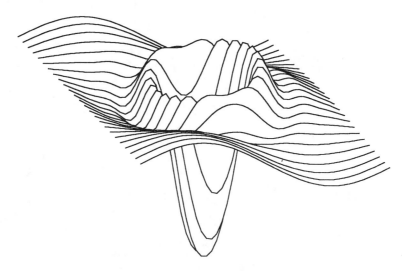

Figure 11.25   Williamson's example plotted with the macro of Figure 11.23.

where

$$\psi = \tan^{-1} \frac{\sqrt{1 - \zeta^2}}{\zeta}$$

Figure 11.25 is the example of Williamson's paper showing visible maximum and minimum features of the equation

$$y(z) = y_o \cos(z) - 1.5 e^{-((x-\pi)^2 + (z-\pi)^2)} \cos(1.75((x - \pi)^2 + (z - \pi)^2))$$

We can describe the algorithm with the aid of Figure 11.26 where we show two piecewise linear functions G and Y, represented as arrays with the same names in the macro. G is our current visual maximum function while Y is the next function to be tested for contributions to a new visual maximum function. We will advance our test in the direction of the increasing X and XG axes, also arrays with the same names in the macro. The figure shows that the test, already in progress, requires computation of the difference between the two functions, G − Y, to determine the intervals within which one or the other function is the maximum. The arrows indicate whether the difference is negative (down arrow), in which case Y is the greater, or positive (up arrow), in which case G is the greater. The product of advancing pairs of these differences will be negative, signifying that the curves crossed between their computed locations, or positive, signifying that the curves did not cross. The differences are computed only at the abscissa values of X and XG, with linear interpolation used to compute the corresponding value of Y or G if the abscissa values in the X and XG arrays are not equal at that point.

When the curves cross, we then delineate the abscissa range by computing its new crossing point coordinates (we already know the previous crossing point

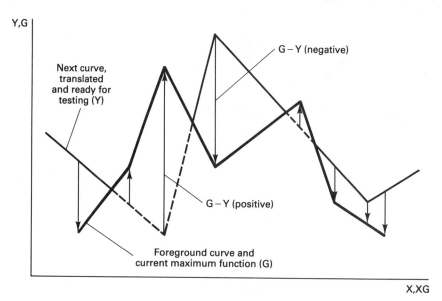

Figure 11.26   Hidden-line elimination macro principle.

coordinates) and make a calculation to determine which curve is the greater in this range. If the Y curve is the greater, we will modify the new visual maximum function, which is being formed in arrays XH and H, by adding the values of Y to it and by also adding them to the plot arrays XPlot and YPlot. If the G curve is the greater, we copy the relevant portion of it to the new visual maximum function but do not add it to the plot arrays, since it has already been plotted. We then continue progressing along the Y and G curves until reaching their ends. Upon completion, we plot the new contribution to the visual maximum function and save the new maximum function as the current one and begin the computation again for a new Y curve, if desired.

11.2.2 The Macro Implementation

The Hide.curve function macro does not compute the function to be plotted nor does it do the plotting. Command macros, called drivers, are used for the function computation. Macros Test.2ndO, for the second-order system, and Test.A420, for Williamson's example, are shown in Figures 11.27 and 11.28, respectively. The Make.plot macro of Figure 11.29, called from Test.2ndO and Test.A420, plots the new visual maximum function increments computed during the last call to Hide.curve. The function macros of Figure 11.30 are used for linear interpolation (Fctn), table lookup (T.Lookup), and for building the plot file for new visual maximum function increments (Pdata). Comments on our macros follow.

	D	E
1		Test.2ndO
2		Driver for 2nd order closed loop response to step function.
3		Shortcut key = "s"
4	curves	=19
5	stpX	=0.1
6	stpY	=0.1
7	mm	=0
8	delZ	=0.05
9	zeta	=0.95
10	wn	=4
11	delT	0.1
12		=FOR("m",1,curves,1)
13		=SET.VALUE(xypt,0)
14	t	=0
15		=FOR("p",1,60,1)
16		=SET.VALUE(INDEX(X,p),(p-1)/10)
17	rad	=SQRT(1-zeta^2)
18	angle	=wn*rad*t+ATAN(rad/zeta)
19		=SET.VALUE(INDEX(Y,p),1-1/rad*EXP(-zeta*wn*t)*SIN(angle))
20		=SET.VALUE(t,t+delT)
21		=NEXT()
22		=Hide.curve(60,curves,stpX,stpY,1,mm)
23		=Make.plot()
24		=SET.VALUE(mm,1)
25		=SET.VALUE(zeta,zeta-delZ)
26		=NEXT()
27		=RETURN()

Figure 11.27   Driver to produce the plot of Figure 11.24.

Test.2ndO and Test.A420.   Test.2ndO is a straightforward implementation of the formula of Section 11.2.1. We step ζ within an external FOR-NEXT loop to compute 19 curves. After setting up the pointers for plot curve storage, we compute 60 values for each curve by stepping the time t within the internal FOR-NEXT loop, after which we call Hide.curve followed by Make.plot. Test.A420 is similar to Test.2ndO except that it is executed twice so as to plot the minimum curves also. Variable Sgn is changed from $+1$ (for the maximum curves) to -1 (for the minimum curves). We use the chart window for storage of the maximum curves, to which we then add the minimum curves.

Hide.curve.   We retained variable names from Williamson's paper to the extent possible. The principal variables are defined in Table 11.1. The first time we enter Hide.curve we save the input function from arrays X and Y, the foreground curve, as the current visual maximum (or minimum) function in arrays XG and G. Subsequent entries cause new visual maximum function increments to be

	D	E
74		Test.A420
75		Driver for Williamsons' example.
76		Shortcut key = "w"
77	Sgn	=1
78	numcrv	=25
79	Step	=PI()/25
80		=SET.VALUE(INDEX(XR,1),0)
81		=SET.VALUE(INDEX(YR,1),0)
82		=FOR("m",2,50,1)
83	Tmp	=INDEX(XR,m-1)+Step
84		=SET.VALUE(INDEX(XR,m),Tmp)
85		=SET.VALUE(INDEX(YR,m),0.2*SIN(INDEX(XR,m)))
86		=NEXT()
87		=FOR("ij",1,2,1)
88	kk	=0
89	z	=0
90		=SET.VALUE(Step,PI()/12.5)
91		=FOR("m",1,numcrv,1)
92		=SET.VALUE(xypt,0)
93	CZ	=COS(Z)
94		=FOR("p",1,50,1)
95	Const	=(Z-PI())^2
96	Aux	=(INDEX(XR,p)-PI())^2+Const
97		=SET.VALUE(INDEX(Y,p),INDEX(YR,p)*CZ-1.5*EXP(-Aux)*COS(1.75*Aux))
98		=SET.VALUE(INDEX(X,p),INDEX(XR,p))
99		=NEXT()
100		=Hide.curve(50,numcrv,Step/2,Step/5,Sgn,kk)
101		=Make.plot()
102		=SET.VALUE(kk,1)
103		=SET.VALUE(Z,Z+Step)
104		=NEXT()
105		=SET.VALUE(Sgn,-1)
106		=NEXT()
107		=RETURN()

Figure 11.28 Driver to produce the plot of Figure 11.25.

	D	E
109		Make.plot
110		Plots multiple curves.
111		=IF(xypt<=1,RETURN())
112		=ACTIVATE("EX11P2A.XLM")
113		=SET.NAME("ColA",COLUMN(XPlot))
114		=SET.NAME("ColB",COLUMN(YPlot))
115		=SET.NAME("RowA",ROW(INDEX(XPlot,1,1)))
116		=SET.NAME("RowB",ROW(INDEX(XPlot,xypt,1)))
117		=SELECT("R"&RowA&"C"&ColA&":R"&RowB&"C"&ColB)
118		=COPY()
119		=ACTIVATE("EX11P2A.XLC")
120		=PASTE.SPECIAL(2,FALSE,TRUE,FALSE)
121		=RETURN()

Figure 11.29 Macro for plotting new maximum function increments.

	D	E
29		Fctn
30		Linear interpolation function
31		=ARGUMENT("AA")
32		=ARGUMENT("BB")
33		=ARGUMENT("CC")
34		=ARGUMENT("DD")
35		=ARGUMENT("EE")
36	Fval	=CC+(AA-BB)*(EE-CC)/(DD-BB)
37		=RETURN(Fval)
38		
39		T.Lookup
40		Table lookup function
41		=ARGUMENT("XF")
42		=ARGUMENT("XTBL",64)
43		=ARGUMENT("ptr")
44	Ind	=ptr+1
45	Adv	=IF(XF<=INDEX(XTBL,Ind),GOTO(NxtT))
46		=SET.VALUE(Ind,Ind+1)
47		=GOTO(Adv)
48	NxtT	=IF(XF<INDEX(XTBL,Ind),,GOTO(EndLK))
49		=SET.VALUE(Ind,Ind-1)
50	EndLK	=RETURN(Ind)
51		
52		Pdata
53		Builds plot file.
54		=ARGUMENT("XP",64)
55		=ARGUMENT("YP",64)
56		=ARGUMENT("LL")
57		=ARGUMENT("Len")
58		=ARGUMENT("Syn")
59		=IF(xypt=0,GOTO(Pd1))
60		=SET.VALUE(xypt,xypt+1)
61		=ACTIVATE("EX11P2A.XLM")
62		=SET.NAME("ColA",COLUMN(XPlot))
63		=SET.NAME("ColB",COLUMN(YPlot))
64		=SET.NAME("RowA",ROW(INDEX(XPlot,xypt,1)))
65		=SELECT("R"&RowA&"C"&ColA&":R"&RowA&"C"&ColB)
66		=CLEAR(1)
67	Pd1	=FOR("kpd",1,Len,1)
68		=SET.VALUE(INDEX(XPlot,xypt+kpd),INDEX(XP,kpd+LL-1))
69		=SET.VALUE(INDEX(YPlot,xypt+kpd),Syn*INDEX(YP,kpd+LL-1))
70		=NEXT()
71		=SET.VALUE(xypt,xypt+Len)
72		=RETURN()

Figure 11.30 Function macros for computation within Hide.curve.

TABLE 11.1 HIDE.CURVE VARIABLES

Williamson's variable	Excel variable	Function
IT	IT	Pointer for arrays X and Y.
IG	IG	Pointer for arrays XG and G.
X1	Xa	⎤ Abscissa values at which Fa and Fb, respectively, are calcu-
X2	Xb	⎦ lated.
F1	Fa	⎤
F2	Fb	⎦ G-Y values for curve crossing test purposes.
ITT	JT	⎤ Pointers for updating the visual maximum function for Y and G
IGG	JG	⎦ values respectively.
Z1	Za	⎤ Abscissa values for trailing and leading curve crossings respec-
Z2	Zb	⎦ tively.
ZZ	ZZ	Abscissa value at which to compute values on Y and G for visibility test purposes.
K1	Kt	⎤ Pointers to Y and G, respectively, for interpolating the values
K2	Kg	⎦ on the curves at ZZ.
IndexT	IndexT	⎤ Trailing pointers for use in copying from Y or G, respectively,
Index G	IndexG	⎦ to the new maximum function arrays XH and H.
N1	Na	Number of data points in the X and Y arrays during this call to Hide.curve.
JJ	JJ	Pointer for arrays XH and H.
X vs Y	X vs Y	The curve to be plotted during this call to Hide.curve.
XG vs G	XG vs G	The current visual maximum function.
XH vs H	XH vs H	Working arrays that hold the new visual maximum function as it is being developed.

computed and combined with current visual maximum function values to form a current visual maximum function for the next entry. Arrays X, Y, XG, and G are global variables.

The Hide.curve macro is shown in Figure 11.23. The first time entry code is in rows 11 through 27. On subsequent entries, we update values and initialize in rows 29 through 57. Then, in rows 59 through 64, we compute a value for G − Y when following the G curve while in rows 65 through 69 we do the same when following the Y curve. Testing for curve crossing is done in row 70. If the curves cross, we compute the crossing point abscissa in rows 72 through 79. Otherwise, we update pointers in rows 80 and 81 and either go back to row 58 or continue through rows 83 through 87 because we have reached the end of the Y curve. We are now ready to determine if the segment we have processed is visible and should be plotted or skipped in favor of the current visual maximum values.

In rows 88 through 93, we compute the values that determine whether a new visible part must be plotted according to the test of row 94. If it is not visible, we perform the operations of rows 95 through 105 to update the new visual maximum function. Otherwise, we perform the operations of rows 106 through 119 to up-

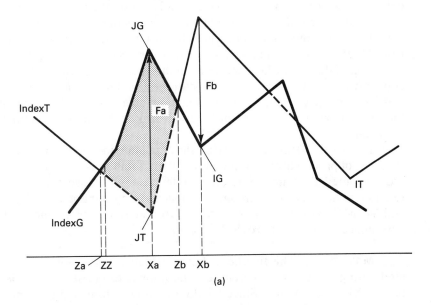

(a)

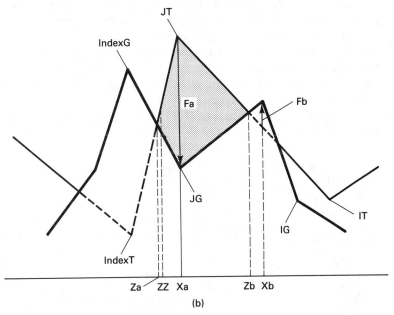

(b)

Figure 11.31   Snapshots of pointer locations after processing the curves for two consecutive intervals.

date the new visual maximum function and to enter the values in the plot array for later plotting. In either case, we update pointers in rows 120 and 121 and test for completion of input data processing. If not finished, we update more pointers in rows 123 through 125 and go back to either row 58 or row 83 to continue sweeping across our data. If finished, we perform the operations of rows 127 through 147 to copy any remaining values from the current visual maximum function (arrays XG and G) to the new visual maximum function (arrays XH and H), then finally copy the entire new visual maximum function back to XG and G for the next call to Hide.curve.

Figures 11.31(a) and 11.31(b) show pointer locations for two consecutive intervals of processing at the time visibility is about to be tested. Minimum values are computed the same as for maximum values because the sign of the input function is first inverted through multiplication by the argument Sign in rows 13 and 34, while also being passed to macro Pdata, and initial and final values are determined according to rows 20 and 146.

Make.plot. This function, shown in Figure 11.29, plots the curve(s) generated during one call to Hide.curve. The x-y values are stored in adjacent arrays named XPlot and YPlot. Since we do not know beforehand how many points of each curve to plot, we must determine this on-the-fly. Pointer xypt is used for this purpose. However, because there may be multiple curve segments, each representing a new visual maximum segment, we delimit the curves by clearing the XPlot-YPlot pair of cells after each curve segment. The cleared cells cause a break in the plotted curve between the x-y pairs of points bracketing the cleared cells. Figure 11.32 shows this array arrangement as well as other arrays used in this example.

We delineate the values to plot by getting the row and column numbers with the SET.NAME functions of rows 113 through 116 of Figure 11.29, then construct

	K	**L**	**M**	**N**	**O**	**P**
1	XPlot	YPlot	XG	G	XH	H
2	-1.999999	3	-3	-1	-3	-1
3	1.9565217	1.30434782	-2	-1	-2	-1
4			-1.999999	3	-1.999999	3
5	6.6666666	3.3333333	1.9565217	1.3043478	1.9565217	1.30434782
6	8	6	3	2	3	2
7	12.1860465	3.6744186	5	5	5	5
8			6.6666666	3.3333333	6.6666666	3.33333333
9	13.8235294	2.7647058	8	6	8	6
10	17	1	12.1860465	3.6744186	12.1860465	3.6744186
11	20	2	13	4	13	4
12			13.8235294	2.7647058	13.8235294	2.7647058
13			17	1	17	1
14			20	2	20	2

Figure 11.32 Various arrays used with the hidden-line elimination macro.

the selection range via concatenation in row 117. Plotting is simply done by copying this range, activating the chart sheet preformatted for a scatter chart, and pasting the data series into it. Therefore, we merely select all cells in the range XPlot(1) : YPlot(xypt) and paste them into the preformatted scatter chart.

Fctn, T.Lookup, and Pdata.   Macros Fctn and T.Lookup of Figure 11.30 are given in Williamson's paper. Fctn performs the linear interpolation operation mentioned at the beginning of this section according to the formula

$$Fctn = y = y_0 + \frac{(x - x_0)(y_1 - y_0)}{x_1 - x_0}$$

where all values on the right hand side are arguments to the function. Macro T.Lookup performs the table lookup function described by Williamson. It is used during re-entry to Hide.curve to obtain subscripts for relative alignment of X and XG, to get the lower subscripts for X and XG to interpolate for curve crossing purposes, and before leaving Hide.curve to process the input data from the last zero crossing to the end of the input data.

Macro Pdata, also in Figure 11.30, is our version of Williamson's subroutine of the same name. We use it to place x-y values into the XPlot and YPlot arrays for later plotting and to separate curve segments with cleared cells to inhibit line segment plotting as described above.

11.2.3 Discussion

The hidden-line elimination macro just presented is the second major macro we developed from a program written in another language. We used as many Excel features as seemed reasonable to implement the macro. Occasionally, during conversion of such programs, it is appropriate to retain some features of the other language to aid in error-free development and to produce a macro that executes in a respectably short time without consuming much memory. We preferred to use one-dimension arrays rather than converting to two-dimension arrays to retain speed of execution. We also preferred to disperse variable definition cells according to their relative location in the FORTRAN program to aid macro checkout through familiarity and association with other parts of the macro, and we retained the FORTRAN variable naming convention for distinguishing integers (mostly pointers in our macro) from real numbers in order to conveniently recognize the variables without making them long to consume space in the formulas (there are advantages to seeing entire formulas at one time without placing them in the formula bar).

However, we did take shortcuts for various reasons. First, to keep the macro short, we omitted parts of the FORTRAN subroutine. We did not incorporate axes, border, or title display, and we omitted error checking for array overflow. Instead of the latter, we rely on Excel checking for out-of-bounds conditions, even though it gives no clue that it occurred. We found it necessary to use the STEP( ) function temporarily to determine the paths of the macro being executed, and we had to perform some hand walkthroughs to find elusive errors. We miss using a trace function to help us while debugging (so we wrote our own), and we find it inconvenient to not be able to pan over our macro sheet while single stepping.

It is very convenient to repeatedly display curves on a graph set up for automatic axes scaling, since, no matter how far the values may be from being correct, we always have something to view. Changing the aspect ratio of a window also resizes the graph, which avoids the need to recompute with new scale factors while experimenting for different presentations. The Excel chart formatting features also allow convenient experimentation to achieve maximum effect.

11.3 BALANCED BINARY TREE

Engineering applications often require data structures other than arrays and data types different from real and integer values. For example, earlier we worked with complex numbers which are quantities more conveniently manipulated as paired values. Three-dimensioned vector and various coordinate system quantities should also be stored and manipulated in their own type of structure. At times, we might need a binary tree structure to accelerate calculations such as searching and sorting, or we may need a list structure for associating values with a particular entity. Unfortunately, in Excel, we must still use arrays for these structures. Consequently, we must contend with pointer manipulation and other aspects of record processing normally made easier and more conveniently with the proper data structure. Despite the limitations of Excel, we are about to demonstrate that binary tree manipulation is possible.

11.3.1 The Algorithm

We implemented the balanced binary tree algorithm given as algorithm A in Chapter 6 of Knuth [6] to insert records in sorted order into a tree and to rebalance the tree as needed. The flowchart is in Figure 11.33 and its macro in Figure 11.34. This algorithm requires a stack from which we obtain storage for records added to the tree. The pointer to this stack is called Avail. Our records, actually locations in arrays, consist of fields called Point1 and Point2 (each holding (x,y,z) coordinate triplets), Pl.num (a geometric plane number), Bal (a tree node balance factor), rev.ind (a data reversal flag), and LLink and RLink (left and right tree node links). These fields are shown in Figure 11.35(a), where sample entries are included. The plane equations arrays, Figure 11.35(b), are not part of the records stored in the tree. The plane equations are keyed to the numbers in the Pl.num field of Figure 11.35(a) where, for example, the polygon corresponding to Pl.num = 1 produced the equation in the first row (row 23) of Figure 11.35(b), that for Pl.num = 2 in the second row (row 24) and so on. We avoided using two-dimension arrays because of the extra processing time and because the names of the one-dimension arrays better convey their purpose.

Detailed discussions of algorithms for traversing binary trees are described in Knuth [6]. We modified one of the algorithms slightly to suit our purpose. The search portion of the flowchart is implemented in rows 4 through 25 of the macro. Here we determine the location within the tree where our record is to be placed. We must have entered this macro with at least one record in the tree, which we placed there with the driver macro that we discuss in Section 11.3.2. The RLink field of node 1 points to the node that is the root of the tree. This first record is not one of our data records. We go to the stack for the storage location pointed to by Avail. Entries are placed into the new record by the call to macro Store.seg in row 26. Our stack is really the rest of the over-dimensioned arrays that later become records of the tree.

The algorithm maintains a balanced tree (right and left branch heights for each node within one level of each other) to realize an $O(\log N)$ operations count possible with binary trees. Admittedly, our interpretive routine is nowhere near as fast as Knuth's assembly language routine. The degree of balance, or unbalance, is given in the Bal field for each node (0 means equal height left and right branches; -1 means the left branch is the longer by one level; $+1$ means the right branch is the longer by one level). The Bal field of node 1 is a counter for the total number of levels in the tree. It is used for information purposes only. The macro code of rows 28 through 80 is for the purpose of adjusting the balance factors after a new node is added to the tree, for determining whether a rebalance of the tree is necessary, and for rebalancing, when required, by performing a single or double rotation as shown in Figure 11.36, where the node to be added in the dotted location of the left diagrams really ends up in the location as shown in the right diagrams.

11.3.2 An Application

We will use our binary tree macro for storing in sorted order the endpoint coordinates of straight line segments. This operation, among others, is required for further processing by a plane-sweep algorithm for hidden line elimination graphics (see Nurmi [9]), for integrated circuit design rule checking (see Bentley and Wood [1] and Nievergelt and Preparata [8]), for polygon intersection testing (see Swart and Ladner [12] and Ottmann and Widmayer [10]), and for other applications. We will also perform transformation operations for applying the plane-sweep algorithm to the hidden-line application.

We first describe the plane-sweep algorithm to appreciate what we are about to do and to place in perspective the need for sorted binary trees. Consider the three-dimensional object of Figure 11.37 where, given the line segments for the polygons outlining each facet (actually a plane), we expect to process the segments such that, when plotted, the portions of each segment that are hidden (the

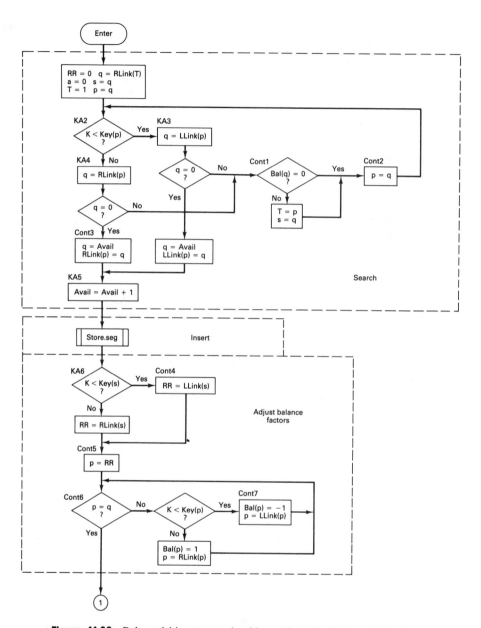

Figure 11.33 Balanced binary tree algorithm. Adapted with permission from D. E. Knuth, *The Art of Computer Programming: vol. 3, Sorting and Searching,* Addison-Wesley Publishing Co., © 1973.

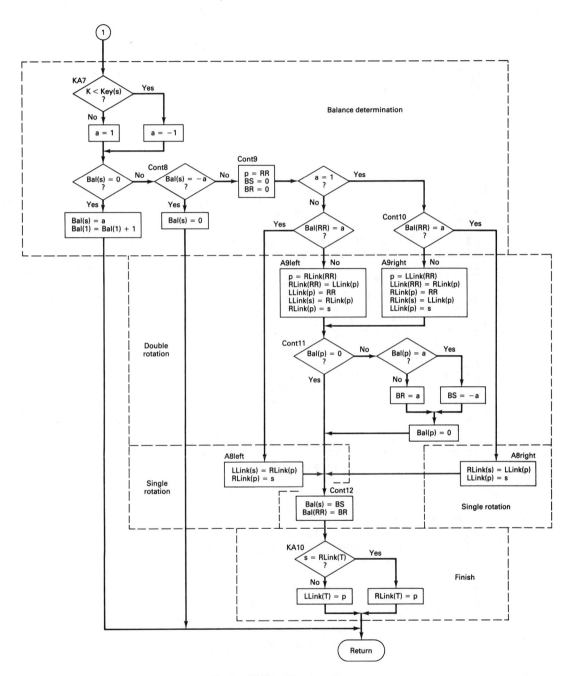

Figure 11.33 (Continued)

	D	E
1		Tree.sort
2		Builds a binary tree in ascending sorted order.
3		=ARGUMENT("K")
4	RR	=0
5	a	=0
6	T	=1
7	q	=INDEX(RLink,T)
8	s	=q
9	p	=q
10	KA2	=IF(K<INDEX(Key,p),,GOTO(KA4))
11	KA3	=SET.VALUE(q,INDEX(LLink,p))
12		=IF(q=0,,GOTO(Cont1))
13		=SET.VALUE(q,Avail)
14		=SET.VALUE(INDEX(LLink,p),q)
15		=GOTO(KA5)
16	KA4	=SET.VALUE(q,INDEX(RLink,p))
17		=IF(q=0,GOTO(Cont3))
18	Cont1	=IF(INDEX(Bal,q)=0,GOTO(Cont2))
19		=SET.VALUE(T,p)
20		=SET.VALUE(s,q)
21	Cont2	=SET.VALUE(p,q)
22		=GOTO(KA2)
23	Cont3	=SET.VALUE(q,Avail)
24		=SET.VALUE(INDEX(RLink,p),q)
25	KA5	=SET.VALUE(Avail,Avail+1)
26		=Store.seg()
27		=SET.VALUE(INDEX(Bal,q),0)
28	KA6	=IF(K<INDEX(Key,s),GOTO(Cont4))
29		=SET.VALUE(RR,INDEX(RLink,s))
30		=GOTO(Cont5)
31	Cont4	=SET.VALUE(RR,INDEX(LLink,s))
32	Cont5	=SET.VALUE(p,RR)
33	Cont6	=IF(p=q,GOTO(KA7))
34		=IF(K<INDEX(Key,p),GOTO(Cont7))
35		=SET.VALUE(INDEX(Bal,p),1)
36		=SET.VALUE(p,INDEX(RLink,p))
37		=GOTO(Cont6)
38	Cont7	=SET.VALUE(INDEX(Bal,p),-1)
39		=SET.VALUE(p,INDEX(LLink,p))
40		=GOTO(Cont6)

Figure 11.34   Macro for Figure 11.33.

	D	E
41	KA7	=IF(K<INDEX(Key,s),SET.VALUE(a,-1),SET.VALUE(a,1))
42		=IF(INDEX(Bal,s)=0,,GOTO(Cont8))
43		=SET.VALUE(INDEX(Bal,s),a)
44		=SET.VALUE(INDEX(Bal,1),INDEX(Bal,1)+1)
45		=GOTO(End)
46	Cont8	=IF(INDEX(Bal,s)=-a,,GOTO(Cont9))
47		=SET.VALUE(INDEX(Bal,s),0)
48		=GOTO(End)
49	Cont9	=SET.VALUE(p,RR)
50	BS	=0
51	BR	=0
52		=IF(a=1,GOTO(Cont10))
53		=IF(INDEX(Bal,RR)=a,,GOTO(A9left))
54	A8left	=SET.VALUE(INDEX(LLink,s),INDEX(RLink,p))
55		=SET.VALUE(INDEX(RLink,p),s)
56		=GOTO(Cont12)
57	A9left	=SET.VALUE(p,INDEX(RLink,RR))
58		=SET.VALUE(INDEX(RLink,RR),INDEX(LLink,p))
59		=SET.VALUE(INDEX(LLink,p),RR)
60		=SET.VALUE(INDEX(LLink,s),INDEX(RLink,p))
61		=SET.VALUE(INDEX(RLink,p),s)
62		=GOTO(Cont11)
63	Cont10	=IF(INDEX(Bal,RR)=a,,GOTO(A9right))
64	A8right	=SET.VALUE(INDEX(RLink,s),INDEX(LLink,p))
65		=SET.VALUE(INDEX(LLink,p),s)
66		=GOTO(Cont12)
67	A9right	=SET.VALUE(p,INDEX(LLink,RR))
68		=SET.VALUE(INDEX(LLink,RR),INDEX(RLink,p))
69		=SET.VALUE(INDEX(RLink,p),RR)
70		=SET.VALUE(INDEX(RLink,s),INDEX(LLink,p))
71		=SET.VALUE(INDEX(LLink,p),s)
72	Cont11	=IF(INDEX(Bal,p)=0,GOTO(Cont12))
73		=IF(INDEX(Bal,p)=a,SET.VALUE(BS,-a),SET.VALUE(BR,a))
74		=SET.VALUE(INDEX(Bal,p),0)
75	Cont12	=SET.VALUE(INDEX(Bal,s),BS)
76		=SET.VALUE(INDEX(Bal,RR),BR)
77	KA10	=IF(s=INDEX(RLink,T),GOTO(Cont13))
78		=SET.VALUE(INDEX(LLink,T),p)
79		=GOTO(End)
80	Cont13	=SET.VALUE(INDEX(RLink,T),p)
81	End	=RETURN()

Figure 11.34   (Continued)

Figure 11.35 (a) Data storage area for the balanced binary tree example and (b) plane equation coefficients for transformed facets.

(a)

	G	H	I	J	K	L	M	N	O	P	Q
	Point1			Point2							
22	x1	y1	z1	x2	y2	z2	Pl.num	Bal	rev.ind	LLink	RLink
23											
24	-1.4855627	1.11417202	-0.7427813	0	0	0	1	5		0	13
25	-1.4244077	1.44330579	-0.3713906	-1.4855627	1.11417202	-0.7427813	1	1	-1	2	7
26	-1.4244077	1.44330579	-0.3713906	-0.6816263	0.88621977	5.55111512	1	0	1	0	29
27	-0.4981614	1.87362106	1.11417202	-0.6816263	0.88621977	5.55111512	1	-1	-1	3	0
28	-0.4981614	1.87362106	1.11417202	0.24461993	1.31653504	1.48556270	1	0	1	0	10
29	0.24461993	1.31653504	1.48556270	0	0	0	1	0	1	0	0
30	-0.4981614	1.87362106	1.11417202	0.24461993	1.31653504	1.48556270	2	0	-1	6	9
31	0.16010610	2.37992042	0.55708601	-0.4981614	1.87362106	1.11417202	2	0	-1	0	0
32	0.16010610	2.37992042	0.55708601	0.90288745	1.82283440	0.92847669	2	0	1	8	15
33	0.90288745	1.82283440	0.92847669	0.24461993	1.31653504	1.48556270	2	-1	1	33	0
34	0.16010610	2.37992042	0.55708601	0.90288745	1.82283440	0.92847669	3	0	-1	0	0
35	0.28241607	3.03818794	2.99867364	0.16010610	2.37992042	0.55708601	3	0	-1	5	22
36	0.28241607	3.03818794	2.99867364	1.02519742	2.48110193	1.67125804	3	0	1	0	0
37	1.02519742	2.48110193	1.67125804	0.90288745	1.82283440	0.92847669	3	0	1	12	32
38	0.28241607	3.03818794	2.99867364	1.02519742	2.48110193	1.67125804	4	-1	-1	14	0
39	2.91548617	5.06338537	-0.92847669	0.28241607	3.03818794	1.29986736	4	1	-1	25	20
40	2.91548617	5.06338537	-0.92847669	3.65826752	4.50629935	-0.55708601	4	0	1	0	0

(b)

	R	S	T	U
21	Planes			
22	pl.a	pl.b	pl.c	pl.d
23	0.658267	0.506299	-0.55708	-5.55111
24	-0.12230	-0.65826	-0.74278	2
25	0.658267	0.506299	-0.55708	-1
26	-0.12230	-0.65826	-0.74278	3
27	-0.65826	-0.50629	0.55708	5
28	0.742781	-0.55708	0.37139	2
29	-0.12230	-0.65826	-0.74278	0.5
30	-0.12230	-0.65826	-0.74278	0.500000

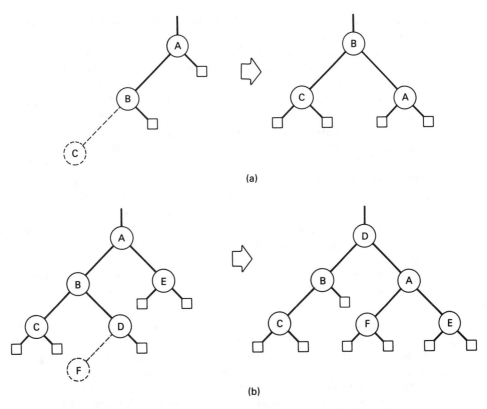

(a)

(b)

Figure 11.36 Binary tree before and after rebalancing with (a) single rotation and (b) double rotation.

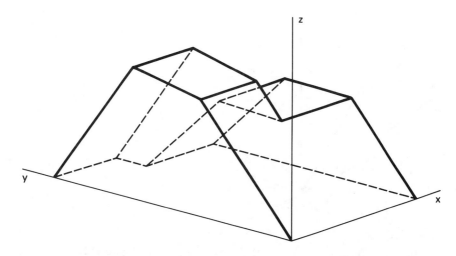

Figure 11.37 Object for demonstrating the plane-sweep algorithm.

dashed lines) will be eliminated and the object plotted will be formed only of those lines now shown solid.

First, we establish a coordinate system (x,y,z) for the object, number the facets (planes) for identification, and write the end-point coordinates of each segment for each polygon representing a facet. Then, we determine the point from which we view the object. The object of Figure 11.37 is already drawn from that viewpoint, whose coordinates are (−a, −b, c). For convenience, we will rotate the object about the axis w through angle θ of Figure 11.38, after which we view the object from above. If we were to project it onto the xy-plane, we would, in effect, strip off its z-coordinate at this time and have a projection that a drafts-man calls an *auxiliary view*. We will not do that because we want to preserve the z-coordinates for later calculations. We now relabel the axes (x′, y′) as shown in Figure 11.39, where we added thin horizontal lines to help explain the plane-sweep algorithm (the dots at the corners of the object were added for emphasis and are the segment endpoints). The x′-axis is the axis of rotation w shown in Figure 11.38.

In the plane-sweep algorithm, we move a plane downward along the y′ axis of Figure 11.39 beginning at y′ = +∞. The plane is perpendicular to the x′y′-plane so it appears as a line in that figure. These lines pass through beginning and ending points of our polygon segments which represent stopping points for the sweeping plane. In the figure, our first stopping point occurs at point 1, where six segments intersect (two for each of the three facets) as shown in Figure 11.40. If we store the segments in decreasing y′ order in a sorted binary tree, it is not difficult to retrieve them from the tree for processing at this time. This tree is usually called the *priority queue*. Our purpose is to determine which segments, or parts thereof, are visible and are to be output for plotting. We cannot yet deter-mine this until we have processed both ends of a segment or until we determine an

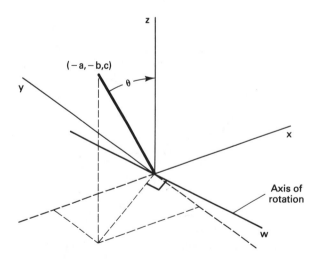

Figure 11.38 Determining the rotation angle θ.

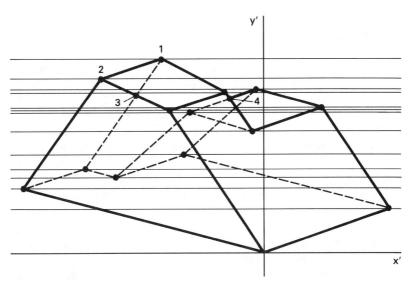

Figure 11.39 Transformed and projected view with plane-sweep stopping points (at thin horizontal lines).

intersection point for that segment as described in the following paragraph. According to Figure 11.39, this would not occur until we process the segments at point 2, at which time we would do something about segments a and b as marked in Figure 11.40. These segments are coincident, and we do not want to plot both of them. So, with a depth calculation (we still know the z' coordinates of the segments and we have the equations of each transformed facet), we can eliminate that segment on the facet not visible (the one with a smaller z' coordinate) and plot only one segment. We proceed by sweeping from point to point until we have processed the lowest y' point (at the origin in our example).

We must have an algorithm for processing the segments at each plane-stopping point. This algorithm is application dependent and requires a suitable

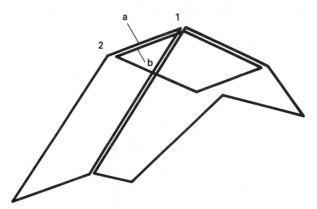

Figure 11.40 Intersection of object facets at point 1.

data structure to hold the segments in work. These segments are also called *active edges*. This data structure, often another sorted binary tree, would contain the active edges sorted in ascending x'-coordinate value. The active edges would be processed in order to determine facet, hence segment, visibility. This process is complicated by the fact that segments which cross create new plane-stopping points. Two such crossings occur at points 3 and 4, through which we did not draw thin lines in Figure 11.39 but where we did add dots. These new stopping points must be computed on-the-fly and inserted into the priority queue, hence the need for initially inserting the segments into a sorted binary tree. In due time, these new stopping points will be reached and the created segments processed. At point 3, no new visible segment is created. However, both visible and invisible segments are created at point 4. It is implicit that each active edge has associated with it information regarding the depth of planes that cover common areas as seen from the viewpoint. Such information often is also stored in another binary tree. At this time, it is not hard to imagine the demands that the plane-sweep algorithm imposes on memory space.

We implemented the beginning of the plane-sweep application only. Its flowchart is in Figure 11.41 and the macro in Figure 11.42. We first prompt for the coordinates of the viewpoint in rows 4, 5, and 6 of Figure 11.42, then compute the transformation matrix (rows 7 through 26) as given by Rogers and Adams [11]. After we input the viewpoint (a,b,c), we compute the axis of rotation w with the cross product as follows.

$$\mathbf{w} = \mathbf{N} \times \mathbf{k} = \begin{vmatrix} \mathbf{i} & \mathbf{j} & \mathbf{k} \\ a & b & c \\ 0 & 0 & 1 \end{vmatrix} = b\mathbf{i} - a\mathbf{j}$$

where

$$\mathbf{N} = a\mathbf{i} + b\mathbf{j} + c\mathbf{k}$$
$$\mathbf{k} = \text{unit vector along the z' axis}$$

To simplify the transformation matrix, we have, for the direction cosines and the rotation angle

$$n_1 = \frac{b}{\sqrt{a^2 + b^2}}$$

$$n_2 = \frac{-a}{\sqrt{a^2 + b^2}}$$

$$n_3 = 0$$

$$\theta = \cos^{-1}\left|\frac{-c}{\sqrt{a^2 + b^2 + c^2}}\right|$$

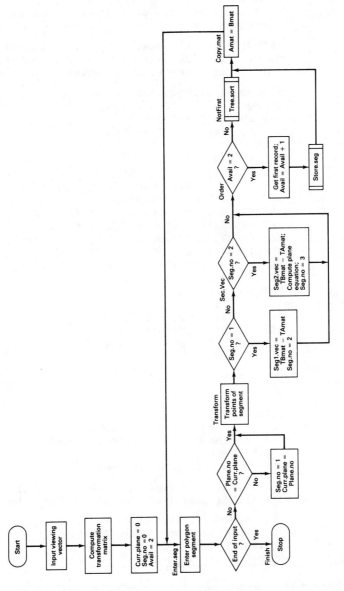

Figure 11.41 Plane-sweep application flowchart.

	A	B
1		Input.data
2		Enter polygons and build priority queue.
3		Shortcut key = "i"
4	va	=INPUT("Enter the viewing vector x-coordinate:",1)
5	vb	=INPUT("Enter the viewing vector y-coordinate:",1)
6	vc	=INPUT("Enter the viewing vector z-coordinate:",1)
7		=IF(AND(va=0,vb=0),GOTO(View.z))
8	nn1	=vb/SQRT(va^2+vb^2)
9	nn2	=-va/SQRT(va^2+vb^2)
10	costh	=-vc/SQRT(va^2+vb^2+vc^2)
11	theta	=ACOS(costh)
12	sinth	=SIN(theta)
13		=SET.VALUE(INDEX(Rot.mat,1,1),nn1^2+(1-nn1^2)*costh)
14		=SET.VALUE(INDEX(Rot.mat,2,1),nn1*nn2*(1-costh))
15		=SET.VALUE(INDEX(Rot.mat,3,1),nn2*sinth)
16		=SET.VALUE(INDEX(Rot.mat,1,2),INDEX(Rot.mat,2,1))
17		=SET.VALUE(INDEX(Rot.mat,2,2),nn2^2+(1-nn2^2)*costh)
18		=SET.VALUE(INDEX(Rot.mat,3,2),-nn1*sinth)
19		=SET.VALUE(INDEX(Rot.mat,1,3),-INDEX(Rot.mat,3,1))
20		=SET.VALUE(INDEX(Rot.mat,2,3),-INDEX(Rot.mat,3,2))
21		=SET.VALUE(INDEX(Rot.mat,3,3),costh)
22		=GOTO(Curr.plane)
23	View.z	=IF(vc>0,1,-1)
24		=SET.VALUE(INDEX(Unit.mat,2,2),View.z)
25		=SET.VALUE(INDEX(Unit.mat,3,3),View.z)
26		=SET.VALUE(Rot.mat,Unit.mat)
27	Curr.plane	=0
28	Seg.no	=0
29	Avail	=2
30	Enter.seg	=DIALOG.BOX(Input.seg)
31		=IF(Enter.seg=16,GOTO(Finish))
32		=IF(Plane.no=Curr.plane,GOTO(Transform))
33		=SET.VALUE(Seg.no,1)
34		=SET.VALUE(Curr.plane,Plane.no)
35	Transform	=SET.VALUE(TAmat,MMULT(TRANSPOSE(Amat),Rot.mat))
36		=SET.VALUE(TBmat,MMULT(TRANSPOSE(Bmat),Rot.mat))
37		=IF(Seg.no<>1,GOTO(Sec.Vec))
38		=SET.VALUE(Seg1.vec,TBmat-TAmat)
39		=SET.VALUE(Seg.no,2)
40		=GOTO(Order)

Figure 11.42 Input data macro for the plane-sweep application flowchart of Figure 11.41.

	A	B
41	Sec.Vec	=IF(Seg.no<>2,GOTO(Order))
42		=SET.VALUE(Seg2.vec,TBmat-TAmat)
43	axbi	=ay*bz-az*by
44	axbj	=-ax*bz+az*bx
45	axbk	=ax*by-ay*bx
46	denom	=SQRT(axbi^2+axbj^2+axbk^2)
47	ux	=axbi/denom
48	uy	=axbj/denom
49	uz	=axbk/denom
50	plane.d	=-ux*x1a-uy*y1a-uz*z1a
51		=SET.VALUE(INDEX(pl.a,Curr.plane),ux)
52		=SET.VALUE(INDEX(pl.b,Curr.plane),uy)
53		=SET.VALUE(INDEX(pl.c,Curr.plane),uz)
54		=SET.VALUE(INDEX(pl.d,Curr.plane),plane.d)
55		=SET.VALUE(Seg.no,3)
56	Order	=IF(Avail<>2,GOTO(NotFirst))
57	1stTime	=SET.VALUE(INDEX(RLink,1),Avail)
58		=SET.VALUE(q,Avail)
59		=SET.VALUE(Avail,Avail+1)
60		=Store.seg()
61		=GOTO(Copy.mat)
62	NotFirst	=Tree.sort(MAX(y1a,y1b))
63	Copy.mat	=SET.VALUE(Amat,Bmat)
64		=GOTO(Enter.seg)
65	Finish	=RETURN()
66		Store.seg
67		=IF(y1a>=y1b,GOTO(Store))
68		=SET.VALUE(INDEX(Point1,q,0),TBmat)
69		=SET.VALUE(INDEX(Point2,q,0),TAmat)
70		=SET.VALUE(INDEX(rev.ind,q),-1)
71		=GOTO(Store.last)
72	Store	=SET.VALUE(INDEX(Point1,q,0),TAmat)
73		=SET.VALUE(INDEX(Point2,q,0),TBmat)
74		=SET.VALUE(INDEX(rev.ind,q),1)
75	Store.last	=SET.VALUE(INDEX(Pl.num,q),Curr.plane)
76		=SET.VALUE(INDEX(LLink,q),0)
77		=SET.VALUE(INDEX(RLink,q),0)
78		=SET.VALUE(INDEX(Bal,q),0)
79		=RETURN()

Figure 11.42 (Continued)

so that the matrix, which we call Rot.mat, simplifies to

$$
\begin{bmatrix}
n_1^2 + (1 - n_1^2)\cos\theta & n_1 n_2 (1 - \cos\theta) & -n_2\sin\theta \\
n_1 n_2 (1 - \cos\theta) & n_2^2 + (1 - n_2^2)\cos\theta & n_1\cos\theta \\
n_2\sin\theta & -n_1\sin\theta & \cos\theta
\end{bmatrix}
$$

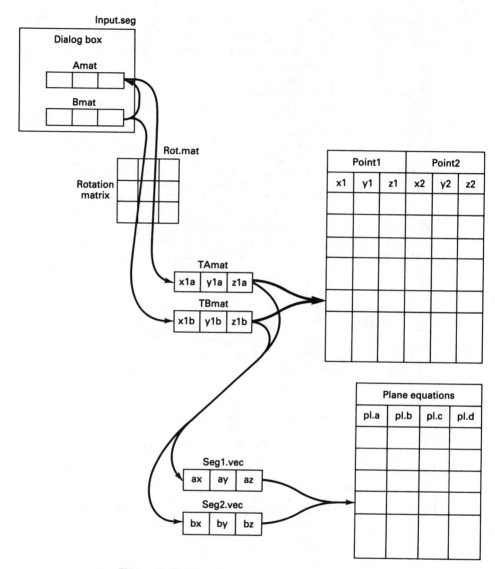

Figure 11.43   Data flow for the plane-sweep example.

If our viewpoint is on the xy-plane, our transformation matrix is the unit matrix, Unit.mat.

The plane equation for each facet is computed from the vector representation of two of the facet's segments **a** and **b** as follows (see Kral [7] for vector manipulation of geometric entities):

$$\mathbf{u_n} = \frac{\mathbf{a} \times \mathbf{b}}{|\mathbf{a} \times \mathbf{b}|} = u_{x'}\mathbf{i} + u_{y'}\mathbf{j} + u_{z'}\mathbf{k}$$

where

$$\mathbf{a} \times \mathbf{b} = \begin{vmatrix} \mathbf{i} & \mathbf{j} & \mathbf{k} \\ a_x & a_y & a_z \\ b_x & b_y & b_z \end{vmatrix}$$

$$= (a_y b_z - a_z b_y)\mathbf{i} - (a_x b_z - a_z b_x)\mathbf{j} + (a_x b_y - a_y b_x)\mathbf{k}$$

Then, for the plane equation

$$ax' + by' + cz' + d = 0$$

we have

$$a = u_{x'}$$

$$b = u_{y'}$$

$$c = u_{z'}$$

$$d = -ax' - by' - cz'$$

where, given a segment endpoint, we compute d. The plane is computed in rows 43 through 54 of Figure 11.42. It is obvious from what we have done that vector operations and an appropriate data type are needed as built-in capabilities of the spreadsheet.

Data flow corresponding to the flowchart appears in Figure 11.43, where the role of the matrices and their components is shown. We used the custom dialog box of Figure 11.44 to input the segments and the plane (facet) number to which they belong, later used as a subscript for storage of the plane equation coefficients. Input cells of the Init/Result column of Figure 11.45 are Plane.no (N5), Amat (N10:N12), and Bmat (N14:N16). Amat and Bmat are shown with the same values because we copy the endpoint of the previous segment, Bmat, to the beginning point of the next segment, Amat, so that one fewer set of point values usually need be entered, provided we enter the polygon segments in order. The statement of row 63 of Figure 11.42 does the copying. Our macro restriction is that all segments of a facet polygon be input before inputting segments for another polygon. Other variable storage locations are shown in Figure 11.46, where the

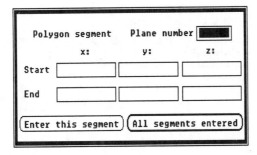

Figure 11.44 Dialog box for entry of polygon segments.

	Element	Item	X pos	Y pos	Box width	Box height	Text	Init/Result
2	Dialog box		0	0	345	157		
3	Text	5	24	19	124	12	Polygon segment	
4	Text	5	173	19	100	12	Plane number	
5	Integer box	7	272	17	55	18		1
6	Text	5	96	40	20	12	x:	
7	Text	5	191	40	20	12	y:	
8	Text	5	286	40	20	12	z:	
9	Text	5	10	62	44	16	Start	
10	Number box	8	60	60	90	18		3
11	Number box	8	155	60	90	18		5
12	Number box	8	250	60	90	18		1
13	Text	5	10	92	28	12	End	
14	Number box	8	60	90	90	18		3
15	Number box	8	155	90	90	18		5
16	Number box	8	250	90	90	18		1
17	OK	1	3	123	160	21	Enter this segment	
18	OK	1	167	123	176	21	All segments entered	

Figure 11.45 Dialog box definition area.

	O	P	Q	R	S	T
1			x1a	y1a	z1a	
2		TAmat	0.133131	3.150151	1.028991	
3						
4			x1b	y1b	z1b	
5		TBmat	3.040963	4.969277	-1.02899	
6						
7			ax	ay	az	
8		Seg1.vec	-0.68599	0.514495	-0.51449	
9						
10			bx	by	bz	
11		Seg2.vec	2.907831	1.819126	-2.05798	
12						
13		Rot.mat:	0.030722	0.726957	0.685994	
14			0.726957	0.454781	-0.51449	
15			-0.68599	0.514495	-0.51449	
16						
17		Unit.mat	1	0	0	
18			0	1	0	
19			0	0	1	
20						

Figure 11.46 Several working arrays with their individually named components.

names to the left pertain to the adjacent array while those above pertain to individual cells of the array below.

Output of macro Input.data is a balanced tree with transformed segments sorted in decreasing order of the largest y value of the segment endpoints. If necessary, the segment endpoints are reversed so that Point 1 always has that endpoint with the largest y' value. The data reversal flag rev.ind is set to +1 for no endpoint reversal and to −1 where a reversal has been made. A plane-sweep algorithm would now start processing this tree as the priority que.

11.3.3 Discussion

The array data structure has been adapted in clever ways to many needs where other data structures would have been preferable. Such was the case for the example of this section. However, when no other choice is available, one can always adapt to the restrictions. Eventually, demand causes enhancements to make up for the deficiencies. A record data type is needed. We must be able to define fields of our choice for purposes such as our binary tree application. In the absence of such a data type, we suggest single subscript array definitions for speed advantages.

Although some Excel array operators perform vector mathematical operations (e.g., for A and B column or row arrays, A − B and A + B perform vector subtraction and addition, respectively, and SUM (A*B) performs the vector dot product), the vector cross product would be a suitable addition to the mathematical function library. User-supplied macros cannot be as efficient as system-supplied routines. We chose to implement a special case of the cross product because of the restricted application.

11.4 POLAR COORDINATE GRAPH

The purpose of this example is to present a polar coordinate graph grid generation function and to demonstrate that complex appearing graphs do not have to be displayed in segments, as was done in the hidden-line elimination routine of Section 11.2. We do not incorporate all the refinements in our graph grid, such as axes tick marks, scale labeling, and the like. Instead, we let the reader customize the graph as desired.

11.4.1 The Polar Coordinate Grid Macro

Our macro computes data points for a single data series that causes a polar coordinate grid to be displayed, such as shown in Figure 11.47. We allow, within limits, user control of the number of grid circles and their scale values.

The density of points defining the circles is affected by the desire to reduce the faceting appearance. Since the radius of the circle exaggerates, or suppresses, this effect, we manually determine the number of points for a pleasing visual effect and control circle generation by referencing this predetermined point count in a

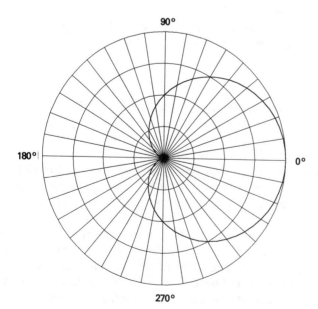

Figure 11.47 Output of macro Plot.polar with the cardioid generated by the Polar driver routine.

loop. It is apparent that fewer points are required for small radius circles. The number of points used for each circle is stored in array Npt. These numbers correspond with their angular separations, in degrees, given in array DAng. The arrays are shown in Figure 11.52. The selection of grids possible with our macro is shown in Figures 11.47 and 11.48, where faceting is hardly apparent. We allow no more than five circles with our macro.

Our plan is to first compute the points of the top half of the inner circle and to reflect them through the origin to generate the bottom half-circle. This is done in rows 21 through 30 of the macro of Figure 11.49. We could have computed them for a quarter-circle only but feel the complexity in managing pointers to generate the full circle not worth the trouble for this example. We then work outward to successively larger circles. The code for these circles is given in the loop of rows 17 through 35, within which we find the circle generation loop just described. Incoming macro argument delrho is the value difference in radius between successive circles while argument NumCir specifies the number of circles for the grid. The code described above generates the grid shown in Figure 11.50, with no gaps at the transition from one circle to the next.

The radial lines are generated by the code of rows 36 through 50 of Figure 11.49. Because we want to avoid selecting values on the macro sheet and pasting them into the chart individually for each radial, and we do not want to insert empty cells as we did in Section 11.2, we must be sure that connecting lines between radials do not appear in unwanted locations on the graph. For this reason, we will ping-pong between opposite sides of the outer circle to generate opposing radial lines and stop at the center only to change direction for the next radial line, which will be at a different angle. The code in rows 42 and 43 returns us to the origin from a circumferential point, that in rows 45 and 46 takes us to a new circumferential point but at a new angle, while that of rows 48 and 49 cause a radial line to be formed on a circle diameter. Rotating incrementally for new radial lines is required until we have computed them over a 180-degree sector. During this time, we will have also computed the radial lines in the opposite sector to complete the radial lines grid. The general scheme is indicated in Figure 11.51. Overwrite of parts of the radial line does not alter the display. Lines are not widened nor are screen intensities varied.

Plotting of the polar grid is done on a preformatted scatter chart with the statements of rows 51 through 59 in the same manner as was done in the hidden-line elimination example of Section 11.2.

The Plot.polar macro is self-contained except for the arguments. Argument SkipSel is a flag to bypass the XPlot and YPlot array definition statements once the arrays have been defined. This saves time during subsequent calls to the macro but the statements, rows 7 through 10, must be executed at least once before the grid can be computed. Arrays XPlot and YPlot do not appear in any of our figures. Label Cont is used for bypassing while NCir, DelTh, Rho, Theta, Rcos and Rsin are temporary variables and xypt, Hpt, hrpt, rpt and Np are pointers and control variables.

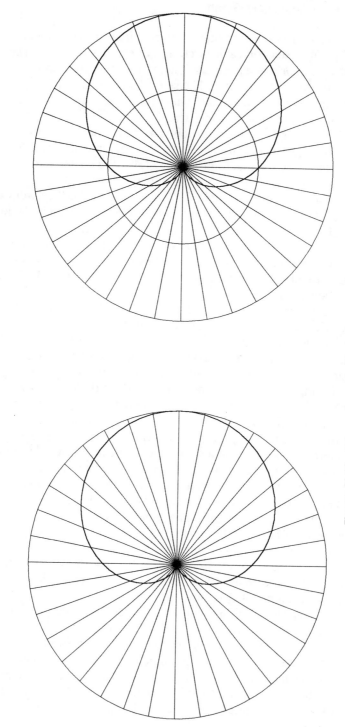

Figure 11.48 Other polar grids possible with macro Plot.polar.

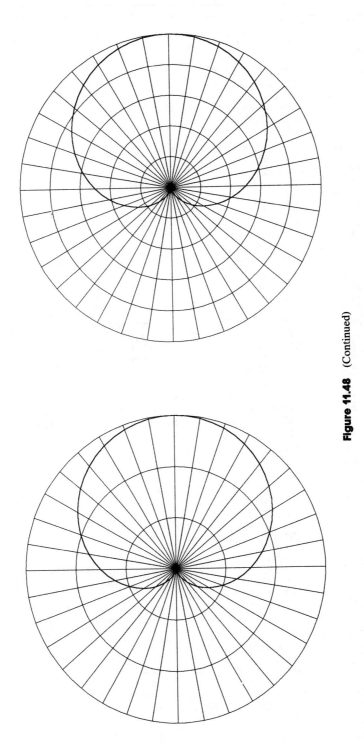

Figure 11.48 (Continued)

	A	B
1		Plot.polar
2		Draws polar coordinate grid.
3		=ARGUMENT("delrho")
4		=ARGUMENT("NumCir")
5		=ARGUMENT("SkipSel")
6		=IF(SkipSel>0,GOTO(Cont))
7		=SELECT(!J2:J700)
8		=DEFINE.NAME("XPlot",SELECTION())
9		=SELECT(!K2:K700)
10		=DEFINE.NAME("YPlot",SELECTION())
11	Cont	=SET.VALUE(INDEX(XPlot,1,),0)
12		=SET.VALUE(INDEX(YPlot,1,),0)
13	NCir	=NumCir
14		=IF(NCir>5,SET.VALUE(NCir,5))
15	xypt	=2
16	jk	=IF(NCir=5,5,4)
17		=FOR("j",1,NCir,1)
18	Rho	=j*delrho
19	DelTh	=INDEX(DAng,j+jk-NCir)*PI()/180
20	Hpt	=(INDEX(Npt,j+jk-NCir)-1)/2
21		=FOR("k",1,Hpt,1)
22	Theta	=(k-1)*DelTh
23	Rcos	=Rho*COS(Theta)
24	Rsin	=Rho*SIN(Theta)
25		=SET.VALUE(INDEX(XPlot,xypt),Rcos)
26		=SET.VALUE(INDEX(YPlot,xypt),Rsin)
27		=SET.VALUE(INDEX(XPlot,xypt+Hpt),-Rcos)
28		=SET.VALUE(INDEX(YPlot,xypt+Hpt),-Rsin)
29		=SET.VALUE(xypt,xypt+1)
30		=NEXT()
31		=SET.VALUE(xypt,xypt+Hpt)
32		=SET.VALUE(INDEX(XPlot,xypt),INDEX(XPlot,xypt-2*Hpt))
33		=SET.VALUE(INDEX(YPlot,xypt),INDEX(YPlot,xypt-2*Hpt))
34		=SET.VALUE(xypt,xypt+1)
35		=NEXT()
36	hrpt	=xypt-Hpt-1
37	rpt	=hrpt-Hpt
38		=SET.VALUE(INDEX(XPlot,xypt),INDEX(XPlot,hrpt))
39		=SET.VALUE(INDEX(YPlot,xypt),INDEX(YPlot,hrpt))
40		=FOR("j",4,Hpt,4)
41		=SET.VALUE(xypt,xypt+1)
42		=SET.VALUE(INDEX(XPlot,xypt),0)
43		=SET.VALUE(INDEX(YPlot,xypt),0)
44		=SET.VALUE(xypt,xypt+1)
45		=SET.VALUE(INDEX(XPlot,xypt),INDEX(XPlot,rpt+j))
46		=SET.VALUE(INDEX(YPlot,xypt),INDEX(YPlot,rpt+j))
47		=SET.VALUE(xypt,xypt+1)
48		=SET.VALUE(INDEX(XPlot,xypt),INDEX(XPlot,hrpt+j))
49		=SET.VALUE(INDEX(YPlot,xypt),INDEX(YPlot,hrpt+j))
50		=NEXT()
51		=ACTIVATE("EX11P4A.XLM")
52		=SET.NAME("ColA",COLUMN(XPlot))
53		=SET.NAME("ColB",COLUMN(YPlot))
54		=SET.NAME("RowA",ROW(INDEX(XPlot,1)))
55		=SET.NAME("RowB",ROW(INDEX(XPlot,xypt-1)))
56		=SELECT("R"&RowA&"C"&ColA&":R"&RowB&"C"&ColB)
57		=COPY()
58		=ACTIVATE("EX11P4A.XLC")
59		=PASTE.SPECIAL(2,FALSE,TRUE,FALSE)
60		=RETURN()

Figure 11.49 Polar coordinate grid macro.

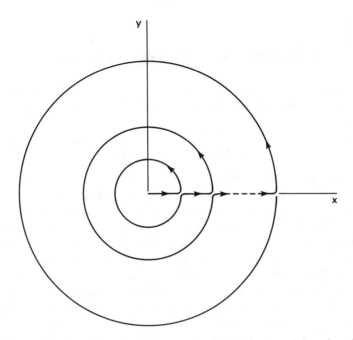

Figure 11.50 Path followed while generating the circular part of the polar grid.

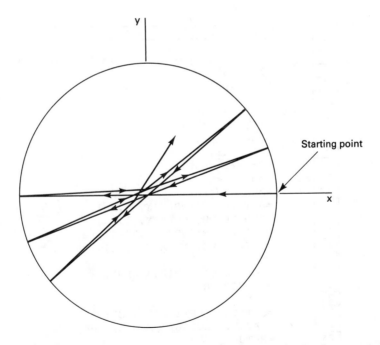

Figure 11.51 Sequence for generating the radial grid lines (lines are displaced for clarity of understanding; they all pass through the origin).

535

11.4.2 A Polar Coordinate Plotting Application

Our polar coordinate grid driver command macro called Polar is shown in Figure 11.52. We compute and display a cardioid function with the parametric equations

$$x = 2a \cos \phi(1 + \cos \phi)$$
$$y = 2a \sin \phi(1 + \cos \phi)$$
$$-\pi \le \phi \le \pi$$

We do not have true polar plotting, since our data points are still represented in (x,y) form rather than in (r,θ) form. The cardioid is shown on the polar grid of Figure 11.47, where we manually entered the degree labels.

We call the Plot.polar macro at the beginning of Polar, compute the cardioid points in rows 5 through 17, then display the figure with the statements of rows 18 through 22. Because the cardioid is an even function as we choose to plot it, we compute only half the points and transform them to complete the other half of the figure. Our points, stored in arrays X and Y, are not shown in any of our figures.

When plotted with a laser printer, the center of the polar coordinate grid does not darken appreciably due to density of radial lines there. For other printers, the radial lines should probably be shortened to terminate on the inner-most circle rather than at the center. This requires more ingenuity to develop a

	D	E	F	G
1		Polar		DAng
2		Driver for polar coordinate function.		10
3		Shortcut key = "p"		7.5
4		=Plot.polar(1.3333,3,1)		5
5	a	=1		2.5
6	dphi	=5*PI()/180		2.5
7		=FOR("j",1,37,1)		
8	Phi	=(j-1)*dphi		
9	cost	=COS(Phi)		
10	Aux	=2*a*(1+cost)		Npt
11	xa	=Aux*cost		37
12	ya	=Aux*SIN(Phi)		49
13		=SET.VALUE(INDEX(X,j),xa)		73
14		=SET.VALUE(INDEX(Y,j),ya)		145
15		=SET.VALUE(INDEX(X,74-j),xa)		145
16		=SET.VALUE(INDEX(Y,74-j),-ya)		
17		=NEXT()		
18		=ACTIVATE("EX11P4A.XLM")		
19		=SELECT(!H2:I74)		
20		=COPY()		
21		=ACTIVATE("EX11P4A.XLC")		
22		=PASTE.SPECIAL(2,FALSE,TRUE,FALSE)		
23		=RETURN()		

Figure 11.52 Cardioid function generator macro.

plot file for display only once as we have done; otherwise, multiple reactivation of the macro sheet and chart are required as in Section 11.2.

Because of symmetry, our polar coordinate grid will satisfy all requirements for a full circle grid. By transforming curve points, a curve can be rotated to any convenient angular orientation.

11.4.3 Discussion

The chart window sizing capability affects aspect ratio adjustment that allows our polar chart to be conveniently made circular after it is generated. Thus, we need not worry about axes scale factors so long as we use a preformatted scatter chart with automatic axes scaling.

We could have displayed interrupted line segments as we did in the hidden-line elimination example. However, operations that involve cell selection are inherently slower than retracement of some lines as we did in forming the radial lines.

We still prefer a polar paired data type rather than having to compute x-y pairs for plotting purposes. Engineering data is often available in r-θ form so we should be able to use it directly. Although our parametric equations allowed convenient coordinate value computations, in general we would have to transform from r-θ form to x-y form for the spreadsheet as it is now constructed.

11.5 ABOUT VERSION 3.0

All examples of this chapter run under version 3.0 without change. This is not surprising since we have applied many basic principles of programming successfully used with other computer programming languages. But, spreadsheets are different and we expect to uncover useful features that are unmatched by the traditional languages. Unfortunately, there are no programming standards for spreadsheets, and what we accomplished can be transported to other spreadsheet programs only with substantial conversion effort.

We do not profit much from a new version of Excel, since we could welcome only the Form 2 IF construct with a structured programming characteristic. The macro debugger provides little help for complex program logic and it does not automatically give us a history of the macro operation. Only our custom debugging routines provided the record needed to uncover the cause of anomalous behavior.

No new data structures of the type commonly used in engineering as we discussed in Chapter 1 appear in the new version. We still do not have routines that manipulate and display data in cylindrical and spherical coordinate systems, and we have no built-in complex numbers computation routines. Scatter charts are now easier to construct but we cannot plot three dimensional data on continuous axes and we cannot display surfaces. However, there are reasons for using a dependency based calculation structure, a linked data generation and presentation vehicle, and a display scheme compatible with human visual recognition and concurrent mental processing ability. So, we still believe spreadsheet development will advance to provide capability that technical disciplines need.

REFERENCES

[1] Bentley, J. L., and D. Wood, "An optimal worst case algorithm for reporting intersections of rectangles," *IEEE Trans. Computers,* July 1980, pp. 571–577.

[2] Berry, R. D., "An optimal ordering of electronic circuit equations for a sparse matrix solution," *IEEE Trans. Cir. Th.,* vol. CT-18, no. 1, January 1971, pp. 40–50.

[3] Chang, A., "Application of sparse matrix methods in electric power system analysis," *Proc. 1968 Symp. on Sparse Matrices & Their Appl.,* R. A. Willoughby, ed., IBM Res. Rept. RA1, Yorktown Heights, NY, 1969, pp. 113–121.

[4] Doolittle, M. H., "General method of solution of normal equations," Report of the Superintendent of the U.S. Coast and Geodetic Survey Showing the Progress of the Work During the Fiscal Year Ending with June, 1878, Appendix 8, Paper 3, 1881, pp. 115–120.

[5] Eisenstat, S. C., et al., "Yale sparse matrix package," Res. Rept. #114, Dept. Computer Sci., Yale Univ, undated.

[6] Knuth, D. E., *The Art of Computer Programming: Vol. 3, Sorting and Searching,* Reading, MA: Addison-Wesley Pub. Co., 1973.

[7] Kral, I. H., *Numerical Control Programming in APT,* Englewood Cliffs, NJ: Prentice-Hall, Inc., 1986.

[8] Nievergelt, J., and F. P. Preparata, "Plane-sweep algorithms for intersecting geometric figures," *Comm. ACM,* October 1982, pp. 739–747.

[9] Nurmi, O., "A fast line-sweep algorithm for hidden-line elimination," *BIT,* vol. 25 (1985), pp. 466–472.

[10] Ottmann, T., and P. Widmayer, "Solving visibility problems by using skeleton structures," *Proc. 11th Symp. on Mathematical Foundations of Computer Sci.,* Lecture Notes in Computer Science, v. 176, Springer-Verlag, 1984, pp. 459–470.

[11] Rogers, D. F., and J. A. Adams, *Mathematical Elements for Computer Graphics,* New York: McGraw-Hill Book Co., 1976.

[12] Swart, G., and R. Ladner, "Efficient algorithms for reporting intersections," Tech. Report No. 83-07-03, Computer Sci. Dept., Univ. of Washington, Seattle, WA.

[13] Williamson, H., "Hidden-line plotting program," *Comm. ACM,* February 1972, pp. 100–103. (Also see Remark on Algorithm 420[J6] by (a) I. D.G. Macleod and A. M. Collins, *Comm. ACM,* July 1973, pp. 448; (b) H. Williamson, *Comm. ACM,* September 1973, pp. 578–579; (c) B. Gaither, *Comm. ACM,* June 1974, p. 324; (d) T. M. R. Ellis, *Comm. ACM,* June 1974, pp. 324–325; (e) T. M. R. Ellis, *Comm. ACM,* December 1974, p. 706.)

Index